ROAD

TO

DISASTER

ROAD

TO

DISASTER

A NEW HISTORY OF AMERICA'S DESCENT INTO VIETNAM

BRIAN VANDEMARK

ch.
CUSTOM
HOUSE

HarperCollins books may be purchased for educational, business, or sales promotional use. For information, please email the Special Markets Department at SPsales@harpercollins.com.

FIRST EDITION

Designed by Leah Carlson-Stanisic

Maps by Nick Springer, copyright © 2018 Springer Cartographics LLC

Photograph by AP/REX/Shutterstock

Library of Congress Cataloging-in-Publication Data has been applied for.

ISBN 978-0-06-244974-0

18 19 20 21 22   LSC   10 9 8 7 6 5 4 3 2 1

To all those touched by the Vietnam War

Contents

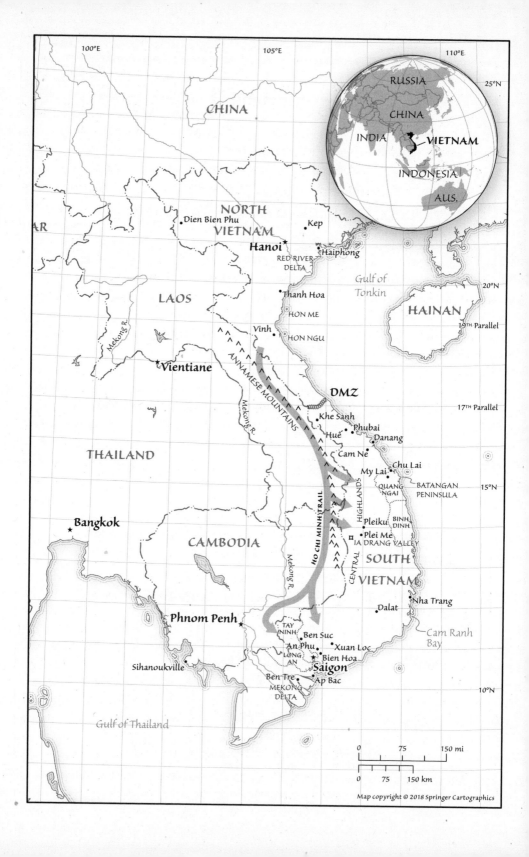

Map copyright © 2018 Springer Cartographics

30°N

85°W   80°W   75°W

UNITED STATES

ATLANTIC
OCEAN

USA

CUBA

SOUTH
AMERICA

Gulf of Mexico

Miami

25°N

Key West

Nassau

Straits of Florida

THE BAHAMAS

Mariel   Havana

San Antonio de los Baños

Jaguey Grande

Bejucal

San Cristobal

INSET
AREA

ESCAMBRAY MTS.

Trinidad

Yucatan Channel

MEXICO

Bahia de Cochinos
(Bay of Pigs)

CUBA

20°N

CAYMAN ISLANDS

Guantánamo

HAITI

Port-au-Prince

JAMAICA

Kingston

CARIBBEAN   SEA

Jaguey Grande

0   10 mi

0   10 km

Zapata Swamp

HONDURAS

15°N

Tegucigalpa

Playa Larga

Puerto Cabezas

NICARAGUA

Girón

Playa
Girón

Managua

Bahia de Cochinos
(Bay of Pigs)

COSTA RICA

10°N

San Jose

PACIFIC
OCEAN

Panama City

0   75   150 mi

0   75   150 km

PANAMA

Golfo de
Panamá

COLOMBIA

Map copyright © 2018 Springer Cartographics

A Very Human Culprit

They were not bad men. But they made some very bad decisions. Certainly, their decisions illustrate a disturbing disconnect between intent and effect, a chilling contrast not uncommon at the highest levels of government—then and now. There is overwhelming evidence that their decision-making was not always rational and logical. But people, as each of us knows deep down, are not always rational and logical. Mental mistakes are inherent in human nature. People have trouble seeing how their minds can mislead them. Our decision-making often has more to do with our desires than it does with reality. Yet the consequences are very real and, in the case of these men and those whose lives they affected, tragic.

These were the men of the Kennedy and Johnson administrations who presided over the Bay of Pigs invasion, brought the United States to the brink of nuclear Armageddon during the Cuban Missile Crisis, and led the country into the quagmire of Vietnam. Extraordinarily bright and able, their judgments and decisions on Cuba and Vietnam—more linked than commonly assumed—make them appear blind, slow, and altogether inadequate in dealing with problems that inflicted terrible suffering on millions of people. It is an unnerving puzzle: How and why did such intelligent and patriotic men not only make such unwise decisions but continue to make them despite circumstances and their previous professional accomplishments? What are the implications of their experience for the process of decision-making generally? These are the questions that drive the investigation—a sort of detective story—at the heart of this book.

Their example exposes the limitations of the "rational actor" model of decision-making, which assumes that decision-makers take account of available information, potential costs, and benefits in defining options, and act consistently in choosing the best course of action. Arrogance and ignorance help explain their mistakes, to be sure, but their failure goes deeper, and has more relevance, than that. Only by drawing upon recent findings of psychologists, cognitive scientists, and behavioral economists can we gain a more complete sense of what went wrong. This research sheds considerable light on the errors that people make in judgment and choice, showing how the cognitive constraints of decision-makers, combined with the complexity of their tasks, undermine their capacity to navigate toward a more objective assessment of reality. Such shortcomings, as Nobel Prize–winning psychologist Daniel Kahneman of Princeton University and the late Amos Tversky of Stanford University observed, are "too widespread to be ignored [and] too systematic to be dismissed as random error."[1] The harder the problems, moreover, the more binding cognitive constraints become.[2] The pioneer in this field, Nobel Prize–winning economist Herbert Simon of Carnegie Mellon University, put it well: "The capacity of the human mind for formulating and solving complex problems is very small compared with the size of the problems whose solution is required for objectively rational behavior in the real world."[3] Simon labeled this "bounded rationality." An analytical approach based on an understanding of these flaws inherent in human decision-making does not excuse the serious mistakes that Kennedy's and Johnson's men made, but it does make them comprehensible and coherent, accounting more fully for why they made the mistakes they did, and why they so often repeated the same errors despite manifestly unfavorable results.

In this light, we can see that their story is not a simple cautionary tale of hubris. It is the more complex and sobering tale of *well-intentioned* individuals making bad decisions. The pages that follow help us better understand both why good people sometimes make decisions that lead to big trouble and what happens when they begin to lose control of events. Such dynamics, if we are honest with ourselves, can apply to anyone. We all know people who continue to make foolish decisions in the face of bad consequences. The reason is that more often—and in more ways than we like to admit—people rely on things other than available information and logic to make decisions. Even the best minds are prone to such errors. Highly intelligent and accomplished people, when dealing with complex problems under stressful conditions, are no less immune to cognitive foibles than are we in our own lives. "We are," concludes Daniel Kahneman, "prone to overestimate how much we understand about the world."[4] They certainly were.

Deep down, we know that each human being can err, inflicting suffering and themselves suffering in turn—the pain of the world. But error and suffering have their purpose if they can help others gain insights into the glitches of human nature and profit from those insights. The ancient Greeks called this *pathei mathos*, "learning by suffering." Perhaps the best place to begin solving the puzzle of good intent producing disaster is by looking at the story of Robert McNamara.

Robert McNamara spent decades running away from Vietnam. The longest continually serving secretary of defense in American history (from January 1961 through February 1968), McNamara led the Pentagon with more force and vision than anyone before or after him. Under presidents John F. Kennedy and Lyndon B. Johnson from 1961 to 1968, he became one of the chief architects of the Vietnam War, the most divisive conflict in twentieth-century American history. For a generation of Americans, Vietnam became known as McNamara's War and McNamara became the face and living symbol of a struggle fought half a world away in the jungles of Southeast Asia. Eventually Americans of all ages and political persuasions associated him with what went wrong in Vietnam— and a great deal went wrong: the conflict led to the death and wounding of millions of Indochinese and hundreds of thousands of Americans; damaged American prestige; exposed the limits of American virtue, wisdom, and power; poisoned and polarized American politics; and deeply and lastingly divided the American people. It inflicted a lingering toll of incalculable anguish and hurt—physical and emotional—on countless people in the United States and Southeast Asia. For many of these people, the suffering has never ended—in fact, can never end.

The singling out of McNamara for blame and condemnation, regardless of the contribution of others, was a powerful and understandable reaction deeply rooted in human experience. More than twenty-five hundred years ago in ancient Greece, a cripple or beggar or criminal was stoned, beaten, and cast out of the community in response to a natural disaster such as a plague or famine. In ancient Israel on Yom Kippur, the Day of Atonement and the holiest day of the year for Jewish people, the High Priest ascended the Temple Mount and ritually slaughtered a goat as an offering to the Lord. The High Priest then laid his hands on a second goat, confessed the sins of the people of Israel, and sent the goat off "to the wilderness." To ensure it never returned, the goat was led to a cliff outside the city walls of Jerusalem and thrown over the precipice. In the aftermath of Vietnam, Americans sought someone on whom to focus their anger and rage at the sins inflicted and endured as a result of the war. Antiwar protestors and Vietnam veterans often shared nothing in common—except this: they wanted, even needed, to find psychological relief for their fury and enduring suffering. They found it by vilifying Robert McNamara. The man with slicked-back hair and rimless glasses became a kind of toxic talisman. For many people, he still is—even almost a decade after his death and nearly half a century after the war ended.

This reaction to McNamara began early on. In 1965, the United States escalated its involvement in the war in order to avert the collapse of its South Vietnamese ally. That escalation boosted casualties of soldiers and innocents alike and increased physical destruction throughout Vietnam. Newspapers and televisions brought vivid images of death and devastation into America's living rooms. Such images profoundly disturbed an intense, sensitive thirty-one-year-old Quaker husband and father from Baltimore named Norman Morrison. Deeply committed to Quaker principles of pacifism and personal witness, Morrison felt compelled to take an extreme, even desperate step. "What can we do that we haven't done?" he asked his wife, Anne. The next day, November 2, 1965, he wrote her a note after she had gone to work. "For weeks . . . I have been praying only that I be shown what I must do. This morning with no warning I was shown."[5] At twilight that day, Morrison drove fifty miles from his home in Baltimore to the River Entrance of the Pentagon in Arlington, Virginia, and parked forty feet below the window of McNamara's office.

Morrison wanted McNamara to see and remember what happened next. Hearing a commotion outside, McNamara moved to his window and witnessed the clean-cut, all-American–looking Morrison, dressed in a tweed jacket, douse himself with kerosene from a gallon jug and then immolate himself in self-sacrificial protest at the human suffering caused by the war, as Buddhist monk Thích Quảng Đức had done at a busy intersection in Saigon in June 1963. Morrison held his eleven-month-old daughter Emily in one arm but tossed her at the last moment before a rising column of orange flame consumed him.

Though the defense secretary was popularly viewed as emotionally impervious, Morrison's ghastly death deeply shook McNamara. He later wrote that he "understood and shared some of [Morrison's] thoughts," but he could never bring himself to discuss its emotional effect on him even with his own family. Recalling the incident nearly thirty years later still brought him to tears. When queried about it by Vietnamese officials in Hanoi in 1997, he frankly admitted it had "devastated" him. It was an overwhelming reminder of the intensity of emotion created by the war. But if Morrison's death brought the pain caused by the war home to McNamara in an immediate and horrifying way, it did not prompt an immediate and fundamental reconsideration of what he could and should do.

On November 7, 1966, McNamara traveled to Boston, Massachusetts, to speak at his alma mater, the Harvard Business School, and then with Harvard undergraduates across the Charles River

in Cambridge at Quincy House, one of Harvard College's undergraduate residences. As McNamara, unaccompanied by security,
left Quincy House that afternoon, several hundred young people
whose lives had been touched by the war—including members of
Students for a Democratic Society, a national protest group radicalized by American involvement in Southeast Asia—swarmed his
vehicle. People in the crowd began rocking the station wagon,
shouting obscenities at the man sitting in the back seat, spitting
and banging at the window separating him from them. Seeking
to avert an outbreak of violence, McNamara got out of the station
wagon, climbed atop the hood, and started to speak, only to be
interrupted with shouts of "Murderer!" McNamara, his voice and
legs trembling, lost his composure and blurted that he had been
both tougher and more courteous as a college student at Berkeley
in the 1930s. Just then, university officials hustled McNamara from
atop the vehicle through a Quincy House door and down into a
maze of underground steam tunnels. He emerged in safety a few
minutes later in Harvard Yard. The next day, Harvard publicly
apologized to McNamara for the ugly confrontation. McNamara,
who by then had regained his composure, replied that no apology
was necessary. "I understand," he said.

Six years later, on September 29, 1972, long after McNamara
had left the Pentagon but before America had left Vietnam, Mc-
Namara stood in the lounge of a ferry one rainy Friday night as
it crossed Vineyard Sound from Woods Hole, Massachusetts, to
the island of Martha's Vineyard, where he had a vacation home. A
bearded, twenty-seven-year-old artist in sneakers approached Mc-
Namara and said, "Mr. McNamara, there's a phone call for you.
Please follow me." The young man was full of pent-up humiliation
and fury, partly because his decision to avoid the draft had es-
tranged him from his family—his uncle had been a navy admiral
who received the Congressional Medal of Honor in World War II
and his two brothers had served in Vietnam. He led McNamara
outside onto a narrow walkway. On one side of the walkway lay
the pilothouse; on the other, a four-foot railing with a metal grate
that separated the ferry from the dark open water of Vineyard

Sound. The young man suddenly turned and grabbed McNamara by his belt and shirt collar and tried to throw him overboard. McNamara's glasses flew off as he clawed for the railing. A trim and strong fifty-six-year-old man, he desperately interlocked his long fingers in the metal grate as the young man repeatedly jabbed at his throat with the heel of his hand and tried to pry loose McNamara's fingers. A crewmember grabbed the young man from behind and wrestled him down onto the walkway as another crewmember rescued McNamara from danger. He returned to the lounge badly shaken. When the ferry reached Martha's Vineyard, McNamara refused to press charges. He later told a close friend that the incident came close to unhinging him. But he said it in a way that suggested he bore no grudge against the young man who attacked and nearly killed him. It was as if McNamara understood his rage.

Such incidents might make McNamara seem like a character in a tragedy by Aeschylus or Sophocles, doomed to ignominy by a chorus of unforgiving critics, a singularly despised focus for what was ultimately a collective failure. These personal confrontations burdened McNamara as the war stumbled to its tragic conclusion in 1975. While the fall of Saigon marked an inglorious end to America's long and unsuccessful involvement in Vietnam, its ghosts continued to haunt Americans for years afterward. During all of those years, McNamara stayed silent about Vietnam, the trauma intensifying his desire for a private, untouchable zone. While he had not left the public eye, serving as president of the World Bank from 1968 to 1981, he never discussed the war's impact on him or how he dealt with his emotional wounds. He kept his grief and guilt tightly locked up as a means to protect himself emotionally and psychologically. He also feared that whatever he said would hurt someone—Americans, Vietnamese, and others— without changing anything; the wounds of Vietnam were just too raw and too deep.

But McNamara's heart ached to express the heavy feelings of grief and guilt that he had buried deep inside himself, and his acute awareness of all that had gone wrong in the jungles of Vietnam compelled him to try to understand and explain why he and others had failed so utterly with such tragic consequences for so many people. Amid profound internal turmoil and conflict, he struggled to look squarely at what had happened, to come to terms with the disastrous decisions he had made and how those decisions had affected so many others. The hardest things to talk about are the ones that we ourselves can't understand, and bewilderment often accompanies these internal deliberations.

After years of painful distancing, McNamara finally decided to come to grips with the past and confront his (and the country's) demons. In the early 1990s, with the help of a young historian, he set out to write his memoir of the war. He knew that after his death, he would no longer be able to answer the lingering questions and that who he was, what he thought and felt, would be defined by others and that secondhand conception would be entombed in people's memories and perceptions. Assisted by the young historian, he began to reconstruct the story of his involvement with Vietnam based on the contemporaneous record rather than flawed memory or wishful recollection. Though tethered by documents and timelines, it was a deeply personal and painful journey of self-reflection and self-criticism, an act of severe introspection. Along the way, he took a hard look at loss, guilt, accountability, and, at last, acceptance, in an effort to find relief from unpleasant truths. Nothing went excused or unexamined, including the heretofore unspeakable and almost unbearable responsibility he had for those whom he had sent into harm's way and had perished or been irreparably scarred as a result of decisions he had directly made or heavily influenced. Over many months of work, telescope became microscope and increasingly he struggled as he approached the most sensitive and painful of topics, his speech slowing, thick with emotion. At times, he began to tear up, almost out of panic, overwhelmed with shame. At one point, he halted altogether, incapacitated by perplexity and despondency. The young historian listened intently but quietly—to say anything seemed inappropriate, even impious at such a poignant moment. An awkward silence followed. The young historian did not want to intrude on McNamara's silence, not knowing what to say. At last, McNamara brought himself to ask, "Do you think 58,000 Americans died in vain?" He labored to get each word out and wept in humiliation when he finished.

I was that young historian. I came in time to understand Robert McNamara as a human being who showed a capacity to learn, to grow, and to change, who epitomized the complexities and ambiguities of the human condition, but also as a powerful and enduring symbol to an entire generation of Americans who came of age during the Vietnam War and whose lives became forever intertwined with the tragedy and its lingering aftermath. Whatever one's feelings about Robert McNamara—and I fully understand there are some people on the Left as well as the Right who, for entirely different reasons, will simply never forgive him—his role as secretary of defense during the Vietnam War offers a—perhaps *the*—prime example of how intelligent and well-intentioned individuals can make decisions that lead down the road to disaster. Yet people sometimes forget that McNamara represented only one individual of a broader group and Vietnam only one episode of a broader era when very good, very smart people made very bad decisions.

Over the years since, I became an older (and hopefully wiser) historian who devoted a considerable portion of my time to explaining America's involvement in world affairs to young men and women at the United States Naval Academy in Annapolis. My students prepare to serve their nation as newly commissioned navy ensigns on warships deployed to trouble spots around the globe or as marine corps second lieutenants on the front lines of danger. Many of these young men and women (known at Annapolis as midshipmen) went on to fight in the post–September 11, 2001, wars in Afghanistan and Iraq and several—heartbreakingly—were wounded or killed. Such a prospect hovers in the mind and consciousness of every midshipman and makes him or her intent on understanding the history of America's involvement in the world, including the conflict-ridden decade of the 1960s. Many of these midshipmen have parents who, like me, were just children at the time. Yet the Bay of Pigs, the Cuban Missile Crisis, and the Vietnam

War are powerful touchstones because they realize that some of them will become senior military officers and public servants who may have to deal with their own dangerous, high-stakes crises and wars. For many students, study of these events is a primarily academic pursuit. For those in the seats in front of me, it is shop class.

When I began teaching the course at Annapolis more than a quarter century ago, I hardly knew where or how to begin. I joined the faculty of the Naval Academy not because I believe that war is the best solution to differences between human beings with a capacity to reason or that problems are best solved militarily rather than politically—quite the opposite—but because I admired the ethos of service to which midshipmen dedicate themselves as they risk their lives on others' behalf and their commitment to devote their lives to something larger than themselves. I wanted midshipmen to learn from the great crises of the 1960s so that their generation of military leaders could learn how to avert wars, not just how to fight and win them. As a historian aware of the complexities and contradictions that color decisions confronting those who actually wield power, I initially found it hard to give the midshipmen "the gouge" (the takeaway point in navy lingo) they wanted and needed.

What lessons could be drawn from events as complex but interrelated as the Bay of Pigs, the Cuban Missile Crisis, and the Vietnam War? I believe the threads that bind these disparate events together can be reduced to two simple but powerful paradoxes: good leaders can make bad decisions, even terribly bad decisions, and moral clarity—the ability to judge decision-makers in terms of black or white—is often diminished by increased understanding. These are sobering contradictions that at first unsettle midshipmen. Yet as midshipmen delve into the crises of the 1960s and the characters involved in them, the contradictions slowly sink in because they see themselves as good people who will one day be leaders, too. They come to realize that they—"the best and the brightest" of their generation—are, with the very best of intentions, also capable of making very bad decisions and that humans are capable of follies and blunders, but also resilience and reconciliation.

My own insights came partly through an unusual combination

of circumstances. In September 1987, as I neared completion of my Ph.D. in history at the University of California, Los Angeles (UCLA), Richard Holbrooke telephoned me. Then an investment banker in New York who had served as President Jimmy Carter's assistant secretary of state for East Asian and Pacific affairs, Holbrooke asked if I was interested in working as the research assistant on Clark Clifford's memoir, which Holbrooke had agreed to coauthor. I jumped at the chance. Clifford was a legendary figure in Washington, D.C., dating back to the end of World War II. An elder statesman of the Democratic Party, he had worked for four presidents, most famously serving as Johnson's secretary of defense during the pivotal and tumultuous year of 1968, when the Vietnam War reached its climax and intensifying violence and division wracked America.

I moved to Washington a few months later. For the next three years, Clifford, Holbrooke, and I carefully reviewed and reconstructed the great moments in Clifford's legendary public career: when he had been at Truman's side at the beginning of the Cold War and the creation of the containment policy that guided American strategy toward the Soviet Union from 1947 to 1991, when he served as the chairman of Kennedy's Foreign Intelligence Advisory Board during the tense years of the early 1960s, and when he became one of Johnson's closest advisors as LBJ wrestled with the war that destroyed his presidency and sundered the country for a generation. I vividly remember our work conferences in Clifford's spacious wood-paneled office overlooking Lafayette Square across Pennsylvania Avenue from the White House. The White House, especially when illuminated at night, seemed so close that I could almost reach out and touch it. The silver-haired and courtly Clifford sat behind his desk with his long fingers pointed in a steeple, recalling the agony of LBJ and his advisors as they made one disastrous decision after another on the war. Our host still harbored deep affection for Johnson—Clifford kept a small bronze bust of LBJ in his private anteroom adjoining the office, where he took his afternoon naps. He especially admired Johnson for securing civil and political rights for African Americans that had been denied them since the country's founding—a signal and lasting achievement in U.S. history—but Clifford frankly acknowledged the magnitude of Johnson's failure on Vietnam. LBJ was long dead and Clifford, having entered his eighties, had left his ambitions behind him, so he had no reason to pull his punches or disguise the anguished expression on his chiseled face as he remarked again and again on the irony of intelligent and well-intentioned men leading the country into disaster. Clifford, Holbrooke, and I spent countless hours analyzing, trying to explain and come to terms with this paradox.

As we neared completion of Clifford's memoir in 1990, I accepted a teaching position at the United States Naval Academy and shortly thereafter published my Ph.D. dissertation with Oxford University Press, *Into the Quagmire: Lyndon Johnson and the Escalation of the Vietnam War* (1991). Soon, I embarked on a new book project: a biography of Clifford's predecessor as secretary of defense, Robert McNamara. Undeniably important, McNamara seemed, in a sense, the Greta Garbo of America's greatest twentieth-century tragedy, an intriguing figure made more so by his deafening silence. I interviewed him many times in the course of my research, yet during each of our discussions, the one topic he steadfastly refused to discuss was the one that mattered the most and was the most sensitive for him—Vietnam.

A year and a half into my work, a thorough and very critical biography of McNamara was published—Deborah Shapley's *Promise and Power: The Life and Times of Robert McNamara*. By now, he and I had grown to know one another well and felt comfortable talking with each other. McNamara asked me to read Shapley's biography and tell him what I thought of it. A week later, I went to see McNamara at his office next to the Willard Hotel on Pennsylvania Avenue, just east of the White House. The afternoon January sun casting a lengthening shadow through the window, McNamara sat at his large oak desk, clothed in a worn oxford-cloth shirt and khakis. He turned his lean, tightly coiled six-foot frame and intense hazel eyes toward me and asked in a clear, forceful voice, his body language carefully controlled, "What is your opinion of Shapley's work?" I looked him in the eye and declared she had written a fundamentally good book. I told him what I thought, rather than what I assumed he might want to hear, because I had come to believe that McNamara was the sort of man—a big man rather than a little one—who respected (indeed, expected) honesty and criticism from those around him, a rare breed in the often egocentric and unreflective world of Washington. I then told McNamara that I would abandon my project and help him write his own memoir about Vietnam if he would address what had happened rather than what he wished had happened and if he would base his account on the record rather than on fallible human memory. Such a memoir would be far more significant and enduring than anything I could write about him.

McNamara agreed and we proceeded. Our collaboration was taxing and intense. For McNamara, the process of reconstruction was like reliving a nightmare, triggering powerful memories and emotions. The intensity and fragility of his demeanor both impressed and disconcerted me. His recollections were intimate and self-revealing, tangibly both painful and purgative. My tape recorder captured his words when he spoke, yet the transcribed pages were inevitably incomplete as they could not convey the look in his eyes, the movement of his hands. As we went deeper and deeper, I got the impression that McNamara *had* to talk, that this was more than shedding—it was part of his attempt to truly, directly confront himself. And as he spoke, his feelings and insights finally broke through the fetters that had restrained them. The burden that had been locked up inside him for years achieved release at last—not by absolution but by acceptance and deliberation.

Two years later, in the spring of 1995, McNamara published the memoir everyone thought he would never write. *In Retrospect: The Tragedy and Lessons of Vietnam* rocketed to number one on the *New York Times* bestseller list, garnering commendatory reviews from unlikely corners of the media. But while I thought speaking frankly and honestly would be cathartic for McNamara and for the nation, along with the praise came an intense storm of criticism and controversy. The book tore open old wounds, provoking a volcanic eruption of emotion among many people on both the Left and the Right. I utterly failed to anticipate this perhaps inevitable reaction on the part of people who lived through the crucible of the Vietnam years because I had been too young to experience that period as an adult. For millions whose lives were touched—intimately and enduringly—by the war and for whom it remained living history, Vietnam will never be over. I understood that the roots of such anger deserve understanding and respect, and that expressing such feelings can be therapeutic, but the ferocity of the *In Retrospect* storm had been unexpected—though perhaps not so much by McNamara himself. Meanwhile, I returned to my teaching duties and academic life at the Naval Academy.

More than two decades have passed since then. All that time, I hesitated to talk or write about my close relationships with Clark Clifford and Robert McNamara and what I learned from them. After all, they had let me into their confidence and shared very private, very personal insights and had said what they wanted to say in their published memoirs. I respected the ethos of discretion they had imparted to me, and I did not wish to criticize—and therefore hurt—men who had let down their guard before me. I feared deep down that I could not do their memories justice, partly because, like them, I had not fully been able to solve the general mystery of why they, who had been so right in so many pre-Vietnam decisions, could get the war so, so wrong. And I felt sensitive and anxious about adding to the pain of Vietnam by whatever I said, even in the spirit of investigation to further understanding.

As the years went by, Clifford and McNamara passed away (Clifford in 1998, McNamara in 2009), I went on with my life, and wrote books on other subjects. Yet the experience of working with Clifford and McNamara never left me. There was so much I got to ask them, so much I learned from them. All of it remained vivid and undiminished in my memory. Again and again I wondered, how *could* such decent men (and their colleagues) make such extraordinarily dangerous yet successful decisions as those made by Kennedy during the Cuban Missile Crisis and such deliberate and utterly disastrous ones as those made by Kennedy at the Bay of Pigs and by Johnson during the Vietnam War? That question haunted me as I sought to convey the lessons of recent American history to midshipmen in my classroom. For them, I wanted—almost needed—to go beyond the powerful cliché of arrogant and ignorant men stumbling blindly into danger and disaster, to search for a deeper and more fundamental truth that explained their mistakes and failures in a way that took account of what I knew to be their essential decency and humanity. That was the essential task—daunting and yet compelling. I came to realize that their story was not a superficial morality tale of bad leaders making bad decisions, but a much more sobering, cautionary, and very human tale of good leaders making bad decisions. The road to disaster was indeed paved with good intentions—a truth that speaks to how Americans of every generation make foreign and military policy.

The fallibility of human nature under pressure and certain circumstances is universal and timeless. Yet we can also learn valuable lessons by examining what made those who took America down the road to disaster exceptional and distinct. Their decisions illustrate a troubling human tendency when it comes to judgment and choice: "our excessive confidence in what we believe we know," in the words of Kahneman, "and our apparent inability to acknowledge the full extent of our ignorance and the uncertainty of the world we live in."[6] More than most, these men felt reason to be confident, and that confidence, justified by previous professional triumphs and remarkable intelligence, became a blindfold instead of a clarifying lens.

This book aims to do many things, but by no means everything. That is impossible, especially when treating subjects as complex and contentious as Cuba and Vietnam during the 1960s. Readers expect and deserve to know the limits of this study. It is not a detailed operational history of air and ground campaigns related to the Bay of Pigs invasion, the Cuban Missile Crisis, or Vietnam. Showdowns and battles are described, but from a high altitude, with the drama of engagement and those who did the fighting treated in general rather than specific terms. This reflects the discipline of focus rather than any lack of appreciation for the human face of war. In this book, Cuba and Vietnam are largely executive pursuits: high-level American officials; U.S. military commanders; Russian, Cuban, and Vietnamese leaders; and how things were seen in Washington, Moscow, Havana, Saigon, and Hanoi. Such individuals were certainly not the only actors, but their choices broadly shaped the course of events. In this process of decision-making, things went around in circles much more than straight ahead. Just as in regular life, questions were debated over and over—like a record stuck in a scratched groove—often without resolution.

In researching and writing this book, I utilized the voluminous records of the Kennedy and Johnson presidential libraries—including the recently completed release of recorded meetings and telephone conversations between presidents Kennedy and Johnson and others and the entire audio diary of Lady Bird Johnson. I also relied on materials in my possession that have never been made public: hundreds of hours of interviews that Richard Holbrooke and I conducted with Clark Clifford in 1987 through 1990 and that I conducted with Robert McNamara and some of his closest associates, like McGeorge Bundy, in 1991 through 1994. These interviews were recorded, transcribed at the time, and comprise more than a thousand pages. Some material from them was used in Clifford's and McNamara's memoirs, but other details and insights revealed in the interviews were not used—either because Clifford and McNamara considered them to be too personal or critical, or because they did not seem to be relevant when Clifford and McNamara wrote their books more than two decades ago. Clifford's daughters, Joyce Clifford Burland and Randall Clifford Wight, and McNamara's widow, Diana Masieri McNamara—convinced that their father and husband would want to help future generations avoid the mistakes of the past—allowed me to use these recordings without restriction.

Those interviews, along with the abundant records at the Kennedy and Johnson presidential libraries, enabled me to more fully understand and explain why JFK, LBJ, and their advisors made the dangerous and disastrous decisions they did. But, as noted earlier, I was also able to draw upon something earlier scholars could not:

groundbreaking research conducted over the last three decades into how we make decisions based upon neuroscience, psychology, and other behavioral investigations. Novel experiments have led to major discoveries, including that people who use heuristics (cognitive shortcuts or simplifying rules of thumb) in uncertain and stressful situations often make flawed decisions. These cognitive tools are utilized automatically and unreflectively. "Heuristics facilitate rapid inferential processing and often produce correct answers," note psychologists Susan Fiske of Princeton University and Shelley Taylor of UCLA. "However, they may also be vulnerable to a number of serious errors of which the perceiver is usually unaware."[7] As a result, people keep (mis)applying them. "Once a simple heuristic has been used," social psychologists Richard Nisbett of the University of Michigan and Lee Ross of Stanford explain, "subsequent considerations fail to exert as much impact as common sense or normative considerations might dictate that it should." In this way, judgments can become resistant to logical or evidential challenges.[8] These discoveries help better explain how people perceive and define problems, and why they can exhibit unfounded overconfidence, ignore essential information, and become blind to their own errors. This cognitive and behavioral research not only illuminates the decisions made, but allows us to see ourselves in their limits because we are shown that they are our limits, too. Every serious scholar or journalist who has studied Vietnam has drawn upon psychology in an attempt to decipher decision-making. But most of them did so well before the current era of social scientific research, and many of those who have written about the war more recently continue to apply familiar means of assessment.

It is important to note here that psychology, cognitive science, and related models of decision-making are lenses—not perfectly polished or all encompassing, but generally neglected when it comes to understanding America's descent into Vietnam. This is partly a function of the fact that such theories have been developed relatively recently, after most major studies of the war were written. But it goes beyond that. Historians have always considered the mindset of individuals and societies they study. But the complexity of that consideration has been limited by a reluctance to fully engage in an interdisciplinary manner with science that is often either deemed too "hard" (neuroscience) or too "soft" (psychology). This is a serious shortcoming. To use astronomy as an example, we study the stars through different sorts of telescopes, each calibrated to perceive a portion of the whole (X-ray, reflector, infrared, radio, gamma ray), and only upon integrating such distinct data do we acquire a fuller understanding of the universe. Such is the case with this book: an account of the historical record is combined with our deepened understanding of how people think, a combination that provides the foundation for more comprehensive—and thus more illuminating—conclusions. If an admixture of telescopic observations helps us understand how stars formed, in this case an admixture of history and cognitive science allows us to better understand how a different set of stars fell.

As McNamara himself said, "We screwed up." They most certainly did, but concluding that is hardly novel or useful. The war had been lost, millions of lives had been lost, and in his way, McNamara too was lost. But he retained a stubborn hope. "How in God's name did it happen? And how can we avoid it in the future? That's the question." Here, perhaps, is an answer. "I owe an explanation to those whom I killed," he added.[9] Pain inflected McNamara's face as he spoke these words and lingered in his voice after he finished. His feelings of regret and sorrow hadn't changed, would never change.

CHAPTER 1

The Danger of Unquestioned Assumptions
(January–April 1961)

When David Halberstam coined the phrase "the best and the brightest" in his 1972 book about Vietnam by the same name,[1] he did so with caustic irony. But eleven years earlier, in the heady days at the beginning of the Kennedy administration in January 1961, the label seemed a fitting description. Among those appointed to serve in senior national security posts of the new administration were Dean Rusk, former Rhodes scholar and president of the Rockefeller Foundation, who became secretary of state; Robert McNamara, first nonfamily president of Ford Motor Company, who became secretary of defense; and McGeorge Bundy, wunderkind dean of Harvard University's faculty, who became special assistant for national security affairs. The troika of Rusk, McNamara, and Bundy, along with their key subordinates, constituted an extraordinary assemblage of genius and talent— eminently worthy stewards of the national interest. These men came to Washington to serve John F. Kennedy. The young new president had sought the most able and decent people he could find, top-notch problem solvers regardless of political affiliation, and he had found them.

In the more than half century since his assassination in Dallas, Texas, on November 22, 1963, Kennedy has grown into a mythic figure, a kind of vessel into which people pour their hopes, expectations, and dreams for what might have been. People forget that Kennedy won the 1960 election by a razor-thin margin over Republican Richard Nixon—less than 113,000 votes out of more than 68.3 million votes cast. Handsome, articulate, and charismatic, Kennedy raised people's hopes and expectations, but he understood the narrowness of his election victory and his Democratic Party base—a fragile and uneasy coalition of northern urban liberals and southern conservatives—and this made him more cautious than his activist rhetoric suggested. He was a cool pragmatist sensitive to political pressures who took steps to satisfy conservatives without risking major war and who preferred to play for time. His supporters called this "keeping one's options open." His critics called it indecisiveness. Kennedy approached foreign policy determined to avoid a nuclear conflagration, which he dreaded above all else, without giving ground to Communists in the Cold War that would invite grave charges of appeasement. Having experienced combat as a junior officer in the Pacific during World War II, he understood the pain, confusion, and heartache of battle and instinctively sought to avoid war if at all possible. But he was also a risk-taker whose luck had always been good. He had never lost an election and, at the age of forty-three, was the youngest person ever elected president.

The men Kennedy surrounded himself with comprised an activist generation eager to get the country "moving again." They had grown up in and survived the Great Depression, answered the call of duty during World War II, and they had won. After the war, their enthusiasm, intelligence, and energy had helped to build the richest and most powerful of nations, and they were eager to demonstrate their excellence. They had been part of molding the history of the previous decades and believed with every fiber of their beings that they could fix any problem because they had been able to fix those they had encountered in the past. Fundamentally, they were convinced that every problem had a solution—one just had to find it; it simply required sufficient energy, imagination, intellect, and resources. It was a glittering era and they dazzled.

Kennedy disarmingly admitted to a Washington acquaintance shortly after his election victory that he had spent so much time getting to know people who could help him become president that he knew very few people who could help him *be* president. The team of advisors that he assembled to help him deal with issues of national security had not worked with one another before—in fact, they barely knew one another, strangers to him as well as to each other (a troublingly common phenomenon at the start of a new administration). Kennedy valued—perhaps overvalued—raw intellect, and he paid more attention to their professional accomplishments than to their specific wisdom related to their new assignments, which usually comes with time and experience. None of these men were the sort to engage in a painful, and even existentially challenging, self-assessment of possible weaknesses. Indeed, their evident prior successes made them even less likely to do so than might have been the case with someone who had struggled and stumbled. Such achievement almost perversely left them exposed and blind to such exposure.

Their vulnerability reflected what social scientists call the "availability bias." Amos Tversky and Daniel Kahneman, exploring the methods people use to form judgments under conditions of uncertainty, found that people adopt heuristics to help them find adequate (though often imperfect) answers to complex and difficult questions. When evaluating an issue or making a decision, individuals use the heuristic of recent experiences. The number of such experiences recalled, moreover, is used to infer the future frequency with which such experiences occur.[2] In the case of the men on Kennedy's team, their recent experiences—their readily accessible memories—were a string of problems successfully solved. This fostered an inadequate appreciation of what they could not fix that would lead them to take risks they should have avoided. At the time, however, their optimistic outlook was highly valued by both Kennedy and those who enthusiastically boosted the Camelot narrative.

Kennedy had never met Dean Rusk before he offered him the top cabinet post in his administration. An unassuming and laconic

Dean Rusk, JFK, and Robert McNamara
Abbie Rowe/JFK Library

man with a balding pate above a round, genial face freckled like
a shake of nutmeg that made him look, one journalist said, "like a
friendly neighborhood bartender," Rusk possessed intellect and
ability as deep as his gravelly voice. Born on a small, red-clay farm
in rural Georgia, he had traveled a long road to success and prom-
inence. He won a Rhodes scholarship to Oxford during the 1930s,
where he personally witnessed Hitler's rise to power during a trip
to the continent. He then served as an army staff officer in the
China-Burma-India Theater during World War II; worked as assistant secretary of state for Far Eastern affairs under George Marshall in the late 1940s; and then became president of the Rockefeller
Foundation in the 1950s. Rusk's bland demeanor and sense of duty
made him discreet and loyal—but also diffident. Even close colleagues found it difficult to get to know the man behind his stoic,
Buddha-like facade.

Three historic events in Rusk's life shaped his outlook: Munich, the fall of China, and Korea. Munich meant appeasement would never work. China meant beware the domestic backlash of foreign policy failure. And Korea meant limited war for limited objectives could avert defeat even if it might not bring victory. Kennedy chose Rusk to head the State Department because he had substantive administrative experience and his lack of vanity appealed to a new president who relished foreign affairs and intended, in many ways, to be his own secretary of state. Rusk was not oblivious to the fact that his new job was likely to be much more challenging than anything he'd previously done and confessed to JFK, "There is no way to be adequately prepared to become Secretary of State." ("How do you think I feel?" the president-elect replied.[3]) The difference in their backgrounds and styles meant their relationship began awkwardly, each groping to understand the other. Together, they would set the course of American foreign policy, but they began as strangers to one another.

Self-contained but driven, with a pug-nosed face, rimless glasses, and slicked-back dark brown hair, Robert McNamara possessed a towering reputation for analytical prowess in identifying problems and finding solutions, whether in business or government. He had developed an expertise in statistical analysis of quantitative data that he had applied with great effectiveness as an instructor at Harvard Business School before the war; as an officer in the army air corps during World War II, when he maximized the efficiency of U.S. bombing operations against the cities of Germany and Japan; and as an executive at Ford Motor Company in the 1950s. An independent thinker, McNamara called things the way he saw them—within the framework of loyalty to the boss, because he prized loyalty and respected the administrative chain of command. He exuded a brilliance and intensity that intimidated some and a disdain for flattery that offended others. But while he firmly believed that objectivity could be achieved by careful analysis and deliberation, the rigorous logic that he displayed to the world in making and carrying out tough decisions competed with an emotional sensitivity and introspection—"the protective covering with which each of us guards his inner thoughts,"[4] he called it—that he kept carefully hidden from the world.

Although Ford was one of the biggest companies in America at the time and Michigan a swing state that he visited on the campaign trail (including only a day before the election), surprisingly Kennedy had not even known who McNamara was until his brother-in-law Sargent Shriver mentioned his name during a December briefing he gave Kennedy on possible candidates to lead the Pentagon. Both men were extraordinarily gifted—in different ways—but also extraordinarily inexperienced at governing. McNamara had been a successful executive in the private sector, far from the nation's capital. In Kennedy's case, he knew Washington but as a junior senator with greater celebrity than accomplishment and a much closer view of camera lenses than the inner workings of the executive branch.

At the beginning of the Kennedy administration, McGeorge Bundy was, by his own later admission, "a forty-one year old governmental greenhorn who had come to this particular job largely by accident."[5] The two had met in the 1950s when Kennedy served on Harvard's Board of Overseers and Bundy headed the university's Faculty of Arts and Sciences. A crisp and concise man with penetrating light blue eyes set behind clear-plastic-frame glasses, his prominent forehead accentuated by thinning sandy-brown hair, McGeorge Bundy looked very much the astute Ivy League professor he had been for more than a decade. Beneath the scholastic exterior, however, lurked an ego of iron self-confidence. With razor-sharpness he could rapidly analyze, synthesize, and summarize an extraordinary amount of information—an activity not always incorporating a desire for amity. "He could be impatient with people whose minds weren't as quick as his," said an associate who knew him well. "He did not suffer fools gladly."[6] The president and his national security assistant shared a common New England heritage, urbane sophistication, and interest in foreign affairs that facilitated rapport. But the two men were not close—Kennedy was a "lace-curtain" Irish-Catholic Democrat and Bundy was a Boston Brahmin Republican. That distance was amplified by the fact that

Bundy's office initially was not in the West Wing of the White House, but instead in the Old Executive Office Building (now the Eisenhower Executive Office Building) next door. Further highlighting both the gap and more broadly the alacrity of appointments in the new administration, Kennedy initially had difficulty learning Bundy's name. (One morning shortly after taking office, Kennedy said to his secretary, "Tell McB—McBundy that I would like a copy of any memoranda, minutes, notes, and such which he might make for our files."[7]) Nevertheless, Kennedy held his national security assistant's opinions in high regard because Bundy knew how to cut to the point.

On paper, these men were some of the most capable individuals ever to serve in government—a formidable team, but one that had never tackled and solved a problem together. Most observers in their enthusiasm overlooked the lack of hard-earned insight and seasoning at the time, but not House Speaker Sam Rayburn of Texas. When his protégé, Vice President Lyndon Johnson, described the Kennedy men's intellect to Rayburn in terms bordering on awe, Rayburn replied, "Well, Lyndon, you may be right and they may be every bit as intelligent as you say, but I'd feel a whole lot better about them if just one of them had run for sheriff once."[8]

Kennedy insider Arthur Schlesinger captured the atmosphere of excitement and confidence that marked the new team's arrival in Washington in January 1961:

> The capital city, somnolent in the Eisenhower years, had suddenly come alive. The air had been stale and oppressive; now fresh winds were blowing. There was the excitement which comes from an injection of new men and new ideas, the release of energy which occurs when men with ideas have a chance to put them into practice. The pace was frenetic . . . Everyone came early and stayed late . . . Telephones rang incessantly. Meetings were continuous. The evenings too were lively and full. The glow of the White House was lighting up the whole city. Washington seemed engaged in a collective effort to make itself brighter, gayer, more intellectual, more

resolute. It was a golden interlude . . . A new breed had come to town, and [they] carried a thrust of action and purpose wherever they went . . . Euphoria reigned; we thought for a moment that the world was plastic and the future unlimited.[9]

"They were brand-new," recalled Clark Clifford, who worked closely with Kennedy during the transition and had served five years in the Truman White House. "My God they were cocky."[10] Yet while they believed they had (or could certainly find) the answers to most problems, in this new environment they had yet to learn how to ask the right questions. They had brains and ability, good intentions and self-confidence all in considerable measure, but they lacked awareness of the realities and complexities of the world beyond America's shores, the limits as well as the reach of American power, and the dilemmas and burdens of decision-making at the highest levels of government. These newcomers, including their boss (a newcomer himself) did not suffer from a lack of brainpower; in fact, ironically that was to some extent their weakness. Nothing but hard and bitter experience could teach them these important but intangible things.

Their education began with the disastrous Bay of Pigs invasion in April 1961, when the Central Intelligence Agency (CIA) landed 1,543 exiles on the island of Cuba with the intention of toppling the regime of Fidel Castro. Instead, the aborted invasion led to the death or capture of the invasion force and the humiliation and humbling of the Kennedy administration. The invasion failed because Kennedy and his advisors neglected to question two deeply flawed assumptions underlying the plan: that America's role in the operation could be kept "plausibly deniable" (the reason the CIA, rather than the military, had been put in charge of it), and that a tiny exile force could trigger the downfall of a regime with an army and militia nearly 130 times its size and with considerable popular support. In hindsight, these assumptions seem remarkably naive, even preposterous. How could these intelligent men premise such consequential decisions on them? Their failure stemmed from inexperience and wishful thinking that discouraged them from questioning their assumptions, a pattern that would repeat itself in the realm of Vietnam decision-making.

Decision researchers Baruch Fischhoff of Carnegie Mellon University and Paul Slovic and Sarah Lichtenstein of the University of Oregon found that people frequently "fail to ask, 'What were my assumptions in deriving that inference?' or 'How good am I at making such inferences?' . . . People tend to treat the results of inferential processes as though there was no uncertainty associated with the early stages of the inference." Adds Cornell University psychologist Thomas Gilovich, "People's preconceptions [tend] to bias their interpretations of what they see."[11] Erroneous assumptions are not formulated through a series of logical steps, but swiftly, almost unconsciously, without subjecting them to critical analysis. This can produce a dangerous overconfidence that contrary evidence is irrelevant. And overconfidence can lead to disastrous miscalculations.

Vietnam was "not the top problem, to us or to the country, as we began," McGeorge Bundy later reflected. "That doubtful honor belonged to the communist regime in Cuba."[12] The superpower rivalry rooted in suspicion and mistrust between the United States and the Soviet Union after World War II had entered its most dangerous phase at the time of Kennedy's inauguration in January 1961. An "iron curtain" had descended across the continent of Europe and a nuclear arms race was underway that threatened not just mutual destruction but the destruction of the entire world. The Berlin Blockade of 1948, the "fall" of China the following year, the Korean War of 1950–1953, the domestic anti-Communist hysteria of McCarthyism, the Soviets' violent putdown of uprisings in East Germany in 1953 and Hungary in 1956—all of these developments influenced and defined America's fear of the Soviet Union and its allies in the years leading up to Kennedy's election.

"The basic adversary everywhere was seen to be the Soviet Union," Bundy later wrote. "The existence of a world-wide contest was an assumption of life and thought."[13] This assumption became a shibboleth akin to religious dogma, the very word "Communism" understood without nuance, reinforced through the actions of the USSR, the rhetoric of its leadership, the existential fear of nuclear war, and American pop and political culture. Indeed, there was no personal or professional advantage to opposing this binary conception. Such a rigid ideological conception of the world set in motion a fateful dynamic best described by sociologist William Graham Sumner at the beginning of the twentieth century. Sumner warned of "the danger of having a doctrine lying loose about the house, and one which carries with it big consequences . . . You accede to it now, within the vague limits of what you suppose it to be; therefore you will have to accede to it tomorrow when the same name is made to cover something which you never heard or thought of. If you allow a political catchword to go on and grow, you will awaken some day to find it standing over you, the arbiter of your destiny, against which you are powerless, as men are powerless against delusions."[14] This way of seeing the world becomes internalized.

The power of political catchwords reflects the tendency of our preconceptions to influence our interpretation of new information. "When examining evidence relevant to a given belief," observes Thomas Gilovich, "people are inclined to see what they expect to see, and conclude what they expect to conclude. Information that is consistent with our pre-existing beliefs is often accepted at face value, whereas evidence that contradicts them is critically scrutinized and discounted. Our beliefs may thus be less responsive than they should be to the implications of new information."[15] This effect has been demonstrated by two experiments. In the early 1960s, psychologist Edward Engel conducted the "Face A–Face B" experiment in which an observer was asked to look through a prism stereoscope, a device for presenting different images simultaneously to the two eyes through two lenses of equal power. One eye saw Face A, the other eye saw Face B. At the start, only the lens showing Face A was opened. Then both lenses were opened, showing both Face A and Face B, Face B very faintly. In successive exposures, Face B increased in brightness until it matched the brightness of Face A. During each exposure, the observer reported seeing Face A. Then the procedure was reversed: Face B was kept at the same level of brightness while Face A was dimmed until only Face B remained. And yet the observer continued to report seeing Face A.[16] In 1999, cognitive scientists Christopher Chabris of Union College and Daniel Simons of the University of Illinois devised the Invisible Gorilla experiment in which participants were asked to watch a video of two teams—one wearing white shirts, the other wearing black shirts—passing basketballs and to count the number of times those in white passed balls. In the middle of the video, a person dressed in a gorilla suit unexpectedly crossed the court. Only half of the participants who watched the video noticed the gorilla. "People typically do not consciously perceive aspects of their world that fall outside of the focus of their attention," notes Simons of what he and Chabris call "inattentional blindness." "These events can be dramatic enough that the vast majority of people are convinced that they would notice. In reality, though, many people do not."[17] The new Kennedy administration was no less immune to this tendency to see what one expects to see—and therefore to miss important things.

Two weeks before Kennedy's inauguration, Nikita Khrushchev, the Soviet Union's blunt-spoken and mercurial leader since Stalin's death in 1953, delivered a speech to party officials in Moscow proclaiming the inevitable triumph of Communism through "national liberation wars" in the Third World. Citing Cuba as an example, he called Latin America one of the "most important centers of revolutionary struggle against imperialism" and pledged Soviet support.[18] Khrushchev intended his blustering rhetoric to rally party officials and burnish the Soviet Union's standing in its competition with China for leadership of the Communist world rather than to provoke the United States, but most Americans heard only evidence of Soviet aggressiveness and nefarious intentions because suspicion of such intentions was the filter through which they perceived Soviet actions.

Kennedy was no exception. He wanted a better relationship with the Soviets but he interpreted Khrushchev's speech (which followed the premier's famous shoe-banging speech at the United

Nikita Khrushchev
Sputnik/Alamy Stock Photo

Nations) as a zero-sum call to arms, an authoritative statement of
Soviet motives, and a personal challenge to his presidency before it
even started. Kennedy made his top national security staff read the
speech, himself quoted frequently from a translated version that
he carried around with him, and devoted most of his inaugural
address as a response to it, dramatically announcing, "Let every
nation know, whether it wishes us well or ill, that we shall pay
any price, bear any burden, meet any hardship, support any friend,
oppose any foe, in order to assure the survival and the success of
liberty."[19] Ten days later, Kennedy delivered one of the most alarm-
ist State of the Union Addresses in American history. Using language he had drafted himself, Kennedy said, "Each day, the crises
multiply. Each day, their solution grows more difficult. Each day,
we draw nearer to the hour of maximum danger . . . The tide of

events has been running out—and time has not been our friend."[20] Kennedy's hard-line rhetoric illustrated the tenor of the times and led him to overlook the conciliatory gestures that Khrushchev made in the early days of the new administration when the Soviet premier offered a New Year's toast to Kennedy's presidency as "a fresh wind" in U.S.-Soviet relations, released captured U.S. airmen from a downed RB-47 reconnaissance plane,[*] published Kennedy's unedited inaugural address in Soviet newspapers—something no Soviet leader had ever done before—reduced jamming of Voice of America radio broadcasts, and called for an early summit between the two leaders before Kennedy established his course toward Moscow. Kennedy did not test the implications of Khrushchev's unilateral gestures signaling a new willingness to cooperate with the United States because his assumptions made him devalue and distrust them. Khrushchev responded by reverting to a more guarded stance toward Kennedy and his administration.

Animosity between the United States and Cuba had been building for almost two years. Washington viewed new Cuban leader Fidel Castro, who had led a popular revolution that toppled American-supported dictator Fulgencio Batista from power in January 1959, as an emerging despot who had subverted the democratic promise of the anti-Batista revolution and sought to move Cuba into the Communist orbit. During an April 1959 goodwill visit to the United States, the big, bearded Castro, wearing an open-collared olive-green uniform, had assured television audiences of his opposition to Communism and his enthusiastic support for a free press and democratic elections.[†] At the time, Americans assumed that

---

[*] Khrushchev, however, continued to keep captive U.S. pilot Francis Gary Powers, whose high-altitude U-2 reconnaissance plane had been brought down by a surface-to-air missile over Sverdlovsk (since renamed Yekaterinburg) on May 1, 1960, and who had then been convicted of espionage in a show trial. Powers would eventually be released in a prisoner swap for Soviet spy Rudolf Abel on February 10, 1962.

[†] Castro's 26th of July Movement printed millions of stickers in English and Spanish proclaiming, "We Are Humanists and Not Communists." Karl E. Meyer and Tad Szulc, *The Cuban Invasion: The Chronicle of a Disaster* (Frederick A. Praeger, 1962), p. 17.

democratic elections equaled a pro-American outcome; a corollary assumption was that those subject to Communist regimes inevitably preferred to live in alliance with the United States, following its commitment to free markets and fair elections. But soon Castro began to move away from his assurances, a troubling shift that blinded Washington to another fact: Castro's commitment to land reform and universal education and health care appealed to many Cuban peasants, the urban working class, and students. Indeed, the young, energetic, forceful, and charismatic Castro possessed considerable popular appeal, whatever his broken promises and authoritarian politics. There was also historical context that was played down by the American leadership. Castro's regime in Havana viewed the United States ("the great power of the North") as a neighborhood bully that had traditionally dominated and exploited Cuba through "Yanqui imperialism"* and seemed determined to strangle its socialist revolution in its crib. Castro understood that depicting the United States as the enemy of the revolution would facilitate his drive to consolidate power by allowing him to label his political opponents as American-inspired. That, in turn, would help justify his increasingly authoritarian control as necessary to preserve Cuba's independence in the face of growing hostility from the Yankee colossus to the north.

Outgoing President Dwight Eisenhower, fearful that the new leader intended to transform Cuba into a Soviet outpost on America's doorstep, severed U.S. relations with Havana two weeks before Kennedy succeeded him. The year before, Eisenhower had imposed a partial trade embargo on Cuba, terminated the island's economically important sugar quota to the United States, and initiated a covert CIA operation to recruit and train a paramilitary force of Cuban exiles to overthrow Castro, admonishing the CIA that "the

---

* Passed by Congress in 1901 following the Spanish-American War, the Platt Amendment gave the United States the self-appointed right to intervene in Cuba; it marked the beginning of a long era when navy gunboats and marines were regarded as indispensable tools of American diplomacy in the Caribbean. After the Platt Amendment's repeal in 1934, the United States would continue to intervene in Cuba—indirectly.

Fidel Castro
*Ian Dagnall
Computing/Alamy
Stock Photo*

main thing was not to let the U.S. hand show."[21] Having enjoyed
Batista's anti-Communist stance, the United States had overlooked
a great deal of his nastiness, so there was no small irony in the
American conception of Castro as the greater dictatorial threat.

Planning for the covert operation accelerated throughout the
election year of 1960. That summer, the tweedy, pipe-smoking CIA
director Allen Dulles briefed then candidate Kennedy on the outlines of the operation at the Kennedy family compound in Hyannis
Port, Massachusetts. Kennedy, far more concerned and knowledgeable about winning elections than running covert operations, harbored no sympathy for Castro, asked few questions of Dulles, and
expressed no misgivings about the operation. During the fall election campaign, Kennedy publicly attacked the Eisenhower administration (and, by extension, his opponent, Vice President Richard
Nixon) for "inaction, retreat, and failure" that had "permit[ted] a
Communist menace to arise only ninety miles from the shores of
the United States." "If you can't stand up to Castro," he taunted

Nixon at one debate, "how can you be expected to stand up to Khrushchev?"[22]

Kennedy did not have a simplistic view of Cuba. As senator, he had acknowledged that the United States historically seemed "more interested in the money we took out of Cuba than in seeing Cuba raise its standard of living for its people."[23] He also recognized the need to address the economic and political conditions in Latin America that made Communism attractive to the dispossessed, and would launch the Alliance for Progress within weeks of his inauguration in an effort to promote development throughout the hemisphere. But he considered Castro an emerging threat that must be addressed.

The same month that Kennedy narrowly won election as president, the CIA, because it had failed to organize an effective underground against Castro, broadened the Cuba plan from a guerrilla infiltration operation to a much more ambitious and risky amphibious invasion supported by air cover. That the CIA had as of yet been so thoroughly unable to compel the Cuban people to rise up against Castro was a telling fact, yet there is little evidence that anyone of note in the CIA or the new Kennedy administration took the time to consider its implications. Dulles and his deputy for covert operations, CIA deputy director for plans Richard Bissell, men of monumental self-assurance who savored the sense of being secret makers of history, briefed Kennedy on the expanded operation at his father's winter home in Palm Beach less than two weeks after the election. Dulles and Bissell laid out maps and papers on a large table by the swimming pool. Kennedy seemed impassive. He raised few questions—the responsibility was still Eisenhower's—and indicated he would go along with it for now. The two men returned to Washington with a qualified go-ahead.

As the scope of the operation increased—its budget and personnel expanded tenfold from the original plan—its bureaucratic momentum increased accordingly and the plan began to take on a life of its own. Two months later, on the day before his inauguration, Kennedy and his new team of advisors met with the outgoing Eisenhower team in the Cabinet Room at the White House to dis-

Kennedy and Eisenhower
Robert Knudsen/JFK Library

cuss various issues, including Cuba. Eisenhower told Kennedy and his lieutenants that they must support "to the utmost" any effort to remove Castro, that planning for the CIA operation was going very well, and that the new administration had a responsibility "to do whatever is necessary" for the operation to succeed. As he had in November, Kennedy neither questioned nor challenged any of these assertions. He had only a vague understanding of the operation, had bigger problems on his mind, like the Soviet Union itself, and hesitated to second-guess Eisenhower, even as the still popular commander in chief was on the way out. (As Kennedy privately acknowledged at the time, he would have been roundly defeated in the recent election if Eisenhower had been allowed to run for a third term.[24]) Thus, at the meeting and more generally, Kennedy and his senior advisors uncritically accepted Eisenhower's judgment that Castro represented an intolerable threat to the Western Hemisphere. Beyond deference to rank and public opinion, they had no basis on which to question the outgoing administration's judgment. None of Kennedy's men possessed thorough knowledge and understanding of Cuban history and culture; Rusk's government experience had involved the Far East, and McNamara and Bundy were effectively novices. None of them knew much about covert operations, which had become a frequent tool of U.S. foreign policy under Eisenhower, notably when the CIA had successfully (if, in the long run, disastrously) engineered the downfall of Mohammed Mossadegh in Iran in 1953 and Jacobo Árbenz in Guatemala in 1954. And all of them lacked expertise in the history of U.S.–Latin American relations—especially the deeply troubled history between Washington and Havana (the United States had supported not only Batista but previous Cuban dictators and dominated the island's economy for sixty years since the end of the Spanish-American War). Like most Americans at the time, what they did have extensive history in was viewing events everywhere through a Cold War prism that starkly divided the world between "free" countries that supported the United States and "unfree" countries that were hostile to it. They accurately assumed Castro to be a Marxist—he declared himself one in a secret speech in Havana in November 1960[25]—but by doing so, they could not imagine that Marxist ideology was not at the heart of his motivations. "He was," said someone who knew him well before he came to power in 1959, "above all a man with a firm will and an extraordinary ambition. He thought in terms of winning power and keeping it."[26] His program of land expropriations and nationalization of private businesses and foreign assets testified to his socialist agenda, but he was a Marxist who hung crucifixes and images of the Virgin Mary on his office walls and whose ferocious nationalism defined his worldview as much as anything.

When Kennedy became president, the CIA had been running for

months a secret training camp for the Cuban exiles, known as Brigade 2506, in the mountains along Guatemala's Pacific coast. The endeavor fit into a by now well-established pattern. Eisenhower had turned often to the CIA during the 1950s to implement and advance his policies through covert means, as in Iran and Guatemala. These results had enhanced the prestige and influence of Dulles and Bissell, so much so that they had become almost legendary figures, their success—the coin of the realm in Washington—an aura added to by the mystique of their golden doings. It was widely believed—including by them—that their "double signature on the check"[27] of a CIA operation was a guarantee of its effectiveness and success. But these results also made them intoxicated by their past triumphs, temperamentally and intellectually unwilling to assess their plans with critical detachment.

Bissell, the official formally in charge of the Cuban operation, had close ties to Kennedy and Ivy League members of his team, who knew him personally, respected his intellect and gentlemanly

JFK, Richard Bissell, and Allen Dulles
Everett Collection/Alamy Stock Photo

manners, and admired his past successes. Bissell had supported
Kennedy for president. Kennedy, in turn, considered Bissell "one
of the four or five brightest guys in the whole administration" and
intended to make Bissell CIA director when Dulles retired.[28] Bissell indeed possessed impressive credentials. A graduate of Groton
School and Yale University, he had taught economics at his alma
mater before World War II, where his students had included Mc-
George Bundy; Bundy's brother William, whom Kennedy had
appointed deputy assistant secretary of defense for international
security affairs; and Bundy's National Security Council (NSC) deputy, Walt Rostow. After the war, Bissell had helped administer the
highly successful Marshall Plan in Western Europe before returning to the United States in the mid-1950s and joining the CIA, where
he became a favorite of Dulles. Bissell oversaw a revolution in information gathering, directing the agency's technically brilliant
and spectacularly effective U-2 and Corona satellite reconnaissance
programs, which led America's intelligence services from the age of
spooks into the space age and propelled the CIA to the pinnacle
of its power and prestige. He exuded an aura of exceptional competence and confidence that deeply impressed the new arrivals.
"All of us—Kennedy and Bundy and the rest—were hypnotized by
Dick Bissell to some degree," recalled Arthur Schlesinger.[29] Many
considered him not only the true brains at the CIA but the smartest
man in Washington.

A smooth, seasoned, and effective bureaucratic advocate with
a long face framed by dark-rimmed spectacles, Bissell once said, "I
admire and believe in the use of power, when it's available, for purposes that I regard as legitimate." Such a conceit could border on a
frigid utilitarianism. "My philosophy during my last two or three
years in the agency," he frankly acknowledged in his memoirs,
"was very definitely that the end justified the means, and I was not
going to be held back."[30] Dulles granted his star subordinate feudal
prerogatives and independence, which fit well with Bissell's priorities and personality. An activist with bright ideas, Bissell "wanted
all the reins in his own hands," said a CIA colleague who knew
him well.[31]

Although he had little knowledge of spy tradecraft and little direct experience with on-the-ground covert action, Bissell decided to limit knowledge of the Cuban plan to a small number of people within the agency on a need-to-know basis, thereby denying himself the expertise of old hands in the Directorate of Operations (such as his eventual successor Richard Helms) and Directorate of Intelligence analysts who understood the situation inside Cuba far better than he did. In a January 1961 study, the Intelligence Directorate's Board of National Estimates concluded "that while Castro will probably continue to lose popular support, this loss is likely to be more than counterbalanced by the regime's increasingly effective controls over daily life in Cuba and by the increasing effectiveness of its security forces." In a follow-up study two months later, it concluded that Castro remained "firmly in control" on the island.[32] Bissell studiously ignored these estimates because he believed passionately in his own projects. "If Dick has a fault," Bundy wrote in a February memo to the president, "it is that he does not look at all sides of the question."[33] But both Bundy and Kennedy, trusting and admiring of Bissell and disdainful of what they considered a plodding bureaucratic approach they associated with the State Department but not the CIA, let this shortcoming, too, go unaddressed and therefore unremedied. Machinery existed within the CIA to independently evaluate the operation (the Intelligence Directorate's Office of National Estimates), as well as the State Department's Bureau of Intelligence and Research, the Pentagon's Defense Intelligence Agency, and the White House's National Security Council, but Bissell utilized none of them. Utterly self-assured and undoubting, Bissell—like his boss, Allen Dulles—had become dangerously overconfident. Bissell (with Dulles's consent) gave himself sole responsibility for estimating his own plan's likelihood of success. Self-interest and emotional attachment tend to be the enemies of good decision-making and by his own later admission, Bissell became "deeply committed emotionally"[34] to the operation.

Beyond predicating the Cuban operation on an appallingly inadequate and inaccurate understanding of the indigenous resistance to Castro, they also convinced themselves that the American-supported operation could be kept plausibly deniable—despite the mounting evidence that the CIA's "secret" training camp in Guatemala had been infiltrated by Castro's agents and stories about it had been published in newspapers throughout Latin America and the United States. Here two priorities, both of which obscured their view, coincided. For the sake of the invasion's success, they *wanted* to believe that their hand in the operation could be kept hidden. Yet for the sake of their own professional standing, they wanted the echo heard within the larger chamber of Washington—an example of how multiple priorities can become conflicting ones leading to bad decisions. University of Michigan psychologist David Dunning has emphasized the tendency of "people's motivational states—their wishes and preferences—to influence their processing" of information. What is more, notes Dunning, people "remain unaware of the distortions they place on their thinking" because "self-serving biases . . . remain outside of conscious awareness, monitoring, or control."[35] Cognitive experiments have confirmed this tendency. In one experiment, participants drew cards from a deck that portrayed either happy or angry faces; they greatly underestimated the percentage that displayed angry faces. In a similar experiment, participants won points if they drew a marked card and lost points if they drew an unmarked card. When asked to guess what kind of card they would draw next, they overestimated the probability of drawing a marked card.[36] Kennedy and his team similarly overestimated desired outcomes and underestimated undesired ones. They conflated desirability with probability. As a result, their ill-informed preconceptions—central to the operation's later failure—went unquestioned in the days leading up to the invasion.

A man-in-a-hurry who liked shortcuts—he had not "waited his turn" for the presidency—Kennedy, like Eisenhower before him, wanted a quick, low-cost way of deposing Castro and as soon as he was inaugurated, Dulles and Bissell set out to sell the new president and his advisors on the existing operation. Polished, articulate, and effective advocates, the two gave their first comprehensive briefing on the planned invasion, complete with detailed charts and colored maps set up on easels, just eight days after Kennedy assumed office. Pointers in hand, Dulles and Bissell walked the receptive and impressionable audience gathered around the cabinet table through the scenario. Kennedy had considerable confidence in the CIA. ("If I need some material fast or an idea fast, CIA is the place to go," he said. "The State Department takes four or five days to [give me] a simple yes or no answer.") He even went so far as to proclaim that those involved in the intelligence business possessed skills "not available to ordinary mortals."[37] The agency's cultivated secrecy was seductive and convenient.

Though Kennedy had known of the plan in general terms since the previous summer, this was the first he heard of the enlarged scale of the operation—now the biggest in CIA history. It envisioned a dawn amphibious landing of the exile force at Trinidad, a large town on the southern coast of Cuba near the Escambray Mountains, that its advocates said would trigger a popular uprising with the "active support" of one-fourth of the population and snowballing defections, resulting in Castro's overthrow. (Rival leaders of the Miami-based Cuban exile community, seeking CIA support and funding for their particular factions as they constantly competed and maneuvered with one another for influence, had consistently and intentionally claimed to have large followings on the island—assertions they knew Washington wanted to believe but that later proved to be grossly exaggerated.) If an uprising did not occur, Bissell and Dulles explained, the exiles could take refuge in the Escambray Mountains and subsequently conduct guerrilla operations from there against Castro, just as Castro had done from the Sierra Maestra against Batista. Neither Kennedy nor any of his advisors asked if the exiles had received amphibious warfare and guerrilla training, which they had not.

Bissell concluded his briefing by advising Kennedy that the plan stood "a good chance of overthrowing Castro"[38] and urged Kennedy not to delay. "You can't mañana this thing," Bissell told the president. ("It will be infeasible to hold all these forces together

beyond early April," he wrote him a short time later. "Their motivation for action is high but their morale cannot be maintained
if their commitment to action is long delayed.") When Kennedy
said he wanted more time to consider the invasion plan, Dulles
rushed him, saying, "That's understandable, Mr. President, but
there isn't much time." He and Kennedy then retired to the Oval
Office, where Dulles moved to close the deal. "I stood right here
at Ike's desk and told him I was certain our Guatemalan operation
would succeed," said Dulles, pausing for effect, "and, Mr. President,
the prospects for this plan are even better than they were for that
one." "They didn't just brief us on the Cuban operation," said one
of those in the Cabinet Room that day, "they sold us on it."[39]

Kennedy and his advisors met with the Joint Chiefs of Staff
three days later to hear the chiefs' evaluation of the CIA's invasion
plan. Older men with distinguished war records, the chiefs, in full
medaled regalia and tiers of service ribbons advertising their experience and accomplishments, deeply impressed Kennedy and his
team, who had been junior officers in World War II. That view of
the four-star generals and admirals as larger-than-life military leg-
ends vastly reduced the odds of the chiefs' evaluation being questioned. ("How impressive it was to see the Joint Chiefs of Staff
show up with all that fruit salad,"* Kennedy told an aide afterward. "And they had colonels carrying their pointers and maps!"[40])
At this early stage of his presidency, McGeorge Bundy later recalled, Kennedy "tended to ask the Chiefs" rather than McNamara
for advice on military matters.[41] Fresh to the Oval Office, he had
no awareness of what the chiefs might *not* tell him. Kennedy also
hesitated to start off on the wrong foot with them at a time when
McNamara was asserting real (and therefore sensitive) control
over the military's roles, missions, and budgets.

Though the chiefs had been tasked with assessing the CIA plan's
military feasibility, they had not analyzed it as carefully and thoroughly as they would have a plan of their own. This hesitancy was
rooted in both a sense of possession and political and methodical

---

* Gold braid, medals, and ribbons on their caps and uniforms.

positioning. They hadn't dreamed up the plan and weren't in charge of it. It wasn't their responsibility and therefore didn't feel obliged to strongly criticize it.* Joint Chiefs of Staff chairman General Lyman Lemnitzer and his staff director, Lieutenant General Earle Wheeler,† eventually conceded as much. "You couldn't expect us to say this plan is no damn good, you ought to call it off; that's not the way you do things in government," claimed Lemnitzer several decades later, quickly adding: "The responsibility was not ours."[42] The military "didn't step forward and say, 'This ain't going to go,'" admitted Wheeler, because "this was not per se a military operation."[43] Although McGeorge Bundy did not perceive it at the time, he explained the military's outlook in hindsight: "The individual services in the Pentagon survived by tolerance of one another's favorite weapons and deployments; they were bureaucratically cautious about dissecting another agency's most cherished enterprise."[44] The chiefs' failure to thoroughly vet the plan also reflected the restrictions imposed by the CIA's compartmentalization ("need-to-know") rule, which precluded use of Joint Staff personnel for the usual detailed operational analysis. Without a comprehensive briefing and without the commonplace fat, tabbed binder of documents containing all the elements of the plan (which did not even exist), the operation's crucial military dimensions—how long the exile force could hold the invasion beaches, how they would get ammunition ashore from freighters quickly, how they could keep the airstrip adjacent to them open, how they could prevent Castro's troops from approaching the beaches—therefore went almost entirely unaddressed and unassessed.

---

* The military did speak up, however, when *its* interests were at stake. At one point, Rusk suggested landing the exiles in southeastern Cuba, where they could retreat to the nearby U.S. naval base at Guantanamo Bay if necessary. Joint Chiefs of Staff chairman General Lyman Lemnitzer and chief of naval operations Arleigh Burke protested vigorously. "Rusk later said," wrote a White House aide, "that they would be perfectly ready to put the President's reputation on the block but wouldn't let anyone touch their precious Guantanamo." Arthur M. Schlesinger Jr. to Robert Kennedy, Robert F. Kennedy Papers, JFKL.

† Wheeler would become chairman himself in 1964 and serve in the position until 1970.

The chiefs were not without an opinion: noting the operation's logistical vulnerabilities, they asserted that the only course of action certain to succeed would require overt American air support of the invasion—which Eisenhower had dismissed and now Kennedy again ruled out in order to avoid inflaming Latin American popular resentment against a long history of U.S. armed intervention in the Western Hemisphere. Presuming the exile invasion would meet light resistance and a popular uprising quickly would follow*—crucial and optimistic assumptions that again no one closely questioned—the chiefs told the president the plan stood "a fair chance of ultimate success." Kennedy and his civilian advisors interpreted the chiefs' remarks to mean they endorsed the plan and believed it would work. The chiefs had carefully and cagily hedged, however. No one had asked them precisely what they meant by "fair chance"—and the chiefs had not volunteered their assessment: 30 percent. Rusk later wrote that the chiefs should have "come clean with an honest, professional, military judgment regarding its probability of success."[45] Yet he, too, had not pushed for clarification.

Wanting the greater confirmation and perhaps the political cover, Kennedy ordered the chiefs to review the CIA's plan in greater detail. The chiefs set up a committee comprising two air force and two navy officers—but none of the military intelligence agencies' Latin American specialists—under the chairmanship of Major General David Gray. Although the CIA retained control of invasion planning, Bissell later wrote that the Gray Committee "nevertheless effectively had the power to pass or reject the operation as it took shape."[46] The committee visited the CIA and traveled to Guatemala for a firsthand look at the exile combatants—for all of forty-eight hours. They reported that the invasion force seemed capable enough, a carefully worded assessment. They remained in daily contact with the CIA, assisted in operational planning by

---

* No one noticed the contradiction between this assumption and the fact that the operation had been planned, in part, because of the *absence* of organized resistance inside Cuba.

the air force, and regularly updated the chiefs. The air force, still smarting from the CIA's running the U-2, SR-71, and Corona satellite reconnaissance programs, which it thought should have been under its jurisdiction, participated reluctantly and with no particular motivation to help the CIA. The committee's air force officers met with Brigade 2506's Cuban and volunteer Alabama Air National Guard pilots, examined their planes—old, slow-moving B-26 light bombers whose limited fuel capacity meant they could spend only a short time over the invasion beaches—and even flew on a practice mission with them. "There was no expression on [Gray's] part in any way that he felt the mission couldn't be accomplished the way we had planned it," recalled the CIA official in charge of air operations.[47] Following Gray's shuffle, the chiefs muted their lingering doubts about the plan—the CIA "had the action" in bureaucratic parlance and the military didn't want to second-guess it.[48] McGeorge Bundy later summarized this sensibility: "It's the other fellow's property . . . The Joint Chiefs really didn't regard this as their main business, and therefore if they responded honestly and straightforwardly to the President's questions, they didn't have a campaigner's need to go on and say, 'Please don't do this.'"[49] As a result, their concern about the likelihood of achieving surprise, and its negative consequences, was buried in the annexes of the report—excluded from the executive summary read by busy government officials—that they submitted to McNamara on March 11. They did not frankly advise what most of them believed: the self-imposed limitations robbed the venture of a chance to succeed. A postmortem inquiry into the debacle chaired by General Maxwell Taylor concluded that the military "took active part in considering changes to the plan as it developed into final form, did not oppose the plan and by their acquiescing in it gave others the impression of approval."[50]

Rusk, McNamara, and Bundy served Kennedy no better. All of them harbored reservations about the plan, but kept those reservations to themselves. Deferential, the three of them relinquished their chance to ask tough questions and to offer a cold and objective appraisal of the proposed course of action. If they had done so, they probably would have identified the fatal weaknesses in the CIA's plan. "I was uneasy," McNamara later said. "Neither Dean Rusk nor I were enthusiastic about it, but neither one of us said, 'Don't do it.'"[51] Unsure in their new jobs, they were reluctant to express vague (and potentially embarrassing) doubts in front of a new boss with whom they had not yet established a close bond. "We were just freshmen," Bundy later admitted, "and as freshmen you don't go in and say, 'Dammit, Mr. President, you're not getting the right kind of information.'"[52] "At that time I was feeling my way in my relations with President Kennedy," Rusk would confess. "We had just taken office [and] we were still trying to arrange our relationships with each other." Rusk felt "highly skeptical" about the operation "from the very beginning" and he claimed that he registered that skepticism with the president—but only privately. At the many meetings on the operation, however, Rusk limited himself to raising relatively softball questions. "Looking back on it, I made a mistake in being so tactful. I should have made my opposition clear in the meetings themselves and taken a position in front of those who were proposing the operation." He concluded, "I failed [Kennedy] in not making my own opposition more dramatic and more forceful."[53]

"The truth is I did not understand the plan very well and did not know the facts," McNamara later confessed. "I let myself become a passive bystander."[54] He assumed that because the chiefs did not oppose the plan, they approved it. Bissell, who observed McNamara at the White House meetings, assessed him perceptively in his memoirs: "It is my feeling that at that very early moment in the administration McNamara was probably diffident about voicing opinions on strictly military matters in the presence of the chairman of the Joint Chiefs, which is understandable. He was a civilian; he had no recent military experience . . . and none at high levels of command. In the presence of a uniformed representative of the Joint Chiefs, a civilian newly arrived in office did well to keep a low profile."[55] McNamara came to deeply regret his assent and believed the chiefs should have been more forthright in pointing out their reservations about the shortcomings in the

CIA's plan. Thereafter, he became acutely conscious of his responsibility to scrutinize all recommendations the chiefs submitted to the president. McNamara would never again automatically accept the chiefs' opinions without carefully probing the underlying assumptions and facts on which the recommendations were based and pressing them to explain what they really meant. When he left the Pentagon seven years later, McNamara publicly stated that he still felt burdened for having misadvised Kennedy on the Bay of Pigs. It was, he later said, "a *serious* error of judgment."[56] While the lessons he drew from the experience were admirable, at least one of them would turn out to be hazardous: "Don't rely on advice from anybody"[57]—which could sometimes mean listen to nobody but yourself.

Kennedy bore a considerable degree of responsibility himself. He had a casual, informal, ad-hoc operating style and didn't like elaborate structures and cumbersome red tape. Determined to reduce the size and complexity of the NSC in order to make it leaner and more responsive—to get the NSC, like the country, "moving again" to use the slogan of his election campaign—he dismantled the NSC's planning and operations coordinating boards in the first days of his presidency. This action made the NSC smaller, as Kennedy intended, but it also eliminated half of its staff, thereby greatly reducing the ability to thoroughly vet prospective plans and policies such as the proposed exile invasion of Cuba. What is more, the president's brother and closest confidant, attorney general Robert Kennedy, admonished doubters that once the president made up his mind, they had a duty to open their mouths only in support of the operation.

Not everyone remained silent. William Fulbright of Arkansas, a Washington veteran and chairman of the Senate Foreign Relations Committee, shared his adamant opposition with Kennedy privately, warning that such an enterprise risked undoing Latin American goodwill toward the United States and strengthening Castro's appeal throughout the hemisphere by making him appear as a beleaguered underdog bullied by its big neighbor to the north. In the executive branch, only Arthur Schlesinger, a relatively low-level White House assistant, explicitly counseled the president against the operation. "However well disguised any action might be," he wrote Kennedy, "it will be ascribed to the United States." He added, "Worst of all, this would be your first dramatic foreign policy initiative. At one stroke, it would dissipate all the extraordinary good will which has been rising toward the new Administration through the world. It would fix a malevolent image of the new Administration in the minds of millions." Fulbright and Schlesinger's misgivings carried far less weight with Kennedy than did the CIA's confidence and the Joint Chiefs' apparent endorsement, but their warnings about the plan's potential political fallout in Latin America did prompt the president to direct Dulles and Bissell to "reduce the noise level" of the operation and make America's role in it more "quiet."[58]

That Kennedy gave the agency only four days to rework the plan and come up with a "less spectacular" alternative seems foolish—as does the fact that the CIA agreed to it. Still, things rolled forward. Bissell now prepared a nighttime amphibious landing at the Bay of Pigs, a sparsely inhabited area on the Caribbean coast south of Havana with good beaches and a few scattered cottages and hamlets that lay a hundred miles west of Trinidad. Both were chosen because they addressed Kennedy's determination to reduce the noise level of the operation, but nighttime amphibious landings are notoriously difficult—only one had been successfully accomplished throughout all of World War II—and the Bay of Pigs lay eighty miles west of the Escambray Mountains, thereby mooting the escape-to-become-guerrillas fallback option. In fact, there would be no place for the brigade to go if the landing failed. Bissell did not appreciate or emphasize the significance of these changes when he briefed the president on the revised plan on March 15, and neither Kennedy nor any of his advisors picked up on them or their implications as they discussed the plan for all of twenty minutes. After the meeting, Bundy still believed "a substantial portion of the force would almost certainly be able to survive for a prolonged period in guerrilla operations," while McNamara thought that if a popular uprising failed to occur, the exiles "would be split up into a guerrilla force and moved into the Escambrays."[59] Bissell did nothing to disabuse Kennedy and his advisors of this notion. But they might have disabused themselves if they had studied the geography of southwestern Cuba.

As before, the lack of curiosity and analysis among Kennedy and his team was devastating. The invasion beaches around the Bay of Pigs were surrounded by the Zapata Swamp, which the CIA asserted would actually be a positive by providing a natural defense perimeter for the exiles once they landed, as well as a small airstrip at the nearby town of Jagüey Grande for supporting air cover. Dulles and Bissell again described Castro's army as a low-grade military force, poorly equipped and trained, weakened by dissension, and unprepared to resist even a small-scale invasion. They estimated that "approximately 75 to 80 percent of militia units will defect when it becomes evident that the real fight against Castro has begun" and dismissed the Cuban air force as "entirely disorganized" with "for the most part obsolete and inoperative" aircraft and "almost non-existent" effectiveness. This contradicted an assessment of Castro's military capability by British intelligence (London still had an embassy presence in Cuba). "In spite of the alienation of the middle class," Britain's Joint Intelligence Committee informed the CIA before the invasion, "the hard core of fanatical support for the regime, backed by an efficient propaganda and security apparatus, is likely to be able to resist attempts, from within or from outside Cuba, to overthrow the regime."[60] Emotionally invested in the success of their invasion plan, and carried along by the momentum generated by their strong commitment to resolving the Cuban problem, Dulles and Bissell chose to ignore this conflicting and troubling assessment as they did any internal concerns. When CIA inspector general Lyman Kirkpatrick—hearing gossip about the operation's haphazard organization from mid-level members of the task force who feared it would blow up in the agency's face—had gone to Dulles with his concerns, Dulles waved Kirkpatrick off, telling him he "didn't want to hear about it."[61] Kennedy and his advisors did not probe deeply enough to become aware of either contention. Instead, Bundy told the president that the CIA had "done a remarkable job of reframing the landing plan so as to make it unspectacular and quiet, and plausibly Cuban in its essentials."[62]

There was more. The CIA had broadened the original plan from a guerrilla infiltration to an amphibious invasion *precisely because* it had been unable to organize effective internal resistance to the Castro regime. Indeed, the chief of the CIA Analytical Division's Western Hemisphere Desk, whom Bissell did not consult, had received reports that resistance units in the Escambray Mountains were starving to death because the local peasants refused to feed them.[63] ("If there was a resistance to Fidel Castro," Kirkpatrick later acidly noted, "it was mostly in Miami."[64]) No one involved in the deliberations noted or analyzed this glaring and fundamental contradiction. Former secretary of state Dean Acheson, who did not participate in the deliberations, punctured the wishful thinking and self-delusion—temporarily—when Kennedy informed him of the plan at a private meeting on another matter in the Oval Office in late March. "Are you serious?" Acheson asked. "It isn't necessary to call in Price Waterhouse [an accounting firm] to discover that 1,500 exiles aren't as good as 25,000 Cubans."[65] Despite Acheson's warning, planning for the invasion moved forward to its tragic denouement.

Meanwhile pressure for a decision mounted. Cuba's rainy season neared, East Bloc arms shipments continued to increase Castro's military strength, Guatemalan president Miguel Ydígoras wanted the exiles out, the exiles themselves were growing restless—some had begun complaining that the United States was preventing them from liberating their homeland, and prompted by leaks and lack of subterfuge newspapers had begun running front-page stories about an impending invasion. Kennedy also faced what Dulles called "the disposal problem": If Washington did not unleash the brigade, what to do with it? Where would it go? Kennedy did not want 1,500 disgruntled Cuban émigrés ending up in Miami complaining that the president was weak and vacillating.* Domestic

---

* Ironically, this is precisely what would happen after the failure of the invasion.

politics contributed, too: thwarting or dismantling a major CIA initiative to unseat Castro could invite a storm of conservative criticism of the narrowly elected president. For a former navy lieutenant junior grade to cancel an operation initiated and supported by a former five-star general who had commanded the largest—and most successful—amphibious invasion in history (D-Day) would, as Arthur Schlesinger later put it, "have been hard to explain" to the Republican opposition.[66]

Kennedy acknowledged the difficulties and dangers. When Arthur Schlesinger asked him, "What do you think about this damned invasion?" he replied, "I think about it as little as possible."[67] But the enormous benefits that would accrue if the operation succeeded, combined with the CIA's powerful advocacy and the chiefs' ostensible endorsement, outweighed whatever doubts remained in the mind of a president who, in the words of an aide, "did not yet feel he could trust his own instincts against the judgments of recognized experts."[68] There was something else at work, too. Whatever the risks of the operation, deep down Kennedy believed in his own good fortune. "When Jack Kennedy was elected," Clark Clifford recalled, "he had everything going for him. Within a month after he became President, if he had run again [the excitement about the new, young, dynamic administration meant that] he would have been elected by [a margin of] ten or fifteen percent instead of by one tenth of one percent." "He had won the [1960 Democratic] nomination and election against all the odds," wrote Arthur Schlesinger later. "Everyone around him thought he had the Midas touch and could not lose."[69]

At a meeting on April 3 in the small conference room just off the secretary of state's office on the seventh floor of the new State Department Building on the west end of the Mall near the Lincoln Memorial, Kennedy went around a crowded table, jabbing his finger in a typical gesture, and asked each of those present in turn whether he favored or opposed the impending operation. Everyone except Fulbright and Rusk—who remained silent—endorsed the plan. Kennedy slept on the matter that night. The next morning, he called a smaller meeting in the Oval Office attended only by Dulles, Rusk, and McNamara. Kennedy told them to go ahead, with the understanding—to be made explicitly clear to the Cuban exiles beforehand—that there would be no U.S. military support for the invasion and that he reserved the right to cancel the invasion up to the last minute.

Still, discussions continued. Kennedy's explicit ban on U.S. military support for the invasion prompted Bissell's two planning assistants, Jacob Esterline of the CIA's Operations Directorate and Jack Hawkins, a marine corps colonel and World War II veteran whom the Pentagon had assigned as liaison to the agency for this operation, to threaten resignation because they believed the prohibition made it "impossible to win." Bissell met with Esterline and Hawkins at his home in the upscale Cleveland Park neighborhood of northwest Washington on Saturday morning, April 8. Bissell sat them down in his living room and urged them not to resign, telling them the operation would go ahead with or without them—in effect, "Be good soldiers." "He talked us into continuing," Esterline ruefully recalled.[70] Two days later, Bissell called on Robert Kennedy at his Justice Department office and told the attorney general that the impending invasion's chance of success was two out of three, and in the worst case the exiles could take to the mountains and become guerrillas.[71]

Bissell based this conclusion, in part, on earlier experience. When the 1954 Guatemalan operation appeared about to fail, Eisenhower had actually reversed his prohibition and authorized use of American military aircraft to ensure victory. Bissell assumed that Kennedy would, too; the pressure of events would compel him to intervene with U.S. forces. "It never occurred to Bissell that if push came to shove, Kennedy wouldn't put in his stack," Bundy said later. "Once engaged," Bissell believed, "Kennedy wouldn't allow it to fail."[72] Dulles certainly thought so; as he later wrote in an unpublished article, "I [had] seen a good many operations which started out like the B[ay] of P[igs]—insistence on complete secrecy, non-involvement of the United States—initial reluctance to authorize supporting actions. This limitation tends to disappear as the needs of the operation become clarified." Tactically, pushing Kennedy now would be counterproductive. "We did not want to raise issues which might only harden the decision against the type of actions we required," Dulles elaborated. "We felt that when the chips were down—when the crisis arose in reality, any request required for success would be authorized rather than permit the enterprise to fail . . . We believed that in a time of crisis we would gain what we might lose if we provoked an argument" about restrictions they deemed unwise.[73]

For this reason, Dulles and Bissell may have directed their subordinates to go even further than discussed with the president and his core deputies. According to journalist Haynes Johnson, CIA operatives told the Cuban exile force that if Kennedy decided to call off the invasion at the last minute, they should stage a fake mutiny and go ahead anyway.[74] (Looking back, Esterline always assumed that "we couldn't stop the Cubans even if we wanted to," but insisted "flat out" that Dulles and Bissell did not act as rogue elephants.[75]) Bissell and Dulles (and later the chiefs) did, however, misread and misjudge Kennedy, continuing to see things as they had always wanted to see them, assuming particulars were universal patterns. Anticipating just such pressure to directly engage, Kennedy confronted it head-on at a press conference he held in the State Department auditorium on April 12 in order to put the CIA and the chiefs on notice and to inoculate himself in the event the invasion did not go according to plan. During the press conference, he obliquely but unequivocally warned the CIA and the chiefs that "there will not be, under any conditions, an intervention in Cuba by the United States armed forces." Kennedy privately explained his thinking to close aides. "The minute I land one Marine," he said, "we're in this thing up to our necks. I can't get the United States into a war and then lose it, no matter what it takes. I'm not going to risk [it] . . . *Is that understood gentlemen?*"[76]

Meanwhile, Bissell dispatched Colonel Hawkins to Puerto Cabezas on the Caribbean coast of Nicaragua, where the exiles had been moved to board the ships that would take them to Cuba, to reiterate to the men Kennedy's caveat that it could not expect any U.S. military support and to provide a final assessment on the eve of the invasion. Hawkins delivered the message and then cabled Washington: "My observations the last few days have increased my confidence in the ability of this force to accomplish not only initial combat missions, but also the ultimate objective of Castro's overthrow." The amphibious invasion expert on Bissell's team, and the man on whom Kennedy relied to make a final on-the-spot assessment, Hawkins had participated in *one* amphibious landing in his entire military career—at Iwo Jima in February 1945, as part of three marine divisions comprising 60,000 men supported by a massive U.S. naval and air bombardment. "The Brigade and battalion commanders now know all details of the plan and are enthusiastic. They say it is a Cuban tradition to join a winner and they have supreme confidence they will win against the best Castro has to offer. I share their confidence." He added, "The Brigade is well organized and is more heavily armed and better equipped in some respects than U.S. infantry units . . . The Brigade now numbers 1,400; a truly formidable force."[77] His optimism was ridiculous but for the lack of anyone willing to ridicule him. The colonel's upbeat appraisal allayed the president's lingering concerns, wishful thinking on the part of both Hawkins and Kennedy ruling the day. Kennedy became so assured that on the day before the invasion, he directed Bissell to reduce the scale of the planned exile air strikes— make it "minimal," he said—in order to reduce the invasion's visibility.[78] This decision revealed just how deluded he was about the pending operation, that cutting back on the exile air strikes would fool the world that America was an innocent bystander. Furthermore, Kennedy did not grasp the integral role that air strikes would play in the invasion plan, and Bissell did not explain it to him at this critical moment; instead, the CIA man merely responded by cutting the planned sixteen aircraft to eight.

The larger a covert operation, the greater the likelihood there is of leaks. The "plausibly deniable" plan—an ambitious military undertaking clandestine in name only—was known to at least 1,543 exiled Cubans. Only a single CIA officer was assigned counterintelligence responsibility for the operation. Not surprisingly, spies working for Castro's Dirección Generale de Inteligencia learned of the operation almost as soon as planning for it began. In a widely publicized speech on April 23, 1960, Cuban foreign minister Raúl Roa declared, "I can guarantee categorically that Guatemalan territory is being used at this very time . . . as a bridgehead for an invasion of our country." Six months later, on October 7, Roa publicly revealed the location of the exile training camp in Guatemala, based on intelligence obtained through Cuban espionage.[79] Three weeks after that, the Guatemalan newspaper *La Hora* published an article describing the CIA training base and indicating that preparation for an "invasion" of Cuba was "well under way." By the end of 1960, the invasion plan had become an open secret in Miami's loquacious Cuban exile community, which according to local police included at least a hundred Castro agents. One Cuban exile offered the name and phone number of the CIA's Miami station chief to a reporter friend in a bar within an hour of the journalist's arrival in Miami.[80]

About the same time, Stanford University professor Ronald Hilton, a Latin American specialist conducting research in Guatemala, learned that the "secret" base's existence and purpose were common knowledge throughout the country. The town near the base at Rancho Helvetia, Retalhuleu, had more than a hundred residents who belonged to the Guatemalan Communist Party, including the mayor. A railroad ran alongside a field just outside the base's fence and exiles often waved to people on passing trains. Hilton's discovery, first published in Stanford's *Hispanic American Report*, made its way into an editorial published by *The Nation*, a liberal national weekly critical of American foreign policy, on November 19, titled, "Are We Training Cuban Guerrillas?" The *New York Times'* executive editor instructed the paper's Central American correspondent to look into the story. On January 10, 1961, the *New York Times* published a front-page story with a three-column headline that read: "U.S. Helps Train an Anti-Castro Force at Secret Guatemalan Air-Ground Base." The article, accompanied by a map, reported that "commando-like forces are being drilled in guerrilla warfare tactics by foreign personnel, mostly from the

United States . . . The United States is assisting this effort not only in personnel but in material and the construction of ground and air facilities." Articles appeared identifying the former naval air station near Miami, Opa-Locka, used to ferry exiles to the training camp. On April 7, the *Times* ran another page-one story that said exile training had been discontinued because an invasion was "imminent." "I can't believe what I'm reading," Kennedy exploded to his press secretary, Pierre Salinger, after going through the article in the Oval Office that morning. "Castro doesn't need agents over here. All he has to do is read our papers!"[81] Kennedy kitchen cabinet member Robert Lovett proclaimed that given press coverage, "it became apparent that it was going to be the best advertised assault ever made."[82]

Those who planned the ostensibly covert operation were "all aware of what was coming out in the press," Bissell later noted, adding "the whole world accepted what was going on as a U.S. government operation." How could it not? "You can't say that 1500 Cubans got together and acquired aircraft and ships and ammunition and radios all by their little selves," noted Bissell's CIA colleague Robert Amory after the operation. "The American hand would clearly show in it." Bissell himself understood this, but as he later admitted, "I was very much afraid of what might happen if I said, 'Mr. President, this operation might as well be made open because the role of the United States certainly cannot be hidden.'" Kennedy and his advisors, for their part, stubbornly continued to believe—despite mounting evidence to the contrary—that the fig leaf of "plausible deniability" based on the Guatemala model remained in place. None of them could bring themselves to see that "plausible deniability," as the CIA's Inspector General wrote in his postmortem of the disaster, "was a pathetic illusion." Wishful thinking became self-delusion, reinforced by the silence of those like Bissell who knew better, Washington's eagerness to get rid of Castro, and Kennedy's naïve assumption that the newspapers already writing about the pending invasion would let it drop afterward.[83]

Thus, on April 17, when the invasion commenced, Fidel Castro grasped what was coming. He knew a great deal about the CIA's earlier operation against Árbenz—his deputy Ernesto "Che" Guevara had been living in Guatemala when it occurred, his spies had infiltrated the exile training camp, and he could read U.S. and Latin American newspaper reports about the preparations. Having learned that the two-stage invasion plan included preliminary air strikes from Guatemala against the Cuban air force base at San Antonio de los Baños south of Havana and the military base at Camp Libertad on the western outskirts of the city, Castro ostentatiously parked his obsolete planes in plain view, wing tip to wing tip, and dispersed and camouflaged his small fleet of operable Sea Fury fighter-bombers and T-33 jet trainers,* surrounding them with anti-aircraft batteries. As a result, the exiles destroyed only five of the obsolete aircraft on the runway and damaged a dozen more, but only one each of the deadly Sea Furies and T-33s was disabled—a near total failure of the CIA's plan to soften up the Cuban defenses before the full-on invasion. Afterward, Castro had more planes than pilots to fly them.

One of the exile planes displaying the markings of Castro's Revolutionary Air and Air Defense Force flew on to Miami, where, per the plan, the pilot proclaimed himself a defector who had single-handedly just bombed Castro's airfields. As with secretary of state Colin Powell in February 2003 on the eve of the American invasion of Iraq, the CIA persuaded U.S. ambassador to the United Nations Adlai Stevenson to unwittingly repeat the unfounded defector story at an emergency session of the United Nations the next day called by Cuban foreign minister Roa to denounce the United States as an aggressor, a sneak, and a liar. The press immediately began asking embarrassing questions about the pilot—his plane had a solid-metal nose (while Cuban air force planes of the same type had Plexiglas noses), the machine guns had tape over the barrels (and therefore had not been fired), and on closer examination the plane's markings differed noticeably from a recent genuine defector's identical aircraft.

---

* MiG jets had also reached Cuba by April 1961, but they were still in crates, unassembled, with no pilots trained to fly them.

The widely publicized Cuban attack in the United Nations against American foreign policy and administration credibility compelled Kennedy to cancel a planned second strike the night before the invasion. This had the effect of reducing the number of air strikes by 80 percent. (Even without this reduction, the total would have been only forty sorties*—hardly a substantial aerial campaign.) Bissell protested to Rusk, who, opposing a second air strike because of the political damage the first one had done at the United Nations, and speaking for the president (who was at his weekend retreat, Glen Ora, in Northern Virginia's hunt country), told Bissell that while the exile pilots were allowed to use the airstrip adjacent to the beach after the invasion began for close air support of the invasion force, they were not to bomb Cuban airfields or harbors or radio stations. Rusk offered Bissell the chance to argue his case directly with Kennedy over the phone, but Bissell mollifyingly—not permanently—demurred. Bissell and the chief of naval operations, Admiral Arleigh Burke, later lobbied Kennedy aggressively in person for direct American air support to save the invasion (the carriers USS *Boxer* and USS *Essex* with naval aircraft steamed offshore), assuming that the president would give in to the pressure of events. But Kennedy steadfastly refused, reiterating his earlier insistence—well known to Bissell and Burke—that U.S. forces would not be committed. Burke continued to press Kennedy nonetheless:

BURKE: Can I not send in an air strike?

KENNEDY: No.

BURKE: Can we send a few planes?

KENNEDY: No, because they could be identified as United States.

BURKE: Can we paint out their numbers on any of this?

KENNEDY: No.

BURKE: Can we get something in there?

KENNEDY: No.

---

* A sortie is one aircraft flying one mission.

BURKE: If you'll let me have two destroyers, we'll give gun-fire support and we can hold that beachhead with two ships forever.

KENNEDY: No.

BURKE: One destroyer, Mr. President.

KENNEDY: No.[84]

Admiral Burke seemed unwilling to accept a no order from his commander in chief, and Kennedy eventually consented to allow six unmarked navy jets from the U.S. carriers to provide an hour's air cover over the beach for the lumbering, propeller-driven B-26s. But because of a timing mix-up—Cuba was one hour ahead of Nicaragua—the B-26s arrived over the Bay of Pigs an hour before the jets. Two of the exile bombers were shot down and the others fled before the navy planes reached the scene. That was all Kennedy would do. He had explicitly pledged—both publicly and privately to the exile brigade—that U.S. military forces would not be involved and if the Cuban people would not rally to support the exile landing, he would not try to impose a new regime on them through American arms, with all the unpredictable and uncontrollable consequences that entailed.

A tragic fiasco ensued. On the eve of the landing, a tipped-off Castro rounded up and incarcerated nearly 100,000 opposition members, negating whatever likelihood of a spontaneous uprising existed. During the landings at Playa Girón (Blue Beach), just east of the entrance to the Bay of Pigs, and Playa Larga (Green Beach), at the apex of the bay, in the predawn hours of April 17, the small fiberglass boats carrying the camouflage-uniformed exiles ashore hit razor-sharp coral reefs that CIA charts had erroneously marked as sea grass and the invaders had to wade hundreds of feet laden with equipment in order to reach the beaches. Castro's small but lethal fleet of T-33s, armed with 20 mm cannons, and his Sea Furies, armed with rockets, pummeled the exile troops on the beaches and their two rust-bucket supply ships offshore, sinking the brigade's crucial ammunition reserves and communications equipment, along with vital food and medical supplies. The other two freighters fled to the open sea. Instead of taking out Cuban positions, the exiles' B-26s—some of them secretly piloted by Alabama Air National Guardsmen working for the CIA and skirting Kennedy's express prohibition on the use of U.S. personnel*—flew defensive missions over the next few days and suffered heavy casualties; four American pilots were killed. Castro mobilized his soldiers and militiamen faster than expected and took command at the scene—it was his favorite fishing spot and he knew the area well—by quickly moving 20,000 troops, tanks, and anti-aircraft artillery down the only highway in the area to the beaches, allowing him to isolate the invasion force. (Just as any realistic evaluation would have concluded, Castro's forces did not desert in any significant numbers and—especially with 100,000 opposition members behind bars—there was no popular uprising.) Aroused by what they perceived as another U.S. violation of Cuban sovereignty and independence, people rallied to Castro after the invasion began. Within three days, it was all over.

The Bay of Pigs invasion proved an utter disaster and a human tragedy. The exiles fought with great bravery against a vastly superior force, but 140 died fighting on or near the landing beaches and Castro captured and imprisoned nearly 1,200 of the exile invasion force—more than 80 percent of the total sent. The survivors endured twenty months in captivity, including televised humiliations, before eventually being exchanged for a ransom of food and medical supplies in December 1962. Rather than topple Castro, the invasion galvanized Cuban sentiment against the United States and enhanced Castro's reputation with the Cuban people as the brave David who had successfully thwarted the aggressive Goliath. "Castro's position is stronger than before the invasion attempt," the CIA reported ten days after the invasion, adding: his "hard-core supporters are more heavily armed and more enthusiastic on his behalf, and the widespread support which he has received abroad

---

* The CIA also skirted Kennedy's prohibition by using agency operatives as pathfinders to mark the invasion beaches for the first wave of the brigade to come ashore.

Front-page Headline of Bay of Pigs Invasion
John Frost Newspapers/Alamy Stock Photo

has probably increased his stature among many other Cubans." At a secret meeting in Uruguay four months later, Che Guevara sarcastically thanked NSC Latin American expert Richard Goodwin, who participated in the deliberations leading to the invasion, for the Bay of Pigs.

The failed invasion also drove Castro closer to the Soviet Union—precisely what the U.S. government had sought to prevent by launching it. On April 16, Castro for the first time publicly proclaimed a "socialist revolution" during his funeral oration in Havana's Revolution Square for Cubans killed in the CIA's pre-invasion air strikes. He said later: "Our Marxist-Leninist party was really born at Girón."*[85] The following year, Castro sent Che Guevara to Moscow to sign a defense pact that included the installation of Soviet nuclear missiles in Cuba to protect his regime against a second Bay of Pigs invasion—a development that led directly to the Cuban Missile Crisis of October 1962.

In the aftermath, Kennedy wondered in stunned humiliation, "How could anybody involved have thought such a plan would succeed?"[86] "The whole enterprise from beginning to end," concluded one Washington insider, "was a shocking example of what not to do as well as how not to do it."[87] It was an unmitigated disaster—a "perfect failure" in the apt words of historian Theodore Draper.[88] The debacle left Kennedy "almost in a state of shock," said one associate.[89] Robert Kennedy privately called it the darkest moment in his brother's life. "We got a big kick in the ass—and we deserved it," a chastened president admitted shortly after the disaster. "But maybe we'll learn something from it."[90]

An orgy of self-recrimination followed. Rusk, McNamara, and Bundy all told Kennedy they had failed him miserably and tendered their resignations. McNamara even volunteered to publicly acknowledge his responsibility. "After it was over," McNamara later recalled, "I went into the Oval Office and told the President, 'I knew where I was at the time the decision was made. I was at the table and nineteen out of twenty people said, "Go ahead." I am fully prepared to say I was one of those, and to say it publicly.'"[91] Kennedy brushed aside McNamara's offer. He did accept Dulles's and Bissell's resignations, telling Bissell (who was allowed to stay until

---

* The town closest to the invasion beaches, which Cubans have always used—rather than "the Bay of Pigs"—to refer to the invasion.

February 1962), "If this were a parliamentary government, I would have to resign and you, a civil servant, would stay on. But being the system of government it is—a Presidential government—you will have to resign."[92] He then went on national television, famously declared, "Victory has a hundred fathers and defeat is an orphan," and took sole public responsibility for the debacle.

In his mind, though, Kennedy felt the CIA had led him astray and the chiefs had skirted the line of insubordination. The latter conclusion stuck in McNamara's mind, too. Both he and Kennedy thereafter became reluctant to accept the military's advice at face value and grew guarded about its judgments. In this respect, the Bay of Pigs had a lasting effect not just on American policy toward Cuba but on American policy toward Vietnam in the years to come. This link between the Bay of Pigs and Vietnam would carry over to the Johnson administration because LBJ's senior advisors would be the same ones who served Kennedy.

Kennedy and his advisors emerged from the humiliating fiasco battered and bruised and wiser than when they had entered office three months earlier. Their naive confidence, certainty, and optimism had been tempered by experience. But the ill-considered invasion had inadvertently and unknowingly set in motion a chain of events that eighteen months later would trigger the gravest crisis of the Cold War, the closest the world has ever come to nuclear Armageddon—and which in turn, in tremendously important if not obvious ways, would shape America's descent into Vietnam.

CHAPTER 2

The Limits of Imagination

(April 1961–October 1962)

For most people, the Cuban Missile Crisis—the Cold War's most dangerous episode—seems unfathomably distant. But for people who lived through October 1962—both anxious participants and helpless bystanders—it was an episode of extreme tension and uncertainty. Because the missile crisis remains *the* most perilous moment in human history, the importance of understanding why it happened and what lessons it taught—both at the time and today (not one and the same)—remains undiminished, and essential to exploring what went wrong in Vietnam.

Kennedy and his advisors, encountering an unfamiliar situation fraught with danger, struggled at first to understand Soviet intentions and behavior. The turbulence and urgency of the situation disoriented and destabilized them and initially triggered emotional and impulsive reactions. But as the thirteen days of the Missile Crisis unfolded and they began to consider the situation more calmly and dispassionately, they began to overcome their failure of imagination. This enabled Kennedy and his advisors to look at things from the other side's perspective, and thus to understand motivations and dangers more clearly and fully. They came to think themselves into their adversary's shoes. Robert McNamara emphasized the cardinal importance of imaginative understanding when he drew retrospective lessons about the crisis. "Potential adversaries [must] take great care to try to understand how their actions will be interpreted by the other party," McNamara stressed. "We all performed poorly in this respect during the Missile Crisis."[1]

In fact, they ultimately performed well enough, in that the crisis was resolved without great loss of life. The failure would come later. Kennedy and his advisors overcame their limitations and acted with greater understanding of their adversary. In this way, they triumphed. But their triumph also deepened their anxiety about the intemperate judgment of senior military officers formed at the time of the Bay of Pigs. This anxiety, along with the illusion of control over events engendered by the successful resolution of the crisis, created its own legacy of unperceived dangers and limitations that would profoundly affect Vietnam decision-making.

The Bay of Pigs fiasco had humbled Kennedy and his fledgling administration. The new president and his team of advisors, who had engendered such anticipation and expectation upon entering office, now seemed bumbling, self-righteous, and stupid. Reflected Richard Goodwin, "The first adventure of the New Frontier had been a failure, and not an ordinary failure, but one that reeked of incompetence, of naïve and therefore dangerous militance; one that weakened the new president's pretension, so eloquently proclaimed just a few months before, to leadership of the free world."[2] "Kennedy has lost his magic," one European leader bitingly observed.[3] Kennedy himself worried, as he confided to journalist James Reston after the Vienna Summit with Khrushchev in June, that Khrushchev "thought anyone who was so young and inexperienced as to get into that mess could be taken. And anyone who got into it and didn't see it through had no guts," adding, "I've got a terrible problem."[4]

Nevertheless, by stoically accepting blame for the debacle immediately afterward, Kennedy increased his popular approval, astonishingly, from 72 to 82 percent. ("The worse I do, the more popular I get," he sardonically remarked. "If I had gone further, they would have liked me even more."[5]) Some of this public forgiveness reflected the fact that the failed operation had no direct and immediate consequences for Americans outside of Washington. But privately, Kennedy seethed with anger at himself and had uncharacteristically personal animus toward Castro for the humiliating setback. The most famous offspring of a famously competitive family, John Kennedy hated to lose, and was unaccustomed to defeat—particularly a self-inflicted one, the most painful kind. His pride, confidence, luck, and reputation had all been deeply wounded. Beneath his calm facade, he was furious—full of frustration, ire, and vengeance. JFK recognized that the Bay of Pigs had been the worst defeat of his career, and he had handed his critics a stick with which to beat him.

Dean Rusk was astonished that "this man with ice water in his veins" was so "emotional" about Castro. Kennedy "had no intention of allowing the likes of Castro to hand him his hat," observed Richard Bissell's successor at the CIA, Richard Helms. Kennedy decided to apply a family maxim: "Don't get mad, get even." "It was almost as simple as, goddammit, we lost the first round, let's win the second," recalled McGeorge Bundy.[6]

Disenchanted by the advice he had received from the CIA and the military, Kennedy turned to his brother Bobby, whom he trusted and who also lived by the family's retaliatory maxim. The president knew that he could expect the unvarnished truth from his brother. "Jack would never have admitted it," his close friend Lem Billings later wrote, "but from that moment on the Kennedy presidency became a sort of collaboration between them."[7]

This new arrangement became apparent at a White House meeting the morning after the failed invasion. Under Secretary of State Chester Bowles, who had let it be known to the press that he had opposed the exile landing, announced that the Bay of Pigs had secured Castro's regime from all but a U.S. military invasion. As Bowles spoke, Bobby Kennedy's eyes grew steely and his jaw set. "That's the most meaningless, worthless thing I've ever heard," he said, tearing into Bowles. "You people are so anxious to protect your own asses that you're afraid to do anything. All you want to do is dump the whole thing on the President. We'd be better off if you just quit and left foreign policy to someone else!" Throughout

Robert F. Kennedy
Everett Collection/Alamy Stock Photo

his brother's tirade, John Kennedy sat tapping a wooden pencil on his front teeth, saying nothing. "I suddenly became aware," recalled Goodwin, "that Bobby's harsh polemic reflected the President's own concealed emotions, privately communicated in some earlier, intimate conversation. I knew, even then, there was an inner hardness, often volatile anger beneath the outwardly amiable, thoughtful, carefully controlled demeanor of John Kennedy."[8]

The Kennedy brothers were not alone in their emotional reaction to the debacle. "We were hysterical about Castro at the time of the Bay of Pigs and thereafter," McNamara later acknowledged.[9] In the fall of 1961, the president and Bobby met with Bissell and "chewed him out"—"raked [him] stem to stern"—for "sitting on his ass and not doing anything about getting rid of Castro and the Castro regime."[10] Shortly thereafter, the president authorized a covert program of harassment and sabotage against Cuba code-named Operation MONGOOSE, predicated on the assumption that the economic embargo combined with covert operations would trigger an uprising against Castro—another example of wishful thinking.

"Bobby was his brother's wire-brush man," recalled Helms, "and he was tough as nails on Cuba." Though distant from the CIA in the government flow chart, RFK had no compunction about asserting himself, and his home, Hickory Hill, lay just a few miles down the road from agency headquarters in Langley, Virginia, which made it easy for him to drop in. On January 18, 1962, Bobby summoned Helms and several other senior CIA officials to his cavernous wood-paneled Justice Department office on Pennsylvania Avenue between the Capitol and the White House. Using "the most forceful language," according to Helms, the attorney general declared that Operation MONGOOSE had become "the top priority in the United States Government." "All else is secondary—no time, money, effort, or manpower is to be spared," emphasized Bobby in a low, precise voice. The president had told his brother that "the final chapter on Cuba has not been written—it's got to be done and will be done" and Bobby conveyed this warning loud and clear to everyone at the meeting.

Many in the CIA considered Bobby in particular "a wild man" on the subject of Castro. Bobby would "sit there, chewing gum, his tie loose, feet up on his desk, daring anyone to contradict him," recalled one official. "He was a little bastard, but he was the President's brother, the anointed guy, and you had to listen to him. Everybody felt that he would tell Big Brother if you didn't go along with what he was proposing." "Robert Kennedy's involvement in organizing and directing MONGOOSE became so intense," Richard Bissell recalled, "that he might as well have been deputy director for plans for the operation."[11] No one doubted for a minute that Bobby spoke directly for the president. RFK "meticulously followed the instructions of his brother," Rusk recalled of their relationship. "He never freewheeled; he [did] exactly what the President wanted him to do."[12]

Among those who had gathered with Bobby that day was Edward Lansdale. An air force brigadier general with a pencil-thin mustache, matinee-idol good looks, and considerable experience in the political dimension of warfare, he had helped Philippine leader Ramon Magsaysay suppress the Communist Hukbalahap insurgency in the early 1950s through a successful land reform program that had won back much of the countryside. He had also advised South Vietnamese leader Ngô Đình Diệm as head of the Saigon Military Mission. Lansdale became the model for Colonel Edwin Hillendale, a character in the best-selling 1958 political novel *The Ugly American* by William Lederer and Eugene Burdick, which traced U.S. failure in the Third World to disregard of local languages, cultures, and customs—a book that Kennedy so deeply admired that he sent a copy of it to each of his colleagues in the Senate. Kennedy believed Lansdale's sensitivity to these things and knowledge of counterinsurgency operations* in Asia would prove useful in developing a strategy against Castro and personally selected him to lead the effort.

Under the Kennedy brothers' prodding and pressure, Lansdale and the CIA went to work. Lansdale devised a plan focused on political and psychological warfare as well as proposed "attacks on the cadre of the regime, including key leaders"—such attacks to range from economic disruption to physical destruction.[13] MONGOOSE quickly became the agency's biggest clandestine operation, involving nearly 600 CIA and 5,000 contract employees, a budget of nearly $100 million, and a private armada of speedboats that regularly crisscrossed the Florida Straits; Miami grew into the largest CIA station in the world. The MONGOOSE activities seemed to entail little risk—CIA analysts doubted the Soviet Union would aid Cuba militarily in response to the covert operations. And "almost certainly," they concluded, "the USSR would not resort to general war for the sake of the Castro regime."[14]

"The Kennedys wanted action and they wanted it fast," one CIA official put it. "The President and his brother were ready to avenge

---

* Counterinsurgency (popularly known today as COIN) operations stressed the integration of military and civil efforts to win the "hearts and minds" of people among whom guerrilla warriors move, not only the targeting of guerrillas themselves. A comprehensive history of this subject is Max Boot, *Invisible Armies: An Epic History of Guerrilla Warfare from Ancient Times to the Present* (Liveright, 2013).

their personal embarrassment by overthrowing their enemy at any cost."[15] Spurred on by the Kennedys, Lansdale exhorted the CIA: "We want boom-and-bang on the island." The agency responded by shifting its emphasis away from refugee interrogations and intelligence collection to sabotage missions by infiltrating agents; planting bombs; attacking sugar refineries, oil storage facilities, and copper mines; circulating counterfeited pesos and ration books; and contaminating sugar exports and industrial imports. Helms described these activities as "nutty schemes born of the intensity of the pressure."[16] Yet the hectoring from the White House and the attorney general's office continued unabated. "My God, these Kennedys keep the pressure on about Castro," Helms told an associate.[17] "If anybody wants to see the whiplashes across my back inflicted by Bobby Kennedy, I will take my shirt off in public," he grumbled at CIA headquarters.[18]

The Bay of Pigs invasion gave Castro a pretext to crack down on his remaining domestic political opposition. In the months after the invasion, he consolidated his control by arresting another 20,000 people for counter-revolutionary activities and instituting a block surveillance program—in effect, a neighborhood spy system—that allowed the regime to keep a close eye on its citizens. From this strengthened position, Castro tentatively reached out to Kennedy in a way he never had before but could afford to do so now. At a conference of the Inter-American Economic and Social Council in Punta del Este, Uruguay, in August 1961, Castro's deputy Che Guevara asked to meet Richard Goodwin. They secretly rendezvoused at a private apartment in nearby Montevideo on August 16. "Che was wearing green fatigues and his usual scraggly beard," Goodwin wrote the president about their meeting. "Behind the beard his features are quite soft, almost feminine, and his manner is intense. He has a good sense of humor, and there was considerable joking back and forth during the meeting." Guevara told Goodwin that Cuba wanted a modus vivendi with the United States and said Cuba, in return, could agree not to make any political or military alliance with the USSR.[19]

Goodwin reported the overture to Kennedy upon his return to Washington. Preoccupied by the Berlin Crisis,* still smarting from the Bay of Pigs humiliation, and acutely aware that responding to an outreach from Communist Cuba would provoke fierce conservative criticism at home, Kennedy, too vulnerable and defensive after his string of foreign policy mishaps, ignored Guevara's overture. (When journalist Elie Abel sought Kennedy's cooperation on a book that August that he wished to write about JFK's first year in office, Kennedy responded, "Why would anyone want to write a book about an administration that has nothing to show for itself but a string of disasters?"[20]) Kennedy's decision to ignore Guevara's offer had fateful consequences. Just weeks later, on September 4, Castro petitioned Khrushchev for increased Soviet military assistance in the form of tanks and anti-aircraft missiles.[21]

Castro's request to the Soviets languished unanswered as Operation MONGOOSE got underway in the fall of 1961. Political leaders, like ordinary people, perceive things in ways that reinforce their preconceptions and fears. The sabotage operations unnerved Castro, who saw them as a precursor to another, much bigger invasion—which he believed the Americans would not abandon the next time. He believed a second invasion would involve the full force of the American military, not just 1,500 or so anti-Castro exiles. These fears compelled Castro to step up his request for So-

---

* A confrontation between the United States and the Soviet Union over the divided city of Berlin came to a head in the summer and fall of 1961. Hemorrhaging refugees from Communist East Germany, Khrushchev demanded the withdrawal of Allied occupation forces from West Berlin in order to unify the city under East German control. Kennedy responded by insisting on maintaining Allied access to West Berlin (per the Potsdam Agreement of 1945), calling up the reserves, increasing the draft, and expanding the nation's system of fallout shelters. Khrushchev closed the border between East and West Berlin through the construction of a wall to keep people in—a step that Kennedy tacitly accepted in order to defuse the crisis. "It's not a very nice solution," he told aides, "but a wall is a hell of a lot better than a war." After U.S. and Soviet tanks came face-to-face at Checkpoint Charlie dividing East from West Berlin, the crisis finally abated when Kennedy and Khrushchev mutually agreed to withdraw their tanks. The Berlin Wall finally came down in November 1989, when the Soviet Union imploded and the Cold War ended.

viet protection from what, to him, seemed an imminent American attack. On December 17, Castro conveyed his anxiety about "the expected U.S. aggression against Cuba" to the KGB Havana station chief and, later, Ambassador Aleksandr Alekseyev. Where were the tanks and missiles he had requested? Castro anxiously asked Alekseyev.[22] Soviet intelligence, meanwhile, observed the increased U.S. clandestine operations tied to MONGOOSE.

President Kennedy made two moves in early 1962 that heightened fears of a second American invasion in both Havana and Moscow. In a private meeting at the White House with Khrushchev's son-in-law Aleksei Adzhubei, editor of the newspaper *Izvestia*, on January 30, Kennedy told Adzhubei that Americans resented a hostile regime so close to their shores and then compared Cuba to Hungary (where Khrushchev had sent in tanks and troops in 1956 to suppress an anti-Soviet uprising). Kennedy's Hungary analogy implied his intent to defend America's sphere of influence in the Caribbean with force, just as the Soviets had defended theirs in Eastern Europe six years earlier.[23] Five days later, Kennedy broadened Eisenhower's partial embargo against Cuba into a total embargo, a measure clearly designed to cripple Castro's economy. These two events finally pushed Khrushchev to answer Castro's long-pending request. On February 8—more than five months after Castro had submitted it—he approved the request for increased Soviet military aid. "We were quite certain," Khrushchev later wrote, "that the [Bay of Pigs] invasion was only the beginning and that the Americans would not let Cuba alone . . . We were sure that the Americans would never reconcile themselves to the existence of Castro's Cuba . . . It was clear to me that we might very well lose Cuba if we didn't take some decisive steps in her defense."[24]

The United States, which created the first atomic bombs during the wartime Manhattan Project in 1945, made nuclear weapons the centerpiece of its postwar security posture. America possessed the scientific and technological know-how, nuclear weapons were relatively inexpensive to build and maintain, and they substituted for a politically and economically costly large standing army in peace-time. The Soviet Union had ended America's nuclear monopoly by detonating its first atomic bomb in 1949, but it continued to rely more heavily on the massive Red Army for its security. Hence-forth, the United States and the Soviet Union embarked on an arms race that accelerated during the 1950s as the relationship between Washington and Moscow deteriorated amid an atmosphere of mutual fear, suspicion, and distrust. By 1962, the Soviet Union had far fewer—one-sixth as many—nuclear intercontinental ballistic missiles (ICBMs) capable of striking the American homeland as the United States had ICBMs capable of striking the Russian home-land. (The disparity in overall destructive power was even greater: Russia had 300 nuclear warheads against America's 5,000.[25]) But Moscow had an equivalent number of nuclear medium-range bal-listic missiles (MRBMs) with a range of 1,200 nautical miles. In late April, while vacationing on the Black Sea coast of Crimea, Khrushchev met with Soviet defense minister Marshal Rodion Malinovsky. Malinovsky pointed over the Black Sea and noted that the United States had recently deployed MRBMs (Jupiter missiles)—which the Americans considered (and called) "defensive"—at Çiğli Air Base in western Turkey; each carried a 1.5-megaton nuclear warhead and could reach Moscow in just under seventeen min-utes. The United States had also agreed through the North Atlantic Treaty Organization (NATO)* to send Polaris ballistic missile sub-marines to patrol off the Turkish coast. Khrushchev, an impulsive man who feared and resented America's nuclear superiority and was thus particularly alarmed by the deployment of the MRBMs in Turkey, said: "Rodion Yakovlevich, what if we throw a hedge-hog down Uncle Sam's pants?"[26] Khrushchev had hit upon the idea of deploying Soviet MRBMs and supporting military person-nel to Castro's Cuba. Such deployments, he believed, would deter the United States from invading Cuba, eliminate the imbalance in nuclear striking power between America and Russia by doubling the number of Soviet missiles that could reach the United States,

---

* America's military alliance with its Western European allies.

give America a taste of its own medicine (stationing nuclear missiles near its adversary's homeland), and discourage Castro from seeking mainland China's help, the Soviet Union's increasingly assertive rival within the Communist camp.* Such a bold and unprecedented move—Moscow had never deployed nuclear weapons outside of Eurasia—might solve four of Khrushchev's problems in a single stroke.

Khrushchev had no intention, however, of using the missiles. When Anatoly Dobrynin, head of the Russian Foreign Ministry's American Department, prepared to leave Moscow in early March to take up his new ambassadorial post in Washington, Khrushchev "plainly told me," Dobrynin later wrote, "that I should always bear in mind that war with the United States was inadmissible; this was above all." Khrushchev emphasized to Kremlin associates that the Soviet missiles in Cuba would "not in any case be used."[27] "Any fool can start a war," he told them, but "once he's done so, even the wisest of men are helpless to stop it—especially if it's a nuclear war . . . The main thing was that the installation of our missiles in Cuba would restrain the United States from precipitous military action against Castro's government. In addition to protecting Cuba, our missiles would [equalize] what the West likes to call 'the balance of power.' The Americans had surrounded our country with military bases and threatened us with nuclear weapons, and now they would learn just what it feels like to have enemy missiles pointing at [them]."[28] An earthy Ukrainian—his grandfather had been a serf, his father a coal miner, and he had been illiterate into his twenties—Khrushchev loved to make points through parables. The situation, he explained, reminded him of one of his favorite stories, about the man who fell on hard times and had to live with a goat: he hated the smell but he got used to it. The Soviets had been living with goats in Turkey. The Americans would now have to live with goats in Cuba.

Khrushchev raised his idea with Kremlin colleagues. Sharing Castro's assumption about the likelihood of a second American

---

* Beijing and Havana had signed a Chinese-Cuban trade treaty in March 1962.

invasion, Khrushchev emphasized this danger to his comrades. "The only way to save Cuba is to put missiles there," he told them. Most of his Kremlin associates "either shared his assessment," a high-ranking Soviet official later explained, "or feared to voice their doubts."[29] (This behavior mirrored that of Kennedy's men during the Bay of Pigs—which, as will be discussed later, says something deep about the inhibiting effect of power on bureaucracy.) The Russian military endorsed the deployment. The Foreign Ministry, however, which understood the impact of domestic political pressures on American foreign policy, did not. Foreign Minister Andrei Gromyko told Khrushchev that "putting missiles in Cuba would cause a political explosion in the United States. I am absolutely certain of that." Khrushchev did not understand the United States and American politics nearly as well as Gromyko did, but Gromyko was Khrushchev's subordinate and Khrushchev had already made up his mind. Khrushchev had "no intention of changing his position," Gromyko later wrote.[30]

People often ignore or belittle advice that contradicts their assumptions. This is known as "confirmation bias." Cornell University's Thomas Gilovich and Margit Oswald and Stefan Grosjean of the University of Bern in Switzerland, among others, have stressed the pervasiveness of this "mother of all biases." Most people, these researchers found, do not seek to question their beliefs but rather to confirm them. Unsurprisingly, doing so can lead them to become overconfident in those beliefs, which can produce faulty judgments and counterproductive courses of action.[31] A famous experiment by cognitive psychologist Peter Wason of University College, London, in the 1960s brought this reasoning bias to light. In what's known as the "2–4–6 Problem," Wason asked participants to determine the rule in a sequence of three numbers. (It was any ascending sequence.) As an example, he told them that 2–4–6 satisfied the rule. Most participants formed the hypothesis that it was a sequence of ascending even numbers—and tested it by proposing similar sequences of even numbers such as 10–12–14, which Wason did not tell them was wrong. A great majority of them then stopped, believing they had discovered the rule. Very

few composed a sequence of ascending odd or consecutive numbers that might disprove their hypothesis yet reveal the actual
rule.[32]

Khrushchev did just this; he listened to information that validated his preconception and ignored information that undermined
it. His decision also reflected his impulsive nature and penchant
for bold improvisation, such rapidity further eroding opportunities for more removed appreciation. He did not anticipate the
intensity of American fear of—and the domestic political firestorm
triggered by—Soviet missiles in the Western Hemisphere. Without deeper consideration, the deployment, codenamed Operation
ANADYR, proceeded.

Khrushchev and his colleagues sent a delegation led by Marshal Sergei Biryuzov, head of the Soviet Strategic Rocket Forces
to Havana to secure Castro's agreement to the deployment and
determine if it could be implemented without detection by the
United States. Moscow always masked the movement of its nuclear
deployments—even those within the Soviet Union—but the Soviets knew that American U-2 high-altitude reconnaissance planes
flew regularly over the Caribbean island. Khrushchev planned
to reveal the presence of the missiles to Kennedy soon after the
November 6 congressional elections. Faced with a fait accompli,
Kennedy, the Soviet leader believed, would grudgingly accept their
presence in Cuba just as Khrushchev had grudgingly accepted
the American Jupiter missiles in Turkey. "Once the elections are
over and electoral tensions have eased," he told the Politburo, "the
Americans will have no choice but to swallow this bitter pill. Aren't
we compelled to put up with the American missiles in Turkey?"[33]
Castro quickly accepted the offer and the condition that the missiles and their nuclear warheads would remain under Soviet command and control.

Upon returning to Moscow in early June, Biryuzov told Khrushchev the deployment could be accomplished without American
U-2 detection. (Some of this confidence came from the fact that
unbeknownst to the West, the Soviet Union had deployed nuclear
missiles to East Germany in the spring of 1959 and removed them

a few months later.³⁴) Biryuzov said the missiles could be disguised as palm trees with fronds covering the warheads. Deputy Premier Anastas Mikoyan laughed at the suggestion. Biryuzov "wasn't very bright," Mikoyan later recalled. "I myself had seen those palms, and there was no way you were going to hide rocket launch sites under them."³⁵

In early July, Fidel's brother Raúl and his close aide Emilio Aragonés traveled to Moscow to work out the details of the missile deployment as part of a defense treaty between the two countries. The Cubans urged Khrushchev to announce the missile deployment publicly; the Soviet Union had as much of a right to send missiles to Cuba, they argued, as the United States had to send missiles to Turkey. The Cubans, who understood American leaders and American politics much better than the Soviets, warned that the Kennedy administration might react violently to a move that it perceived as deceptive. Khrushchev dismissed their suggestion and their concern as he had dismissed Gromyko's warning, telling Raúl and Aragonés there would be no problems—the missiles would not be discovered before November. Khrushchev was wrong.

By August, the pressure from the Kennedy brothers for results in Operation MONGOOSE had grown so intense that the possibility of solving the Cuba problem through the "liquidation" of its leaders became a subject of discussion.³⁶ Bobby pushed the idea, but not everyone shared his enthusiasm. McNamara was "very skeptical," recalled deputy defense secretary Roswell Gilpatric, who represented McNamara at most Operation MONGOOSE meetings, "but because this was such a deeply-felt project of the Attorney General—Castro must be destroyed—McNamara accepted that the Kennedy brothers, particularly Robert, was going to pursue this line. McNamara thought Robert Kennedy's position vis-à-vis the President made it very important that the two of them got along."³⁷

The Kennedy brothers wanted to avoid creating a paper trail—their wily father had taught his boys "Never write it down"—so CIA officials put little in writing about assassination attempts. As with the Bay of Pigs, they operated on the principle of "need to know" in order to protect themselves and to insulate the president and the attorney general from explicit knowledge of their efforts.* Information was strictly compartmentalized, orders given face-to-face in private meetings. In the end, however—despite all the resources allocated—Operation MONGOOSE produced negligible results. It did little to weaken Cuba's economy or to destabilize Castro's regime. Instead, it paradoxically strengthened Castro's hold on power by prompting him to impose stricter security measures throughout the island that interfered with American intelligence collection. As Richard Helms later concluded, the CIA's efforts "never amounted to more than pinpricks."[38] Looking back, Robert McNamara said "the whole damned MONGOOSE operation was one of the most irresponsible things I've ever seen."[39] White House special assistant Arthur Schlesinger put it more bluntly: "It was total nonsense."[40]

U-2 flights over Cuba that summer had revealed evidence of increased Soviet military activity on the island. Reconnaissance photos, combined with reports from Cuban agents and refugees, suggested the Soviets were building anti-aircraft surface-to-air missile (SAM) sites—a sophisticated air defense system that often presaged the installation of nuclear missile sites. Conservative Republican senators Homer Capehart of Indiana and Barry Goldwater† of Arizona soon learned of this intelligence through their sources in the Pentagon and began attacking Kennedy for failing to confront the "Red Menace" ninety miles from America's shores. Then, on August 31, a moderate Republican senator running for reelection, Kenneth Keating of New York, added credibility to the chorus of right-wing critics when he gave a speech on the Senate floor accusing Kennedy of ignoring evidence of a Soviet military

---

* Similar conversations had been held during the final year of the Eisenhower administration. See Thomas Powers, *The Man Who Kept the Secrets: Richard Helms & the CIA* (Alfred A. Knopf, 1979), pp. 147–148.

† A major general in the air force reserves, Goldwater had many contacts in the active-duty air force, which conducted the U-2 reconnaissance flights over Cuba that summer.

buildup in Cuba. These charges suggested trouble for Kennedy in the upcoming midterm elections and perhaps even for his own reelection prospects in 1964. Kennedy responded by summoning congressional leaders to the White House on September 4 and promising to take action if he found that the Soviets had deployed nuclear missiles in Cuba. The White House issued a public statement later that day warning that the introduction of "offensive ground-to-ground missiles" in Cuba would raise "the gravest issues."[41]

That same afternoon, Kennedy sent his brother Bobby to meet privately with Ambassador Dobrynin at the Soviet Embassy. Located on 16th Street, NW, just three blocks up from the White House, the embassy occupied a four-story turn-of-the-century brownstone mansion that had been purchased by Tsar Nicholas II's government in 1913 from the family of George Pullman, the famous railroad sleeping car manufacturer. Arriving "highly agitated" according to Dobrynin, Bobby quickly steered the conversation to the issue of Soviet aid to Cuba. He told Dobrynin that Washington had been monitoring the shipment of Soviet military equipment to the island with growing concern. Bobby then voiced what he anticipated would happen next: the delivery of nuclear missiles capable of reaching the United States. He feared they might fall into the hands of "impulsive Cubans" and that his brother would not tolerate this. Since Dobrynin had not been informed about the missiles, he neither confirmed nor denied Bobby's allegation. As Bobby rose to leave, he remarked, "I only wish that in the Soviet Union it was understood what feeling was stirred up in American society as a result of the reports of Soviet military supplies to Cuba, a distance of only 90 miles from the United States."[42]

After the meeting, Dobrynin cabled Moscow for direction. "In talking to the Americans," Moscow replied, "you should confirm that there are only *defensive* Soviet weapons in Cuba [italics in original]."[43] Khrushchev tried to convey this same message to President Kennedy when he met visiting interior secretary Stewart Udall two days later at Pitsunda, the Soviet leader's summer retreat in the Caucasus Mountains. "A lot of people are making a big fuss because we are giving aid to Cuba," Khrushchev told Udall. "But you are giving aid to Japan. Just recently I was reading that you have placed atomic warheads on Japanese territory, and surely this is not something the Japanese need. So when Castro comes to us for aid, we give him what he needs for defense. He hasn't much military equipment, so he asked us to supply some. But only for defense."[44] Khrushchev was clearly hinting that he intended to send nuclear arms to Cuba for defensive purposes.*

Why did Kennedy miss Khrushchev's signals? The answer lies in the fact that, as negotiation researchers Roger Fisher and William Ury of Harvard Law School pointed out, negotiators are first and foremost people—often with differing cultural backgrounds and temperaments. Such cultural and temperamental differences can lead to misunderstanding, frustration, and anger that inhibit one's ability to see that other people's interests are an attempt to satisfy something they value, a key principle in understanding negotiation behavior. Fisher and Ury further noted that feelings are as important as substance during negotiation because fear—a common human emotion—can lead negotiators to incorrectly judge the intention of the other party.[45] These dynamics are what blinded Kennedy to Khrushchev's hints during the critical days of early September.

The following day, September 7, Kennedy called up 150,000 army reservists to active duty. Less than a week later, in response to growing pressure from Republicans and even Democratic senators at risk in the upcoming congressional elections—who sent word on September 12 through Majority Leader Mike Mansfield of Montana that they might "have to leave [him] on this matter" unless there were "at least a 'do-something' gesture of militancy"[46]— Kennedy declared at a press conference the next day that if Cuba

---

* To drive home the point, Khrushchev arranged the release of a Soviet news agency TASS statement on September 11 affirming that Soviet intentions on the island were purely defensive.

should "become an offensive military base of significant capacity for the Soviet Union, then this country will do whatever must be done to protect its own security and that of its allies."[47] Kennedy's statement did nothing to ease the political pressure. On September 20, the Senate passed a resolution 86 to 1 authorizing the president "to prevent the creation or use of an externally supported offensive military capability endangering the security of the United States." (The one dissenting senator voted no because he thought the resolution was not strong enough.) The House of Representatives passed a similar resolution 384 to 7 on September 26. Former vice president Richard Nixon and a quartet of conservative Republican senators—Goldwater, Hugh Scott of Pennsylvania, Strom Thurmond of South Carolina, and John Tower of Texas—accused Kennedy of weakness and fecklessness and demanded that he impose a blockade on Cuba to prevent further Soviet arms shipments. The political pressure on Kennedy to get tough on Cuba intensified daily.

Eleven days earlier, on September 15, the Soviet cargo ship *Poltava* had docked at the port of Mariel just west of Havana carrying the first MRBMs for Cuba. After the dismantled missiles were unloaded under cover of darkness, a convoy of tarpaulin-covered trucks had transported them to San Cristóbal in the interior western part of the island. That same day, nuclear warheads for the missiles had left the Soviet Union by ship. They reached Mariel on October 4. From there, special KGB guards transported the warheads to underground storage bunkers concealed from American reconnaissance that had been built into wooded hillsides near the towns of Bejucal twenty miles south of Havana and Managua five miles to the northeast. The warheads stored at Bejucal and Managua represented more than two thousand times the destructive capacity of the atomic bombs that destroyed Hiroshima and Nagasaki in 1945. The missiles and their nuclear warheads remained

---

* Kennedy's statement closely paralleled President Barack Obama's "red line warning" to Syrian president Bashar Assad on August 20, 2012, against use of chemical weapons in the Syrian civil war—a statement that also generated its own pressures and that Obama also later came to regret.

under strict Soviet control, with multiple precautions taken to prevent Cubans from accessing them.

The day after the warheads' arrival in Cuba, Khrushchev again tried to signal his defensive intent to Kennedy. That day, October 5, Moscow sent Georgi Bolshakov—a Soviet Military Intelligence (GRU) colonel posing as an embassy information officer and editor of the English-language Soviet propaganda magazine *USSR*—to the attorney general's office. Bolshakov had served as a secret liaison between Kennedy and Khrushchev via Bobby since May 1961* and in their previous meetings, Bobby had always affected nonchalance—loose tie, rolled-up sleeves, and casual conversation. This time, Bobby's tie was carefully knotted at the neck, his shirtsleeves were buttoned, and there were no pleasantries or small talk. Bolshakov told Bobby he had a new message for the president from Khrushchev. Usually Bobby delivered the messages to his brother orally. Not on this occasion. "The weapons that the USSR is sending to Cuba will only be of a defensive character," Bolshakov told Bobby as the attorney general carefully took notes. Kennedy deliberately asked Bolshakov to repeat the key sentence in the message, which he did.[†48]

Nine days later, in the early morning of October 14, a U-2—its high-resolution camera whirring—flew south to north over western Cuba where SAM sites had earlier been spotted. The supersonic, high-altitude flight lasted just six minutes and took nearly a thousand photographs. Intelligence officials in Washington developed and carefully analyzed the photos the following day. McGeorge Bundy delivered the U-2 photos to Kennedy in the White House living quarters at 8:30 on the morning of October 16. Kennedy, who had returned late the night before from a campaign trip to Pennsylvania and New York, sat in his bedroom in a wing chair eating breakfast from a tray and reading the morning newspapers

---

* Bolshakov had also passed correspondence between Khrushchev and Kennedy through White House press secretary Pierre Salinger.

† The notes that Bobby took of his meeting with Bolshakov on October 5, 1962, have never been found.

through horn-rimmed glasses that he never wore in public. A front-page headline in the *New York Times* read, "Eisenhower Calls President Weak on Foreign Policy." Kennedy frowned and his face darkened as he flipped through the photos. Khrushchev seemed to be deliberately challenging and testing him, and, JFK concluded, if he did not respond forcefully, the Soviet leader might poke and prod the United States even more aggressively in other places down the road, with dangerous consequences for world peace and stability. What was more, the domestic political reaction would be volcanic. Kennedy told Bundy to gather his close advisors— what would come to be known as the Executive Committee of the National Security Council (ExComm)—in the Cabinet Room at midday.

.White House staffers sensed Kennedy's shock, bewilderment, and anger when he walked into the Oval Office later that morning. To speechwriter Ted Sorensen, the president seemed unusually cold and detached—his way of showing displeasure. Personal aide Dave Powers thought, "God, he looks like someone has just told him the house is on fire."[49] Just before noon, Kennedy convened the ExComm in the Cabinet Room. "I don't recall a time when I saw him more preoccupied and less given to any light touch at all. The atmosphere was unrelieved by any of the usual asides," Roswell Gilpatric later recalled.[50] Kennedy sat at the center of the large oblong Cabinet table on the side nearest the windows beneath the Presidential Seal, his back to the Rose Garden. Rusk sat on his immediate right, McNamara on his immediate left. At first they had been strangers to one another, but now Kennedy had a very informal relationship with his advisors, which encouraged them to be open and frank with him. Kennedy and his advisors began by discussing the U-2 photographic evidence. Everyone around the Cabinet table viewed the missiles as a threatening provocation. "Mr. President," said Rusk, "this is an overwhelmingly serious problem . . . I do think we have to . . . eliminate this base. I don't think we can stand still."[51] McNamara agreed, arguing that air strikes should be carried out against the missile sites followed by an invasion—unless

ExComm Meeting
Cecil Stoughton/JFK Library

the missiles already had been armed with nuclear warheads—in which case, McNamara said, "I would strongly urge against the air attack [and an invasion] because I think the danger to this country in relation to the gain would be excessive."

Kennedy followed the discussions that went on around him with a sometimes sardonic expression. Turning the discussion to the cardinal question of motivation, he surmised that Khrushchev sought to gain an "advantage." It "must be that they're not satisfied with [the range limits of] their ICBMs," he speculated. Yet while Kennedy had identified one of Khrushchev's motives, it was not the central one. At this stage, he could not imagine that Khrushchev's primary motive in deploying the missiles had been to defend Cuba from another invasion. Bundy voiced the mindset of everyone in the room when he quoted from—and peremptorily dismissed—Khrushchev's statement to Interior Secretary Udall on September 6 that any Soviet weapons sent to Cuba would be purely defensive. The president asked Vice President Lyndon Johnson what he thought. "The country's blood pressure is up, they are fearful, and they're insecure," noted Johnson. His comment applied equally well to Kennedy and the ExComm that morning.

Cognitive researcher Emile Bruneau of the Massachusetts Institute of Technology has found that when someone contemplates the motivations and behavior of an adversary as opposed to someone not perceived as antagonistic, the mind creates what Bruneau calls an "empathy gap." His research involving the responses of Arabs, Israelis, and South Americans to one another's misfortunes demonstrated that when two groups are in conflict, psychological biases drive people to delegitimize the other group's perspective. Arabs and Israelis reported feeling significantly less compassion for each other's pain and suffering, but no such diminution of compassion for South Americans, with whom they were not in conflict.[52] Such an empathy gap discouraged Kennedy and his advisors from perceiving a defensive intent on Khrushchev's part. As a result, none of them initially focused on a nonmilitary solution to his action; they focused instead on strictly military options for physically removing what they perceived as offensive missiles by force. Kennedy himself sketched the alternatives: an air strike against the known missile sites; a larger air strike against a wide array of targets; a naval blockade to prevent nuclear warheads and more missiles from reaching Cuba; and an all-out American invasion. "We're certainly going to do number one," Kennedy announced. "We're going to take out these missiles . . . We ought to be making *those* preparations." In their initial reaction to the Soviet missiles, a mindset of anger and retaliation dominated Kennedy's and others' thinking.

At the next ExComm meeting that evening, Bundy raised the issue of the missiles' strategic effect. "Quite aside from what we've said—and we're very hard-locked onto it—I know," said Bundy, "what is the strategic impact on the United States of MRBMs in Cuba? How gravely does this change the strategic balance?" "Mac, I asked the Chiefs that this afternoon," said McNamara. "In effect, they said 'substantially.'* My own personal view is not at all." Kennedy agreed. "You could say it doesn't make any difference if you get blown up by an ICBM flying from the Soviet Union or one that was ninety miles away. Geography doesn't mean that much . . . They've got enough to blow us up now anyway." Strategic realities differed vastly from political pressures, however; congressional imperatives had precipitated Kennedy's September warnings against offensive missiles in Cuba and now he felt boxed in by his statements. "Last month I said we weren't going to [allow it]," he said. "I should have said that we don't care. But when we said we're not going to [allow it], then they go ahead and do it,† and we do nothing . . . then I think our risks increase." Failure to act now in light of such warnings would generate "a ton of instability in this country," said assistant secretary of state for hemispheric affairs Edwin Martin. "Oh, I understand that," Kennedy knowingly replied.

The situation's gravity had begun to sink in for McNamara as well. Only that morning, he had advocated air strikes followed by an invasion, but the unpredictable consequences of military action now made him hesitant. "I don't know quite what kind of a world we live in after we've struck Cuba and we've started [a nuclear war]. How do we stop at that point?" he mused anxiously. "Why does he put these in there?" Kennedy continued to wonder. "It's just as if we suddenly began to put a major number of MRBMs in Turkey. Now that'd be goddamn dangerous, I would think." "Well, we did it, Mr. President," Bundy pointed out: Kennedy himself had authorized the Jupiters' deployment and, despite the fact that he had expressed skepticism about their strategic value at an NSC meeting in August, failed to order their removal—an

---

* This judgment derived from the common belief among American military officers of that generation that nuclear weapons were simply bigger bombs in the nation's arsenal. More nuclear weapons meant more usable military power.

† He could not imagine that Khrushchev had made his deployment decision long before his September warning.

indication of just how casually he took the possibility of Soviet upset.*

Like any astute politician, Kennedy had always sought to comprehend the motivation of his adversary, but in this case "I can't understand their viewpoint," he confessed. Kennedy slapped his knee in anger and frustration. "It's a goddamn mystery to me," he conceded, unable to fathom Khrushchev's motivation. "I don't know enough about the Soviet Union, but if anybody can tell me any other time since the Berlin Blockade† where the Russians have given us so clear a provocation, I don't know what it's been." Kennedy nervously tapped his two front teeth with his right forefinger, which he often did when trying to concentrate. "Maybe our mistake was in not saying sometime before this summer that if they do this we must act." Defensive and affronted, he could not imagine that Khrushchev had deployed the missiles to Cuba in reaction to the Bay of Pigs invasion and Operation MONGOOSE rather than in defiance of Kennedy's public warnings.

Kennedy left the meeting at that point, but several advisors remained behind to deliberate further. McNamara raised the possibility of alternative courses of action. This reflected McNamara's growing concern over the unpredictable consequences of military action—and something else. "I'll be quite frank," McNamara said. "I don't think there is a military problem here. This is a domestic political problem. In our [September 4th] announcement, we didn't say we'd go in and . . . kill them. We said we'd act. Well, how will we act? We want to act to prevent [the missiles'] use." The idea of risking nuclear war to remove missiles that in his opinion did not change the strategic balance seemed needless and reckless to McNamara, who proposed going simply with Kennedy's third option, a naval blockade, which would prevent

---

* First generation liquid-fueled ballistic rockets, the Jupiters were unstable, unreliable, unprotected, and therefore vulnerable to attack.

† In 1948, the Soviet Union had abruptly cut off American access to West Berlin. President Truman responded by implementing an airlift that flew food and supplies into West Berlin over the land blockade, avoiding a military confrontation. A year later, the Soviets lifted the blockade.

more Soviet missiles from reaching Cuba while addressing the dilemma created by Kennedy's public warnings—and avoid direct military action.

The next day, Kennedy decided to bring U.N. ambassador and former Democratic presidential candidate Adlai Stevenson into the deliberations as well. Stevenson was a Democratic mandarin and stalwart of its liberal wing—he had been the party's unsuccessful nominee for president against Eisenhower in both 1952 and 1956—whose voice Kennedy respected. Kennedy shared the missile photos with Stevenson the next morning. Because of his U.N. experiences and because he was no longer subject to significant political pressure, Stevenson was able to think differently, and he responded as no one else had thus far, factoring Russia's perspective into his thinking. "We must be prepared for the widespread reaction that if we have a missile base in Turkey and other places around the Soviet Union surely they have a right to one in Cuba," Stevenson wrote the president in a memo the same day. Stevenson also urged Kennedy not to rush into military action. "To start or risk starting a nuclear war is bound to be divisive at best and the judgments of history seldom coincide with the tempers of the moment," he warned. Instead, he recommended Kennedy make it clear to Khrushchev "that the existence of nuclear missile bases anywhere is negotiable before we start anything."[53] Stevenson's recommendation would sink in slowly over the following days.

The next morning, October 18, Kennedy met with former defense secretary Robert Lovett in the White House residence.[*] During their meeting, Kennedy expressed frustration and anger at the Soviets'"bare-faced lies."[54] He remained convinced the Soviets had put offensive missiles in Cuba to challenge him rather than out of fear of an American invasion of an ally and as a shortcut to strategic missile parity. That he could not understand why the

---

[*] In his 1964 oral history for the Kennedy Library, Robert Lovett recalled his meeting with Kennedy after the president's 5 P.M. meeting with Soviet foreign minister Andrei Gromyko. But presidential secretary Evelyn Lincoln's contemporaneous appointment book confirms the two met at 10:45 A.M. See President's Appointment Books, JFKL.

USSR would care so much about a far-away island was mirrored by his dismissal that the Soviets would care much about America's placement of its own missiles in far-away Turkey.

Kennedy reconvened the ExComm at 11 A.M. U-2 reconnaissance had identified additional Soviet arms in Cuba: intermediate-range ballistic missile (IRBM)* launch sites and IL-28 strategic bombers—both capable of delivering nuclear bombs against nearly the entire continental United States. This new evidence increased the sense of danger and thus the impetus for military action. Normally reticent to speak and reluctant to advocate force, Rusk now forcefully recommended that very step. The buildup was not "just an incidental" case of a few missiles, he said, but "a formidable military problem." With the president sitting right next to him, Rusk read from the September 4 White House statement "that the gravest issues would arise" if the Soviets deployed offensive nuclear missiles to Cuba. He said the Soviets "would consider [it] a major backdown" if Washington did not respond. "I think they would be greatly encouraged to go adventuring, to feel that they've got it made as far as intimidating the United States is concerned." Inaction "would undermine and undercut the enormous support that we need for the kind of foreign policy that will eventually secure our survival." Rusk urged military intervention despite acknowledging that doing so involved "very high risks" of a reprisal "against the United States itself" and that "no one can surely foresee the outcome."

While the growing pressure unsettled Rusk, it had the opposite effect on Kennedy, cooling him off, calming him down, and making him less emotional. This made a deep impression on the president's advisors. "I was walking along the porch of the White House to the Cabinet Room for one of the critical discussions," McNamara later remembered. "Caroline was running in toward the Mansion [the White House], perhaps a hundred feet away from the President. He watched her run, and called to her, 'Caroline,

---

* IRBMs were larger than MRBMs and therefore could reach more targets in the United States.

have you been eating candy?' And, as is so typical of a four- or five-year old, she gave no answer at all and no indication she had even heard the question. He called again, 'Caroline, have you been eating candy? Answer me.' Again she paid no heed to his question. And finally, with a smile on his face, he said, 'Caroline, have you been eating candy? Answer me. Yes, no, or maybe.'"[55] The momentary, trivial exchange had a nontrivial effect on Kennedy: not only did it allow him to shift roles (to one more comfortable and with much, much lower stakes) but it allowed him to step out of the rising waters. The personal exchange with Caroline seemed to take a weight off his mind; in his confidence as a parent and in his playful interrogation of his daughter, he was once again the confident, self-assured Jack Kennedy who had charmed and out-thought others on his way to the top. Pausing, getting out of the moment, gave him the chance to put the crisis in some perspective.

This quality enabled Kennedy for the first time since the Bay of Pigs to view the Cuba situation with some detachment—"to see himself in perspective," as McNamara later put it.[56] It reawakened Kennedy's sense of irony that normally accompanied his confidence and enabled him to question himself. America's allies, he now acknowledged, regarded Cuba "as a fixation of the United States and not a serious military threat . . . They think that we're slightly demented on this subject." Kennedy believed they would regard military action "as a mad act by the United States because they will argue that, taken at its worst, the presence of these missiles really doesn't change" the balance of power. Up until now, the growing danger had blurred and enraged—now it focused and sobered Kennedy's thinking. He had begun to view the crisis from others' perspectives—not yet Khrushchev's perspective, but at least that of America's friends.

Thus far, the ExComm deliberations had focused exclusively on military action. State Department Soviet expert Llewellyn Thompson shifted the focus to diplomatic action. Recently returned from Moscow, where he had served as U.S. ambassador for five years, Thompson had gotten to know Khrushchev well during his time in the Soviet Union. Thompson counseled Kennedy that whatever he did, "make it as easy as possible" for Khrushchev "to back down." If Kennedy did so, Thompson predicted, Khrushchev might reply, "This is so serious, I'm prepared to talk to you about it." Thompson's suggestion challenged conventional thinking and prevailing opinion, particularly regarding the Soviet premier's absolute obstinance—and spoke to Kennedy's generally innate caution. ("Never shove your opponent against a closed door," he liked to say.[57]) Like Stevenson the day before, Thompson got Kennedy thinking about a diplomatic solution. An idea came to mind: "The only offer we would make" that would give Khrushchev "some out," Kennedy speculated, "would be our Turkey missiles." That it had taken this long for him to make the connection was indicative of just how focused he had been on counterpunching. Certainly Kennedy felt compelled to demonstrate resolve because of his September warnings, but to him "the question really is what action we take which lessens the chances of a nuclear exchange, which obviously is the final failure." The hierarchy of objectives had been revised. This apocalyptic prospect compelled Kennedy to raise a question no one else had thought—or perhaps dared because they were scared of the president's response—to ask. "Is there anyone here who doesn't think that we ought to do something about this?" His question was answered with deafening silence.

At five o'clock that afternoon Kennedy met in the Oval Office with Soviet foreign minister Andrei Gromyko.[58] Gromyko had traveled to the United States to attend the annual autumn session of the United Nations General Assembly in New York and had arranged a White House visit while in the country. Late afternoon sunshine poured through the French doors leading to the Rose Garden as Gromyko, Ambassador Dobrynin, and Soviet interpreter Viktor Sukhodrev entered the room. They took seats on the cream-colored sofa to the right of Kennedy's famous cushioned rocking chair that eased his chronic back pain. Rusk, Thompson, and U.S. interpreter Alexsander Akalovsky sat on another sofa across from the Russians. The dour, stony-faced, but perceptive Gromyko noticed that the president "was nervous, though he tried not to show it." Gromyko was too; his face, according to Rusk, was as red as "a crab."

Dobrynin, Gromyko, and JFK in the Oval Office
Robert Knudsen/JFK Library

They talked for two hours. Reading from notes he had prepared in consultation with Khrushchev before leaving Moscow, Gromyko cited Washington's unabated anti-Cuba campaign—which he compared to a giant threatening a baby—and said the Soviet Union would not sit idly by in the face of it. He had been instructed, however, "to make it clear" that Soviet aid to Cuba was "by no means offensive." It had been extended solely for "the purpose of contributing to the defense capabilities of Cuba. If it were otherwise, the Soviet Government would never have become involved in rendering such assistance."

Kennedy, who knew how to contain his emotions during

conversations in order to avoid excessive tension, listened patiently until Gromyko finished. Then, conspicuously ignoring Operation MONGOOSE, he asserted he had not "pressed the Cuban
problem"—in fact, had "attempted to push it aside." Implicitly acknowledging error at the Bay of Pigs, he told Gromyko he had "no
intention" of invading Cuba and therefore did not understand why
Khrushchev had shipped arms to Castro, which he pointed out
only inflamed American sentiment against Havana and Moscow.
Kennedy soberly declared that he did not know where things were
headed or how they might end. He said it was "the most dangerous
situation" since the end of World War II.

Gromyko noted there had already been a U.S.-supported invasion of Cuba. This led Kennedy to admit what he had only implied
before, bluntly declaring the Bay of Pigs "a mistake." He said he
would have given a public no-invasion pledge had the Soviets not
begun arming Cuba over the summer. Gromyko replied that Moscow's steps had been taken to protect Castro's government and
reiterated that Soviet arms sent to Cuba "were only defensive"—
and he stressed the word "defensive"—in character. Gromyko's
words finally seemed to register. Kennedy paused a moment,
reached into his coat pocket, took out a piece of paper, and read
aloud a portion of his September 4 announcement and *twice* called
Gromyko's attention to his October 13 statement on the campaign
trail implicitly criticizing conservatives' "intemperate remarks"
about Cuba as well as "self-appointed generals and admirals who
want to send someone else's son to war . . . and ought to be kept
at home by the voters and replaced by those who understand what
the twentieth century is all about"[59]—implicitly referring to both
the domestic political pressures he faced and the danger of escalation to nuclear war. Kennedy was signaling Gromyko that he
had to respond to Soviet missiles in Cuba in *some* way because
of his public warnings but that he intended to do so in a manner
that minimized the risk of triggering war between America and
Russia. He finished by telling Gromyko that he would proceed
on the "presumption that the armaments supplied by the USSR
were defensive." Kennedy and Gromyko's two-hour meeting had

produced a breakthrough of sorts, enabling Kennedy for the first time in the crisis to begin seeing things from Russia's perspective. Whether Gromyko came away seeing things from Kennedy's standpoint was less clear.

That night, Rusk hosted a diplomatic dinner for Gromyko in the large reception room on the top floor of the State Department. The strain of the crisis had begun to take its toll on him, and he, Gromyko noticed, drank a lot during the dinner. "I never saw him in such a state—he was not himself," Gromyko reported to Khrushchev. Unguarded by drink, Rusk told Gromyko, "We know everything," confessing, "You are accustomed to living with our missiles encircling you, but this is the first time that we face such a threat. That's why we are in such a state of shock and cannot overcome it."[60]

Later that night, Kennedy met with Rusk and other ExComm members in the Oval Sitting Room on the second floor of the Executive Mansion. The president presided in a rocker, while his advisors sat on the surrounding gold-and-white Louis XVI French furniture. The emerging consensus favored a naval blockade. Believing no response at all "would divide our allies* and our country," as he dictated in a memo after the meeting, Kennedy decided to go forward with what was clearly the least dangerous and bloody of the options under consideration. He explained his reasoning to a White House governors' conference later that week. "I chose the quarantine† because I wondered if our people are ready for the bomb."[61] He might have said the same about himself.

His decision did not go down well with the military, as became clear at a meeting he and McNamara held with the Joint Chiefs the next morning in the Cabinet Room. The Bay of Pigs had shaken

---

* Kennedy particularly worried that U.S. military action against Cuba would provoke Soviet military retaliation against West Berlin (deep inside Communist East Germany), which Washington would find very difficult to defend against.

† Kennedy's preferred term for the naval blockade, which State Department lawyers had told him might be viewed as an act of war under international law.

Kennedy's faith in the military's advice and reawakened the former junior naval officer's skepticism toward top brass. The chiefs, in turn, resented Kennedy's verdict not to provide air support at the Bay of Pigs—which they believed would have saved the invasion—and now his decision not to bomb the missile sites. Overall, they thought the young president lacked the nerve and steel to confront Khrushchev. Their point of view—that a clash between the United States and Russia was inevitable and zero-sum—seems extreme today, but at the time it reflected the sentiment of many, perhaps a majority of, Americans who had been conditioned over seventeen years of the Cold War to view the Soviet Union as an aggressive and expansionist totalitarian empire that had to be confronted and vanquished. The resulting tension, with the commander in chief and his secretary of defense on the one side and the country's highest-ranking military officers on the other, intensified the political sensitivity of the crisis—a dynamic that would play out again later regarding Vietnam.

Kennedy began by explaining his decision to implement a naval blockade. A savvy politician, he also wanted to establish a record that he had consulted the chiefs. McNamara remained largely silent throughout the meeting. Kennedy told the chiefs he intended to demonstrate American resolve while minimizing the risk of a nuclear war. The chiefs had no interest in diplomatically demonstrating resolve; they *wanted* to eliminate what they considered an intolerable threat to U.S. security—that would show the Soviets what American resolve really was. Military men educated and trained throughout their careers to solve disputes through force, they leaned reflexively toward military action. "Are we really going to do anything except talk?" one of them had asked the others the day before, disgusted by the administration's "political shenanigans."[62] Aside from General Maxwell Taylor, appointed JCS chairman just two weeks earlier, the chiefs harbored barely concealed contempt for Kennedy's judgment.

Sixteen years older than the president, Taylor had known Kennedy since the late 1940s, when the former had headed the United States Military Academy at West Point and Kennedy focused on military issues as a young veteran representing Massachusetts's 11th Congressional District. Handsome, thoughtful, articulate, and physically courageous—he had gone hundreds of miles behind enemy lines in uniform to Rome in 1943 and had parachuted into Normandy in the early morning hours of D-Day as commander of the 101st Airborne Division—Taylor grasped the political dimension of national security, knew how to communicate with political leaders, and understood the pressures they confronted—unusual in his generation of general officers. Polite and straightforward in the manner of his native Midwest, Taylor was in many ways a diplomat in uniform. As army chief of staff during the late 1950s, he had, like (then senator) Kennedy, championed conventional forces over nuclear weapons, and the president and McNamara felt comfortable with Taylor in a way they did not with the likes of Curtis LeMay, a fact that led LeMay and many of his senior military colleagues to consider Taylor "too political."

Maxwell Taylor with McNamara and JFK
Abbie Rowe/JFK Library

Speaking in monosyllables through gritted teeth as he puffed on his ubiquitous cigar, air force general Curtis LeMay, a highly opinionated, intensely conservative, and blunt-spoken warrior a decade older than Kennedy whom one observer called "a rogue elephant barging out of a forest,"[63] lectured the president that he had no "choice except direct military action." A "blockade and political action," LeMay pronounced, would "lead right into war." The general then presumed to offer a political judgment. "This is almost as bad as the appeasement at Munich," he gruffly declared (a cutting reference to the president's father Joseph Kennedy's proappeasement stance as U.S. ambassador to Britain in 1938–1940). LeMay ended by urging "direct military intervention right now." Navy admiral George Anderson also insisted there was no "solution to the Cuban problem except a military solution." Army general Earle Wheeler argued that only an invasion could protect the Ameri-

General Curtis LeMay
World History Archive/Alamy Stock Photo

can people. Marine corps general David Shoup was even blunter. Shoup banged his fist on the Cabinet table and declared, "You'll have to invade the place!"

Kennedy listened to all of this without losing his composure or his temper. He tried to rebut the chiefs' criticism with logic, pointing out that "no matter what [missiles] they put in there, we live *today*" under threat of Soviet ICBMs—"you're talking about the destruction of the country." Having missiles in Cuba, he said, "*adds* to the danger, but doesn't create it." LeMay would have none of it. Staring at Kennedy beneath bushy eyebrows and with his chin jutting out, he pointedly reminded the president of his public warnings against offensive missiles in Cuba, then pronounced, "I think that a blockade and political talk would be considered by a lot of our friends and neutrals as being a pretty weak response to this. And I'm sure a lot of our own citizens would feel that way too. In other words, you're in a pretty bad fix at the present time." "What did you say?" the president asked, stunned by LeMay's insolence. "I say, you're in a pretty bad fix," LeMay repeated. "You're in with me—personally," Kennedy acidly replied. He ended the meeting by politely thanking the chiefs for their views—and pointedly reminding them that he wanted above all "to avoid nuclear war by escalation." After the meeting, Kennedy told Dave Powers, "These brass hats have one great advantage in their favor: if we listen to them and do what they want us to do, none of us will be alive later to tell them they were wrong."[64]

Kennedy met with his advisors again on the afternoon of October 20 in the Oval Sitting Room. "Gentlemen, today we're going to earn our pay," he remarked upon entering the room. Although he had settled on a blockade, he wanted to review the alternatives a final time before publicly announcing his decision. None of the options—including a blockade—were without risk and danger, a point Kennedy drove home with sardonic humor. "You should all hope that your plan isn't the one that will be accepted," he quipped as he began the discussion.[65] McNamara spoke first, forcefully advocating a blockade.[66] He acknowledged it would create "serious political trouble" at home (especially among conservatives

in Congress and the military who demanded that Kennedy take
more forceful action), but it ran far less risk of provoking a Soviet
response that could result in "escalating actions leading to general
war." It offered a path toward removal of the Soviet missiles and
the eventual withdrawal of the obsolete Jupiter missiles from Turkey. Like Kennedy, McNamara had cooled off since the beginning
of the crisis four days earlier and come to see that resolution of
the crisis lay in reciprocity between Washington and Moscow, not
in punitive military action against Cuba. "We [can] obtain the removal of the missiles from Cuba only if we [are] prepared to offer
something in return during negotiations," he argued.

General Taylor disagreed. He argued just as forcefully for air
strikes, asserting that destroying the Soviet missiles posed less
danger than allowing them to remain in Cuba. He dismissed
McNamara's argument that such action would trigger a Soviet
response leading to general war. McNamara warned that the air
strikes advocated by the Joint Chiefs would kill thousands of Russians and Cubans—and eventually large numbers of Americans
as well. "In such an event, the United States would lose control of
the situation which could escalate to general war." Taylor flatly and
vehemently disagreed: a blockade would not eliminate the missiles; military force "was inevitable"; and it would simply be more
costly the longer it was delayed.

While Rusk had advocated air strikes just two days before,
with the passage of hours he had come to share Kennedy's and
McNamara's concern that such an attack risked escalation to nuclear war. He also recommended a naval blockade followed later
by air strikes if necessary. Others—including McGeorge Bundy—
expressed continued support for air strikes. But with Rusk's shift,
the two most senior officers in Kennedy's Cabinet—the secretary
of defense and the secretary of state—now opposed direct military
action. That meant those arguing for direct military action were
edged toward the sidelines. Predicting that "the domestic political
heat would be terrific" (because many Americans would see his
action against Cuba as too little), Kennedy approved a naval block-

ade. He then turned to General Taylor and said, "I know that you and your colleagues are unhappy with this decision, but I trust you will support me in this decision." That Kennedy as commander in chief felt compelled to say such things at this juncture revealed a great deal about the intense Cold War atmosphere in Washington and throughout the country at the time. Taylor reiterated that he and the military chiefs were "against the decision," but he said they would "back him completely"—obedience to civilian authority had been bred into their bones. When Taylor returned to the Pentagon and informed his colleagues of the president's decision, General Wheeler sniffed, "I never thought I'd live to see the day when I would want to go to war."[67]

After the meeting, Kennedy stepped out onto the Truman Balcony with Bobby, Dave Powers, Ted Sorensen, and a few others to get some fresh air and relieve the tension. It was a crisp autumn evening, and the sun was a golden disk sinking on the horizon. The view south to the Washington Monument and, beyond it, the Jefferson Memorial, was magnificent, the beautifully clear air a tonic to the near stifling atmosphere inside. But Kennedy was distracted and pensive. "We are very, very close to war," he said quietly. Then he mordantly deadpanned, "I hope you realize there's not enough room for everybody in the White House bomb shelter."[68]

The next day, October 21, Kennedy asked British ambassador David Ormsby-Gore to lunch with him in the family quarters of the White House. Kennedy and Ormsby-Gore had first met as young men in the late 1930s, when Ormsby-Gore was an undergraduate at Oxford and Kennedy was an undergraduate at Harvard visiting his father, then serving as Franklin Roosevelt's ambassador to the Court of St. James's, and remained good friends over the years. When Kennedy won election as president, Prime Minister Harold Macmillan sent Ormsby-Gore to Washington as ambassador. Smart, sophisticated, and discreet, Ormsby-Gore had Kennedy's ear and his trust, and Kennedy felt particularly comfortable leveling with Ormsby-Gore because he had no competing ambitions and he never tattled to the press. "I trust David as I would my own Cabinet," Kennedy once said.[*69]

Kennedy spoke candidly to Ormsby-Gore about the Cuban situation, and the latter reported to London afterward that the president's statements "in some instances were so frank that I doubt very much whether he would repeat them to any member of his administration except his brother Bobby." Cabled Ormsby-Gore, "He [Kennedy] said with great seriousness that the existence of nuclear arms made a secure and rational world impossible." The only sane solution, Kennedy declared, involved a negotiated compromise with Khrushchev, which JFK believed meant swapping the Jupiter missiles in Turkey for the Soviet missiles in Cuba. Strategically, removing the Jupiters meant giving up little, he added, because deploying Polaris submarines off the coast of Turkey would provide a more secure deterrent and more broadly the insanity of using nuclear weapons in a general war made them "more or less worthless." Domestic pressure remained an abiding concern for Kennedy, which became clear when he wondered aloud to Ormsby-Gore "whether political developments would enable him to do a deal on the reciprocal closing of bases"[70] and that the American public might view a naval blockade as too little too late—to say nothing of a trade. But he had traveled the distance, and was now firm and self-assured.

Kennedy met with the ExComm again the following afternoon, October 22,[71] prior to publicly announcing the naval blockade. "I don't think there was anybody *ever* who didn't think we shouldn't respond," he plaintively declared, making room for those who disagreed with him while at the same time subtly revealing a glimmer of defensiveness. He acknowledged the considerable risk that even a naval blockade entailed—"Khrushchev will not take this without a response," he predicted—and admitted that if it proved the wrong choice, they might not have "the satisfaction of knowing what would have happened if we had acted differently." It was

---

[*] Ironically, Ormsby-Gore kept Kennedy regularly supplied with Cuban cigars via the British diplomatic pouch between Havana and Washington.

a sobering admission not lost on anyone. Kennedy then explained "why we must act" despite the risks and the fact that Western Europeans had been living in the close shadow of Soviet missiles for years. "In September, we said we would react if certain actions were taken in Cuba. We have to carry out commitments which we had made publicly at that time." If he did not, Khrushchev and others would doubt his word in the future—and this would pose an even greater danger to stability and peace. He also stressed the Soviets' covert deployment of missiles outside Russia, which his ignorance of the Soviet deployment of nuclear missiles to East Germany three years earlier led him erroneously to call the USSR's actions in Cuba "a complete change in their previous policy," an aggressive "probing action to find out what we would be prepared to do in Berlin."

Scattered across the country on recess and on campaigns, congressional leaders had been summoned to Washington that afternoon for a 5:30 P.M. secret briefing an hour and a half before the president planned to go on television to deliver a national address about the Cuba crisis. What Kennedy told them shocked most of the senators and representatives present—though not Richard Russell of Georgia, the powerful conservative chairman of the Senate Armed Services Committee, who had been briefed by the White House (and likely informed through leaks by the military chiefs) beforehand. "Mr. President, I could not stay silent under these circumstances and live with myself," Russell pronounced. "I think that our responsibilities to our people demand stronger steps than [a naval blockade]." Russell demanded an immediate American attack on Cuba. "We're either a first-class power or we're not." Noting that even a naval blockade was *one hell* of a gamble," Kennedy told Russell that "if we invade Cuba, there is a chance these weapons will be fired at the United States." Russell was unmoved. A war with Russia "is coming someday," he pronounced with certainty—better to have it now. Several others—including Fulbright, who had argued eloquently against the Bay of Pigs invasion—seconded Russell's demand for an invasion of Cuba. Nevertheless, most present said they would back the president in public despite their

Senator Richard Russell
Frank Wolfe/LBJ Library

misgivings that Kennedy wasn't doing enough. "Whatever we do is filled with hazards," Kennedy emphasized with caution. Kennedy told Bobby afterward that the meeting had been "a tremendous strain" and "the most difficult meeting" of the entire week.[72]

A hundred million Americans tuned in to the speech on television and radio that night—the largest audience ever for a presidential address. The White House had requested airtime from the networks for an address to the nation on a matter of "the highest national urgency." Kennedy's anxiety and exhaustion showed in his sallow complexion, the grim look on his face, and the dark rings under his eyes. Looking directly into the black-and-white television camera, he solemnly accused the Soviets of "false statements," "deliberate deception" and "offensive threats." "This sudden, clandestine decision to station strategic weapons for the first time outside of Soviet soil is a deliberately provocative and unjustified change in the status quo which cannot be accepted by this country, if our courage and our commitments are ever to be trusted again by either friend or foe . . . These actions may only be the beginning," he warned. "I have directed the Armed Forces to prepare for any eventualities," Kennedy chillingly added, making terrifyingly clear what one of those eventualities was: "It shall be the policy of this nation to regard any nuclear missile launched from Cuba against any nation in the Western Hemisphere as an attack by the Soviet Union on the United States, requiring a full retaliatory response upon the Soviet Union."[73]

Kennedy's fearful address spread across the country like a squall across a field of wheat. Americans rushed to corner markets and grocery stores, where they cleared the shelves of food, water, and other essentials in anticipation of the worst. They filled their basements and garages with these and other emergency provisions such as flashlights, battery-powered radios, and nonperishable goods. Many thought their worst nightmare—an all-out nuclear war between America and Russia—was near.

Kennedy's speech set things in motion. The navy began deploying warships off Cuba. The air force put its nuclear bomber force on alert. The army and marine corps moved troops and supplies to southern Florida in preparation for a possible invasion. State and local governments placed civil defense systems and fallout shelters in readiness. Unbeknownst to Washington, four Soviet cargo ships carrying thermonuclear warheads and four Soviet attack submarines armed with nuclear torpedoes neared Cuban waters, and Moscow authorized the commander of Soviet military forces in Cuba to protect the missiles and the nearly 43,000 Soviet troops[*] on the island by using battlefield nuclear weapons in the event of an American amphibious invasion. Believing such an invasion to be imminent, Castro mobilized 350,000 Cuban troops and militiamen and raised their alert status to its highest level.

As Kennedy gave his speech, a personal letter was delivered to Khrushchev via the U.S. embassy in Moscow. "The one thing that has most concerned me," Kennedy wrote the Soviet leader, "has

---

[*] U.S. intelligence agencies grossly underestimated Soviet troop strength on Cuba, assuming the number to be 8,000 to 10,000.

been the possibility that your Government would not correctly understand the will and determination of the United States in any given situation, since I have not assumed that you or any other sane man would, in this nuclear age, deliberately plunge the world into war which it is crystal clear no country would win and which could only result in catastrophic consequences to the whole world, including the aggressor."[74] Khrushchev reacted to Kennedy's letter and speech with agitated bewilderment. "We were not going to unleash war," he plaintively told his Kremlin colleagues. "We just wanted to intimidate them, to deter the anti-Cuban forces." "You blew it," he angrily told Malinovsky, the defense minister, who had raised the deployment idea. When Malinovsky rose to speak, Khrushchev cut him off with a wave of his hand. "There's nothing to say. Stay in your seat." Khrushchev's failure to anticipate how sharply Kennedy would react had contributed to the escalation of tensions that now threatened disaster. Like Kennedy, Khrushchev felt constrained by his earlier decisions and yet compelled to show resolve. "It is tragic," he bemoaned. If the Americans "attack us, we shall respond. This may end in a big war."[75]

Fearing the worst, Khrushchev spent that night in the Kremlin. "I slept on a couch in my office—and I kept my clothes on." He recalled later, "I was ready for alarming news to come any moment and I wanted to be ready to react immediately."[76] On the other side of the world, in Washington, Dean Rusk harbored similar fears. Waking up the next morning, October 23, the first thing he thought to himself was, "Well, I'm still here. This is very interesting."[77] He had lived to see another day; Russia had not reacted with a preemptive strike against the United States. But Soviet ships continued steaming toward Cuba, and McNamara announced at a Pentagon briefing that the blockade would take effect at 10 A.M. the next day.

The momentum of events—especially those related to military operations—can generate unexpected scenarios with sobering and irreversible consequences of their own. Sensing this, Kennedy sent another, more temperate letter to Khrushchev that afternoon. He stressed the responsibility that both leaders carried, urging "that we both show prudence and do nothing to allow events to make the situation more difficult to control than it already is"—an implicit acknowledgment of the misperceptions and misjudgments that had gotten them into this predicament.[78] Having set in motion a naval blockade, Kennedy urged Khrushchev to help him avert a bloody and potentially irreversible confrontation.

At seven o'clock that evening, Kennedy, at his large oak desk made from the timbers of the HMS *Resolute* in front of a pool of press photographers who had been ushered into the Oval Office to record the event, formally signed the blockade proclamation that authorized the U.S. Navy to intercept and "take into custody" Soviet ships bound for Cuba with "offensive weapons." Normally jaunty and eager to mix with reporters, Kennedy this evening appeared somber and harried. He was usually meticulous about his appearance, but now one side of his shirt collar jutted over his coat lapel and a handkerchief looked hastily stuffed into his breast pocket. Kennedy distractedly asked the date as he signed the proclamation. For the first time he could remember, one reporter thought, John Kennedy looked and acted much older than his age.

After signing the proclamation, Kennedy walked through his secretary Evelyn Lincoln's small office to the Cabinet Room, where he talked alone with Bobby. "Well, it looks like it's gonna be real mean, doesn't it?" the president said. "But on the other hand, there's really no choice." "No choice," Bobby echoed. His brother remained apprehensive. "I don't think there was a choice," the president repeated, as if struggling to persuade an uncertain part of himself that he had made the right decision. "No, there wasn't any choice," Bobby reassured him, saying if he had done nothing, "you would've been impeached." "Well, that's what I think—I would've been impeached," the president agreed. It was a frank exchange that highlighted the political pressures on Kennedy that had contributed to the outbreak of the crisis and constrained him from appearing weak.

After talking with his brother, he met in the Oval Office with

Charles Bartlett, a Washington journalist and one of his closest personal friends,* who had helped set up Bobby's secret channel with Georgi Bolshakov beginning in May 1961. Bartlett was there to report on his lunch with Bolshakov at the National Press Club earlier that day. Bartlett had told Bolshakov that the president had authorized the meeting. "He is very angry about what has happened in Cuba," Bartlett had told the GRU colonel. "It reminds him of the Japanese deception before Pearl Harbor." Bartlett had then asked how Moscow would respond to the blockade. Bolshakov had replied that Soviet ships would go through it. To avoid an apocalyptic showdown, Kennedy had directed Bartlett to float the idea of withdrawing the Soviet missiles from Cuba in exchange for withdrawing the American Jupiter missiles from Turkey—precisely what JFK had privately outlined to David Ormsby-Gore two days earlier.[79]

Kennedy sent Bobby back to the Soviet embassy later that night. Dobrynin met Bobby at the front door at 9:30 P.M. and escorted him to a third-floor sitting room, where they talked alone over a tray of coffee. Dobrynin reported later that Bobby was visibly upset. Bobby conveyed his brother's anger and betrayal at perceived Soviet duplicity. "You have deceived the President and you have deceived me," he announced. His explanation revealed the monumental misunderstanding and erroneous assumptions at the heart of the crisis. "From the start, the Soviet side—Khrushchev, the Soviet government in its statements and the ambassador in confidential discussions—stressed the defensive character of the weapons being supplied to Cuba," he said. Looking straight at Dobrynin, he added, "You, for example, particularly told me about the defensive goals behind the supply of Soviet arms, in particular missiles, at the time of our meeting at the beginning of September. I understood you as saying that what was involved—at that point and in the future—was purely the sending of missiles of a comparatively short range for the defense of Cuban territory and the approaches

---

* Bartlett had arranged the blind date between John Kennedy and Jacqueline Bouvier in 1952.

to the island and not the sending of missiles that could strike all of the continental United States." Dobrynin, who actually had said nothing about missiles at their earlier meetings—he did not know about them—asked why the president had not raised his concerns when he met with Gromyko "before embarking on such a dangerous path, fraught with the first military confrontation between our countries." Bobby replied by asking why Gromyko had not told his brother about the missiles. He got up and started to leave. Suddenly he stopped in the doorway, turned around, and asked a final question: What instructions had been sent to Soviet ship captains? Dobrynin repeated what Bolshakov told Bartlett: Soviet ships would not stop; the United States had no right to search vessels in international waters. "I don't know how all this will end," Bobby said, "since we are determined to stop your ships." "But that would be an act of war," Dobrynin replied.[80]

Bobby returned immediately to the White House. He found his brother sitting on a sofa with Ambassador Ormsby-Gore in the center hallway of the family quarters on the second floor. Aware of JFK's desire to avoid a conflict with the Soviet Union, Ormsby-Gore suggested moving the naval blockade line from eight hundred to five hundred miles off Cuba in order to give Moscow more time to consider its response. Kennedy immediately phoned McNamara at the Pentagon and ordered him to move back the blockade line in order to buy more time.

At ten the next morning, October 24—the moment when the blockade took effect—Kennedy reconvened the ExComm. The atmosphere in the Cabinet Room was tense and grave. Soviet ships continued on course; two of them would reach the blockade line within an hour. The alert status of U.S. nuclear bombers had been raised to only one level below readiness for war. "This was the moment which we hoped would never come," Bobby later wrote. "The danger and concern that we all felt hung like a cloud over us all. These minutes were the time of greatest worry by the President. His hand went up to his face and covered his mouth and he closed his fist. His eyes were tense, almost gray, and we just stared at each other across the table. Was the world on the brink of a holocaust and had we done something wrong? I felt we were on the edge of a precipice and it was as if there were no way off."[81]

Khrushchev's initial reaction to the naval blockade mirrored Kennedy's angry and emotional response upon learning of the missiles, when he impulsively leaned toward bombing the missile sites: Khrushchev wanted to run the blockade. The Soviet leader ordered ships' captains to ignore the blockade and hold their course for Cuban ports. That decision made, Khrushchev invited an American businessman visiting Moscow, William Knox of Westinghouse Electric International, to the Kremlin. Knox found Khrushchev "friendly and frank" but looking "very tired." Using Knox—whom he had met in New York during his visit to the United States two years earlier—as his conduit, Khrushchev declared that Moscow would sink any U.S. warships that harassed Soviet ships at sea.[82] As the hours passed, however, emotions diminished and passions cooled in the Kremlin just as they had in the White House. Khrushchev and his colleagues had time to reflect and calm down. Later that day, Deputy Premier Mikoyan—with Khrushchev's implicit consent—modified the premier's order to Soviet ships at sea: vessels carrying military cargo were directed to stop just short of the blockade line—the Soviet equivalent to the American shift from direct military confrontation to something in a lower gear.[83] All such vessels slowed down, stopped, or turned around just minutes before the blockade took effect.

The news reached Washington during the ExComm meeting. CIA director John McCone interrupted, "I have a note just handed to me. It says we've just received information through ONI [Office of Naval Intelligence] that all six Soviet ships currently identified in Cuban waters have either stopped or reversed course." "We're eyeball to eyeball," Rusk murmured to Bundy, "and I think the other fellow just blinked."[84] "Everyone looked like a different person," Bobby later recalled. "The world had stood still, and now it was going around again."[85] The news came as a relief, but no one believed this meant the crisis had ended. Would the Soviet ships later resume their course toward Cuba? If they did, what would happen if a navy warship tried to stop and board one of them? Things could still go terribly wrong.

Even at this precarious moment, the antagonism of some in the military toward civilian authority that would later handicap the American effort in Vietnam was evident. When McNamara returned to the Pentagon after the meeting he learned that the navy had received preliminary intelligence* about Soviet ships stopping and reversing course *before* he had left for the White House meeting but had not shared the intelligence with him until it had been confirmed. He was furious about the delay. The crisis had also begun to affect the tightly controlled McNamara, a driven man who always worked hard to contain and conceal his emotions. He was bone tired. For a week now, he had been working from 6 A.M. to midnight, taking meals at a card table next to his desk, and sleeping on a cot in the dressing room of his third-floor Pentagon office. He had witnessed the military chiefs' impertinence toward the president at the October 19 Cabinet Room meeting, and now this. He summoned Roswell Gilpatric and together they marched from the secretary's suite of offices on the outermost E-Ring of the Pentagon to Flag Plot, the navy's command center one floor up where the blockade was being directed.

Naval officers and enlisted men milled about as the two civilian leaders walked past a marine guarding the door and entered the room dominated by a huge wall map of the Atlantic plotting the locations of all U.S. and Soviet ships. The color rising in his face, McNamara began "chew[ing] out one officer after another as they were attempting to explain their actions," recalled an eyewitness.[86] The duty officer summoned Admiral Anderson, chief of naval operations. When Anderson arrived, McNamara began interrogating him about procedures for intercepting Soviet ships. Like most military officers, Anderson resented what he considered civilian officials' meddling in operational matters—what they derisively called

---

* This intelligence came from the navy's Field Operational Intelligence Unit at the National Security Agency at Fort Meade, Maryland, naval air reconnaissance, and surface ships in the area.

"micromanagement." (The navy ethos was, "You tell someone to do something, not how to do it.") His own temper rising, the admiral replied that ship captains on the scene would decide how to respond, curtly and gratuitously adding, "We've been doing this ever since the days of John Paul Jones." Anderson waved the *Law of Naval Warfare*, a soft-cover manual that described procedures for boarding and searching enemy warships, at McNamara, saying, "It's all in there."

"I don't give a damn what John Paul Jones would have done," said McNamara, "I want to know what you are going to do, *now*." He reminded Anderson of the president's overriding objective—which Kennedy had made clear to the chiefs on October 19—to avoid escalation to nuclear war. What would the navy do if a Soviet ship reached the blockade line? Anderson explained that the navy would hail it; if the ship did not stop, they would fire a warning shot across its bow; if it still did not stop, they would fire into its rudder, disabling it. "Now, Mr. Secretary," he declared in a loud and patronizing voice, "if you and your deputy will go back to your offices, the Navy will run the blockade." "You're not going to fire a single shot at anything without my express permission," said McNamara. "Is that clear?" "Yes," the admiral replied. "That's the end of Anderson," McNamara told Gilpatric as they walked back to their offices. "He's lost my confidence."[*][87]

At 9:30 that night, Kennedy received a personal letter from Khrushchev. The letter was less strident than his remarks to the businessman Knox earlier that day, but still unyielding. The Soviet leader urged Kennedy to look at things from his *defensive* perspective—what both leaders had conspicuously failed to do during the months leading up to the crisis. "Just imagine, Mr. President, that we had presented you with the conditions of an ultimatum which you have presented us by your action. How would you have reacted to this? I think that you would have been indignant at such a step on our part. And this would have been understand-

---

[*] Kennedy did not reappoint Anderson chief of naval operations when his term expired the following year. He became ambassador to Portugal.

able to us." Khrushchev then dug in his heels and said the Soviet Union did not recognize the legitimacy of the naval blockade and would not "retreat one step." Kennedy responded four hours later with an equally unyielding letter reiterating the theme of broken promises and deception. "I ask you to recognize clearly, Mr. Chairman, that it was not I who issued the first challenge in this case, and that in light of this record these activities in Cuba required the responses I have announced." Neither leader had given ground, but each had begun to explain his perspective directly to the other.[88]

At midday October 25, Moscow time, Khrushchev convened a meeting of the Presidium, a council of top officials that met when important decisions had to be made, in the wood-paneled conference room down the corridor from his office. He told his colleagues that he did not want to trade any more "caustic remarks" with Kennedy. He had decided the missiles would not remain in Cuba if this meant a nuclear war with the United States. Like America's leader, the Soviet Union's leader viewed this as a final failure to be avoided at all costs. He would tell Kennedy to "give us a pledge not to invade Cuba, and we will remove the missiles." That, after all, was the primary reason he had installed the missiles in the first place. The Presidium members talked things over and quickly agreed. "Comrades," Khrushchev then said, "let's go to the Bolshoi Theater this evening. Our own people as well as foreign eyes will notice, and perhaps it will calm them down." He later wrote, "We were trying to disguise our own anxiety, which was intense."[89]

Kennedy also began taking steps to diffuse the escalating crisis. He and his advisors did not know if the Soviets would continue to avoid a confrontation at sea or would challenge the blockade as suggested in Khrushchev's latest letter. Kennedy decided to delay a confrontation. "We don't want to precipitate an incident," he told the ExComm on the morning of October 25. The destroyer USS *Gearing* intercepted and hailed the Soviet tanker *Bucharest* that morning, but since its declared cargo of petroleum did not include missiles or other offensive weapons, the *Bucharest* was not stopped and inspected but allowed to pass through the blockade.

At the ExComm meeting that afternoon, McNamara reported

that the destroyer USS *Pierce* had begun trailing the *Völkerfreund-schaft*, an East German passenger ship with fifteen hundred people aboard that would soon reach the blockade line. Jeopardizing lives on a passenger ship would make the United States appear to have "acted irresponsibly," McNamara argued, and "would be absurd." Kennedy agreed and decided to let the East German ship pass, though he worried about the political fallout of letting ships through the blockade; domestic political pressure was still weighted toward acting *more* forcefully, not less. That afternoon, the State Department held closed-door briefings on the blockade for members of Congress. Republican representative James Van Zandt of Pennsylvania, running for the Senate, emerged from a briefing and, violating the rules of the briefing, fumed to reporters that the president had let the *Bucharest* through the blockade. It was an attack without nuance or sympathy—and a preview of what might be a ruthless, widespread line should Kennedy fail to resolve the crisis.

Work on the missile sites continued despite the naval blockade. "We're not gonna get these missiles out of there without either fighting to get 'em out or commit[ting] ourselves not to invade Cuba," Kennedy told the ExComm the next morning, October 26. He preferred the second course and used Adlai Stevenson, who had flown to Washington for the meeting, to argue for it before the ExComm. "Governor,* do you want to give us your thoughts?" Kennedy's question was rhetorical; he already knew Stevenson's thinking and wanted others to hear it. Stevenson argued for the removal of the Soviet missiles in exchange for a no-invasion pledge and the removal of the U.S. missiles in Turkey. Most ExComm members loudly criticized the proposal and even Stevenson personally.† "What other devices are we gonna use to get 'em out of

---

* Stevenson had served as governor of Illinois from 1949 to 1953.

† After the crisis ended, one ExComm member anonymously smeared Stevenson in the press, saying, "Adlai wanted a Munich," a cutting reference to the Western democracies' appeasement of Hitler before World War II. Quoted in Stewart Alsop and Charles Bartlett, "In Time of Crisis," *Saturday Evening Post*, December 8, 1962, p. 20.

[Cuba]?" Kennedy pointedly asked. Stevenson's argument "needed to be stated," Kennedy told Kenny O'Donnell later. "I admire him for saying what he said."[90]

At 9:15 that night, a new letter[91] from Khrushchev reached the White House. Delivered by special courier several hours earlier to the American Embassy in Moscow—a highly unusual step*—it contained handwritten deletions, corrections, and insertions penned by Khrushchev in violet ink. Khrushchev had dispatched the letter in urgency without reviewing it with Kremlin colleagues, as was his normal practice. Long, disjointed, and yet intensely personal, it conveyed Khrushchev's thoughts and feelings in simple and powerful language. He began with conciliatory remarks to Kennedy. "From your letter, I got the feeling that you have some understanding of the situation which has developed and some sense of responsibility," he wrote. "I value this." The two leaders stood at a precipice and Khrushchev described the black chasm that lay just over it. "If war should break out," he observed, "then it would not be in our power to stop it, for such is the logic of war." "I have participated in two wars [the Russian Civil War and World War II] and know that war ends when it has rolled through cities and villages, everywhere sowing death and destruction." What had brought them to this point? "We were very grieved by the fact that a landing took place in Cuba as a result of which many Cubans perished. You yourself told me [at Vienna] that this had been a mistake. I respected that explanation." However, admitting a mistake was insufficient. Continued Khrushchev, "But you also declared that you sympathized with the Cuban counter-revolutionary emigrants and would help them to realize their plans against the present Government of Cuba. It is also not a secret to anyone that the threat of armed attack continues to hang over Cuba. It was only this which impelled us to respond to the request of the Cuban Government to furnish it aid for the strengthening of the defensive capacity of this country."

---

* U.S. diplomats normally picked up official correspondence at the Soviet Foreign Ministry.

Khrushchev then turned to the fundamental dispute. "I assure you that your conclusions regarding offensive weapons in Cuba are groundless. It is apparent from what you have written me that our conceptions are different on this score, or rather, we have different estimates of these or those military means. Indeed, in reality, the same forms of weapons can have different interpretations." Khrushchev had captured and accurately articulated the essence of the crisis. "However, let us not quarrel now. It is apparent that I will not be able to convince you of this," he admitted. Disagreement, however, must not give way to irrationality. "You can regard us with distrust, but you can be calm in this regard, that we are of sound mind and understand perfectly well that if we attack you, you will respond in the same way. Only lunatics or suicides, who themselves want to perish and to destroy the whole world before they die, could do this. We, however, want to live and do not at all want to destroy your country." After this heartfelt statement, he proposed a solution. "If assurances were given by the President and the government that the USA would not participate in an attack on Cuba and would restrain others from actions of this sort and if you would recall your fleet, this would immediately change everything.

"I don't know whether you can understand me and believe me," Khrushchev confessed, "but I should like you to believe in yourself and to agree that one cannot give way to passions; it is necessary to control them . . . If people do not show wisdom, then in the final analysis they will come to a clash, like blind moles, and then reciprocal extermination will begin." He stressed that such an outcome must be avoided. "Mr. President, we and you ought not now to pull on the ends of the rope in which you have tied the knot of war, because the more the two of us pull, the tighter that knot will be tied. And a moment may come when that knot will be tied so tight that even he who tied it will not have the strength to untie it, and then it will be necessary to cut that knot, and what that would mean is not for me to explain to you, because you yourself understand perfectly what terrible forces our countries possess." Khrushchev ended his long and moving letter on a constructive note. "If there is no intention to tighten that knot and thereby to doom the world to the catastrophe of thermonuclear war, then let us not only relax the forces pulling on the ends of the rope, let us take measures to untie that knot. We are ready for this."

Kennedy carefully read the letter and then shared it with his closest advisors. Kenny O'Donnell was "deeply moved" by it. Ted Sorensen found the letter "long, meandering, full of polemics, but in essence appearing to contain the germ of a reasonable settlement." Bobby agreed it "had the beginnings perhaps of some accommodation." Rusk believed it showed Khrushchev "trying to find a way out" of a dangerous predicament. Rusk's deputy, George Ball, sensed Khrushchev's "anguish in every paragraph." General Taylor and the Joint Chiefs, ever suspicious of the Soviets and their intentions, saw it very differently—as an attempt to stall for time to complete the missiles' installation. General LeMay dismissed it as "a lot of bullshit," saying Khrushchev must think "we are a bunch of dumb shits, if we swallow that syrup." Kennedy met with the ExComm at ten o'clock that night to discuss the letter. Unlike LeMay, most ExComm members felt that it "seemed to be the break in the clouds we had been waiting for."[92]

Overnight, Castro received a warning from Brazilian president João Goulart, at Kennedy's behest, that if the Soviet missiles in Cuba were not dismantled within forty-eight hours, the United States would destroy them. Convinced the American military intended to strike within twenty-four to seventy-two hours, Castro cabled Khrushchev urging that "if they actually carry out the brutal act of invading Cuba, that would be the moment to eliminate such danger forever through an act of legitimate defense, however harsh and terrible the solution would be." Castro's apocalyptic tone and implied suggestion of a Soviet preemptive strike appalled and unsettled Khrushchev. "Fidel totally failed to understand our purpose," he later wrote. "We had installed the missiles not for the purpose of attacking the United States, but to keep the United States from attacking Cuba."[93]

The Soviet leader admitted to colleagues that he had initially interpreted Kennedy's radio and television address announcing the naval blockade as evidence the Americans "wanted to present us as the guilty ones and then invade Cuba." But five days had passed since Kennedy's speech and the United States had not attacked Cuba. "I think that they won't venture to do this now," he had concluded. Khrushchev urged moderation and restraint to his comrades, as he had to Kennedy in his personal letter. "We cannot liquidate the conflict, if we don't give some satisfaction to the Americans. We must not be obstinate."[94]

Khrushchev then raised the proposal that Bartlett had passed to Bolshakov four days earlier: the removal of Soviet missiles in Cuba in exchange for the removal of U.S. missiles in Turkey. (Bolshakov's report of the meeting had reached Moscow only two days earlier, a dismaying indicator of how, even in the most precarious of times, crucial information could get bottled up—a tendency that would haunt American leadership during Vietnam.) Kennedy's proposal offered a face-saver to Khrushchev *and* a way for the Soviet leader to mollify his annoyed colleagues. (When Khrushchev had raised the prospect of withdrawing the missiles from Cuba with Malinovsky, the general had loudly complained that he was "upsetting the whole Soviet military offensive structure" with a "stupid" and "senseless" move.[95]) "If we could achieve additionally the liquidation of the bases in Turkey," Khrushchev told the Presidium, "we would win." In fact, Khrushchev had already decided to remove the Soviet missiles from Cuba in return for a U.S. no-invasion pledge* and to prevent a nuclear war, but the removal of the missiles from Turkey would allow him to assuage his colleagues by demonstrating that he had wrested a parallel and symbolically important concession from Kennedy. Khrushchev then dictated a new letter to Kennedy in the presence of the Presidium, which was promptly broadcast over Radio Moscow.

At that same moment (10 A.M. in Washington), Kennedy reassembled the ExComm. McCone reported that the missiles had be-

---

* Kennedy had intimated this formula to Gromyko during their October 18 meeting in the Oval Office.

come fully operational and the Soviets had installed anti-aircraft batteries around them, increasing the danger to American pilots flying reconnaissance missions. McNamara reported that the Soviet tanker *Grozny* had begun to move toward the blockade line. Kennedy interrupted the discussion to read a wire story handed to him: "Premier Khrushchev told President Kennedy in a message today he would withdraw offensive weapons from Cuba if the United States withdrew its rockets from Turkey." Was it a new letter from Khrushchev? No one could be certain at this point.

McNamara and Bundy recommended intensifying reconnaissance over Cuba. Kennedy deflected their recommendation and instead returned to the issue of the Jupiter missiles in Turkey. Nearly every ExComm member—including Rusk, McNamara, Bundy, and even Bobby (none of whom knew of Bartlett's proposal to Bolshakov)—opposed trading the missiles in Turkey for those in Cuba, believing Khrushchev had upped the ante at the last minute and fearing it would undermine NATO's confidence in American resolve. Kennedy did not retreat, however. "To any rational man, it will look like a very fair trade," he said. "Most people will regard this as not an unreasonable proposal." "What 'most people'?" pressed Bundy, a man of ample skepticism and self-esteem. "I think you're gonna find it very difficult to explain why we are going to take hostile military action in Cuba, when he's saying, 'If you get yours out of Turkey, we'll get ours out of Cuba,'" Kennedy shot back. "We have to face up to the possibility of some kind of trade over missiles."[96]

The situation seemed to be stabilizing a bit. Then, shortly before 2 P.M., McNamara notified the White House of a report from Eielson Air Force Base in Alaska that a U-2 on a routine air-sampling mission* had accidentally strayed into Siberian airspace over the Chukot Peninsula as a result of a celestial navigation error triggered by the aurora borealis (the northern lights). The pilot, air

---

* The U.S. Air Force flew regular reconnaissance missions in the North Pole region using U-2s equipped with sensitive filtering instruments to detect radioactive particles in the atmosphere as a way of monitoring Soviet nuclear tests on Novaya Zemlya Island high above the Arctic Circle.

force captain Charles Maultsby, made an emergency call on open radio for navigational assistance. Soviet warplanes scrambled to intercept, but the U-2 exited Russian airspace before Soviet warplanes could reach it and Maultsby returned safely. When informed of the potentially catastrophic incident, the president noted that he had ordered such air-sampling missions suspended as a result of the crisis, then mordantly observed, "There's always some son-of-a-bitch that doesn't get the word."[97] Outwardly, Kennedy remained calm, but underneath he saw the incident as chilling evidence that unforeseen and totally unrelated events might lead the crisis to spin out of control at any moment. Later that afternoon, he summoned Gilpatric to the Oval Office and privately instructed him to draft a plan for withdrawing the U.S. missiles from Turkey if Khrushchev agreed to stop work on the Soviet missiles in Cuba.[98]

Kennedy reconvened the ExComm at four o'clock. Everyone had grown tired and weary. The days had been tense and nerve-racking and exhaustion had set in. Many had not gotten a good night's sleep in more than a week. The accumulated stress and fatigue had begun to wear down even the strongest of men, making them wonder about the outcome of the crisis. McNamara, whose stamina exceeded most others', later recalled his feelings when he walked out on to the West Wing portico during a break in the ExComm discussions later that evening. "I thought then that I might never live to see another Saturday night."[99]

The group took up Khrushchev's latest letter,[100] which had been received by the White House several hours earlier. The one drafted in the presence of the Presidium and polished by the Foreign Ministry, it was more formal than the previous day's personal letter. It echoed the earlier one in substance, adding the Cuba-Turkey missile swap suggested by Kennedy via Bartlett and Bolshakov. "You are disturbed over Cuba," Khrushchev's latest letter began. "You say that this disturbs you because it is 90 miles by sea from the coast of the United States of America. But Turkey adjoins us; our sentries patrol back and forth and see each other. Do you consider, then, that you have the right to demand security for your own country and the removal of the weapons you call offensive, but do not accord the same right to us?" Khrushchev went on with a proposal. "We are willing to remove from Cuba the means which you regard as offensive" and "you will make a declaration to the effect that the United States, for its part, considering the uneasiness and anxiety of the Soviet State, will remove its analogous means from Turkey." Unbeknownst to Washington, at the same time that Khrushchev released this formal letter, he instructed the Soviet ambassador in Havana, Aleksandr Alekseyev, to persuade an agitated Castro to publicly endorse a Cuba-Turkey missile trade.[101]

Nearly all of the ExComm continued to oppose a Cuba-Turkey missile trade, but the president nonetheless held firm. "Most people will think [Khrushchev's] offer is rather reasonable," he declared. Bundy warned a trade would damage America's relationship with Turkey and the NATO alliance. "Mac," Kennedy firmly replied, "this trade has appeal. If we reject it out of hand, and then have to take military action against Cuba, then we'll also face a decline" in NATO and a loss of support around the world. Bobby (who had met with his brother after the morning meeting) now endorsed a trade. "People are gonna think it's quite reasonable," Bobby said, echoing JFK's earlier comment. "We just can't out of hand reject this and after 24 hours go and make a bombing attack." Bundy, Rusk, and others continued to resist. Kennedy's frustration mounted as he listened to all of the criticism of a missile trade. His patience broke and he said in an uncharacteristically raised voice, "Because we wouldn't take the missiles out of Turkey, we're gonna either have to *invade* or have a *massive* strike on Cuba which may lose Berlin! That's what concerns me!"

Opposition within the ExComm continued, however. General Taylor told Kennedy a trade meant "you're deeply in trouble with NATO." Bundy recommended intensifying the naval blockade. Rusk urged "shaking Khrushchev off" his latest position by calling up additional reserves and declaring a national emergency. Even Ambassador Thompson, who had persistently advocated a diplomatic solution, criticized a missile trade. Kennedy, sure in his own mind and determined to avoid a nuclear war with the Soviet Union, stood his ground. "I just tell you," he said, exasperation evident in his voice, "I think we're better off to get those missiles out of Turkey and out of Cuba because I think the [other] way of getting 'em out of Cuba is gonna be *very, very* difficult and *very* bloody."

But Taylor would not give up, telling Kennedy the Joint Chiefs urged striking Cuba in two days (October 29) unless "irrefutable evidence" emerged "that offensive weapons are being dismantled and rendered inoperable." McNamara reported that Cuban antiaircraft batteries had begun firing on low-level U.S. reconnaissance flights and the *Grozny* was nearing the blockade line. Then, he received word and announced in a dismal tone that a U-2 had been shot down over Cuba by a Soviet surface-to-air missile (SAM)* and the pilot, Air Force major Rudolph Anderson, killed. Taylor urged retaliating immediately against the SAM site—something that Kennedy had agreed to, in principle, earlier in the crisis. But now Kennedy, nervously tapping his fingers on the Cabinet table, deflected the general's suggestion and instead stressed quickly removing the Jupiter missiles from Turkey. "We oughta get moving on it," he emphasized. "The fact is, time's running out."

Leadership sometimes means going against prevailing opinion, however strongly held and forcefully expressed. It involves trusting one's judgment and holding to it in the face of immense pressure and criticism—what management experts call "good stubbornness." Such adamancy can serve a constructive purpose. However, if stubbornness causes one to pursue destructive avenues or to ignore wise advice, then it can become a hindrance or even a disaster—what management experts term "bad stubbornness." Bad stubbornness, notes Muriel Wilkins in the *Harvard Business Review,* "is the ugly side of perseverance." Wilkins cites the example of a senior-level executive whose stubbornness made him "unable to see other courses of action that were in the best interest of the com-

---

* After trying unsuccessfully to reach their superior, two Soviet deputy commanders gave the order to fire. When Moscow received the news, Defense Minister Malinovsky immediately reprimanded them for "hastily" shooting down a plane "while agreement for a peaceful way to deter an invasion of Cuba was already taking shape." Quoted in Michael R. Beschloss, *The Crisis Years: Kennedy and Khrushchev, 1960–1963* (HarperCollins, 1991), p. 532.

pany."[102] Such bad stubbornness would apply to Lyndon Johnson regarding Vietnam.

Kennedy showed good stubbornness at this moment of the crisis. He stuck to his position in favor of a missile swap despite the almost unanimous opposition of his ExComm advisors because he saw it as the key to resolving a rapidly destabilizing situation. His go-it-alone stubbornness called to mind his predecessor Abraham Lincoln's during the second year of the Civil War (a story Kennedy liked to tell himself). In September 1862, Lincoln polled his Cabinet whether or not to issue the Emancipation Proclamation. A straw vote revealed that every Cabinet officer opposed issuing the proclamation. Lincoln thought things over a moment, then said, "Seven nayes and one aye—the ayes have it."

After the meeting, Kennedy gathered his closest and most trusted advisors, an inner ExComm—Bobby, McNamara, Rusk, and Bundy—around his desk in the Oval Office. He told them Bobby would meet Dobrynin that night and tell him the Jupiters would be removed as part of the deal to end the crisis. Sensitive to the domestic political pressure on Kennedy and, to a lesser degree, the potential fallout on the NATO alliance, Rusk proposed that Bobby tell Dobrynin a public quid pro quo was impossible but the Jupiter missiles would be removed from Turkey within a few months of the removal of the Soviet missiles from Cuba. Bobby would stress that the American end of the missile trade would be voided if the Soviets ever publicized it. Later that evening, Kennedy and Rusk devised a second secret fallback plan that would be implemented if all else failed: a back-channel U.S. representative—former UN official Andrew Cordier, now dean of Columbia University's School of International Affairs—would signal UN secretary general U Thant to announce a "neutral" public trade of the missiles in Cuba and Turkey, thereby allowing Kennedy to avoid the political burden of having initiated the swap. It was a secret two-tier negotiating strategy that offered a way out of the crisis while allowing Kennedy to save face domestically.

Bobby phoned Dobrynin and arranged to meet the ambassador at his cavernous Justice Department office, which the attorney general had decorated with his children's watercolor paintings. Their tête-à-tête began just after 8 P.M. and lasted barely fifteen minutes. Bobby appeared "very nervous" and disturbed to Dobrynin, "the first time I had ever seen him in such a condition." Bobby wasted no time. He told Dobrynin the president faced "strong pressure" to retaliate for the downing of the U-2 earlier in the day, and "if we start to fire in response—a chain reaction will quickly start that will be very hard to stop." His brother wanted to avoid this outcome and believed Khrushchev did, too. To end the crisis, the Soviets must stop work on the missiles. In exchange for removing them from Cuba, his brother would pledge not to invade and quietly withdraw the U.S. missiles from Turkey within a few months. This had to be done quietly because "the greatest difficulty for the President is the public discussion of the issue." Bobby stressed that the crisis must be resolved soon because there were "hotheads among the generals, and in other places as well, who were spoiling for a fight" and events were "developing too quickly." An irreversible turn could occur at any moment. He urged Khrushchev to reply by the next day. "Time will not wait," he stressed. "We must not let it slip away."[103]

He was right. While the president was grinding his way toward a peaceful solution, on the ground and in the sea there was little calm. The Soviets had dispatched four Foxtrot-class diesel-electric submarines to protect surface shipping, each carrying twenty-one conventional torpedoes—and one shiny gray ten-kiloton nuclear-tipped torpedo, which theoretically could be fired only by coded instruction from Moscow but practically could be fired by agreement between the ship captain and the torpedo officer. Unlike U.S. nuclear-powered Polaris submarines, which could remain submerged for months, Soviet Foxtrot submarines needed to surface daily to recharge their batteries and communicate with Moscow. The U.S. Navy urged using sonar buoys and warning depth charges to force any Soviet submarines to surface. McNamara had warned of "many, many uncertainties" related to the procedure but Kennedy had reluctantly approved it at the ExComm meeting on the morning of October 24 as he and his advisors braced themselves for a confrontation on the blockade line with Soviet ships. Washington had cabled Moscow that same day informing it about the surfacing procedure, but the Soviet government inexplicably never relayed this information to its submarines, nor did it inform Washington that nuclear missile launch authority had been delegated to the captain and torpedo officer of its submarines.

Now, on the night of October 27, the navy found submarine B-59 under the command of Captain Valentin Grigorievich Savitsky. B-59's batteries had run dangerously low, it had missed its scheduled communication with Moscow that afternoon because it had been forced into an emergency dive when American planes appeared overhead, its ventilation system had broken down, creating dangerous levels of carbon dioxide and temperatures of 122 degrees Fahrenheit inside the submarine, crewmen had begun to pass out from heat and exhaustion, and U.S. Navy warning depth charges detonating next to the hull created explosions that felt like "sledgehammers on a metal barrel." An officer aboard later described what happened next. "A totally exhausted Savitsky became furious. He summoned the officer in charge of the nuclear torpedo and ordered him to ready it. 'Maybe the war has already started up there while we are doing somersaults down here!' shouted Valentin Grigorievich emotionally, justifying his order. 'We're going to blast them now! We will perish ourselves, but we will sink them all! We will not disgrace our Navy!'"

B-59's other officers persuaded Savitsky to calm down. Then shortly before 10 P.M., B-59 surfaced, surrounded by destroyers, helicopters buzzing overhead with powerful searchlights, and a constellation of brightly flashing sonar buoys bobbing in the choppy Atlantic waters. Tracker planes dropped flares. Savitsky ordered his crew to run up the Soviet flag. One of the U.S. destroyers signaled the B-59, asking if it needed assistance. "This ship belongs to the Union of Soviet Socialist Republics," B-59 replied. "Halt your provocative actions." After an hour, B-59 received a radio message from Moscow instructing it to move away and slip its pursuers.

After two days of continuous surveillance, the submarine finally did so and the U.S. Navy abandoned the chase.[104]

As the *B-59* incident occurred, news of the downing of the American U-2 over Cuba reached Khrushchev at 10:45 A.M., October 28, Moscow time, seven hours ahead of Washington. The Soviet military also told him the United States might attack Cuba the next day. Realizing, like Kennedy, that the situation was rapidly deteriorating and time was short, he ordered members of the Presidium to meet him at noon at the government dacha in Novo-Ogaryovo outside Moscow. The atmosphere at the dacha, a two-story neoclassical mansion in a leafy birch forest near the meandering Moscow River, was "highly electric" recalled a participant; everyone was "on edge from the outset."[105] As soon as the meeting began, Khrushchev got right to the point. "We find ourselves face-to-face with the danger of war and of nuclear catastrophe, with the possible result of destroying the human race," he told those seated around a long, polished oak table in the dacha's large dining hall. "In order to save the world, we must retreat." That retreat must have certain conditions, including face, he explained, stressing the need for "a dignified way out of this conflict." At that moment, an urgent call came in from the Foreign Ministry reporting Dobrynin's meeting with Bobby. "The contents of the dispatch increased the nervousness in the hall by some degrees," noted an aide.[106] Khrushchev immediately summoned a stenographer and dictated his acceptance of Kennedy's proposal: "I express my satisfaction and thank you for the sense of proportion you have displayed . . . In order to eliminate as rapidly as possible the conflict which endangers the cause of peace . . . the Soviet Government, in addition to earlier instructions on the discontinuation of further work on weapons construction sites, has given a new order to dismantle the arms which you described as offensive, and to crate and return them to the Soviet Union." Khrushchev ordered the letter rushed to Radio Moscow for immediate release, so fearful that something could go wrong, that some Soviet captain or rogue Pentagon general or admiral might decide to take matters into his own hands. Khrushchev's letter was simultaneously broad-cast in both Russian and English even before the editing of its final passages had been completed.

Khrushchev then sent two short messages to Kennedy to be de-livered by Dobrynin orally through Bobby. The first confirmed the contents of the radio broadcast. The second was more sensitive: "In my letter to you [today], which was designed for publication, I did not touch on [the] matter [of the missiles in Turkey] because of your wish, as conveyed by Robert Kennedy. But all of the offers which were included in this letter were given on account of your having agreed to the Turkish issue raised in my letter of October 27 and announced by Robert Kennedy, from your side, in his meeting with the Soviet ambassador."

Finally, Khrushchev sent four urgent cables to Cuba. The first forbid firing any more SAM missiles and grounded all Soviet jets in order "to avoid a clash with U.S. reconnaissance planes." The second rescinded the prior authorization to use tactical nuclear weapons in the event of an invasion. The third ordered the *Grozny* to stop dead in the water. The fourth implored Castro to cease fir-ing immediately on American reconnaissance planes. Castro was furious—Khrushchev had cut a deal with the United States with-out consulting him—but the Cuban leader quickly regained his composure, at least publicly. Castro told his colleagues later that day that "Cuba will not lose anything by the removal of the mis-siles, because she has already gained so much." Privately, he com-plained to the Soviet ambassador that the Cuban people viewed the agreement "unfavorably."[107]

A transcript of Radio Moscow's broadcast was rushed to the White House at 9 A.M., October 28, Washington time. Bundy, who had brought news of the missiles to Kennedy thirteen days ear-lier, now brought him news that they would be removed. "It was a very beautiful morning," Bundy later wrote, "and it had suddenly become many times more beautiful." Red, orange, and yellow autumn leaves shimmered in brilliant light against an azure sky. "It reminds me of the Georgia O'Keefe painting that has a rose growing out of an ox skull," an ExComm member told McNamara.

"Everyone knew who were the hawks and who were the doves,"
Bundy graciously remarked later that morning, and "today was the
doves' day."[108] Kennedy told Dave Powers, "I feel like a new man.
Do you realize that we had an air strike all arranged for Tuesday?
Thank God it's all over."[109] That afternoon, he ordered Operation
MONGOOSE suspended immediately.

The Joint Chiefs reacted with stunned outrage. They immediately convened in "the Tank," their meeting room at the Pentagon
dominated by a huge map of the world, at midday and prepared
a memorandum to President Kennedy blasting Khrushchev's radio
statement as a disingenuous effort "to delay direct action by the
United States while preparing the ground for diplomatic black-
mail." They urged Kennedy to begin bombing Cuba the next
day, followed by an invasion within a week, unless Washington received "irrefutable evidence" that dismantling of the missiles had
begun. General Taylor forwarded their recommendation without
endorsing it.[110] Taylor, who had vigorously advocated air strikes at
ExComm meetings, later noted "that if I was classified as a hawk
in the arena of the ExComm, I was definitely viewed as a dove in
the arena of the Joint Chiefs of Staff."[111] One military leader, when
informed of Khrushchev's willingness to remove the missiles,
asked, "Does this mean our air strike has to be called off? Why
can't we attack on Tuesday anyway?"[112]

Kennedy met with the chiefs the following week. Adroit and
discerning, he did not want them jeopardizing the deal he had
struck with Khrushchev by publicly criticizing it or privately undermining it with their conservative allies on the Hill or in the
media. "I want to tell you how much I admire you and how much
I benefitted from your advice and your counsel and your behavior
during this very, very difficult period," the president told them.
His soothing words did no good. "We've been had!" Admiral
Anderson responded. General LeMay denounced Khrushchev's
statement as "a charade" and pounded his fist on the Cabinet
table. "It's the greatest defeat in our history, Mr. President. We
should invade today!" LeMay's comment left McNamara speech-
less. The defense secretary glanced at Kennedy and noticed that

he was "absolutely shocked. He was stuttering in reply."[113] But the aye still had it.

The resolution of the Cuban Missile Crisis proved a spectacular success for the United States. Kennedy had forced a showdown, and Khrushchev had publicly removed Soviet missiles from Cuba. Kennedy had simultaneously demonstrated resolve and restraint toward the Soviet Union and the deterrent power of American arms and pressure, while also burnishing his anti-Communist political credentials. Kennedy could not be creditably accused during the upcoming 1964 reelection campaign of being "soft on Communism." These were positive results. But the resolution of the crisis produced significant negative effects as well, especially in relation to Vietnam. The specter of nuclear war in Cuba made Kennedy and his advisors less attentive to the specter of conventional war in Vietnam after October 1962, and created an abiding fear of escalation that would influence Vietnam policymaking. It intensified their anxiety about the judgment of senior military officers—an anxiety that would inhibit open, candid discussion of fundamental strategic differences and make it difficult for civilian leaders and service chiefs to level with each other when it came to Vietnam. And it confirmed their conviction that the gradual application of force could achieve results without provoking the unlimited war they feared and dreaded. Success was essentially a matter of crisis management, which meant signaling an adversary to desist through gradual and controllable escalatory steps while maintaining tight operational control over the military.

To Kennedy and his advisors, this strategy had worked decisively during the Cuban Missile Crisis and carried the day. Such beliefs, principles, and precedents would heavily influence American military strategy in Vietnam in the years to come. This approach had its merits in the context of the hair-trigger superpower nuclear rivalry of the Cold War. But the successful resolution of the standoff also made Kennedy and his advisors dangerously overconfident in themselves, and—most important and fateful—in their ability to anticipate and control events. "We had seen the gradual application of force applied in the Cuban Missile Crisis," said Cyrus Vance, Roswell Gilpatric's successor as deputy defense secretary (and later President Jimmy Carter's secretary of state), "and had seen a very successful result. We believed that if this same gradual and restrained application of force were applied in Vietnam, that one could expect the same kind of result: that rational people on the other side would respond to increasing military pressure and would therefore try and seek a political solution."[114] The assumption (and illusion) of control became fixed in their minds and actions. Beneficiaries of a stunningly fortuitous outcome, these men of such brilliance and promise, said McGeorge Bundy, looking back, "foolishly exaggerated the ability of men to control events."[115]

CHAPTER 3

The Failure of Anticipation

(October 1962–November 1963)

The American war in Vietnam ground on for eight long years, from 1965 to 1973. It notoriously and voraciously consumed both lives and reputations on its way to becoming an iconic cautionary tale: hubris—arrogance and pride that ancient Greeks warned against twenty-five hundred years ago—led the United States at the height of its power into the quagmire of Vietnam. The resulting war grew into a disastrous and divisive conflict that devastated the land of Indochina, killed an estimated 3 million Vietnamese and more than 58,000 Americans, exposed the limits of America's massive military power, sapped American treasure, polarized American politics, shook Americans' faith in their country and themselves, and cast a shadow that persists to this day.

This is how people inevitably view Vietnam—backward, as history. Viewing Vietnam in this way, one clearly sees all of the blunders committed by Presidents Kennedy and Johnson and their advisors, understandably judging them in the harsh light of the war's consequences. But Søren Kierkegaard's famous insight about philosophy applies to history as well. "Philosophy is perfectly right in saying that life must be understood backward," he wrote. "But then one forgets the other clause—that it must be lived forward."[1] Viewing the Vietnam War as it unfolded is difficult because it requires suspending knowledge of the outcome—hard to do because that outcome was such a debacle. But the effect is more poignant because looking at Vietnam forward rather than backward enables one to observe, in painful and chillingly comprehensible detail, how and why intelligent and well-intentioned individuals made woeful errors of judgment. It allows one to embrace incongruities and plumb them one by one. It means looking at a much-treated subject again—but in a new way that recalls Gustave Flaubert's advice to the young Guy de Maupassant, when Flaubert sat Maupassant down in front of a tree and told him to describe it: "There is a part of everything that remains unexplored," Flaubert said, "for we have fallen into the habit of remembering whenever we use our eyes, what people before us have thought of the thing we are looking at. Even the slightest thing contains a little that is unknown. We must find it."[2] Doing so brings fresh perspective even for those who already know the story of Vietnam well.

Hubris certainly played a part. But it did so in concert with miscalculation that grew out of ignorance, blindness, pressure, fear, denial, and wishful thinking. Like all human beings, Kennedy, Johnson, and their advisors approached problems with the tools available to them: their beliefs, their values, their experiences, their hopes, their fears, their prejudices. Who they were, where they came from, and when they lived all mattered. Like all policymakers, they acted on uncertain assumptions and incomplete information. Their grasp of the present and wisdom concerning the future remained necessarily limited. Readers of history do not share the same perspective as makers of history. We know what will happen—all of the twists and turns of the story—but they do not.

Inevitably, some retrospection is impossible to avoid when looking at events as those at the time understood them. Sometimes it is necessary to discuss ideas and events those participants did not know about—indeed, that may be the point. To best navigate this story both map and compass are required. The Vietnam catastrophe resulted from a very human but flawed process that constrained and imprisoned Kennedy, Johnson, and their advisors. Aspects of their environment nudged them toward some courses rather than others. This process made mistakes inevitable. It encompassed the real world of Washington decision-making at one end and events in Southeast Asia at the other. That real world of Washington decision-making—then and now—prioritized conventional over unorthodox thinking; reactive, short-term choices in response to immediate crises in an environment where multiple events often unfolded simultaneously and developed quickly; and intemperate sensitivity to the domestic political implications of national security decisions. In a sense, those prosecuting the war were always playing catch-up—they were behind, not ahead of the curve. They learned all too slowly they could not control affairs in the field and at the same time confronted mounting pressures for deeper U.S. involvement they found increasingly difficult to navigate and resist. This dynamic discouraged—but did not prevent—attention to long-term consequences and careful consideration of alternative choices and outside perspectives. But once ensnared, Kennedy, Johnson, and their advisors found it difficult to escape; the contours they established entrapped them. As a consequence, good and intelligent men made grievous errors of judgment that cost countless lives and inflicted immeasurable suffering. Whether anyone might have done better than they did is arguable, given the times in which they lived and the pressures they confronted. We all have blinders of one sort or another and each of us is limited by our sense of what is possible. But that does not absolve Kennedy, Johnson, and their advisors of responsibility for their decisions—or us of responsibility for learning from them.

The United States came out of World War II the richest and most powerful of the combatant states, marking the true beginning of the American Century. Americans had always been aggressive in approach; good, smart, tough, and highly motivated problem-solvers, they believed they could accomplish anything if they worked hard enough. Americans had survived the Great Depression and led the Allied coalition to victory over Nazi evil in the greatest war in human history, dominating events through the sheer force of their industrial capacity. The resulting immense optimism gave America's approach to the world its concrete shape and substance. The country's mistakes and failings (at least those popularly recognized as failings), and those of its friends, were things that the United States could, should, and would fix. But while that confidence in America's ability to repair was very strong, the sense that some things could not be fixed was very weak.

America's sense of mission was clarified by continental fissures. As the Cold War with the Soviet Union set in during the late 1940s, the United States sought to build order in a world ravaged by World War II. As part of this effort, it assumed leadership of a western alliance whose European junior partners lacked the ability to defend their interests in Africa and Asia, as Cold War rivalries collided with postcolonial nationalism. This included the French colony of Indochina (comprising Vietnam, Laos, and Cambodia). France had first taken over Vietnam in the 1860s. Like other imperial powers, Paris had ruled Vietnam for its own benefit, exploiting Vietnam's natural resources economically and repressing its people politically. The Vietnamese wanted the French out. Since 1945, France had struggled to reassert control over its former colony of Indochina amid a nationalist revolt led by the Communist Việt-minh, a Vietnamese political movement led by the popular, avuncular, and charismatic Hồ Chí Minh (the adopted name of Nguyễn Sinh Cung). This had led to the Franco-Việtminh War which, in the words of its preeminent chronicler, Fredrik Logevall, "was simultaneously an East-West and North-South conflict, pitting European imperialism in its autumn phase against the two main competitors that gained momentum by midcentury—Communist-inspired revolutionary nationalism and U.S.-backed liberal internationalism."[3]

The Việtminh had fought Japanese occupation during World War II (with American help) and now sought independence from the returning French. Inspired by President Roosevelt's anticolonialist rhetoric, Hồ had written his successor, Harry Truman, on October 22, 1945, for help against the reimposition of French colonialism in Vietnam, but neither Truman nor anyone of influence in Washington at the time ever saw Hồ's letter, much less answered it.[4] Preoccupied with the reconstruction of Germany and

Hồ Chí Minh
Everett Collection/Alamy Stock Photo

Japan and the conversion of the American economy to peacetime, the pleading of an obscure anti-Japanese guerrilla leader in Indochina seemed relatively unimportant in the fall of 1945 and was not forwarded up the chain; government machinery filters according to current priorities and interests, and in this case no one with Southeast Asian expertise possessed the sway needed for Hồ to be heard.

Vietnam remained of marginal significance to the United States in the years that immediately followed World War II. The doctrine of containment, first enunciated by President Truman in 1947, became a policy that both Democrats and Republicans endorsed as a sensible and sustainable response to the threat of Communist expansion. Fearful of alienating French cooperation with the Marshall Plan and Western European defense—particularly the creation of NATO with Paris at its core (France had the largest army in Western Europe)—Truman at first tolerated France's neocolonial effort in Vietnam, then indirectly aided it, and finally began actively assisting it after Communist North Korea invaded South Korea in June 1950. Just a few months later China intervened against U.S. forces and inflicted heavy casualties, intensifying Americans' belief that all Communist actions comprised elements of a single, implacably aggressive, global war against freedom.* Driven by this perception, U.S. military aid by 1954 financed 80 percent of the French war effort in Indochina. Truman's acceptance of the reimposition of French rule in Indochina seemed an unpleasant but minor trade-off at the time, with no thought given to the long-term implications for his successors.

Indeed, Truman had bigger things on his mind. Less than a year before the Korean War, the Soviet Union had detonated an atomic bomb and Mao Zedong's Communists had won the Chinese Civil War. The resulting anti-Communist hysteria in America led by Republican senator Joseph McCarthy (one of whose staff assistants was Bobby Kennedy) froze perceptions and attitudes. Constantly reinforced anti-Communism had what cognitive scientists call a "priming effect" among Americans, evoking information that was compatible with it and discarding that which was not.[5] Incidents in people's lives that are especially vivid, or recent, are likely to be recalled with special ease, and thus to be disproportionately weighted in any judgment. Amos Tversky and Daniel Kahneman called this the "availability heuristic," which leads to systematic biases. Tversky and Kahneman demonstrated this bias through their K experiment. Participants were asked, "If a random word is

---

* The reality, contrary to the perception at the time, was less sinister. Rather than initiating the invasion of South Korea, the Soviet leader at the time, Joseph Stalin, only slowly consented to North Korean leader Kim Il Sung's plan that both men expected would be over before the United States could come to the aid of South Korea. Chinese leader Mao Zedong decided to intervene early in the conflict because he feared the Americans would use Korea as a springboard to invade China—but waffled on implementing the decision for several months and tied it to Soviet military assistance. See Donggil Kim, "China's Intervention in the Korean War Revisited," *Diplomatic History*, v. 40, n. 5, 2016, pp. 1002-1026.

taken from a text in English, is it more likely that the word starts with a K, or that K is the third letter?" Participants overestimated the number of words that began with K and underestimated the number of words with K as the third letter—even though it is possible to make three times as many words with K as the third letter than words with K as the first letter, and texts in English typically contain twice as many words beginning with K than words with K as the third letter. It is easier to think of words that begin with K than words with K as the third letter. People's judgments are informed by how easily they recall things.[6] The priming effect and the availability heuristic made American policymakers prone to believe too strongly what they already believed. These combined with a tendency of policymakers—like people in general—to share basic assumptions that they rarely questioned.[7]

Another troublesome factor was what cognitive scientists call "theory-induced blindness": the fact, writes Kahneman, that "once you have accepted a theory and used it as a tool in your thinking, it is extraordinarily difficult to notice its flaws . . . You give the theory the benefit of the doubt, trusting the community of experts who have accepted it."[8] Because established theories give a coherent view of reality, contradictory facts are often overlooked or ignored until the theory is displaced.[9] Said simply, once people adopt a particular interpretation, they find it very difficult to see things any other way. Theory-induced blindness led nearly all Americans to uncritically assume the monolithic nature of Communism. A stereotype warped their judgment (as happened to many Communists who had a stereotypical view of the United States). Reinforcing these tendencies was the habit of people to reach conclusions on the basis of limited evidence—what Kahneman calls "WYSIATI" (What You See Is All There Is). WYSIATI leads people to focus on existing evidence and ignore absent evidence. People do so because this makes it easier to fit things into a coherent pattern. "It is the consistency of the information that matters for a good story," notes Kahneman, "not its completeness." He continues, "We often fail to allow for the possibility that evidence that should be critical to our judgment is missing—what we see is all there is." Almost perversely, it is by incompleteness that we complete: we construct interpretations on the basis of partial evidence because this facilitates achievement of consistency and coherence, which makes an interpretation plausible. Explains Kahneman, "You build the best possible story from the information available to you, and if it is a good story, you believe it . . . Our comforting conviction that the world makes sense rests on a secure foundation: our almost unlimited ability to ignore our ignorance."[10]

Limited knowledge can make for a compelling story and sometimes that story can lead (even by accident) to a favorable outcome. Indeed, since we can almost never know "it all," most of our decisions are to some extent based on information that, while fragmentary, can be sufficient. But WYSIATI also generates a limited set of basic assessments, reinforces biases, dulls the pursuit of completeness, and feeds overconfidence.[11] Afflicted by the priming effect, the availability heuristic, theory-induced blindness, and WYSIATI, American policymakers did not realize just how little they really knew about Vietnam—including that there was much more to know.

As a result, American policymakers failed to grasp, because they did not seek to discover, the historical enmity between China and Vietnam and thus to recognize that there were significant differences between Communists in China and Vietnam and the fact that Hồ Chí Minh, though a Communist, behaved primarily as a Vietnamese nationalist. They did not know the Vietnamese adage that the shape of Vietnam's coastline reflects a spine bent under the weight of China, its great neighbor to the north, with which it had fought more than a dozen wars dating back to 39 C.E. They did not know that, as a result, the Vietnamese developed an unyielding determination to resist foreign occupation at all costs, usually adopting guerrilla warfare to wear down more powerful armies through hit-and-run attacks, avoiding major engagements whenever possible, and using their knowledge of local terrain to establish weapons caches and inaccessible hideouts. They did not know about the Battle of Bach Dang in 938 C.E.—as famous in Vietnamese history as the 1775 Battles of Lexington and Concord are in American history—in which Vietnamese guerrilla fighters dealt a fatal blow to superior Chinese troops through the tactic of feint and strike. They did not know about the Lake of the Restored Sword in the heart of Hanoi, based on the legend that when the Ming dynasty ruled Vietnam, a fisherman named Lê Lợi found in his net a magical sword that empowered him to lead his people in a ten-year struggle that drove the Chinese out in 1428 C.E. and when Lê Lợi offered gratitude to the spirit of the lake, a giant golden tortoise snatched the sword and restored it to the depths. They did not know that when faced with the threat of French domination at the end of the nineteenth century, the Vietnamese had set aside their ancient suspicion of Chinese domination and pleaded with Beijing to come to their aid. American policymakers were conditioned so much that even if someone came to them with such information, they did not pay attention to it or discarded it as irrelevant. The atmosphere of Cold War America did not encourage such attention and awareness, or the perceptions and distinctions that went with them, so government decision-makers in Washington—for not the last time—remained dangerously ignorant and therefore seriously overestimated ideological factors and seriously underestimated historical and nationalistic ones.

It can be difficult to assess just how damaging America's domestic war against Communism was in hindering its foreign struggle against Communism. Come the 1950s, Democrats were on the defensive for having "lost" a major country (China) to Communism, an outcome that led Republicans like Vice President Richard Nixon to label the Democratic Party the party of treason. The Red Scare destroyed the reputations and careers of Foreign Service Officers and ostracized academics with regional expertise who had warned Washington of the weaknesses of Chiang Kai-shek's nationalist regime and the inevitable victory of Mao's Communists. Rising stars in the Democratic Party like John F. Kennedy and Lyndon B. Johnson learned to err on the side of being too tough rather than what might be seen as too soft in their approach to the world. From the China experience they became convinced that a country could not be lost to Communism without astronomical domestic political consequences. They learned not to question or reexamine foreign policy assumptions, at least publicly. If they did, they worried that most Americans would not understand. Kennedy and Johnson, anxious to protect their right flank, consciously took account of these elements, even if they did not share all of their assumptions. Leader or backbencher, any politician thinking about how to win the next election believed he must not lose the fiercely anti-Communist voters and media tycoons and newspaper editors who felt similarly.

National security officials who dominated at the upper levels of the State Department, the CIA, and the military and who continued their work as the White House changed hands—what admirers called the Cold War Establishment and critics today call the Deep State—embraced America's new commitment in Southeast Asia. They had an activist bent and saw the Cold War as their new mission. They became advocates for the commitment rather than analysts of what could be expected to work. It became an article of faith for them that the United States would not be trusted by its allies or respected by its enemies unless it proved its virtue by holding fast to its commitments. Their activist, hawkish attitude was imbedded in the politics of the time and reflected popular opinion in the United States from the late 1940s onward. The insistence by the Joint Chiefs during the Cuban Missile Crisis that if the United States did not pursue military action, America's global credibility would be destroyed was indicative of this line of thinking, and the peaceful conclusion of the crisis did little to change their worldview.

The United States had begun sending modest numbers of military advisors to Vietnam in 1950. Republican Dwight Eisenhower, elected president in 1952, sustained America's commitment in Indochina even as France's hold steadily weakened. Viêtminh forces supported by China and the Soviet Union and commanded by General Võ Nguyên Giáp wore down the French through guerrilla warfare as opposition to the conflict grew at home in France. Although the French enjoyed military superiority and controlled most cities, they were unable to bring the Viêtminh to decisive battle or to cripple its logistical network. In late 1953, the Việtminh laid siege to a French outpost in the remote valley of Điện Biên Phủ in far northwestern Vietnam, seeking to knock France out of the war. Although Eisenhower rejected U.S. military intervention when the siege of Điện Biên Phủ reached its climax in the spring of 1954, he was convinced of a need to contain Communist influence in Indochina. He famously predicted at the time that if Indochina fell, the rest of Southeast Asia would "go over very quickly" like a "row of dominos" and the consequences would be "incalculable to the free world."[12] Eisenhower's metaphor resonated in Cold War America and the domino theory took on a life of its own. It defined a linearly connected world in which weakness anywhere would have bad effects everywhere. This almost binary conception assumed a place in U.S. political discourse that quickly became unquestioned dogma.

Rather than seize the moment created by the French defeat at Điện Biên Phủ to wash its hands of the effort and walk away from the mess in Indochina, the Eisenhower administration essentially replaced the French. This dreadful transfer resulted from assumptions common in America at the time: France was a washed-up colonial power scheming to recapture yesterday's glory that had consequently performed like a junior varsity B team. The United States, on the other hand, was a great power that championed democracy and sought no selfish territorial gains—the varsity A team. America's power and moral virtue would be decisive. France had sought geographical conquest; the United States sought to rescue a beleaguered people from impending tyranny. That assessment was enough for most Americans. (A four-star U.S. general summed up the thinking: "The French haven't won a war since Napoleon. What can we learn from them?") The United States had the power and smarts to prevail where France had failed.

Negotiations to end the war between the Việtminh and the French and their respective allies—the Soviet Union and China on one side, the United States (which refused to have any contact with the Chinese delegation) and Britain on the other—began in Geneva in May 1954. The accords signed in July ended French rule in Indochina; created the separate states of Cambodia, Laos, and Vietnam; established a temporary partition of Vietnam at the seventeenth parallel, dividing a Việtminh-controlled North from a Western-aligned South; stipulated the eventual reunification of Vietnam through countrywide elections scheduled for 1956 for which the Việtminh, in return, agreed to regroup its forces above the seventeenth parallel, thus relinquishing control over much territory south of that line; and prohibited the introduction of additional foreign troops and military supplies into either northern or southern Vietnam, as well as the establishment of foreign bases and alliances. The United States, unhappy with the conference's ratification of Việtminh control over northern Vietnam, was the only major power not to endorse the accords, but it promised to "refrain from the threat or the use of force to disturb them."[13]

Following Geneva, Eisenhower set out to build a strong non-Communist South Vietnam under the leadership of Ngô Đình Diệm, who had lobbied for the job and was installed as prime minister in late June 1954. A fifty-three-year-old nationalist with the temperament of an ascetic aristocrat, a portly build, slicked-down black hair, and a stony face, Diệm belonged to a mandarin family from the old imperial capital of Huế that—unlike most Vietnamese—had converted to Catholicism in the late nineteenth century. In a country of semiliterate village farmers and fishermen, Diệm spoke fluent French, smoked Gauloises cigarettes, and wore tailored Western clothes—in his case, usually double-breasted white suits set off by a narrow black tie. Educated at a French lycée in Hanoi, he worked in the colonial apparatus during the 1920s and 1930s, but his proud family heritage fed a desire for Vietnamese autonomy as strong as his Catholicism's distaste for Communism, which had been intensified by the Việtminh's assassination of his older brother Ngô Đình Khôi in 1945. Diệm denounced Emperor Bảo Đại, who ruled from the French Riviera, as a tool of Paris even as both helped French forces suppress Việtminh revolts. Many of the years that Hồ and the Việtminh spent in the rice paddies and jungles against the French fighting and dying for national independence—and thus gaining priceless street credibility with

Ngô Đình Diệm
Everett Collection/Alamy Stock Photo

the mass of ordinary Vietnamese villagers—Diệm spent in exile in the United States at Francis Cardinal Spellman's Maryknoll
Seminaries in Lakewood Township, New Jersey, and Ossining,
New York, meditating, networking, and cultivating American politicians, journalists, and academics.

By turns autocratic, incorruptible, self-righteous, patriotic, and
aloof, Diệm paternalistically considered himself to have the same
relationship to his countrymen as a Vietnamese father with absolute authority had to his children. He looked down on the rural
masses as "unlettered peasantry," in the words of a CIA officer
who knew him well, and believed maintaining a strong line of
authority kept the country from falling apart.[14] Diệm saw himself
as the leader destined to defend Vietnamese culture and independence, as his country's energetic savior from totalitarian Communism, despite the fact that he lacked personal charisma and

broad popular appeal. Diệm confronted overwhelming problems with little executive experience and little willingness to delegate authority. While he worked sixteen to eighteen hours a day and read everything that crossed his desk—he signed every exit visa himself—to many he seemed ethereal and unworldly, as if more at home in the contemplative atmosphere of the monastery than Saigon's rough-and-tumble political world of religious sects, secret societies, gangsterism, and venal opportunists. Whatever Diệm's limitations, however, Washington believed it could bring him along and build him up over time. "A truly representative government was certainly our objective in the long run," Ambassador Frederick Reinhardt recalled secretary of state John Foster Dulles saying, "but one shouldn't be unrealistic in thinking it was something to be achieved in a matter of weeks or days." Besides—and here was the crucial and telling point—Dulles privately conceded that "no better substitute had been advanced."[15]

The buildup began in the media, much of it through stories directly planted by the U.S. government. The weekly photo magazine *Life* depicted Diệm as a "tough miracle man" who had halted "the red tide of Communism in Asia." The *Saturday Evening Post* called South Vietnam "the Bright Spot in Asia." The *New York Times* trumpeted his "firm concept of human rights." More concretely, the Eisenhower administration lavished Diệm with money—more economic aid per capita than all but two other countries; when his government ran low on funds, he simply asked the Americans for more and got it. The Eisenhower administration set up the U.S. Military Assistance Advisory Group, comprising American advisors, to organize and train the South Vietnamese army (ARVN). It funded the work of the Michigan State University Vietnam Advisory Group under the direction of professor Wesley Fishel, which administered an economic development program. It flew Diệm to Washington, where the president met him at the airport before he addressed a joint session of Congress. The CIA provided offstage counsel from Edward Lansdale, the counterinsurgency and nation-building expert who had advised Ramon Magsaysay after the Philippines gained its independence in 1946.

France had ruled Vietnamese society indirectly, through a local Catholic elite that derived influence from its connection with
the French and the faithful support of their rule. This neoman-
darin class substituted for the independent Vietnamese polity that
France never permitted; elective institutions for channeling political conflict had been forbidden. With America's money, Diệm per-
petuated a social and political structure that had been fashioned
under French colonialism and consolidated his control of South
Vietnam. He did so not by attracting widespread participation and
loyalty—as Lansdale advocated—but by stacking his cabinet with
relatives and quelling dissent through repression of civil liberties
and detention of political and religious opponents. He assumed the
people of South Vietnam *ought* to support him; and like any auto-
crat who could not conceive of government as a matter of give-
and-take, he exercised top-down authority through a subservient
bureaucracy—most of whom came from the landowning elite that
had absorbed the habits and values of the French—and the military. Symbolically and ideologically, he rarely walked rice paddies
with his countrymen. "Society functions through proper relationships among men at the top," he declared.[16] "I know what is best for
my people," he endlessly repeated to Lansdale and every American
visitor.[17]

Diệm's sense of entitlement was so great that he did not view
the 1954 Geneva Accords as binding on him because he had not
signed them. In 1956, he thwarted the promised election leading
to reunification, citing the absence of free voting in the North (yet
Diệm himself had rigged a plebiscite ousting Emperor Bảo Đại the
year before with more than 98 percent of the vote*). Eisenhower
endorsed Diệm's decision,† suspecting the South Vietnamese leader
would be crushed in a legitimate contest. As Ike candidly remarked

---

* The official results: Diem: 5,721,735; Bao Dai: 63,017. This included 605,025 votes
for Diem in Saigon, where only 450,000 voters were registered. Even American
officials, such as later CIA Saigon station chief William Colby, called it "the worst
form of manipulated façade." William Colby OHI, LBJL.

† So, too, did Massachusetts senator John F. Kennedy, a supporter of Diem and a
rising star in the Democratic Party during the 1950s.

in his memoirs, "I . . . never talked or corresponded with a person knowledgeable in Indochinese affairs who did not agree that had elections been held as of the time of the fighting, possibly 80 percent of the population would have voted for the Communist Hồ Chí Minh as their leader."[18] By acquiescing to Diệm's decision to abort the 1956 election, however, the Eisenhower administration effectively sealed Vietnam's political division. Eisenhower and most other Americans in the 1950s simply could not imagine a Third-World Communist independent of Moscow and Beijing. Through this filter, Hồ was not a Communist nationalist wary of traditional Chinese domination of Southeast Asia and eager to establish and protect Vietnam's independence, but a cunning and obedient acolyte of the Sino-Soviet camp serving its larger purpose of aggressive expansion. They did not know that Moscow and Beijing had actually counseled Hanoi against supporting armed struggle in South Vietnam out of fear that it might draw the United States directly into the conflict, and continued to do so through the early 1960s.[19] Yet even without that intelligence, it was remarkable how easily America's leaders ignored knowable history.

Washington came to believe that a two-Vietnams solution was possible just the way two Germanys and two Koreas had been. In this sense, assisting a small, pro-Western, anti-Communist government seemed a logical and appropriate extension of earlier Cold War policies that had proven successful. But while Diệm committed to develop democratic institutions, his authoritarian rule and prioritization of loyalty over competence in the government continued to undercut this stated goal. By 1958, Diệm-related unrest among non-Communists and former Việtminh in South Vietnam alike had given way to open rebellion. Shortly thereafter, in 1959, North Vietnam reactivated its support of southern Communists who had remained behind after Geneva. They, along with non-Communist opponents of Diệm, formed a popular front that in December 1960 became known officially as the National Front for the Liberation of South Vietnam (NLF), which Diệm and the Americans derisively called the Vietcong (a derogatory contraction of "Vietnamese Communists"). The NLF adopted guerrilla warfare against the Diệm regime.

Hanoi's decision to support the NLF resulted from several factors. By 1959, it had lost hope of achieving reunification through diplomacy because of Saigon's and Washington's steadfast intransigence toward countrywide elections. At the same time, having ended its war with France, consolidated its internal position, and recovered from a disastrous land reform program that had set back the Hanoi regime for several years, North Vietnam had developed sufficient strength to pursue militarily what it had been denied politically. Finally, Diệm's tightening repression had generated an enticing degree of political disaffection within South Vietnam, which Hanoi could exploit through the small but dedicated cadre of underground Vietcong who saw themselves as fighting to liberate the country and redistribute the land while Diệm represented "the rich, the landowners, the city."[20]

During this same period, Eisenhower increased U.S. support for the Diệm regime. Assuming responsibility for training and equipping the ARVN after the full French departure in 1955, Washington structured the ARVN along conventional lines based upon America's most recent war in Korea rather than unconventional lines based upon Vietnam's most recent war between France and the Việtminh. Washington also bolstered its military advisory forces. From 1955 to 1959, the number of American military advisors to the ARVN increased, as did opposition to Diệm's regime. By the close of Eisenhower's tenure in January 1961, the United States had poured more than $7 billion in economic and military assistance into South Vietnam and publicly allied itself with Diệm.

Eisenhower's successor maintained the commitment despite considerable misgivings based on personal experience. Kennedy's Irish heritage, instinctive skepticism, and detachment sensitized him to anticolonialist sentiment and when he visited Indochina during a seven-week trip across Asia in the fall of 1951, he came away doubting France's ability to quell Vietnamese nationalism, whatever its ideological persuasion. ("We are more and more becoming

colonialists in the minds of the people," he noted in a trip diary.)
Kennedy supported the Vietnamese hunger for independence in
speeches after he returned home. ("This is going to cost me some
votes with my French Catholic constituents," he said privately,
"but it seems like the right thing to do.") Telling a nationwide radio audience that "we have allied ourselves to the desperate effort
of a French regime to hang on to the remnants of empire," Kennedy warned that Communism in Vietnam could not be checked
"only through reliance on the force of arms" and that to act "in
defiance of innately nationalistic aims spells foredoomed failure."
At the time of the climactic Việtminh siege of Điện Biên Phủ in the
spring of 1954, he had proclaimed: "To pour money, materiel, and
men into the jungles of Indochina without at least a remote prospect of victory would be dangerously futile and self-destructive."[21]
To preserve the old order and ignore the national aspirations of the
Vietnamese, Kennedy made clear, spelled doom.

Yet Kennedy moderated his criticism as the decade went on and
he rose from the House of Representatives to the Senate and began preparing to run for the White House. The robust American
conservative tendencies of the 1950s had not diminished and they
reinforced Kennedy's Catholic anti-Communism—a sensibility he
shared with Diệm. Events in Asia were understood through a lens
of recent casting: Truman's beating over the "loss of China" in 1949
continued to instruct every Democratic politician aspiring to national office not to appear soft on Communism. Kennedy understood the damaging effect of such charges because he had helped
to inflict them. "The responsibility for the failure of our foreign
policy in the Far East," he had pronounced on the House floor on
January 25, 1949, "rests squarely with the White House and the
Department of State. Our policy of vacillation, uncertainty, and
confusion has reaped the whirlwind."[22] In a keynote address to a
lobby group called the Americans Friends of Vietnam in June 1956,
Kennedy publicly declared that "Vietnam represents the cornerstone of the Free World in Southeast Asia, the keystone in the
arch, the finger in the dike"—in short, "a test of American responsibility and determination." "This is our offspring," he concluded.

"We cannot abandon it."[23] Kennedy saw (or wanted to see) Diệm as an indigenous nationalist who would trump both French colonialism and Việtminh Communism. His detachment—so valuable in some circumstances—isolated him at times, preventing him from learning more, and his attachment to his own political future sometimes did the same.

"It is very hard to recapture the innocence and confidence with which we approached Vietnam in the early days of the Kennedy administration," Robert McNamara lamented three decades later.[24] Unlike cabinet members in a parliamentary system such as Great Britain's who before assuming office have studied the issues for years as shadow ministers in the political opposition, McNamara and his senior colleagues possessed scant knowledge and even less understanding of Southeast Asian history, language, and culture. What did they know about Vietnam? "Not enough to have done what we did," McNamara later confessed.[25] "It was a tiny blip on the radar and we didn't understand at the beginning how it would develop," McNamara admitted, looking back.[26]

While by 1961 many of the early dynamics of the Cold War—Stalinist brutality, Sino-Soviet cooperation, Moscow's considerable influence on other Communist movements—had begun to fade, American perceptions, assumptions, and political rhetoric remained rooted in an earlier mindset. (The Soviet Union suffered from its own simplistic myopia about the West during this period.) As a result, Kennedy and his advisors made policy on Vietnam by relying on Cold War blueprints that assumed the monolithic nature of Communism, defined Communism and nationalism in mutually exclusive terms, and understood the domino theory as a given, filtering it all through fear of a domestic political firestorm that would follow the loss of a country to Communism. They feared the costs of what they termed a "cut-and-run" policy "too much and too automatically," said Bundy retrospectively.[27] More fundamentally, "we never fully explored each other's views about Communism and the danger of it in Asia, particularly Southeast Asia," McNamara later acknowledged.[28]

JFK with Map of Vietnam
Cecil Stoughton/JFK Library

The dysfunction and inadequacies of the national security bureaucracy only made matters worse. The CIA had precious little expertise in Southeast Asia. Its World War II forerunner, the Office of Strategic Services, had appointed as head of its Southeast Asia Division a man whose Indochinese experience amounted to bird-watching along the Chinese-Vietnamese border.[29] The State Department failed to train any Vietnamese-speaking foreign service officers until the early- to mid-1960s, relying instead on French speakers who could communicate only with urban elites—a symptom of the lack of knowledge of the underlying cultural and political forces at work in Vietnam. "Those who did know" more than a little about Vietnam, wrote CIA official Richard Helms, looking back, "were too far down the line of command to have impact on the national-level policymakers."[30] The American academic world shouldered some of the blame, too: after World War II and even up through the late 1960s, universities as great as Harvard relegated study of the Francophone world, including Indochina, to French scholars.[31]

As a result, the Kennedy administration came to the conclusion that while Diệm headed a strong-man government for a people not yet prepared for democracy, he sincerely sought "to move his people forward toward freedom," as McNamara later said. As they "got closer and closer to the situation," in McNamara's words, they began to realize that "he sure as hell wasn't a democrat and surely the people around him weren't and even if they were, they hadn't been able to convey their thoughts to their people and develop a bond with them. We were just *totally wrong* in that." In addition, they "totally underestimated the nationalist aspect of Hồ Chí Minh's movement," admitted McNamara. "We saw him first as a Communist and only second as a Vietnamese nationalist."[32] This combination of unexamined assumptions and entrenched convictions—perhaps *the* fundamental failure of America in Vietnam—would prove disastrous and deadly.

The beginning of Kennedy's presidency also marked a time of intense Sino-Soviet competition for leadership of the Communist bloc. As the people of Africa and Asia asserted their independence from European rule, the Soviet Union and China curried their favor by championing "wars of liberation" from colonial oppression. Interpreting this exhortation and its heated rhetoric as a challenge to the United States rather than to each other, Kennedy stepped up American efforts in the Third World, including Vietnam. "He was deeply interested in Vietnam," wrote McGeorge Bundy, looking back, and "inclined from the first to believe that the United States should do more there, and do it better."[33] A series of international crises during his first year reinforced his concerns. In April 1961, Kennedy experienced the Bay of Pigs disaster; in June, sparred with Khrushchev at a stormy summit in Vienna; in July, began sensitive negotiations on the neutralization of Laos; and in August, the world had witnessed the construction of the Berlin Wall. "There are limits to the number of defeats I can defend in one twelve-month period," JFK confided to an aide that fall. "I've had the Bay of Pigs and pulling out of Laos, and I can't accept a third."[34]

The contrast between the American focus on Vietnam and Laos was striking. A civil war had been underway in Laos since 1950 between the Communist Pathet Lao, supported by the Soviet Union and North Vietnam, and the royalist government, supported by the United States. At their Vienna summit, Kennedy and Khrushchev agreed to the neutralization of Laos. Kennedy did not want to become involved in landlocked Laos with its mountainous terrain and ready access from China, and thought he could hold the line against Communist expansion better in neighboring South Vietnam, where the U.S. presence had been greater for longer and whose coastline along the South China Sea and better logistical infrastructure afforded more favorable conditions for the projection of American power. The Declaration on the Neutrality of Laos signed at Geneva on July 23, 1962, led to the de facto partition of the country, with the royalist government controlling the cities along the Mekong River and the Pathet Lao the mountainous eastern region that included North Vietnam's infiltration routes into South Vietnam (the Trường Sơn Strategic Supply Route or Highway 559*—later known to Americans as the Hồ Chí Minh Trail). The Soviet Union and the United States agreed to withdraw their military aid to the country. North Vietnam also signed the declaration, but soon began violating it by expanding the Hồ Chí Minh Trail. In response, the United States resumed covert aid to the royalist government and the Hmong mountain tribes who opposed Hanoi's presence in Laos.

Diệm's position, meanwhile, had declined markedly by the fall of 1961. Facing heavier Vietcong attacks and eroding support throughout the country, he petitioned Washington for more help.

---

* The number 559 commemorated the month (May) and year (1959) that Hanoi resumed active support of the southern insurgency.

Kennedy, a great believer in fact-finding missions, sent White House military advisor* General Maxwell Taylor and Deputy National Security Advisor Walt Rostow to Saigon to assess conditions and recommend appropriate action. The two men arrived in South Vietnam on October 18 and submitted their report when they returned to Washington on November 3. They urged a substantial increase in U.S. support, including more military advisors and even limited numbers of combat troops under the guise of flood control relief—all part of a fundamental "transition from advice to partnership" by expanding American participation in counterinsurgency operations.[35] The combat troop request took Kennedy by surprise and reawakened his skepticism. "The troops will march in; the bands will play; the crowds will cheer," he told Arthur Schlesinger, "and in four days everyone will have forgotten." "It's like taking a drink," Kennedy explained. "The effect wears off, and you have to take another."[36]

Instinctively opposed to involving American troops on the Asian mainland, Kennedy refused Taylor's—and, by extension, the military's—request for combat troops. "The President did not," McNamara later noted, "wish to make an unconditional commitment to preventing the fall of South Vietnam to Communism."[37] He did his best, however, to conceal his refusal. "There was no announcement of it," Bundy later noted. "Instead there was deceptive backgrounding with selected members of the White House Press to the effect that no such proposal had been made"[38]—a reflection of Kennedy's abiding concern not to appear insufficiently anti-Communist.

Yet precisely *because* Kennedy refused the combat troop request, he felt compelled to grant the request for more American advisors. The number of U.S. military advisors increased dramatically over the subsequent two years. In November 1961, the number stood at 948. By January 1962, it rose to 2,646. In June of that year, it climbed to 5,579. At the end of 1962, it reached 11,300. By October 1963, the month before Kennedy's death, it stood at 16,732—more

---

* Taylor would become chairman of the Joint Chiefs in October 1962.

than twenty times as many as when Kennedy had taken office, and far more than the 685 permitted under the Geneva Accords. Ominously, under Kennedy U.S. military advisors began accompanying South Vietnamese into battle, also in violation of the Geneva Accords.

The man who knew Kennedy's thinking on Vietnam better than anyone else except perhaps his brother Bobby, Robert McNamara, later reflected that Kennedy "was influenced by two factors. First, the nearly unanimous view of his advisors that without such assistance, South Vietnam would be lost and, with it, all of Southeast Asia—these would be two devastating blows to the West's containment policy." Then there was Kennedy's own political containment strategy: "Secondly, he undoubtedly believed that the damage to the [Western] alliance and his domestic political standing would be less if he tried to help the Vietnamese help themselves and they proved incapable of doing so than it would if he failed to make such an effort."[39] This was JFK's hedge: no matter what, don't let the critics say you didn't try, and if the effort failed, make it clear that the fault lay in others.

The same month that Kennedy approved a substantial increase in American military advisors, November 1961, McNamara—Kennedy's most energetic and, after Bobby, loyal lieutenant—volunteered to become his point man on Vietnam. McNamara's reputation in Washington had reached dizzying heights. In less than a year, he had quickly and effectively wrested control of the Pentagon from parochial generals and admirals—the first secretary of defense, with the possible exception of James Forrestal, to actually do so. The president thought "most highly of McNamara," Bobby later said of his brother, "more than any other cabinet member."[40] There seemed to be no problem that he could not fix on behalf of the president—at least, he believed so. The military advisory effort in South Vietnam lay within the Pentagon's jurisdiction, and no one else at the top of the administration had deep knowledge of Indochina, so no else seemed a better candidate.

McNamara quickly became the administration's key person on Vietnam in the eyes of the bureaucracy, Congress, Washington's political class, and the American public. Choose the right people, give them the right terms of reference, and hold them accountable—that was how McNamara believed things should be done. When he believed in what he was doing, he was relentless—he drove everyone, most of all himself, very hard. "He felt very sure of himself," his deputy Roswell Gilpatric later said, but he also felt "a very heavy responsibility because he knew the President's reluctance about the whole operation."[41] McNamara believed he could make productive judgments and recommendations about Vietnam based on enough information and then delegate responsibility for carrying out those decisions to the military. But while confident—perhaps overconfident—he was no fool. McNamara was exceptionally intelligent, forceful, earnest, and intense—a man who strived with perseverance to get things done. McNamara had brought to the Defense Department the formidable executive skills he had developed in marshaling Ford's huge platoons of managers and factory workers. But he was fundamentally ill-equipped and ill-prepared to deal with Vietnam because his experience was administrative and managerial, not political and regional. He had never even visited Indochina before he became secretary of defense. He did not know how to penetrate to the core of Vietnam's complex problems because he lacked expertise, intuition, and insight about Southeast Asia.

At this point, Vietnam was a hard subject but in comparative terms not a big one. Yet those who could recognize the shades of red were beyond McNamara's field of vision. The Pentagon had few specialists on Vietnam. Officials far more knowledgeable about the history, culture, and politics of Vietnam and Indochina existed at the lower levels of the State Department, the Agency for International Development (AID), and the CIA, but those with the most extensive firsthand, long-term knowledge and understanding worked in the field thousands of miles from the corridors of power in Washington. Established structures and procedures channeled the experts' information and insights up through their respective departments, not directly to the Office of the Secretary of Defense. Within the Defense Department, understanding of the political dynamics of Vietnam was very limited—military, not political, affairs was its bailiwick—and this shaped the information and insights available to McNamara as he initially confronted and defined the problem; where he sat inevitably influenced what he saw. The separation between the field-based, street-level Vietnam experts who understood the gritty nuances of the country inside out and McNamara's office in the outermost ring of the Pentagon facing the Potomac River literally and figuratively spanned an immense ocean. The insights and wisdom of Vietnam experts would have helped him to ask better questions and to anticipate and concentrate on fundamental issues that McNamara in his ignorance failed to see or overlooked.

Instead, McNamara approached Vietnam the way he had successfully approached challenges throughout his career, whether logistical bottlenecks in the army air corps during World War II or production and profit issues at the Ford Motor Company after the war: through the careful analysis of numbers. "All you're giving me are conclusions," he often said. "You're not giving me any evidence. Where's the hard evidence? Where are the statistics?" McNamara was skeptical of people assessing themselves— "individuals reporting on their own performance are generally optimistic," he observed[42]—so he put much greater emphasis on "objective" quantitative measurements than on anecdotal reports of progress. It was a familiar and time-tested process to him: identify the key variables, collect and evaluate the relevant findings, then move to fix things. The more he could quantify, the better; to do otherwise seemed an imprecise and inferior approach. When a CIA analyst expressed doubts to McNamara about the effectiveness of statistically assessing a guerrilla war, "it was as if I had been talking to a devout Catholic and had questioned the Virgin Birth," the analyst later recalled.[43]

McNamara had been an "organization man" his entire adult life. In the 1950s, *Fortune* magazine editor William H. Whyte Jr. published a penetrating sociological study titled *The Organization Man*. Organization men, noted Whyte, subscribed to a collective ethos and considered serving an organization preferable to advancing one's individual opinions. They committed to the organization over and above their personal interests. McNamara was no different. He believed an individual should dedicate his talents to serving the organization to which he belonged. He had learned to operate within the context and constraints of large corporate entities not by challenging their foundations, but by making them work. In his current organization, the Pentagon, he would translate its military vocabulary and grammar into the language of numbers familiar and useful to him. And in a war without battle lines on a map, how else to measure progress except through quantitative measurements of casualties, engagements, weapons seizures, desertions, and so forth? He would slowly and painfully learn that Vietnam would not prove so amenable to quantitative analysis, and he would personally feel the consequences for years to come.

Like most quantitative analysts of his generation, McNamara assumed that he could correctly estimate probabilities of various outcomes or at least avoid estimating probabilities in a biased way. But empirical research has demonstrated that this is not true: the vast majority of people misjudge probabilities based on what Kahneman and Tversky called the "law of small numbers"—that is, they tend to extensively generalize from small amounts of data; they have too much faith in what they learn from a few observations; and they are prone to exaggerate the meaning and consistency of what they see.[44] McNamara exhibited this tendency. He had limited data on Vietnam with which to work, but he persuaded himself that given his intellect he could estimate probable outcomes based on that limited data. This led him toward what Kahneman and Tversky call "the illusion of validity," a cognitive bias in which people overestimate their ability to interpret and predict outcomes when analyzing a set of data, in particular when the data analyzed show a consistent pattern—that is, when the data "tell" a coherent story. This effect persists even when people are aware of what they don't know, which is often a great deal.[45] McNamara's faith in a limited amount of questionable data was his great misestimation, not his calculus. He could get the right number, but he overestimated his ability to ask the right questions. It was not the brilliance of his mind, but how he applied it.

Before making his first of what would prove to be many visits to South Vietnam in May 1962, McNamara received a briefing from Edward Lansdale in his capacity as deputy assistant for special operations to the secretary of defense. At the briefing, McNamara asked Lansdale to critique a list of factors he had drawn up to evaluate progress in the war against the Vietcong. All of them involved statistical measurement: number of enemy killed, number of weapons captured, number of operations launched, number of aircraft sorties flown, number of additional troops trained and equipped—the list covered many areas. Lansdale looked over the list and replied, "Your list is incomplete. You've left out the most important factor of all." "What is it?" asked McNamara. "Well, it's the human factor," Lansdale said. "You can put it down as the x factor"—without it, the list would be inevitably misleading. McNamara penciled an x on his graph paper and asked Lansdale what it consisted of. "What the people out on the battlefield really feel; which side they want to see win and which side they're for at the moment. That's the only way you're going to ever have this war decided." "Tell me how to put it in," replied McNamara. "I don't think any Americans out there at the moment can report this to you," Lansdale answered. McNamara knitted his brow and began erasing the x. Although Lansdale had provided no ready and convincing answer, he urged McNamara to leave it in.*[46]

---

* Two months later, Lansdale sent McNamara a list of questions for American advisors working in the field, such as "What [are] the villages' attitude toward [South] Vietnamese troops?" and "What are the feelings of [ARVN] troops at being in military service?," that led to the creation of the Hamlet Evaluation System (HES), a database of information on South Vietnamese villages and ratings of security conditions. The HES had fatal flaws from the start. David Donovan, a first lieutenant in a remote district of the Mekong Delta, later wrote: "I saw District Senior Advisors [DSAs] give the [HES] reports they should have filled out themselves to their less informed and less experienced subordinates. Sometimes the instructions would be to just fill in the blanks with anything that seemed reasonable. Meeting the deadline for submission of the report was the important thing, not accuracy. Often reports on hamlets were filled in when the hamlet had never been seen by the DSA or any of his team members." Max Boot, *The Road Not Taken: Edward Lansdale and the Amer-*

McNamara began his initial trip to Vietnam in Saigon, where he held a series of meetings with senior officials of the American mission at the U.S. embassy on Lê Văn Duyệt Street, where the Arroyo Chinois flowed into the muddy Saigon River. At these meetings, he stressed that (per Kennedy): South Vietnam had become America's "number one priority" but the United States should not carry the burden of combat—ARVN must learn to do it themselves. He also spent considerable time at U.S. Military Assistance Command, Vietnam (MACV) headquarters located in a converted colonial-era hotel on Rue Pasteur in downtown Saigon. There, he received a long series of carefully prepared and elaborate military briefings complete with flip charts and graphs in the Combat Operations Center, a conference room containing a large, long table rimmed with chairs, at the end of which stood a lectern. McNamara sat at the head of the table. The briefings left him unimpressed and cold. "He didn't like men in uniform with pointers reading off things," his deputy, Roswell Gilpatric, observed. "He wanted to ask his own questions, and he wanted un-stereotyped answers."[47]

McNamara then toured the countryside by helicopter. Strapped in a jump seat, wearing padded earphones to protect his hearing from the loud whoosh of the rotor blades, he pored over data and scribbled notes as he flew from one destination to another. Dressed in rumpled khaki shirt and pants and dusty leather, lug-soled hiking boots, McNamara visited corps headquarters, province headquarters, district headquarters, and rural communities hidden behind bamboo hedges surrounded by electric-green rice paddies. At each stop, armed with a lined notepad on which he scratched notes (his left-handed script almost indecipherable), he fired questions at everyone he met, from unassuming villagers to American generals. To his great credit, McNamara did not believe that good ideas came from just one person or one place. He quickly grasped the unconventional nature of the war against the Vietcong. "He saw the humblest sort of military force in Vietnam, which is the

ican Tragedy in Vietnam (Liveright, 2018), p. 367; and David Donovan, *Once a Warrior King: Memories of an Officer in Vietnam* (McGraw-Hill, 1985).

little hamlet militia," a military officer traveling with him recalled, "and perceived that they were the least trained, the least organized, the poorest armed of everybody in Vietnam and said to me, 'These are important people. We should put money into them instead of larger forces.'"[48] But while McNamara was perceptive and adaptable, and not wide of the mark in many of his assessments, because he felt tasked to find a solution within the well-established parameters regarding Cold War and American political dynamics, his analysis was processed via equations that were incomplete and biased.

Sensitive to Kennedy's desire to limit American military involvement,* even as the number of U.S. military advisors increased—a contradiction that went unnoticed and unaddressed by both the president and his defense secretary—McNamara asked the head of MACV, General Paul Harkins, how long it would take to conclude the advisory effort. "I was operating on the belief that we were there to train the Vietnamese to defend themselves," McNamara later observed, "and that we should be thinking about an end to that training support."[49] Harkins frankly—and tellingly—replied that he had not thought about an exit strategy. McNamara told the general to prepare such a plan and submit it at their next conference. When they met again at Camp H. M. Smith, the former Pearl Harbor naval hospital outside Honolulu, Hawaii, on July 23, Harkins presented a withdrawal blueprint, called the Comprehensive Plan, drafted by military experts in Washington and Saigon and formulated for reducing the rapidly rising number of U.S. advisors in South Vietnam from 7,500 to 1,600. Harkins told McNamara it would take "one year from the time that we are able to get [the Saigon forces] fully operational and really pressing the VC† in all areas." McNamara, whom experience had taught to be conserva-

---

* Roswell Gilpatric later recalled that Kennedy "made clear to McNamara and me that he wanted to not only hold the level of U.S. military presence in Vietnam down, but he wanted to reverse the flow." Roswell Gilpatric OHI, LBJL.

† "VC" became the acronym—a common feature of military jargon—for Vietcong in U.S. military circles during the Vietnam War.

tive in making estimates, tripled the timeframe to the end of 1965 and urged Harkins to work toward the 1965 target. Believing the monitoring of progress to be a bedrock principle of good leadership, he set the Comprehensive Plan's schedule as the metric defining the general's performance.[50]

McNamara's decision-making approach to Vietnam at this early stage made no allowance for the unquantifiable but crucial intangibles of war, the human and political factors that lay at the root of the conflict, that drove it in fundamental respects, but that could not be counted, such as the disconnect between the South Vietnamese people and their government and the Việtminh's fanatical drive to unify the country under their banner of Communist nationalism. No metric existed to gauge the intense élan and willingness to sacrifice of the Vietcong and the North Vietnamese. These particular and considerable advantages could not be perceived, much less expressed, in numbers or percentages. To this extent, McNamara's comment to a journalist at the end of his first visit to South Vietnam—"Every quantitative measurement we have shows that we're winning this war"[51]—revealed an ultimately devastating truth about the inadequacy of McNamara's conceptual framework.

McNamara's reliance on quantitative measurement echoed the approach he had used as a statistical control officer assessing the efficacy of U.S. Army Air Corps bombing operations against Germany and later Japan during World War II. His approach in that conflict had been the same toward Western Europeans as it had been toward East Asians. But McNamara's unfamiliarity with Vietnam and its people played a part: it reinforced his simplistic reliance on that earlier approach. McNamara's cultural ignorance discouraged him from considering, and weighing, the all-important political complexities of Vietnam that could not be expressed in numbers, and yet would prove so decisive.

McNamara sought to broaden his base of information by meeting with ARVN generals and South Vietnamese government officials. However, cultural differences between Americans and Vietnamese created an unspoken dynamic that McNamara failed to detect and therefore to compensate for or to remedy. McNamara expected ARVN generals to be blunt like American commanders and clinically analytical like him. But that was not how Vietnamese communicated with those whom they did not know well. Candor in Vietnamese culture grew out of personal relationships and trust built up slowly over a long period of time, and ARVN generals did not feel comfortable being frank in formal meetings with visiting foreign dignitaries, however important, earnest, and inquisitive they were. Exhibiting the traditional Vietnamese tendency to keep unpleasant matters confidential within the extended family, the ARVN officers often told McNamara what they thought he wanted to hear and believed would meet his expectations. Those who knew the country, its people, and its customs well—such as Rufus Phillips, an old Vietnam hand who headed AID's Rural Affairs Program—understood much better how Vietnamese communicated. Phillips explained—not to McNamara but in his memoirs many years later—that "[South] Vietnamese officers would never reveal their true thoughts to a high-ranking American whom they did not know personally, certainly never in front of other [South] Vietnamese officers."[52] Phillips could have told McNamara at the time, so some of the blame was his. McNamara's ignorance of Vietnamese culture and manners blinded him to this practice.

This lack of cultural awareness and his heavy reliance on statistics increased McNamara's vulnerability to the exploitation of statistics by others. Much of the numerical data that McNamara sought and used to inform his understanding of the conflict, his private recommendations to President Kennedy, and his public statements to the press and the American people, originated from South Vietnamese sources. He did not ask ARVN officers probing and searching questions like "Where do your statistics come from?" and "How did you compile them?" because he assumed those he asked would be frank. One indicator—killed by air, or KBA—illustrated the limitations and vulnerabilities of relying on "objective" statistics. Because the Vietcong made a practice whenever possible of carrying away their dead from the battlefield,

South Vietnamese pilots routinely estimated rather than actually counted the number of KBA when flying over after a battle. One American advisor privately reckoned that this process inflated the KBA count by 40 percent.

The data contained in the South Vietnamese's excessively optimistic reports, moreover, often reflected more than the human impulse to please an important and demanding stranger whose organization funded most of their operations and their salaries. There were other benefits of positive reporting: McNamara did not know it at the time, but he later learned that Diệm's government distributed resources to the provinces not in proportion to need but in proportion to reported success in the war. CIA analysts later concluded that "province and district chiefs felt obliged to 'create statistics' which would meet the approbation of the Central Government." "How many villages are there in your district?" a village chief was asked shortly after Diệm's government fell. "Twenty-four," he said. "And how many do you control?" "Eight," answered the chief. "And how many did you tell Saigon you controlled?" "Twenty-four," the chief sheepishly replied.[53] "To understand a good story," notes psychologist Thomas Gilovich, "it is necessary to examine the needs of the speaker and listener, and the goals they try to achieve in their interaction"—"goals that are most likely to introduce bias and distortion in the content of the communication." Explains Gilovich, "A person's conclusions can only be as solid as the information on which they are based. Thus, a person who is exposed to almost nothing but inaccurate information on a given subject almost inevitably develops an erroneous belief, a belief that can seem to be 'an irresistible product' of the individual's secondhand experience."[54] The South Vietnamese told McNamara a good story.

General Harkins proved equally susceptible to such reports. Fifty-seven years old with short-cropped gray hair, deep blue eyes, a strong nose, and a chiseled chin, the West Point graduate looked "every inch the professional soldier," as Time described him. A protégé of General George S. Patton, whom he had served as deputy chief of staff of the U.S. Third Army during World War II, the quiet and proper Harkins stood ramrod straight in his crisp khakis and carried a swagger stick like his flamboyant mentor, but he had a more reserved demeanor and a staff officer's aversion to the limelight and determination to please his civilian boss. Harkins recognized that ARVN officers gained promotion through bribery or political influence,* but he—like the Joint Chiefs and McNamara—uncritically accepted their reporting because they knew more about their country than he did, because he assumed them to be honest, and because their reporting reinforced his (and McNamara's) assumptions and expectations. On one visit to the Mekong Delta, a local South Vietnamese commander told Harkins that he had built three times as many "protected hamlets"† as originally planned because the population desperately wanted to be brought into them. Harkins's job was to train ARVN to help defeat the Vietcong and what ARVN officers told him seemed to confirm it was doing just that. Harkins congratulated the South Vietnamese commander on his success, did not question the inhabitants of the protected hamlets, and took the intelligence they provided him and fed it to his operations staff.

Such ARVN reporting conditioned the overly optimistic assessments that Harkins regularly delivered during afternoon briefings to the American press at MACV headquarters. Most journalists who attended had independent sources of information‡ and often

---

* The slogan that junior U.S. military officers in South Vietnam used privately to describe the ARVN promotion system: "Fuck up and move up." Quoted in David Halberstam, *The Best and the Brightest* (Random House, 1972), p. 281.

† Designed to isolate the rural population from the Vietcong, protected hamlets aimed to provide protection and economic support, thereby strengthening ties with Saigon and increasing loyalty to the government.

‡ One source was junior Foreign Service Officer Richard Holbrooke, assigned to Ba Xuyen Province in the Mekong Delta. "Sometimes when I asked [the province chief] to visit a particular hamlet or village that was shown on our official maps as Saigon-controlled," Holbrooke later wrote, "he would tell me that we could not go there until he got a battalion of troops to escort us. 'Well then,' I'd say, 'it isn't very safe, is it?'" Quoted in Harvey Neese and John O'Donnell, eds., *Prelude to Tragedy: Vietnam, 1960–1965* (Naval Institute Press, 2001), p. ix.

General Paul Harkins
*Keystone Pictures USA/
Alamy Stock Photo*

reported from the field themselves, filing articles critical of the war effort. The difference between what Harkins announced and what journalists had learned made them at first skeptical and then cynical, so much so that they began referring to Harkins's briefings as "the Five O'clock Follies"—in effect, a deliberate charade. Journalists derisively nicknamed Harkins "General Blimp"—another later labeled him "a compelling mediocrity"[55]—for what they considered his inflated and misguided assessments of U.S.-supported ARVN operations and the war effort. But the truth was both less sinister and more disquieting than that: the ARVN generals had cunningly told Harkins what he wanted to hear and Harkins ingenuously repeated it, which made the journalists doubt his integrity.

"It wasn't dishonesty, intending to deceive the people back home," a Defense Intelligence Agency analyst who came to know Harkins and other senior American military officers well later reflected. "It was self-delusion, magnified by the 'can-do' spirit that pervades military organizations, the Boy Scouts, and the Salvation Army."[56] One high-ranking military officer put it more diplomatically, but no less revealingly: "Every enterprise that a government or an organization undertakes can be acclaimed as having some success. And the degree of success that you claim for it is largely a function of your personal enthusiasm."[57] Such "can-do" optimism was bred into the bones of Paul Harkins and every other American military officer, who learned from the moment they arrived as young cadets at West Point and young midshipmen at Annapolis not to belly-ache but to "accomplish the mission." That was paramount— perhaps *the* central ethos of military culture. It was their fundamental task and it made sense in a profession that carried great inherent risks to human life. Negativism was counterproductive. The weekly dispatches that Harkins submitted to the Joint Chiefs and McNamara conveyed this spirit from the first page: its title did not read "Weekly Evaluation," but "Headway Report." "Harkins had the feeling that if you're a general, and you have troops out there in the field dying, you must be optimistic," said a member of the Kennedy administration well acquainted with the general. "This is the way you keep up morale."[58] Harkins himself put it bluntly: "I am optimistic, and I am not going to allow my staff to be pessimistic."[59] A critical attitude did not get the mission accomplished and it did not lead to rapid promotion.

The U.S. military's conventional grasp of the Vietcong's unconventional approach compounded the problem. The Vietcong sought to win the support of the South Vietnamese people; the U.S. military sought to kill Vietcong. American generals believed in large-unit offensive operations designed to trap and destroy the enemy. At one point, they arranged for an ARVN division to conduct a large-unit sweep through the iron triangle north of Saigon, a long-time Vietcong stronghold. Armored personnel carriers and troops moved through the area and when they finished, no Vietcong could be found. "We drove them out," the U.S. colonel attached to the division concluded and reported triumphantly at a briefing afterward.[60] Rufus Phillips, who attended the briefing, was dumbfounded. "I approached the colonel . . . and asked him how he could call the operation a victory when, according to his own unit advisors, not a single Viet Cong had been encountered. He said, 'But we drove them out.' I said, 'What do you think is going to happen when our side leaves?' He was nonplussed."[61] An officer schooled in the conventional battlefield dynamics of World War II, the colonel—along with his generational contemporaries Harkins and McNamara, to whom the U.S. military reported their assessments—failed to grasp that the Vietcong did not behave the way that Nazi German and Imperial Japanese soldiers had acted on the battlefields of Europe and the Pacific Islands two decades earlier. Contrary to the colonel's conclusion, the Vietcong had not been driven out of the iron triangle; they had temporarily retreated into the jungle or gone underground into tunnels until the sweep had ended. The two wrongs—the idea that numbers were revealing and the distortion of the numbers provided—did not make for a right.

The Kennedy administration's emphasis on counterinsurgency (unconventional warfare based on the premise that people are the key to be secured and defended rather than territory won or enemy bodies counted) further exposed the American military's conventional thinking and stubborn resistance to change. "It is fashionable in some quarters to say that the problems of Southeast Asia are primarily political and economic, rather than military," the army chief of staff, General Earle Wheeler, declared in a widely publicized speech at Fordham University on November 7, 1962. "I do not agree. The essence of the problem in Vietnam is military."[62] Senior military officers like Wheeler viewed the Vietcong as irregulars of enemy main-force units, rather than as traditional hit-and-run guerrillas who moved among the people, relied on local recruitment, and chose where, when, and how long to fight—

thereby controlling their casualties.* To senior American military officers, the nonmilitary aspects of counterinsurgency missed the point because they believed that fighting insurgents did not differ fundamentally from fighting regular soldiers. Unsurprisingly, when they looked at their ragtag Vietcong opponents through the filter of conventional weaponry and traditional large army strategy, they thought, "We're better than they are." It was almost as if they were bragging about their down-filled winter coats at the start of the Indochinese summer.

Nothing illustrated their complacency and conventional thinking more vividly and dramatically than the fact that only *three* members of the entire American military advisory team in South Vietnam at the beginning of 1961 were "skilled in guerrilla warfare operations" according to Wheeler's own predecessor as army chief of staff, General George Decker.[63] The military's persistent "reservoir of ignorance" about counterinsurgency, admitted another general looking back several years later, "was almost unlimited."[64] As McNamara later said of senior U.S. military officers—a comment that he retrospectively acknowledged applied in equal measure to himself as well—"They didn't speak the language, they didn't know the values, the culture, the habits of thought" of the Vietnamese and therefore "the great majority of them were not competent to judge progress other than in the terms they normally examined military operations."[65] Harkins's own chief of staff, Richard Stilwell, spoke just as bluntly. "Most of the players, myself included, simply had not grasped the immensity of the problem that we were confronting."[66]

As the U.S. military advisory effort grew—there were twenty-two American generals in South Vietnam by the beginning of 1963—the MACV establishment quickly became very large and very powerful. Nothing those advisors saw kept the U.S. military from remaining settled into deeply ingrained instincts and famil-

---

* When the Vietcong launched attacks, they usually did so against vulnerable civil guard and self-defense corps outposts, which enabled the Vietcong to inflict more casualties than they suffered.

iar habits, to what it knew best, what it had been structured and equipped to do for decades, and—perhaps most important—what had brought it success and victory in World War II, the crucible in which most generals of the early 1960s had been formed. If all one has is a hammer, everything looks like a nail. (Social scientists call this the "law of the instrument": an overreliance on a familiar tool or methods, ignoring or undervaluing alternative approaches.) Characterized by a strong culture of conformity that clung to traditional and familiar patterns of behavior, the military had become accustomed to a particular way of fighting. The organizational logic and inertia of that way had become so great that it constrained senior MACV officers from adapting readily and effectively to the Vietcong's very different approach of relying on minimal logistical demands, night-time movement, and hit-and-run tactics in order to control its casualties. Racism further added to American certainty: surely these primitives so removed from whiteness and Western culture could not think beyond the most basic and predictable. In their vanity and complacency, senior military officers assumed their materiel superiority over the Vietcong gave them superiority over all other aspects of the war. The U.S. military's lack of adaptability would prove crippling.

Increased U.S. air and artillery also sapped the motivation of ARVN, which increasingly relied on American firepower to do their job for them. The use of defoliants such as Agent Orange containing the contaminant dioxin* destroyed villagers' crops and large-unit operations' preattack artillery fire all too often forewarned the Vietcong (who escaped by carefully planned routes) but killed noncombatants, who described their predicament as being "on the anvil and under the hammer."[67] This proved particularly true in the rich rice-growing Mekong Delta south of Saigon, the most populated area of South Vietnam and a traditional center of Vietcong strength. It also applied to the ethnic mountain tribes

---

* Over the course of the war, U.S. and ARVN forces sprayed 19.4 million gallons of herbicide throughout South Vietnam, 11.7 million gallons (60 percent) of it dioxin. See Paul Frederick Cecil, *Herbicidal Warfare—The RANCH HAND Project in Vietnam* (Praeger, 1986).

of the Central Highlands—the Montagnards, the Rade, the Jarai, and the Nnong—on whom ARVN depended to control North Vietnamese infiltration from the Hồ Chí Minh supply trail, a network of rudimentary foot paths and dirt roads that snaked through the densely forested and sparsely populated hills along the Laotian and Cambodian borders that the Việtminh had created during the First Indochina War because French troops seldom patrolled there.

And then there was the Strategic Hamlet Program. Devised to protect the majority rural population of South Vietnam, improve their well-being, and deny support for the Vietcong by depriving them of the ability to collect food and taxes and manpower, the program became the focus of the counterinsurgency effort in 1962. It moved villagers into armed stockades as a way of denying support to the Vietcong. Mao had famously compared guerrillas to "fish in the sea," and the United States saw strategic hamlets as a way to drain the sea. Proposed by counterinsurgency expert Sir Robert Thompson, who headed the British Advisory Mission in Saigon, the program replicated a tactic of creating new villages that separated guerrillas from the larger population that Thompson had successfully implemented when he directed Britain's counterinsurgency struggle in Malaya during the 1950s. But unlike South Vietnam, Malaya was more a geographically self-contained country, and its guerrillas comprised ethnic Chinese separate from the Malay majority. In South Vietnam, no such difference existed between the rural population and the Vietcong, which made physical differentiation between South Vietnamese villagers and the Communist Vietcong impossible. Furthermore, the strategy assumed South Vietnamese villagers *wanted* strategic hamlets, would willingly join them, and sustained the Vietcong only out of fear or indifference. Such premises reflected a projection of hopeful assumptions more than they did a confirmation of local sentiment. When ARVN cleared the Bến Cát district in Bình Dương province near Saigon in late March 1962, it rounded up villagers, tore down or burned their thatched huts and storehouses to deny them to the Vietcong, and prepared to resettle them. But only 70 of 205 families volunteered to move into the half-built hamlets.

Enclosed within thick bamboo hedges, villages were the essential units of Vietnamese society. This made village identity and loyalty of central importance. "The laws of the emperor are less than the customs of the village" went a popular Vietnamese adage. To be displaced from one's village was to be lost, literally and figuratively. Many South Vietnamese villagers, who simply wanted a good rice crop and the ability to keep it, viewed strategic hamlets as concentration camps. Furthermore, in Malaya, the British had paid ethnic Chinese to resettle. Under Diệm, the cost of constructing hamlets came out of money set aside to pay villagers. In some instances, local officials sold villagers sheet-metal roofing provided to the government free of charge by the United States. In several provinces construction included six-foot-high earthen ramparts running across food-producing rice paddies and arduously built over many weeks by forced laborers who complained bitterly about unpaid work. One official charged relocated villagers for the barbed wire strung in front of their new homes.[68]

Above all, the Strategic Hamlet Program sought to win popular support—the "hearts and minds" of the South Vietnamese people, in the parlance of the day—by providing physical security through the construction of safe villages surrounded by barbed wire, bamboo spikes, parapets, and moats—to keep the Vietcong out. But all too often the forced relocations alienated ordinary people who previously had seldom ventured more than a day's walk from their villages; now they had to tread long distances every day to work their rice paddies. Relocation separated them from their village đình (the shrine to the god of the earth beneath each village) and disrupted the ancient tradition of ancestor worship that closely bound villagers to their locality as the source of intergenerational immortality. The Strategic Hamlet Program upended the traditional order, disturbed the all-important cycle of rice growing, and undercut the ancient custom of self-governing at the village level. It disrupted the social harmony necessary for Diệm to claim the Mandate of Heaven.

Diệm insisted on implementing the program in the heavily populated provinces of the Mekong Delta, an intricate web of marshes,

canals, irrigation ditches, and dikes where 60 percent of the country's population lived and which was a Vietcong stronghold. But
concentrating on the Delta increased the number of Vietcong sym-
pathizers placed *inside* strategic hamlets. As a result, the Vietcong
more effectively penetrated the villages to distribute leaflets, access
food and intelligence, and recruit manpower.

By the end of September 1962, the Diệm regime claimed to
have resettled 4,322,034 villagers—33.39 percent of the country's
population—into strategic hamlets. This number later proved to be
wildly inflated, but its alleged precision appealed to the Americans'
penchant for statistics. The limited number of strategic hamlets
actually built proved, more often than not, to be little more than
Potemkin villages. Designed to drive a wedge between rural South
Vietnamese and the Vietcong, the Strategic Hamlet Program instead
drove a wedge between villagers and the government. Throughout
Vietnamese history, mandarins had found it difficult to assert their
dominance over villages, and Diệm was no exception.

Relations with the Soviet Union and events leading up to the Cuban Missile Crisis dominated the Kennedy administration's overseas attention during 1962. Yet a steady flow of newspaper stories
and confidential cables reached the White House that year reporting that Diệm's position continued to weaken, and the Vietcong's
to strengthen, despite America's increased aid and the thousands of
additional military advisors sent to the country. The contradiction
troubled Kennedy, who understood the fundamentally political
nature of the war. He and his team had expected more military advisors to prevent the need for U.S. combat troops. But their stationing intensified the pressure for greater U.S. involvement as ARVN's
campaign against the Vietcong deteriorated. The larger American
advisory presence also paradoxically aggravated the political tension between Washington and Saigon it was meant to relieve because the fiercely independent Diệm resented, at the same time
that he needed, increased American military assistance. And the
expanded U.S. advisory effort *weakened* South Vietnam's already
limited capacity for self-reliance—the very quality that Kennedy

**Senate Majority
Leader Mike
Mansfield**
*Everett Collection/
Alamy Stock Photo*

had sought to strengthen in the first place. Kennedy's anxiety and pessimism spilled over during a conversation with an NSC aide when he lamented, "We've got to face the fact that the odds are about a hundred-to-one that we're going to get our asses thrown out of Vietnam."[69] That he was even considering the possibility of failure was revealing.

To help sort things out, Kennedy asked Senate Majority Leader Mike Mansfield of Montana to take a firsthand look and report back to him. Fellow Democratic Irish-Catholic politicians, Kennedy and Mansfield had joined the Senate the same year, 1953. They shared back-row desks and an interest in French Indochina during their eight years together in the upper chamber and remained close after Kennedy became president. Kennedy relied on Mansfield to steward his legislative program through the Senate, and he respected

Mansfield's long experience in Asia—the Montanan had served as a marine in the Philippines and China in the 1920s and taught East Asian history at the University of Montana in the 1930s—as well as his familiarity with South Vietnam. Mansfield (an early supporter of Diệm) made his tour of South Vietnam, including two long talks with Diệm, in early December and shared his findings with Kennedy the day after Christmas in Palm Beach, where the president spent the 1962 holidays. Joining Kennedy that day for a sail on nearby Lake Worth, Mansfield discussed his report, which Kennedy had read carefully. "He questioned me minutely," Mansfield later recalled, "and it wasn't a pleasant picture that I had depicted for him."[70]

What Mansfield learned during his first trip to South Vietnam since 1955 sobered both men. "Although it is seven years and billions of dollars later . . . the fact [is] that we are once again at the beginning of the beginning." Diệm had effectively subordinated defeat of the Vietcong to preservation of his personal rule. If this continued, Mansfield foresaw "a truly massive commitment of American military personnel and other resources—in short, going to war fully ourselves against the guerrillas—and the establishment of some form of neocolonial rule in South Vietnam." He added, "That is an alternative which I most emphatically do not recommend." Mansfield urged a negotiated exit from South Vietnam along the lines of the neutralization of Laos, which the president had accepted just five months earlier.[71]

Mansfield's assessment hit a nerve with Kennedy. "I got angry with Mike for disagreeing with our policy so completely," he told Kenny O'Donnell after their meeting, and then "I got angry with myself because I found myself agreeing with him." The process repeated itself when Mansfield expressed his views at a White House congressional leadership breakfast in the spring of 1963. Kennedy reacted with annoyance, then invited Mansfield to the Oval Office for a talk. In that private setting, Kennedy confided his agreement with Mansfield's conclusion. "But I can't do it until 1965—after I'm reelected." Kennedy explained why in terms that his fellow Democrat understood: if he announced an exit from Vietnam before the

1964 election, conservative Republicans would howl for his scalp and likely deny him a second term. Kennedy's agitation continued after Mansfield left the room. "If I tried to pull out completely now from Vietnam," he explained to O'Donnell, "we would have another Joe McCarthy red scare on our hands, but I can do it after I'm reelected." There would be a cost, but he would still be president. "In 1965," Kennedy asserted, "I'll become one of the most unpopular Presidents in history. I'll be damned everywhere as a Communist appeaser. But I don't care."[72]

JFK's friend and advisor Clark Clifford later described Kennedy as having "splendid political instincts" and "a detachment, a determination not to get caught up too much in something so that your judgment is adversely affected."[73] Yet Kennedy had a broader agenda than Vietnam, and detachment in one case might lend itself well to avoiding trouble, and in another to drifting into it. Rather than grasp the nettle and make hard choices in early 1961, when the slate—at least for him—was clean, Kennedy's narrow election victory, the conservative mood in Congress, and the anti-Communist atmosphere in the country would lead Kennedy for the next two and a half years to repeatedly improvise and temporize regarding Vietnam. He and his advisors took steps intended to stabilize the situation for the moment, leaving its resolution to the longer future, always conscious that harder decisions lay ahead. This ad-hoc approach never forced Kennedy and his advisors to confront and resolve fundamental issues; rather, they postponed hard choices that only grew more difficult and more intractable over time. "When he didn't know which way to go," recalled Harvard political scientist Richard Neustadt, who knew Kennedy well, "he tried to be a little bit pregnant on both sides and steer along until he could find an out—but he was doing that while the situation [in Vietnam] was fundamentally changing underneath him."[74]

Kennedy's plaintive assertion to O'Donnell in the spring of 1963 assumed that he could mark time until the 1964 election—that events in South Vietnam would allow him to finesse the issue in the meantime. This crucial assumption proved wrong. Feeling increasingly besieged, Diệm intensified his repression during the

spring of 1963, diminishing his already limited popular support
and generating still more recruits for the Vietcong. Diệm particularly feared and distrusted the power of South Vietnam's Buddhist
monks, a powerful elite with a shrewd grasp of public relations
that had never reconciled itself to his rule. (The vast majority
of South Vietnamese were rural villagers who mixed Buddhism
with animism, ancestor worship, and Confucianism.) Dating back
to the eleventh-century Lê dynasty, when a Vietnamese Buddhist
emperor's army defeated China's Song dynasty during a forty-
day battle, Vietnamese had traditionally associated Buddhism
with nationalism and Catholicism with foreign (particularly
French) domination. Buddhists also felt the sting of discrimina-
tion: Diệm officially recognized Catholicism—which comprised no
more than 10 percent of the population—as a religion, but classified
Buddhism—which comprised nearly 80 percent—as an "association," which allowed the government to control its acquisition of
land for pagodas and permits for political rallies. Catholics often
gained exemption from labor conscriptions necessary to build
strategic hamlets and in land redistribution programs received the
safest and best land near the coast. Diệm once told an ARVN general, unaware the general was Buddhist, "Put your Catholic officers in sensitive places. They can be trusted."[75]

Buddhist protestors carrying signs in both Vietnamese and English began demonstrations in Huế in May that spread to Saigon
by June. A fierce government crackdown provoked a cri de coeur
by one impassioned monk, Thích Quảng Đức, who on June 11
stepped out of a squat Austin Westminster sedan at the busy Saigon intersection of Phan Đình Phùng Boulevard and Lê Văn Duyệt
Street, a few blocks southwest of the presidential palace built by the
French in the late nineteenth century to house the colonial governor. Đức calmly sat down in the meditative lotus position on a
cushion as another monk pored five gallons of diesel fuel over him.
A crowd of passersby and tipped-off journalists gathered to watch,
transfixed by the unfolding drama. Đức rotated a mala of wooden
prayer beads and chanted an homage to the Buddha as a third
monk lit a match, then dropped it on a trail of fuel leading to Đức.

Associated Press Saigon bureau chief Malcolm Browne snapped photographs as flames consumed Đức's saffron robe and flesh and black smoke rose from his burning, motionless body before it eventually toppled backward onto the street. Several people prostrated themselves in homage before the burning monk. Within hours, Browne's horrific images splashed across newspapers and televisions around the world. Kennedy remarked that "no news picture in history generated so much emotion in the world as that one."

To Americans, Đức's immolation seemed an act of crazed desperation. But to Vietnamese Buddhists, it had a powerful religious and political significance, the extreme gesture of an exceptional individual free of physical needs and seeking a wholly spiritual existence. Fire served as the rite of passage to an eternal state of enlightenment (as represented by the flame emanating from the heads of Buddha statues), and many believed that via such an act of ritual purification Đức had become a bodhisattva (bồ tát), one who selflessly helps others along the path to enlightenment. As was surely intended, Đức's sacrifice carried great political symbolism, powerfully contrasting his virtue with the corruption and repression of Diệm's regime, and through his gesture, Buddhists had thrust themselves into the role of providing moral and political leadership for the South Vietnamese people. But Washington grasped none of this. What the Vietnamese saw as sanctification, Washington saw as psychosis. The uncorking of the Buddhist crisis caught it completely by surprise. "We didn't know who [the Buddhists] were," an NSC official admitted, "we didn't have . . . the faintest idea what their organization was all about."[76] In a country populated mostly by Buddhists, this admission revealed a great deal about what America did not know about Vietnam.

Nevertheless, recognizing that this enigmatic (to them) religious group was disrupting ARVN progress, the U.S. embassy urged Diệm and his younger brother, presidential counselor Ngô Đình Nhu, to compromise with the Buddhists. The brothers bridled at any outside pressure; they smiled politely and stiffened their resistance—sometimes with undisguised nastiness. Nhu's wife and self-styled first lady—Diệm had never married—Trần Lệ Xuân (better known as Madame Nhu or the Dragon Lady to her critics), was glamorous and outspoken with a brusque, imperious manner, meticulously coiffed hair, and long lacquered red nails as pointed as her tongue. After another monk immolated himself, she said that Buddhist leaders had "simply barbecued a bonze [monk] with imported gasoline." She further crowed, "Let them burn! . . . And we shall clap our hands."[77] She then gave an interview accusing the U.S. embassy of conspiring with the Buddhists and the Vietcong to overthrow her brother-in-law's government. After ordering Madame Nhu to make no more public statements and promising outgoing Ambassador Frederick Nolting that his government would take no further repressive steps against the Buddhists, a week later Diệm declared martial law and Nhu's security forces raided pagodas across the country, arresting and detaining more than fourteen hundred monks. The security forces disguised themselves in regular military uniforms, in order that blame be put on ARVN generals rather than the Ngô brothers. The photos of South Vietnamese "soldiers" clubbing Buddhist monks that appeared in American newspapers did little to help the impression made by the Diệm regime.

The international publicity generated by the Buddhist crisis moved Vietnam from the back burner to the forefront of Kennedy's attention for the first time in his presidency. By now, however, the issues regarding Diệm had become so severe that the chances of resolving them successfully had dwindled dramatically. From the beginning of his presidency, Kennedy had assumed that he could avoid the hazard of deeper American military involvement in Vietnam while postponing the political storm he believed would be triggered by a withdrawal. Events in the summer of 1963 exposed the limits of that straddling act.

Kennedy's stance toward Diệm illustrated the problem. Kennedy had instructed Nolting not to pressure Diem—pressure had not worked in the past, it did not fit Kennedy's view of productive relationships, and, most important, it did not encourage the partnership that Kennedy considered essential to success in the war against the Vietcong. Instead, he had bolstered the South Vietnamese leader and his shortcomings because, as Kennedy himself put it privately, "Diem is Diem and the best we've got,"[78] a comment that hauntingly echoed similarly tortured reasoning of the Eisenhower administration. But while the two presidents had championed Diệm for almost a decade, the political situation in Saigon had not improved—it had only worsened. By propping up the South Vietnamese leader, moreover, Kennedy and his advisors inadvertently encouraged his intransigence. As a result, serious leadership problems festered into critical ones whose solution courted either the deeper involvement Kennedy sought to avoid or a retreat with undesirable domestic consequences.

All of this came to a head in the late summer of 1963. Diệm's already limited popular support had eroded alarmingly, his repression had antagonized the Buddhists, and his failure to confront corruption—for example, he did nothing when informed that palace officials had skimmed public money by selling national lottery tickets on the black market—had alienated many on whom he relied to run the government. Many of these problems resulted from the growing influence of the astute and ruthless Ngô Đình Nhu, who personally directed the secret police, in effect the Ngô family's private army. Diệm needed his brother's skill at manipulating and controlling information—he created ten separate intelligence agencies and the special forces (a paramilitary praetorian guard) to keep the disgruntled opponents in check. Ambitious, cunning, and suspicious, the lean and pale Nhu had progressively isolated Diệm from the rest of the government and the people, with whom Diệm had never had the common touch to begin with. Nhu's mother-in-law considered him "absolutely drunk with power," and he exercised extraordinary influence over his shy and withdrawn older brother. "Until surgery invents a technique for operating on Siamese twins," noted one American diplomat, "they cannot be separated." Diệm relied on Nhu for many of his ideas and used his brother as his executive agent. Nhu wrote all of the president's speeches as well as his answers to press inquiries. As one palace official put it, "If one hundred people came to Diem and called something white and Nhu called it black, Diem would believe

Nhu." Diệm became "completely a prisoner of his own family," lamented another.[79]

A quartet of Kennedy administration officials—Under secretary of state Averell Harriman, assistant secretary of state for Far Eastern affairs Roger Hilsman, NSC staff member Michael Forrestal in Washington, and newly appointed ambassador Henry Cabot Lodge Jr. in Saigon—agreed that Diệm and Nhu would never put defeat of the Vietcong above preservation of their own rule. The four Americans viewed the Ngô brothers as millstones around the neck of the war effort who would never make the changes necessary to save the country. As a result, they believed the time had come for the Ngôs to go. The same thing had been done with Syngman Rhee of South Korea three years earlier, and they thought such a maneuver would succeed again.*

Seventy-two years old, Harriman seemed out of place among the Young Turks of the Kennedy administration, but the blunt, tough-talking patrician born to wealth but drawn to public service understood how Washington worked, having served Democratic presidents since Franklin D. Roosevelt. Harriman wore a hearing aid that he conspicuously turned off when listening to people that he found boring or arguments that he considered foolish but quickly switched it back on when it came time to aggressively assert his own point of view. This behavior led McGeorge Bundy to liken Harriman to a cagey old crocodile that feigned somnolence—until he suddenly sprang to life with snapping jaws. Harriman loved the comparison—indeed, he deliberately cultivated it, often using "Crocodile" as his code name when sending State Department cables. Harriman considered Ngô Đình Diệm "a losing horse in the long run" who had passed "beyond the point of no return."[80]

Hilsman succeeded Harriman as assistant secretary of state for Far Eastern affairs in April 1963, and he shared the older man's views about Diệm. An army brat, West Point graduate, and wounded

---

* As protests mounted against Rhee in the spring of 1960 for rigging election to his fourth term as South Korea's president, the CIA flew him out of the country to exile in Hawaii.

combat veteran of World War II who became an academic in the 1950s, Hilsman had considerable experience in guerrilla warfare, having led partisan operations as an Office of Strategic Services officer behind Japanese lines in Burma. Cocksure, abrasive, and unencumbered by modesty or self-doubt, Hilsman held his own among the strong egos and personalities of the New Frontier, aggressively advocating policies that he favored, sometimes pushing the limits of propriety in the process. One colleague summed him up as a Boy Scout with brass knuckles. But he understood the fundamentally political nature of counterinsurgency war—winning the loyalty of the population rather than killing insurgents.

Thirty-five-year-old Michael Forrestal occupied a key position, responsible for coordinating Vietnam policy on the National Security Council. Son of the first secretary of defense, James Forrestal, he had curly dark hair and wore glasses that made him appear less intense than his driven father, but he had watched his father wield power in the policy wars of the Truman administration and understood how it flowed through the corridors of Washington. Forrestal was particularly close to Averell Harriman, whom he had served as assistant naval attaché during Harriman's ambassadorship in Moscow at the end of World War II and who had become Forrestal's mentor and sponsor after his father's suicide in 1949. Forrestal had been brought down from New York, where he was a partner at the law firm of Shearman & Sterling, at Harriman's request. He shared Harriman's and Hilsman's antipathy toward Diệm and represented their position at the White House.

A lanky, nattily dressed man who walked with an assured gait marked by a slight stoop, Lodge exuded the patrician self-confidence of one of New England's oldest and most distinguished families. The Lodges and the Kennedys comprised one of the storied rivalries in Massachusetts politics: Lodge's grandfather, Henry Cabot Lodge Sr., had defeated John Fitzgerald to hold his U.S. Senate seat in 1916. A generation later, Fitzgerald's namesake and grandson John F. Kennedy unseated Lodge Jr. in the 1952 Senate race. The Boston Brahmin Republican and the Irish Catholic Democrat ambassador's son shared a zest for the game of politics and

Ambassador Henry Cabot Lodge Jr. with JFK
Abbie Rowe/JFK Library

grudgingly respected each other's political talents, but they eyed one another warily and never mixed socially. (Jack Kennedy was president, but Lodge would never invite him to his home in the WASP enclave of Beverly on Massachusetts's North Shore.) When Dean Rusk suggested sending Lodge to Saigon as ambassador to replace the retiring Frederick Nolting, Kennedy found the idea of getting Lodge mixed up in the mess of Vietnam "irresistible," according to his aide Kenny O'Donnell.[81]

Certainly Lodge seemed to have all the right qualifications: he spoke French fluently, so he could communicate directly with Diệm; he had visited Indochina as a reporter in the 1930s; he had excellent relations with the American military—he was a major

general in the army reserves and had known MACV head General
Paul Harkins for decades; and he even had an eccentric Buddhist
uncle. Having the prominent Republican in Saigon promised a political insurance policy as well, providing bipartisan cover in the
event that South Vietnam collapsed. But this arrangement also
gave Lodge leverage over Kennedy, who could not lightly ignore
his ambassador's recommendations.

"A take-charge type accustomed to exercising authority," in
Rusk's words,[82] Lodge arrived in South Vietnam on August 22
well aware of the domestic American reaction to the Buddhist im-
molations and well informed about Kennedy's basic thinking that
something had to be done about Diệm and Nhu. Lodge had been
sent to Saigon to help resolve the crisis, and he intended to do so,
but he and Diệm did not hit it off. "The chemistry between the
two didn't work at all," said a CIA official familiar with South Vietnam.[83] At their first meeting, Lodge later recalled, "I could see a
cloud pass across his face when I suggested that he get rid of Nhu
and improve his government. He absolutely refused to discuss any
of the topics that President Kennedy had instructed me to raise,
and that frankly jolted me. He looked up at the ceiling and talked
about irrelevant subjects. I thought it was deplorable."[84] Lodge's
broader engagement was inconsistent and shallow. Another American with long experience in Vietnam who came to know Lodge
well observed that the ambassador tended to view the South Vietnamese as "a set of enigmatic figures to be dealt with arbitrarily."[85]

Lodge, Harriman, Hilsman, and Forrestal believed they could
pressure Diệm to mend his ways and dismiss Nhu before the situation became irretrievable. But they misread this obstinate and
supercilious and stubborn man, who even his adversary Hồ Chí
Minh called "a patriot in his way."[*] Consistent with his earlier relations with Washington, Diệm's personal pride and national sensitivity made him bristle at taking orders from anyone—whether
French or American—and the traditional Vietnamese duty to family

---

[*] Hồ once remarked with sympathy that Diệm's independent character made it
hard for him to deal with the overpowering embrace of the Americans.

made the idea of throwing Nhu under the bus highly unpalatable and even dishonorable. His carefully cultivated image of independence also stood at risk. "Diem seemed to understand that Nhu was causing him harm," a South Vietnamese official later observed, "but he was afraid if he sent Nhu abroad, the Vietnamese people would think the Americans had made him do it."[86]

Thus rather than change Diệm's behavior, the growing American pressure only increased his implacability—which in turn aggravated popular resentment and intensified the sense of disorder. South Vietnamese villagers began wearing bits of saffron cloth to symbolize their support for the Buddhist monks. Fearful that Diệm and Nhu's repression jeopardized American military support for the war, ARVN generals began plotting a coup, which diverted their attention and efforts from military operations. The Vietcong took advantage of the lull in ARVN operations to step up their attacks. The situation in South Vietnam seemed to be unraveling.

Harriman, Hilsman, Forrestal, and Lodge were convinced that success in South Vietnam hinged on Diệm's ability to win and maintain the support of the people. By late August 1963, they had concluded that Diệm had lost that ability, that the war against the Vietcong could never be won under Diệm. Whether the South Vietnamese president wanted it or not, he—or at least his brother Nhu—had to go.

Blackbelts in the bureaucratic jiujitsu of Washington policy battles, Harriman, Hilsman, Forrestal, and Lodge knew how to circumvent established procedures and cut corners in order to move an idea up on the government agenda and position it for enactment via an action-forcing event, expert practitioners of bureaucratic circumvention that obviated serious debate of a policy move with major implications. Over the hot, humid weekend of August 24–25—when most senior officials had gone on vacation and escaped Washington's swelter—Hilsman drafted and Harriman approved a State Department cable to Lodge suggesting a coup. The key part of the cable read: "We wish [to] give Diem reasonable opportunity to remove [the] Nhus, but if he remains obdurate, then we are prepared to accept the obvious implication that we can no longer support Diem. You may also tell appropriate [ARVN] military commanders we will give them direct support in any period of breakdown of [the] central government mechanism."[87]

Forrestal phoned the president at Hyannis Port. "JFK had an amiable weakness," recalled McGeorge Bundy, "which was he was afraid of being caught taking the weekend off."[88] Forrestal read the vacationing Kennedy the "relevant passages." "Can't we wait until Monday, when everybody is back?" Kennedy asked. Harriman and Hilsman "really want to get this thing out right away," Forrestal replied. "Well," said Kennedy, "go and see what you can do to get it cleared."[89] Harriman and Hilsman tracked down acting secretary of state George Ball on the golf course at the Chevy Chase Club in suburban Maryland. Refusing to OK the cable until he talked to Kennedy, Ball called Hyannis Port. "If Rusk and Gilpatric* agree, George, then go ahead," the president told him.[90] Ball then phoned Rusk in New York, where he had gone for a special U.N. session, and the secretary gave his OK on the assumption that Kennedy had approved it. Forrestal reached Gilpatric at his farm on Maryland's Eastern Shore. "I was suspicious of the circumstances in which it was being done," Gilpatric later said, but after learning that Kennedy and Rusk had approved the cable, he reluctantly cleared it for the Defense Department as McNamara's deputy in his absence.[91] Richard Helms, viewing it as a policy decision, cleared the cable on behalf of the CIA, and it went out to the U.S. embassy in Saigon that night at 9:36.

When McNamara and CIA director McCone returned to their offices on Monday, August 26, and learned of the cable's transmission, they were furious at what they considered, and Taylor explicitly termed, an "egregious 'end run'" perpetrated in the absence of the president and his senior advisors. Kennedy expressed his own anger at Forrestal that day for hurrying transmission. Kennedy elaborated his thoughts in a private memo he dictated two months later, in which he partly blamed himself for not paying close at-

---

* McNamara was away from Washington on vacation, climbing the Teton mountains in Wyoming with his family.

tention to details over a summer weekend. "In my judgment, that wire was badly drafted. It should never have been sent out on a Saturday. I should not have given my consent to it without a round-table conference in which McNamara and Taylor could have presented their views." "He always said that it was a major mistake on his part," his brother Bobby later said. "The result is we started down a road that we never really recovered from."[92]

Kennedy did not want a change in government in Saigon so much as he wanted Diệm to change his ways, which was a stall more than a decision. Sharp divisions among his advisors only reinforced Kennedy's vacillation. One group—the quartet—focused on the dangers if Diệm remained; the other group—led by Nolting, McNamara, Taylor, and McCone—focused on the dangers if Diệm was removed. "I was disturbed by the repression," McNamara later observed, "but I thought there was a far better chance of achieving [success] with him in control than with any alternative that was on the scene or in prospect."[93] The quartet and its opponents defined the problem differently, yet both sides believed the war could be won. No one at the top posed the question of what would happen if it could not because no one at this point thought to contemplate such an outcome. Competing groups of men with towering egos, they battled one another at a series of contentious meetings the following week, pulling Kennedy in one direction and then the other.

Conflict among his advisors produced what cognitive psychologists call "deferred decision-making" or "choice deferral" by Kennedy. Psychologists Amos Tversky and Eldar Shafir showed that people tend to delay decisions when conflict over options is high through an experiment involving two groups of college students. One group was told, "Suppose you are considering buying a compact disc (CD) player, and have not yet decided which model to buy. You pass by a store that is having a one-day clearance sale. It offers a popular Sony player for just $99, well below the list price. Do you buy the Sony player or wait until you learn more about the various models?" While 66 percent chose to buy the Sony player, only 34 percent chose to wait. The second group was told, "Suppose you are considering buying a compact disc (CD) player, and have not yet decided which model to buy. You pass by a store that is having a one-day clearance sale. It offers a popular Sony player for just $99, and a top-of-the-line Aiwa player for just $159, well below the list price. Do you buy the Aiwa player or the Sony player?" Some 27 percent chose the Aiwa player, an equal percentage the Sony player—while 46 percent chose to wait until they learned more about the various models. "Many things never get done," conclude Tversky and Shafir, "not because someone has chosen not to do them, but because the person has chosen not to do them *now*."[94] As a consequence of choice deferral, important but difficult decisions are often delayed, and in an environment where the ground is shifting all the while, the likelihood of an undesirable default option is increased. The result can be everyone's least desired outcome, what everyone sought to avoid from the start. This is what unfolded during the weeks of debate over Diệm that followed.

Kennedy held the first of these meetings on Monday, August 26. He began by questioning Hilsman about developments in Saigon since the cable had gone out. Hilsman described plotting by ARVN generals against Diệm and Nhu. "Who would be qualified to replace Diem?" McNamara asked, adding: "If we put a weak man in there, we're going to be in *real* trouble." Hilsman had no ready answer, but Rusk implicitly supported Hilsman by arguing the status quo was unsustainable. "Unless there's a major change in Diem and Nhu's approach," Rusk told the president, "we're on the road to disaster." "If [Diệm] is thrown out, we don't know who will replace him," warned McNamara. Kennedy asked what Ambassador Nolting thought. "Nolting believes that if Diem goes, we're finished," Harriman accurately reported—then dismissed Nolting as "full of emotion." "Maybe logically," Kennedy coolly replied.[95]

The president made sure that Nolting attended the meeting the following afternoon. He sent a government car to pick up the former ambassador at his home in rural northern Virginia and bring him to the White House. A career foreign service officer who spoke in the slow cadences and soft twang of his native Virginia, Nolting felt a special burden and sensitivity as the U.S. ambassador to

Saigon for the last two and a half years to explain what he thought South Vietnam without Diệm would be like. He told Kennedy the ARVN generals lacked "the guts and the sang-froid and the drive" of Diệm and Nhu, and predicted that if they seized power, "they won't have the leadership" talent to govern the country. He then related an incident that had occurred just before he left Saigon. Nolting had pleaded with Diệm to send away his brother and Madame Nhu. Immediately after their meeting, Diệm had summoned the Australian ambassador and asked if his government would issue an invitation to the Nhus to visit the country. Nothing had come of his request, but it seemed evidence that Diệm might separate himself from his brother. "Do you think we can continue the momentum against the Vietcong with the present government?" Kennedy asked. Nolting recommended "tak[ing] it slow and easy and see if that prospect exists over the next several weeks." He said the August 24 cable had created "a problem because we've already, in effect, given our word through [the CIA] to the generals to get cracking" but "since we don't have a good place to jump to, we shouldn't jump right now." Rusk doubted events would allow a wait-and-see approach. "We've been carrying a tremendous load on our back in Vietnam given the nature of this regime," the secretary said, "and this just multiplies that load many times over." Kennedy ended the meeting by directing that Lodge and Harkins be asked "whether we should proceed with the generals or wait."[96]

Lodge and Harkins recommended going ahead. George Ball did, too. At the first of two meetings on August 28, Ball told Kennedy "it would be difficult, if not impossible, to live with Diem," and that "we have no option but to try to bring about a change," in part because the August 24 cable had moved events "beyond the point of no return." Kennedy disagreed. "I don't think we should take the view that this has gone beyond our control," he said. But Ball, joined by Harriman, continued to urge the president to support Diệm's ouster. "I think we've lost South Vietnam if we don't succeed in launching a coup," Harriman said, adding flatly: "We cannot win with the combination of Diem and Nhu . . . We created them and they have betrayed us." "There's no one I know of who has a reasonably good prospect of holding this fragmented and divided country together except Diem," countered Nolting. The back-and-forth between Harriman and Nolting went on for some time. Eventually a furious Harriman in full-on Crocodile mode ridiculed Nolting as a "god-damn fool," tongue-lashing him in a way that embarrassed everyone in the room. After the meeting, Kennedy told a friend in mock despair, "My God, my administration is coming apart."[97]

But while Harriman had humiliated Nolting, the former ambassador's reservations had registered. Kennedy began the next day's meeting by asking whether he should withdraw support for a coup. McNamara urged one last attempt to separate Diệm from Nhu. Deposing Diệm meant a military junta, McNamara said, and the generals "aren't capable of running a government." "I agree with you that we're not going to have much of a government" if the generals take over, Bundy responded, "but on the other hand, how much of a government is there" now? Nolting proposed telling Diệm that Washington would end its support if Nhu remained. Kennedy's response to Nolting's proposed ultimatum revealed as starkly as anything in the record of his administration how anxious he felt about both getting in deeper *and* getting out of Vietnam. "For us to go through with that—it would be hard to withdraw our assistance and pull out of there," he said. Kennedy cited a cardinal reason why at a later, smaller meeting with his inner-circle that followed. Rusk reported the feeling in Congress "that we're up to our hips in the mud out there." "I know everybody is mad at this situation," Kennedy acknowledged, "but they'll be madder if South Vietnam goes down the drain, just like Congress got mad about Chiang Kai-shek." Even neutralization—a much less radical step—entailed great political risks. (Only a few weeks after the meeting, *Newsweek* ran an article about neutralization describing "this type of solution" as "laden with domestic political dynamite."[98]) Looking back, McNamara regretted that "we didn't properly analyze the *idea* of a neutral solution. It wasn't taken seriously. It was simply rejected. And that, I believe, was a basic mistake—a failure of imagination, a failure to explore the possibilities, to test the limits of the option in each concrete situation where it arose, from whatever source."[99] All of this was true. But in the fall of 1963, domestic political considerations and the mood of the country made neutralization unimaginable to Kennedy.

After the meeting Kennedy left for Hyannis Port to spend the Labor Day weekend. That evening, he phoned Bundy at the White House and approved a cable to Lodge conditionally agreeing to a U.S.-backed coup. The quartet had carried the day, Kennedy concluding that Diệm could not be separated from Nhu* and indicating he was less willing to risk the loss of Vietnam than to take the risk of removing Diệm. "Until the very moment of the go signal for the operation by the Generals," the president's message to Lodge said, "I must reserve a contingent right to change course and reverse previous instructions." The Bay of Pigs fiasco fresh in his memory, he went on: "I know from experience that failure is more destructive than an appearance of indecision . . . When we go, we must go to win, but it will be better to change our minds than to fail. And if our national interest should require a change of mind, we must not be afraid of it." Lodge replied the next morning, expressing his understanding of the president's reservation. But he added an important caveat: he warned that a coup would be "essentially a Vietnamese affair with a momentum of its own. Should this happen, you may not be able to control it, i.e. the 'go signal' may be given by the Generals."[100] It was a fateful insight.

On Labor Day, Monday, September 2, the president sat down for a taped television interview with Walter Cronkite of the *CBS Evening News*,† facing one another in wicker chairs on the sun-drenched back lawn of the Kennedy family compound. Kennedy addressed two different audiences in his remarks. To the Saigon

---

* At the small meeting on August 29, Kennedy told Rusk, McNamara, Bundy, and Taylor regarding the effort to separate Diệm from Nhu: "I don't think it will work." Tape 108, PRC, POF, JFKL.

† Kennedy's appearance marked the inaugural broadcast of the network's expanded thirty-minute newscast that evening.

government he said, "I don't think that unless a greater effort is made by the government to win popular support that the war can be won out there . . . and in my opinion, in the last two months, the government has gotten out of touch with the people . . . It is my hope that this will become increasingly obvious to the government, that they will take steps to try to bring back popular support for this very essential struggle." To the American people Kennedy explained, "In the final analysis, it is their war. They are the ones who have to win it or lose it. We can help them, we can give them equipment, we can send our men out there as advisors, but they have to win it, the people of Vietnam, against the Communists." He then went on to declare, "I don't agree with those who say we should withdraw. That would be a great mistake. I know people don't like Americans to be engaged in this kind of effort . . . but this is a very important struggle even though it is far away." One hardly had to read between the lines to notice that he believed two different and even opposing things at the same time.[101]

Kennedy publicly addressed the subject of Vietnam again a week later in an interview broadcast on the NBC Evening News *Huntley-Brinkley Report*. His remarks that evening were the most extensive about Vietnam that he had ever made publicly (and ever would) as president, and thus deserve to be quoted at length:

CHET HUNTLEY: Are we likely to reduce our aid to South Vietnam now?

KENNEDY: I don't think we think that would be helpful at this time. If you reduce your aid, it is possible you could have some effect upon the government structure there. On the other hand, you might have a situation which could bring about a collapse. Strongly in our mind is what happened in the case of China at the end of World War II, where China was lost, a weak government became increasingly unable to control events. We don't want that.

DAVID BRINKLEY: Mr. President, have you had any reason to doubt this so-called "domino theory," and that if South Vietnam falls, the rest of Southeast Asia will go behind it?

KENNEDY: No, I believe it. I believe it. I think that the struggle is close enough. China is so large, looms so high just beyond the frontiers, that if South Vietnam went, it would not only give them an improved geographic position for a guerrilla assault on Malaya, but would also give the impression that the wave of the future in Southeast Asia was China and the Communists. So I believe it . . . The fact of the matter is that with the assistance of the United States, SEATO, Southeast Asia, and indeed all of Asia has been maintained independent against a powerful force, the Chinese Communists. What I am concerned about is that Americans will get impatient and say because they don't like events in Southeast Asia or they don't like the government in Saigon, that we should withdraw. That only makes it easy for the Communists. I think we should stay. We should use our influence in as effective a way as we can, but we should not withdraw.[102]

The contradictory assessments of Vietnam that Kennedy received at a White House briefing the following day, September 10, reinforced the conflicting imperatives implicit in his public statements the week before. A few days earlier, Kennedy had dispatched the Pentagon's counterinsurgency expert, marine corps major general Victor "Brute"* Krulak, and State Department Vietnam specialist Joseph Mendenhall on another fact-finding mission. The two men visited South Vietnam September 8 and 9. During their thirty-six-hour tour, Krulak canvassed opinion among U.S. military advisors and their ARVN counterparts while Mendenhall interviewed U.S. embassy personnel and South Vietnamese government officials in the four largest cities of Saigon, Huế, Da Nang, and Nha Trang. Krulak and Mendenhall approached Vietnam from vastly different perspectives and reached vastly different conclusions, which they presented in turn to Kennedy at a meeting that began at 10:30 that morning. It was almost like watching Akira

---

* Krulak—a ferocious wrestler despite his diminutive size—had been nicknamed "Brute" by his fellow plebes (first-year midshipmen) at Annapolis in 1930.

Kurosawa's 1950 film *Rashomon* based on the classic short story by Ryūnosuke Akutagawa in which various characters provide subjective and contradictory versions of the same incident.

Krulak began his presentation by telling Kennedy the war effort continued "ahead at an impressive pace." "It has been affected adversely by the political crisis," he conceded, "but the impact is not great." Krulak's bottom line: "The Vietcong war will be won if the current U.S. military and sociological programs are pursued, irrespective of the grave defects in the ruling regime." It was an upbeat analysis that reflected his best efforts to examine the situation, but it also reflected how Krulak had gathered the information on which he based that assessment (a methodology that he did not share with Kennedy and others at the meeting). "Although I just wanted to talk to advisors," Krulak later said of his trip, "often the advisors would bring their Vietnamese counterpart in and say, 'You tell General Krulak about the dedication of your men to their country and so on.'"[103] Mendenhall gave Kennedy a radically different appraisal. He described a "virtually complete breakdown of the civil government" and "a pervasive atmosphere of fear in Saigon." The war against the Vietcong had become secondary, Mendenhall told the president; the primary concern of the South Vietnamese now was the "war against the regime." Nhu had become "the focal point of hate—I really mean *hate*—on the part of the people." Mendenhall had no doubts: "Nhu must go," he concluded. "We will not be able to win the war if he stays."

"You both went to the same country?" Kennedy asked, frustration and impatience apparent in his voice. "What is the reason for the difference?" he wanted to know.* Krulak, a little spark plug of a man who liked to have the last word and to win every argument, quickly offered an answer. "It would seem difficult to make sense between these widely divergent views," the general said, "until our attention is focused on our purpose in Vietnam, which is to *win*." It was a matter of determination and proper focus. "We can still

---

* After mulling things overnight, Kennedy concluded that "they were both right." Meetings: Tape 110. Meeting on Vietnam, 11 September 1963, PRC, POF, JFKL.

stagger through and win the war if somehow we can be permitted to tolerate their conduct," he declared. "I feel sure that we could."

Another sobering observation came from John Mecklin, the head of the United States Information Agency in Saigon and public affairs officer for the embassy, who had returned to Washington with Krulak and Mendenhall. A former *Time* correspondent who had covered the French-Indochina War a decade earlier, Mecklin had seen the French similarly frustrated in Vietnam. He urged Kennedy to think about "what we're going to do when everything else fails, because in my opinion everything else will fail"—and then called for the introduction of American combat troops. Mecklin's suggestion caused a stir around the Cabinet table. Kennedy listened but said nothing.[104]

At the next day's meeting, Kennedy's three senior national security officials—Rusk, McNamara, and McCone—all urged caution in forcing Diệm's removal. Rusk advised continuing to pressure Diệm while cautioning against "using American forces to go in and take over" South Vietnam "if we don't get what we want in the short run." McNamara also urged moving "carefully and slowly," rather than "start on a course of action" that would prompt a coup, which Lodge and other members of the quartet favored and Kennedy tacitly accepted. McCone felt "very much the same way"—"that we should move cautiously . . . We ought to weigh very carefully the effect of a move" against Diệm, because removing the South Vietnamese president "might seriously damage important aspects of the war effort." He later remarked to Kennedy, "Mr. President, if I was manager of a baseball team, and I had one pitcher, I'd keep him in the box whether he was a good pitcher or not."*[105]

Kennedy continued to equivocate for the next several weeks, qualifying and hedging. As part of this process, he decided to send

---

* McCone delivered an even more sobering assessment when he met with the president's Foreign Intelligence Advisory Board (PFIAB), a panel of former senior government officials and top scientific experts who advised Kennedy on intelligence matters, two days later in a high-ceilinged room of the Old Executive Office Building across West Executive Avenue from the White House. Privy to the CIA's analytical assessments, McCone saw the immense problems involved in Vietnam

McNamara and Taylor back to Saigon on a high-level mission to gather more information on the circumstances there. Kennedy explained his reasoning at a meeting with his closest advisors on the evening of September 17. The trip "seems to me to have two advantages," Kennedy told them. "Domestically, we would have the advantage of having the military look at it"* and "we'd be able to operate ourselves with a little better judgment." He acknowledged the deep and abiding division among his own advisors, but noted that "If this thing fails, everybody is going to be wrong. So let's see what we need to do to get it to succeed." He made a comment toward the end of the meeting that cogently summarized the situation (and indirectly revealed his fundamental consent to a coup). "Until a coup comes along," he said, "what we're going to do is to be living with Diem in a state of friction."[106]

Two days later, as McNamara and Taylor prepared to depart, Kennedy gathered them and the other members of his inner circle in the Cabinet Room to frame the mission's agenda. The president told McNamara and Taylor to assess the situation and define "what we should do to make them do what they have to do." Taylor proposed telling Diệm, "'It's not only that we have to win with you, Mr. President, but we have to win very soon. We can't continue on this basis because of the pressures we're seeing being generated at home.'" (Public sympathy for Diệm's regime had begun crum-

---

better than most. The CIA's June 1963 Special National Intelligence Estimate had concluded that "the relations between the Diem/Nhu regime and the public and also the relationship between the regime and the United States are so disturbed that victory over the Vietcong is doubtful if not impossible." (McCone had read from this estimate at one of the September White House meetings.) "If the Diem regime were to be disposed of," McCone told the PFIAB, "there is no one to replace him" and "even if a military coup were pulled off, the CIA does not believe it could stay in power." "The situation is so bad," McCone concluded, "we may have to get out of the war." "Memorandum for the File, Meeting of the President's Foreign Intelligence Advisory Board, September 12 and 13, 1963," September 19, 1963, "New Board Meetings (9–12–1963), #9," PFIAB Records, Washington, D.C.

* This would insulate the administration from conservative criticism that the military's viewpoint was being ignored—an important consideration at a time when Kennedy sought the Joint Chiefs' support for, and the Senate's approval of, the Limited Atmospheric Test Ban Treaty. Kennedy needed to keep the chiefs on board.

bling and influential members of Congress had begun criticizing
U.S. policy.) Tell him "'we're not here forever,'" added Bundy.
Furthermore, Taylor resumed, "'we have a plan—the Secretary
[of Defense] has—showing how we expect to phase out of here.
We need to do this in some finite period of time.'" McNamara reinforced the point. "I'd like particularly to tell Diem that," he told
Kennedy. "I'd like to show him that we *do* have a plan for getting
out of there, that the time is set, and we have worked it out in some
detail." (McNamara had initiated a withdrawal plan[*] after query-
ing British counterinsurgency expert Sir Robert Thompson in late
March about the advisability of reducing U.S. forces in Vietnam.
Thompson had suggested reducing the number of military advisors by a thousand at year's end if progress continued in the war
effort and Harkins had confirmed that progress to McNamara at
their last meeting in Honolulu in May.[107]) Kennedy listened to all of
this but said nothing.[108]

The president met a final time with McNamara and Taylor on
the morning of their departure, September 23. This time, Kennedy spoke frankly and at length. He expressed frustration at the
depth of division in his administration and apprehension about
the future in Saigon. "If the situation there continues to unwind,"
he said with consternation, "then what the hell do we do?" He
imagined a long list of situations, possibilities and scenarios, then
mused with eerie foresight that "we'll have to take some rather
desperate measures because we're going to bear responsibility six
months from now." He seemed contemplative but he also felt im-
mobilized by anxiety about the future. For the first time he conjec-
tured that "we're beginning to lose." Since the summer, Kennedy
had frequently talked in a restless way about Vietnam. McNamara
and Taylor sought to help him. "We have plans for withdrawal
of our forces when military success warrants it," McNamara reminded Kennedy, and "we hope that before the end of the year, we
can be withdrawing military personnel if the military situation

---

[*] McNamara confirmed in an interview with the author in July 1993 that he—not
Kennedy—originated the phased withdrawal plan.

improves." A man of intense personal loyalty and, like Dean Rusk, deep respect bordering on reverence for the presidency itself, Mc-Namara wanted to ease Kennedy's anxiety. Perhaps slanted by that emotional dimension, he presented his withdrawal plan as more feasible than it would turn out to be. Still, McNamara did not see himself as a wishful thinker, because he operated on the mistaken assumption that what he had outlined was possible under current circumstances.[109]

Later that day, McNamara, Taylor, and the other members of their party boarded a chopper on the helipad in the inner court-yard of the Pentagon and hopped over to Andrews Air Force Base just east of Washington, where they climbed aboard a spartanly outfitted and windowless air force KC-135 tanker, originally de-veloped to refuel B-52s in flight, equipped with desks, bunks, and wing fuel tanks for long-distance travel known as the poor man's 707 (and to the press as the "McNamara Special" because of his frequent overseas trips). Saigon was twelve thousand miles away, and after a refueling stop that evening at Anchorage, they headed southwestward over the Pacific. During the long flight, McNamara pored over memo after memo, including hamlet reports and province summaries by U.S. AID and Rural Affairs officers in the field. These reports indicated that conditions in the all-important Mekong River delta had begun to deteriorate markedly. In Long An province immediately south of Saigon, one of the most heavily populated areas of the country, the Vietcong had destroyed sixty strategic hamlets in the past few weeks, forcing the inhabitants to cut the barbed-wire defenses and remove the thatch from their roofed huts to make them uninhabitable. ARVN troops intended to defend the hamlets had been confined to quarters by an increas-ingly apprehensive government for fear they might be used for a coup. McNamara "read no document more carefully than he did the field representatives' province summaries on the way out," re-called a member of the traveling party, "and thereafter he took it and reread it before each of the field trips and used it as a basis for many of his questions."[110]

McNamara carried these hamlet reports and province summaries with him when he and Taylor went out into the field—to Long An province—a few days after their arrival in South Vietnam. There they met with a U.S. Army major who served as the provincial advisor to ARVN. McNamara asked the major if he had read the report of his civilian counterpart in Long An. Yes, the major replied. Did he agree with the appraisal? McNamara asked. The officer paused and finally said yes. Why, McNamara asked, hadn't the major reported these problems himself in his own dispatches? Because his responsibility was limited to reporting on ARVN military operations, the major replied; his reports had been accurate as far as they went, which was not very far. This exchange sharpened McNamara's awareness of the complexity of how understanding what was going on required more than simply analyzing operational statistics, the indicators he had relied on up to now to gauge success in the war, partly because the military's tunnel vision discouraged the reporting of unflattering facts that cast light on the overall effort.[111] And it revealed how difficult it was for McNamara and others in Washington to get to the bottom of what was happening in Vietnam because so much took place below the surface. What it did not do was shake McNamara's belief that fruitful quantification was possible, only that the inputs required were badly distorted and the equation in need of refinement.

Reports that McNamara received in Saigon reinforced the picture of a regime in decline. On September 26, he met with Vietnam expert Patrick Honey, a lecturer at the University of London's School of Oriental and African Studies, who had first visited Saigon in 1945, spoke Vietnamese fluently, and maintained close contacts with the leaders of both South and North Vietnam. Honey had been invited to Saigon by Lodge to advise the U.S. embassy. "His comments carried special weight with me," McNamara later wrote, "because of his strong background and because he had previously supported Diem."[112] Honey told McNamara it was impossible to liberalize the regime or to prevail in the war as long as Diệm remained in power. But he also told McNamara that if the Communists took control of South Vietnam, no Asian political leader would trust the word of the United States. Honey's contradictory conclusion: the United States could not win with Diệm but also could not afford to lose South Vietnam. It was an acute dilemma to which Honey offered no solution, perhaps because there was no solution.[113]

McNamara received an equally sobering assessment from the CIA's Saigon station chief, John Richardson, who knew Diệm and Nhu well and had excellent contacts in the presidential palace. Richardson explained the Buddhist crisis had crystallized discontent that had lain dormant for a long time. Night arrests of students and a pervasive climate of suspicion particularly troubled him. He described Diệm as patriotic, but said Nhu threatened to ruin him. Richardson saw no one in the military with sufficient ability and leadership to replace Diệm. To save South Vietnam, he urged McNamara to press Diệm to end the repression and force Nhu's departure. Otherwise, a coup (that, paradoxically, the CIA had already begun encouraging) would occur and "this would be disastrous."[114]

Finally, on the afternoon of September 29, McNamara and Taylor, accompanied by Lodge and Harkins, called on Diệm at the presidential palace. They sat down in brocade armchairs for a three-hour meeting beneath the whirring ceiling fans and gilded cornices of the president's cavernous office. "Diem was an enigma to me," McNamara later confessed, "because he was from such a different cultural background."[115] The voluble Diệm began the meeting, as was his custom, by launching into a marathon soliloquy. "Purring French in somnolent tones and chain-smoking cigarettes," McNamara observed, "Diem spent the first two and a half hours delivering a monologue about the wisdom of his policies and the progress of the war, frequently springing up and referring to maps to make his case. His serene self-assurance disconcerted me." During a pause in Diệm's lecture, McNamara finally spoke. With Lodge translating his words into French, McNamara told Diệm that the United States wished to help South Vietnam, but that it was basically a Vietnamese war and all the United States could do was help, stressing the second "help" intended to make clear the limitations. McNamara forcefully expressed Washington's disapproval of the current unrest, emphasized that repression jeopardized the war effort, and described a crisis of confidence in the United States about supporting the war against the Vietcong. Diệm reacted as inflexibly as ever. "You could just see it bouncing off him," Taylor later recalled. Feeling isolated and defensive, Diệm sarcastically said that he bore some responsibility for the Buddhists' unrest because, in hindsight, he had been "too kind" to them. McNamara pressed him to muzzle Madame Nhu, reading from a newspaper clipping that he pulled from his pocket quoting her latest inflammatory remark that American junior officers in South Vietnam were "acting like little soldiers of fortune." Diệm squirmed in his armchair as McNamara read the clipping, suggesting that the warning had registered, but he offered no assurance that he would take steps to address McNamara's criticism. At the official dinner that evening, however, Diệm said to McNamara as he walked into the room, "We have much work to do on a few of the suggestions you made this afternoon."[116] "It was, I felt," McNamara said later, "the start of a dialogue."[117]

McNamara and Taylor left South Vietnam on October 1. They prepared their report to Kennedy during their twenty-seven-hour flight back to Washington. Based on conversations with more than 150 American and South Vietnamese officials, they concluded that the war effort—excluding the Delta provinces—continued to make progress. They noted that the political situation under Diệm continued to decompose, but warned that a replacement military regime "would be apt to entail a resumption of the repression at least of Diệm, the corruption of the Vietnamese Establishment before Diệm, and an emphasis on conventional military rather than social, economic and political considerations." They made two key recommendations: first, that "a program be established to train Vietnamese so that essential functions now performed by U.S. military personnel can be carried out by Vietnamese by the end of 1965. It should be possible to withdraw the bulk of U.S. personnel by that time"; and second, that "in accordance with the program to train progressively Vietnamese to take over military functions, the Defense Department should announce in the very near future presently prepared plans to withdraw 1000 U.S. military personnel by the end of 1963."[118] McNamara and Taylor believed (as they had told Kennedy before their trip), that the war effort was going well enough that the United States could wrap up its involvement in two years, but their report was a classic expression of wishful thinking about the present and, especially, the future. As social psychologists David Dunning of the University of Michigan and Emily Balcetis of New York University demonstrated through research, people are indeed more likely to believe things they want to believe. Dunning and Balcetis conducted an experiment involving two ambiguous images that could be perceived as either a loosely formed capital letter B or the number 13. They associated B with a desirable outcome (freshly squeezed orange juice) and 13 with an undesirable outcome (an untasty health food smoothie). Participants more often perceived B than 13.[119] Explained Ziva Kunda of the University of Waterloo, "People do not realize that the [inferential] process is biased by their goals." We see things based on our own desires, but the best way to avoid this trap is to be aware of it.[120]

McNamara and Taylor arrived back at Andrews Air Force Base in the early hours of October 2. Later that morning, after catching a few hours of much-needed sleep, they went to the White House and briefed the president on their trip. Thumbing through their report, Kennedy quickly focused on their recommended withdrawal of a thousand advisors by year's end. "This one thousand reduction—is that going to be an assumption that [the war] is going well? And if it doesn't go well . . . ?" As much as actual progress, Kennedy worried that his administration might be accused of overconfidence. "We believe we can complete the military campaign" by the end of 1965, McNamara told him, "and if it extends beyond that period, we believe we can get the Vietnamese to take over the essential functions and withdraw the bulk of our forces." Later in the meeting he added, "We need a way to get out of Vietnam and this is a way of doing it. To leave forces there when they're not needed I think is wasteful and complicates both their problem and ours."[121] McNamara elaborated his thinking many years later, looking back. "I believed that introducing a phased withdrawal

beginning in 1963 and extending into 1965 would permit completion of the training program by the Vietnamese forces *were they
trainable*."[122] Yet he had given little thought to how that might happen.

Despite his hopes regarding the ARVN training challenge, the
trip had planted doubts in his mind about South Vietnam's political
future. "I was depressed by the evidence of internal political conflict in the society at a time when what was needed was unity," he
later observed.[123] Tension existed between McNamara's desire to
disengage the United States from Vietnam through a phased withdrawal of military advisors and his fear that political disorder in
Saigon posed a potentially serious threat to that effort. He resolved
this tension by assuming that circumstances would enable the first
thousand-man withdrawal by year's end and its completion by the
end of 1965. "One way [that people] resolve conflicts between beliefs and desires," notes social psychologist Lee Ross of Stanford
University, "is to engage in biased reasoning in a way that brings
beliefs about facts in line with heartfelt desires."[124] McNamara did
just this when he presumed that the withdrawal of U.S. military
advisors could be completed by the end of 1965.

Kennedy convened a National Security Council meeting that
evening to discuss McNamara and Taylor's report further and to
prepare a press release about its recommendations. He began by
summarizing where things stood, expressing concern that the political situation might begin to hurt the war effort (as McNamara
and Taylor had warned), and said the United States should try to
change the atmosphere in South Vietnam—another indication of
his implicit support for a coup. "We've pretty much got our policy
now," he announced with some relief, then stepped momentarily
from the room. In his absence, Bundy—whom Kennedy had spoken to privately about McNamara and Taylor's report—told the
others that "the President is concerned about this sentence [in the
report] that the major part of the U.S. military task can be completed by the end of 1965 and asked whether we wouldn't do better
to say that is the judgment reported by Secretary McNamara and
General Taylor. The President wants to be sure that the document
as a whole reflects the notion that the object here is to win the

war." Kennedy's objective—victory—had been made crystal clear to everyone at the meeting, including Lyndon Johnson, who would become president less than two months later.

When he rejoined the gathering, Kennedy again expressed skepticism about the thousand-man target. "If the war doesn't continue to go well, it looks like we were overly optimistic," he said, adding, "I'm not sure what benefit we have at this time in announcing" it. "The advantage of taking them out," McNamara said, determined to push through the withdrawal plan, "is that we can say to the Congress and people that we *do* have a plan for reducing the exposure of U.S. combat personnel to the guerrilla actions in South Vietnam—actions that the people of South Vietnam should gradually develop a capability to suppress themselves. I think this will be of great value to us in meeting the very strong views of [Senate Foreign Relations Committee chairman William] Fulbright and others that we're bogged down in Asia and we'll be there for decades." "All right," Kennedy finally said. The White House statement released after the meeting included mention of the withdrawal of a thousand U.S. military advisors by the end of the year; most of the others would be out of the country by the end of 1965, "when the major part of the U.S. military task can be completed." While Kennedy had accepted McNamara's phased withdrawal plan in principle, he did not share McNamara's optimism that it could be achieved. JFK did, however, understand its domestic political benefits and hoped it might be a spur to improve ARVN's performance.[125]

A few days later, events in Saigon soon took a decisive turn. On October 5, the CIA station chief, John Richardson, boarded a plane at Tan Son Nhut airport and returned to the United States. Richardson's long-standing close relationship with the Ngô brothers and his past support of the regime irritated Lodge, who resented and suspected the station chief had a confidential channel to the palace. In fact, Lodge had been gunning for Richardson from the moment he arrived as ambassador, and had leaked Richardson's identity to sympathetic American reporters, blowing the CIA officer's cover, precipitating his recall, and signaling an end to the close American relationship with the Ngô brothers. Richardson out of the way, the ambassador stood in unchallenged command of U.S. policy in Saigon. Just as important, the South Vietnamese generals plotting Diệm's overthrow could now be confident that no American would tip off the Ngô brothers if they planned a coup.

Just hours after Richardson departed, General Dương Văn "Big" Minh met with CIA liaison Lucien Conein in a French-era bungalow at Saigon garrison headquarters. An unusually burly Vietnamese officer with missing front teeth who served as Diệm's military advisor, Minh had fought with the French against his own people in the First Indochina War and had helped bring Diệm to power in 1954. Lodge authorized Conein's meeting with Minh. Americans had been waiting for the generals to make a move since late August, and Minh revealed that he and his colleagues were ready at last. A cabal of senior ARVN generals had resolved weeks earlier, in mid-September, to mount a coup against Diệm. In addition to Minh, the conspirators included Trần Văn Đôn, ARVN chief of staff; Nguyễn Khánh, the young and ambitious commander in the Central Highlands; and Trần Thiện Khiêm, the president's godson and operations officer at ARVN headquarters, who controlled troops in the Saigon area. Calculating and mutually suspicious, Minh, Đôn, Khánh, and Khiêm had been plotting for weeks but had held back, uncertain whether the Americans would support their action. Financially dependent on the United States, they hesitated to act without Washington's approval. The Kennedy administration's cutoff of commodity aid on October 5 (which affected the business community on whom Diệm relied for much of his funding), combined with the White House's promise of continued support to the military, now led the generals to act.

On the night of October 24, Conein met with General Đôn at a dentist's office in downtown Saigon. The CIA dossier on Đôn captured his character succinctly: "Real loyalty uncertain and probably an opportunist. Seems to be in all camps: reported close to French, to Nhu, impressive to many Americans, and close to chief military critics of [the Diệm government] but not fully trusted by them."[126] Đôn told Conein to expect a coup no later than November 2. ("Lou," Đôn told him, "don't leave town within the next week."[127]) Conein passed along the information to Lodge, who authorized Conein to station himself at rebel headquarters during the upcoming insurrection to communicate developments to Lodge at the embassy. "In the event that the coup aborts," Lodge cabled Washington the next day, "our involvement to date through Conein is still within the realm of plausible denial."[128]

A day later at the White House, the coup debate recommenced. While acknowledging that we may "have passed a point of no return," McCone urged Kennedy to reconsider his tacit support for an overthrow. "Our appraisal—the people in the Agency who have experience there—is that if a coup did come off, they would expect a very serious interregnum in political affairs and some period of political confusion. They don't think that General Don has the strength of leadership necessary and therefore we look forward to this period of confusion and possibly a second coup." Instead of going through with it, McCone suggested another attempt "to make a further positive effort to try to bring about some arrangements at the top with Diem. I think this is going to be preferable to what we see as the consequences of the alternative course." But there were no concrete proposals, just apprehensions. "The appraisal of our intelligence people is that we're entering a period of political confusion that might have consequences for the war effort," he warned. "I would hope that Lodge, in his weekend with Diem, might be able to reach some kind of understanding—or the commencement of a series of understandings—that would permit us to go forward with this government."[129] Kennedy discounted McCone's warning because he believed McCone harbored personal animus toward Lodge for forcing the recall of his Saigon station chief.[130]

Yet clarity remained absent. Kennedy did not abandon his tacit support for a coup, but he instructed Lodge to urge Diệm to end the repression and remove Nhu before it was too late. On the morning of October 28, Lodge encountered General Đôn at the Dalat airport on his way back to Saigon. Đôn told him a coup was imminent. That night, Conein in Saigon met a second time with Đôn. Đôn told Conein that rebel headquarters would be the Joint General Staff headquarters at Tan Son Nhut airport, and to remain available beginning in two days. Đôn promised Conein prior notice of the coup. When this information reached Washington, Kennedy again called together his advisors. Taylor and McCone repeated their warning that a coup would trigger prolonged political instability damaging to the war effort; better to stick with Diệm despite all of his faults and limitations. Harriman—this time supported by Rusk—vehemently disagreed. Kennedy did not take sides in the ongoing debate over the wisdom of a coup but concentrated on whether or not it would succeed. Kennedy's decision to let things stand effectively reinforced his tacit consent.[131]

Diệm had been slow to respond to American entreaties and pressures, but with coup fever building and alarmed by a detected shift in the weather, he tentatively reached out to Lodge, inviting the ambassador to join him over the weekend of October 27 at the presidential villa in Dalat, a cool, lush mountain retreat in the Central Highlands. The South Vietnamese leader had not communicated with Lodge in nearly a month, since the ambassador had accompanied McNamara, Taylor, and Harkins to the palace on September 29. Now Diệm treated Lodge to ritual tea followed by a seven-course lunch before they sat down to talk—their first real conversation since Lodge had taken up his post in late August. Lodge found Diệm as unresponsive as ever, though he conceded that without U.S. economic aid he could not continue to govern. "When it was evident that the conversation was practically over," Lodge reported afterward, "I said, 'Mr. President, every single specific suggestion which I have made, you have rejected. Isn't there some one thing you may think of that is within your capabilities to do and that would favorably impress U.S. opinion?' As on other previous occasions when I asked him similar questions, he gave me a blank look and changed the subject." He is "simply unbelievably stubborn," Lodge concluded.[132]

Never one to react on the spot to pressures and prodding, Diệm waited two days, then began to show signs of movement. At a meeting at Gia Long Palace on October 29 with Trần Văn

Dĩnh, Saigon's chargé in Washington, Diệm told Dĩnh that upon his return to Washington on November 1, he should call a press conference and announce that "agreements have been reached between the Vietnamese government and Ambassador Cabot Lodge regarding . . . changes in both personnel and policies." In terms of a timetable, Diệm proclaimed that "the next few days will see the materialization of these agreements." He asked Dĩnh to convey the same message directly to Kennedy,[133] but Diệm did not inform Lodge of those instructions to Dĩnh.

Meanwhile, momentum carried things forward. At the eleventh hour, Diệm and Nhu had realized the precariousness of their situation. Diệm invited Rural Affairs director Rufus Phillips, an old friend who was aware of the generals' plotting, to the palace on the morning of October 30. Aides ushered Phillips right in to see the president. "There was none of the agitation I had seen in him during the height of the Buddhist crisis," Phillips later wrote. "He seemed philosophical about whatever fate might bring. We sat in silence for a moment while he looked down and puffed on his ever-present cigarette. There was no more to say, I thought. Then he looked up directly at me and asked softly, 'Do you think there will be a coup?' I looked him in the eye. I couldn't lie to him, 'I'm afraid so, Mr. President.' I felt like crying and wanted to take him aside out of the room, which I thought might be bugged, to tell him, 'For God's sake, talk to Lodge and reach some agreement.' Then I thought I couldn't do that; I had already said more probably than I should have. Further words might endanger the lives of Conein and the generals, because of how Nhu might react. Reading the emotion in my face, he tried to comfort me without words by putting his hand on my arm. He stood up, took my hand, said . . . goodbye—*au revoir* not *adieu*, but I had the feeling it might be the last time I saw him."[134]

Later that same day, Nhu requested a private meeting with Lodge—the first time he had ever done so. When they met, Nhu told Lodge what Washington had been waiting to hear for two months: that he would leave South Vietnam if personally asked to do so by President Kennedy, whom he said it would be impossible to refuse. But Lodge interpreted Nhu's remark as a slight against himself as Kennedy's personal emissary; he did not grasp that it was Nhu's way of trying to save face.[135] Lodge's lack of cultural awareness blinded him to the subtle (and not so subtle) signals of compromise that Diệm and Nhu had begun conveying to him. It also reflected Lodge's patronizing attitude toward the South Vietnamese that the ambassador's critics saw clearly and regretted, then and later.* "My general view," Lodge cabled Washington that evening, "is that the U.S. is trying to bring this medieval country into the 20th century and . . . to gain victory we must also bring them into the 20th century politically." His pride offended and his perception obtuse, Lodge did not report Nhu's offer in his cable.[136] That same day, Generals Minh, Đôn, Khánh, and Khiêm met secretly at a private club in Cholon, the Chinese quarter of southern Saigon, and made the decision to launch the coup on November 1.

Hours later, at 2 P.M., October 30, Washington time, Kennedy met again with his advisors in the Cabinet Room to discuss developments. McNamara handed him a telegram from Harkins complaining that Lodge had not informed him about the impending coup and strongly advising against it. Harkins, who knew senior ARVN officers as well as anyone, bluntly declared, "Certainly there are no generals qualified to take over in my opinion."[137] Kennedy read aloud as he perused the cable, though skipped the last paragraphs, which said, "I would suggest we not try to change horses too quickly, that we continue to take persuasive actions that will make the horses change their course and methods of action . . . Rightly or wrongly, we have backed Diem for eight long hard years. To me it seems incongruous now to get him down, kick him around, and get rid of him."[138] Harkins's warning rekindled JFK's lurking reservations. Lodge "is much stronger for [a coup] than we are here," he declared. Rusk moved to reassure an uncertain Kennedy. "We're on a downward slope at the present time," he re-

---

* Senate Armed Services Committee chairman Richard Russell said of Lodge the following spring: "He thinks he's dealing with barbarian tribes out there, that he's an emperor and he's gonna tell 'em what to do." Michael R. Beschloss, ed., *Taking Charge: The Johnson White House Tapes, 1963–1964* (Simon & Schuster, 1997), p. 366.

minded the president, predicting that "the chances are very high there's an outcome that will change a situation that is deteriorating." "I would associate myself with that," Bundy quickly chimed in. Harriman did the same.[139]

On October 31, General Đôn called on Diệm at the presidential palace. Fearing Diệm might leave the city the next day, he wanted to keep the president at the palace. Đôn told Diệm that Admiral Harry Felt, commander of all U.S. forces in the Pacific (and technically Harkins's superior in the chain of command), planned to visit Saigon the following day and asked Diệm to officially receive him. Diệm expressed surprise at the suggestion, but agreed to meet the admiral. He then wrote a personal letter to Lodge, who would be accompanying Felt to the palace, asking the ambassador to remain behind for fifteen minutes after Felt left so that Diệm could talk privately with him. Later that day, Nhu agreed to free the thousands of imprisoned Buddhists and announced the news in an official press release. The issue that had triggered the plot against Diệm and Nhu had been resolved very late—too late.

At 10 o'clock Friday morning, November 1, Felt and Lodge called on Diệm at the presidential palace. Diệm greeted them in an ornate salon. He spoke politely but with unusual directness. "I know there is going to be a coup," he said, "but I don't know who is going to do it."[140] Lodge told Diệm he did not think there was anything to worry about; he had no intention of revealing what he knew concerning the coup. At 11:45 A.M., Felt bid farewell and left for Tan Son Nhut airport. Lodge stayed behind to talk privately with Diệm. Lodge listened impassively as Diệm spoke. When Lodge got up to leave, Diệm—aware that the ambassador intended to visit Washington soon—told him what he had told Dinh three days earlier. "Please tell President Kennedy that I am a good and frank ally," Diệm said, "that I would rather be frank and settle questions now than talk about them after we have lost everything. Tell President Kennedy that I take all his suggestions very seriously and wish to carry them out . . . Tell us what you want and we'll do it." Lodge returned to the embassy and drafted a cable about this critical meeting. The category "Critical Flash"—which Lodge had used before and which the CIA station used regularly during the coup that followed—would have ensured the message's immediate transmission to Washington. Instead, he slow-walked it by labeling it "Priority," the lowest category possible. It would not reach the White House for many hours.[141]

Meanwhile Đôn signaled Conein, who hurried to Vietnamese General Staff Headquarters near Tan Son Nhut and installed himself there with direct telephone lines to the embassy and the CIA station. The generals notified Harkins and MACV of the coup at 1:45 P.M. Fifteen minutes later, the coup was underway. Coup forces stormed special forces headquarters, took control of Tan Son Nhut and communications facilities in Saigon, and prepared to attack the presidential guard barracks near Gia Long Palace. At 3 P.M., Diệm phoned Đôn from the air-conditioned cellar of the palace and announced his willingness to implement reforms. "Why didn't you tell me that yesterday?" Đôn said. "It is too late now."[142] He urged Diệm to surrender unconditionally and promised safe conduct for the president and his brother. The other three generals got on the phone and repeated the offer. Nhu received the same message when he phoned Đôn minutes later. Firing on the presidential palace began at 4 P.M. Thirty minutes later, Diệm telephoned Lodge at the ambassador's residence. Lodge could hear intermittent gunfire as he picked up the receiver.

DIỆM: Some units have made a rebellion and I want to know: what is the attitude of the United States?
LODGE: I do not feel well enough informed to be able to tell you. I have heard the shooting, but am not acquainted with all the facts. Also it is 4:30 A.M. in Washington and the U.S. government cannot possibly have a view.
DIỆM: But you must have some general ideas. After all, I am a chief of state. I have tried to do my duty. I want to do now what duty and good sense require. I believe in duty above all.
LODGE: You certainly have done your duty. As I told you this morning, I admire your courage and your great contributions

to your country. No one can take away from you the credit for all you have done. Now I am worried about your physical safety. I have a report that those in charge of the current activity offer you and your brother safe conduct out of the country if you resign. Had you heard this?

DIỆM: No. You have my telephone number.

LODGE: Yes. If I can do anything for your safety, please call me.

DIỆM: I am trying to reestablish order.[143]

At 4:45 P.M., the generals called Diệm, put special forces commander Colonel Lê Quanh Tung* on the phone, and made him tell Diệm that the special forces had surrendered and the situation was hopeless. They then took Tung outside and shot him. An hour later, Minh called Diệm and told him the palace would be bombed if he and his brother did not surrender. Diệm hung up on him, enraging Minh, who felt humiliated in front of the other generals. At 9:30 P.M., the generals broadcast a radio announcement warning all members of the government to surrender before 11 P.M. or suffer the consequences. The ground assault on the presidential palace began at 3:30 A.M. the next morning, supported by artillery, tanks, and mortars. It was all over before 7 A.M. When troops entered the gutted building, they found Diệm and Nhu had vanished. The brothers, dressed in dark gray business suits, had slipped away at nightfall through the palace's back gate on Cong Ly Street, climbed into a waiting Land Rover that drove them to Cholon, switched to a black Citroën sedan, and via a circuitous route through a warren of narrow streets arrived at the villa of Ma Tuyen, a Chinese merchant who had grown wealthy on their patronage. Tuyen's villa had a phone connection to the palace switchboard, which allowed Diệm and Nhu to hide their whereabouts. There, chain-smoking cigarettes and sipping tea, they tried unsuccessfully to contact ARVN commanders whom they thought might still be loyal. At daybreak, the brothers moved to Saint Francis Xavier, a French

---

* Tung's special forces had carried out the late August raid on the Buddhist pagodas wearing regular army uniforms.

mission church on the southern edge of Cholon, where they had attended mass over the years, and took Communion. At 6:20 A.M., Diệm, his voice husky with fatigue, phoned Đôn and offered to surrender "with the honors due a departing president." Đôn only promised Diệm and his brother safe conduct. Diệm accepted and requested that his godson Khiem be sent to escort them to rebel headquarters. Minh and Đôn asked Conein for a U.S. plane to fly them out of the country into exile. Conein, who had overlooked that vital detail, told them it would take twenty-four hours to bring in a long-range aircraft from Okinawa. He then left rebel headquarters for his home to shower and change clothes.

When Conein got home, the CIA station directed him to report to the embassy. There, he received instructions sent directly from President Kennedy to find Diệm and protect him. It was a tragically belated command: after Conein left rebel headquarters, Minh had called a meeting at which the conspirators decided to assassinate the Ngô brothers. ("To kill weeds, you must pull them up at the roots," one of them said.[144]) Minh dispatched a convoy to pick up Diệm and Nhu at the church. It did not include Khiêm, but Minh's bodyguard, instead—designated to be the executioner. As the convoy set off in two jeeps and an armored personnel carrier, Minh raised two fingers of his right hand—a prearranged hand signal to his bodyguard. The convoy reached the church shortly after 8 A.M. and took Diệm and Nhu into custody. The brothers were ordered to get in the armored personnel carrier. When Nhu objected, saying it wasn't dignified enough, they were shoved into the carrier and their hands bound tightly behind their backs. On the way to rebel headquarters, the convoy stopped at a railroad crossing on Hong Thap Tu Avenue at the edge of the downtown. At this point, the end finally came. Minh's executioner boarded the armored carrier, knifed Nhu, bloodied Diệm's face, then shot both of them in the back of the neck at point-blank range. "Why are they dead?" Đôn asked Minh when the convoy returned to rebel headquarters. "What does it matter?" replied Minh. "What would we [the U.S.] have done with them if they had lived?" a clinical Lodge later said.[145]

News of Diệm's and Nhu's deaths reached Washington a few hours later, at 12:24 A.M. on November 2. The CIA station in Saigon reported the brothers had committed suicide "en route from

Front-page Headline of the Coup Against Diệm
John Frost Newspapers/Alamy Stock Photo

city to General Staff Headquarters." The message went immediately to the White House and Michael Forrestal awakened Kennedy. The president spent the rest of the night in the Situation Room in the basement of the West Wing. The brothers' deaths "shook him personally," Forrestal recalled, "bothered him as a moral and religious matter." He seemed more depressed than at any time since the Bay of Pigs, noted Arthur Schlesinger, who saw Kennedy later that morning. Taylor perceived "a look of shock and dismay" on Kennedy's face "which I had never seen before." "The thing that is of concern is what happened to Diem and Nhu," Kennedy told his advisors when he met with them at 9:30 A.M. "That is what bothers me about this . . . I do not believe he committed suicide, given his strong religious career."[146] A sophisticated and worldly man, Kennedy had nonetheless willfully and naively persuaded himself that a coup could be carried out without endangering their lives. Struggling to absorb the shock, Kennedy tried to convince himself that he and his administration were not responsible for what had happened. "The suggestion"—no one had yet made such a suggestion—"is that the United States made the coup inevitable by applying pressures which developed the atmosphere," he mused to those gathered around the Cabinet table that morning. "I think that certainly in September after the conclusion of the McNamara-Taylor visit, our intention was to apply pressure to persuade Diem to modify his course of action. At that time, we were not pushing a coup. He didn't give at all and the coup developed. I would say that was our policy—and we ought to stick with it."[147] This story would stand in place of a disturbing reality. "There's this nice theory that keeps coming through [the cables]: that it's really the generals who are going to decide, and not us, about the removal of Diem," a CIA official later said. "There's an unreality to it when you think of the enormous importance of the American position."[148]

Privately, however, Kennedy could not shake a sense of responsibility and even guilt for the Ngô brothers' deaths, which he definitively learned several hours later had not been suicides. "I feel we must bear a good deal of responsibility for it beginning with our cable of [late] August in which we suggested the coup," he confessed in a private memo he dictated two days later. "I was shocked by the death of Diem and Nhu . . . [Diệm] was [an] extraordinary character and while he became increasingly difficult in the last months, nevertheless over a ten-year period he had held his country together to maintain its independence under very adverse conditions. The way he was killed made it particularly abhorrent. The question now is whether the generals can stay together and build a stable government."[149] Kennedy had failed to thoroughly probe this cardinal question—Could the generals who sought to replace Diệm do better?—before tacitly encouraging and then sanctioning their coup. Subsequent events would answer his question with a resounding no.

McNamara later addressed the Kennedy administration's responsibility for the coup. "It's very clear we were responsible for the overthrow and death of Diem," he admitted. "Certainly it would not have occurred at that moment in time had we not either stimulated or indicated support for the military coup. Events might have evolved in such a way that popular unrest and/or military dissatisfaction with his leadership would have led to his overthrow at some date. But it certainly wouldn't have occurred then. And I'm inclined to believe based, again, on the last comment he made to Lodge, that we could have negotiated with him a series of changes that would have reduced the pressure from the military and other groups to overthrow him. In any event, I'm certain we could have prevented the overthrow at that particular time. And not only could we have prevented it, but I think that it occurred in large part because of what the military believed was our support for it"—which, of course, was a correct assumption.[150]

Diệm's assassination sobered Kennedy, vividly reminding him of what he always suspected: that the United States could affect events in Vietnam but not determine them. The realization that the United States had lost whatever control it might have had over circumstances in that country rekindled his skepticism about American involvement in Indochina. The day before he left on the political trip to Texas that tragically ended in his own assassination on November 22, Kennedy wondered aloud to Michael

Forrestal about South Vietnam's long-term prospects and viability and even the American commitment itself. "I want you to organize an in-depth study of every possible option we've got in Vietnam, including how to get out of there," he told Forrestal. "We have to review this whole thing from the bottom to the top."[151] Diệm's death had taught Kennedy the dangers and limits of American power in Vietnam. Its consequences would confront his successor, Lyndon Johnson.

President Kennedy regularly asserted two contradictory propositions about Vietnam: that the South Vietnamese must do the job for themselves and yet the United States must not quit there. Unable to reconcile the conflicting imperatives of avoiding another American ground war on the Asian mainland and avoiding the loss of South Vietnam, he remained indecisive. It was uncharacteristic of him. "When he knew what he really wanted," McGeorge Bundy said of Kennedy, "he had no problem" making a decision. Kennedy did not live to see the consequences of removing Diệm, but his advisors did, and most of them came to view it as a grave mistake. "It was not well handled," Bundy later admitted. "There was no victory for the United States in the fall of Diem" and "still less in his death." That mishandling was rooted in naïveté. "The consequences were so unpredictable, including the death, which was no part of our intent or expectation, which was pretty stupid," Bundy concluded. "We should have guessed that these people would feel that if you strike at a king, you strike to kill, which they did." That there was no evacuation plan for Diệm was only one of the wretchedly telling signs that the American consideration of the coup's possible outcomes was shallow and incomplete. In hindsight, Mike Mansfield was probably right when he said that Diệm "was the only one, despite his frailties, who could have kept South Vietnam together." None of the generals who followed Diệm did better at leading South Vietnam, and most did worse. All of them would be equally if not more dependent on the United States. "The only durable result of the coup against Diem," Bundy noted, "was durable political instability in Saigon."[152]

Myopic decision-making is a common human foible. People tend to overvalue short-term payoffs and discount long-term consequences. A choice might have adverse effects down the road, but people somehow persuade themselves those effects "won't be *that* bad." Diệm and Nhu were Kennedy's immediate concern, and this ultimately blinded him to the long-term consequences of a coup by generals whom Kennedy admitted he did not know.[153] The military coup that Kennedy sanctioned achieved his immediate goal, but it also ushered in a host of unanticipated and unattractive consequences, many of which undermined the goal he had set in the first place: to bolster the war effort. What Kennedy had done did not foreclose later choices, but it made those later choices much more difficult.

For their part, the Vietcong and the North Vietnamese were flabbergasted when they learned of Diệm's and Nhu's deaths as a result of an American-inspired coup; they could not believe the Americans would allow South Vietnam to be disrupted in this way. "They were gifts from heaven for us," said a senior Vietcong official.[154] "Both Ho Chi Minh and he (Mao) thought that Ngo Dinh Diem was not so bad," wrote journalist Edgar Snow, based on an interview with Mao Zedong in January 1965. "After all," said Mao, "following his assassination, was everything between Heaven and Earth more peaceful?" Even Nguyễn Văn Thiệu, who participated in the coup that brought down Diệm, later said that "he actually ran the country pretty well" given the circumstances confronting him.[155] Diệm had many faults, but his pride meant that he "didn't want us in there fighting his war," noted McNamara.[156]

Kennedy refused throughout his presidency to commit U.S. combat forces to Vietnam. "JFK saw the U.S. support for Vietnam as strictly limited to helping the Vietnamese help themselves," McNamara later said. Kennedy never deviated from this position, even as the situation in South Vietnam steadily deteriorated during his three years in office. He had always been dubious about the effectiveness of Western military power on the Asian mainland. He knew from the Bay of Pigs the limits of what the generals recommended. He understood the basic principle of guerrilla warfare:

that the object was not killing enemy soldiers, but winning the allegiance of the people—that the solution in Vietnam was fundamentally political, not military. He never accepted the premise that the United States should save South Vietnam at all costs and he never made an unqualified commitment to maintain its independence. If the South Vietnamese were not capable of defending themselves, "he thought it impossible to do so with U.S. military forces," said McNamara. He went on: "At the time of Kennedy's death, I think he was very concerned about the dominoes. But when he got to a point where he had to choose between the risk of the dominoes falling and adding 400,000 men," McNamara surmised, "he wouldn't have done it." Perhaps Bobby Kennedy, who knew the president better than anyone, put it best. "Nobody can say for sure what my brother would actually have done, in the actual circumstances of 1964 or '65. I can't say that, and even he couldn't have said that in '61. Maybe things would have gone just the same as they did. But I do know what he *intended*. All I can say is that he was absolutely determined not to send ground units."[157]

McNamara's successor as secretary of defense, Clark Clifford—who knew Kennedy quite well—agreed. "In judging matters of this kind," said Clifford, Kennedy "was a real cold fish. He could be totally objective." There was a JFK smile, and behind doors, also a set of gritted teeth. "Under that façade of charm and attractiveness . . . President Kennedy could be as coldly analytical as anybody I ever saw . . . He was cold, calculating, and penetrating," with "the ability to step away" and "with a surprising degree of objectivity look at the problem." Clifford could imagine Kennedy eventually saying, "I'm not willing to take the chance. I don't like what I see ahead. I'm suspicious of the people who are involved. I just don't think I ought to accept the representations of the military with full faith and credit extended. I'm going to be more cautious. I'm just not going to get more deeply involved in what is obviously a stinking mess."[158] Kennedy was not, as his aide and historian Arthur Schlesinger dryly observed, "inclined to heavy investments in lost causes."[159] McNamara concurred: "In the most basic terms— avoiding risk—I'll guarantee you, that moved him."[160]

Kennedy's last public comments on Vietnam support such conclusions. At his final Washington press conference on November 14, eight days before his assassination, a reporter asked Kennedy to "give us your appraisal of the situation in South Vietnam now, since the coup." Kennedy replied that "our object [is] to bring Americans home, permit the South Vietnamese to maintain themselves as a free and independent country." Later during the press conference, Kennedy asked rhetorically, "Are we going to give up in South Vietnam?" and answered his question: "The most important program, of course, is our national security, but I don't want the United States to have to put troops there."[161]

Kennedy did, however, publicly and privately acknowledge the difficulty of ending America's involvement in Vietnam, and his sensitivity to the political climate had been evident from his first campaign for Congress. Far more skeptical in his private comments than in his public pronouncements, he seriously questioned whether the United States could do what the French had failed to do, and in the last days of his life wondered whether the United States should be there at all. But he never shared his doubts and concerns with the American people or educated them about the limitations that he saw. Kennedy perceived the dangers of deepening American involvement, yet his actions paradoxically contributed to this very result. As McGeorge Bundy admitted in retrospect, "When you put your thumb on the scales of domestic politics" as Kennedy did by sanctioning the generals' coup, "you're pretty far in."[162] Thus one president who intuitively understood the limits of American military power in Southeast Asia, who possessed the security and self-confidence to resist calls by generals and advisors to apply that power, set in motion during his last months in office an event whose unanticipated repercussions would create immense pressures for greater American military involvement. These pressures would confront another president who lacked Kennedy's intuitive understanding, security, and self-confidence.

CHAPTER 4

The Peril of Short-Term Thinking
(November 1963–July 1965)

The November 1963 coup that toppled Ngô Đình Diệm triggered political turmoil in South Vietnam that in less than a year swept the country to the brink of collapse. In response to this turmoil, President Lyndon Johnson and his advisors made a series of decisions that sucked the United States into the vortex of a major, bloody, and unsuccessful war. Why did intelligent and well-meaning men embark on such a futile enterprise so costly in human lives and suffering? They did so because short-term thinking made them far more confident than they should have been about dealing with the problems they confronted and far less attentive than they should have been to the long-term consequences of their decisions. It shifted their attention from a careful examination of alternatives to a groping for means of overcoming difficulties. It also left them psychologically ill-equipped to deal with the accelerating force of events as the deterioration of South Vietnam deepened throughout 1964 and into the spring and summer of 1965. They failed to recognize the tiny changes in circumstances that carried them from one decision to another. As a result, they found themselves facing pressures they had not anticipated and that resulted in outcomes they had not intended. "It gets harder to see straight as you get more deeply committed," confessed McGeorge Bundy, looking back.[1] In this environment, the absence of careful attention to the implications of small decisions became magnified. Myopic decision-making turned a series of those small decisions into a large blunder.

President Johnson and his team confronted numerous forces and circumstances they did not create and could not ignore. Some implications of their decisions could not be discerned at the time, becoming apparent only later. But their persistent lack of reflection—reinforced by Johnson's fear of an international and domestic political firestorm that "losing Vietnam" would provoke, especially the possible failure of his cherished Great Society* reform agenda—inhibited a comprehensive, creative, and conscientious reckoning. It is not that Johnson and his advisors did not foresee serious problems—they did. It is that they failed to ponder the long-term consequences of the serious problems they did see. Whatever control they possessed began to slip away as events generated their own momentum, took on a life of their own, and ultimately overwhelmed those leading the war effort, carrying them like rafters who lose their oars down a swiftly moving river littered with waterfalls. Short-term thinking blunted their ability to anticipate obstacles and gave them less time to react to hidden rocks. Each step deeper in, moreover, made extrication harder. As a result, Johnson and his advisors got an outcome they did not plan and that brought them and the American and Vietnamese people to grief. They demonstrated a striking lack of foresight, judiciousness, and reflection that circumstances demanded. Thirty years after, Rob-

---

* Johnson used the term "Great Society" to describe his ambitious legislative agenda to eliminate social injustice and poverty. He first used the term during speeches in Athens, Ohio, and Ann Arbor, Michigan, in May 1964. The Great Society meant a lot to Johnson. "The reason," explained Clark Clifford, who came to know Johnson as well as anyone outside of his family, "was that he'd grown up with minorities in the area of Texas where he lived. He saw what their lives were like. Their lives had no hope. Their lives were just to live out their days in the most unfortunate circumstances and then die. They were part of that great one-third of our population that Franklin Roosevelt referred to as ill-fed, ill-clothed, and ill-housed. Johnson saw that and he determined as a boy and as a young man that if he ever got in a position where he could be helpful to those people, he intended to do so. And he followed through on it magnificently." Author's interviews with Clark Clifford, June 3, 1988, Tape One; and August 18, 1988.

ert McNamara saw to the heart of the matter. "The problem was that we did not adequately foresee the implications of our actions."[2] There is a powerful lesson in their experience for all of us.

President John F. Kennedy's public murder on November 22, 1963, instantly transformed him into a martyred icon. During the days of grief and mourning that followed his assassination, a profound sense developed throughout the country that it had not only lost a graceful, confidant leader but all of its hopes for the future. The countless images of the glamorous JFK on television screens, front pages, and magazine covers inevitably invited unflattering comparisons to his successor's overbearing demeanor and unvarnished manner. A man of labyrinthine mind, mountainous ambition, and Shakespearean contradictions, Lyndon B. Johnson could range from soaring exhibitions of brilliance and sensitivity to oppressive melancholy and vulgar abrasiveness. He could persuade, flatter, cajole, intimidate—depending on the person and the circumstances. He displayed both great depth and great shallowness, combining piercing insights with self-deception on the grandest scale, but none of the celebrity cool that had made for Camelot. He was, noted a long-time aide, at once "a man bedeviled by grand and innocent visions almost beyond mortal reach, and a man beset by petty doubts and cynical suspicions of himself."[3] "I am no more bewildered by Lyndon," his wife, Lady Bird, once said, "than he is bewildered by himself."[4] "The well of ambition and aspiration flowed out of him like an explosive force," a close friend said. Whenever that explosive force was frustrated, the friend explained, Johnson "behaved like a youngster with a temper tantrum."[5] It was an extraordinary mixture of good and bad qualities, all manifest on a larger-than-life scale.

At once cruel and compassionate, sensitive and profane—his speech filled with the colorful rhythms and sometimes crude similes of those born on the land—Johnson's patois of coarseness, magnified by the microscope of critical examination, masked a quick and incisive mind. He was a man of gargantuan ego, a consummate wheeler-dealer whose boorishness, braggadocio, and drive to

LBJ and JFK
Abbie Rowe/JFK Library

control and humiliate others masked a deep sense of personal insecurity. Johnson had harnessed this extraordinary mix of qualities
as a legendarily effective Senate majority leader from 1955 to 1961
when, in the words of a Washington insider, "he played senators
like a violinist would play a Stradivarius."[6] His physical movements
were equally calculated: "The voice swelled as he went along,
arms pumped, hands clapped against his forehead, eyes turned
heavenward . . . He would not let the conversation begin until he
knew how it would end."[7] "He twisted a lot of arms," recalled one
long-time aide, and "he did it not only with zest, but with a good
deal of confidence that he would win."[8] "He was a con man," his
close friend Clark Clifford remembered, "but I'd see him use the
con approach in a good cause and bring people along. He'd go up
and put his arm around some senator—he'd get his nose about that
far away from his face—and pretty soon this senator would just

wilt, almost as though he was being physically bombarded by some kind of atoms that were coming out of Johnson onto the fellow."[9] There was a pitiless side of his character, too, which Clifford also witnessed. "Lyndon Johnson believed you dominate those you can dominate, and you suck up to those that you can't dominate."[10]

But the same qualities that made Johnson an effective Senate majority leader (arguably the greatest in history)—his habit of pursuing his goals through manipulation and secrecy; his willingness to be elusive and downright disingenuous when it served his purposes; his obsession about not showing the cards in his hand; his reluctance to reveal his hand even to favored advisors at sensitive moments; his conviction that everyone had their price, it was simply a matter of finding it; and his compulsion to personalize every issue—made him particularly ill-equipped to deal with Vietnam. McGeorge Bundy, who saw Johnson warts and all in his role as national security advisor, put it well. "He was a great, wonderful man, and he did accomplish an awful lot of good things. But he got stuck with a really bad problem for which he was not the design solution."[11]

Johnson possessed as much intelligence and political savvy as Kennedy, but he lacked Kennedy's privileged background and schooling and, perhaps more important, the self-confidence and self-possession that went with it. (This sense of marginalization was what fed Johnson's superstitious respect for education—and his determination that all Americans should receive its benefits.) His ascension to the presidency magnified and accentuated a tragic aspect of his character: his lack of inner security. Johnson "did not have the smoothness and control over his actions that John F. Kennedy did," said Clark Clifford.[12] Kennedy of Choate School, Harvard College, and Palm Beach, Florida, felt secure in his dealings with the world; Johnson of small-town Central Texas felt uncertain in the same. "I think his problem in foreign affairs at the beginning was 'I'm going to show these guys I'm not a Texas provincial,'" said Bundy, looking back. "That kind of 'I'll show them' [attitude] was a part of it . . . Foreign affairs wasn't his home country." "Foreigners are not like the folks that I am used to," Johnson once said self-consciously and only half jokingly.[13] As a result, he did not trust his own political instincts on international issues, he did not buck the opinion of his foreign policy advisors, and he took almost everything personally. These frailties of character would have important consequences.

Following Kennedy's assassination, Johnson pursued a policy of continuity. "A nation stunned, shaken to its very heart, had to be reassured that the government was not in a state of paralysis," he wrote in his memoir. "I had to convince everyone everywhere that the country would go forward . . . Any hesitation or wavering, any false step, any sign of self-doubt, could have been disastrous . . . The times cried out for leadership."[14] Johnson was right: Americans were rooting for him. They mourned Kennedy, but they wanted Johnson to succeed—his progress would be restorative as well as beneficial in its own right. For them, Johnson harkened back to his political idol Franklin D. Roosevelt and a time when government could do things to help ordinary people. Johnson intended to push Kennedy's stalled civil rights legislation on behalf of disenfranchised African Americans through Congress in order to both secure the martyred president's legacy and election in his own right in 1964. Until then, he wanted to keep Vietnam at bay and off the front pages, and to make as few decisions about it as possible for as long as possible. "I'm building the Great Society, don't bother me," he told one White House aide during this period.[15] But Johnson would soon learn, like Kennedy, that Vietnam would not wait on him and that he could not control events in that country.

Johnson's desire for continuity applied to Kennedy's foreign policy advisors as well. "I want you to stay on," he implored the troika of Dean Rusk, Robert McNamara, and McGeorge Bundy in the days immediately following the assassination. "I need you."[16] "Without them," Johnson later told biographer Doris Kearns, "I would have lost my link to John Kennedy, and without that I would have had absolutely no chance of gaining the support of the media or the Easterners or the intellectuals. And without that support I would have had absolutely no chance of governing the country."[17] It was not the troika's expertise in national security affairs, tellingly, that was decisive in LBJ's judgment, but the domestic impact of their reputation. In short, Johnson felt deeply dependent on Rusk, McNamara, and Bundy, and while he could be rude and insulting to his closest Texas aides, he rarely was to them.

The circumstances of Kennedy's death, the continuing attraction of being at the center of power, and, not least, the disarming candor of the new president's personal plea for help made it hard for veterans of JFK's inner circle to say no to Johnson. Rusk, McNamara, and Bundy shared a lofty sense of civic duty and a stake in decisions they had helped to make and policies they had helped to set. They had become attached to the problem of Vietnam and obsessed with finding a solution. They had not gotten to where they were by being iconoclasts or troublemakers; they were company men in a company town in an era of establishment solidarity. All of them had survived the Cuban Missile Crisis, and thought, as Rusk said, "How can Hanoi stand up to us when we have just made Khrushchev back down?"[18] All of them believed that unchecked aggression invited war down the road and that what Washington did and did not do mattered a great deal in terms of balancing, stabilizing, and protecting the world. Johnson believed these things, too. But years later, after he had left the White House—his presidency scarred by Vietnam—Johnson confided to an aide that he should have brought in his own advisors and taken a fresh look at the war.[19] But in his insecurity and his own lack of reflectiveness, he did not.

So Kennedy's men became Johnson's men. But each man's relationship with the new president and their influence changed dramatically. Although Kennedy had respected Rusk and trusted his counsel, he found Rusk excessively formal and diffident, and this kept their relationship a distant one. Rusk and Johnson, on the other hand, felt comfortable with one another and shared a natural rapport. Johnson had been miserable as vice president—often ignored, marginalized, and ridiculed behind his back—but the secretary of state had always shown him deference, which the proud and prickly Johnson welcomed and did not forget. He liked that Rusk wasn't flashy like many other Kennedy men; he was quiet,

Rusk, LBJ, and McNamara
Yoichi Okamoto/LBJ Library

unflappable, *and* a former Rhodes scholar. The two men shared similar rural Southern roots, similar ages—both had been born in the first decade of the twentieth century—and similar up-by-the-bootstraps life stories that convinced them that hardships existed to be overcome. "This is my kind of man," Johnson said of Rusk privately. "I can get along with him, I understand him, he understands me, and we both are aware that the country is full of Yankees."[20] Yet these common backgrounds made them more inclined to accept the received wisdom about the United States in the world than to question it; America's image as the resolute and reliable leader of the West mattered a great deal to both of them. More subtly but importantly, Rusk and Johnson also shared "a kinship on the issue of the right wing and the injury done to the body politic by that right wing attack over China and Korea," recalled one of the new president's closest aides, Bill Moyers.[21] In the late 1940s they had seen towering figures—Harry Truman, George Marshall, Dean Acheson—brought low by the demagogic McCarthy, their effectiveness savaged by accusations of weakness in the face of Communist aggression in East Asia. "God Almighty, what they said about us leaving China would just be warming up, compared to what they'd say now," Johnson remarked early in his presidency.[22] In particular, as assistant secretary of state for Far Eastern affairs, Rusk had underestimated China's intentions prior to Beijing's intervention in the Korean War in late 1950. He was determined not to repeat the mistake he had made a decade earlier. In the process, he made the opposite one, overcorrecting as secretary of state by overestimating China's intentions in Vietnam.

Robert McNamara's considerable influence with Kennedy carried over to Johnson—and, remarkably, grew even greater. McNamara became, in Clifford's words, "the second most important citizen in the country after the President."[23] Kennedy had come to view McNamara as the choicest pick of all the glittering men of talent he had attracted to Washington in 1961, and Johnson did, too. At Kennedy's first Cabinet meeting, it was "the fellow from Ford with Stacomb on his hair" who had impressed Johnson most. "The ablest man I ever met," he called McNamara.[24] "There is nobody he is more at home with, more fond of, more respectful of in this Administration than Bob McNamara," Lady Bird wrote in her diary. Johnson could be a bully toward others, but never toward McNamara. "He knew he couldn't rule me," said McNamara later, "and he knew goddam well that I would leave if we didn't develop a constructive relationship."[25] "If I got word that Bob had died or quit," Johnson confided to Lady Bird, "I don't believe I could go on with this job."[26] Every time he sent McNamara to Vietnam, noted Lady Bird, "Lyndon spoke of how frightened he was. 'I lie awake until he gets back.'"[27]

Kennedy had also relied heavily on McNamara, but he had tempered his defense secretary's drive with his own skepticism and coolness, sense of history, and awareness that McNamara's analytical acuity often exceeded his political judgment. Lacking Kennedy's self-confidence and experience in foreign affairs, Johnson relied on McNamara more unreservedly and uncritically—at least initially. As a result, McNamara became even more assertive, more willing to press his own opinions with Johnson than he had with

Kennedy, even as he resolved to protect Johnson as he had tried to protect Kennedy. Temperamentally, they were very different— McNamara was an intellectual who loved ideas and books and was reluctant to enter the Washington fray, Johnson was an utterly political animal who rarely read beyond newspapers and magazines and instead loved manipulating people and exercising power. Over time, as their differences over Vietnam took root and grew, their relationship would become more complicated, tense, and ultimately unsatisfactory, and the evolution of their relationship from its warm beginning in November 1963 to its cold conclusion in February 1968 would become a metaphor for the course of American involvement in Vietnam during these fateful years. But that was in the future.

McGeorge Bundy's easy relationship with John Kennedy did not carry over to his successor. "There was a tension in Mac" toward Johnson, said Francis Bator, who served as Bundy's deputy, "because of his prior relationship with Kennedy. They had been like brothers. They could finish each other's sentences."[28] "It was more complicated between [Johnson] and me," Bundy later acknowledged[29]—"he and I came from different worlds," he added[30]—but Bundy went out of his way to confirm the impression in Johnson that his loyalty was to the presidency. Bundy was an operational man with an instinct for how power worked and his influence in the realm of policy under Johnson increased substantially. He had been an expediter and fixer under Kennedy, who more often than not relied on his own knowledge of the world and his own judgment about foreign policy when evaluating Bundy's contributions. Lacking these strengths, from his first day in office Johnson leaned heavily on Bundy's advice, though he found him faintly patronizing. "I think he's a brilliant man, I'm attached to him, and he's indispensable to me," Johnson confided to a close friend.[31] Still, Johnson felt painfully removed from the Establishment that Bundy personified. Many people, he once noted plaintively, "say I am not qualified in foreign affairs like Jack Kennedy and those other experts. I guess I was just born in the wrong part of the country."[32] The self-contained Bundy, in turn, found it hard to swallow Johnson's boorishness, as when he demanded that Bundy continue his briefing in the bathroom as Johnson relieved himself. Johnson's legendary skills as a showman, schemer, and bully of men—the alternation of flattery and intimidation that he deployed to work his will on others—generally failed when he trained them on the coolly detached and supremely confident Bundy. An uneasy codependence nonetheless developed between these very different men—one too confident and the other too insecure—that Johnson both resented and relished. After all, the graduate of Southwest Texas State Teachers College had the former faculty dean of Harvard University working for him. "A small amused smile would come to his face," wrote David Halberstam, "like a hitting coach watching a fine batter or a connoisseur watching a great ballet dancer. Mac was dancing, and dancing for *him*."[33]

Johnson inherited many of Kennedy's men, and he shared many of Kennedy's convictions, too. He had in fact articulated these convictions in his report to Kennedy of the one trip he made to South Vietnam as vice president, in May 1961. "The battle against Communism must be joined in Southeast Asia with strength and

McGeorge Bundy and LBJ
Yoichi Okamoto/LBJ Library

determination," Johnson wrote Kennedy. Otherwise, the United States might as well "throw in the towel in the area and pull back our defenses to San Francisco and a 'Fortress America' concept." He predicted dire consequences stemming from American with-drawal from the region. "Without [Washington's] inhibitory influ-ence," Johnson warned, "the vast Pacific becomes a Red Sea." Yet his overheated rhetoric—during the trip he publicly hailed Diệm as "the Winston Churchill of Asia"—did not mean that he favored a military solution in South Vietnam. (And Diệm himself had told Johnson he did not want U.S. troops.) He even downplayed the rel-evance of U.S. troops, whose commitment to South Vietnam was "not only not required" but "not desirable." He believed the funda-mental problems plaguing Vietnam mirrored what he considered were the world's fundamental problems—"hunger, ignorance, poverty and disease," not "the momentary threat of Communism itself"—and posed the "greatest danger" to Southeast Asian stabil-ity. "We must—whatever strategies we evolve—keep these enemies the point of our attack," Johnson stressed in conclusion.[34] In this, he had his finger on what were ultimately the wiser priorities, pur-suit of which in the long run would have left America stronger and better depressed the spread of Communism in Asia. But John-son always remained deeply concerned, as McGeorge Bundy later put it, "with what the average American voter is going to think about how he did in the ball game of the Cold War. The great Cold War championship gets played in the largest stadium in the United States and he, Lyndon Johnson, is the quarterback, and if he loses, how does he do in the next election? So don't lose . . . He's living with his own political survival every time he looks at these questions."[35] Shrewdly, Johnson first considered the weakness of any proposed policy or tactic, but his filter was such that the merits of a particular foreign policy interested Johnson less than the domestic consequences of changing it. During the 1940s and 1950s—Johnson's formative years in Congress—most of the power-ful figures on Capitol Hill from whom he had learned the art of national politics had been conservative hawks with an emotional attachment to American involvement in Asia. His own fidelity was

more modest; instead, he dispassionately believed no serious con-
tender for political office could afford letting go of Vietnam—the
repercussions would be devastating. For him, the domino theory
was largely a matter of domestic politics. Yet not letting go carried
enormous risks, too. "If this winds up bad and we get in a land war
in Asia," he said, "there's only one address they will look for, and
that is mine."[36]

Like Kennedy, Johnson defined his objective in Vietnam as
winning the war. But unlike Kennedy, he did not qualify that
objective; he did not publicly put limits on U.S. support of South
Vietnam; he did not emphasize, as Kennedy had, that the United
States could help the South Vietnamese but only the South Vietnamese could win the war. Johnson's mindset was rooted in his
assumption that the loss of South Vietnam would entail greater
risks and costs than would the introduction of U.S. combat forces.
This reflected his greater sensitivity to the political consequences
of failure in South Vietnam than to the dangers and unpredictable
consequences associated with the application of American military
power. Johnson—like Rusk, McNamara, and Bundy—had not experienced the chaos and heartache of war up close as Kennedy had
as a junior naval officer in the Pacific during World War II, and
they therefore lacked an intuitive understanding that war does
not always go according to plan—and the instinctive caution that
goes with that bloody recognition. This difference would become
important as the pressure of events mounted in Vietnam after the
November 1963 coup and forced more momentous choices.

Johnson's thinking came through clearly in the first meeting
he held with his Vietnam advisors just two days after Kennedy's
assassination. Gathering in a high-ceilinged room of the Old Executive Office Building while workers readied the Oval Office for
its new occupant, said new occupant expressed his misgivings
about the coup against Diệm (particularly the political turmoil
it had unleashed), but in remarkable contrast to his May 1961 report stressed that he wanted priority given to military operations
over "do-gooders'" social reforms, and made clear his objective
to "win the war!" He instructed Lodge (back in Washington for

consultations) to "tell those generals in Saigon that Lyndon Johnson intends to stand by our word."[37] "He really laid down the law
that first day," Bundy recalled.[38] His advisors, in turn, painted a
gloomy picture of the situation he faced. Johnson learned, Mc
Namara later wrote, that he had "inherited a god-awful mess eminently more dangerous than the one Kennedy had inherited from
Eisenhower."[39] "It's going to hell in a hand basket out there," Johnson told an aide after the meeting, as he tilted back in the big chair
behind the desk in the office he had occupied for three years as vice
president. "If we don't do something, [Lodge] says, it'll go under
any day," he said as he stared at the ice cubes in his glass. "They'll
think with Kennedy dead, we've lost heart. So they'll think we're
yellow and don't mean what we say." "Who?" asked his aide. "The
Chinese. The fellas in the Kremlin. They'll be taking the measure of us. They'll be wondering just how far they can go . . . I'm
not going to let Vietnam go the way of China. I told them to go
back and tell those generals in Saigon that Lyndon Johnson intends
to stand by our word . . . I want 'em to get off their butts and get
out in those jungles and whip hell out of some Communists. And
then I want 'em to leave me alone, because I've got some bigger
things to do right here at home." He swiveled in the chair, looked
at the far corner of the ceiling, and said, "I feel like I just grabbed a
big juicy worm with a right sharp hook in the middle of it."[40] The
words seemed to make Johnson close in on himself.

One of Johnson's biggest problems involved coming to terms
with the real nature of the war. He soon learned from McNamara
that Diệm's regime had fed grossly misleading statistics to the
Americans, including the defense secretary himself. (After Diệm's
death, the number of secure hamlets in Long An province was revised downward from over 200 to 10.) The Defense Intelligence
Agency reported to McNamara for the first time in mid-December
that new, more honest and accurate statistics uncovered by MACV
showed that, in reality, the Vietcong had sustained and even improved their capability over the past year, and would probably step
up their military operations in the coming year. ARVN stopped
conducting operations in Vietcong-controlled areas of the Mekong

Delta. With increased access to villages, the Vietcong collected taxes and recruits for an intensified push to topple the government before the United States could intervene militarily. "The structure of the [South Vietnamese] regime in the countryside," wrote journalist Neil Sheehan, "was like a beam that has been eaten from inside by wood-boring beetles. The instant the beam is stressed it snaps in two and reveals the powdered residue within."[41]

McNamara's trip to South Vietnam on December 19 and 20 confirmed all of this. Harkins reported that Diệm had submitted considerable falsified data to the American military. And now Washington had to deal with a junta of a dozen generals that represented an ineffective instrument of government and that kept the group away from their real military duties. McNamara walked into a conference with the generals, looked around "with blood in his eye" according to one observer, and asked, "OK, which one of you here is the boss?" (The fact that he had to ask such a question spoke volumes.) After a long pause, Minh replied that Đôn headed the army. Well, who then is chief of state? asked McNamara. Minh reluctantly raised his hand—then added: "I am not Naguib, and there is no Nasser."*[42] It was a telling admission that should have given McNamara pause if he had stopped to reflect on the implications of Minh's remark. Instead, McNamara lectured the generals on the need for unity and leadership: utterly inexperienced in political leadership, they looked to the Americans to help them run the country and the war effort just as they had, as junior officers, looked to the French. They earnestly admitted that a great deal needed to be done and that they must work harder for their country. Then they went back to their squabbling for hours over patronage (who would control promotions) before adjourning, having accomplished nothing.

McNamara laid out all of this in his trip report. "The situation is very disturbing," he told Johnson upon his return to Washington.

---

* Muhammed Naguib and Gamal Abdel Nasser had staged a military coup in Egypt in 1952. Soon after, Nasser shoved aside Naguib and became the forceful ruler of the country for fourteen years until his death in 1970.

"Current trends, unless reversed in the next two to three months, will lead to neutralization at best [a prospect that Johnson, like Kennedy, found unpalatable*] and more likely to a Communist-controlled state. The new government is the greatest source of concern. It is indecisive and drifting." Worse yet, McNamara reported, "there is no organized government in South Vietnam," inside the capital and beyond. Continued McNamara, "Viet Cong progress has been great during the period since the coup, with my best guess being that the situation has in fact been deteriorating in the countryside since July to a far greater extent than we realized because of our undue dependence on distorted Vietnamese reporting." He admitted that the statistics on which he had based his earlier conclusions had been "grossly in error." The Vietcong controlled "larger percentages of the population, greater amounts of territory, and have destroyed or occupied more strategic hamlets than expected."[43]

"In Texas we say it's better to deal with the devil you know than the devil you don't know," Johnson had privately grumped in the weeks leading up to the coup.[44] As vice president, he had been invited to few meetings on Vietnam and at those he did attend, he withheld his counsel in deference to Kennedy so his dissent had been muted and therefore discounted. The coup had realized Johnson's worst fears. "That was a *tragic* mistake," he would moan the following spring. "It was awful and we've lost everything."[45]

McNamara had concluded his report by saying, "We should watch the situation very carefully, running scared, hoping for the

---

* An idea promoted by President Charles de Gaulle of France, other Western European allies, and liberal American pundits, neutralization, the logic went, had not worked in Laos—North Vietnam had not withdrawn its forces per the 1962 Geneva Accords, so why should it work in Vietnam? As Bundy remarked to Johnson in a telephone conversation on February 6, "You cannot neutralize the bottom half with the top half waiting to eat it up." Beschloss, ed., *Taking Charge*, p. 226. Johnson and his advisors did not want to negotiate the neutrality of South Vietnam while the country remained perilously weak. They feared it would have a negative effect on the generals who had succeeded Diệm and would be tantamount to surrender. Perhaps at some point in the future, but not now.

best, but preparing for more forceful moves if the situation does not show early signs of improvement." A few days later, Johnson asked McNamara, along with Rusk and Bundy, for their reactions to a memo he had received from Mike Mansfield—something that Kennedy had never felt the need to do when the Senate majority leader wrote him. (LBJ and Mansfield had worked together closely when the Montanan served as Senate majority whip under him from 1957 to 1961.) Mansfield made many of the arguments to Johnson that he had made to Kennedy. "As you remarked on the telephone," Mansfield wrote the man, now president, that he had known since their days together in the House in the 1940s, "'we do not want another China in Viet Nam.' I would respectfully add to this observation: Neither do we want another Korea. It would seem that a key (but often overlooked) factor in both situations was a tendency to bite off more than we were prepared in the end to chew. We tended to talk ourselves out on a limb with overstatements of our purpose and commitment only to discover in the end that there were not sufficient American interests to support with blood and treasure a desperate final plunge. Then, the question followed invariably: 'Who got us into this mess?' and 'Who lost China?' etc." He urged Johnson to pursue negotiations leading to neutralization and American withdrawal.

The troika unanimously counseled Johnson to stand firm. McNamara announced that "Senator Mansfield is challenging what he regards as the gross imbalance between the extent of our involvement in Southeast Asia and our narrow self-interests in the area. My assessment of our important security interests is that they unquestionably call for holding the line against further Communist gains." Rusk added, "Peace will not prevail in Southeast Asia until aggression is frustrated." And Bundy argued, "The political damage to Truman and Acheson from the fall of China arose because most Americans came to believe that we could and should have done more than we did to prevent it. This is exactly what would happen now if we should seem to be the first to quit in Saigon."[46] Their unanimous advice hardened Johnson's preexisting attitude.

Of the three, McNamara had shifted his position most dramatically. In just two months, he had swung from advocating a phased withdrawal of U.S. military advisors to stressing the essential truth of the domino theory. McNamara's abrupt shift reflected his accommodation to Johnson's goal (echoing Kennedy's)—clearly stated at his first Vietnam meeting—to "win the war!" His long immersion in bureaucratic and corporate culture had instilled in him a strong sense of duty to the institution and the person who headed it, and despite his hard-driving personality, McNamara had learned to put his boss's views above his own—whether it was in the army air corps, at the Ford Motor Company, or now at the highest level of the United States Government. He had not been elected to office—only the president who appointed him had—"and this affected the way I behaved as Secretary, particularly concerning Vietnam," he later explained.[47] (That LBJ had been vice president until now made no difference—it had been the ticket that Americans had voted for and the office that mattered.) McNamara's loyalty had been strengthened by witnessing the near insubordination of senior military officers like Admiral Arleigh Burke during the Bay of Pigs and General Curtis LeMay and Admiral George Anderson during the Cuban Missile Crisis, and this defiance made McNamara more committed to standing by first President Kennedy and now President Johnson instead of confronting Johnson when disagreeing with him. "How loyal is that man?" Johnson once asked about a potential staffer. "Well, he seems quite loyal, Mr. President." "I don't want loyalty," Johnson replied, "I want *loyalty*." He got that from McNamara. "If you asked those boys in the Cabinet to run through a buzz saw for their President, Bob McNamara would be the first to go through it," he proudly said.[48] Placing loyalty to the presidency above loyalty to personal beliefs and principles would, in time, exact a heavy emotional and psychological toll on this most allegiant deputy.

During the first months of his presidency, Johnson acted like the proverbial ostrich that buries its head in the sand when it sees dan-

ger. He wanted to keep Vietnam at arm's length, to delay confronting vexing problems, and to postpone difficult decisions until after
the November election. In a phone conversation with McNamara
early in the year, Johnson spelled out his options as he saw them.
"We could send in our divisions—our own Marines in there and
they could start attacking the Vietcong . . . We could come out of
there . . . and as soon as we get out, they [North Vietnam] could
swallow up South Vietnam . . . Or we can say this is the Vietnamese's war—they've [the ARVN] got 200,000 men." Nothing stood
out as an obvious course. "After considering all of these," Johnson
said, "it seems that the latter offers the best alternative for America to follow." It was a conclusion thick with equivocation. "If the
latter option failed," he conceded with trepidation, "then we have
to make another decision. But at this point, it has not failed."[49] Johnson hoped it would not.

"The only thing I know to do is do more of the same and do it
more efficiently," Johnson said privately.[50] But he faced growing
pressure from the Joint Chiefs. LeMay, who hated the restraints
imposed by civilian leaders, had begun to argue that North Vietnam should be bombed on the grounds that "we are swatting flies
when we should be going after the manure pile."[51] Kennedy had
heard out LeMay and the other chiefs, but he had in the end never
been intimidated by them or felt compelled to follow their hawkish advice. In turn, the chiefs had come to recognize, and grudgingly accept, their limited influence with Kennedy—particularly
with regard to sending U.S. combat troops to Vietnam. Now Kennedy was dead and Johnson was president, and the chiefs wasted
little time in probing to see what influence and pressure they
could exert on the new occupant of the Oval Office when it came
to dealing with what they had always considered a fundamentally
military problem and their solution to it: the application of more
force.

Johnson had served for years on the House and Senate Armed
Services Committees and he understood the military's parochialism as well as its patriotism. He recognized and feared the military's

LBJ, McNamara, and the Joint Chiefs of Staff
Yoichi Okamoto/LBJ Library

ties with the political Right* and Congress; indeed, what gave the chiefs influence with Johnson was not their rank but their influence and support on the Hill. "Lyndon Johnson could not afford to have the Joint Chiefs on record against him, in his own eyes," recalled McGeorge Bundy, "and they were using that political power" in a "very offensive" way. "They tried to gang up on" Kennedy too, Bundy noted, but Kennedy had resisted them on the big issues and at moments of crisis,[52] choosing to have McNamara and Taylor mediate between him and the chiefs.

The chiefs began their pressure campaign in late January with a memo urging Johnson to "put aside many of the self-imposed restrictions" on U.S. operations in South Vietnam and undertake bolder action, including bombing and even U.S. ground operations against North Vietnam—a significant escalation of military involve-

---

* "Twice," recalled close aide Horace Busby, Johnson "sat through *Seven Days in May*, the [1964 movie] of a president fighting to prevent a military takeover of the United States; and when a guest asked his reaction, the president said, without smiling, 'It scares me.'" Horace Busby, *The Thirty-First of March: An Intimate Portrait of Lyndon Johnson's Final Days in Office* (Farrar, Straus, and Giroux, 2005), p. 7.

ment. "We must prepare for whatever level of activity may be required and, being prepared, must then proceed to take actions as necessary to achieve our purposes surely and promptly," they categorically declared. It was an endorsement for using the maximum force necessary, whatever the consequences. The chiefs premised these recommendations on their belief that "a more aggressive program would enhance greatly our ability to control the degree to which escalation will occur" and "our conviction that if support of the insurgency from outside South Vietnam in terms of operational direction, personnel, and material were stopped completely, the character of the war in South Vietnam would be substantially and favorably altered."[53] But could escalation be controlled once it started and could North Vietnamese infiltration be completely stopped? The chiefs had not thought to ask and answer these crucial questions at anything beyond a superficial level, and as a result they based their entire Vietnam strategy on what would prove to be fallacious assumptions.

The chiefs continued their pressure campaign when they met again with Johnson in early March. Arguing that "preventing the loss of South Vietnam" was of "overriding importance" to the United States (a political judgment properly made by the president, not the chiefs, and one which Johnson had never articulated), they insisted that Johnson be prepared to destroy North Vietnamese military and industrial targets, mine harbors, and impose a naval blockade—even if this led to Chinese intervention and the use of nuclear weapons to cope with that consequence. In addition, they privately complained to the White House through military aide Major General Ted Clifton about the level of force recommended by McNamara, comparing it to the Bay of Pigs.

Johnson had no intention of triggering a larger war with China. "Can you imagine the United States being at war with Red China in the jungles of Southeast Asia with a population of a billion contiguous to North Vietnam?" he said. "If we get into that situation, we will bleed to death over there in South Vietnam. I am not going to do it."[54] So Johnson deflected the chiefs' pressure for the time being. "It is quite apparent that he does not want to lose South

Vietnam before next November," JCS chairman Taylor wrote afterward in a memorandum of the meeting, "nor does he want to get the country into the war."[55] The chiefs had not gotten what they wanted, but they had staked out their position and made it abundantly clear to the president. While Johnson did not want to do what the chiefs recommended, he also did not want to be in conflict with them—especially in an election year. Their incessant pressure for heavier American involvement would lodge itself in Johnson's mind and have a significant cumulative impact. Repetition would have its effect.

Johnson felt anxious and frustrated as political conditions in South Vietnam continued to deteriorate and the Vietcong grew stronger, making it harder and harder for him to finesse the problem. Denied a competitive, pluralistic process, South Vietnam had never developed a tradition of responsible political opposition. Dissent had expressed itself, instead, in conspiracies of small, clandestine groups distrustful of one another and the government. Freed from Diệm's authoritarian restraints, Buddhists, religious sects such as the Cao Đài and Hòa Hảo, non-Vietnamese minorities like the Montagnards of the Central Highlands and the urban Chinese of Cholon, and students all battled, often violently, to define South Vietnam's political direction independently of their rivals. (In Saigon, wags said, two people constituted a party, three people a party and a faction.) Amid this chaos, professional soldiers with no background or training in politics except experience at petty infighting struggled to rule the country. No one had anticipated the magnitude of the centrifugal political forces that had been kept under control by Diệm's iron rule.

The junta of generals certainly had not. Though they were locals (unlike the Americans in Washington), they read the political situation badly because they had no experience at governing a country and had eliminated the one man who did. Confronting many more problems than they had expected and sensitive to charges of dictatorship, the generals preoccupied themselves with self-justification and mutual recrimination. They bickered endlessly, offered no unified vision, and relied heavily on cronyism.

They did little to improve the lives of villagers and the urban poor. Popular euphoria over Diệm and Nhu's removal soon gave way to frustration over the junta's incompetence and corruption. Uncertainty and fear about the future grew. The generals watched passively as political anarchy set in.

After just three months, on January 30, 1964, General Nguyễn Khánh seized power, underscoring the intense political maneuvering in South Vietnam. Short, stocky, and taciturn, the thirty-six-year-old Khánh compensated for his natural reticence with a peacock's display of aviator sunglasses, goatee, and red beret. Also noticeable was his rigorous practice of always taking care to keep Nguyễn Khánh's interests uppermost in his ambitious mind. When the Buddhist crisis erupted, Khánh had encouraged Diệm to declare martial law. Then, as Diệm's fortunes declined, Khánh began plotting with other ARVN generals to oust him and his brother. The junta rewarded Khánh's participation by appointing him a corps commander, a position from where he laid plans for his own seizure of power. Washington recognized the new Khánh regime, but with few illusions. To one senior U.S. official, Khánh seemed "a skillful if unscrupulous croupier in the political roulette as played in Saigon, one who knew how to give the wheel a new spin whenever the ball seemed about to settle on the wrong number."[56]

Johnson and his advisors did not focus on Khánh's weaknesses but, rather, on what they imagined to be his strengths: his opposition to neutralization talks (which he—like Washington—believed would simply lead to North Vietnam's takeover of South Vietnam) and his potential to rally his people and reinvigorate the war effort. Anxious to keep South Vietnam from unraveling, Johnson swallowed his anger and irritation at the latest coup and fixed on Khánh as someone who would somehow hold together the fractious and disintegrating country. Wanting "no more of this coup shit," Johnson ordered McNamara and Taylor to travel to South Vietnam to "make Khanh 'our boy,' and proclaim the fact to all and sundry," wrote Taylor. "He wants to see Khanh in the newspapers with McNamara and Taylor holding up his arms" like a winning boxer. In his parting instructions to McNamara, Johnson said,

"Bob, I want to see about a thousand pictures of you with General Khanh, smiling and waving your arms and showing the people out there that this country is behind Khanh the whole way."[57]

McNamara and Taylor arrived in South Vietnam on March 8, and the following day, like politicians on the hustings, barnstormed the countryside with Khánh trying to promote the general to his own people. Heavily protected by troops and helicopters, they posed for news cameramen and photographers as Johnson had instructed, standing on either side of Khánh and holding up his arms, creating a tableau that evoked a presidential nominating convention. *"Việt Nam Muôn Năm!"* shouted McNamara in fractured Vietnamese to crowds of mystified onlookers with blank expressions on their faces. He meant to say, "Vietnam Ten Thousand Years!"—the Vietnamese equivalent of "Long Live Vietnam!"—but his improper intonation of the memorized phrase made it sound like "Vietnam wants to lie down!"[58] A gesture that had been intended to boost Khánh's popular appeal instead made the general look like an American puppet to his South Vietnamese countrymen—exactly what the Vietcong and the North Vietnamese had been arguing since late January.

"The greatest gift for us was when McNamara came and toured the countryside, holding up Nguyen Khanh's hand and shouting, 'This is our man!'" said the leader of the Vietcong's political wing, the National Liberation Front. "This saved our propaganda cadres a great deal of effort."[59] The episode illustrated American policymakers' shocking lack of cultural awareness and insensitivity to Vietnamese sensibilities, and the appalling disparity between American intentions and their effects. An individual (Nguyễn Khánh) and an institution (ARVN) utterly dependent on the United States had become the preponderant political forces in South Vietnam. And while Johnson and his advisors saw them as bulwarks against the chaos gripping the country, the South Vietnamese, who traditionally perceived professional soldiers as lacking the Confucian moral and political authority to govern, saw them quite differently.

When McNamara returned to Washington, he told Johnson that conditions in South Vietnam had "unquestionably" worsened since

Khánh took power. The Vietcong had benefited from the turmoil following the November and January coups and now controlled nearly 90 percent of the key Delta provinces. They had also begun driving ARVN from the Central Highlands, home to numerous spurs of the Hồ Chí Minh Trail that infiltrated troops and supplies from the North. Khánh had taken little action to confront and reverse these trends. The government lacked broad political appeal, the war effort continued to deteriorate (ARVN desertions were skyrocketing), and North Vietnamese infiltration had increased due to more support from China, which wanted to drain American resources without risking another armed confrontation as in Korea. The chiefs were again pushing for air attacks against North Vietnam. McNamara opposed, noting that Khánh opposed them, too, because he believed South Vietnam lacked the strength to withstand North Vietnamese retaliation. "Unless and until the Khanh government has established its position and preferably is making significant progress in the South," he wrote, bombing the North "carries the risk of being mounted from an extremely weak base which might at any moment collapse and leave the posture of political confrontation worsened rather than improved." Johnson agreed with McNamara. Wanting to play for time, he told McNamara on March 21 to keep doing "more of the same" and on April 14, he told Bundy that "what we're trying to do is get 'em [the South Vietnamese] to protect themselves."[60]

When grappling with domestic issues such as the landmark Civil Rights Act that he was then steering through Congress, Johnson enjoyed—even relished—a sense of challenge, confident that he could master the situation. But with Vietnam, Johnson saw no thread to guide him through what seemed a frightening labyrinth. On the one hand, he wanted to avoid making decisions about Vietnam. On the other, he wanted to win the war. His fear battled with his proud ego, which became apparent in a phone conversation with McNamara on April 30. "Let's get somebody that wants to do something besides drop a bomb," Johnson told McNamara, someone "that can go in and go after these damn fellows and run them back where they belong." But this was not the Senate, where he

knew precisely which levers to pull. "We're not getting it done,"
he fretted. "We're losing. So we need something new . . . What I
want is somebody that can lay up some plans to trap those guys
and whup hell out of them, and kill some of them. That's what I
want to do."[61] Conflict between his anxiety about deepening the
war and his determination to win it would characterize Johnson's
attitude toward Vietnam throughout his presidency.

As the spring progressed, mounting frustration heightened the
dilemma that Johnson and his advisors faced between avoiding
direct U.S. military involvement and preventing the loss of South
Vietnam. This fed a "desperate energy," wrote McNamara, looking
back, to do something, try something to halt the rapid deterioration
in South Vietnam. Their desperation discouraged them from carefully considering whether things could be turned around, because
homefront pressures did not allow for travel on that path; in concert
with this, there would be no consideration of what victory would
ultimately cost.[62] A bleak intelligence assessment in mid-May reinforced this inclination. "The overall situation is South Vietnam
remains extremely fragile," the CIA reported. "Although there has
been some improvement in GVN [Government of South Vietnam]/
ARVN performance, sustained Viet Cong pressure continues to
erode GVN authority throughout the country, undercut US/GVN
programs and depress South Vietnamese morale. We do not see
any signs that these trends are yet 'bottoming out.' . . . If the
tide of deterioration has not been arrested by the end of the year,
the anti-Communist position in South Vietnam is likely to become
untenable."[63] The CIA predicted dire consequences should South
Vietnam fall. Such an outcome, it concluded, would be "profoundly
damaging" to American prestige "and would seriously debase the
credibility of U.S. will and capability to contain the spread of Communism elsewhere in the area. Our enemies would be encouraged
and there would be an increased tendency among other states to
move toward a greater degree of accommodation with the Communists."[64]

As their anxiety and desperation mounted, Johnson and the
troika began to internalize and, more insidiously and dangerously,

to personalize the issue. Social scientists call this "the IKEA Effect": the tendency for individuals to place a disproportionately high value on objects—or, in this case, policies—they assembled themselves (such as furniture from IKEA), regardless of the quality of the end result. Michael Norton of Harvard Business School, Daniel Mochon of the University of California, San Diego, and Dan Ariely of Duke University conducted a study that demonstrated this effect: participants with no carpentry experience who built their own products saw their products as similar in quality to those of professional carpenters—and expected others to share this opinion—because they had made these products themselves.[65] So, too, with policy: individuals sometimes become so bound up in a certain course that it becomes difficult to know where objectivity stops and personal involvement begins. Increasingly identified with Vietnam in the public mind and increasingly cognizant that their reputations had become hostage to the issue, the foursome's detachment slowly gave way to personal investment in a commitment for which none of them countenanced failure. America's war was becoming *their* war. A reporter asked McNamara for his response to the conflict being called "McNamara's War." "I don't object to it being called McNamara's War," he said. "I think it's a very important war and I am pleased to be identified with it and do whatever I can to win it."[66]

The increasingly personal language that McNamara and others used when talking about Vietnam and one another's relationship to it underscored this shift. "I don't believe the American people ever want me to run [from Vietnam]," Johnson told his old mentor, Senate Armed Services Committee chairman Richard Russell of Georgia. (Russell had taken Johnson under his wing when the Texan entered the Senate in 1949 and helped guide his career.) "If I lose it, I think that they'll say *I've* lost, *I've* pulled in. At the same time, I don't want to commit us to a war. I'm in a hell of a shape." Even the famously logical McNamara began to mix emotional appeals with analytical reasoning. "I just don't believe we *can* be pushed out of there," McNamara told the president. "We just *can't* allow it to be done. You wouldn't want to go down in history as

having—" "Not at all," Johnson quickly replied. McNamara's uncharacteristic willingness to play on Johnson's personal insecurity
revealed his own.[67]

These factors, combined with continuing pressure from the
chiefs, led the troika to recommend—and Johnson to authorize—
contingency planning for air attacks against North Vietnam. "I
don't want for us to be responsible for escalating this thing and
appear that we're on a bombing campaign because we're not," he
privately told Senator Hubert Humphrey of Minnesota in early
June.[68] So Johnson gave the chiefs the chance to *plan* for what they
wanted, failing to realize the momentum and pressure that would
generate. Johnson believed he had held off the chiefs, but he had
actually energized them by giving some of the most aggressive
and effective lobbyists in Washington a chance to privately tell
their hawkish allies in Congress and the press that the president
had forbidden them to do what they wanted and yet allowed them
to prepare by identifying targets in a country they claimed with
relentless certitude would be extremely vulnerable to bombing.

Rusk, McNamara, and Bundy were not *entirely* in disagreement
with the chiefs on the utility of air power. Filtering their analysis
through their own experience, the troika assumed that the threat
of graduated air attacks would dissuade North Vietnam in the
same way, they believed, that the naval blockade had dissuaded the
Soviet Union during the Cuban Missile Crisis only eighteen months
earlier. Limited force—"controlled escalation" in the parlance of
the day—would sober the North Vietnamese, while allowing them
to back down from a larger engagement. Maxwell Taylor, now outgoing as chairman of the Joint Chiefs, whom Johnson had recently
selected to succeed Lodge as ambassador in Saigon, shared the
troika's thinking. He liked to quote Polybius, the Greek historian
of Republican Rome, who wrote, "It is not the purpose of war to
annihilate those who provoke it, but to cause them to mend their
ways." Taylor believed, as he wrote early the following year, that
"as practical men," the leaders of North Vietnam "cannot wish to
see the fruits of ten years of labor destroyed by slowly escalating air
attacks (which they cannot prevent) without trying to find some

accommodation which will exorcise that threat. It would be to our interest to regulate our attacks not for the purpose of doing maximum physical destruction but for producing maximum stresses in Hanoi minds."[69] Limited bombing seemed the most prudent and flexible of all possible courses of action—far less risky that obliterating North Vietnam or getting out. Such bombing represented a mere intimation of the massive force America could unleash against North Vietnam should it hesitate to yield on Washington's terms. Hanoi could not possibly resist this pressure.

Yet because they viewed Vietnam as a limited war (as it certainly was from America's perspective), Taylor and the three others mistakenly assumed the North Vietnamese would view it as limited, too. But for the North Vietnamese, it was much more than that: it was a total war—almost a sacred crusade—for national unification and social justice, one that had been going on for decades. The troika and Taylor could not imagine that a small country vastly outgunned by the United States would meet force with force, responding to air attacks by actually *escalating* the fighting in South Vietnam. This would prove a fundamental miscalculation rooted in their failure to see the conflict from Hanoi's perspective.[70] Similar logic applied to a draft congressional resolution the troika had been working on that supported U.S. military operations in Southeast Asia should they become necessary. "While we weren't certain that we would recommend to the President that we undertake such action," McNamara later said, "we were certain that since it was a possibility, we should go forward with a resolution that would itself have some deterrent effect" on North Vietnam.[71]

At the heart of this reckless assumption that North Vietnam could be intimidated into compromise was profound ignorance of political currents in Hanoi. Hardliner Lê Duẩn, who had taken control of the Politburo from Hồ Chí Minh at the Ninth Plenum of the Vietnamese Workers' Party in late 1963, was far less amenable to a compromise solution than Hồ had been. Lê Duẩn and his fellow militants, in fact, severely criticized Hồ as a half-hearted temporizer who had compromised too much with the French in 1946 and 1954. They had no intention of compromising on reunification with the Americans now. Hồ feared that a confrontation with the United States would turn Vietnam into a battlefield between Americans and Chinese, as had happened a decade earlier in Korea. Lê Duẩn, on the other hand, believed recent events—particularly the Battle of Ấp Bắc* in January 1963 and the coup that overthrew Diệm in November 1963—proved the vulnerability of South Vietnam's military forces and the instability of its political structure, which could be effectively exploited by stepping up the war in the South. To this end, Lê Duẩn (himself a southerner†) steered a resolution through the Politburo that granted the authority to wage war in the South‡ and ordered a buildup of the North's conventional army to bring the war to a speedy end before the Americans could successfully intervene militarily. Going forward, political struggle would support military struggle, not vice versa as had been true to date.[72]

All of this was unknown to Johnson and his advisors, who believed that contingency planning would leave them in control, and that if it came to the use of force, they could turn it up or down, on or off as quickly and easily as adjusting a thermostat. But this assumption was an illusory coping mechanism on the part of increasingly desperate men. Control had begun to slip away from them. McNamara's assistant for Vietnam, John McNaughton, hinted at the self-delusion of those in LBJ's inner circle who felt unable to control a rapidly deteriorating situation. "The trouble with you," McNaughton told Bundy aide Mike Forrestal that spring, "is that you always think we can turn this thing off, and that we can get off of it whenever we want. But I wonder. I think if it was easy to get off of it, we would already have gotten off. I

---

* At the Battle of Ấp Bắc, the Vietcong bested a much larger (ten-to-one) and better equipped ARVN force that failed to sustain contact with the enemy, and downed five U.S. helicopters flown in support of American advisors assisting the ARVN operation.

† He was from the village of Bich La in Quảng Trị province.

‡ One historian called this resolution—passed nine months before August 1964—"Hanoi's equivalent of Washington's Tonkin Gulf Resolution." See Pierre Asselin, *Hanoi's Road to the Vietnam War, 1954–1965* (University of North Carolina Press, 2013), p. 175.

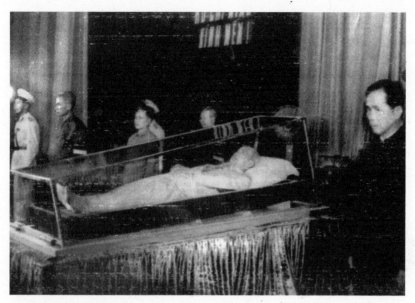

Lê Duẩn (on far right)
Keystone Pictures USA/Alamy Stock Photo

think it gets harder every day, each day we lose a little control, each decision that we make wrong, or don't make at all, makes the next decision a little harder because if we haven't stopped it today, then the reasons for not stopping it will still exist tomorrow, and we'll be in even deeper."[73] What McNaughton said to Forrestal applied just as well to Johnson and the troika. This hallucination of command, rooted in their confidence that all equations were solvable and that they were smart enough to do so now, gulled men vexed by an intransigent problem.

Rusk, McNamara, and Bundy discussed these contingency plans among themselves and presented their recommendation to Johnson on May 26. They told Johnson that worsening circumstances might soon force him to initiate military action against North Vietnam. Johnson often talked through his deliberations both for nervous relief and to think out an issue and, hesitant to make such a decision, he turned to others for advice the next day. First he called U.N. Ambassador Adlai Stevenson. "I shudder at getting too deeply involved over there, and everybody thinks that's the only alternative," he lamented. Stevenson sympathized: "I've been shuddering on this thing for three years and I'm afraid that we're in a position now where you *don't* have any alternatives. It's a hell of an alternative and it really gives me the shakes."

As soon as Johnson hung up with Stevenson, he called Richard Russell. An astute politician, whose low-key manner masked razor-sharp political judgment, Russell—called "Mr. Defense" by his Senate colleagues—had followed developments in Vietnam since the first Truman commitments in the late 1940s. Their exchange was so telling that it deserves to be quoted in detail.

> JOHNSON: What do you think of this Vietnam thing? I'd like to hear you talk a little bit.
> RUSSELL: . . . It's the damn worst mess I ever saw . . . I knew that we were going to get into this sort of mess when we went in there and I don't see how we're ever going to get out of it . . . I just don't know what to do.
> JOHNSON: That's the way I've been feeling for six months.
> RUSSELL: It appears that our position is deteriorating and it looks like the more that we try to do for them, the less that they're willing to do for themselves. It's just a sad situation. There's no sense of responsibility there on the part of any of their leaders . . . It's a hell of a situation. It's a mess. And it's getting worse. And I don't know what to do . . . You've got over there McNamara . . . he's a can-do fellow. But I'm not sure he understands the history and the background of those people out there as fully as he should . . . The damn thing ain't getting any better and it's getting worse . . .
> JOHNSON: I spend all my days with Rusk and McNamara and Bundy . . . and all those folks that are dealing with it and I would say that it pretty well adds up to them now [telling me] that we've got to show some power and some force . . . Their feeling is that . . . we haven't got much choice . . . that we are there, that this will be a domino that will kick off a whole list of others, that we've just got to prepare for the worst . . . Now

I have avoided that for a few days. I don't think the American people are for it . . . I don't think the people of the country know much about Vietnam and I think they care a hell of a lot less.

RUSSELL: Yeah, I know, but you go to send a whole lot of our boys out there—

JOHNSON: Yeah, that's right. That's exactly right. That's what I'm talking about . . . I don't want to do anything on the basis of just the information I've got now . . .

RUSSELL: It's a tragic situation. It's just one of those places where you can't win. Anything you do is wrong . . . I have thought about it. I have worried about it. I have prayed about it.

JOHNSON: I don't believe we can do anything—

RUSSELL: It frightens me 'cause it's my country involved over there . . . If you . . . bring North Vietnam into it too, it's the damndest mess on earth. The French report that they lost 250,000 men and spent a couple billion of their money and two billion of ours down there and just got the hell whipped out of them . . .

JOHNSON: . . . The whole question, as I see it, is, is it more dangerous for us to let things go as they're going now, deteriorating every day . . . than it would be for us to move in?

RUSSELL: We either got to move in or move out.

JOHNSON: That's about what it is.

RUSSELL: . . . It would be consistent with the attitude of the American people and their general reactions to go in, because they could understand that better. But getting out, even after we go in and get bogged down in there . . . it's going to be a hell of a mess. It would be worse than where we are now, to some extent, and that's what makes it so difficult . . . McNamara is the smartest fellow that any of us know, but . . . he is opinionated as hell, and he's made up his mind on this.

JOHNSON: . . . I think he's a pretty flexible fellow. He's gone out there. He got Khánh to agree that we cannot launch a counteroffensive or hit the North until he gets more stabilized and better set in the South and he thought he was buying us time and we could get by till November. But these [Republican] politicians got to raising hell . . . All the Senators, Nixon and Rockefeller and Goldwater all saying, "Let's move, let's go into the North!" . . . They say pick out an oil plant or pick out a refinery or something like that. Take selected targets. Watch this [Hồ Chí Minh] trail they're coming down. Try to bomb them out of the[re] when they're coming in.

RUSSELL: Oh, hell! That ain't worth a hoot! That's just impossible.

JOHNSON: McNamara said yesterday that in Korea that LeMay and all of 'em were going to stop those [North Korean] tanks. There's 90 came through. They turned all the Air Force loose on them. They got one. 89 come on through.

RUSSELL: We tried it in Korea. We even got a lot of old B-29s to increase the bomb load and sent 'em over there and just dropped millions and millions of bombs . . . They would knock that road at night and in the morning, the damn people would be back traveling over it . . . We never could actually interdict all their lines of communication although we had absolute control of the seas and the air, and we never did stop them. And you ain't gonna stop these people either.

JOHNSON: Well, they'd impeach a President they thought would run out, wouldn't they? . . . Wouldn't that pretty well fix us in the eyes of the world, though, and make it look mighty bad? . . . I've got a little old sergeant that works for me over at the house and he's got six children and I just put him up as the United States Army, Air Force, and Navy every time I think about making this decision and think about sending that father of those six kids in there. And what the hell are we going to get out of his doing it? And it just makes the chills run up my back . . . I just haven't got the nerve to do it, and I don't see any other way out of it.

RUSSELL: I wish I could help you. God knows I do 'cause it's a terrific quandary that we're in over there. We're just in the quicksands up to our very heads. And I just don't know what the hell is the best way to do about it.

Sharing LBJ's doubts and sympathizing with his predicament, Russell had not offered a solution to his problem, and Johnson's anxiety about Vietnam remained undiminished. Feeling cornered and frustrated, he turned next to Bundy, who, along with Rusk and McNamara, had begun pressing him to take action. Johnson the decider wanted Bundy the recommender to feel the pressure and burden weighing on him.

JOHNSON: I'll tell you the more that I stayed awake last night thinking of this thing, the more . . . it just worries the hell out of me. I don't see what we can ever hope to get out of there with, once we're committed . . . I don't think it's worth fighting for and I don't think that we can get out. It's just the biggest damned mess that I ever saw.

BUNDY: It is. It's an awful mess.

JOHNSON: . . . What is Vietnam worth to me? . . . What is it worth to this country? . . . Of course, if you start running from the Communists, they may just chase you right into your own kitchen.

BUNDY: Yeah, that's the trouble. And that is what the rest of that half of the world is going to think if this thing comes apart on us. That's the dilemma.

JOHNSON: But everybody I talk to that's got any sense in there says, "Oh, my God, PLEASE give this thought." . . . This is a terrible thing we're getting ready to do.

BUNDY: . . . I'm not telling you today what I'd do in your position. I just think the most we have to do is to pray with it for another while . . .

JOHNSON: Did you see the poll this morning? 65% of 'em don't know anything about it and of those that do, the majority think we're mishandling it. But they don't know what to do. That's Gallup. It's damned easy to get in a war but it's gonna be awfully hard to ever extricate yourself if you get in.

BUNDY: It's very easy. I'm very sensitive to the fact that people who are having trouble with an intransigent problem find
it very easy to come and say to the President of the United
States go and be tough.[74]

Griping to Bundy did no better at helping Johnson solve his
problem.

Locked in his dilemma, Johnson took refuge in self-pity, a common response in times of stress that encourages people by virtue
of a sense of impotency to defer hard decisions and to project a
preemptive alibi for failure. This hindered Johnson from coming
to terms with the predicament confronting him. Such irresolution
soothed Johnson in the short run but would prove harmful in the
long run. Johnson "was not so stupid that he didn't know that he
was pushing his problem ahead of him," Bundy later said. "And
he knew that it was going to be there as a great big nuisance."[75]
Nevertheless, Johnson huddled.

At the same time that Johnson authorized contingency planning
for air attacks against North Vietnam, he initiated secret diplomatic contact with Hanoi through J. Blair Seaborn, Canada's representative on the International Commission for Supervision and
Control, the body established to monitor compliance with the 1954
and 1962 Geneva Accords. Seaborn relayed a combination of car-
rots and sticks, telling Hanoi that if it agreed to cease its support
for the Vietcong, Washington would provide it economic aid and
diplomatic support; otherwise, it could anticipate American air attacks. Hanoi—still confident it could win a stepped-up war in the
South—had no intention of abandoning its goal of reunification or
responding to what it perceived as coercive U.S. threats: compromise amounted to a demonstration of weakness that would only
embolden the Americans. ("The more concessions we make, the
more insatiable they will be," said a secret resolution passed by the
Politburo the previous December.[76]) Foreign Minister Pham Van
Dong told Seaborn that the precondition for settlement would

be American withdrawal from South Vietnam and acceptance of Vietcong participation in a "neutral" coalition government. He hastened to note, however, "that there was no reason to fear that the [Vietcong] would take over a coalition government."*[77] Dong ended by stressing, prophetically, that Hanoi and the Vietcong would "struggle regardless of sacrifice."[78]

Neither side stood ready to compromise or, just as important, to define mutually satisfactory options—a key ingredient to success. Defining mutually satisfactory options does not come naturally, note negotiation experts Roger Fisher and William Ury. "People involved in a negotiation rarely sense a need for them. In a dispute, people usually believe that they know the right answer—their view should prevail . . . Judgment hinders imagination."[79] Thus, Washington and Hanoi remained determined to do and endure whatever might be necessary to see the war to a conclusion satisfactory to it. This meant no negotiations for the foreseeable future. The Seaborn mission, moreover, only provoked the chiefs to step up their campaign for escalation. "The time for continuing a monologue of 'messages' that repeat the substance or maintain the intensity of our past effort seems to us to be well past," they wrote McNamara and the president on June 2. "We should not waste critical time and more resources in another protracted series of 'messages,' but rather we should take positive, prompt, and meaningful military action to underscore our meaning that after more than two years of tolerating this North Vietnamese support we are now determined that it will stop."[80]

In this atmosphere of growing pressure from the chiefs, Johnson authorized extension of a covert action program against North Vietnam, codenamed PLAN 34A, first discussed at Honolulu on

---

* Hanoi echoed this point to French Communist Party visitors that summer, stressing it was prepared to accept an indefinite separation of North and South Vietnam if the Americans left and the two halves of the country enjoyed normal relations and freedom of movement for civilians. See Gareth Porter, "The Tonkin Gulf Crisis Reconsidered: Unwitting Provocation in U.S. Coercive Diplomacy," October 28, 1988, pp. 10–11.

November 20 and begun in early February. Intended to counter
North Vietnamese infiltration of men and materiel into South
Vietnam along the Hồ Chí Minh Trail in neighboring Laos and
Cambodia and from barges along the coast, PLAN 34A included
sabotage and propaganda missions against North Vietnam by
South Vietnamese commandos as well as Taiwanese and Filipino
mercenaries advised by U.S. personnel. Aircraft dropped agents
into North Vietnam to blow up rail and highway bridges and
high-speed boats launched hit-and-run attacks along the North
Vietnamese coast. Electronic intelligence-gathering patrols by specially equipped U.S. naval vessels in the Gulf of Tonkin, codenamed DESOTO, intercepted North Vietnamese radio and radar
signals triggered by the PLAN 34A missions and relayed them to
a marine corps signals intelligence (SIGINT) unit at Phú Bài and
a navy SIGINT unit at San Miguel in the Philippines. (Similar
DESOTO patrols had been conducted for years off the coasts of
China, North Korea, and the Soviet Union, which paralleled Soviet
intelligence-gathering patrols off America's East and West coasts.)
Although by June PLAN 34A had accomplished very little—the
rigid Communist control structure of block committees in towns
and villages detected and reported all unusual movements—the
chiefs nonetheless asserted its potential "remains high" and urged
its extension.[81] They especially wanted to gather information on
the location and frequency of Soviet anti-aircraft missile and radar stations along North Vietnam's Tonkin Gulf coast as part of
their contingency planning for air attacks against North Vietnam.
Johnson acceded to their request.

PLAN 34A raids against North Vietnam resumed in July on instructions from the chiefs, as did DESOTO patrols operating in
international waters. The closest approach to North Vietnam of the
DESOTO patrols was set at eight miles to the mainland and four
miles to the offshore islands—distances informed by the conclusion
of legal experts that international waters extended to three miles
offshore. This was the same limit established by France when it
controlled Indochina, as well as by other Communist countries like

Cuba, Poland, and Yugoslavia.* PLAN 34A and DESOTO operated in the same general area at the same general time—a convergence that led the North Vietnamese to mistakenly assume they were connected. In fact, the approval process and operational scheduling of each was compartmentalized: the CIA controlled PLAN 34A and the Joint Chiefs, through MACV, controlled DESOTO. In Washington, each department and agency of government (then and now) zealously guards and fences off its turf—an abiding fact of bureaucratic life that inhibited senior Johnson administration officials from looking at PLAN 34A and DESOTO in an integrated way, which might have led them to see the danger that the North Vietnamese could reasonably associate the programs and therefore view DESOTO patrols as a provocation. The chiefs had ordered the commander of DESOTO patrols to maintain contact with the CIA so that they could avoid "mutual interference," but senior administration officials did not know this and therefore did not ponder its possible implications from a North Vietnamese perspective because no senior civilian official had followed the planning for either PLAN 34A or DESOTO. In hindsight, senior officials should have viewed PLAN 34A and DESOTO as operationally in unison and weighed the implications before approving the patrols. Their negligence proved a fateful error.

On the night of July 30–31, South Vietnamese boats on a PLAN 34A mission raked the offshore islands of Hon Me and Hon Ngu with machine-gun and cannon fire, triggering radar signals and radio traffic that was picked up by the USS *Maddox*, a destroyer then steaming into the Tonkin Gulf on a DESOTO patrol. The *Maddox* passed near Hon Me Island the next day[82] and continued monitoring North Vietnamese communications. In the early afternoon of August 2, as the *Maddox* approached ten miles off the Red River Delta, three North Vietnamese torpedo boats emerged from the estuary. A local North Vietnamese naval commander acting

---

* Hanoi did not claim a twelve-mile limit until September 1, 1964—three weeks *after* the Tonkin Gulf incident.

on his own initiative, without orders from Hanoi,[83] connected the American ship with the shelling of Hon Me and Hon Ngu and struck back, attacking the *Maddox* in international waters sixteen miles from the coast, inflicting slight damage.

Word reached Washington a few hours later. Johnson initially seemed "bewildered about what had happened," recalled a State Department official who briefed him on the attack that morning. "He couldn't understand why they had done it."[84] Maxwell Taylor, now fully installed as U.S. ambassador to South Vietnam, spoke for himself and the chiefs when he urged the president to retaliate, arguing that failure to do so would be construed as an "indication that the U.S. flinches from direct confrontation with the North Vietnamese."[85]

Johnson chose not to strike back. Instead, he ordered the DESOTO patrol continued with a second destroyer at a further distance from the North Vietnamese coast, and sent Hanoi a diplomatic note through Seaborn warning that "grave consequences would inevitably result from any further unprovoked offensive military action" against U.S. ships in international waters. Johnson thought these steps would keep the incident from escalating into a confrontation and would deter—not invite—further North Vietnamese attacks. Even if, as McNamara now realized and pointed out to him the following day, the North Vietnamese might have associated PLAN 34A with DESOTO, it seemed fantastic to Johnson that such naval lightweights would take on the massive destructive forces of the United States.

Amid all this, Johnson's overriding concern remained the election three months away. Just weeks earlier, on July 16, the Republican Party had nominated ultraconservative senator Barry Goldwater of Arizona at its convention in San Francisco. Goldwater had won the nomination on a right-wing platform that included a hard line on Vietnam (America should be "carrying the war to North Vietnam") and a withering condemnation of Johnson's "Munich-like appeasement" in foreign policy. In his acceptance speech, Goldwater had declared that "failures infest the jungles of Vietnam . . . I needn't remind you, but I will, it has been during Democratic years that a billion persons were cast into Communist captivity and their fate cynically sealed. Today we have an administration which seems eager to deal with Communism in every coin known . . . even human freedom itself." Goldwater then added: "I would remind you that extremism in the defense of liberty is no vice." His words had drawn loud applause from the audience. Johnson felt extraordinarily sensitive to Goldwater's criticism and made this clear when speaking with McNamara on the morning of August 3: "The people . . . want to be damned sure I don't pull 'em out and run . . . That's what all the country wants because Goldwater is raising so much hell about how he's gonna blow 'em off the moon. And they say that we oughtn't to do anything that the national interest doesn't require, but we sure ought to always leave the impression that if you shoot at us, you're gonna get hit."[86]

Within hours, another PLAN 34A operation took place. Less than a day later—at 7:40 P.M., August 4, Vietnam time—the commander of the *Maddox*, Captain John Herrick, reported intercepting North Vietnamese communications* that, combined with radar readings and sonar soundings†, indicated preparations for a second attack on his ship and its companion destroyer, the *C. Turner Joy*. Johnson received word of these concerns shortly afterward (just after 9 A.M., August 4, in Washington), and two hours later, the *Maddox* reported being under attack. Having absorbed the first attack without retaliating, Johnson felt stung by an apparent second one. This time he responded swiftly, ordering a retaliatory strike against the North Vietnamese bases that had launched the torpedo boats and a nearby oil storage depot. As McNamara later put it, "How in God's name did they think we would react to the idea that

---

* These intercepted North Vietnamese messages had been interpreted as attack orders by the marine SIGINT unit at Phú Bài, but passed along to Herrick as established fact.

† These readings and soundings resulted from the high-speed evasive maneuvers of the American warships in response to a perceived attack in the pitch-black night. Every time the destroyers suddenly changed course, their propellers' turbulence caused high-speed returns on their sonars.

North Vietnam could attack a U.S. naval vessel in international waters and not receive some response from the United States?"[87] Johnson's anxiety to preempt any accusation that he was "soft on Communism" and irresolute on Vietnam reinforced his decision.

A canny politician with a keen sense of timing, Johnson understood how to exploit a situation to his advantage, and the moment seemed an ideal one to submit the draft resolution the troika had been working on to Capitol Hill. "You know that resolution?" he told Bundy shortly after receiving reports of a second attack on the morning of August 4. "Well, now's the time to get it through the Congress." Johnson knew that Congress hesitated to question the president in an atmosphere of crisis—the flag had been challenged on the high seas—and he liked having as many fingerprints on his policies as possible. Congressional support for his Vietnam policy would blunt pressure from the Right, defusing the fragile and volatile issue as he went into the fall presidential campaign. It would also protect him later if things went wrong—which he remembered Truman had failed to do in Korea. (As Johnson vividly put it, "I want Congress in on the take-off as well as any crash landing.") Bundy wondered about the rush and urged Johnson to slow down and lay the groundwork for a resolution of such import by building public and congressional understanding and support first. But Johnson wanted no argument from his national security advisor; he had made up his mind. "I'm not asking you for a discussion," he told Bundy in a voice edged with anger. "I asked you for the resolution. I want you to do it."[88] Johnson made himself equally clear to McNamara.

Within a few hours, however, information reached Washington that raised doubts about the second attack. Low clouds and thunderstorms made visibility in the Tonkin Gulf that moonless night extremely difficult. Crewmembers of the *Maddox* were young, inexperienced, and jittery. At 1:27 P.M., Captain Herrick cabled Washington: "Review of action makes many reported contacts and torpedoes fired appear doubtful. Freak weather effects on radar and overeager sonar men may have accounted for many reports. No actual visual sightings by *Maddox*. Suggest complete evaluation before any further action taken."[89] Throughout the afternoon, messages flew back and forth between the Pentagon and U.S. Pacific Fleet headquarters in Honolulu trying to nail down exactly what had happened. Shortly before 5 P.M., McNamara met with the chiefs to review everything that had been learned. Three factors stood out: one of the destroyers had allegedly observed torpedo boat cockpit lights; the *Maddox* had intercepted and decoded a North Vietnamese message apparently indicating that two boats had been sunk; and U.S. Pacific Fleet commander Admiral U. S. Grant Sharp told McNamara that no doubt now existed that a second attack on the destroyers had been carried out.*[90] When Johnson informed congressional leaders of his decision in the Cabinet Room at seven o'clock that evening and the American people by televised address at 11:30 P.M., he treated the attack—despite a lack of hard evidence—as a given. Johnson did not have all of the facts, nor had he waited for them before making a firm judgment. "What really mattered to Lyndon Johnson in 1964 was the election politics of these events," Bundy later explained. "He had decided to hold back from retaliation after the attack of August 2. That left him less firmly and effectively anti-Communist than he wanted to be. The report of the second attack gave him a second chance. He had been patient, and people liked that; now he could also be firm, and most people would like that even better."[91] McNamara's interrogation of the chiefs had been done "on behalf of a president who had already committed himself to having a resolution and a speech and had air time."[92] "For God's sake, tell me this thing happened," LBJ told Bundy that night, "because I have scheduled a speech to say it happened, I have told the Congress I am going to go after a resolution, and if I cancel this speech, the press is going to say, 'What the hell are you doing?' So I sure as hell hope this is right."

---

* Sharp was considerably less certain when he recalled the episode six years later. "We asked the *Maddox* to confirm absolutely that the ships were attacked and told them to get word to us as quickly as possible. We got a report from the ships which neither absolutely confirmed or denied that they'd been under attack, but the weight of evidence still was that an attack had occurred, so I told Mr. McNamara that." U. S. Grant Sharp OHI, LBJL.

"The Lyndon Johnson pressure to get the answer 'Yes, it happened' was on very heavy," recalled Bundy.[93]

As noted earlier, it is rarely possible to have all of the facts. We live in a world of considerable complexity and uncertainty, and we simply don't have the time or capacity to calculate all of the probabilities and risks inherent in every choice. Cornell University's Thomas Gilovich has explained this dilemma. "Instead of providing us with clear information that would enable us to 'know' better," notes Gilovich, the world "presents us with messy data that are random, incomplete, unrepresentative, ambiguous, inconsistent, unpalatable, or secondhand . . . It is often our flawed attempts to cope with precisely these difficulties that lay bare our inferential shortcomings and produce the facts that just ain't so."

This produces the "illusion of validity"—people's tendency to "be overly impressed by data that, at best, only *suggests* that a belief may be true." National Public Radio reporter Gregory Warner's account of the terrorist attack on the Westgate Mall in Nairobi, Kenya, in September 2013 is a case in point. Warner based his account on eyewitness interviews—including with his personal friend Puni, who was at the mall that day. The eyewitnesses described ten to fifteen multiethnic gunmen (Somalis, Kenyans, Arabs—even a British woman they called "the white widow"), two wearing short-sleeved shirts, and one who escaped by dropping his gun and blending in with fleeing shoppers. When an FBI forensic team arrived in Kenya to investigate the attack, they gained access to all closed-circuit television (CCTV) footage taken in the mall during the attack. The footage revealed there were only four gunmen—all of them Somalis, none wearing short-sleeved shirts, and no evidence that any of the gunmen escaped. When Warner told his friend Puni what the FBI had learned through the CCTV footage, she still resisted accepting the evidence because it did not match her emotions from that day.[94] "Willingness to base conclusions on incomplete or unrepresentative information is a common cause of people's questionable and erroneous beliefs," concludes Gilovich.[95] As a result, people conclude too much from too little.

People exhibit the related tendency to focus on confirmatory evidence when they gather information relevant to a particular belief. When trying to assess whether or not a belief is valid, explains Gilovich, "people ask questions or seek information" that "lend credence to their hypothesis."[96] Peter Wason of University College, London, conducted an experiment a few years after Tonkin Gulf that confirmed this tendency. Participants received four cards, each with a letter and a number—A, B, 2, or 3—on opposite sides. Participants were asked to determine, by turning over one card at a time, whether all cards with a vowel on one side had an even number on the other. Most participants turned over the A card first, then the 2 card—even though a B on the other side of the 2 card proved nothing, while turning over the 3 card and finding an A on the other side would invalidate the hypothesis.[97]

Cognitive scientists Hugo Mercier of the French National Center for Scientific Research in Lyon and Dan Sperber of the Central European University in Budapest observe that deciding without all the facts makes evolutionary sense, given that humans do not have the luxury to analyze "big data" prior to every decision. People think about a situation only to the extent necessary to make sense—but perhaps only superficial sense—of it. Such "early closure" can lead to premature drawing of conclusions.[98] Reinforcing this is what Steven Sloman of Brown University and Philip Fernbach of the University of Colorado have identified as the "illusion of explanatory depth"—people's belief that they know much more than they actually do.[99] An experiment conducted at the University of Liverpool known as the "bicycle problem" illustrates this phenomenon: participants who rode bicycles and were deemed good artists were asked to sketch an image of a bicycle. A majority of them drew bicycles that would be nonfunctional, such as attaching both wheels to the chain.[100] As we have seen before, "confirmation bias" compounds the problem. Raymond Nickerson of Tufts University notes that people tend to embrace information that supports their beliefs and reject information that contradicts those beliefs. This unconscious selectivity in the acquisition and use of information leads people to dismiss evidence of new or underappreciated threats. "People can and do engage in case-building

unwittingly, without intending to treat evidence in a biased way
or even being aware of doing so," writes Nickerson.[101] Much of this
bias is rooted in the fact that humans are social creatures. "The
main role of reasoning in decision-making," observes Sperber, "is
not to arrive at [a] decision but to be able to present the decision"—
the heart of LBJ's dilemma—"as something that's rational." Johnson behaved in this fashion in response to events in the Tonkin
Gulf, with fateful consequences.

Three decades later, North Vietnamese officials confirmed what
many had long suspected: no second attack occurred on August 4.[102]
Evidence that emerged in the intervening years buttressed this
conclusion. NSA and CIA officials concluded after careful study that
the intercepted North Vietnamese message had actually pertained
to the confirmed August 2 attack,* and nearby carrier USS *Ticond-
eroga* pilot James Stockdale wrote in his memoir that he had seen
no North Vietnamese boats when he flew over the *Maddox* and
C. Turner Joy on August 4 and believed no attack had occurred.
Johnson's concern about appearing tough and resolute had discouraged him from patiently and exhaustively analyzing the uncertain
evidence. The resulting hastiness contributed to later accusations
that he had fabricated or provoked a second attack in order to secure Congress's support for a war that he secretly planned.

On August 7, Congress passed the Tonkin Gulf Resolution granting the president the power "to take all necessary steps, including
the use of armed force" to repel attacks against U.S. forces and to
"prevent further aggression" in Southeast Asia. The Senate voted

---

* The fullest study of SIGINT related to the Tonkin Gulf affair—Robert J. Hanyok's
"Skunks, Bogies, Silent Hounds, and the Flying Fish: The Gulf of Tonkin Mystery, 2–4 August 1964," *Cryptologic Quarterly*, Winter 2000/Spring 2001—concludes:
"Through a compound of analytic errors and an unwillingness to consider contrary
evidence, . . . SIGINT information was presented in such a manner as to preclude responsible decisionmakers in the Johnson administration from having the
complete and objective narrative of events of 4 August 1964. Instead, only SIGINT
that supported the claim that the communists had attacked the two destroyers was
given to administration officials . . . This mishandling of SIGINT was not done in a
manner to be construed as conspiratorial . . . Rather, the objective was to support
the Navy's claim that the DeSoto patrol had been deliberately attacked by the North
Vietnamese."

88–2; the House of Representatives, 416–0. In order to secure its near unanimous passage, Johnson had Rusk assure the bill's sponsor and floor leader, Senate Foreign Relations Committee chairman William Fulbright, that the administration would not use the vast power granted by the resolution without further close consultation with Congress. Johnson had no secret escalatory agenda; "I don't want to get in a land war in Asia," he flatly told Fulbright's Senate colleague Mike Mansfield earlier that summer."[103] Johnson's objective was more immediate and less sinister. Polls showed 85 percent of Americans approved of his reprisal against Hanoi, and afterward support for Johnson's handling of Vietnam jumped from 58 to 72 percent. "In a single stroke," pollster Louis Harris wrote on August 10, "Mr. Johnson has, at least temporarily, turned his greatest political vulnerability in foreign policy into one of his strongest assets."[104]

Looking back, Bundy used baseball parlance to explain Johnson's behavior. LBJ saw it as a clever "triple play": "the right response for the election" (appearing firm), "the right response for the war" (preventing a larger conflict by deterring Hanoi from further action), and the right response for the future (giving him discretion and license to act later if necessary).[105] But his short-term thinking planted the seeds of a long-term military problem: he intended the retaliatory air strikes to deter North Vietnam, but instead they prompted Hanoi, who interpreted them as evidence the United States intended to escalate the war, to begin dispatching North Vietnamese army (NVA) troops to the South. The first NVA units departed in September and reached South Vietnam by the end of the year.[106]

Johnson's normally long face brightened after Labor Day. As the fall election campaign got under way, he plunged into the race, fueled by his renowned, deep reservoir of energy. Johnson thrived on the hectic, joyous confusion and the adulation that fed his large and insecure ego. He drew big crowds everywhere he went and, casting aside Secret Service admonitions, sporadically waded into the teeming throngs of well-wishers lining his motorcades, giving and getting the warmth and energy—the external validation—that he so desperately wanted and needed. For this brief period, Johnson relaxed and actually enjoyed being president. The unflattering comparisons to Kennedy evaporated, replaced by a popular image of Johnson as a man of moderation rather than extremism like Goldwater: he had transcended his provincialism to become a national leader, the Great Healer of the nation's wounds created by Kennedy's assassination, the man who would build a Great Society on behalf of all the people. Polls suggested he was going to win and win big, giving him large Democratic majorities in both houses of Congress that would enable him to pass his ambitious legislative agenda over the objections of Republicans and conservative southern Democratic barons controlling the key Senate and House committees, who had always blocked such legislation in the past.

None of this meant Vietnam had gone away as an issue. He understood Washington as well as—or better than—anyone and viewed it as a gigantic shark tank teeming with cunning predators (like himself) waiting to pounce on rivals and adversaries at the first scent of blood in the water. This made him obsessed and terrified about being blamed for "losing" South Vietnam, because he feared losing South Vietnam meant losing something precious to him: his ambition and dream of building a Great Society of equal opportunity for all Americans as a monument to the country and his own place in history. This fear coincided with his aversion to going against the grain and being out front alone on an issue without the protective cover that a consensus provided, a strategy that he had made a habit as Senate majority leader, and one that he believed would protect him against any attacks. It seemed political suicide to challenge the prevalent anti-Communism of the day. Vietnam might not do you a lot of good, he liked to say, but it sure as hell could do you a lot of harm.[107]

Like Kennedy during the last months of his presidency, Johnson whispered behind closed doors about avoiding Truman's fate. It wasn't a domestic issue that had doomed Truman, Johnson often reminded his aides—it was a foreign one. "I am not going to lose Vietnam," he said privately, "I am not going to be the President who saw Southeast Asia go the way China went."[108] Johnson spelled out his dilemma vividly and at length in an interview with a biographer years later. "I knew Harry Truman and [his secretary of state] Dean Acheson had lost their effectiveness from the day that the Communists took over in China. I believed that the loss of China had played a large role in the rise of Joe McCarthy. And I knew that all these problems, taken together, were chicken shit compared with what might happen if we lost Vietnam."[109]

As a result, Johnson walked a tightrope on Vietnam during the fall campaign—seeking to deflect Goldwater's charge of weakness while capitalizing on Americans' fear of Goldwater's hawkishness. In a speech to the American Bar Association in New York City shortly before the Democratic National Convention, Johnson warned that "others are eager to enlarge the conflict" by supplying "American boys to do the job that Asian boys should do." He rejected this course, stressing that "such action would offer no solution at all to the real problem of Vietnam" and vaguely promised to maintain the U.S. commitment to South Vietnam while avoiding the dangers of an expanded war.[110] In his first appearance after winning the nomination, he declared, "I have had advice to load our planes with bombs and drop them on certain areas that I think would enlarge the war and . . . result in our committing a good many American boys to fighting a war that . . . ought to be fought by the boys of Asia to help protect their own land . . . For that reason, I haven't chosen to enlarge the war. Nor have I chosen to retreat and turn it over to the Communists." He repeated this formulation over and over during the campaign—in Oklahoma and New Hampshire, in Kentucky and Ohio. As Election Day neared, Johnson moved even further, toward an outright rejection of American combat involvement. In a speech on October 21, though dismissing retreat from South Vietnam, he assured his audience that he was "not about to send American boys nine or 10,000 miles away from home to do what Asian boys ought to be doing for themselves."[111]

Johnson himself wanted to believe his campaign formulation about preserving South Vietnam's independence without widening the war, but (kept hidden from the electorate) he was well aware that the Joint Chiefs had been pushing their air campaign against North Vietnam for months and the CIA had growing doubts that South Vietnam could continue much longer to defend itself. To reveal these unsettling things would be to expose his dilemma—something Johnson could not summon the courage to do. ("If you have a mother-in-law with only one eye and she has it in the center of her head," he later said in explaining his lack of candor, "you don't keep her in the living room."[112] Johnson's remark was pungent and also very defensive.) "He wasn't fully candid," McNamara later said. "He didn't disclose that he might have to consider moves beyond what he indicated and he didn't disclose that the Chiefs at various times had recommended action beyond what he discussed."[113] Like any politician, Johnson was focused on getting elected. Political expediency and personal insecurity led him to convey an impression and expectation during the 1964 presidential campaign that would come back to haunt him.

Transparency is unnatural among most in power because they usually gain a competitive advantage and succeed by withholding information from their opponents. People try to hide the pressures on them because it makes them appear vulnerable. And people—especially politicians—fear being exposed as seemingly feeble and thin-skinned. Johnson could not understand the fundamental truth that a president must trust the public if he wants the public to trust and follow him. He could not understand this because deep down he did not trust his own judgment.

Of course, politicians frequently sacrifice candor during election campaigns. Woodrow Wilson ran on the slogan He Kept Us Out of War in 1916—only to seek a declaration of war against the kaiser's Germany the following spring. And Franklin Roosevelt, Johnson's role model in the 1930s and 1940s, did not level with the public during the 1940 presidential campaign, when he vowed not to send American boys to fight in a foreign war—just a year before the United States entered World War II. But Wilson's and Roosevelt's transgressions were forgiven because America succeeded in the World Wars I and II. Johnson's transgression was not because the United States failed in Vietnam. By failing to level with the public, he only dug a deeper hole for himself, planting the seeds of a "credibility gap" that would dog him for the rest of his presidency. It's never easy for politicians to share unpalatable facts with the electorate, but sharing his dilemma with the public hardly could have served Johnson any worse.

All of that lay in the future. For now, in the fall of 1964, Johnson reveled in an exhilarating and undeniably successful campaign. As Election Day approached, pollsters and pundits began predicting a landslide victory of historic proportions for the accidental president who desperately wanted the validation of election in his own right. He got it: the dimensions of Johnson's triumph on November 3, 1964, proved staggering. LBJ garnered the largest popular vote margin in American electoral history—61 percent of a record 70 million votes cast. He carried 44 states and swept the Electoral College by 486 to 52, and riding his coattails, the Democrats gained 37 seats in the House, giving them a stunning 295 to 140 advantage, making for a filibuster-proof supermajority of 68 in the South-dominated Senate. Johnson carried every part of the country except Goldwater's home state of Arizona and the Deep South—Alabama, Georgia, Louisiana, Mississippi, and South Carolina—whose white voters punished Johnson and the Democratic Party for supporting passage of the Civil Rights Act over the summer.

Despite his margin of defeat, Goldwater's success in the heretofore solidly Democratic South alarmed Johnson. As a white Southerner, he understood the depth and intensity of the anger and resentment spurred by his aggressive championing of civil rights. "He made a good deal of enemies in doing so," Clark Clifford said later. "Conservatives did not like him. They hated him for it."[114] Johnson understood that while white Southerners might not be able to stop him from implementing civil rights reforms, they could punish him and his party for doing so, using any pretext—like the loss of South Vietnam—to exact their revenge. "When you win big, you can have anything you want for a time," Johnson said. "You come home with that big landslide and there isn't a one of them who'll stand in your way." That would not last. "No," he sneered, "they'll be glad to be aboard and to have their photographs taken with you

and be part of all that victory. They'll come along and give you almost everything you want for a while, and then"—Johnson paused
for a moment—"they'll turn on you. They always do." He could almost see it. "They'll lay in waiting, waiting for you to make a slip
and you will. They'll give you almost everything and then they'll
make you pay for it."[115] He told civil rights leader Martin Luther
King Jr. early the following year, "We've got to get [voting rights
legislation] passed before the vicious forces concentrate."[116]

Johnson had been living on borrowed time. The campaign had reinforced his (and, indeed, most politicians') natural inertia in facing
hard choices, but with the election over, he realized that he could
not continue postponing critical decisions about Vietnam. "God,
I hate for it to be over, because the hell starts then," a curiously
morose Johnson said on the evening of his election victory, when
most newly elected presidents would be euphoric and savor the
moment.[117] His fate, despite his triumph, seemed companioned
by disaster. Johnson sensed only too well what awaited him, Mc-
Namara having spelled it out in no uncertain terms in a phone call
several weeks earlier. "It *doesn't* look good, Mr. President," the defense secretary told him on September 21. "I think the odds are
we can squeeze through between now and the [election] but it certainly is a weak situation . . . After the election, we've got a real
problem on our hands."[118] Avoidance had shielded Johnson from
decisions that he found difficult to face.

The chiefs, who hated the idea of "controlled escalation," had
begun pushing a bombing program against North Vietnam known
as the 94 Targets List. Comprising an array of military and economic targets whose destruction the chiefs confidently argued
would destroy Hanoi's will and ability to support the Vietcong,
the list represented an operational manifestation of their underlying belief, in LeMay's words, that we "should bomb them into the
Stone Age" even if this made Chinese intervention "more than
likely."[119] The goal of LeMay and the chiefs reflected wishful thinking based on their World War II experience more than it did careful
analysis of conditions in North Vietnam. "I understand that there

are Americans who believe that early, massive strikes on the North would have won the war for the U.S.," said a North Vietnamese anti-aircraft artillery officer after the war. "Maybe this would have been a good strategy for [the United States] in World War II, against heavily industrialized countries like Germany and Japan, but when you are bombing an almost totally agricultural country like Vietnam, then your bombs just hit the ground and kill a little rice."[120] The chiefs could simply not imagine—or accept—this reality.

Far from it: LeMay and his cohorts urged the immediate implementation of the 94 Targets List starting in the southern panhandle of North Vietnam and moving northward in a pattern of ever-increasing air attacks. The chiefs also chafed to begin bombing because they saw it as a solution to Saigon's political dysfunction. We "do not agree that we should be slow to get deeply involved until we have a better feel for the quality of our ally," they wrote Johnson in late August. "The United States is already deeply involved. [We] consider that only significantly stronger military pressures on [North Vietnam] are likely to provide the relief and psychological boost necessary for attainment of the requisite [South Vietnamese] governmental stability and viability."[121]

JCS chairman General Earle Wheeler—an army officer with thirty-two years of service but only five months of combat duty who had never led soldiers in battle—had succeeded Taylor in June. Wheeler told McNamara on November 1 that the chiefs felt so strongly about the target list that if the president decided against implementing it, most of them believed the United States should withdraw from South Vietnam. They delivered this de facto ultimatum despite the conclusion of their own Joint Staff that "industrial and military bombing" of North Vietnam "would not quickly cause cessation of the insurgency in South Vietnam" and, indeed, "might have but minimal effect on the (low) living standard" of the adversary.[122] These findings reinforced McNamara's own doubts and strengthened his resistance to the chiefs' pressure. "I had served in World War II in the Army Air Corps," McNamara later explained. "I knew something about" the military limitations of bombing, and "I had absolutely no hesitancy in saying, 'You're just wrong on that.'"[123] The Joint Staff would have agreed, but the chiefs didn't care.

South Vietnam's accelerating decline during the fall of 1964 only intensified the pressure. Johnson's wishful, desperate illusion that Nguyễn Khánh could turn things around had been shattered. When he had issued a decree in late August granting himself sweeping powers, students and Buddhist monks took to the streets, forcing him to withdraw his edict and fatally undermining his author-ity. The ceaseless intrigue among South Vietnam's politicians and generals—so inimical to political stability and military success—persisted. ARVN generals continued to fight among themselves rather than against the Vietcong, which continued to grow stron-ger as North Vietnam boosted its men and supplies sent south. In December, the CIA reported for the first time that regular NVA units had been infiltrated into South Vietnam. A South Vietnamese observer put it well. "The American policy of boosting whoever happened to grab power, for the sake of an elusive stability, was now reaping its harvest."[124]

To cope with looming decisions, the day before the election Johnson had authorized creation of the Working Group to frame policy choices. The Working Group met every day for the next two weeks. Its chair, McGeorge Bundy's older brother Bill, the assistant secretary of state for Far Eastern affairs, later described the Work-ing Group as conducting "the most comprehensive" Vietnam pol-icy review "of any in the Kennedy and Johnson Administrations."[125] But the options that the Working Group crafted under the troika's guidance—continuing along present lines; escalating immediately and heavily against North Vietnam; and escalating gradually—did not include any alternative involving diplomatic negotiations or an outright American withdrawal. Created to define options, the Working Group generated information and estimates tailored to make the exercise of particular policies more likely. In policy-making, it is vital that all alternative courses of action be analyzed, but in this case, the selection of premises controlled the conclusions reached. United around the conviction that Washington could not allow a defeat, the Working Group framed a narrow range of choices that excluded any diplomatic or political initiatives. Critic Dorothy Parker's caustic remark that Katharine Hepburn ran "the gamut of emotions from A to B," applied in a sense to the Working Group's deliberations as well.

Partly, this reflected a problematic human response to complex problems. Nobel Prize–winning economist Richard Thaler of the University of Chicago and Harvard Law School professor Cass Sunstein have demonstrated that as choices become based on more and more factors, people are likely to adopt simplifying strategies as a way of coping with numerous variables, and these simplifying strategies often mislead. An experiment known as the Stroop Test illustrates this principle. Shown words flashed on a computer screen, participants faced a simple task: to press the right button if they saw a word displayed in red, to press the left button if they saw a word displayed in green. Participants handled this task easily and with great accuracy. But when the task become more complex— when they saw the word "green" displayed in red or vice versa— their reaction time slowed and their error rate increased.[126]

When framing choices, moreover, people often suffer from belief perseverance, the tendency to maintain beliefs despite explicit conflicting evidence.[127] An experiment conducted by social psychologists Lee Ross and Mark Lepper of Stanford University in 1975 showed this process in action. Three groups of participants were asked to distinguish authentic suicide notes from false ones. Group A received a very high evaluation, Group B received an average evaluation, and Group C received a very low evaluation. Each group then learned that the evaluations did not correspond to their actual performance but were precooked as part of the experiment. Nevertheless, when subsequently asked to rate their ability to judge the authenticity of suicide notes in a postexperiment questionnaire, those in Group A continued to rate themselves higher than those in Group B did and far higher than those in Group C did.[128]

What made matters worse was the troika's unwillingness or inability to confront the feasibility and consequences of getting out. They could not bring themselves to consider, as McNamara later put it, "that getting out will lead to all these problems, but that's better than the problems we'll face staying in." This failure reflected their abiding aversion to what McNamara called "a break in the containment dike"—the loss of South Vietnam. "None of us wanted to do anything that would lead to that as long as there was something else we could do," he explained. Fashioned at the outset of the Cold War, containment had become an unquestioned axiom that none of them thought to reexamine even though the constellation of international forces had shifted amid diffused authority and power among Communist states and nationalist upheaval in the postcolonial world. The troika treated containment as if it was religious dogma, an entrapment that inhibited them from recognizing their bias and therefore addressing fundamental questions: Could South Vietnam be saved without political stability? What would happen if the bombing began and where might it lead? It was a grievous failure painfully apparent to McNamara looking back. "With hindsight," he acknowledged, "the course that would have led to the least cost to the United States in lives lost and erosion of the containment dike would have been simply pursuing the present program to the point where the South Vietnamese asked us to leave or it became so politically unstable that a chaotic situation developed and it was obvious that we should pull out our advisors. That was the course we should have chosen."[129]

There was another "containment dike" that in many ways superseded the international one, and that was the short-term effort to contain domestic opposition to Johnson's broader agenda and political standing. The Cold War containment axiom may have been the lens through which the political elite viewed the world, but the focal target was the American ballot box and Capitol Hill. Here, too, another sort of conventional focus created a kind of conceptual dungeon: not only were they unable to think unconventionally about what might be done regarding Vietnam, but they were unable to think unconventionally about how a decision that might appear to risk current political momentum might be only a short-lived political setback—but a long-term triumph. Everyone is limited by his or her sense of what is possible and conceivable, and this proved true of Bundy, McNamara, and Rusk at this crucial juncture.

On November 19, the troika, along with Bill Bundy, briefed Johnson about the Working Group's progress. They made it clear the group had begun focusing on a graduated bombing campaign and would continue doing so unless Johnson instructed otherwise. He voiced no objection to the absence of a political option and no desire to broaden the Working Group's deliberations in order to extend his range of choices. Yet Johnson sensed that the troika had gravitated toward their recommendation out of desperation—they did not know what else to do to solve a deepening problem—and his political instincts made him skeptical that bombing would make Hanoi amenable. Johnson dreaded the options before him, but not enough to consider withdrawal. That seemed too dangerous—too politically explosive—to merit serious attention. However, the troika told him that bombing would, in effect, buy time and *that*—more than anything else—is what Johnson still wanted even though the election had passed: more time to postpone making difficult choices, to hope that before he was absolutely forced to act the situation would have magically resolved on its own.

Johnson called a meeting on December 1 to decide about the Working Group's recommendations. All of the principals had been assembled—a sign of the meeting's importance. In addition to Johnson and the troika, Vice President–elect Hubert Humphrey[*] and JCS chairman General Wheeler attended, as did Ambassador Taylor, who had flown back to Washington for five days of consultations with the Working Group. Taylor opened the meeting by describing South Vietnam's political woes in all-too-familiar detail. Johnson's anxiety and frustration mounted as he listened to Taylor. "The day of reckoning is coming," Johnson grumbled, and he wanted to be sure that Washington had done everything it could "to pull a stable government together" in Saigon. "Hadn't we better shape up *before* we do anything?" he wondered—otherwise, it would be like "sending a widow to slap" a boxer. Finally, Johnson

---

[*] Johnson had been operating without a vice president since becoming president upon Kennedy's assassination.

tentatively agreed to go ahead with bombing, but he told Taylor to "do his damndest" to improve political conditions in South Vietnam first. "If that doesn't work," the president said, turning toward Wheeler, "then I'll be talking to you, General."[130]

Still, while Johnson had agreed to bombing in principle, he hesitated to take the fateful step, grasping at anything to buy more time. "I still do not feel we are making the all-out effort of political persuasion that is called for," he told Taylor, wondering whether Americans in Saigon were "communicating sensitively and persuasively" with their South Vietnamese counterparts.[131] Johnson explained that he wanted a stable government in South Vietnam before he raised the stakes by moving against Hanoi. Taylor took Johnson's message back with him to Saigon, where he told the ARVN generals that U.S. action against the North required political stability in the South, and that meant the generals must stop their scheming against one another and the government. Taylor's warning did no good. Within days, the generals dissolved a major arm of the South Vietnamese government, effectively ending the beginning of civilian rule with another military coup. This infuriated Taylor and reinforced Johnson's reluctance to carry the war to the North.

By early January 1965, Taylor had concluded that Johnson's prerequisite of political stability in South Vietnam could never be met. The chronic dysfunction he had witnessed for six months as ambassador in Saigon had exasperated him. Disgusted and disillusioned with the game of political musical chairs and the incompetence of ARVN leadership, he turned to bombing of the North as a form of political therapy for the South. Taylor understood the limitations better than most—as Eighth Army commander during the last year of the Korean War he had witnessed bombing's limited effectiveness at interdicting China's movement of men and supplies to the battlefront—but he saw no other way. "We are faced with a seriously deteriorating situation," he cabled Johnson on January 6. "We cannot expect anything better than marginal government and marginal pacification progress unless something new is added to make up for those things we cannot control." Re-

signed, he admitted, "I know that this is an old recipe with little attractiveness," but "we are presently on a losing track and must risk
a change," warning that "to take no positive action now is to accept
defeat in the fairly near future . . . The game needs to be opened
up and new opportunities offered for new breaks which hopefully
may be in our favor. The new breaks may also be unfavorable but
scarcely more so than those we have been getting thus far."[132] For
an old warrior like Taylor, giving in to despair seemed like giving
up to the enemy.

Similar desperation gripped Robert McNamara and McGeorge
Bundy. The two had watched as Johnson postponed troublesome
choices for almost a year. "McNamara and I were deeply frustrated
by a year of doing nothing," Bundy recalled, and "we believed
continuing to do nothing would be worst of all."[133] They had a
"stored-up eagerness to act"—to do *something*—"that came" from
"6+" months of "inaction."[134] During that time, his and McNamara's
hope for political stability in Saigon had been dashed. Intelligence
indicated that Vietcong infiltration had doubled and NVA regulars
had begun entering the South in significant numbers. The Vietcong had begun mauling entire ARVN battalions. There was almost nothing contradicting the notion that South Vietnam seemed
about to fall.

Much later, McNamara would admit, "You can't create a nation
by military means."[135] At the time, he and Bundy embraced bombing both because they did not know what else to do and because for
can-do problem-solvers like them, the instinct was not to throw in
the towel and let things go down the drain but to continue working a problem until they figured out how to get it right. Unable to
redefine what "throwing in the towel" meant, they were despon-
dent, and grasped for long chances based on a forlorn hope. Their
minds like propellers running at high speed out of water, Johnson's men searched frantically and erratically for a solution. In
the end, McNamara and Bundy reached the same conclusion as
Taylor: bombing as a solution to problems that otherwise they did
not know how to fix.

McNamara and Bundy laid out their case in a joint memo to

Johnson—something they had never done before—to maximize
the impact of their argument. "Both of us," Bundy wrote the president, "are now pretty well convinced that our current policy can
lead only to disastrous defeat." He summarized that policy: "What
we are doing is to wait and hope for a stable government. Our
December directives make it very plain that wider action against
the Communists will not take place unless we can get such a government." That effort had failed. Now Bundy and McNamara
urged Johnson to change "policy and priorities" and seek stability
through escalation. Bombing would buck up the South Vietnamese
and create "a bargainable instrument,"[136] in Bundy's words, in any
future negotiations with Hanoi. McNamara agreed. "I am absolutely certain in my own mind," he told Johnson several months
later, that "bombing represents a political pressure which we benefit from . . . The bombing represents something we'll give up in
return for something they'll do—at some point."[137]

Theirs was a fateful departure, and they knew it. "Both of us
understand the very grave questions presented by any decision
of this sort," Bundy wrote. "We both recognize," he added, "that
the ultimate responsibility is not ours." But convinced the present
course spelled defeat, he and McNamara felt "the time has come
for harder choices." Bundy admitted that Rusk did not share their
judgment, though the secretary of state did not deny "that things
are going very badly [or] that the situation is unraveling." "What
he does say is that the consequences of both escalation and withdrawal are so bad that we must simply find a way of making our
present policy work"—in other words, neither act nor react.[138] In
a choice between action and inaction, with risks in either direction, Bundy and McNamara preferred doing something rather
than nothing at all, more comfortable feeling their way through
a problem without being certain of the outcome. So they pressed
Johnson hard. "His notion of what was ready for decision would be
almost anybody else's view of over-ready for decision," Bundy later
remarked.[139] They believed Johnson could dither no longer. "We
took some initiative—unfortunately, in the wrong direction," said
McNamara, looking back.[140]

Dean Rusk rarely wrote the president, preferring to speak privately with him. This reticence only heightened the impact of a letter he subsequently wrote to Johnson. Knowing Johnson faced a momentous choice, Rusk felt it "desirable and timely to put down an outline of my own thinking about South Viet Nam." "I am convinced that it would be disastrous for the United States and the free world to permit Southeast Asia to be overrun by the Communist North," he told Johnson. "I am also convinced," he added, "that everything possible should be done to throw back the Hanoi-Viet Cong aggression"—even at "the risk of major escalation."[141]

McNamara and Bundy met with Johnson and Rusk on the morning of January 27 to discuss their joint memo. Barely a week had passed since the president's inauguration. Johnson had been strangely blue the day he took the oath of office on the East Portico of the Capitol, despite what should have been one of the happiest moments of his life. He seemed preoccupied, irritable, and frustrated. In private, he moped and lashed out at those closest to him. "This week's mood is not good," Lady Bird noted in her diary. "The obstacles indeed are no shadows. They are real substance— Vietnam the biggest."[142] Johnson could not shake his feeling that the jaws of a bear trap were about to close on him. In his mind, doing nothing seemed preferable to the alternatives of withdrawal or escalation. But doing nothing no longer seemed a viable option. He did not see how he could win, but he believed he could not afford to lose. Political insecurity fused with personal insecurity— Lyndon Johnson would not cut and run, he would not be the first president to lose a war. He told McNamara and Bundy that he would go forward with military action against Hanoi. "Stable government or no stable government, we'll do what we have to do—we will move strongly." He had chosen his path at the fork. "I'm prepared to do that," he at last declared. Johnson's abiding fear of failure in Vietnam had finally made him accept bombing, overriding the hesitation he still harbored about Saigon's instability.[143]

It was also a capitulation to southern Democrats in Congress, who, if unwilling to challenge the president publicly on voting rights, would exact their political revenge should Johnson stumble

and lose Vietnam. "If I don't go in now and they show later that I
should have," Johnson confided to friends, "then they'll be all over
me in Congress. They won't be talking about my civil rights bill, or
education or beautification." As a former chieftain of the Senate,
he knew well how a minority voting bloc could ravage political
legislation. "No," Johnson added with certainty, those Democrats
and their Republican allies will "push Vietnam up my ass every
time. Vietnam. Vietnam. Vietnam. Right up my ass."[144]

Once it started, the long postponed bombing of North Vietnam
boomeranged wildly. Johnson and his advisors believed it would
encourage the South Vietnamese by boosting morale and popular
support for the government and discourage the North Vietnamese by increasing the cost of supporting the war in the South and
thereby providing an incentive for Hanoi to negotiate a settlement.
It did neither. Rather than stabilize South Vietnam, it unleashed
escalatory pressures that advocates of bombing never intended
or imagined. Rather than intimidate North Vietnam, bombing
"strengthened our resolve," said a North Vietnamese diplomat,
looking back. "It also strengthened world support for our cause."[145]
Influenced by strategic theories of the day—advanced most prominently by Harvard economist Thomas Schelling*—that conflicts
were essentially bargaining situations, that one could signal an adversary that he should in his own interest avoid certain courses
of activity, and that participants in a conflict coolly and rationally
calculate costs and benefits and arrive at consistent expectations
of each other, Taylor, McNamara, and Bundy had assumed bombing would be perceived by North Vietnam as limited and would
be controllable—something that could be turned on and off like

---

* Schelling's 1960 book elaborating these theories, *The Strategy of Conflict*, influenced the outlook of many members of the Kennedy-Johnson national security
team, several of whom had served with Schelling on the Harvard faculty and
introduced Schelling to McNamara and his civilian aides in the Office of the Secretary of Defense. War gaming had been practiced by some elements of the U.S.
military—for example, the United States Naval War College—for decades, but such
war games did not assume collaboration between adversaries, as Schelling's bargaining theory did.

a faucet. "It's something you can stop. It's a bargaining chip," Mc-Namara would say of bombing—one that seemed to have the advantages of both flexibility and control.[146] Taylor, McNamara, and Bundy thought bombing would not last long, perhaps a few months at most. They made the cardinal error of assuming that the North Vietnamese agreed with them. They did not contemplate what would happen if Hanoi did not perceive bombing as a limited gesture and proved willing to absorb its costs because they did not believe bombing would fail, making such considerations moot. They might not have agreed on when to start a bombing campaign, but nobody doubted it would work. None of them foresaw that bombing would instead feed demands for greater military action, that it would be only the first step in what would become a massive American military effort in Vietnam. When an associate asked Bundy whether the North Vietnamese might match American air escalation with their own ground escalation, Bundy replied, "We just don't think that's going to happen."[147] Bundy never imagined "in early 1965," he later acknowledged, "that we'd still be bombing three and a half years later . . . I don't think any of us thought or believed that it would be that long, that inconclusive, that big, or should be."[148] Looking back years later, Bundy saw all of this as "self-deception."[149]

Bundy's confession reflected a larger failing on the part of Johnson and his advisors: their woeful inattention to possible consequences and ultimate costs. Each step they took generated unforeseen demands for another, bigger step that unsettled Johnson and his team and that they found increasingly difficult to anticipate, control, or resist. The unanticipated consequences of bombing "sent a shock wave through all of us," McNamara said. "We were totally unprepared for thinking in such terms."[150] By late July 1965, they had committed the United States to fight a major land war on the Asian mainland despite the accepted wisdom after Korea that such a war should never again be fought.

The same day Johnson received Bundy and McNamara's memo, he ordered Bundy to Saigon to assess the situation on the ground and come back with recommendations. Bundy had never been to

Vietnam. In fact, Bundy had never been to Asia—a shocking but revealing demonstration of the Eurocentrism of the president's national security team, whose judgments about Vietnam influenced him heavily. Bundy arrived in Saigon on February 4 and what he learned from embassy and MACV briefings confirmed the fears he had brought with him from Washington. "The current situation among non-Communist forces," he cabled Johnson, "gives all the appearances of a civil war within a civil war."[151] The bombing of North Vietnam that Bundy had urged as a way to avert Saigon's political collapse appeared, on the scene, more necessary than ever. On the third day of Bundy's visit, the Vietcong attacked a U.S. air base near Pleiku in the Central Highlands near the Laotian and Cambodian borders about 240 miles north of Saigon. Eight American servicemen died and over a hundred suffered injuries. The Vietcong had attacked other American targets in recent months—Bien Hoa Air Base in November and the Brinks Hotel in December—without American reprisals. But Pleiku afforded an occasion to begin bombing.

Johnson now moved quickly. He convened a meeting with congressional leaders in the Cabinet Room. "We have kept our gun over the mantel and our shells in the cupboard for a long time now," Johnson said, and the time had come to act. The president's forcefulness silenced most of those present—but not Mansfield. Looking straight at Johnson across the Cabinet table as he puffed on his pipe, the senator cautioned that, even if Hanoi had directed the attack, it should have "opened many eyes." "The local populace in South Vietnam is not behind us," Mansfield warned, or "else the Vietcong could not have carried out their surprise attack." He urged Johnson to weigh this fact carefully, because the beginning of bombing meant that America would no longer be "in a penny ante game." Johnson heard Mansfield out, then ordered a reprisal air strike against North Vietnam.[152]

Late the next evening, Bundy arrived back in Washington with a report he had written in the dimly lit cabin of an air force transport plane high above the Pacific Ocean. Bundy went straight to the White House with this eight-page document and delivered it personally to Johnson, who read it before he went to bed that night. Bundy's report aimed at turning the reprisal air strike into a sustained bombing campaign. "The situation in South Vietnam is deteriorating," Bundy opened, "and without new U.S. action defeat appears inevitable." South Vietnam's problems were grave, he argued, because of the American interests intertwined with them. "The stakes in Vietnam are extremely high. The American investment is very large, and American responsibility is a fact of life which is palpable in the atmosphere of Asia, and even elsewhere. The international prestige of the United States, and a substantial part of our influence, are directly at risk in Vietnam." Given this, Bundy dismissed the idea of a negotiated withdrawal, which he termed "surrender on the installment plan," and a policy of graduated and sustained bombing of North Vietnam seemed to him "the most promising" option. "Our primary target," he stressed, "is the improvement of the situation in *South* Vietnam." He also hoped the new strategy would affect the North's will, moving them to reduce their support of the Vietcong and/or negotiate. But even if the bombing failed, Bundy wrote the president, "the policy will be worth it": "At a minimum, it will damp down the charge that we did not do all that we could have done, and this charge will be important in many countries, including our own." Here, in different language, was Johnson's own concern, that bombing, whatever its limitations, would offer protection against conservative attacks in the wake of a South Vietnamese collapse. Bundy ended his report with a plea for presidential frankness. "At its very best the struggle in Vietnam will be long," he wrote. Therefore, "it seems important," he concluded, "that this fundamental fact and our understanding of it be made clear to our own people." Bundy urged Johnson to acknowledge the costs of escalation in order to win and maintain the American people's support.[153]

Bundy presented his report at a meeting attended by congressional leaders the next day, February 8. Johnson opened the gathering by saying he had decided to implement a program of "further pressure" against North Vietnam. But rather than describe bombing as Bundy had described it to him—an "extensive and costly" expansion of the war entailing "higher and more visible" American casualties—Johnson characterized it to congressional leaders as an effort to defeat North Vietnamese aggression "without escalating the war." His vagueness prompted the House minority leader, Republican Gerald Ford of Michigan, to ask Johnson exactly what he intended to do. Vietcong attacks called for a "response," Johnson replied, but he did not intend to limit his actions to a single act of retribution, vaguely implying a policy of sustained bombing. The Senate minority leader, Republican Everett Dirksen of Illinois, asked Johnson what he could tell the press. Johnson had agreed to begin bombing, but in order to limit its impact on his domestic agenda and avert hard-line pressure for even greater military action that might trigger Chinese intervention, he decided to conceal its dimensions and he urged Dirksen not to say that Washington was "broadening the war." Once again, short-term considerations negated attention to ultimate costs—in this case, the consequences of not leveling with Congress and the American people about deeper U.S. involvement.[154]

After wavering for several more weeks, Johnson finally gave the order to commence the sustained bombing of North Vietnam in late February. The long-contemplated air campaign against Hanoi, codenamed ROLLING THUNDER, began with a hundred-plane raid on March 2. The bombers that roared over the seventeenth parallel dividing North and South Vietnam that day symbolized a deeper crossing for the United States. Johnson had committed America to direct participation in the war—something that Truman, Eisenhower, and Kennedy had never done. It marked a fateful step. "Once the bombers were sent north," recalled Bundy's NSC aide Chester Cooper, "there was no turning back."[155]

The American people strongly supported the move at first: 83 percent approved of the air strikes and 69 percent favored bombing North Vietnam in order to prevent South Vietnam's collapse—even though 58 percent believed bombing might provoke Chinese intervention. Americans' strong support for military action reflected the importance they attached to the U.S. commitment to South Vietnam, which a majority of respondents considered necessary "to win victory over aggression" (56 percent); "to defend the security of the United States" (63 percent); and "to keep the Communists from taking over all of Southeast Asia" (79 percent). Against these results, Johnson actually seemed *more* reluctant than most of his countrymen to deepen America's involvement in Vietnam. His hesitancy, in fact, explained much of the public's earlier dissatisfaction with his policy. Before Pleiku, Johnson's approval rating on Vietnam had hovered at 41 percent; after the air strikes began, the figure jumped to 60 percent.[156] "I am far more afraid of the right wing than I am of the left wing," Johnson had confessed to an aide. To deputy secretary of state George Ball he remarked, "George, don't pay attention to what those little shits on the campuses do. The great beast is the reactionary elements in this country. Those are the people we have to fear."[157] The poll results seemed to confirm his anxiety—and quantify the wisdom of his choice.

Johnson's decision to begin bombing North Vietnam had been slow and agonizing but once made, it unleashed unexpected consequences with frightening alacrity. Taylor, McNamara, and Bundy had endorsed bombing because they believed it would prevent the need for U.S. troops. But even before ROLLING THUNDER began, General William Westmoreland requested two Marine battalions* to protect the U.S. air base at Danang. Westmoreland had replaced Harkins as MACV commander the year before. Born in South Carolina, where the Confederacy's martial ethic endured long after the Civil War, he settled on a military career as a boy. He had checked all of the traditional boxes for promotion to the army's highest ranks: first captain of cadets at West Point, combat command during World War II and Korea, graduate study at Harvard Business School, leadership of the fabled 101st Airborne Division, superintendent of the United States Military Academy. Tall and ramrod straight, with a square, jutting jaw, he looked handsome,

---

* A battalion is a military unit consisting of 300 to 800 soldiers. A brigade is composed of 3 to 6 battalions—approximately 3,200 to 5,500 troops. A division is composed of several brigades, usually between 10,000 and 20,000 soldiers.

William Westmoreland
Yoichi Okamoto/LBJ Library

spoke well, and understood how to relate to civilian authority. He projected the perfect image of a strong and decisive military leader, and if he lacked the brilliance of a Douglas MacArthur, whose insubordinate challenge to Washington's limited war policy in Korea had led to his dismissal by President Truman in the spring of 1951, he also lacked the towering ego and political ambition that had led to so much trouble. Johnson had chosen Westmoreland to lead MACV on McNamara's and Taylor's recommendations. He seemed a safe choice, not a troublemaker, someone who would grasp the president's problems and would not go public with any complaint. (He had "neither Patton's boastful flamboyance nor LeMay's stubbornness," in McNamara's words.[158]) Westmoreland worked hard, played by the rules, and went by the book. "Duty, Honor, Country" meant something real to him. He was a team player—a quality greatly valued in the military—who understood his place in the chain-of-command. Plainspoken and optimistic, Westmoreland epitomized American values, among them confidence and certainty. Westmoreland had both when it came to considering his own talents. ("He never got over being first captain of cadets," observed a fellow West Pointer who knew Westmoreland well.[159]) More a good leader than a great intellect, he thought and acted in predictable and conventional ways, and he saw the war as he had been trained and taught: as a military rather than a political struggle, and a conventional one at that. As a result, Westmoreland believed the key to military success in Vietnam lay in targeting the enemy's main-force units and destroying them; winning the hearts and minds of the South Vietnamese people took a distant second place. Like most other American officials, he would vastly underestimate Hanoi's and the Vietcong's will to fight, to endure punishment, to replace their losses, and to sustain the war effort despite massive suffering and hardship.

Although there were 23,000 U.S. advisors in South Vietnam by the spring of 1965, their mission remained unchanged from the first arrivals in the 1950s: to assist and train ARVN to fight its own war against the Vietcong. They were not allowed to engage in combat. Westmoreland now wished to introduce American combat forces, albeit in a defensive role—something Johnson and his advisors had sought to avoid. In their downcast longing to save South Vietnam without committing American troops, they had adopted a course that quickly and unexpectedly generated demands for just that. During the many months they had contemplated bombing, they had never considered what consequences might flow from it, other than the very linear "we bomb, they retreat" variety. They had not even considered basic logistics, such as a need for troops to protect the airfields from which bombing missions would be flown. Had they done so, McNamara later observed, it "might have influenced our decisions with respect to the initial deployments."[160]

When Taylor learned of Westmoreland's request, he immediately cabled Washington advising against it. "Such action would be a step in reversing the long-standing policy of avoiding the commitment of ground combat forces to South Vietnam," he wrote. "Once this policy is breached, it will be very difficult to hold the line."

These were strong words coming from a retired four-star general and former chairman of the Joint Chiefs of Staff. McNamara also felt uneasy about Westmoreland's request. "This is a recommendation that I would be very reluctant to accept," he told Johnson, "but frankly I doubt we have any alternative." It was a revealing statement. In the past, Taylor's and McNamara's warnings would have been decisive. But a line had been crossed, and now the voice of the commander in the field was a substantial counterweight. Westmoreland had direct responsibility for the lives of American boys in South Vietnam, and he had tied the security of U.S. personnel to approval of his troop request. Had not Johnson already approved the bombing, whose planes and pilots Westmoreland now sought to protect? "I'm scared to death of putting ground forces in," Johnson told McNamara, "but I'm more frightened about losing a bunch of planes from lack of security."[161] Again, Johnson's fear overrode his caution.

Although no student of war, Johnson possessed keen intuition. The shifting dynamics shocked and frightened him, and he had an uneasy feeling about what lay ahead. "I think everybody's going to think, 'We're landing the Marines. We're off to battle,'" he confided to his old mentor, Senator Russell. "Of course, if they come [in] there, [the chiefs] are going to get them in a fight—just sure as hell. They're not going to run. Then [we're] tied down. If they don't [go in] though, and [the Vietcong] ruin those airplanes, everybody is going to give me hell for not securing them." Russell sympathized with Johnson's predicament, but offered him no solution. "We've gone so damned far, Mr. President, it scares the life out of me. But I don't know how to back up now. It looks to me like we just got in this thing, and there's no way out. We're just getting pushed forward and forward and forward and forward and forward." "That is exactly right," Johnson lamented.[162] Later the same day he told McNamara, "All right, we'll just go with it." Ensnared by his approval of the bombing and lacking the self-confidence to trust his instincts, Johnson felt compelled to grant the request. "We know what we're walking into, and rather than have it said, 'We wanted protection for our planes—you wouldn't give it to us,' my answer is yes. But my judgment is no."[163] Yet having taken the big step to begin bombing, Johnson felt locked on a perilous course.

On the morning of March 8, 1965, a flotilla of amphibious landing craft slowly chugged toward "Nam O" Beach on the western rim of crescent-shaped Danang Bay. The landing craft, struggling against stiff winds and rough surf, carried the first American ground troops to the Asian mainland since the end of the Korean War twelve years earlier. The young marines aboard the transports, dressed in full battle gear with fresh faces full of optimism, determination, and vigor, splashed ashore as if reenacting the legendary landing on Iwo Jima two decades before. But instead of hostile enemy troops, on this occasion the marines encountered only a cordial welcoming committee. Local South Vietnamese officials hailed their arrival. Danang's mayor had mobilized a bevy of pretty young Vietnamese women wearing close-fitting silk *áo dài* tunics, who showered the newcomers with garlands of yellow dahlias and red gladiolas. Spectators silently watched the spectacle beneath darkening skies. An elderly Vietnamese villager muttered, "Ah, the French are back."[164]

The marine deployment to Danang marked an immediately invisible but crucial turning point. Up to this time, civilians had dominated policy, controlling the direction and pace of decision-making on the war. Now that began to change. Once the first American combat troops splashed ashore, the initiative implicitly but ineluctably shifted toward the military. The long-standing taboo against committing American ground forces to South Vietnam, once breeched—however slightly—broke an important psychological barrier and began generating powerful pressures for more troops. Suddenly, with almost natural inevitability, the military began setting the agenda and the terms of debate. Once combat troops had been committed, there was no such thing as being a little pregnant. This shift unsettled civilians accustomed to their privileged perch, throwing them back on their heels and on the defensive, forcing them to respond to the demands of the generals, whom even Taylor from his far-away post in Saigon could not stop now. None of this had been anticipated by Johnson and his advisors. Instead they were skidding toward the sobering realization that wars generate their own momentum and are governed by the iron law of unexpected and unintended consequences.

The first sign of this appeared within days of the Danang landing. Westmoreland had initially proposed using two marine battalions—3,500 men—in patrol sweeps around the air base. Johnson and his advisors had rejected his proposal, restricting the marines to static defense. But base security quickly evolved into an enclave strategy that enabled the marines to fight up to fifty miles from the air base. Then, barely a week after their arrival, Westmoreland cabled Washington asking for more troops. He wanted another battalion to protect the air base at Phú Bài. Around the same time, the army chief of staff, General Harold K. Johnson, returned from South Vietnam with a recommendation to increase the American military effort there substantially. General Johnson urged intensifying the bombing of North Vietnam, creating an anti-infiltration force along the demilitarized zone below the seventeenth parallel, and deploying an army division—16,000 men—in the Central Highlands. General Westmoreland's and General Johnson's requests marked the beginning of a ceaseless campaign by the military for ever more troops.[*] The door had been unlocked, and now the military was leaning hard against it.

On March 20, the chiefs submitted their own request that upped the ante still further: two combat divisions—40,000 men—to Vietnam. This juggernaut of demands shocked officials in Washington. Bombing had been underway for less than a month, and already the military had submitted three troop requests, each one bigger than the one before it. The process resembled sand falling through an overturned hourglass, a scattering of grains quickly becoming a cascade. Unprepared for what was happening, civilian

---

[*] This push would continue, and intensify, for three years, until by early 1968 the number of American troops in Vietnam had reached nearly 550,000. The breaking point came when the military asked for another 205,000 more during the Tet Offensive in February of that year.

leaders did not know how to slow down or control the process once it got started. Events were beginning to get away from them. The president and his inner circle had hardly discussed whether to send combat troops, and already the discussion had become how many.

Now that Washington had crossed the threshold of war, the military began to push full throttle. Their logic was simple and inescapable (in their opinion): in for a penny, in for a pound, and if you resorted to force, you used maximum force. They absolutely did not want to relive the frustrations of the "no-win" policy of the Korean War, with its limited objectives and restrictions. That meant a heavy bombing campaign, up front, to prevent the North Vietnamese from dispersing their resources and committing as many American troops as necessary to do the job as quickly as possible to prevent the enemy from adapting to the increased military presence. General Johnson and his team also knew that speed was key on the home front. Putting the country on a war footing meant mobilizing the reserves[*] and increasing draft calls[†] in order to drive home the seriousness of the endeavor and the imperative of shared sacrifice—support of which would be eroded as American casualties increased.

Johnson and his advisors had anticipated or prioritized little of this. As noted, their goal was not to win the war as quickly (and ruthlessly) as possible, but to prevent the loss of South Vietnam through "controlled escalation"—slow and carefully measured increases in military pressure—in the belief this would logically persuade Hanoi that its costs exceeded its potential gains, thus averting a war with China that might draw in the Soviet Union and trigger a nuclear World War III. But there was no such thing as a rational application of power that would control events in Vietnam, and civilian and military leaders' unwillingness to candidly share their

---

[*] Mobilizing the reserves, a force of men who had civilian jobs and families that would be disrupted by their call-up, would make the impact of the war felt far more acutely in neighborhoods and communities throughout the country.

[†] The U.S. government had instituted the draft (Selective Service) on the eve of Pearl Harbor in 1941. It remained in effect until repealed in 1973 as a result of popular antipathy generated by the Vietnam War.

fears and expectations with one another only made matters worse. This fundamental conflict in goals generated friction and resentment between the two groups that would intensify over time as the war dragged on and U.S. casualties mounted.

Vietnam has been used as a great example of asymmetric warfare, yet in a stark sense a similar inversion had just happened far from Southeast Asia. Constitutionally, Johnson commanded the military and it thus was mandated to follow his agenda. But his own psychological constitution—his emotional disposition and makeup—had allowed the generals enormous leverage and, eventually, control. He could scarcely imagine what had been set in motion or what was to come; he thought his worst nightmare—a war with China "that would start World War III"—meant "I'd have to send three or four hundred thousand men there."[165] Still, the prospect of more than a half million American troops fighting the Vietcong and the North Vietnamese alone—what came to pass by the beginning of 1968—would have seemed absurd to him in the spring of 1965, despite his mounting dread. His vice president, Hubert Humphrey, confided to a Democratic senator that spring that "there are people . . . [in] the Pentagon who want to send *three hundred thousand* men out there." Humphrey paused. "The President will *never* get sucked into anything like *that*."[166] And yet, he would.

It soon became apparent that bombing had not stiffened South Vietnamese morale, nor had it curtailed North Vietnamese infiltration, and it had not forced Hanoi to the bargaining table. Whatever results bombing might yield, it now seemed they would take some time to achieve. In the meantime, how to shore up South Vietnam's declining fortunes if not with more American troops? The chiefs certainly felt this way. At a White House meeting on April 1, JCS chairman Wheeler stressed the urgency of the situation— "We are losing the war out there"—and pressed Johnson to approve the chiefs' two-division proposal. Rusk, McNamara, and Bundy all questioned the wisdom of the request. Resentment of foreigners lay just beneath the surface in South Vietnam, they said, and committing large numbers of American troops risked bringing it to the surface in potentially disastrous ways. Sharing their concern, an almost totally paralyzed Johnson deflected the chiefs' proposal, but he agreed to Westmoreland's two-battalion request and, more important, to change the marines' mission from base security to active combat. The troop numbers had been moderated, but their mission had been changed aggressively. He also agreed to pave the way for future deployments by approving the dispatch of a logistics command and an engineering battalion construction group. Johnson thought he had held the line, but in fact he had made crucial concessions with fateful consequences in the months to come.[167] He had parried the chiefs' larger force proposal, but given up something tremendous to the chiefs in return.

Approving the first troop request created a subtle but powerful psychological dynamic that made it harder for Johnson to deny subsequent approaches in order to remain consistent with his initial approval. People desire to maintain consistency between their past and future actions. Research on the foot-in-the-door (FITD) effect has demonstrated that individuals are significantly more likely to comply with a large request after they have first agreed to a small request. In an experiment conducted only a year after Johnson received the chiefs' request, a group of stay-at-home mothers were contacted by telephone to answer a brief survey about their household kitchen items. Only 22.2 percent agreed to participate. Three days later, those who had participated in the survey were presented with a larger, more intrusive request—to allow someone to come into their home to catalog all of the items in their kitchen cabinets—and 52.8 percent agreed to the second, larger request.[168] Self-consistency and the FITD effect mean that engaging in an initial act of support for a cause leads to an increased propensity to make further contributions to the cause, particularly on the part of individuals connected publicly with support of that cause.[169] Johnson now found himself entrapped in such a dynamic with the chiefs.

The April 1 meeting also exposed a growing split within the government over bombing, which had been underway barely a month. Johnson's agreement to commit more U.S. troops to the

South and to change their mission—without at the same time increasing air strikes—troubled CIA director John McCone. ROLLING THUNDER had failed to appreciably curtail Hanoi's infiltration of men and supplies into the South. Unless Washington intensified the bombing, McCone argued, sending more American troops would prove futile. "In effect," he wrote in a memo to the troika the next day, "we will find ourselves mired down in a combat effort that we cannot win, and from which we will have extreme difficulty in extracting ourselves."[170] Many in the military agreed with McCone; the air force and navy had been advocating "will-breaking" strikes against North Vietnam for more than a year. But neither McCone nor the air force nor the navy could define what it would take to break Hanoi's will, and the troika doubted that bombing ever would—short of a nearly genocidal bombardment that might well trigger Chinese intervention.

This fear of crossing the "flash point"—of sparking, through heavy bombing, a direct confrontation between the nuclear superpowers—constantly worried Johnson. "In the dark at night," he later recalled, "I would lay awake picturing my boys flying around North Vietnam, asking myself an endless series of questions: What if one of those targets you picked today triggers off Russia or China? What happens then?"[171] Hindsight validated Johnson's concern. He and his advisors did not know it at the time, but Beijing had pledged support troops* and war materiel to Hanoi, grudgingly opened its railroads to the transit of Soviet weaponry and supplies for North Vietnam, and secretly promised Hanoi that if the United States invaded North Vietnam, it would intervene with combat forces (as it had done during the Korean War).[172] Mao saw aid to North Vietnam as a response to what he perceived as American encirclement of China. He also believed Communist success in Vietnam would prevent the United States from moving

---

* Chinese engineering troops constructed anti-aircraft batteries, built and rebuilt roads and airfields, and stored massive amounts of ammunition in caves invulnerable to American bombing. As many as 300,000 Chinese eventually served in North Vietnam. A. J. Langguth, *Our Vietnam: The War, 1954–1975* (Simon & Schuster, 2000), pp. 374–375.

closer to China's southern border. Unlike the military, which with its own limited mindset and priorities preoccupied itself with the operational theater immediately at hand (Southeast Asia),* Johnson and his civilian advisors necessarily weighed broader concerns, including America's global security and protection of the homeland from nuclear attack. These different perspectives would become a source of growing disagreement in the years ahead as American casualties increased the pressure to ratchet up the air assault against North Vietnam.

The generals moved quickly to exploit Johnson's decision. Within days, Westmoreland and the chiefs peppered the White House with a flurry of still more troop requests. On April 10, the chiefs requested another two-brigade deployment. The next day, Westmoreland renewed his bid for an army division, while seconding the chiefs' two-brigade proposal. The two battalions approved by Johnson had yet to arrive in South Vietnam, and already the generals told him they wanted thirteen more. Johnson's predicament now included not only the military's increased voice in policy councils but the political sensitivity of his dealings with the generals. He grew "scared of what Wheeler and Westmoreland could do to him," noted Richard Neustadt, a Harvard political scientist who knew Johnson well and advised him throughout his presidency.[173] Having put U.S. troops directly at risk, Johnson now found himself compelled to constantly feed mouths he had seated at the table.

This became apparent when McNamara and senior military leaders gathered in Honolulu on April 20 for a conference to discuss future troop commitments. The men sat at a large conference table beneath a bank of clocks in the cavernous War Room at the navy's Pacific Command headquarters. Outside, through enormous picture windows, spread a panoramic view of Pearl Harbor, where America's isolationist illusions had been shattered on a Sunday morning in December 1941. The setting seemed an eerily ironic

---

* The military either did not think China would intervene on North Vietnam's behalf or had not considered what to do if it did.

one, for this day's conference on Vietnam would shatter the increasingly brittle belief held by McNamara and other civilians that they could hold back the surging tide of troop requests. Indeed, the decisions and forecasts agreed to at this conference dramatically confirmed this trend, marking the beginning of a long slide toward a major American combat commitment with no clear strategy in mind and no upper limit in sight, though the decision-makers lacked awareness of this threshold at the time.

In many ways, this ignorance was predictable. People are less sensitive to gradual rather than rapid change and often fail to notice when a threshold is crossed bit by bit rather than in one abrupt move. Researchers call this "creeping normality"—the way a major change may be accepted if it happens slowly, in increments, when it would be regarded as objectionable if it happened rapidly in a single step. UCLA geographer Jared Diamond used this concept to explain why Easter Islanders would, seemingly irrationally, chop down the last tree on their island: "Gradually trees became fewer, smaller, and less important. By the time the last fruit-bearing adult palm tree was cut, palms had long since ceased to be of economic significance. That left only smaller and smaller palm saplings to clear each year, along with other bushes and treelets. No one would have noticed the felling of the last small palm."[174] Insensitivity to changes occurring at a slow pace, combined with their failure to anticipate the implications of those changes, had led policymakers little by little into accepting what they had sought to avoid: a major American troop commitment. "We were on a slippery slope," McNamara admitted, looking back—and they had helped grease it.[175]

Taylor, McNamara, and Bundy not only underestimated the pressures that bombing would generate, they also overestimated the results it would produce. Bombing had not reduced North Vietnamese infiltration—it had increased—nor had bombing coerced Hanoi to the bargaining table. North Vietnamese leaders had no intention of pursuing negotiations at the moment.[176] Hanoi sensed a growing advantage in the South, which steeled its determination to withstand whatever pressure was inflicted by American air strikes.

As bombing would not do the job alone, the war in the South

assumed decisive importance. The Honolulu Conference participants agreed that what happened in the South would determine
the outcome of the war, but ARVN continued to languish, losing
more soldiers to desertions and more territory to the Vietcong—
compounding the pressure for more U.S. troops. As the troop requests increased, so did the pressure on civilian leaders to accept
at least some of them. All of this led McNamara at the end of the
conference to endorse a marked increase in U.S. forces—from
33,000 advisors to 82,000 combat troops. This vault transformed
Washington's relationship to the war. It not only increased America's dangers and responsibilities but meant inevitably higher casualties and closer public attention to the conflict. When McNamara
returned to Washington the next day, he urged Johnson to inform
Congress and the American people about the pending deployments and the change in mission of U.S. forces. To do otherwise,
he implied, courted serious trouble in the future.[177]

Johnson accepted McNamara's recommendation about troops
because it moderated the military's larger requests he feared while
forestalling the South Vietnamese collapse he dreaded. But he did
not follow his defense secretary's advice about candidly explaining
his decision to Congress and the American people. Johnson had his
Great Society legislation moving—the historic Voting Rights Act
neared completion in the Senate—and he did not want Congress being aroused about Vietnam in a way that might endanger passage.
During a press conference on April 27, a reporter asked Johnson
about whispers of impending escalation. "Mr. President," he asked,
"could there be circumstances in which large numbers of American
troops might be engaged in the fighting of the war rather than in
the advising and assistance to the South Vietnamese?" "Our purpose in Vietnam," Johnson replied, "is to advise and assist these people in resisting aggression." He neglected any mention of the new
combat mission or the 50,000 additional forces.[178] Journalists got
wind of the changes nonetheless; the increased American military
presence in South Vietnam could not be missed. Less than a month
later, for the first time a major American newspaper, the *New York
Herald-Tribune*, alluded to Johnson's emerging "credibility gap."[179]

Nguyễn Cao Kỳ and Nguyễn Văn Thiệu
RBM Vintage Images/Alamy Stock Photo
Everett Collection/Alamy Stock Photo

Johnson feared conservative pressures, but he was beginning to provoke liberal criticism that would intensify dramatically over the next three years. What people really fear is not always what most endangers them.

The month of May witnessed a host of new troubles in South Vietnam. Another military coup brought a pair of politically ambitious young generals to power: Nguyễn Văn Thiệu* and Nguyễn Cao Kỳ. "People ask me who my heroes are," Kỳ told an interviewer. "I have only one—Hitler. I admire Hitler because he pulled his

---

* Thiệu became president (number one) and Kỳ premier (number two). Thiệu would eventually force Kỳ from power and rule unopposed until the country's collapse in 1975.

country together. But the situation is so desperate now that one man would not be enough." He went further: "We need four or five Hitlers in Vietnam," Kỳ said. Such comments reinforced the image of the new leaders, in the understated words of one South Vietnamese observer, as "individuals with no discernible concept of government." To officials in Washington like William Bundy, they were evidence that South Vietnamese politics had hit "the bottom of the barrel, absolutely the bottom of the barrel."

Meanwhile the southwestern monsoons began, pelting the Indochina Peninsula with heavy rains from the Gulf of Thailand and grounding air operations. The Vietcong seized the opportunity to launch assaults on an unprecedented scale. Bigger and better equipped than ever, they began defeating undermanned, illtrained, and poorly led ARVN battalions with frightening speed, inflicting alarming losses along the way. These setbacks only prompted the chiefs to urge prosecuting the war even more vigorously. On a tour of South Vietnam, Marine Corps commandant Wallace Greene told reporters that the "Marines' mission is to kill Vietcong." "They can't do it sitting on their ditty boxes," he said, "I told them to find the Vietcong and kill 'em. That's the way to carry out their mission." And Ambassador Taylor, who six months before had pressed Johnson to begin bombing, cabled Washington that "we should like to make very clear that we do not believe that any feasible amount of bombing . . . is of itself likely to cause the DRV [North Vietnam] to cease and desist its actions in the south. Such a change in DRV attitudes can probably be brought about only when there is also a conviction on their part that the tide has turned or soon will turn against them in the south." A charter member of the military's "never-again club" who had warned repeatedly against committing American troops to the fight, Taylor now reversed himself, since he had no expectation the tide would turn if things continued to be left up to ARVN and the South Vietnamese government. Taylor's about-face vividly illustrated how events had overwhelmed the calculations and expectations of those who might have been expected to have the greatest acumen, leading them to abandon their doubts and reservations and embrace a step that they had resisted for years.[180]

A bombshell hit Washington on June 7 in the form of a telegram from Westmoreland. "Of the thousands of cables I received during my seven years in the Defense Department," McNamara later wrote, "this one disturbed me most."[181] Arriving in the Message Room of the Pentagon's National Military Command Center at 3:35 A.M., Westmoreland's message was clear and troubling: the Communist monsoon offensive, gathering strength for weeks, now threatened "to destroy government forces." Although the Vietcong had committed only two of nine regiments to battle, he warned that the ARVN was "already experiencing difficulty in coping with this increased VC capability." Desertion rates had reached "inordinately high" levels and "the steadfastness under fire" of South Vietnamese troops "is coming into doubt." The Vietcong were grinding ARVN units faster than they could be replaced, and had South Vietnamese forces running. "The GVN [Government of South Vietnam] cannot stand up to this kind of pressure without reinforcement," Westmoreland told Washington. He perceived no alternative "except to reinforce SVN with additional U.S. forces." In addition to the thirteen American battalions already committed to South Vietnam, he urged deploying nineteen more. These additions would increase American strength to 175,000 troops. Instead of a "defensive posture," he wished to "take the war to the enemy," for which "even greater forces" might be required. His request effectively meant an open-ended Americanization of the war.[182]

Johnson met with his advisors the next morning to discuss Westmoreland's message. The inexorable pressure of events had become palpable. McNamara captured the mood in the Oval Office when he confessed, "We're in a hell of a mess." George Ball wondered aloud, "Is this the French result?"—the beginning of America's own long and futile Indochina war. "Can you stop it?" Johnson muttered.[183] "The momentum was formidable," said Ball, looking back.[184] Each small troop decision Johnson had made since late February had led to another, bigger troop decision, and now he confronted a potentially unlimited commitment. He had crossed the Rubicon months ago with the bombing, and only now did he recognize the full force of pressures unleashed by that decision. Johnson lamented the consequences in a phone conversation with Mike Mansfield that night. "I'm no military man," he told Mansfield, "but if they get a hundred and fifty [thousand American troops], they'll have to have another hundred and fifty. And then they'll have to have another hundred and fifty . . . I know what the military wants to do." He felt trapped in a dilemma of his own making. "Where do you stop?" Mansfield asked him. "You don't," Johnson replied. "To me, it's shaping up like this, Mike—you either get out or you get *in*." It was the same stark choice he had confronted six months earlier, but now it would be infinitely harder to choose the first option.[185]

Mansfield sent Johnson two memos the next day. In them, he beseeched Johnson to resist "pressures for an irreversible extension of the war." Now was the moment, for "the rate of commitment is accelerating," he noted, "and a course once set in motion, as you know, often develops its own momentum and rationale whatever the initial intentions." Mansfield felt that course flowed directly from Johnson's earlier bombing decision—a decision urged on him by Taylor, McNamara, and Bundy. "I think it is about time you got an accounting from those who have pressured you in the past to embark on this course and continue to pressure you to stay on it . . . What was promised by the initial extension of the war in the air over the North? And what, in fact, has it produced to date?" The disparity should give Johnson pause. Mansfield closed by urging him to approve "the minimum military effort necessary to hold the situation in the South from falling apart altogether and a maximum initiative on our part to get this whole sorry business to a conference table as soon as possible."[186]

Mansfield's memos hit a nerve. When McNamara at a meeting the next day urged Johnson to explain his Vietnam policy more fully to the American people, Johnson retorted defensively with bitter sarcasm. "*His* reason for going North," he said, gesturing toward McNamara, "was to save morale in the South." McNamara

said nothing.[187] McNamara had grown frustrated by Johnson's indecision while Johnson had become irritated by what he considered McNamara's poor advice. Their frustration with each other
paled, however, in comparison to their shared anxiety about the
potential extent of American involvement. "I have a very definite
limitation on the commitment [of U.S. ground troops] in mind,"
McNamara told Johnson by phone that evening. "I don't think the
Chiefs do. In fact, I *know* they don't." "Do you think that this is
just the next step with them up the ladder?" Johnson asked. "Yes.
They hope they don't have to go any further. But Westmoreland
outlines in his cable the step beyond it. And he doesn't say that's
the last." "I don't guess anybody knows," said Johnson nervously.
McNamara agreed, then said, "I'm inclined to think that unless
we're really willing to go to a full potential land war we've got to
slow down here and try to halt, at some point, the ground troop
commitment." The dogs of war had been let loose months ago,
but McNamara believed—or wanted to believe—he still had them
on a tight leash. Johnson had no such illusions. "Not a damn human thinks that 50,000 or 100,000 or 150,000 are going to end that
war," Johnson moaned to McNamara. "We're not getting out," he
insisted with stubborn defiance, then dolefully added, "We're trying to hold what we got."[188]

Johnson decided to commission a secret poll gauging the American public's reaction to larger deployments. The confidential
survey revealed an astonishingly hawkish public. Although U.S.
involvement in the war had expanded considerably, Johnson's
popularity remained extraordinarily high: 69 percent. So did his
handling of Vietnam: respondents supported his policy 65 to 35
percent. The most striking results, however, concerned additional
troops. A heavy plurality, 47 percent, favored sending more—
double those not sure (23 percent), two and a half times those
wishing to keep the present number (19 percent), and more than
quadruple those wanting to take troops out (just 11 percent).[189]
These figures indicated strong support for further action. But they
also indicated deep division over the war—a conclusion Johnson

could not miss. He stressed this point to McNamara a few days later. "It's going to be difficult for us to prosecute a war that far away from home with the divisions we have" in the United States, Johnson accurately predicted. "I'm very depressed about it because I see no program from either Defense or State that gives me much hope of doing anything except just praying and gasping to hold on and hope they'll quit." But "I don't believe they're ever going to quit and I don't see any plan for victory—either militarily or diplomatically."[190] As before, Johnson felt trapped.

The gathering force of events carried along McNamara, too. He had initially been cool to Westmoreland's request. But the ARVN's recent spectacular losses—the Vietcong had annihilated three South Vietnamese battalions and killed nearly 1,000 ARVN soldiers in a massive assault—jolted McNamara and compelled him to endorse Westmoreland's full request of 175,000 U.S. troops in 1965 and an undetermined number more in 1966. The collapsing situation in South Vietnam, combined with the rising tide of un-anticipated troop requests triggered by the bombing he had sold to Johnson, had decisively overwhelmed his long-standing opposition to an American combat commitment in Vietnam. "We were be-ing pushed by events," confessed McNamara, looking back.[191] Yet he and his colleagues had pushed events, too—just in a hazard-ous direction. This became clear during his phone conversation with Johnson on June 30. (Little more than a year and a half earlier, McNamara had aggressively lobbied a reluctant Kennedy to begin withdrawing American military advisors from South Vietnam.) "I don't see anything to do except give them what they need, Bob," said Johnson. "Do you?" "Mr. President, I'm very much of that frame of mind," McNamara replied. "I feel very strongly on that point . . . It is a very heavy risk, but that's my vote."[192]

At times of extreme stress Johnson could become strikingly angry, short-tempered, and morose. One morning in early July, his close aide Bill Moyers entered his bedroom in the family quarters of the White House and found Johnson lying in bed with the cov-ers pulled almost over his head. He told Moyers he felt as if he was in a Louisiana swamp "that's pulling me down." "I have the choice to go in with great casualty lists* or to get out with disgrace," he confided to Lady Bird shortly afterward. "It's like being in an airplane and I have to choose between crashing the plane or jumping out. I do not have a parachute."[193] "I'm pretty depressed," he told McNamara around the same time. "We know it's going to be bad."[194]

At a meeting on July 2, Johnson made clear he wanted to postpone making a decision on General Westmoreland's request until the end of the month—after Congress had voted on his Medicare and Voting Rights bills. He ordered McNamara to go to Saigon in mid-July to discuss specific numbers with Westmoreland and agree on a figure. McNamara met with Westmoreland in Saigon on July 16 and 17. The general told McNamara he wanted 175,000 troops by year's end and another 100,000 in 1966. He predicted that the additional U.S. troops would halt the losing trend by year's end, take the offensive during the first half of 1966, and defeat the enemy within a year to eighteen months (that is, before the 1968 election). McNamara returned to Washington on July 21 with a report recommending approval of Westmoreland's troop request, telling Johnson this course of action "stands a good chance of achieving an acceptable outcome within a reasonable time." McNamara knew this meant a major war, and he urged Johnson to frankly acknowledge its costs to Congress and the country by mobilizing reserves and national guardsmen, increasing conscription, extending tours of duty, and raising taxes.[195]

Johnson decided to review his choices before making a final decision. This review took place in an atmosphere of what cognitive scientists call "loss aversion": the tendency of people to become risk seeking when all their options are bad, as Johnson's certainly were. In such circumstances, people are more likely to accept a gamble than reject it. This imbalance between the power of pos-

---

* At this point in the war, fewer than 500 Americans had been killed in Vietnam. The number would grow to more than 58,000 by the end of U.S. involvement in 1973.

itive and negative expectations is illustrated in the following two experiments. In the first experiment, people were asked to choose between one of two options—a 50 percent chance to win $1,000 or a 100 percent chance to receive $500; a large majority of respondents preferred the sure thing. In the second experiment, people were asked to choose one of two options—a 50 percent chance to lose $1,000 or lose $500 for sure; a large majority of these respondents preferred to take the chance. "People are loss averse," notes Daniel Kahneman. "Losses loom larger than gains . . . In bad choices, where a sure loss is compared to a larger loss that is merely probable, diminishing sensitivity causes risk seeking."[196] Loss aversion was also at work during the 2017 debate over repeal of the Affordable Care Act (the national health insurance program popularly known as Obamacare). Although many Republican voters opposed the Affordable Care Act, Cornell University economist Robert Frank noted, these same voters feared losing their coverage even more.[197] This psychology of loss aversion and sensitivity to the disadvantages of changing policy[198] proved applicable to Johnson and his advisors as they deliberated on Vietnam in July 1965.

At a series of White House meetings over the next week, George Ball—supported by Clark Clifford—argued against escalation, warning that America faced a long and protracted struggle that it could not win and that would produce serious problems at home and abroad. Rather than repeat France's ordeal, Ball and Clifford urged Johnson to leave South Vietnam to its fate. The troika vigorously rebutted Ball and Clifford, arguing that the two underestimated the consequences of withdrawal and overestimated the difficulties of a larger military effort. Joining them against Ball and Clifford were the chiefs, Westmoreland, and a group of elder statesmen known as "the Wise Men"* whom Johnson had invited

---

* Dean Acheson; Omar Bradley, World War II infantry commander and first chairman of the JCS; John Cowles, liberal Republican publisher of the *Minneapolis Star and Tribune* and *Look* magazine; Arthur Dean, Eisenhower's negotiator during the Korean armistice talks in 1953; Roswell Gilpatric, McNamara's deputy defense secretary from 1961 to 1964; Paul Hoffman, wealthy industrialist and administrator of the Marshall Plan from 1948 to 1950; George Kistiakowsky, Harvard chemist,

to Washington in early July to examine the issue and share their judgment. "You can't sit there and have the Secretary of State, the Secretary of Defense, the National Security Assistant, and the Chairman of the Joint Chiefs go right down the line without getting the feeling that the current was running very strongly," said Clifford later. "The odds against the position we were taking were too great . . . There was so much inexorably pushing [Johnson] along this road."[199] It was a lopsided majority, and Johnson ultimately sided with this majority, despite his persistent anxieties, because, in his words, the fall of South Vietnam "would seem to be an irreparable blow" to America's credibility, world security, and—not least—his political standing and therefore the viability of his Great Society legislation. "Losing the Great Society was a terrible thought," he later told a biographer, "but not so terrible as the thought of being responsible for America's losing a war to the Communists. Nothing could possibly be worse than that." So, in the words of one of his advisors, Johnson finally decided "to put in his stack."[200]

Johnson consciously and deliberately underplayed his decision with the American people by revealing it to the nation and the world on July 28 at a midday news conference rather than in a prime-time speech before a joint session of Congress. Although he had authorized a substantial increase in American combat forces—from 75,000 to 225,000 by the end of 1966—he carefully obscured the magnitude of this increase, simply declaring, "I have today ordered to Vietnam certain forces which will raise our fighting strength from 75,000 to 125,000 men," vaguely adding, "Additional forces will be needed later and they will be sent as requested." Johnson also obscured the new, much greater and costlier U.S. combat involvement. When a reporter at the news conference asked him, "Does the fact that you are sending additional forces to Vietnam

---

Manhattan Project veteran, and Eisenhower's scientific advisor; Arthur Larson, Duke University law professor and counselor to Kennedy's and Johnson's State Departments; Robert Lovett; and John McCloy, former president of the World Bank and American proconsul in occupied postwar Germany.

imply any change in the existing policy?" Johnson answered, "It does not imply any change in policy whatever."[201] He also refused to call up the reserves to meet the enlarged troop requirements or to raise taxes to pay for the war.

In some ways, Johnson's obfuscation was consistent with two fundamental aspects of his character: his belief that the end justified the means and his instrumental view of facts. "Lyndon Johnson's view of the truth," McGeorge Bundy privately observed late in life, "was like a Boston trustee's view of capital—it's much too valuable ever to be used."[202] His equivocation also reflected a calculation of short-run goals rooted in three different motives. Given public support for increased American involvement, he worried that declaring the extent of the ramp-up would play into the hands of the hawks. "They'd pressure him to go further," McNamara recalled, "and he didn't want to do that."[203] He thus decided to play down the decision. Desiring to maintain what flexibility he could, he avoided an announcement that committed the United States to winning a ground war; a decision not acknowledged could be more easily reversed, he thought.[204] But the third and largest motive involved his desire to protect passage of his Great Society legislation, which had reached a critical juncture in its congressional odyssey. Speaking about Southern Democrats to friends that summer, he explained, "Those damn conservatives . . . hate this stuff, they don't want to help the poor and the Negroes . . . But the war—oh, they'll like the war. They'll take the war as their weapon. They'll be against my programs because of the war. I know what they'll say, they'll say they're not against it, not against the poor, but we have this job to do, beating the Communists. We beat the Communists first, then we can look around and maybe give something to the poor."[205] "I shuddered" to sound the tocsin of war that summer, he later admitted to McNamara, "because I thought they'd just murder the [Great Society] which then was in its final days up there in the Congress."[206]

Johnson remembered what his political idol, Franklin Roosevelt, had done at the time of World War II when he publicly sent away "Dr. New Deal" and called in "Dr. Win-the-War." So he misled—

not for sinister purposes but for a real and palpable reason: his vision for the country that he alluded to later during his July 28 news conference. "There is something else, too," Johnson told the nation after discussing Vietnam.

> When I was young, poverty was so common that we didn't know it had a name. An education was something that you had to fight for, and water was really life itself. I have been now in public life for 35 years, and in each of those 35 years I have seen good men, and wise leaders, struggle to bring the blessings of this land to all of our people. And now I am the President. It is now my opportunity to help every child get an education, to help every Negro and every American citizen have an equal opportunity, to have every family get a decent home, and to help bring healing to the sick and dignity to the old. As I have said before, that is what I have lived for, that is what I have wanted all my life since I was a little boy, and I do not want to see all those hopes and all those dreams of so many people for so many years now drowned in the wasteful ravages of cruel wars.[207]

His strategy bought him the political breathing room he wanted. Congress passed the Voting Rights Act and the Medicare Act—two cornerstones of his Great Society agenda—within weeks of his July 28 announcement, marking the climax of the most substantial legislative year of any president in history. But this short-term political triumph came at a dear long-term political price. By neglecting to secure the American people's informed consent of his Vietnam policy and thus their support for the human and financial sacrifices that policy would entail, Johnson's extraordinary feat of political legerdemain planted the seeds of failure by mortally jeopardizing both his trustworthiness and affirmative congressional (as well as public) support for the war. It was a serious and tragically self-defeating error. Fearful and vulnerable, Johnson could not bring himself—or felt he dare not allow himself—to share his really bad problem with the American people. His failure to level with them was poignant because it reflected deep-seated insecurity, but it was also poisonous because it violated a cardinal principle of politics: the reciprocal faith between president and public that is indispensable in a democracy. If a president decides to take the nation to war, he must tell the country so and explain why and how he is doing it—that is the essence of democratic leadership. It may be a tall order, but presidents must run the risk. Without popular support and the trust that goes with it, presidents are doomed to failure— as Lyndon Johnson would grievously discover.

CHAPTER 5

The Hazard of Sunk Costs

(August 1965–May 1967)

The United States crossed a divide with the deployment of American troops to Vietnam in the spring and summer of 1965. Lyndon Johnson and his advisors committed the country to war, expecting American military might to wear down the Communists and force them to the peace table. But the United States soon found itself waging a conflict in which a technologically sophisticated modern army got bogged down in a failing state trying to hold the line against cunning adversaries determined to sustain the fight for decades (a familiar theme in more recent wars as well). U.S. casualties began to increase as serious flaws in the American ground strategy and the bombing emerged. Rather than develop a different military strategy or lower the political objective and seek a negotiated exit in light of these serious flaws, Johnson and his advisors escalated the commitment. Looking back, McGeorge Bundy self-consciously and painfully wondered—like so many people have since: "Why did almost no one say, 'This is a loser; the best thing we can do is admit it and quit'?" After all, he went on, "If you are going to lose it is better not to take too long about it—better not to spend too much blood and treasure to achieve that defeat." Robert McNamara put it just as bluntly in hindsight: "The policy was failing and there was an unwillingness to accept it and to admit it and to act on it."[1] Johnson and his advisors did not do this because it would have required charging themselves with, and accepting, failure (in Asia, in Congress, at the ballot box, and, they presumed, in the eyes of history), whereas persisting meant increasing the potential magnitude of failure (in human lives and suffering, in American power, and in other nations' faith in Washington's judgment) but also, they hoped, left open the prospect of ultimate success that would justify the sunk costs in American blood, treasure, and prestige. Greater effort to turn the situation around seemed preferable to enduring a certain defeat, given the losses already sustained. Discouraged from questioning the broader trend toward deeper involvement without perceptible results and failing to think things through, the process became a tyranny of small decisions, each one building pressure and momentum for the next.

Common sense suggests that negative results will cause a change in one's course of action. But we all know people who throw good money after bad in the hope of recouping their original investment or at least postponing the day of reckoning.[2] Individuals and organizations often face the choice between committing more resources to make a costly course of action pay off, or cutting losses. When a person buys stock at $50 a share, then the price falls to $25 a share, does he continue to hold the stock he has (and perhaps buy more at a lower price) in hope of recouping, or sell and cut his losses? When a city government undertakes a transportation project estimated to take twenty years to complete at the cost of $10 billion, then cost overruns and time delays skyrocket, doubling the price and completion date of the project, does the city government abandon the project, or commit even more public funds in order to finish it? Such dilemmas further illustrate a counterintuitive phenomenon: the more invested people and organizations are in a failing course of action, often the more unwilling they are to give up and change their course of action.[3]

This is especially true when individuals feel personally responsible for the negative consequences of previous decisions. That is when, seemingly counterintuitively, they become locked in and commit the greatest amount of resources to an established course of action.[4] Escalated commitment occurs most often when feedback is negative, justification needs are high, and consequences are not easily changed.[5] As a participant in one behavioral study put it, "Once I had invested a certain amount, I had to keep going, otherwise all of that previous investment would have been a waste."[6] That costly mistake illustrates what behavioral scientists call the "sunk cost fallacy":[7] encumbered by damage resulting from previous decisions, people persuade themselves that if they just continue for a while, everything will turn out OK. Thus, awareness that one is in trouble does not always make escape easier—in fact, it can make escape more difficult.

Research corroborates that greater sunk costs in a failing endeavor increase the likelihood of persistence.[8] A prime example was the development of the supersonic Concorde passenger jetliner in the late 1960s and early 1970s. From the start, the Concorde proved far more expensive than anticipated, its financial viability very uncertain. Despite these facts, the French-British consortium Aérospatiale/British Aircraft Corporation (BAC) did not cancel the Concorde but instead invested substantially more money in the project. The original cost estimate had been £70 million; the final cost proved to be £1.3 billion—for only 14 planes. In the end, the extreme overrun forced the French and British governments to absorb a price tag that Aérospatiale/BAC could not afford.[9] The lesson is clear: "People who face very bad options take desperate gambles, accepting a high probability of making things worse in exchange for a small hope of avoiding a large loss . . . The thought of accepting the large sure loss is too painful and the hope of relief too enticing to make the sensible decision that it is time to cut losses."[10] Johnson and his advisors fell into this trap. Frustrated by setbacks and burdened by mounting American casualties, they responded to pressure from Westmoreland and the chiefs and their conservative allies in Congress by reaching for future results. Like gamblers desperate to recoup their losses—in this case, the precious coin of human lives—they pressed onward.

Other factors reinforced this dynamic: a reluctance, and in some an inability, to admit to themselves and others that the lives and resources already committed had been committed unwisely; a decision-making environment in which pressure from the military and the influence it wielded intensified as American involvement grew; the ad-hoc mentality of decision-makers under conditions of uncertainty and stress; and the fact that most people are not good at reasoning into the distant future and seeing what the end result will be. More often than commonly assumed (or comfortable to contemplate), decision-makers operate not as visionary strategists but as emergency responders to the latest fire alarm. The White House is a place where things come hard and fast and don't let up, despite staff support and paperwork. Pressed to solve immediate problems before they become crises, policy-makers often lack the time to question established policies and to notice evidence that prevailing assumptions cannot explain. "The picture that emerges," in the words of Richard Thaler and Cass Sunstein, "is one of busy people trying to cope in a complex world in which they cannot afford to think deeply about every choice they have to make . . . Because they are busy and have limited attention, they accept questions as posed rather than trying to determine whether their answers would vary under alternative formulations."[11]

The experience of one junior official during the Cuban Missile Crisis drives home the point. "During the Cuban missile crisis," he later wrote, "I was a member of two of the working groups under the ExComm [Executive Committee of the NSC]. One was the short-range group, which toward the end of the crisis was working on invasion plans two to three days away. The other, the long-range planning group, looked two weeks ahead. I used to say, when I mentioned the name of that group, that two weeks was 'long-range' for our normal operations, not only for crises, and that wasn't a joke."[12] Preoccupation with the problem of the moment can overtake and overshadow everything else, kicking in bounded rationality and creating pressures that inhibit thinking through the consequences of decisions and engaging in a careful exploration and thorough assessment of alternatives.[13] This tendency to maintain operating procedures impeded Johnson and his Vietnam advisors from viewing each troop decision as part of a larger, failing pattern and led to an outcome they never anticipated: the commitment of more than a half million American troops by early 1968 with no end to the war in sight.

"We believe certain things because they ought to be true," notes Thomas Gilovich. "But many times our sense of what ought to be true obscures our vision of what is actually the case, particularly when the underlying theories that generate this sense of plausibility are rather superficial. This tendency to rely heavily on what seems plausible has contributed to a number of questionable beliefs."[14] In the late summer of 1965, "the Americans came in like bulldozers," said a South Vietnamese observer, and "the war was now indisputably an American enterprise." The enormous weight and mass of American military power—now that it had been committed—further persuaded Johnson and his advisors that the United States could not fail. They believed, as White House aide Bill Moyers later put it, "that if we indicated a willingness to use our power, they [the Communists] would get the message and back away from all-out confrontation . . . There was a confidence that when the chips were down, the other people would fold." Many close observers of Southeast Asia believed this, too. Bernard Fall, a deeply knowledgeable French expert on Vietnam who had covered the First Indochina War, visited South Vietnam in September. "Today in Vietnam there is *so much* of everything available that almost any kind of military error, no matter how stupid, can be retrieved on the rebound," he wrote. "Against that, the teachings of Mao Tse-tung [on guerrilla war], superior tactics, popular support for the VC, or, conversely, poor motivation among the ARVNs and patent ineptness among many of their officers and even the 'mess in Saigon' are totally irrelevant." To those who "thought of the American effort as being somewhat larger and more modern than what the French had been doing; but essentially of the same kind," Fall concluded otherwise. "The truth is that the sheer magnitude of the American effort in Vietnam renders all such comparisons futile," adding that "U.S. air and firepower made the Vietnam War 'militarily unloseable.'"[15]

Initially, the war unfolded as Fall and others anticipated and hoped. An early engagement between U.S. and Vietcong forces, fought amid the dunes and salt marshes of the Batangan Peninsula south of Chu Lai from August 18 through 21, resulted in an American victory, though a marine officer noted how well the Vietcong fought, and U.S. firepower destroyed several villages, killing civilian inhabitants,* damaging crops on which residents depended for their livelihood, and creating the first of an eventual tide of uprooted refugees. Ten days later, on September 1, General Westmoreland laid out his strategy and projected timetable to the civilian leadership in Washington. Westmoreland had never faced a problem this knotty before and remarked that no sand table exercise at Fort Leavenworth's Command and General Staff College had ever included a fraction of Vietnam's complexity.[16] A war without distinct fronts or battle lines, it differed from any conflict the United States had fought since the Filipino insurgency following the Spanish-American War in 1898. (Such fuzziness would consistently confuse the American public as well, which could not follow the war on a map as it had during World War II and Korea.) Order-of-battle analysis was hampered by the amorphous nature of the Communist force structure—an ever-shifting mix of regular troops, guerrillas, political cadres, part-time combatants, and passive collaborators—who spent much of their time dispersed and in hiding, all of which made them difficult to identify, locate, and count accurately.† And the U.S. military could not wage a tra-

---

* The number of South Vietnamese noncombatants killed and wounded from such "friendly action" eventually rose to more than 75,000 a year.

† This led to a raging numbers debate throughout the war between the military and the CIA over the Communist order of battle, which later played out publicly in a 1982 libel suit Westmoreland brought against CBS for broadcasting a television documentary, "The Uncounted Enemy: A Vietnam Deception," based in large part on CIA analyst Sam Adams's allegation that MACV deliberately understated the Communist order of battle. The lawsuit was settled out of court.

ditional war of annihilation by invading North Vietnam because Johnson and McNamara assumed (prudently in hindsight) that such an invasion would trigger China's intervention, as had happened during the Korean War, thereby escalating the war's risks and costs exponentially.

Like most military commanders, Westmoreland had been conditioned to see decisive battle as the goal, and this fed his quest for decisive victories in the field. He defined success as the destruction of enemy main force units. Westmoreland therefore settled on a strategy of attrition intended to bring enemy ground forces to battle and wear them down—what he often termed the doctrine of "find 'em, fix 'em, fight 'em, and destroy 'em." Such an approach had been successfully adopted by the American military before, most notably by Ulysses S. Grant against Robert E. Lee's Army of Northern Virginia during the Civil War and by Dwight Eisenhower against Nazi Germany and Chester Nimitz and Douglas MacArthur against Imperial Japan. World War II admiral Ernest J. King encapsulated the philosophy that had become "the American way of war" when he declared, "War is force—force to the utmost—force to make the enemy yield to our own will—to yield because they see their comrades killed and wounded."[17] Westmoreland intended to do the same through the use of large-unit infantry, the ability to move forces quickly, and overwhelming superiority in firepower and logistics support that reflected the might of a complex machine. He would conduct search-and-destroy operations to inflict losses on the enemy faster than they could replace their losses through recruitment in the South and infiltration from the North. Once this "crossover point" was reached, his thinking went, Hanoi would be forced to settle at the peace table. "We'll just go on bleeding them until Hanoi wakes up to the fact that they have bled their country to the point of national disaster for generations," he said.[18] (Thus the brutal measuring stick of "body counts" came into practice.)

Westmoreland earnestly believed his strategy would end the war faster and require fewer troops than would a drawn-out, manpower-intensive counterinsurgency strategy that would sorely test the patience of a democracy at war.* He also assumed it would mean fewer civilian casualties and less damage to South Vietnamese infrastructure by concentrating the fighting outside of heavily populated urban areas. His projected timetable reflected this confidence: Phase 1—halting the Vietcong's momentum—would be completed by December 31, 1965. Phase 2—taking the offensive against Vietcong and North Vietnamese forces and "winning the hearts and minds" of South Vietnam's rural peasantry—would be completed by June 30, 1966. Finally, Phase 3—destroying remaining Vietcong and North Vietnamese military units or rendering them ineffective—would be completed by December 31, 1967. The tide would be reversed and the war won in less than two and a half years with 275,000 American troops—and importantly for Johnson, before the 1968 campaign.

It was no secret that the French had bogged down in an unsuccessful eight-year war against the Viêtminh from 1946 to 1954, but Westmoreland did not think to apply that experience as a more relevant baseline; indeed, from start to finish the defeat of a much more powerful foe, Nazi Germany, had taken only a year longer. Relying on the U.S. Army's World War II experience instead of considering lessons of the French failure in Indochina, Westmoreland's projected timetable was more a best-case scenario than a realistic assessment.

Such forecasts are a function of what psychologists call the "planning fallacy," a phenomenon in which predictions about how much time will be needed to complete a task display an optimism bias and underestimate the time needed. In a 1994 study, college students estimated how long it would take for them to finish their senior theses. The average estimate was 33.9 days. They also estimated how long it would take "if everything went as well as it possibly could" (averaging 27.4 days) and "if everything went as poorly as it possibly could" (averaging 48.6 days). The average actual

---

* Westmoreland later wrote that he "simply had not enough numbers [of troops] to put a squad of Americans in every [South Vietnamese] village and hamlet." William C. Westmoreland, *A Soldier Reports* (Doubleday & Company, 1976), p. 166.

completion time was 55.5 days, with only about 30 percent of the students completing their thesis in the amount of time they predicted.[19] "When forecasting outcomes," writes Daniel Kahneman, planners "too easily fall victim to the planning fallacy. In its grip, they make decisions based on delusional optimism rather than on a rational weighing of gains, losses, and probabilities. They overestimate benefits and underestimate costs. They spin scenarios of success while overlooking the potential for mistakes and miscalculations."[20]

Westmoreland's choice of an attrition strategy compounded the challenge. Although successful in the past and tailored to the U.S. Army's conventional force structure, material abundance, and superiority in size and weaponry, an attrition strategy also reflected a dangerous (and eventually fatal) complacency and lack of imagination rooted in the army's earlier successes and material advantages. A U.S. Army advisor to ARVN summed it up. "It's just another god-damn war," he flatly declared. "There's nothing mysterious about it. The only thing to do is get American troops and firepower in here, some aircover and artillery, and we'll lay these rubber-sandaled bastards out so fast that Uncle Ho won't be able to get his people out quick enough, except for those we've killed."[21] "We're going to stomp them to death," Westmoreland's operations officer, General William DePuy, confidently predicted to an American reporter. He then tellingly added, "I don't know any other way." Reflecting on his comments years later, DePuy admitted: "We were arrogant, because we were Americans and we were soldiers or Marines and we could do it, but it turned out . . . it was a losing concept of operations."[22]

Westmoreland fell victim to the planning fallacy, but the responsibility for avoiding it ultimately lay with the civilian decision-makers who approved the plan. McNamara—who had been a first-rate logistician in the army air corps during World War II and who knew a great deal about air operations (but later admitted that he "didn't know that much about ground operations")—failed to creatively ask the hard questions that might have exposed the implicit flaws of Westmoreland's attrition strategy. It was not that he

never wondered how long the war would take if something went
wrong; whether attrition was a winning strategy; and what the
price of victory would be. The problem was that he thought about
all of these within a framework bounded by American military or-
thodoxy, racial condescension, resistance to upsetting hierarchy,
and cognitive traps that could only be escaped with extraordinary
attention. This crippling expertise was found everywhere—even
old hands such as Fall could see no further than their confidence;
like those in Washington, his lens was of precise construction but
lacked sufficient field of view. "I didn't know enough . . . to probe
as much as I should have," McNamara later confessed.[23] Had he
further scrutinized Westmoreland's assessments, he would have discovered that two of the chiefs, army's chief of staff Harold Johnson and the marine corps commandant Wallace Greene, had doubts
about the attrition strategy. But McNamara didn't—and Johnson
and Greene did not volunteer their doubts to him or the president.
This reflected many things, including the military's aforemen-
tioned deeply ingrained "can-do" ethos, the chiefs' reluctance to
dictate concepts to a field commander, and their desire to present
a united front to the civilian leadership. It also reflected an un-
written agreement among the chiefs to keep their differences to
themselves that had grown out of their interactions with the civilian leadership. Harold Johnson later explained, "As the adversary
relationship hardened, the opposing factions tended to close ranks,
and differences that ought to be exposed and analyzed didn't appear, and there's a deliberate effort to submerge them so that they
don't appear . . . where they might be exploited."[24]

McNamara's relations with the military establishment had been
stiff, formal, and strained from the start. "Very little good was
said about Mr. McNamara . . . by any Service," recalled an admiral.[25] Most of the military saw only a cold and imperious man, the
rational technocrat who sought to exclude them from the process.
Some privately respected his decisiveness and analytical rigor even
as they roundly criticized him for discounting their perspective and
ramrodding through his larger agenda (supported by Kennedy and
Johnson) of asserting the Office of the Secretary of Defense (OSD)'s

control over the military services by systematizing their roles and missions and budgeting process. An army major general privately called him "a field marshal without qualifications . . . We have worried sometimes about the military man on horseback; now I think we have to worry a little about the civilian on horseback."[26]

McNamara made little effort to assuage such bitterness. He eschewed ceremonial appearances that might bolster military morale and seemed too busy to offer explanations that might salve resentment. For McNamara to be right was more necessary than to be liked. Deeply committed to the ethos of subordination to civilian authority in a democracy, military officers had "grudgingly cooperated" with the OSD nonetheless,[27] but to them, for whom loyalty to those below you is as important as loyalty to those above you, the lack of reciprocal deference was contemptible. McNamara discounted the advice of senior officers who failed to speak his language of logic, facts, and numbers. The admirals and generals, in turn, disliked having their professional experience and judgment questioned by McNamara's "snot nose," "smart alec," and "fast-talking" deputies—particularly the "whiz kids" in OSD's Office of Systems Analysis. The difference in age only made matters worse. Forty-four years old when sworn in as secretary of defense, McNamara was considerably younger than most of the chiefs, who had far outranked him during World War II and now answered to him. All of this fostered a tense and adversarial climate between McNamara and senior officers that neither labored to mitigate.

Morton Halperin, who observed the chiefs closely during these years as special assistant to assistant secretary of defense for international security affairs John McNaughton, noted another reason for the chiefs' silent alliance. "The Joint Chiefs had a compact in which each service got to say what it wanted about what it was doing, and the other services went along in return for the same favor for them," noted Halperin. "McNamara never understood that" even though he was "in the building for seven years." Added Halperin, "You've got to force" the chiefs "to tell you their differences. Otherwise, they hide them."[28] McNamara's failure to sufficiently challenge the chiefs proved a fundamental error. It is not that McNamara lacked the analytical capacity and audacity to ask searching questions—after all, he did not know anything about cars before he went to Ford in 1945, so he quickly educated himself about automobiles. But political leaders don't like second-guessing military men (who in turn detest being second-guessed about military operations by civilian leaders), and this reluctance was reinforced by the constraints that McNamara and Johnson had imposed on Westmoreland and the chiefs, specifically a prohibition on an invasion of North Vietnam and limits on bombing operations in order to avert Chinese or Soviet intervention. As a result, as long as Westmoreland restricted ground operations to South Vietnam, McNamara and Johnson uncritically accepted his attrition strategy. "We can't run this war from Washington," McNamara told a Pentagon staffer. "Let Westmoreland run it." In effect, said Bundy later, the military was allowed to do "whatever they were not forbidden to do." It was "Westy's business."[29] Looking back, McNamara admitted, "I should have forced more discussion and then come to a decision after there had been more debate . . . The uniformed services did not perform well. God knows I didn't."[30]

Like two boxers ascending into the ring before the first-round bell, the Americans and their adversaries in Vietnam spent the months of September and October 1965 fighting small skirmishes to gauge each other's strengths and weaknesses, capabilities and strategies—trying to figure each other out. Then, from November 14 through 18, the first major battle between American and North Vietnamese forces took place amid the dry scrub brush, high elephant grass, and gargantuan red anthills of the Drang River Valley at the foot of the Chu Pong Massif near the Cambodian border where the Hồ Chí Minh Trail fanned out into South Vietnam's Central Highlands. (*Ia* means "river" in the local Montagnard language, thus the engagement became known as the Battle of the Ia Drang Valley.) Led by General Nguyễn Chí Thanh, Hanoi's commander in the South who believed that revolutionary fervor could overcome technology, North Vietnamese forces initiated contact with U.S. forces using close-quarters combat—what they called

"clinging to the belt" (*bam lung dich*) of the Americans—to deny
their enemy use of artillery and close air support. Effectively an
experiment in how to impair the American approach, they clashed
with the elite First Air Cavalry, the army's new heliborne division
with black and gold horse-head shoulder patches, whose superior
mobility and firepower inflicted over 1,300 casualties. But the initial American success at what was officially called Landing Zone
(LZ) X-Ray in the Ia Drang Valley had been followed three days
later by the disastrous ambush of an American unit at nearby LZ
Albany, when a marching column of Air Cavalry troops inadvertently stumbled into a North Vietnamese encampment. The Vietnamese suffered far heavier casualties but nearly 300 Americans
were killed—almost half of all U.S. casualties incurred in Vietnam
up to that time. Westmoreland boasted to his old friend, Democratic senator Fritz Hollings of South Carolina, that U.S. forces
had killed ten NVA soldiers for every one American lost. "Westy,"
replied Hollings, "the American people don't care about the ten,
they care about the one."[31] The general heard but did not listen.

Westmoreland interpreted the battle's results as evidence the
attrition strategy worked. American forces had engaged large-unit
enemy formations, inflicting heavy losses and producing a high
body count. Having fixed on this singular metric, Westmoreland
and his MACV staff, already overconfident, showed no willingness
to test or anticipate the potential limits and vulnerabilities of the
attrition strategy. Westmoreland complacently assumed that the
Vietcong and North Vietnamese would continue to fight (or could
be made to continue fighting) a conventional war according to
American rules. But the Vietcong and North Vietnamese had no
interest in conforming to his conception of proper warfare. Out
of necessity and wisdom, they quickly adapted and began fighting
according to *their* rules—that is, a guerrilla war that played not to
America's advantages but to their own. Unable to best the far larger
and more powerful American military in open battle, the Vietcong and the North Vietnamese infrequently tried to do so after
Ia Drang. Instead, they resorted to ambushes, mines, booby-traps,
hit-and-run attacks, and small surprise skirmishes that harassed,

demoralized, and inflicted steady casualties on the Americans while avoiding sustained confrontation with them—except at times and places and for durations of *their* choosing—taking advantage of support among South Vietnam's rural peasantry and their sanctuaries in neighboring Laos* and Cambodia for supplies and to replenish their losses. They spent most of their time hidden away, not fighting. Less than *1* percent of nearly 2 million U.S. small-unit operations conducted between 1966 and 1968 resulted in contact with the enemy. (For ARVN, the percentage was only one-tenth of 1 percent.) On the infrequent occasions when the Vietcong and North Vietnamese chose to fight, 95 percent of their assaults were conducted by units smaller than a battalion.[32] The Communists were patient, determined to play the long game even if they won few outright battles along the road to ultimate victory. As a result, the Americans found it impossible to pin down and defeat an enemy who chose to evade combat because they had the common sense not to fight in a manner that suited their better-armed and more mobile adversary.

A poor man's blueprint perfectly tailored to the weaker side in a conflict, guerrilla warfare was a time-tested strategy of exhaustion based on popular support and local knowledge that stressed protracted fighting in the hope that the more powerful side, usually a foreign occupying force, would give up and go home. Its foremost exponent in Asia was Mao Zedong, who used it to lead the Communists to victory in China in 1949. The leader of North Vietnam's military, General Võ Nguyên Giáp, a former schoolteacher who had fought against colonial France and now the Americans, followed Mao's famous dictum: "When the enemy attacks, retreat; when he retreats, harass him." Giáp defined the front as "wherever the enemy is found" and vulnerable to a local concentration of forces. In these instances and places, and only these, the North Vietnamese and Vietcong would employ "initiative, flexibility, rapidity, sur-

---

* U.S. interdiction bombing and CIA covert ground operations in Laos made it less of a sanctuary than Cambodia (which the United States also began bombing later in the war). None of this significantly inhibited the movement of Communist troops and supplies down the Hồ Chí Minh Trail.

prise, suddenness in attack and retreat"—all in an effort to exhaust the Americans "little by little by small victories." The point was not to gain territory but to avoid losses while inflicting damage on the adversary; indeed, losses were to be avoided "even at the cost of losing ground."[33] Giáp explained his strategy to an American journalist after the war using an Old Testament metaphor. "David did not kill Goliath just because he was brave," explained Giáp. "He looked up at Goliath and realized that if he fought Goliath's way with a sword, Goliath would kill him. But if he picked up a rock and put it in his sling, he could hit Goliath in the head and knock Goliath down and kill him. David used his mind when he fought Goliath. So did we Vietnamese when we had to fight the Americans."[34]

The general who ranked second to Giáp in North Vietnam's military hierarchy, Nguyễn Chí Thanh, laid out this strategy in a paper titled "Five Lessons Learned in a Highly Victorious Dry Season":

1. Always keep the initiative on your side in battle.
2. Force the enemy to fight on your terms.
3. Try to be always on the offensive, fighting only when the odds favor your side. Otherwise it is better to avoid the enemy, to deflect his attention—to hide, even, while waiting for a time and space of your choosing or a better opportunity.
4. Always try to fight at close range, to fight vigorously and quickly, and to conclude the battle expeditiously; never drag it out or fight an inconclusive battle.
5. Always prepare carefully and understand the enemy, the terrain, and the rules of action, and predict correctly the enemy's reactions. You must also be flexible, always be on the move, concentrating only enough force for the action; assemble and disperse quickly, and move fast. Finally, keep your moves secret and unpredictable, giving special attention to creating diversions and dissimulation to throw off the enemy's calculations.[35]

Such a strategy enabled the Vietcong and North Vietnamese to dictate the tempo and level of fighting and thus to control their casualties—thereby nullifying the fundamental premise and effectiveness of the attrition strategy. Westmoreland's operations chief, General DePuy, came to see this fatal flaw of attrition *after* the war. "They metered out their casualties, and when the casualties were getting too high, they just backed off and waited," he said in retrospect. "I was surprised at the difficulty we had in trying to find the VC. We hit more dry holes than I thought we were going to hit. They were more elusive . . . They were the ones who decided whether there would be a fight."[36] In hindsight, the chiefs themselves acknowledged that "the enemy, by the type of action he adopts, has the predominant share in determining enemy attrition rates."[37] This gave the Vietcong and North Vietnamese the precious commodity of time in a conflict against a militarily superior but adaptively inferior opponent fighting a war half a world away—and they knew it. Instead of a grinding war of attrition, it became a protracted war of endurance that the Vietcong and North Vietnamese would win.

The tendency to project one's thinking onto an opponent—to expect the opponent to play by your rules—is a common shortcoming of individuals and institutions, particularly those accustomed to success. This shortcoming reinforced Westmoreland's and the chiefs' preconceptions, dulled their realization that attrition was not working, and discouraged them from making efforts to win the support of South Vietnam's rural peasantry in order to wage a successful counterguerrilla campaign. When the Americans found themselves fighting on terms set by the opponent, they were stunned, even peeved that their adversary would react in such a way. "What's the matter, general?" a high-ranking U.S. official asked a clearly agitated general officer after one such engagement in Vietnam. "God damn 'em!" the general huffed, on the verge of tears, "they wouldn't come out and fight!"[38] He and other officers did not know what to do or how to develop an alternative strategy—a Plan B. Attrition was the method they knew and they clung to what they were more familiar with, and those up the ladder, consequently, saw no need for a true reevaluation.

Military men who were focused on battlefield techniques and

tactics separate from political context, Westmoreland and his superiors in Washington failed to grasp the Vietcong's and North Vietnamese's intense belief in themselves as the sole legitimate expression of Vietnam patriotism and their fanatical commitment to reunify the country and drive the foreigners out—all of which fed their extraordinary tenaciousness and willingness to absorb extraordinary punishment* from an adversary they knew that they could not defeat by force of arms alone. "When I was a young soldier and a junior officer," North Vietnamese army veteran Bui Tin later wrote, "I took it for granted that ours was a sacred and righteous cause, that . . . it was a national salvation effort. We were fighting against foreign aggression and occupation of our national territory by foreign troops. Nothing could be clearer or simpler!"[39] Looking back, General Richard Stilwell, a senior member of Westmoreland's MACV staff, acknowledged the American military "failure to [recognize]" "that we were confronting a North Vietnam . . . that was committed to total war . . . for as long as it took."[40] Hồ Chí Minh told his countrymen in the summer of 1965, "No matter if we have to fight for five years, ten years, twenty years, or even longer, we are resolved to fight on until we achieve complete victory."[41] No price was too high to pay for reunification and independence; one North Vietnamese leader said that they were prepared to confront and outlast as many as a million American troops.†[42]

The U.S. military possessed a strong organizational culture. A strong organizational culture unites people, offers a shared sense of purpose, and creates a common identity. But "where there is a 'strong' culture," note behavioral economists Mats Alvesson of

---

* North Vietnam's relative casualties tell the story. Based on a very conservative estimate of a million war-related deaths out of a population of approximately 50 million, North Vietnam suffered losses of 20,000 per 1 million people—*fifty-eight times* the rate of U.S. losses (58,000 war-related deaths out of a population of 200 million).

† Ironically, an ARVN officer who had served with the Việtminh against the French conveyed his people's grit best. "You must understand," he said, "that we are a people who think of ourselves as having defeated the Chinese, though it took us a thousand years." Colonel Tran Ngoc Châu, quoted in Daniel Ellsberg, *Secrets: A Memoir of Vietnam and the Pentagon Papers* (Viking, 2002), p. 134.

the University of Lund in Sweden and Andre Spicer of City University, London, "there is also likely to be a strong tendency for people to think in homogenous ways. Culture does the thinking for them. It can give them a sense of integration and direction, but it can also trap them in set ways of understanding the world."[43] It narrows one's outlook, and discourages people from thinking outside of well-defined parameters. American military tradition had always favored aggressiveness and prioritized maintaining an offensive rather than a defensive stance. Search and destroy meant going after the enemy—that is, keeping the initiative. Teamwork and mission accomplishment—not searching self-criticism—was the name of the game. One did not rise through the ranks by being a naysayer, which meant advice (and, more rarely, criticism) was usually limited to the best tactics for executing the accepted strategy. In a culture that valued action and decisiveness, deep analysis and careful reflection—what some in the military derided as "analysis paralysis"—were often avoided. It was hard to discuss problems openly and frankly. Many, including Westmoreland and the chiefs, believed that stopping to reflect would divert attention and resources (including time) from the all-important task of pushing forward. So Westmoreland continued search-and-destroy operations that led to more destructiveness and alienated more South Vietnamese, whose support was crucial to success. "The finger of Death," wrote a CIA officer with long experience in South Vietnam, "pointed too often at the very people who should have been our allies, not our enemies."[44]

Rather than being cowed by U.S. escalation, the Vietcong and North Vietnamese reacted in precisely the opposite way: they pushed back, demonstrating determination rather than intimidation and moving nimbly as mice in response to the lumbering American elephants. Westmoreland struggled to find an enemy that knew how not to be found. And because American forces never held territory, they never denied the enemy an important source of strength and resiliency: access to the rural population. As a result, Vietcong recruitment among South Vietnam's peasantry doubled in the fall of 1965, as did NVA infiltration down the Hồ

Chí Minh Trail. Meanwhile, most ARVN units were so plagued by apathy and poor leadership* that they refused to go out at night patrolling in small units. Westmoreland's troop estimates of July had been based on force ratios that had quickly become dangerously obsolete.

Although McNamara had supported the commitment of U.S. troops during the summer because he believed they—along with bombing—would prevent Saigon's collapse and push Hanoi to the negotiating table, he soon realized their limited effectiveness. Within weeks of their arrival in country, he warned Johnson of "the danger that our forces, effective at preventing any large Vietcong operation, may not be effective in dealing with very small harassing and ambushing and terror operations." On September 12, he told LBJ, "You can't win [the war] with American troops going out after Vietcong terrorists . . . It isn't going to be done that way."[45] Another turn of the screw came when Norman Morrison's self-immolation beneath McNamara's Pentagon window in early November and the hundreds of American dead and wounded at Ia Drang two weeks later further drove home to McNamara the increasingly human costs of the war.

American officials had been right to think about popular reaction to the war and its possible duration. During the late summer and fall of 1965, draft calls† rose along with the casualty rate, in-

---

* Unlike Vietcong, North Vietnamese, and U.S. promotions, ARVN promotions were determined more by bribery and nepotism than by demonstrated leadership in combat.

† Approximately 30 percent of those who served in Vietnam were draftees. Young men ages eighteen to twenty-five (older men were called first) registered with their local draft board, composed of local community members, which determined their draft status (a power that subjected draft boards to intense lobbying by relatives and friends of the better educated and economically advantaged who had greater access to expert advice, psychiatric professionals, and legal counsel). Exemptions existed for those deemed physically and mentally disqualified, married fathers, and conscientious objectors; deferments existed for those enrolled in college and studying to become doctors and ministers. A majority of draftees (approximately 75 percent) were from poor and working-class families; roughly 20 percent were from middle-class families; and relatively few from upper-class families. In response to criticism of the draft's inequities, college deferments were repealed in 1968 and a

creasing young Americans' opposition to the war. Small numbers
of draft-age men began burning draft cards and fleeing to Canada
or Sweden. Domestic and international pressure for a negotiated
settlement began to mount as media coverage, such as CBS News
correspondent Morley Safer's televised report on August 5 of marines using flamethrowers and cigarette lighters to burn thatch-
and-wattle huts and destroy rice stores in the village of Cam Ne
while old men and women begged them to stop, conveyed the
war's destructiveness around the world. A marine commented
about a similar patrol earlier that summer, "Their homes had been
wrecked, their chickens killed, their rice confiscated—and if they
weren't pro-Vietcong before we got there, they sure as hell were by
the time we left."[46]

It was television news coverage such as Safer's segment that
brought the disturbing reality of war home, literally, for the first
time, with unprecedented intimacy, and as a result criticism and
opposition began to crystallize and became increasingly respect-
able. Nearly 100,000 antiwar demonstrators turned out in over
ninety cities across the country on November 27; a crowd of 20,000
gathered for a March on Washington that included protests along
Pennsylvania Avenue in front of the White House. The sponsors of
the Washington march wrote Hồ Chí Minh, urging Hanoi to enter
peace talks. (Hồ replied by reiterating that any settlement must
be "in accordance with the program of the NLF [Vietcong]"—in
effect, acceptance of North Vietnam's terms.) Although 75 percent
of Americans continued to support Johnson's handling of Vietnam
that fall, almost half (and many people elsewhere, particularly in
Europe) believed the president was not doing enough to find peace.

Thrown on his heels by the unexpected North Vietnamese success, Westmoreland reacted by seeking twice the number of addi-

---

lottery system based on birth dates drawn (the lower the number, the higher the
likelihood of being drafted, with 19-year-olds called first) was instituted the following year. Between 1965 and 1973, 2,215,000 men were conscripted; 15,400,000
men were granted exemptions or deferments. Similar inequities existed in socialist
North Vietnam. College students were exempted from the draft. Politburo leader
Lê Duẩn sent his draft-age children to study in the Soviet Union during the war.

tional troops for Phase 2 that he had requested just months before (200,000 rather than 100,000). This would bring the total number of U.S. troops in South Vietnam to 410,000—far more than the general's original estimate of 275,000. Johnson ordered McNamara back to Saigon to assess the new situation and troop request that grew out of it. He arrived on November 28 for a short but sobering visit. Although McNamara remained in country for less than two days, he spent fourteen hours with Westmoreland at MACV headquarters in Saigon and an entire day in the field. Visiting the First Air Cavalry near Plei Me in the Central Highlands near the Cambodian border, he talked with those who had recently fought at Ia Drang. Touring the massive deep-water port under construction at Cam Ranh Bay on the central coast—made of enormous floating pier sections prefabricated in the Philippines and towed across the South China Sea—he witnessed how massive U.S. military spending was distorting South Vietnam's economy, and how decisively America was eclipsing the South Vietnamese role in the war. Helicoptering in and out of Biên Hòa, once a small provincial town that had been transformed into a mammoth U.S. Army headquarters, McNamara saw the landscape of Vietcong-controlled areas northwest of Saigon pockmarked with craters ten feet deep and twenty feet wide created by giant B-52 bombers dropping twenty-ton payloads. Perhaps more impressively, he observed the flag-draped aluminum caskets stacked for loading aboard C-130 Hercules transports for their solemn return home. Jolted, the secretary appeared somber and grim as he left Saigon. Speaking without the confident authority he usually projected, McNamara told the press that the Communists' actions "expressed a determination to carry on the conflict which can only lead to one conclusion—that it will be a long war." The mask had cracked a bit.

"Out of this came an understanding of the situation much more comprehensive than I had before," he told Johnson in a grim voice after he returned, "and the situation [was] much more critical than I had realized."[47] Still, the delusive equation persisted. After South Vietnamese premier Nguyễn Cao Kỳ told McNamara the Saigon government exerted authority over only about 25 percent of the population, Westmoreland requested an increase in U.S. troop strength to 400,000 in 1966 and possibly exceeding 600,000 in 1967—the latter figure more than double the upper limit of troops the general had said would be needed just six months earlier. And even this number of troops, Westmoreland admitted, did not guarantee an American victory.

The trend of events "shook me and altered my attitude perceptibly," McNamara later wrote. His July prediction that a major U.S. troop deployment stood "a good chance of achieving an acceptable outcome within a reasonable time" had proven spectacularly wrong. The crushing realization that he had miscalculated badly was written on McNamara's face both in Saigon and when he had returned to Washington. "Mr. McNamara is beginning to show the strain," observed an officer at one of the briefings.[48] And McNamara "looked different" when he stepped into Bundy's office after the Vietnam trip, recalled NSC staffer Chester "Chet" Cooper, appearing "concerned and grave."[49]

That dispirit was evident when McNamara reported what he had learned in a November 30 memorandum to the president. It was a sobering list: tripled—perhaps quadrupled—NVA infiltration,* improved air defenses around Hanoi and Haiphong, doubled Vietcong recruitment in the South, and an increased logistical flow. (Despite heavy air and sea interdiction, North Vietnam could move 200 tons of supplies a day down the Hồ Chí Minh Trail using pack animals and porters on bicycles.) Saigon's political dysfunction, lack of progress in pacification, and a "very, very high" ARVN desertion rate meant that U.S. forces rested on "a bowl of jelly." All of this meant that Westmoreland's original troop request would "not be enough." McNamara sketched two alternatives for Johnson: "to go now for a compromise solution" and "hold further deployments to a minimum," or "to stick with the war, and provide what it takes in men and matériel," combined with gradually

---

* This shattered his prediction to Johnson on July 28 that "the strikes at infiltration routes have at least put a ceiling on what the North Vietnamese can pour into South Vietnam, thereby putting a ceiling on the size of the war that the enemy can wage there."

intensified bombing. If Johnson chose the latter course, McNamara recommended that he precede it with a three- or four-week bombing pause in order to "lay a foundation in the mind of the American public and in world opinion for such an enlarged phase of the war" and to "give North Vietnam a face-saving chance to stop the aggression." McNamara expressed his serious concern "about embarking on a markedly higher level of war in Vietnam without having tried, through a pause, to end the war or at least having made it clear to our people that we did our best to end it." Even though he conceded that more troops "will not guarantee success," that "US killed-in-action can be expected to reach 1000 a month," and that "the odds are even that we will be faced in early 1967 with a 'no-decision' at an even higher level," he concluded "that the best chance of achieving our stated objectives lies in a pause followed, if it fails, by the [additional] deployments."[50] Even before his trip, McNamara told Johnson that the military situation was "not producing the conditions that will . . . win the war for us." He was not entirely dismissive: "It may," he said, "but it probably won't. Therefore, we're going to have to suggest some alternative solutions."[51] McNamara, with Bundy in support and Rusk more skeptical, settled on a bombing pause as the best solution.

Few people readily admit to failure, particularly failure that results in the loss of human life. When confronted with strong evidence that their conviction is wrong, they will change in some ways, but a fundamental shift in a person's outlook usually occurs incrementally over a long period of time. Compounding the danger, people who receive negative feedback about a decision they have made are actually more likely to make a more costly subsequent decision based on the same premises. Psychologists call this escalation of commitment resulting from "act rationalization." An experiment conducted by Jean-Léon Beauvois of Pierre Mendès-France University, Robert-Vincent Joule of the University of Provence, and Fabien Brunetti of the University of Nancy showed this dynamic at work. Participants who received negative feedback about a questionnaire they had answered were three times more likely to commit an even costlier subsequent act (agreeing to a longer, more detailed at-home interview on the same subject) than were those who received positive feedback about the questionnaire (39 percent versus 13 percent).[52] Individuals strive for internal consistency, and when inconsistencies arise, people attempt to rationalize the incongruities involved not by interrogating their original logic but by digging in their heels. Put in shock by a shattered worldview, they not only cling tenaciously to the original belief because the implications of error are so personally devastating, but double down. This explains why changing one's mind about things that are sensitive or that one holds dear is not usually an abrupt about-face but a slow and painful readjustment. In the fall of 1965, Robert McNamara—having ingested a good deal of evidence contrary to his preconceptions—might have told the president that America was unlikely to succeed in Vietnam and therefore should withdraw. But he did not. Years of bloodshed were to follow.

Johnson had initially been cool to the idea of a bombing pause because he worried about increased North Vietnamese infiltration during a pause that would project an image of desperation to Hanoi, and about the political pressures that would be generated domestically and internationally against resumption. However, Westmoreland's much larger troop request and all of the problems revealed during McNamara's visit to Saigon would soften his opposition.

McNamara launched his campaign for a pause during a December 2 phone call to Johnson at his ranch in the Texas Hill Country west of Austin. He told the president that he had grown "more and more convinced that we ought definitely think of some action other than military action as the only program." To grant Westmoreland's request for additional troops "by itself" would be "suicide," he said. These were disquieting words, and McNamara was not done. "I think pushing 300,000, 400,000 Americans out there without being able to guarantee what it will lead to is a terrible risk and a terrible problem." He pleaded with Johnson to couple more troops with a bombing pause, desperately hoping that a temporary cessation would open the door toward a settlement, noting that the Soviet ambassador in Washington had signaled Moscow's willingness to lobby the North Vietnamese in that direction if the United States stopped bombing for two or three weeks.[53]

Johnson remained decidedly cool toward a pause. "We don't serve the interests of our country by (a) doing it and (b) advertising it," he told McGeorge Bundy, another pause proponent, nine days later. "You hold out hope to a lot of people, you confuse them, you frustrate them—we multiply our problems by doing it."[54] The chiefs expressed even greater opposition, and wanted the additional troops Westmoreland had requested. They sought to advance their position by stressing the issue of casualties—a subject they knew was a sensitive and therefore effective one with the president. During the summer, when Johnson had debated the commitment of major U.S. combat forces, the chiefs had stressed more troops as a means of achieving victory. Now after the limitations of Westmoreland's attrition strategy had become apparent, they changed their rationale and began arguing that more troops were needed to *prevent* a rise in casualties (a logical contradiction that none of the civilian leaders questioned) and that a bombing pause—by relieving the pressure on North Vietnamese infiltration—would *cause* a rise in casualties. General Wheeler, speaking for the chiefs, said a pause would allow the Communists "to repair and move," thereby inflicting a heavier price on U.S. pilots and soldiers. Presuming to opine on domestic politics, he warned of a "violent reaction" among elements of the American public. "Once you stop, it's hard to start again," he argued, adding that such disruption "could shake [the South Vietnamese government] to its toenails."[55]

McNamara directly rebutted Wheeler, telling the president, "Okay, so we stop the damn thing. If they take advantage of us, we can come back, we can hit them hard."[56] But the generals' arguments carried weight with Johnson, who continued to hesitate to do anything that hazarded the lives of American boys or that undermined his military commanders. During a meeting with the troika at his ranch on December 7, he listened morosely as his advisors detailed the mounting problems in Vietnam. Simple logic (as defined within his limited conception of what was possible) dictated that more of something good (American soldiers) would inevitably create the likelihood for more of something good (success in Vietnam—and thus, America). But that wasn't working. Frustrated and confused, Johnson said he felt "bogged down," trapped on a course that was carrying him and the country in deeper and deeper with no promise of progress or victory on the horizon. "Where we were when I came in—I'd trade back to where we were," he lamented, a hint of fear and ruefulness in his voice.[57]

Johnson assembled his advisors in the Cabinet Room on December 17 for two final days of debate. The first day's discussion centered on bombing's effectiveness. George Ball, who had assessed the effectiveness of Allied bombing during World War II as a director of the postwar U.S. Strategic Bombing Survey, told those gathered that bombing never wins a war. He said the bombing of North Vietnam was no different; it was driving Hanoi into greater dependency on Beijing and making the likelihood of negotiations to end the conflict more remote. Johnson did not challenge Ball, but said "the problem is the Chiefs go through the roof when we mention this pause." "I can take on the Chiefs," McNamara told him, anxious as ever to protect the president. "They see this as a total military problem—nothing will change their views." Johnson shared McNamara's opinion and respected his loyalty, but another part of him resentfully traced his current predicament to the secretary's original advocacy of bombing. "We are there now because of the bombing," he snapped at McNamara. "We wouldn't be there without it."[58]

At the next day's meeting, McNamara intensified his push for a pause. For the first time, he soberly estimated "a military solution to the problem" "to be one out of three or one out of two"—therefore "we must search for a diplomatic solution." The president stared hard at his defense secretary as if he was trying with his eyes to bore inside McNamara's brain. "You mean that no matter what we do in the military field, you think there is no sure victory?" "That's right," McNamara confessed in the low voice that he used when fighting back emotion or disappointment. "We have been too optimistic." His nerve and plans for Vietnam were frayed, and if he had not reached his breaking point, something had broken. "I'm saying that we may never find a military solution," he said. "We need to explore other means. Our military approach is an unlikely route to a successful conclusion."

A frown appeared on Johnson's brow and his body stiffened perceptibly. McNamara's assessment "just shocked me and, furthermore, it shocked everybody at the table," Johnson later confided to Dean Rusk. Rusk would have none of it, uncharacteristically and sarcastically disparaging McNamara behind his back two months later. "Bob, frankly Mr. President, hasn't had much experience dealing with crises," Rusk said of his fellow veteran of the Bay of Pigs, Berlin, and Cuban Missile Crises. "I just don't believe [McNamara's conclusion]. I can't pull out a slide rule and prove it, but the boys out in the field are proving that we can do better than that."[59] Clark Clifford, who attended the meeting at Johnson's invitation, opposed a pause because he thought it would fail and once it did, the pressure for escalation would increase. Clifford asked McNamara a piercing question: Why send more troops if military victory was so unlikely? "I know this may seem like a contradiction," McNamara replied. "I have come to you for a huge increase in Vietnam, to at least 400,000 men, yet at the same time our actions may lead to counter-escalation by the North Vietnamese and other undesirable results. Therefore, I am simply suggesting that we look for other alternatives first."[60]

The next day, Johnson revealed his decision: an unannounced bombing pause of unspecified duration, coupled with an intense diplomatic effort to move Hanoi toward negotiations—and approval of Westmoreland's request for additional troops. And once more, rather than risk a congressional debate that would threaten the Great Society or attempt to rally the American public and generate pressures to widen the war, Johnson would obscure the magnitude of the troop increase—a doubling of forces by the end of 1966—through incremental announcements as soldiers were deployed month by month. It was an expedient but risky strategy. If the situation continued to worsen, Johnson would be exposed to charges that he had escalated the war without consulting Congress and informing the American people. It avoided a call-up of reservists but required higher draft quotas, which in the spring tripled from 10,000 to 30,000 a month. This, in turn, stoked more and louder antiwar opposition.

The bombing pause began on Christmas Eve and ran for thirty-seven days through the end of January 1966. Throughout this period, the chiefs clamored for resumption, just as Johnson had anticipated, and in fact the pause did not stop military campaigns outside of Vietnam, so U.S. air strikes in Laos intended to destroy North Vietnamese supply lines intensified and ground operations in South Vietnam continued. No breakthroughs came out of the month-long pause. Radio Hanoi broadcast a letter by Hồ Chí Minh in which he denounced the pause as a "deceitful" and "hypocritical" "trick" and said North Vietnam would not negotiate until the United States halted the bombing "unconditionally and for good." Confirming the predictions of those who had opposed the suspension, Hanoi used the respite to increase infiltration and build up its forces in the South, and Johnson, who told Rusk toward the end of the pause "that you and I both knew this thing wouldn't work to begin with," came to view the pause as a "big mistake."[61]

The bombing and troop deployments McNamara had advocated during the spring and summer had drawn America into a war that had gone awry within months. In 1964, 112 Americans had been killed in action. In 1965, 1,130 had been killed in action. How many more would be killed in 1966? Meanwhile, the likelihood of U.S. military victory rapidly diminished. McNamara believed Washington had to get to the bargaining table. But whatever inclination Hanoi had once had to negotiate* had vanished after the

---

* Shortly after the Tonkin Gulf incident in August 1964, North Vietnam—apparently interpreting the retaliatory American air attacks as the first step in a major military effort and seeking to avoid war with the United States because it wanted to develop its economy and knew such a war would be very damaging economically and very difficult militarily—expressed interest in opening talks with the United States. Evidence of Hanoi's openness to talks in the late summer of 1964 is well summarized

bombing of North Vietnam began, American troops arrived in South Vietnam, Communist forces adapted to superior U.S. mobility and firepower, and growing domestic opposition to the war reinforced Hanoi's determination to erode the will of the American people. Heretofore, McNamara—like Kennedy, Johnson, Rusk, and Bundy—had been reluctant to negotiate with North Vietnam because he feared it only intended to negotiate a weak South Vietnam's surrender. Now, McNamara wanted to negotiate with North Vietnam because he feared America's military limitations. He could not fathom why Hanoi refused to negotiate unless the bombing stopped altogether. "I keep thinking they will give some indication," he told the president a few days before the thirty-seven-day pause ended. "It would just seem smart bargaining on their part to do so. They could get a continuation of the pause with very, very little action. Even if they came in with some questions, we'd almost be forced to extend it."[62]

But Hanoi had no intention of negotiating unless the bombing was permanently halted. The North Vietnamese Politburo, led by Lê Duẩn—a southerner who believed Hồ Chí Minh had allowed the Việtminh to be negotiated out of an imminent military victory at the Geneva Conference in 1954—now believed it would be possible to outlast the Americans and not repeat Ho's earlier mistake. To North Vietnam's leaders, bombing pauses represented not an effort by the Americans to reach out and find a way to end the war diplomatically, but a coercive test to determine if Hanoi's will had at last been broken. They also faced a domestic political difficulty. If "we had begun negotiations with the U.S.," explained Trần Quang Cơ, an American expert in North Vietnam's Foreign Ministry, "we would have had to explain to the people why we could negotiate with the U.S., meet with the U.S., and host the U.S. while bombs fell on us."[63] All of this meant that Hanoi would not talk while the bombs fell. "We did not debate this among ourselves," said Huynh, "because there was no dissent. None. We all

in Walter Johnson, ed., *The Papers of Adlai E. Stevenson, Volume VIII: Ambassador to the United Nations, 1961–1965* (Little, Brown, 1979), pp. 661–666.

felt the same way."[64] "Moreover," recalled Nguyễn Khắc Huỳnh, a
military journalist during the war,

> negotiations did not mean the same thing to us as they did
> to you. For you, the U.S., negotiations would provide a way
> to stop a war that you discover you cannot win. But we can-
> not just walk away from the war, because of what the war is
> *about*—it is about our country, about whether our country
> will continue to exist or not. We felt our backs to the wall.
> Under these circumstances, how could we be "flexible"? We
> did not know how to be "flexible." So every time you "took
> our pulse," either in a bombing pause or by sending some
> intermediaries, we did everything in our power to show
> you that we were alive, that we could still defy you, that we
> could outlast you, and that you could not defeat us.[65]

The fact that the top people in Washington had little idea that
Hồ Chí Minh had become a figurehead and that the much more
militant and uncompromising Lê Duẩn was actually in charge
further reflected their shocking lack of knowledge and understanding about North Vietnamese decision-making. (Southern-
born hardliners on the Politburo for whom reunification was a
sine qua non trumped native Northerners who felt North Vietnam
could cope with the Americans but not a million Chinese who
would stay forever.) Washington had few, if any, experts deeply
knowledgeable about Hanoi. Politburo meetings were veiled in
secrecy and American intelligence did not know who made the
decisions or why. CIA director Richard Helms acknowledged this
fatal shortcoming in his memoirs. "Within the Agency, our failure
to penetrate the North Vietnamese government was the single
most frustrating aspect of those years," Helms wrote. "We could
not determine what was going on at the highest levels of Ho's
government, nor could we learn how policy was made or who
was making it. Along with the entire foreign policy element of
the U.S. government, the Agency could not determine what might
bring Ho or any of his principal officers to the table for face-to-

face negotiations."[66] Partly, this reflected the closed nature of the Hanoi regime. But it also reflected the extraordinary apathy and ignorance of the American government regarding its adversary. Such apathy and ignorance could be seen in the weight attached to trying to determine Politburo and North Vietnamese strategy. In 1968, when nearly a half million U.S. troops were operating in Vietnam, the American embassy's political section numbered merely a dozen "Hanoi watchers."[67] Such a significant and revealing imbalance would plague Washington throughout the war.

Frantically looking for a way out of a terrible mess, the United States initiated on average two contacts a month with North Vietnam. Hanoi's diplomatic intransigence* represented a bitter irony that intensified McNamara's torment. With the U.S. military bogged down and Hanoi unresponsive to U.S. overtures, McNamara did not know what to do to stop the killing and to prevent more killing, and he realized the problem was intensifying. As the United States put in more combat troops and stepped up the bombing, how would Hanoi ever believe Washington wanted peace, that its objective was compromise not victory? McNamara began urging Johnson to lower the U.S. objective in order to get out, "to make it abundantly clear," as Johnson summarized his position to Rusk, "that we did not necessarily have to have everybody of our own choosing in this [South Vietnamese] government, that it could be a Communist government." Johnson told Rusk that McNamara "said to me not once, but I'd guess a dozen times, that if we would moderate our objectives and what we're fighting for there, we'd have more chance of succeeding [diplomatically]. And he said to me a number of times that he thought that we ought to give serious consideration to this." (In his desperation, McNamara had begun to think outside the box, at least as far as American objectives were concerned.) But he later admitted "there wasn't a chance in hell

---

* For example, in December 1966, during the secret diplomatic initiative involving Poland codenamed MARIGOLD, the North Vietnamese were apparently prepared to meet with U.S. ambassador to Warsaw John Gronouski—but only to inform him they would not negotiate until the bombing stopped. See James Hershberg, *Marigold: The Lost Chance for Peace in Vietnam* (Woodrow Wilson Center Press, 2012).

of getting Dean to go along with it, let alone President Johnson."
McNamara was right. Johnson considered his position "a very dangerous one."[68]

The United States was not alone in its lack of insight. Hanoi had
astonishingly few resources with which to inform itself about the
United States, even though its adversary was a much more open
society. (Hard as it may seem to believe, the Politburo found it
difficult to acquire even the *New York Times* on a regular basis.)
Each side's acts were interpreted through the preconceptions held
by the other. As a result, each side projected its own assumptions
and fears onto the other, and each judged the other's posture as
so uncompromising and unreasonable as to preclude meaningful
negotiations. Hanoi viewed the multiple U.S. peace initiatives as
cynical publicity gimmicks to divert world and domestic opinion
away from military escalation, justify the bombing, and coerce
North Vietnam into surrender or face annihilation. Washington,
in turn, felt frustrated and disrespected. "We couldn't even get a
serious answer to our own proposals," Chet Cooper, one of the
American officials responsible for peace initiatives, later asserted.[69]
And while for America's adversary avoiding negotiations may have
been strategically consistent, the cost in blood was atrocious: Vietcong and North Vietnamese deaths eventually totaled more than
3.5 *million*—98.7 percent of all fatalities in the war.[70]

McNamara's growing sense of anxiety and desperation came
pouring out at a private dinner with a small group of former Kennedy administration associates held at historian Arthur Schlesinger's home in Georgetown on January 6, 1966. Speaking among
friends whose discretion he trusted, McNamara spoke candidly
and bluntly in order to relieve his internal torment. He lived in
the anxious state of being unable to effectively counsel Johnson
on how to win or end the war. A man unaccustomed to failure,
he admitted to them what he had told Johnson weeks before: that
he saw no military solution to a war that had begun to spin out of
control. He and Johnson had ruled out genocidal air attacks and
ground invasion of North Vietnam in order to prevent a larger war
with China, and this meant the American effort rested on limited

bombing and the attrition strategy, whose flaws had become painfully apparent to him. His objective, he said, was "withdrawal with honor."* But he did not know how to achieve it. "He seemed deeply oppressed and concerned at the prospect of indefinite escalation," Schlesinger wrote in his journal later that night. "Our impression was that he feared the resumption of bombing might well put us on the slippery slide" toward ever greater involvement.[71] And yet McNamara could not surrender to what he recognized as increasingly probable. There could be no turning back.

The enormity of the dilemma had sunk in for McNamara. He began to reflect on how he and his colleagues had gotten to this point and how he, personally, had contributed to the problem. How had they become trapped in such a mess? The rush of events left him stunned and deflated. "There is no piece of paper—no record—showing when we changed from an advisory effort to a combat role in Vietnam," he plaintively asserted to his close aide John McNaughton, then ruefully acknowledged: "We've made mistakes in Vietnam . . . I've made mistakes." He now went so far as to begin questioning the wisdom of the entire endeavor. "The fact is," McNaughton wrote in his diary in late February, "he believes we never should have gotten into the combat role out there."[72] It was a devastating admission by one of the chief architects of escalation. But now the United States was deeply enmeshed with no easy way out, and more troops were on the way with no prospect of negotiations in sight. By June, McNamara's dread had grown so acute that he believed the United States should "get in direct touch" with the North Vietnamese and Vietcong.[73] But the North Vietnamese and Vietcong had no intention of talking with the United States while the bombing continued, and they had no incentive to do so given their mounting strategic advantages. Thirty-seven days after beginning the pause, Johnson approved the intensification of air strikes.

The torrent of bad news from Vietnam began eroding Johnson,

---

* This phrase hauntingly presaged the later Nixon administration's mantra about a Vietnam exit strategy in the early 1970s (after many more Americans and Vietnamese had been killed): "peace with honor."

too. "The lines in his face are deepening," Lady Bird noted in her diary.[74] He became more sullen and moody, swinging between optimism and pessimism from one day to the next—even one hour to the next. The careful, cautious, and reflective man who had agonized from late 1963 to mid-1965 over deepening the country's involvement had committed himself and the country to a war that now appeared much more difficult, costly, and uncertain than he had ever feared, involving perhaps 600,000 or more U.S. troops, no prospect of victory, and growing domestic opposition. In an upbeat moment, he assured himself and others that "once [the Communists] become convinced that we are not weak; that we are not impatient; that we are not going to falter; that they cannot win . . . then peace will come." Then he moaned, "What am I going to do with 200,000 boys out there and the parents in this country?"[75] Johnson understood what all of this meant for his electoral fortunes and his cherished Great Society reform dreams. "I feel a good deal of the ice cracking under me and slipping on the domestic scene," he confided to a trusted associate.[76] Like McNamara, he felt caught in a terrible dilemma of his own making with no discernible exit. And like McNamara, rather than cut his losses, Johnson plunged in deeper in a desperate effort not to nullify the choices and sacrifices already made. "We cannot turn our back on all we fought for," Johnson declared.[77]

A vivid example of Johnson's emotional delicacy surfaced in his response to a February 19, 1966, letter written by Merriman Smith, UPI's long-time White House correspondent, whom Johnson knew well and considered not just a journalist but a friend. Smith brought up his son's combat death in Vietnam, and his letter cut Johnson to the bone. "Dear Mr. President," it began:

Please accept my deepest gratitude for your most considerate note of last evening concerning the loss of my boy in Vietnam.

While it is hard to explain to his younger brother and sister, and at this point, beyond rationalization for his young wife and her two babies, we all know and accept with some degree of comfort the purpose of his mission.

This young Army captain, husband and father was a profes-
sional, but he was no killer. As I wrote you when he shipped out
last year, he was anything but gung ho, but a well-trained young
American going to work.

And reflecting this attitude was every recorded tape I had from
him. This was the way we communicated once or twice a month.
Not once did he ever refer to combat in a personal sense. I've never
known a man at war who showed less bravado in his communica-
tions with home. When he was not flying missions or working out
of battalion headquarters, he and some of his buddies on their own
visited orphanages as individuals and played with the kids. He was
deeply interested in the Vietnamese people, particularly the peas-
ants, and he told me how sorely they wanted more than anything
else to be left alone in some semblance of freedom to grow their rice
and raise their families.

This good, young American, as thousands like him, was not
on the other side of the world fighting specifically for you or me,
Mr. President. He was fighting in perhaps our oldest American
tradition—taking up for people who are being pushed around. . . .

Please try not to take these things personally, Mr. President.
Yours is the awesome responsibility of command and we want you
to exercise it as surely and confidently as possible.

My boy did not die for an empty cause nor was he a war-maker.
His hope was yours, Mr. President—peace and at least a chance at
a better life for others.

Thanks again. And let us know if there is anything we can do to
help you.

Sincerely,
Smitty[78]

Deeply touched, Johnson read Smith's letter aloud at an NSC
meeting on February 22, and later that day confessed to a close
friend that "by God, I cried, and nearly everybody around the

---

* Smith never got over his eldest son's death in Vietnam. Four years later, still despon-
dent, Smith shot himself to death at his home in suburban Alexandria, Virginia.

[Cabinet] table cried."[79] Merriman Smith's admonition notwith-standing, Johnson had already begun to personalize the war, and the letter deepened that serpentine embrace. At a meeting with congressional leaders, he quoted Abraham Lincoln's remark during the dark days of the Civil War that all the responsibilities of the administration "belong to that unhappy wretch called Abraham Lincoln." Johnson recognized that Vietnam was becoming an ex-tension of himself, a test of his strength and judgment, and the arbiter of his place in history. "I know exactly how Lincoln felt," he added.[80]

Johnson's frustration fed his insecurity, and his insecurity fed his defensiveness. At a moment when his vision was most needed, he could focus only on the walls of the labyrinth and not a path to its exit. Dean Acheson, Harry Truman's secretary of state, had once warned Johnson that a president should never let his ego get between himself and his duties, but the beleaguered commander in chief found it increasingly difficult to follow Acheson's advice. When his leading Senate critic, William Fulbright, still perched as Foreign Relations Committee chairman, announced nationally televised hearings in February questioning the wisdom of the war and further legitimizing opposition, Johnson reacted petulantly, attributing his own failures to circumstances and the failures of others to bad character. He privately complained that Fulbright was "one of the most bitter anti-President men in the Senate" who "never liked me as a person and has always been envious of me" and even impugned his patriotism, claiming Fulbright was "al-most saying to Hanoi, 'If you fellas will just hang on a little bit longer, why there may be some chance for you.'"[81] He then hastily arranged a summit conference in Honolulu on February 7 with premier Nguyễn Cao Kỳ and head of state Nguyễn Văn Thiệu—the first between American and South Vietnamese leaders—to review the political and military situation while distracting media atten-tion from Fulbright's highly publicized hearings, which had begun a week earlier. There, Johnson spoke passionately behind closed doors about helping build "a better life for the common people" of Southeast Asia by focusing more effort on pacification, but then publicly postured about fighting and winning the war.[82]

Johnson's transparent effort to manage the news of Fulbright's hearings with a competing public event backfired, the obvious maneuver becoming a story in its own right, further damaging his credibility. This only intensified Johnson's sensitivity to what journalists printed about him and his complaint that Georgetown's liberal elite was sharpening its knives for him. A reporter who witnessed his increasing truculence put it well: "Critics became enemies; enemies became traitors; and the press, which a year earlier had been so friendly, was now filled with enemies baying at his heels."[83]

Johnson directed similar ire toward members of his White House staff who left. His relationship with McGeorge Bundy had always been based on mutual dependency rather than mutual affection—they had satisfied complementary needs in each other—and the growing problems in Vietnam strained their relationship further. Bundy had advocated escalation and still supported America's commitment to South Vietnam, but he recognized, like McNamara, that things had begun to go wrong. Their chemistry had never been good. Bundy had grown weary after five years in the pressure cooker of the West Wing basement ("I was tired of the job . . . It is a stressful and demanding affair," he later wrote),[84] Johnson had lost his infatuation with the former Harvard dean whose advice, like McNamara's, had proven less than sterling, and Bundy's patience for Johnson's volatility, self-pity, and lack of candor about Vietnam's growing costs had grown thin. Johnson retained his admiration for Bundy's intelligence and analytical acuity and Bundy retained grudging respect for Johnson's commitment to social reforms and sympathy for his Vietnam dilemma, but their close working relationship had run its course. In 1962, when Bundy's alma mater, Yale, offered him the university presidency, Bundy had gone to Kennedy, who said, "Mac, you can't do it, I can't let you do it." When the Ford Foundation—the world's largest philanthropy at the time—offered Bundy its presidency in the fall of 1965, Bundy went to Johnson and said, "I want to tell you, I could leave or I could not." Johnson replied, "Mac, if you feel like you ought to leave, the answer is yes, it's accepted." Bundy would miss being at the center of action and excitement, but not Johnson's ever-shifting moods and posturing nor the deepening frustrations of Vietnam. He set his departure date for the end of February.[85] A part of Johnson hesitated to see Bundy go, but another part resented his departure—"you're going to leave us in the middle of a goddam war . . . to go home and play checkers," he only half jokingly grumbled to Bundy.[86] Johnson could not resist making snide and ungenerous remarks about someone who had the temerity to leave *him*; those who worked for Lyndon Johnson simply did not do such things. (Bundy went from being "my Harvard" to "a smart kid, period."[87])

"The Ford Foundation was a plum," McNamara later said, but "he didn't leave to take a plum. He left because he couldn't get along with Johnson."[88] In addition, said Bundy's sister Hattie, "the fact that his wife, his sister, his brother's wife and so many of his Cambridge friends all opposed the war made it easier to make the decision to leave." Kennedy's *wunderkind* became the first of Camelot for whom Vietnam had made a casualty of his reputation. He would not be the last.

After considering Maxwell Taylor, Johnson settled on Walt Whitman (W. W.) Rostow, NSC deputy under President Kennedy and currently director of the policy planning staff at the State Department, as Bundy's successor (though Bundy had not recommended him* and Ball actively opposed his selection).[89] He chose Rostow for several reasons. Johnson believed, as he told Rusk in a telephone conversation, that Rostow "would give us protection from the intellectual crowd and the college crowd." Rostow had all the right credentials—graduate of Yale, professor of economics

---

* Bundy recommended Robert Komer, a deputy on the NSC staff, who became Johnson's special assistant for pacification and, the following year, pacification czar in South Vietnam. McNamara recommended Johnson's close aide and press secretary Bill Moyers.

Walt Rostow and LBJ
Yoichi Okamoto/LBJ Library

at the Massachusetts Institute of Technology (MIT)—but would
be *his* intellectual, beholden to Johnson, not the Kennedy circle.
"Do you know why I'm doing this?" he somewhat contemptuously
asked deputy national security advisor Francis Bator, who had
been a schoolmate of Bundy's at Groton. "Because I want someone
who isn't part of your crowd."[90]

Rostow had no hesitation about emphasizing his own opinions
in the paperwork he submitted to the president. He had been secretly promoting himself for months through starry-eyed back-
channel memos to the president that bypassed both his boss at
State, Secretary Rusk, and Bundy at the NSC. Rostow was an
idea man, who, Johnson said, "is trying to suggest things all the
time."[91] (Indeed, Rostow loved ideas, particularly his own.) Rostow would bring considerable intelligence and analytical skills
to the demanding job of national security advisor, together with
an open and friendly approach to his colleagues. He would also,
Johnson pointed out to Rusk, "be loyal and he seems to have been

very friendly with you and me." Yet he had a weakness. "Walt was an enthusiast," recalled Bator, who had his office next door to Rostow's at MIT's Center for International Studies in the 1950s. "He was very good at formulating a coherent option, but he was not very good at saying that's *one* possible option but there are others. He wasn't a powerful self-critic. He would create a rich and persuasive story, but he wouldn't reach outside of it."[92] (President Kennedy once remarked that Rostow might have ten ideas, nine of which could lead to disaster, but one of which would be brilliant.) It was via these limits that Rostow was a natural optimist and gifted advocate, serenely confident in his own opinions and judgment, whose unflagging support for the war appealed to a president feeling increasingly besieged and criticized. He would not "turn tail," per Johnson's Texas expression, as the war became tough sledding.

A smart and pleasant man with an owlish face and clear plastic horn-rimmed glasses who always wore a button-down oxford-cloth dress shirt, a herringbone tweed jacket, and a faintly patronizing smile, Rostow, like Bundy before him, looked the Ivy League part. An economist, he viewed Vietnam as a testing ground for his favorite theory of national development, determined to prove that capitalism worked for former colonial peoples like the Vietnamese. Another favorite theory of Rostow's concerned bombing. During World War II, he had selected targets for U.S. bombing missions against Nazi-occupied Europe. This experience made him a true believer not only in the notion that a country could be pounded into submission as a result of a detonated economy and collapsed morale but in the efficacy of transporting the lessons he had learned to Vietnam. As a result, Rostow continually pushed for heavier bombing, convinced this would be the key that would win the war. In August 1965, he told an associate "that the Vietcong are already coming apart under the bombing. They're going to collapse within weeks. Not months, weeks."[93] These ideological convictions were matched by a fierce anti-Communism that made Rostow both a firm believer in the American effort in Vietnam and someone who always looked for evidence that supported his conjecture. He was, said Bundy, "a persistent believer that the real world must have the shape of his own."[94] In turn, he had "a great capacity not to see what he did not choose to see," noted a colleague.[95]

Rostow had invested enormous time, energy, and personal reputation in the war, and like people afflicted by confirmation bias, he was selective in what he was willing to see and pass along to the president. He discarded evidence that did not fit in with "the truth," instead seeking out information that validated his own viewpoint, which he was not interested in reexamining. He neglected ambiguity and suppressed doubt. "He could look at evidence and just see what he wanted," noted a State Department official who worked with him frequently. "He had a terrible ability to flatter Johnson in the worst way . . . day after day after day it was coming in the President's ear—morning, noon, and night." "Whatever he could do to prevent the President from hearing the other side, Walt did," Clark Clifford later reflected.[96] Even when it served Johnson badly, Rostow grasped at any straws that seemed to validate his convictions about the war. On one occasion, Rostow phoned CIA analyst George Allen to request a study of progress in the pacification program. Allen asked Rostow if he sought an assessment of pacification. No, Rostow answered—he wanted a paper that showed progress. Allen told Rostow the CIA could not produce a paper that showed only progress—serious problems with pacification existed in many provinces of South Vietnam. Rostow said he was aware of that, but "the President" needed a summary that showed pacification worked. Allen then explained that any summary would have to include bad news as well as good. Growing impatient, Rostow told Allen he didn't care about unfavorable pacification developments; he wanted a summary of *favorable* developments. Allen refused, saying the CIA wouldn't be a party to "cooking the books." Rostow slammed down the receiver. But he didn't give up. He called another office at the CIA, which produced a memo summarizing progress in pacification. A cover note to the memo by Richard Helms made clear that the report did not include adverse developments in the pacification program, which outweighed the favorable ones, and therefore the memo should not be construed as an assessment of overall trends.

When Rostow received the document, he removed Helm's cover and sent the summary on to Johnson with a slip of paper that read, "At last, Mr. President, a useful assessment from the CIA. WWR."[97]

Without a stable and effective South Vietnamese government, no amount of U.S. help would win the war, and Johnson and his advisors had hoped the introduction of American troops would create breathing room for Saigon to put its political house in order. At the Honolulu Conference, Generals Kỳ and Thiệu, who had few qualifications for the job of governing, promised Johnson they would hold national elections and through them build solidarity and common purpose among the contending South Vietnamese factions. The generals also publicly committed themselves "to formulate a democratic constitution in the months ahead, to take it to the Vietnamese people for discussion and modification, to seek its ratification by secret ballot and finally to create, on the basis of elections, a representative government." Within weeks, however, Kỳ and Thiệu cracked down on Buddhists who opposed the junta's rule and demanded an end to the war, triggering demonstrations, strikes, and civil war in the northern Buddhist strongholds of Danang and Huế. The generals' use of force to suppress the Buddhists further diminished their moral authority. (Under Confucianism, military mandarins had always had less prestige than their civilian counterparts.)

Having committed American troops to the war, Johnson and his advisors hesitated to coerce a regime on which the growing U.S. effort rested and that it viewed as the sole potential source of stability in the troubled country. As Johnson told Rusk, "it's going to be so much more difficult to rebuild a government than it is to hold the one we've got if we can do it."[98] Thus emboldened, Kỳ then postponed promised elections and announced that he would hold power until then. The administration grumbled privately, but responded not by pressuring Kỳ and Thiệu to compromise with the Buddhists, but by providing them transport planes piloted by Americans to suppress the uprisings. Rusk called it "intolerable" that Kỳ had acted "without consultation with us." "It bothered me," McNamara later wrote, "that the South Vietnamese battled one another while the enemy pressed at the gates."[99] Yet by ultimately acquiescing in Kỳ's decision, Washington thereby implicitly legitimized his behavior, even though it violated the Confucian values of dignity, maturity, and virtuous example, and disrespected Buddhist monks who retained a powerful hold on the religious and social life of rural villagers. This acquiescence revealed a great deal about just how little Americans understood Vietnamese attitudes and sensibilities.

South Vietnam's generals had always been dependent on the United States, even as they manipulated it; they needed, at the same time they resented, American help. Now, despite supporting the generals and fighting a war on their behalf, the United States was becoming dependent on *them*—and both sides increasingly knew it, though neither was willing to admit it. The United States had gotten so firmly hooked in Vietnam—there were now more than 350,000 American troops conducting missions and suffering casualties—that nothing the ARVN generals did would prompt American disengagement. The tail had begun wagging the dog. This troubling and deeply constraining paradox exposed the contradiction, as one contemporary writer noted, "between the Americans' desire to put the GVN [Government of South Vietnam] on its own feet and their desire to maintain some control over GVN politics."[100] This mutual dependency, and mutual resentment, that lay beneath the allies' surface harmony, would shape relations between Washington and Saigon for the rest of the war.

The latest Buddhist crisis also deepened the division between those who wanted the United States to get out and those who urged doing more to win. The latter prominently included the chiefs, who deeply resented the limitations that Johnson and McNamara continued to impose. The attitude of the Pacific theater commander, Admiral U. S. Grant Sharp, was typical: "The application of military, war-making power is an ugly thing—stark, harsh, and demanding," Sharp later wrote, "and it cannot be made nicer by pussy-footing around with it."[101] The chiefs had reacted to the failed bombing pause by urging stepped-up bombing of North Vietnam and, led by the air force and navy, who "owned" the air war—their participation in the war, and therefore their all-important budgets and missions, were tied to the bombing—they pressed LBJ and McNamara vigorously. Like Westmoreland and the army, air power advocates in the air force and navy uncritically projected their assumptions onto North Vietnam and the Vietcong. Their assurance reflected their stubbornly abiding perception of the conflict as a conventional war in which the enemy required considerable logistical support rather than as a guerrilla war in which the enemy's requirements were modest and diffuse. This, in turn, reflected the priority of industry to America's own war-fighting capability and their own experiences in World War II, when Allied bombing of Germany and Japan had crippled those industrial economies. They did not pause to ponder that North Vietnam and the Vietcong might be different, and what implications for bombing and its effectiveness flowed from those differences. Reasoning that the vulnerability of rail lines to interdiction increased the value of ground transport as a logistical tool and that Hanoi, which had no oil fields or refineries, relied heavily on imported fuel for the trucks that moved men and supplies to the South, the chiefs urged attacking petroleum reserves and oil-storage facilities (POL, shorthand for petroleum, oils, and lubricants) in the North, and mining the main port of Haiphong where most imported fuel arrived aboard Soviet tankers, asserting this would deal Hanoi a mortal blow.

McNamara adamantly disagreed. He believed the chiefs overestimated bombing's effectiveness and privately remarked in early 1966 that "no amount of bombing"—short of genocidal destruction—"can end the war."[102] He also worried that heavier bombing might draw China into the war. An incident that occurred that spring gave credence to this fear. On May 12, a U.S. aircraft on a combat mission over North Vietnam shot down a Chinese MiG-17 just across the Chinese border, though neither Beijing nor Washington publicized the incident.[103] Assessments by CIA analysts with no stake in the bombing corroborated McNamara's judgment. Statistics showed the air force and navy had dropped 50 percent more tonnage on North Vietnam in the month before the pause began than during the peak month of the Korean War, and yet as was now well known, infiltration had *increased* during the period. The CIA concluded that bombing POL targets and mining Haiphong harbor would not have a "critical impact on the combat activity of the Communist forces in South Vietnam"—but would risk widening the war by accidentally hitting a Soviet ship. The official slated to become CIA director, Richard Helms, told Johnson on January 22 that "increased bombing in the North could not stop movement of supplies to the South." The CIA was right. Despite the stepped-up American strikes, Hanoi nearly tripled its gasoline storage capacity by the end of 1966.[104]

But it remained the case that political pressure, not analytical assessments, touched Johnson most. He keenly felt the chiefs' hot breath of criticism, both in their memos and in their back-channel lobbying of allies on the Hill. The air force chief of staff, General John O'Connell, secretly (and insubordinately) visited senators and complained to them that "his hands [were] tied" in Vietnam.[105] The influential Senate Armed Services Committee chairman Richard Russell, who had counseled both Kennedy and Johnson about Vietnam, announced on the Senate floor on January 24 that "we must decide whether or not we are willing to take the action necessary to win the war in Vietnam and bring a conclusion to our commitment." Such was one side of the equation. "The only other alternative I can see," he declared, "is to pull out—and this the overwhelming majority of Americans are not prepared to do."[106] On that front Russell was correct: a Harris poll published the last day of the month reported that "the vast majority of Americans would support an immediate escalation of the war—including all-out bombings of North Vietnam and increasing U.S. troop commitments to 500,000 men."[107]

In late June, Johnson finally authorized attacks on POL targets. The raids destroyed nearly all surface-storage tanks in Hanoi and most of those in Haiphong. The North Vietnamese quickly adjusted by dispersing fuel in underground tanks and fifty-five-gallon drums scattered throughout the country, soliciting increased oil shipments by rail from China, and by off-loading oil from Soviet tankers anchored outside of Haiphong onto barges that transported the oil to transfer points that dotted the Red River Delta. Such was the ignorance of the chiefs that they did not know that North Vietnamese trains ran on coal or wood, not oil.

The CIA concluded several months later that "bombing increased the cost and difficulty of importing and distributing petroleum, both for the USSR and North Vietnam. There is no evidence, however, that the bombing of petroleum targets seriously weakened the economy of North Vietnam, produced shortages of petroleum, or diminished North Vietnam's capability to support military activities or the infiltration of men and supplies into the South."[108] But the American public backed the raids by a five-to-one margin and they raised Johnson's approval rating by twelve points among Americans anxious for a quick end to the fighting.[109]

The POL issue symbolized a larger problem. During 1966, air force and navy aircraft conducted more than 13,000 interdiction sorties against roads, trucks, railway lines, and marshaling yards throughout North Vietnam, dropping more than 800 tons of bombs, rockets, and missiles *every day*. Total air force sorties increased from 25,000 in 1965, to 79,000 in 1966, and 108,000 in 1967. The air force eventually dropped nearly 7 million tons of bombs—three times the tonnage it dropped in all theaters of World War II, and thirteen times what it dropped in the Korean War.*[110] A report submitted to Giáp later in the war revealed that American bombs hit their targets only 0.19 percent of the time—only two of every thousand U.S. bombs dropped.[111] North Vietnam also possessed a sophisticated air defense system, courtesy of the Soviet Union—8,000 anti-aircraft batteries and more than 200 state-

---

* The consequences of so much bombing persist to this day: an estimated 350,000 tons of unexploded ordnance still litter the landscape of Vietnam. Nearly 40,000 Vietnamese have been killed and 67,000 maimed since the war ended in 1975. At the current disposal rate, it will take the Vietnamese 300 years to defuse and remove all of them. See Ariel Garfinkel, "The Vietnam War Is Over. The Bombs Remain." *NYT*, March 20, 2018.

of-the-art fixed and mobile radar-controlled and computerized surface-to-air (SAM) missile systems—combined with a civil defense network of manhole-like individual shelters that dotted city streets and a system of trenches and tunnels in the countryside that allowed peasants to tend their rice and vegetable crops between air attacks. The effectiveness of Hanoi's Soviet-supplied ground-controlled intercept radar and SAM missiles meant that more than 40 percent of all U.S. sorties flown over North Vietnam had to be devoted to flak suppression rather than to bombing targets. The North Vietnamese's adaptability knew almost no limits: they even placed anti-aircraft batteries inside bomb craters on city streets and on bamboo rafts floating on Hanoi's West Lake. As a result, the U.S. assault was a massive, but futile, effort that also led to the downing and capture of American pilots that gave Hanoi precious hostages it would later exploit to maximum effect in negotiations to end the war. Infrastructure damage was ephemeral. American bombs did sometimes hit noncombatant targets such as schools and hospitals, killing thousands of North Vietnamese civilians. The chiefs neglected this danger in the initial targets they submitted for approval, until McNamara insisted that an estimate of civilian casualties be included in all future ones.[112] All such collateral damage enraged and further alienated the North Vietnamese people from any support for negotiations with the United States.

What in some manner held the North "back" was what inspired its dexterity. The leaders of North Vietnam aspired to "industrialized socialism"[113] in order to complete recovery from the First Indochina War with France and increase its people's standard of living, but in 1966 the country remained an overwhelmingly agrarian society with limited industrial capacity. North Vietnam relied very little on electrical generation and manufacturing to sustain its economy. The Pentagon knew that Hanoi's largest power station generated only 32,500 kilowatts—the capacity of an American power station servicing a community of just 25,000 people.[114] Once the bombing began, Hanoi switched to portable generators and decentralized its production process. Self-sufficiency became the norm. Dispersed underground workshops and storage facilities replaced urban factories, and handicraft production rose significantly.

And on it went: hundreds of thousands of Chinese engineering troops repaired rail lines and roads, and built miles of bypasses and detours around choke points to create redundancy in the transportation system. They also stacked steel rails and wooden ties at regular intervals along important routes in order to speed repairs. U.S. pilots flying through murderous flak frequently disabled the Kep rail yard on the northeast railroad from China, only to find it operational the next day. North Vietnam had ample manpower of its own to keep its logistical network functioning. Highways surfaced with clay meant only shovel brigades were needed to repair them. Families donated wooden doors and beds to cover pockmarked roads so that trucks could get through. When bombs broke a rail line, brigades composed of Chinese-made Phoenix bicycles that could carry 250 kilograms unloaded train cargos, traveled beyond the break, and reloaded the cargo onto another train. When bombs destroyed a bridge, local North Vietnamese promptly repaired it with prepositioned replacement spans or pontoons, or lashed canal boats together sideways and laid wood planks over the top. Some bridges were even built just below the water's surface to avoid detection. Peasants pulling oxcarts, pushing bicycles with bamboo frames containing hundreds of pounds of cargo, and porters balancing heavily laden shoulder poles (*đòn gánh*) replaced destroyed and damaged trucks camouflaged with jungle foliage.

Unlike the American military's profligate logistical consumption—the United States imported 600,000 tons of supplies into South Vietnam each month, the ratio of its support to combat troops was seven-to-one,[*] and only 5 percent of American soldiers carried rifles in the field—Vietcong and North Vietnamese military units in South Vietnam were streamlined and ingenious. Many of their sol-

---

[*] By the summer of 1967, 464,000 U.S. troops had been deployed to South Vietnam; only 50,000 of them were available for offensive ground operations. See John S. Bowman, ed., *The Vietnam War: An Almanac* (World Almanac Publications, 1985), p. 174.

diers wore vulcanized rubber sandals with treaded soles cut from discarded tires. They fought on average just one day a month and the entire Communist force needed only thirty-four tons of supplies a day from sources outside the South—less than 0.20 percent of their American adversaries' demands. Seven 2.5-ton trucks making it successfully down the Hồ Chí Minh Trail could transport that requirement.[115]

The quantities contained in such a small number of trucks paled in comparison to what the Soviet Union and China provided North Vietnam: nearly 6,000 tons of war-making supplies a day by rail links through China, off-loading of ships not just in Haiphong but by shallow-draft barges and sampans that dispersed their cargos through a web of canals and rivers along the coast, and shipments to the port of Sihanoukville in Cambodia. Only 0.57 percent of supplies had to make it down the Hồ Chí Minh Trail or across Cambodia—meaning interdiction bombing could be more than 99 percent effective, and that would not suffice. The supply flow to the South in 1965—*after* the bombing began—equaled the total transported during the previous five years.[116]

Air strikes against troop infiltration proved equally ineffective. When ROLLING THUNDER began in February 1965, air power advocates in the air force and navy who had pushed McNamara and Johnson to begin bombing for a year confidently predicted a successful "LOC [lines of communication] cut program." At that point, much of the Hồ Chí Minh Trail was passable only during the dry season. (Soldiers stretched gunnysacks across muddy sections to avoid leaving footprints for U.S. patrols or reconnaissance aircraft.) That year, Hanoi enlarged the draft, extended the period of military service indefinitely, and recalled all discharged officers and enlisted men. (Each year, 200,000 North Vietnamese reached draft age.) Militia forces rose from 1.4 million to 2 million and the regular army increased from 290,000 to 400,000. By the end of 1966, the number of North Vietnamese regulars reached 700,000, of whom 230,000 had been sent to South Vietnam.[117] Many of these men (and some women) made their way South during a five-week journey down 1,250 miles of the Annamese Mountains through

Laos to join 80,000 Vietcong regulars and 174,000 irregulars.[118] The passage was brutal, and for some, fatal. Each carried a forty-pound "frog pack" containing a shelter tarp, a hammock, a plastic rain poncho, and a few precious medicines along with a mountain stick and a helmet. Almost constantly forced to move, they dug up and ate jungle roots when the sausage-shaped bags of rice they draped around their necks ran out. There were many dangers besides American bombs. Some travelers lost their way in the double- and triple-canopy forest and died of starvation. While sleeping at night, they could be attacked by tigers or bears. Others stepped on poisonous snakes and died from venomous bites. In the rainy season, when streams ran fast, some lost their footing on slippery bridges and fell to their deaths. Jungle leeches proved a constant hazard, attaching themselves to all parts of the body. Still others, famished by hunger, died from eating poisonous mushrooms and leaves.[119]

To avoid detection by American aircraft, the North Vietnamese usually moved at night, often on mountain footpaths built up with bamboo steps and even hand railings, and communicated by word-of-mouth or runners—radios used only in emergencies. During the day, when U.S. warplanes appeared over jungle paths that sometimes limited visibility to five or ten yards, the North Vietnamese would disperse and take cover in foxholes or seek refuge in an elaborate maze of underground caves, tunnels, and bunkers where they stored food and supplies and created hospitals to treat the wounded and the many who contracted malaria and other diseases during the trek down the trail. About 15 percent of those who began the journey never made it, dying of disease much more often than as a result of U.S. air strikes. Despite all of these hardships, replacement troops sent South increased sixfold over the number sent in 1965.[120]

During the years that followed, as American aircraft poured an immense load of ordnance down on the Hồ Chí Minh Trail, the Communists constructed an elaborate highway system comprising an astonishing 9,600 miles of all-weather roads surfaced with crushed rocks or logs in soft places, built pontoon bridges over streams and creeks and rivers that could be removed during daylight hours and towed back into place at night, and even created loops and bypasses at choke points and segments frequently cratered by bombing. Along some portions of the trail, workers blasted caves out of the mountains to shelter supplies from American bombing. The blasted rock, in turn, was used for road repair. Even at the height of bombing, road-building battalions constructed one new mile of road per day.

Lê Duẩn and his hard-line colleagues recognized their adversary's political weaknesses—governmental dysfunction in South Vietnam and popular doubt about the war in the United States— and always kept these advantageous strategic facts in mind. This uncomfortable reality trumped the chiefs' belief that destroying North Vietnam's industry would cripple its economy and persuade Hanoi to yield. The stubborn reality was that an underdeveloped society based on subsistence agriculture could not be bombed into submission short of genocidal destruction, and no one—not even the chiefs—advocated that. Like the London Blitz of 1940–1941, U.S. "strategic" bombing of North Vietnam paradoxically steeled popular determination and national will, generating defiance rather than defeatism. The North Vietnamese had no intention of submitting to American pressure—however sophisticated and punitive. "The Americans thought the more bombs they dropped, the quicker we would fall to our knees and surrender," said one resident of Hanoi after the war. "But the bombs heightened rather than dampened our spirit." Almost the same words had been spoken by Cockneys of London's East End in response to Nazi air attacks. Americans couldn't even put themselves in British shoes, so imprisoned were they by their own World War II experience as those who delivered bombs, not suffered from them.

Westmoreland continued his pursuit of an attrition strategy during 1966 and 1967, vainly seeking to bring the Communists to battle despite mounting evidence that he could not. Few inside the army or in Washington ventured to question or criticize him. He enjoyed Johnson's and McNamara's continued support and considerable popularity with the press and public as the highly touted and pro-moted commander of America's fighting men in Vietnam. (*Time* put him on its cover as "Man of the Year" at the end of 1965.) From August to December of 1966, Westmoreland committed 95 percent of his forces to search-and-destroy operations. In 1967, that percent-age dropped only a little, to 86 percent.[121] Yet far too often "search" was "found": the Communists initiated combat in 85 percent of engagements and enjoyed the element of surprise 80 percent of the time. Only 5 percent of the time did U.S. forces have "reason-ably accurate knowledge of enemy positions and strength" prior to an engagement.[122] The U.S. Army followed the rule "Expend shells, not men." As a result, nearly every operation was preceded by "softening-up" bombardments by artillery or air strikes, which yielded few enemy casualties but resulted in the loss of the element of surprise. Search-and-destroy missions relied heavily on Amer-ica's overwhelming advantage in firepower, often extravagantly and indiscriminately applied—at triple the rate expended during the Korean War—which seemed a way of generating a high enemy body count while minimizing U.S. casualties (though thousands of tons of dud shells became raw material for Vietcong mines and booby traps).

When asked at a press conference how to fight the insurgency, Westmoreland replied with one word: "firepower."[123] As a sign at Fort Polk, Louisiana, where army recruits trained in infantry tactics before being shipped to Vietnam, put it, Aggressiveness and Firepower Will Win. The First Air Cavalry fired more than 132,000 rounds of artillery during its sweep through northern Bình Định province from late January to early March 1966. The sweep resulted in 1,342 enemy killed—1,000 rounds of artillery per one Communist soldier killed—and nearly 130,000 refugees. Neverthe-less, Westmoreland reported in the spring of 1967 that U.S. troops had "spoiled" four enemy offensives and increased the enemy death toll to nearly 8,000 a month. Westmoreland persistently spoke of progress—even as he hit up Washington for more troops every three or four months. Before too long, a general on his MACV staff told *Newsweek* "that with between 500,000 and 700,000 men, we

could break the back of the Communist main forces by 1968–69."[124]
It seemed like another age when Westmoreland had initially fore-
cast the need for a total of 275,000 U.S. troops, but it was but a few
years.

Despite mounting evidence that attrition was not working, Westmoreland bullheadedly persisted in his conviction that he had no
alternative. He did not have enough troops, he repeatedly insisted,
to engage in manpower-intensive pacification and population
control efforts that would require more time than the American
public's patience would allow. So, frantically, American soldiers
continued to chase the enemy around the sparsely populated highlands region or along the Laotian and Cambodian borders, allowing
the Communists to maintain their access to the food, recruits, and
intelligence provided by the rural peasantry in the more populated coastal plain within twenty-five miles of the South China Sea
where more than 85 percent of the South Vietnamese lived. One
frustrated American three-star general later admitted that "it was
often necessary to go back into an area time and time again to
defeat not the same enemy but perhaps the same numbered unit
that had regrouped from local recruits and replacements from the
north."[125] Thus the Vietcong and North Vietnamese wore down
the Americans, as their forefathers had worn down the Mongols,
the Chinese, and the French before them, engaging the Americans
in a game of hide-and-seek while inflicting steady casualties and
sapping U.S. domestic support for the war.

There was some pushback from within the military. In the
spring of 1966, junior officers (with some higher level encouragement) who questioned the wisdom of Westmoreland's strategy
produced a nine-hundred-page study, "A Program for the Pacification and Long-Term Development of South Vietnam" (PROVN
for short), that recommended greater emphasis on pacification
under the U.S. ambassador's control and integrating under American command the ARVN forces responsible for standing guard
over the villages. These junior officers believed there needed to
be much more focus on a population security strategy to deny the
Vietcong food, recruitment, and intelligence rather than continue

large search-and-destroy operations in remote areas in an attempt
to kill enemy forces in big battles.[126] The marine corps also favored
a population security strategy combined with a greater emphasis
on pacification, agreeing that the key lay in providing safety for
those living in South Vietnam's hamlets and villages,* but Westmoreland had operational control over marines deployed in Vietnam, and he and his MACV staff resisted the recommendations.
They feared such a strategy would give the Communists free rein
to attack where and when they chose (which the Communists
already did), disliked subordinating army troops and resources
of whatever magnitude to the civilian ambassador's control, and
worried that placing ARVN under U.S. command would play into
Vietcong propaganda that depicted South Vietnam's army as puppets of the Americans. The first of these concerns may have been
the least important to Westmoreland and his allies; more so it was
protection of bureaucratic turf and negative political ramifications
that doomed both proposals. The army downgraded the PROVN
study to a "conceptual document" nonbinding on Westmoreland
and MACV.

During this same period, the number of American troops in
South Vietnam swelled from 184,300 in December 1965 to 485,600
by December 1967. Tragically, the number of U.S. killed in action
rose sharply as well, from 1,928 in 1965 to 6,350 in 1966 to 11,363 in
1967, statistics at once most stark and most human.[127] The number
of wounded went even higher, nearly triple those killed in action.[128]
The Johnson administration fought the war using draftees rather
than reservists, and it allowed college deferments to the draft
during the early years of the war. These policies, combined with
the growing deployments to Vietnam, quickly depleted the army's
pool of well-trained and experienced junior officers and senior noncommissioned officers, diluting maturity and experience levels.
They also put the burden of fighting on poor and working-class

---

* The marines created Combined Action Platoons (CAPs), a combination of U.S.
Marines and South Vietnamese militia who lived inside villages and worked on
civic action projects as well as providing security.

young men and minorities who lacked the education and financial resources to attend college. (African Americans represented 11 percent of the U.S. population in the mid-1960s, but 16 percent of draftees, 23 percent of U.S. combat troops in Vietnam, and only 2 percent of the officer corps. Latinos comprised 12 percent of America's population, but 19 percent of total casualties.[129]) Such a manifestly inequitable arrangement made America's fighting forces in Vietnam less diverse and less representative of American society as a whole than "the greatest generation" of GIs who served the country in World War II and Korea. It divorced the children of elites from military service and exposure to the danger and sacrifices of war (as during the Civil War, when wealthy Northerners could pay for substitutes to serve in their place in the Union Army), and it inadvertently politicized the rank and file of the army because many of the young men drafted and sent to fight in Vietnam did not want to go there, a proportion that grew considerably as the war dragged on.

"American soldiers in Vietnam faced many obstacles and miserable conditions," McNamara wrote of the servicemen under his charge: "an elusive and deadly enemy, booby traps and ambushes, fire ants and leeches, dense jungles, deep swamps, and sweltering heat . . . They answered their nation's call and endured many hardships—both 'in country' and, sadly, after coming home as well. It was not the valor of American soldiers in Vietnam that was ever in dispute but how they should operate in the field."[130] "Humping" under a hot sun, slogging across muddy rice paddies up to one's knees while trying to keep your rifle out of the water, suffering hit-and-run attacks from an elusive enemy that would disappear into the bush, tripping booby traps and mines*—all of this represented a day in the field.

The military's length-of-tour policy proved counterproductive as well. Established during the advisory era and carried over by Westmoreland because he believed it was "good for morale" in that

---

* Mines and booby traps—which produced no enemy losses—accounted for almost 30 percent of all American casualties.

"it gave a man a goal,"[131] every officer and enlisted man served a one-year tour in Vietnam (except generals, who served for nineteen months). Officers' time in the field proved even shorter; the army assigned them only six months of line command, followed by six months in staff jobs. Even though casualties under an officer's command almost always decreased the more time he spent in the field (firsthand participation the best source of better judgment), the army kept its short-term rotation policy because every career officer wanted a stint in Vietnam as a way to "punch his ticket" for promotion; they then had to move on to make room for the next officer. This meant that just as soldiers and officers acquired a modicum of experience and perspective on the people and culture of Southeast Asia and the war, they rotated out of the country, replaced by green draftees—often derisively referred to as "f—in' new guys" (FNGs) by veteran grunts—who knew almost nothing about Vietnam and had to learn the same hard and bitter lessons all over again. Thus a huge problem for the American military, as former ARVN advisor John Paul Vann acidly put it, was, "We don't have twelve years' experience in Vietnam. We have one year's experience twelve times over."

The brutality that American soldiers in Vietnam—many of them teenagers (their average age was just nineteen)—suffered and inflicted claimed a heavy toll on everyone caught in the tragic vortex of war. "The violence of combat assaults psyches, confuses ethics, and tests souls," explained a decorated marine about his experience in the contested jungles of Southeast Asia. "Warriors suffer from wounds to their bodies, to be sure, but because they are involved in killing people they also suffer from their compromises with, or outright violations of, the moral norms of society and religion . . . The Marine Corps taught me how to kill but it didn't teach me how to deal with killing." There is "a powerful, innate human resistance toward killing one's own species," notes former West Point psychology professor Dave Grossman, but soldiers were "condition[ed] to overcome their resistance."[132] Taking life—and the load of emotional pain it bestowed—became part of the sorrow of war. It compelled young men to live with heavy contradictions. "You can't be a warrior and not be deeply involved with suffering and responsibility."[133] Another marine put it bluntly: "Killing leaves a hole in your soul."[134] "It is the existence of the victim's pain and loss, echoing forever in the soul of the killer, that is at the heart of his pain."[135] "In war," observed Argentine writer José Narosky, "there are no unwounded soldiers."

Young men far from home had been taught a great deal about military tactics but precious little about Vietnamese culture, the realities of guerrilla war, and how to cope with the consequences of violence inflicted by human beings on other human beings. The moral injury being done to young Americans soldiers would grow and by the early 1970s include drug use, emotional breakdowns, and even "fragging" (deliberate killing) of officers—all of which fed intensifying opposition to the war. In 1965, only 6 percent of medical evacuations involved psychiatric casualties. By 1971, half of all medical evacuations did.[136] Over time, the desertion rate rose to more than 7 percent, the absent-without-leave (AWOL) rate to almost 18 percent.[137]

MACV issued rules of engagement (ROEs) concerning avoidance of civilian casualties, but officers were under intense pressure to produce body counts and the difficulty of distinguishing friend from foe in a war without frontlines meant that soldiers often shot first and addressed hearts and minds afterward, resulting in large (and politically devastating) civilian casualties. "If you can't count what's important," said a U.S. Army advisor, "you make what you can count important."[138] With no other way to measure progress in the ground war, body counts became the grisly yardstick. The emphasis on body counts led to the widespread practice of inflating numbers to keep everyone happy (ARVN had been inflating these figures for years). A postwar survey of generals found that more than half believed the body count was "often inflated" and less than a fifth believed that ROEs had been carefully followed.[139] Off-the-record interviews with officers and enlisted men revealed a consistent and troubling pattern: battalions doubled the figures coming in from companies and brigades doubled the figures coming in from battalions. Something also had to be put in for all of the shells and bombs expended, which troops on the ground could not confirm, to give the artillery and air forces their share of the "kill."*[140] Under fire, junior officers often found it hard to think about the moral and political consequences of a situation and responded with massive firepower rather than restraint, reconceiving the South Vietnamese peasant not as someone to be won over but as someone in the way. Villagers in the relatively open country of the Mekong Delta learned to flee at the sound of approaching helicopters; some helicopter gunners, interpreting their flight as evidence of Vietcong activity, sprayed the ground with machine-gun fire. Army chief of staff Harold K. Johnson sadly confided to the army's top noncommissioned officer, Sergeant Major William Wooldridge, that "things like this happen when you are following a policy that is not working and such actions are the result of trying to justify that false policy."[141] Despite all of this, Westmoreland publicly insisted that the body count was "very, very conservative" and "probably represents less than 50 percent" of Vietcong and North Vietnamese actually killed.[142]

Some American units practiced "reconnaissance by fire"—finding out if a particular location, such as a "hootch" (hut) or a rice paddy, had enemy forces in it by shooting into it and seeing whether anyone shot back. Other units used artillery to replace ground patrolling in populated areas. Such tactics seemed safer than walking into what might be an ambush, but also resulted in tremendous civilian casualties. A second lieutenant criticized for ordering reconnaissance by fire (which contradicted the ROEs), said, "Tough shit. They know we're operating in this area, they can hear us, and they ought to be in their bunker. I'm not taking any unnecessary chances with my men."[143]

Artillery and bombs pummeled hamlets and adjacent fields on

---

* A 1969 U.S. Army War College survey of former combat commanders in Vietnam revealed that more than 60 percent reported that a significant portion of the "body count" was routinely "estimated," with the figures regularly "upped" during subsequent evaluations. Edward Doyle, Stephen Weiss, and the editors of Boston Publishing Company, *The Vietnam Experience: A Collision of Cultures* (Boston Publishing Company, 1984), p. 146.

which villagers relied for food, inflicting casualties on enemy forces and civilians alike. Much of it involved unobserved fire directed at areas where the enemy *might* be rather than where the enemy was known to be, because villagers rarely cooperated by pointing out the Vietcong's hiding places. (Only 6 percent of artillery fire was observed.[144]) The army called this "prophylactic firepower," which a British military observer in South Vietnam explained, "means if you do not know where the enemy is, make a big enough bang and you may bring something down." "Ammo kept coming whether or not we had targets for it," recalled an artillery commander, "so the batteries fired their allotments every opportunity they had, whether there was actually anything to shoot at or not."[145] One general admitted with considerable understatement that such practices made it "a little expensive in terms of friendly casualties."[146] General Johnson spoke more bluntly, conceding that a great deal of American firepower was applied "on a relatively random basis" that "just sort of devastated the countryside."[147]

The carnage was in no ways limited to the North. In South Vietnam, U.S. air forces dropped 70 tons of bombs for every square mile of the country, about 500 pounds of explosives for every man, woman, and child. Between 1965 and 1968, American aircraft dropped 2.2 million tons of bombs on the territory of its ally—more than triple the 643,000 tons dropped on its adversary.[148] Ordnance included napalm,* jellied gasoline that stuck to the skin and once ignited could not be put out with water, white phosphorus that burned down to the bone and also could not be extinguished with water, and cluster bombs containing hundreds of steel pellets that scattered in all directions at high velocity upon impact. "We usually kill more women and kids than we do Vietcong," admitted an American officer after a village had been destroyed by firepower, "but the government troops just aren't available to clean out the villages so this is the only way."[149] The excessive and reckless use of

---

* The name derives from *naphthene* and *palmitate*, the primary jellifying agents. Developed and first used by the United States during World War II, napalm had been used in Korea and by the French during the First Indochina War.

force sowed widespread resentment among the South Vietnamese. When asked what he feared most, one villager said U.S. artillery and bombs, ARVN troops, and the Vietcong in that order.[150] By the end of American involvement in the war, the country the United States was fighting for had suffered more than a million civilian casualties—more than half due to American firepower and military operations.

Those not killed or wounded suffered as well. A key part of the pacification strategy involved clearing hamlets and villages in order to "drain the pond [the population] to catch the fish [the Vietcong]." Uprooted from their fields, homes, family altars, and ancestral graves by bombing and shelling that made it impossible for them to continue living and working in their villages and by forced relocation in order to create free-fire zones, wave after wave of alienated and dispirited refugees (mixed with Vietcong infiltrators) migrated to South Vietnam's towns and cities, where the government offered little resettlement assistance; they had to fend for themselves. Such exile had been happening since well before the arrival of the American military, but that had been a trickle; now the dam had broken. Partly due to the influx of American dollars, the cost-of-living in urban areas rose 170 percent from 1965 to 1967, and the price of rice doubled during the same period. Tragically, the traditional Vietnamese ethos of family piety broke down amid the poverty created by such financial pressure. South Vietnamese prostitutes servicing American soldiers* could earn more in a week than their fathers earned as farmers in a year—and more than a government minister. (Saigon alone had 56,000 *registered* prostitutes.) The misery and degradation were immense. More than 3 million refugees moved from the countryside to the cities by 1967. South Vietnam's urban population swelled from 20 percent in 1960 to 43 percent in 1971. By the end of the war in 1975, an astonishing and dismaying 10 million people—over half of the

---

* Mixed-race Amerasian children born as a result of these liaisons were derisively labeled "dust of life" (*bui doi*) and became pariahs in Vietnamese society during and after the war.

country's population—had been made involuntary refugees at one time or another.[151]

The same prejudices that led those at the higher levels of war planning to underestimate the North Vietnamese shaped American engagement in the field. Not a few generals and soldiers had imbibed the racist clichés and stereotypes passed down to them by their parents' generation (and commonly held by many Americans at the time): East Asians as lazy, untrustworthy, and unconcerned about the value of an individual human life. "The Oriental doesn't put the same high price on life as does the Westerner," opined General Westmoreland. "Life is plentiful, life is cheap in the Orient, and as the philosophy of the Orient expresses it, 'Life is not important.'"[152] (The last a fatuous misapprehension of Buddhist principles.) Such thinking explained why many soldiers and marines under Westmoreland's command called the Vietnamese—enemies and allies alike—"gooks," "slopes," and "dinks," and treated most of them with reflexive contempt. This attitude made it easier to kill the Vietnamese. Marine John Musgrove put it bluntly in hindsight: "Turning a subject into an object—Racism 101."[153] By perceiving and acting in accordance with racist stereotypes, American soldiers could rationalize brutal behavior and relieve themselves of guilt for its consequences.

American military officers recognized the destructiveness of the attrition strategy. Some endorsed it. "The solution in Vietnam is more bombs, more shells, more napalm till the other side cracks and gives up," remarked Westmoreland's operations officer, Lieutenant General William DePuy.[154] Others lamented it. Even army chief of staff Johnson grasped the damage being done to America's ally by the military's prosecution of the war. "We act with ruthlessness, like a steamroller," he admitted.[155] During World War II in Europe, the American military rejected use of chemical warfare. But in Vietnam in 1967 alone, specially equipped C-123 transports sprayed 18 million gallons of defoliants and herbicides that denuded more than 1.5 million acres of countryside near exit points of the Hồ Chí Minh Trail and along roads and waterways in order to deny Communist forces access to food and places to hide. The chemicals often drifted over local farmland. One study estimated "that over 500 civilians experience crop loss for every ton of rice denied the VC"—disastrous proportions given American ambitions to win popular support.[156] Defoliation eventually stripped an area the size of Massachusetts of all vegetation. It was later learned that the defoliant Agent Orange contained cancer-causing dioxin that poisoned American soldiers and Vietnamese villagers alike. Such was the effort to win the loyalty of the South Vietnamese.

This destruction made more lofty an already tall order—building a nation in the midst of a war—especially in a country where the focus was traditionally on the family, the hamlet, and the village. But the allocation of resources revealed pacification's relative importance to the overall American effort in South Vietnam. In 1968 alone, Washington spent almost $14 billion on bombing and ground operations, but only $850 million on pacification, offsetting war damage, and developing the economy and social structure of South Vietnam in order to win the allegiance of its people for the Saigon government.[157] In the end, the United States spent sixteen times as much on military operations as it did on pacification.

When issues are left to bureaucracies, it is the institutions whose interests will be most quickly honored. The introduction of U.S. forces in 1965 ballooned the American presence in South Vietnam, particularly in Saigon, and it also expanded the list of government institutions with a stake in the war. Eight bureaucracies—the Agency for International Development (AID), the CIA station, the Office of Civil Operations, the Saigon Liaison Office, the U.S. embassy, the U.S. Information Service, the U.S. Operations Mission, and, biggest of all, MACV (now known as the "Pentagon East")—aggressively competed for resources, influence, and power in a tug-of-war of bureaucratic backbiting and squabbling as American dollars flooded into the country. Cooperation between these autonomous baronies ran counter to the intensely competitive and turf-conscious bureaucratic ethos. Each power center wanted control or at least a piece of the action, and each zealously guarded its piece from the others—"turf protection" in bureaucratic lingo.

When a well-connected journalist informed the CIA station chief, Gordon Jorgensen, in the fall of 1965 that Edward Lansdale would be returning to Saigon to advise Henry Cabot Lodge on pacification, the journalist could see "what was going through [Jorgensen's] mind right away. He was throwing up barricades to protect his turf, and that's what everyone was doing out there at the time. There was a great deal of empire-building or turf-building."[158] Lodge similarly refused to back Lansdale because, by acting independently, Lansdale represented a threat to the ambassador's prerogatives and his turf. Like all bureaucratic black belts, Lodge and his peers at the top of each barony played out their traditional rivalries and bureaucratic games. Self-absorption, parochialism, and constant behind-the-scenes maneuvering and backstabbing produced endless conflicts over resources and priorities, and significantly (even mortally) compromised pacification's effectiveness. Sensitive to the fragility of American public support for the war, Johnson and his advisors had wanted South Vietnam's dysfunctional government and disrupted society stabilized as quickly as possible. "Genuine progress in Vietnam was never susceptible to that kind of time frame," a man with long experience in pacification, Rufus Phillips, later wrote, "but nobody had the guts or the understanding to buck the consensus and say so to the president or to level with Congress and the public about it."[159] Had someone done so early on, before the introduction of American troops and the metastasis of bureaucratic entities, it might have given Washington pause.

Persistent apathy and cynicism on the part of South Vietnamese civilian and military officials toward pacification, which they saw as a threat to their perquisites and power, compounded the problem. Many had either bought their positions or acquired them through nepotism and belonged to the landowning class, meaning that they did not come from, think like, know much about, or feel particularly responsive to the villagers they ruled. (This contrasted vividly with Vietcong cadre, who usually remained in their native villages and hamlets building a support network of relatives and friends.) The prevailing attitude was that the rural population should support the central government, not vice versa. Like the

French and the Americans who had trained them, ARVN officers found it difficult to adapt to the unconventional war confronting them. Ostensibly responsible for providing military protection for pacification efforts, ARVN did little. During one five-day period, the 18th ARVN Division at Xuân Lộc conducted 5,237 patrols and made contact with the enemy all of thirteen times. As U.S. aid and their dependency on it increased, South Vietnamese officials concentrated more on pleasing the rich foreigners rather than their own people. Washington's largesse—not electoral support—maintained their position and determined their future. In an unfortunate but telling echo of the Diệm years, representatives of the Kỳ-Thiệu regime manipulated statistics in order to tell their sponsors what they eagerly and desperately wanted to hear. Very few Americans relied on anything other than written reports coming up through official channels or double-checked what they were being told through confidential face-to-face talks with villagers on the spot. During a visit with a province chief one year, a visiting American VIP asked the chief—not the villagers themselves—how the pacification program was going. "Very well indeed," said the chief. "We've made great gains this year. Eighty percent of the province is pacified." The American VIP returned to the States and extolled progress in South Vietnam. When he returned to the province the following year and put the same question to the chief, the provincial leader replied, "We've been making great progress since you were last here. Seventy percent of the province is pacified."[160]

Continuing to undermine progress was the ongoing corruption among the country's elite, where family loyalty predominated over national loyalty. (Under Confucianism, the family constituted the core of society and obligations to the family trumped obligations to the state. For centuries, Vietnamese emperors had worked to check nepotism and family influence—particularly the tendency for families to seek favors when their sons entered the imperial mandarinate.) Many ARVN officers behaved in the same manner as colonial French officers had: with haughtiness and lack of empathy for the enlisted soldiers who carried out their orders and fought their battles. The circulatory system of corruption that ran through ARVN contrasted vividly with the personal discipline, probity, and loyalty to the state of most (though not all) Communists.* This had become apparent to visiting Americans as early as 1960. That year, CIA analyst George Allen dined in Saigon with two lieutenants on ARVN's intelligence staff. "When you're on the general staff," they explained to Allen, "you have to kick back ten percent of your pay every month . . . for the privilege of remaining assigned to the general staff." "That's incredible," said Allen, naive like most Americans at the time about the ways of the South Vietnamese. "Do all officers on the general staff pay that?" "Oh yes," the lieutenants replied, "NCOs [noncommissioned officers] too . . . If we play our cards right, in a few years we ourselves will be majors and lieutenant colonels, and we'll be in a position where we can get some of this. And you know, it's a pretty good living." A stunned Allen tried to process this. "Aren't you afraid that maybe sooner or later you'll have to go back into combat?" "No," they answered, "that's the thing we think we'd be able to manage to avoid . . . Even if you go back to the troops, it's a five-day-a-week war, nine to five. That's not bad. You can survive in that if you . . . don't take any risks."[161]

ARVN generals, their wives, and their relatives abused the system most egregiously. The South Vietnamese had a saying, "The house leaks from the roof on down." The defense minister, General Nguyễn Huu Co, issued an order that ARVN officers abstain from engaging in corruption and hold accountable those who did. Meanwhile, his own wife gambled away 15 million Vietnamese piasters (about $150,000—or about $1 million in 2018 dollars) of charity funds and pillaged ARVN's operating account to cover the loss.[162] The wife of ARVN chief of staff General Cao Văn Viên monopolized the lucrative beer market in one province that was home to a large American military base. "What was so amazing," said a U.S. embassy officer who spoke with her, "was not the

---

* Corruption beset Americans in South Vietnam as well: massive quantities of goods disappeared from MACV's main post exchange in Cholon—a building the size of a major American department store—and ended up on Saigon's black market.

extent of her financial interest, which was very considerable, but the flagrancy of it—the absolute indifference to what we thought."[163] One district chief stole the food rations of his own militia soldiers. Subordinate officers took these examples as license to do the same. "When you see, from the nature of our leadership, that there is no hope . . . you turn to doing what you can do, which is to take care of your family," said one.[164] The mayor of Qui Nhơn converted his official residence into a private "massage parlor" for American soldiers. A district chief diverted cement supplied by AID intended for school construction and sold it on the black market for private housing. Corruption prospered in part because the South Vietnamese economy benefited those who served the Americans. Outside of the capital city, crowded shantytowns without running water or electricity sprouted up around U.S. military bases. These fetid slums sustained thousands of their residents through prostitution, vending soda, and laundry cleaning. Widows, orphans, and amputees begging for money became a distressingly common sight on the sidewalks of Saigon. Viciously, the rampant disillusionment and cynicism only worsened the behavior of ARVN officers and troops, whose corruption, theft, and maltreatment of civilians further undermined support for the government.

The shortcomings of pacification could be measured by the fortunes of An Phú village in Gia Định province just north of Saigon. Until the summer of 1964, An Phú had been one of the most secure, pro-government villages in all of South Vietnam. Only one company of Vietcong irregulars operated in the vicinity. Two years later, in August 1966, an entire battalion of Vietcong operated in the area and another was being formed. In 1964, almost no families in An Phú supported the Vietcong. By 1966, every family in the village paid the Vietcong tax of 10 percent of the rice harvest.[165] Two years later, the Vietcong would use An Phú as a staging area for its 1968 Tet Offensive against South Vietnamese and American installations in Saigon.

All of this deepened McNamara's anguish and disenchantment during 1966. In May, for the first time American casualties exceeded those of the ARVN as South Vietnam's generals-turned-politicians continued their bickering and their troops failed to perform their assigned role of providing security for pacification. In an unguarded moment during the height of the Buddhist crisis, McNamara had confided to his Vietnam assistant John McNaughton, "I want to give the order to our troops to get out of there so bad that I can hardly stand it."[166] A Gallup poll in June 1966 found that support for the U.S. combat role in Vietnam had fallen 20 percent in a year to 47 percent, while opposition had nearly doubled to 35 percent. And 66 percent of the country said they had lost confidence in Johnson's leadership on Vietnam. Johnson privately called the results "disastrous."[167]

By summer, McNamara's doubts about the efficacy of American military operations had grown acute. He laid out his concerns to Johnson in a phone conversation on June 28 as another of Westmoreland's search-and-destroy operations was getting underway. "It scares me to see what we're doing there," McNamara told the president—"taking 6,000 U.S. soldiers and God knows how many airplanes and helicopters and firepower and going after a bunch of half-starved beggars—2,000 at most, and probably less than that." He saw "great danger" in the Communists' ability to avoid battle and control their casualties: "they can keep that up almost indefinitely." The stark reality was that "we're not killing enough of them to make it impossible for the North to continue to fight."[168]

McNamara next turned to the CIA and its director, Richard Helms, for an assessment of North Vietnam's "will to persist" in the war. Unlike his predecessor John McCone, who had asserted himself in policy debates, Helms believed decision-makers tended to overstate, ignore, or pick and choose facts according to their point of view. As a result, Helms limited his role in policy debates to providing information and analytical assessment, even after he became a member of Johnson's inner circle of Vietnam advisors. That is why McNamara particularly valued assessments by the CIA: the agency had "no dog in the hunt," no vested interest in a particular position or prior commitment to an existing policy, no responsibility for carrying American policy to success. Like

all government agencies, the CIA had its own bureaucratic ambitions, but unlike in the military, Helms and his analysts did not
hinge their careers on simply proving the efficacy of more force.
They could assess the situation more dispassionately and express
misgivings more candidly. The CIA responded to McNamara's request with an exhaustive, 250-page study addressing almost every
aspect of the war. The document concluded that bombing could
inhibit but not prevent Hanoi from functioning and sending reinforcements south, that destroying North Vietnam's industrial
capacity would have little effect on the war because China and the
U.S.S.R. produced its arms and provided the vast majority of its
supplies. Echoing McNamara's fears, the CIA concluded that Hanoi remained willing to continue the war indefinitely. The same
information went to President Johnson through the President's
Foreign Intelligence Advisory Board chaired by Clark Clifford.[169]

After reading the study, McNamara asked to meet with George
Allen (the CIA analyst who had been horrified by his encounters
with corrupt ARVN soldiers six years earlier and had spent the last
two years in Saigon). Allen called on McNamara in his cavernous
Pentagon office. Sitting behind his nine-foot Pershing desk in a
high-backed blue leather swivel chair beneath a portrait of the first
defense secretary, James Forrestal, McNamara began by asking
Allen about his experience. Allen replied that he had worked on
Vietnam for seventeen years, and that the study McNamara had
commissioned was the most comprehensive he had ever read. Mc-
Namara asked Allen what he would do if he were in McNamara's
shoes. Allen said he would stop the buildup of American troops,
halt the bombing, and negotiate a permanent cease-fire with Hanoi. McNamara asked if this would lead to a Communist takeover
of South Vietnam. Allen said it would, but that the same outcome
would likely occur even if the war continued. McNamara then
posed the "sunk cost" question: How could the United States justify
its sacrifices if, in the end, it failed to preserve a non-Communist
South Vietnam? They debated repercussions of such an outcome
for some time. Again and again, McNamara came back to how the
United States could stop after all it had spent in support of pre-

serving South Vietnam? The investment of blood, treasure, and prestige remained, at this stage, an insuperable obstacle for McNamara.[170]

The same loss aversion that had driven Johnson and his advisors in 1965 still ruled the day. They could not step outside of themselves to see this. Imagined future losses were abstract and questionable; tangible and indisputable were the losses already suffered. When great leadership meant anticipating the costs of what seemed likely to come, Johnson and McNamara could not look at anything but a cracked rearview mirror. On a brief unannounced visit to South Vietnam in late October 1966 during a conference with allied countries in Manila, Johnson spoke to U.S. troops at Cam Ranh Bay—the first trip by a president to American soldiers in a war zone since Franklin Roosevelt had visited GIs stationed in Morocco during the Casablanca Conference in January 1943. After reviewing assembled troops then visiting the wounded lying in field hospital beds, Johnson delivered an emotional speech in which he pledged, "We shall never let you down." He later confessed, "I have never been more moved by any group I have ever talked to, never in my life."[171] In a sweeping and impassioned defense of his Vietnam policy the following March, LBJ publicly declared, "If we were prepared to stay the course in Vietnam, we could help lay the cornerstone for a diverse and independent Asia, full of promise and resolute in the course of economic development for her long-suffering peoples. But if we faltered, the forces' of chaos would scent victory and decades of strife and aggression would stretch endlessly before us . . . We will stay the course . . . We must not—we shall not—we will not—fail."[172] Johnson had invested so much of himself, his political standing, his presidency's place in history, and—most painfully—the lives of thousands of American soldiers in the conflict. His persistence had become rigidity, locking him and the nation on a course that he was unwilling to admit to himself and others had proven a grievous misjudgment. LBJ had become, in effect, a prisoner of the war.

Johnson's refusal to confront this painful reality resulted, in part, from his ever-increasing personalization of the war. He began referring to "my troops" and "my pilots"—indicators that he had difficulty separating his identity and ego from the war. Clark Clifford recalled a story that illustrated this. "Johnson was at an Air Force base. Air Force One sat there in its beauty and sleekness along with fifty or a hundred big transport planes and helicopters. An enlisted man told Johnson, 'Your plane is ready, Mr. President.' 'Son, these are all my planes,' said Johnson. 'It's all mine. It's my war. I am the one that they are fighting against and I am going to beat the hell out of them before we are through.'" He had permitted himself to become emotionally involved in the war, asserting, "By God, they can't do this to Lyndon Johnson!"[173]

Johnson similarly perceived opposition to the war as personal attacks. He saw antiwar voices in Congress and on college campuses not as people of goodwill seeking to change American policy in Vietnam based on a very different but equally patriotic assessment of the national interest, but as shallow and vindictive troublemakers out to get him. Johnson included in this category his nemesis, Robert Kennedy, now a senator from New York, who had shifted from supporting the war to increasingly opposing it in the years since his brother's assassination. Johnson's personalization of issues and differences reflected a hypersensitivity rooted in his underlying insecurity. This frailty—although very human—crippled Johnson's ability to view issues with the detachment necessary to make wise decisions and to readily admit error.

Against this backdrop, during the summer of 1966, following a now predictable rhythm, Westmoreland submitted another request for more troops, this time seeking to increase U.S. forces to nearly 543,000 by the end of 1967—a 50 percent increase over the number already there, and nearly double the total he had said just a year before would be needed. By now, Westmoreland's repeated requests for more troops had significantly diminished the credibility of his estimates in McNamara's eyes. There seemed to be no end to the general's demands.

Westmoreland's perpetual appetite helped open McNamara's eyes somewhat wider to the folly of relentless escalation to redeem sunk costs. Ineffective search-and-destroy operations alone were now costing a staggering $100 million a day (nearly $750 million a day in 2018 dollars). McNamara responded to Westmoreland's latest request by telling the chiefs he wanted "a detailed line-by-line analysis for these requirements to determine that each is truly essential to the carrying out of the war plan."[174] Westmoreland, supported by the Joint Chiefs and Admiral Sharp, pushed back, insisting, "I cannot justify a reduction in requirements submitted." McNamara would not budge, and urged Johnson in a phone conversation on September 19 to put "a ceiling on our force levels. I don't think we ought to just look ahead to the future and say we're going to go higher and higher and higher and higher—600,000, 700,000— whatever it takes . . . Somewhere between 500 and 600,000 ought to be the ceiling and after the [midterm] election, we ought to tell that to our military commanders and get them planning on it."[*175]

Johnson ordered McNamara back to South Vietnam to evaluate the situation firsthand. The secretary arrived in Saigon, eleven months after his previous trip to South Vietnam, on October 10 and held three days of meetings at MACV headquarters and the American embassy. There, Westmoreland told McNamara that the tide of the war had been reversed, that U.S. forces had seized the initiative, and that the crossover point would be reached by the coming spring. However, MACV intelligence chief Major General Joseph McChristian[†] implicitly and forcefully contradicted Westmoreland's assertions. In his briefing, he told McNamara the

---

* McNamara also recommended "termination of the bombing in the North . . . after the [mid-term] election" in order to get peace talks with Hanoi started— something Johnson, at this point, would not consider. Telephone Conversation between President Johnson and Robert McNamara, September 19, 1966, Tape 10808 (WH6609.10), MCWHR.

† McChristian, who had become Westmoreland's intelligence chief in mid-1965 was, tellingly, the first ground officer to head up MACV intelligence. The first J-2 [intelligence officer] had been a Strategic Air Command reconnaissance specialist— "totally unequipped, professionally and experience wise," for the job in the words of a CIA analyst who knew him well. His successor had been an air force colonel expert in Soviet ICBMs who "had the good grace, excuse the expression, to have a mental breakdown after about four months, realizing he was totally unequipped for the job." George Allen OHI, II, p. 29, LBJL.

Communists had suffered no loss of will to fight and had boosted their infiltration substantially—from 10,000 to over 13,000 a month within the past year, with the capability of reaching 15,000 a month. Vietcong and North Vietnamese combat battalions had increased from 47 to 149 since the bombing began and U.S. troops had been committed, and would likely reach 199 by the middle of 1967. McChristian concluded that enemy force strength would rise from 131,000 to 202,000 by the end of 1967.[*176]

McChristian's assessment deepened McNamara's skepticism and anguish about pouring in more troops in an elusive effort to reach the crossover point through search-and-destroy operations. When McNamara returned to Washington on October 14, he told Johnson that while the enemy's drive for victory had been blunted by the commitment of American troops, he saw "no reasonable way to bring the war to an end soon." The Communists had stymied and inverted Westmoreland's plan, adopting "a strategy of keeping us busy and waiting us out (a strategy of attriting our national will)." They had suffered enormous casualties—more than 60,000 a year—but they had "more than replace[d]" their losses through recruitment in the South and infiltration from the North, which bombing had slowed but not significantly affected. McNamara acknowledged that pacification had "gone backward," and that "full security exists nowhere"—not even behind American lines. "In the countryside, he lamented, the enemy almost completely controls the night." Saigon had failed, too. "This important war must be fought and won by the Vietnamese themselves," he went on. "We have known this from the beginning. But the discouraging truth is that, as was the case in 1961 and 1963 and 1965, we have not found the formula, the catalyst, for training and inspiring them into effec-

---

* The CIA estimated an even higher number of enemy forces. George Carver, one of the agency's top Vietnam analysts, told the President's Foreign Intelligence Advisory Board on November 30 that "the U.S. has been greatly underestimating the personnel strength of the Vietcong forces . . . The experts are now beginning to believe that there are from 200–300,000 Vietcong in the field instead of the previously accepted figure of 100,000." Memorandum for the File: Subject: Meeting of President's Foreign Intelligence Advisory Board, November 30–December 1, 1966, PFIAB Records.

tive action." These words reflected a return in McNamara's thinking to his position during the Kennedy years. But in the interim
the die had been cast, in considerable measure through his efforts.

All of this led McNamara away from proposing escalation of
America's commitment to trying to stabilize the situation by
"getting ourselves into a military posture that we credibly would
maintain indefinitely—a posture that makes trying to 'wait us out'
less attractive." This meant leveling off U.S. troops at 470,000,[*]
installing an anti-infiltration barrier across the northern neck of
South Vietnam and the Hồ Chí Minh Trail in Laos (which Westmoreland and the chiefs lukewarmly supported), leveling off the
bombing of North Vietnam, placing a greater emphasis on pacification, and pressing for negotiations by implementing an indefinite total bombing halt or a "realistic plan" that allowed Vietcong
participation in the South Vietnamese government. In response to
the chiefs' incessant argument that the solution lay in intensified
bombing, he wrote: "to bomb the North sufficiently to make a radical impact upon Hanoi's political, economic and social structure,
would require an effort which we could make but which would not
be stomached either by our own people or by world opinion; and
it would involve a serious risk of drawing us into open war with
China." On the other hand, leveling off America's commitment in
Vietnam would limit costs and risks, and buy time diplomatically
by maintaining the political support of the American people.[177]

McNamara's visceral awareness that attrition was failing led
him to say, in effect, "Don't do more." But he was—like most of his
colleagues—not built to acknowledge that some issues were un-
conquerable and walk away. "The problem," McNamara lamented,
looking back, was "that I didn't take it the next step and say, 'Oh, my
God' . . . I regret that."[178] He could not yet bring himself to say to
Johnson, "Do less militarily and lower your objective politically
in order to get out." "It was the intractability of the problem that
we confronted in the face of an unwillingness to accept the costs
that would be associated with moving out," he later explained.[179]

---

[*] Still a 40 percent increase over the fall 1966 U.S. force level of 325,000.

"My anguish," McNamara recalled, "was over the fact that we were killing people and not accomplishing our objective, and I didn't know what the hell to do about it."[180] He ground his teeth but did not swallow.

McNamara acknowledged the chiefs did not share his judgment, and they certainly did not, directly challenging both his analysis and his recommendations. Themselves still inmates of their own cognitive prison, they claimed the military situation in South Vietnam had "improved substantially over the past year" and opposed curbing the bombing of North Vietnam. Air attacks represented America's "trump card," they argued, one that should not be bargained away except in return for an end to Hanoi's support of the war in the South. Instead of leveling off the American military effort, the chiefs urged intensifying it, further asserting a political judgment that "the American people, our allies and our enemies alike, are increasingly uncertain as to our resolution to pursue the war to a successful conclusion."[181]

McNamara answered the chiefs' criticism in a second memorandum to Johnson on November 17. "We have no prospect of attriting the enemy force at a rate equal to or greater than his capability to infiltrate and recruit," he told Johnson—and by implication the chiefs—"and this will be true at either the 470,000 U.S. personnel level or 570,000 . . . further large increases in U.S. forces do not appear to be the answer."[182] Johnson grudgingly accepted his defense secretary's recommendation to level off the U.S. troop commitment. But while McNamara had again carried the day, his relationship with the president had begun to change. McNamara had become increasingly pessimistic about the prospects of success in the war and therefore the wisdom of further escalatory steps, while Johnson had become increasingly determined to stay the course given the sunk costs to the country and his political standing—a gap that was becoming ever wider. In late January, Johnson hung up the phone on McNamara midsentence for the first time.[183] People around the defense secretary and the president picked up on the growing distance between the two men. "I notice a diminution of power, of influence, in McNamara's hands," McNaughton observed, speculating "this is mainly because the President is in political trouble . . . But for whatever reason, I sense less harmony between the two men . . . Now I see the President is on the 'hard' side of Bob."[184]

Although Johnson had limited Westmoreland's latest request for more troops, the general continued his stubborn pursuits. In early January 1967, Westmoreland launched Operation CEDAR FALLS, targeted against the Communist stronghold north of Saigon known as the Iron Triangle. U.S. forces uprooted and relocated peasants from Bến Súc and other villages in the area (allowing them to take with them only what they could carry), moved in bulldozers and huge "Rome plows" that destroyed vegetation, collapsed civilian huts and Vietcong tunnels alike, and unleashed unrestricted bombing and artillery fire. The American military designated the Iron Triangle a "free-fire zone," and when CEDAR FALLS ended, the village of Bến Súc* and many others no longer existed. The largest search-and-destroy operation of the war, involving 45,000 soldiers, 2,000 tanks and armored personnel carriers, and 600 aircraft, JUNCTION CITY, followed a month later in Tay Ninh province near the Cambodian border. Aimed to destroy the Vietcong's military headquarters (known as the Central Office of South Vietnam or COSVN) and its propaganda arm Liberation Radio, JUNCTION CITY created another free-fire zone that allowed unrestricted bombing and unobserved artillery fire. An American officer involved in the operation later noted that "it was a sheer physical impossibility to keep him [the enemy soldier] from slipping away whenever he wished if he were in terrain with which he was familiar—generally the case. The jungle is usually just too thick and too widespread to hope ever to keep him from getting away; thus the option to fight was usually his."[185] That was exactly what happened: during the operation, the Vietcong evaded combat with

---

* Journalist Jonathan Schell chronicled the destruction of Bến Súc and the dislocation of its inhabitants in a long article in the *New Yorker*, subsequently published in book form as *The Village of Ben Suc* (Alfred A. Knopf, 1967).

U.S. forces and COSVN relocated across the Cambodian border. And, despite all of the destruction, search-and-destroy operations had little effect on population control because the American military simply moved on and as before ARVN consistently failed to provide security in areas cleared of the enemy by U.S. military operations. Vietcong troops returned to the Iron Triangle and Tay Ninh soon after JUNCTION CITY ended. The number of South Vietnamese refugees more than doubled in that region. The number of civilian—not ARVN or Vietcong—casualties rose to more than 100,000 a year.[186]

Although Westmoreland had told McNamara in October that the crossover point would be reached by the spring of 1967, on March 18 he submitted yet another request for more forces, citing increased enemy strength due to infiltration and "to avoid an unreasonably protracted war." The light at the end of the tunnel Westmoreland had proclaimed in the fall seemed to be ever receding. This time, he requested 200,000 additional troops (100,000 in 1968 and another 100,000 in 1969). His latest request would bring the total number of U.S. forces in Vietnam to 670,000—two and a half times the number he had said in June 1965 would be necessary.[*][187] Westmoreland's latest request arrived in a Washington that had become engulfed in the miasma of Vietnam. The public support that had motivated and reinforced many of Johnson's earlier decisions regarding American involvement was rapidly diminishing. Since the beginning of the year, 2,500 more Americans had been killed. The war dominated the attention of Congress and the media. Almost every day, car traffic slowed as a funeral cortege made its way across Memorial Bridge to Arlington National Cemetery. Thousands of people picketed back and forth on Pennsylvania Avenue in front of the White House every week, many chanting, "Hey, hey, LBJ, how many kids did you kill today?!" and bellowing obscenities at its occupant. Campuses throughout the country seethed with antiwar feeling and demonstrations. Conser-

---

* Westmoreland upped these numbers another 50,000 to a total of 720,000 in late May.

vatives demanded that Johnson do more to win the war. Liberals demanded that Johnson end the war. Just as Johnson had feared, his ability to move forward with the Great Society had been disabled.

These pressures led Johnson to summon Westmoreland to Washington in late April to discuss his latest troop request. The president met with the general and his senior advisors at the White House on April 27. At the meeting, Westmoreland stressed the need for 200,000 more troops to avoid "losing the momentum" and lengthening the war. Westmoreland said "it would be nip and tuck to oppose the reinforcements the enemy is capable of providing" at the current level of 470,000. McNamara doubted that more U.S. troops would increase enemy losses because the Communists continued to control their casualties by choosing where, when, and how long to fight. He believed Westmoreland had sufficient forces to fight the enemy's main-force units, which was all that search and destroy could realistically accomplish. More American troops would only intensify domestic opposition to the war and ARVN's dependence on the U.S. military. Given these limitations, McNamara asked Westmoreland to estimate how long it would take to end the war if this latest request for more was granted versus if it was not. Westmoreland said two years and five years, respectively, implicitly acknowledging the political costs of a prolonged war but also that he did not *need* additional troops. Johnson's own doubts about more troops came through in the questions he asked. Could the Communists match another U.S. force increase? Westmoreland answered in the affirmative. "If so," said Johnson, "where does it all end?" Westmoreland said the Communists could not support more than twelve divisions in South Vietnam (they currently had eight). "At what point does the enemy ask for 'volunteers'" from China, as had happened in Korea? asked LBJ. "That is a good question," came Westmoreland's uncomfortably noncommittal reply.[188] The general then recommended an amphibious invasion* of North Vietnam,

---

* Elements within the military and civilians like Walt Rostow had been pushing an amphibious hook invasion at Vinh in south central North Vietnam for some

which Wheeler and Rostow endorsed. Johnson let that suggestion pass (the State Department and the CIA both had long predicted that China would enter the war if the U.S. invaded North Vietnam).

The advisor on whom Johnson had relied most for advice about Vietnam over the years addressed Westmoreland's request for 200,000 more troops in a twenty-two-page, single-spaced memorandum to the president on May 19. In a detailed and forceful memo argued with a passion missing from his earlier memoranda to Kennedy and Johnson, McNamara echoed the recommendation he had made to Johnson back in October 1966 to level off the American troop commitment in South Vietnam. But for the first time, McNamara, after detailing the current situation in Vietnam, focused on prospective costs of further escalation rather than sunk costs, using language that conveyed his growing frustration and anguish over a war for which he bore so much responsibility. McNamara told Johnson he saw "no attractive course of action." He explained: "Continuation of our present moderate policy, while avoiding a larger war, will not change Hanoi's mind . . . Increased force levels and actions against the North are likewise unlikely to change Hanoi's mind, and are likely to get us in even deeper in Southeast Asia and into a serious confrontation, if not war, with China and Russia." He then bluntly addressed the war's impact in the United States—something he had never done before with LBJ. "The Vietnam war is unpopular in this country. It is becoming increasingly unpopular as it escalates—causing more American casualties, more fear of its growing into a wider war . . . and more distress at the amount of suffering being visited on the noncombatants in Vietnam, South and North. Most Americans do not know how we got where we are, and most, without knowing why, but taking advantage of hindsight, are convinced that somehow we should not have gotten this deeply in. All want the war ended and expect their President to end it. Successfully. Or else. This state of mind generates impatience in the political structure of the United

---

time, claiming it would deal a mortal blow to infiltration—without addressing its consequences in regard to Chinese intervention in the war.

States. It unfortunately also generates patience in Hanoi." The situation in South Vietnam generated even more such patience. "The 'big war' in the South between the U.S. and the North Vietnamese military units (NVA) is going well. We staved off military defeat in 1965; we gained the military initiative in 1966; and since then we have been hurting the enemy badly . . . [but] throughout South Vietnam, supplies continue to flow in ample quantities . . . The enemy retains the ability to initiate both large- and small-scale attacks . . . Regrettably, the 'other war' against the VC is still not going well. Corruption is widespread . . . There is rot in the fabric . . . The population remains apathetic . . . The National Liberation Front (NLF) continues to control large parts of South Vietnam, and there is little evidence that the [pacification] program is gaining any momentum. The Army of South Vietnam (ARVN) is tired, passive, and accommodation-prone, and is moving too slowly if at all into pacification work."

Despite his aggressive advocacy of bombing pauses to stimulate peace talks, circumstances had forced McNamara to concede that Hanoi's leaders "seem uninterested in a political settlement and determined to match U.S. military expansion of the conflict . . . There continues to be no sign that the bombing has reduced Hanoi's will to resist or her ability to ship the necessary supplies south. Hanoi shows no signs of ending the large war and advising the VC to melt into the jungles. The North Vietnamese believe they are right; they consider the Kỳ regime to be puppets; they believe the world is with them and that the American public will not have staying power against them. Thus, although they may have factions in the regime favoring differing approaches, they believe that, in the long run, they are stronger than we are for the purpose." Soviet and Chinese support bolstered their determination. "The dominant Soviet objectives seem to continue to be to avoid direct involvement in the conflict . . . while supporting Hanoi to an extent sufficient to maintain Soviet prestige . . . China remains largely preoccupied with its own Cultural Revolution* . . . [but]

---

* Political and social turmoil racked Communist China from 1966 to 1976, triggered

there is no reason to doubt that China would honor its commitment to intervene at Hanoi's request, and it remains likely that
Peking would intervene on her own initiative if she believed that
the existence of the Hanoi regime was at stake."

He then turned to Westmoreland's request. "Proponents of the
added deployments in the South believe that such deployments
will hasten the end of the war. None of them believe that the added
forces are needed to avoid defeat; few of them believe that the
added forces are required to do the job in due course; all of the proponents believe that they are needed if that job is to be done faster."
But the added deployments entailed risks that Westmoreland and
the chiefs had *not* addressed or answered. "The addition of the
200,000 men, involving as it does a call-up of Reserves and an addition of 500,000 to the military strength,* would . . . almost certainly set off bitter Congressional debate and irresistible domestic
pressures for stronger action outside South Vietnam. Cries would
go up—much louder than they already have—to 'take the wraps
off the men in the field.' The actions would include more intense
bombing . . . of strategic [civilian] targets such as locks and dikes,†
and mining of the harbors against Soviet and other ships. Associated actions impelled by the situation would be major ground
actions in Laos, in Cambodia, and probably in North Vietnam. The
use of tactical nuclear and area-denial-radiological-bacteriological-
chemical weapons would probably be suggested at some point if
the Chinese entered the war in Vietnam or Korea or if U.S. losses
were running high while conventional efforts were not produc-

---

by Mao's drive to purge the party of "counterrevolutionaries." It resulted in the
death, imprisonment, and forced relocation of countless Chinese—as well as the
destruction of many Chinese cultural treasures.

* Increasing troop deployments to Vietnam had considerably drained America's
ability to meet its other military commitments throughout the world—for example, to NATO in Western Europe.

† North Vietnam had an extensive system of locks and dikes along the Red River to
prevent flooding and to channel water to rice crops. The Red River bisected Hanoi,
which lay twenty feet below it during the monsoon season. Bombing locks and
dikes would drown countless civilians and lead to widespread starvation.

ing desired results."[189] Escalation, he later wrote in his memoirs, "threatened to spin the war utterly out of control."[190]

McNamara told Johnson "there may be a limit beyond which many Americans and much of the world will not permit the United States to go. The picture of the world's greatest superpower killing or seriously injuring 1000 noncombatants a week, while trying to pound a tiny backward nation into submission on an issue whose merits are hotly disputed, is not a pretty one. It could conceivably produce a costly distortion in the American national conscious-ness and in the world image of the United States—especially if the damage to North Vietnam is complete enough to be 'successful.'"

As he had before, McNamara insisted that Vietnam be viewed in its larger Asian context, but he pointed out that circumstances had changed. Citing the defeat of the Communists in Indonesia and the current turmoil in China stemming from the Cultural Revolution, he argued that events in Asia were now running in America's favor, thus reducing the strategic importance of South Vietnam. Foregoing any mention of either the containment pol-icy or U.S. credibility—the two pillars on which he and others had based Vietnam policy for so many years—he returned to the position he had advocated during the Kennedy administration (be-fore troops had been committed based, in considerable measure, on his recommendation), urging Johnson to rest his decisions on two principles: "1) Our commitment is only to see that the people of South Vietnam are permitted to determine their own future. 2) This commitment ceases if the country ceases to help itself." He therefore recommended limiting the bombing to interdiction of the infiltration "funnel" south of the twentieth parallel,* limit-ing additional deployments to 30,000 and no more, and adopting a more flexible bargaining position (which he did not spell out but implied through the two principles).

McNamara candidly and disarmingly acknowledged the limita-tions of his own recommendation: "Some will insist that pressure,

---

* A line of latitude that ran through North Vietnam just above Thanh Hóa and roughly bisected the country.

enough pressure, on the North can pay off . . . many will argue
that the denial of the larger number of troops will prolong the
war, risk losing it and increase the casualties of the American boys
who are there; some will insist . . . Hanoi will react [with] increased
demands and truculence; . . . and there will be those who point out
the possibility that the changed U.S. tone may create a 'rush for the
exits' in Thailand, in Laos, and especially in South Vietnam, perhaps threatening cohesion of the government, morale of the army,
and loss of support among the people. Not least will be the alleged
impact on the reputation of the United States and its President."
But there was no good alternative—only a least-bad one, a lesser
evil among even greater evils. McNamara's bottom-line message
to Johnson was: "The war in Vietnam is acquiring a momentum
of its own that must be stopped. Dramatic increases in US troop
deployments, in attacks on the North, or in ground actions in Laos
or Cambodia are not necessary and are not the answer. The enemy
can absorb them or counter them, bogging us down further and
risking even more serious escalation of the war."[191]

McNamara's May 19, 1967, memo considerably deepened the growing wedge between the president and his defense secretary on
Vietnam. Since the spring of 1965, McNamara had slowly and painfully wrestled with the burdensome issue of sunk costs. He had
done so fitfully, in stages, during the intervening two years. In November 1965, those costs had spurred McNamara to recommend a
further deepening of America's commitment in Vietnam. During
the summer and fall of 1966, the same logic had held him back
from questioning the basic commitment amid mounting evidence
of failure. By the spring of 1967, however, sunk costs no longer
governed McNamara's thinking about Vietnam—prospective costs
now did. He had crossed an important psychological divide. Now,
the unwisdom of escalation in the face of failure rather than escalation to avert the prospect of failure took precedence in his
mind, thus fueling his opposition to deeper American involvement
in the months to come.

Johnson had also wrestled with the burdensome issue of sunk

costs since approving the bombing of North Vietnam and committing U.S. troops to combat in South Vietnam. But unlike McNamara, he could not yet bring himself to acknowledge failure, come to terms with its terrible human price, and stop trying to recoup earlier failures by expanding the war still further. He was willing to change course only within a narrowly circumscribed range of options—limiting the bombing and the deployment of more troops. Bending further and more substantively by stopping the bombing in order to get talks with Hanoi started or lowering his political objective in order to get out meant betraying his emotional investment in the American lives already sacrificed and jeopardizing his historical reputation by becoming the first president to lose a war.

Throughout the rest of 1967, the emotional and psychological pressures on McNamara intensified as his anguish over the bloodshed, the unwise advice he had given Johnson during the crucial period of escalation in 1964–1965, and what he saw as his failure at the most important task of his public career grew alongside the estrangement between him and the president over the most important issue of the day. The two men's relationship, once very close and still marked by grudging mutual respect, would become increasingly strained and intolerable for both men. By the end of the year, the relationship would reach the breaking point.

Throughout the remainder of his days at the Pentagon, McNamara kept his growing dissent over Vietnam private out of a sense of personal and institutional loyalty and conviction that he could continue influencing the decision-making process. He and Johnson would resolve their internal discord with McNamara's departure from the Pentagon in late February 1968—a decision that also, ironically, marked the first step in Johnson's own effort to come to terms with the sunk costs of Vietnam, as we shall see in the chapter ahead.

CHAPTER 6

The Jeopardy of Conflicting Loyalties
(May 1967–February 1968)

We live our lives in a set of intersecting circles of attachment. The complexity of loyalty is characteristically human, and in making difficult choices, people can act counter to some loyalties in order to further others. How does one make the right choice under such circumstances, especially when the stakes are immense and the trade-offs of vast consequence?

In Robert McNamara's case, by 1967 personal allegiance to Lyndon Johnson and institutional loyalty to the presidency had begun to conflict with his loyalty to the truth about the war as he saw it and the national interest of the United States as he understood it. McNamara had always been a team player who believed overt conflict between himself and the president undercut the morale of American soldiers and the American people. "He thought . . . it was sinful not to present a united front," recalled a former assistant.[1] "I don't believe the government . . . can operate effectively if those in charge of the departments of the government express disagreement with decisions of the established head of the government," McNamara said in an interview that he authorized for direct quotation. "I never discuss any recommendations I might have made to the President before the policy decision was made. To do so might strengthen my position but would weaken the President's . . . Our responsibility as Cabinet Officers is to the nation *through the President* [emphasis added]."[2] He had to support the president or keep quiet. To do otherwise was sabotage if not treason. "My constituency was one man—the elected representative of the people—and I was to do what he believed the Defense Department should do to carry out his objectives for the nation . . . The contract was that I would be totally loyal, but as part of that, I would tell him what I believed and, finally, I would ultimately do what he decided and support what he decided, or I would leave."[3] So McNamara remained publicly silent about his deepening pessimism, convinced that openly challenging the president would be disloyal and would elicit a more defensive and hostile reaction than would privately expressing his dissent—the logic of one who plays the classic insider's game. McNamara's excuse was less that he was following orders as he was attending to *order*. Yet in waiting for Johnson to set the alarm, McNamara continued to help wind the clock.

By the spring of 1967, McNamara saw Johnson persisting in a failing policy costing more and more American and Vietnamese lives with no successful resolution in sight. Johnson, in turn, sensed McNamara's deepening disenchantment and felt stung by it—after all, McNamara had pressured him to hold the line in Vietnam in 1964–1965. "McNamara's gone dovish on me," Johnson complained bitterly to a visiting Senator,[4] on another occasion muttering, "Bob's got a crew over there at the Defense Department, and they're undercutting us on Vietnam."[5] But the truth was far more complex than the stereotype of a petty, intemperate, and callous chauvinist in the Oval Office. LBJ sometimes indulged spasms of anger toward those around him who voiced unwelcome news, but those he trusted could continue to speak their minds knowing he was ingesting their opinion. In this way, McNamara's insights slowly affected and changed Johnson's thinking on the war. However much he fought the painful truth, Johnson gradually realized with bitterness and fatalism that he had fundamentally miscalculated and had steered himself and the country into a dead end in Vietnam. But that realization came slowly in the latter months of 1967, and Johnson began acting on it only after he engineered McNamara's departure.

As the pressures on McNamara mounted, the intense strain of professional obligation and the agony born of guilt and destroyed illusions erupted to the surface in sudden and unexpected emotional outbursts. A man so precise, so orderly, so logical, so cool on the surface but so sensitive underneath—you can almost hear the computers clicking away, Johnson once said of him—had become tired, emotional, and depressed. Said McNamara, looking back: "Jesus, it was an unbelievably stressful environment."[6]

The unique demands of his position as secretary of defense compounded McNamara's burden. Stuck between two very different stakeholders, he was expected to be assertive toward the chiefs but deferential toward the president, a dynamic that created relentless and conflicting demands. (The perspectives of presidents versus those of four-star generals and admirals can be very different.) It required him to constantly engage in what social psychologists call "vertical code-switching," a process that occurs when those in the middle of a hierarchy—in this case, the chain-of-command—frequently alternate between incompatible roles with very different expectations and very different power dynamics.[7] The Pentagon was not Ford; senior military officers subordinate to McNamara also had a de facto political and networking channel with their allies in Congress and the media, and so at times could effectively be the superior party. This oscillation went on day after day for seven years. It exacted a heavy personal toll on McNamara. Role conflicts and incompatible expectations increased his anxiety and exhaustion. They also generated accumulating frustration and resentment toward McNamara on the part of both Johnson and the chiefs. McNamara found no easy relief from the burdens of his office.

In the halcyon early days of the Johnson administration, before Vietnam became a miasma, Tom Wicker wrote in the *New York Times*, "It can all be said in a sentence: Lyndon B. Johnson and Robert S. McNamara have confidence in each other"—the president and his indispensable right-hand man.[8] But by 1967 McNamara was no longer indispensable—in fact, the opposite. In late August, he revealed his serious doubts about bombing for the first time in public testimony before the Senate Armed Services Committee. Two months later, in early November, he privately broke with Johnson over the war—a break that led to his departure as secretary of defense.

By the spring of 1967, McNamara's misery over America's failure in Vietnam had become acute. A record 274 American soldiers were killed during the last week of April, bringing U.S. fatalities in the war to 8,560. The biggest antiwar demonstration yet brought 125,000 protestors into the streets of Manhattan. Sorties and bomb tonnage dropped had increased enormously the previous year, yet during this period Communist troop strength in the South had risen from 204,000 to 278,000.[9] The ground war, despite many more U.S. troops, had become a stalemate. "I never thought it would go on like this," McNamara confessed to a journalist friend, Emmet Hughes of *Newsweek*, a few months earlier. "I didn't think these people had the capacity to fight this way. If I had thought they could take this punishment and fight this well . . . I would have thought differently at the start."[10]

Pacification efforts had stalled. The ARVN remained passive and dependent on American forces to carry the burden of combat. South Vietnamese government corruption continued unchecked. And mounting social strains caused by the swelling refugee population added to Saigon's burdens. The CIA addressed all of these problems in a comprehensive report in late May. "The strategic balance has not been altered perceptively," its analysts concluded. "Two years of bomb damage in the North and setbacks in the South have not shaken Hanoi's determination to pursue the war. The North Vietnamese have managed to keep pace with the US troop build-up and to improve their logistic position. Hanoi seems confident that it can force a prolonged stalemate which eventually will force the US to scale down its objectives."[11] The chiefs' proposed solution to bombing's ineffectiveness—mining the harbors of North Vietnam—promised no answer in the CIA's judgment. "Almost complete denial of water access to North Vietnam," the report concluded, "could interdict at most 70 percent of North Vietnam's capacity to import, reducing it from about 14,000 tons a day at present to about 3,900 a day." But "the military supplies and essential economic goods needed by Hanoi to continue the war," it noted, "would not exceed an estimated 3,000 tons a day." No amount of bombing could erase a stubborn fact: "The capacity of the highway and waterway systems is far in excess of the comparatively small volume of supplies required."[12]

Like Johnson, by now McNamara was more directly personifying the war effort in his own and in the public imagination. His anguish, combined with his regret over the unwise advice he had given Johnson in 1964–1965, and his self-reproach at having failed at the most important task of his career—admissions difficult for anyone to make—compelled him to try to make sense of how the war had become so open-ended, why things had gone so terribly wrong. And there was another loyalty: to logic, to numbers, to the firm conviction that every equation could be solved via rigorous inquisition. That faith remained.

Unlike most players of the Washington power game, McNamara resisted the temptation to look only for an optimistic or self-justifying interpretation of events, particularly those involving him. He always consciously sought to follow the evidence wherever it led, even at the expense of his ego. He sought to do the same now with Vietnam, by turning to the past. On June 17, he commissioned a top-secret study of U.S. involvement in Indochina dating back to World War II that later became known as the "Pentagon Papers." McNamara envisioned an "encyclopedic and objective" compilation of primary source documents "for the purpose of throwing light on the decision-making process so that lessons could be drawn"[13] by historians once the emotions stirred by Vietnam had subsided. He passed along the idea to his assistant, John McNaughton, and his military aide, Colonel Robert Gard, telling them, "I want a thorough study of the background of our involvement in Vietnam."[14] He did not want any whitewashing. "Tell your researchers not to hold back . . . Let the chips fall where they may."[15] McNamara did not tell Johnson, Rusk, or Rostow about the project because, as one of his Pentagon staffers later explained, he "did not want the collecting and weighing of the documents to be influenced by anyone."[16] In one of his last decisions,* McNaughton assigned the project—along with more than one hundred questions he had drawn up—to his special assistant, Morton Halperin, who in turn assigned the project to his deputy, Leslie Gelb. Gelb decided to not only compile a documentary record but to produce an ambitious analytical study, a decision that McNamara later tacitly approved.†

Halperin and Gelb thought the study would take seven people six months to complete.[17] Working in a room across from the secretary's suite filled with desks and classified file safes, Gelb and eventually more than thirty other researchers, including Daniel Ellsberg and Richard Holbrooke, spent a year and a half producing a massive, forty-three-volume study based on many (but certainly not all‡) key Vietnam-related documents going back to 1945. The result ran to more than 7,000 pages and 2.5 million words. The top-secret study was not completed until early 1969, nearly a year after McNamara left the Pentagon—but it became hugely controversial when Ellsberg leaked it to the *New York Times* in the summer of 1971, prompting a Supreme Court decision on press freedom and contributing to Richard Nixon's downfall as president.§ The notoriety occasioned by the publication of classified documents on the

---

* McNaughton, his wife, and his youngest son died in a plane collision in the skies over North Carolina in July 1967.

† Gard sent early draft chapters of the analytical study to McNamara in the fall of 1967. McNamara never responded, but also never questioned or opposed the broadened nature of the enterprise. Author's interview with Robert Gard, August 18, 2016.

‡ They did not have access to many top-level State Department or White House files, nor any of President Kennedy's and President Johnson's recordings of meetings and telephone conversations.

§ A clandestine unit working for the Nixon White House, known as "the plumbers," broke into the California home of Lewis Fielding, the psychologist treating Ellsberg, seeking damaging information to discredit Ellsberg. This same clandestine unit later broke into the Democratic National Committee headquarters in the Watergate building in Washington, D.C., triggering the scandal that led to Nixon's resignation in August 1974.

war obscured the significance of McNamara's decision to commission it. By doing so, he had implicitly acknowledged the magnitude of America's failure in Vietnam and his own culpability in that failure. He had also begun questioning the fundamental premises of U.S. policy toward Vietnam going back more than two decades. "You know," he later told a friend, "they could hang people for what's in there."[18]

Before making his decision about Westmoreland's latest troop request, Johnson sent McNamara back to South Vietnam in early July, his ninth visit to the war-torn country since 1962. Westmoreland viewed McNamara's latest trip as his "last chance" to get more troops, said one of his senior staff officers, and "enormous energy was used in making the briefings for McNamara as persuasive as possible."[19] MACV staff rehearsed their presentations for weeks. When McNamara arrived on July 7, a sign on the door into the MACV briefing room read, appropriately, "High Noon." The military delivered an aggressive sales pitch—a full-court press of sorts—to McNamara that day. "The situation is not a stalemate," Westmoreland assured him. Ellsworth Bunker, who had succeeded Lodge as U.S. ambassador in April, echoed Westmoreland. A flinty and laconic seventy-three-year-old Vermonter with a thin and erect bearing who had succeeded in a variety of diplomatic posts, Bunker had a cool demeanor that quickly earned him the nickname "Old Man Refrigerator" among South Vietnamese. "There was an air of impenetrability about him," wrote one Saigon official, "a shield of dignity that marked him instantly as an aristocrat."[20] Bunker tempered Westmoreland's optimism, however, with a crucial qualification: "In the end, they [the South Vietnamese] must win it themselves." "We are winning slowly but steadily and this pace can accelerate if we reinforce our successes," Westmoreland concluded.[21]

McNamara seemed unaffected by Westmoreland's forceful presentation. His patience with the general's repeated requests—each seemingly the last increase that would be needed—had grown very thin, as had his faith in the accuracy of both MACV's order-of-battle, which counted enemy main-force units but excluded

Ambassador Ellsworth Bunker
Yoichi Okamoto/LBJ Library

part-time village guerrillas, and its body count as an indicator of progress.* "If the reports of enemy casualties are correct," he said that summer, "we would have destroyed the North Vietnamese Army two times over."[22] McNamara also believed that Westmoreland was not effectively using the considerable number of troops al-

---

* McNamara had come to feel much the same about the civilian pacification program, which included the number of refugees within the total of the "increase of people living in secure areas." See Francis FitzGerald, *Fire in the Lake: The Vietnamese and the Americans in Vietnam* (Atlantic–Little, Brown, 1972), p. 363.

ready at his disposal. Sitting at the MACV briefing table in pressed khakis scrawling notes on a lined notepad, McNamara seemed unusually quiet and withdrawn. He asked Westmoreland why Saigon could not supply the additional troops needed by lowering its draft age from twenty to eighteen (as the United States had done). One of Westmoreland's staff officers replied, "Psychologically, we hope they [the Government of South Vietnam, GVN] would accept this." At this, McNamara exploded.

> Let me just say this, general: psychologically, *I* cannot accept it. I am sick and tired of having problems in what the GVN accept when the American society is under the strain it is under today. And, you men out here are under a strain. There is no damn reason in the world why we should worry about whether the GVN will accept it psychologically . . . They are under a strain, I realize that, but there are certain things that they are just going to have to face forcefully. And one of them is that our government is not going to send additional tens of thousands of U.S. personnel over here until they get fully mobilized. That's all there is to it. It just is not going to be done. It is politically impossible. The people won't stand for it. So they are going to have to get this done out here.[23]

The defense secretary's unexpected outburst stunned everyone in the room accustomed to his normally restrained and methodical style. Such an eruption would never have come from the crisp and unemotional McNamara of earlier years.

McNamara met with the president and his other senior advisors at the White House the day after he returned to Washington. Johnson began the July 12 meeting by noting "an attitude in this country today that we are not doing all we should to get the war over" with "quickly." The number of casualties in the first half of 1967 had already equaled all of those the year before. In May, Senator Russell privately warned Johnson that "we've got to finish it soon because time is working against you both here and there."[24] Recent polls corroborated Russell's warning, showing Americans deeply split between escalation (45 percent) and withdrawal (41 percent), but united in their resentment of a lengthening war with no resolution in sight. Gallup surveys released at the end of the month showed 52 percent of Americans disapproved of Johnson's handling of the war—his highest negative rating to date—and only 34 percent saw progress in the fighting.[25] "The U.S. people," he added, "do think, perhaps, that this war cannot be won." Protests against the war mounted throughout the country. "Are we going to be able to win this goddamned war?" It was a startling question coming from Johnson, a small, first crack in his facade of resolution and determination to stay the course in Vietnam. Clifford asked McNamara if he thought it was true that the war could not be won. McNamara's answer seemed to contradict his May 19 memo to the president. "For the first time" since U.S. troops had been committed in 1965, the note taker recorded, McNamara "felt that if we follow the same program we will win the war and end the fighting."[26]

What explained the apparent contradiction in McNamara's assessments regarding the prospect of victory in Vietnam? Partly, it reflected the aggressively optimistic briefings he had received from Westmoreland and others in Saigon just days earlier. At these meetings, every senior American official and many junior American officers—dozens in all—derisively labeled assessments of the war being a stalemate as "the most ridiculous statements they ever heard."[27] McNamara did not fear their disagreement or disapproval, but the number and authority of those who had strongly voiced this opinion challenged and undermined confidence in his own judgment and added to his stress. "I was in a minority," he later explained. "The majority thought we were winning."[28] And how, he wearily pondered, could he know that *his* judgment was the right one? Perhaps *he*—not the dozens of American officials and military officers in Saigon—was wrong. "When we think or believe differently from those around us, we are not sure that we are right," observes University of California, Berkeley, psychology professor Charlan Nemeth. "In fact, we are prone to think that 'truth lies in numbers.'"[29] Finally, and most tellingly, McNamara's apparent about-face reflected his inner conflict as he struggled to reconcile what the facts told him with his sense of personal and institutional loyalty to President Johnson and the fighting men in Vietnam. Attrition had succeeded in this instance: the defense secretary had been ground down to the point of abdication.

At a meeting the next day, Johnson decided to send Westmoreland a limited number of more soldiers. The additional forces—45,000, which would bring U.S. troop strength to 525,000 by the beginning of 1968—represented a quarter of Westmoreland's latest request. But that 45,000 was all that Johnson, struggling to reconcile the pressures of the war with his problems at home, would tolerate. He had decided to set a troop limit on Westmoreland, as Truman had set a troop limit on MacArthur in Korea. Tellingly, before the meeting had ended, Johnson asked if South Vietnam would fall if the U.S. terminated the bombing of North Vietnam—an idea he had never raised before. No one could be sure, but the fact that Johnson had raised the question for the first time indicated that his own thinking was changing.[30]

Wheeler and Westmoreland, who attended the meeting, understood that 45,000 more troops were the most they were going to get, so they embraced the lower figure and resolved to get the job done with the forces their civilian superior had authorized, without complaint or threatened resignation. At a White House press conference afterward, Wheeler, with Johnson standing next to him, said "this meets the need for Vietnam," and Westmoreland— who had returned to the United States for his mother's funeral before coming to Washington—said he was "delighted with the outcome," "that progress can be accelerated once the troops are deployed," and that his recommendations "have been honored."[*]

Despite his question about South Vietnamese resilience, pressure mounted on Johnson that summer to intensify the bombing. This issue came up at a meeting of the "Tuesday Lunch Group" on

---

[*] The army chief of staff, General Harold Johnson, echoed this assessment when he told a White House press briefing on August 12 that 45,000 additional troops "should be adequate to provide a degree of momentum that will see us through to a solution in South Vietnam." Diary Backup, August 12, 1967, LBJL.

July 18. When in Washington, Johnson lunched every Tuesday with his senior Vietnam advisors on the second floor of the Executive Mansion. His guests gathered for glasses of sherry in the family living room at the west end of the main hallway to await the president, who invariably arrived a few minutes late. Johnson would bound into the room, briefly acknowledge everyone's presence, then herd the group into the adjacent family dining room, whose walls were decorated with a mural of British general Cornwallis surrendering at Yorktown in 1781. Johnson sat at the head of the table and, following protocol, Rusk sat to Johnson's immediate right, McNamara to his immediate left. Walt Rostow, Richard Helms, White House press secretary George Christian (who succeeded Bill Moyers in February 1967), and notetaker Tom Johnson rounded out the group. At this Tuesday Lunch, Johnson read aloud a letter he had received from an Arizona man who complained the administration was not serious about ending the war because it refused to escalate the bombing to a level that would force Hanoi's capitulation. Americans like him, the man wrote, "believe that civilian heads have ignored the advice of the military." Unaccustomed to and frustrated by a limited war, such citizens regarded air strikes against the enemy's homeland—as had been conducted against Germany and Japan during World War II—as the proper way to fight, and if the United States was unwilling to assume greater risks, then it should get out of Vietnam. Johnson said the Arizona man's sentiments reflected the pressures he would face in Congress and the country in coming months.

Johnson reiterated this point two months later to Deputy National Security Advisor Francis Bator, a dove on the subject of Vietnam. "You doves think the pressures on me come from you," he told Bator. "You are all wrong. The *real* pressures on me are coming from people who want me to go North, mine the harbors, bomb Hanoi, get into a war with the Chinese—they're crazies. That is where the real pressures are. I am the boy with his finger in the dike protecting you doves from the crazies." After he finished, Johnson walked around his desk, picked up a bumper sticker, and showed it to Bator, almost with tears in his eyes. The bumper sticker read "All The Way With LeMay."[31]

A public opinion survey conducted that fall corroborated Johnson's anxiety. The widespread dissatisfaction it showed with the administration's Vietnam policy came as no surprise. But the reasons for the dissatisfaction did: while 44 percent of Americans favored withdrawal from Vietnam, an even larger number—55 percent—favored a *tougher* policy, including some who advocated using nuclear weapons in Vietnam.[32] Such pressures and the concerns they generated fed Johnson's willingness to approve heavier bombing of North Vietnam.

McNamara's opposition to intensifying the aerial assault, on the other hand, worsened the growing split between him and Johnson. During a Tuesday Lunch on August 8, McNamara opposed the chiefs' recommendation for increased air attacks around Hanoi and Haiphong, saying such actions risked Chinese intervention, threatened to kill hundreds of civilians, undercut the prospect of sparking negotiations, and were certain to inflame domestic protests. He advocated limiting the bombing to the panhandle of southern North Vietnam below the twentieth parallel, arguing that targeting this funnel would be more effective at interdicting the flow of men and supplies to the South, less costly to U.S. pilots, less apt to widen the war, and more consistent with the effort to begin negotiations, an idea he had first broached in his May 19 memorandum to the president. "It doesn't look as though we have escalated enough to win," countered Johnson. McNamara replied that heavier bombing "would not necessarily mean that we would win." "We have got to do something to win," Johnson shot back.[33]

Johnson's impatience reflected his anxiety about Senate hearings on ROLLING THUNDER scheduled to begin the following day. McNamara planned to testify at the hearings. The president, his face darkening, warned McNamara about the heat he would face. "I am not worried about the heat," McNamara replied, "as long as I know what we are doing is right." "It was quite a scene," a White House aide recalled, both men going back and forth,

tempers rising. Finally, Johnson told McNamara, in effect, you are
on your own—I won't pull the rug out from under you, but I am
not accepting your argument, in just that way, right now.[34]

The next morning, the Preparedness Investigating Subcommittee
of the Senate Armed Services Committee, chaired by Democrat
John Stennis of Mississippi, a quintessential Southern conservative implacably opposed to civil rights legislation and hawkishly
anti-Communist—he demanded that Great Society programs be
"relegated to the rear" in order to release resources to win the war—
began closed-door hearings on the air war against North Vietnam.
The hearings came close on the heels of a blistering critique of the
administration's bombing policy on the House floor by Minority
Leader Gerald Ford, who, primed by frustrated and unhappy admirals and generals, chided Johnson and McNamara for "hand-
cuffing" U.S. air operations over North Vietnam. Ford lambasted
"secret restraints" imposed by Washington civilians and chastised
the White House for preventing American planes and pilots from
hitting "hard enough and convincingly enough" to bring Hanoi to
its knees. Ford saw "no justification for sending one more American" soldier to South Vietnam until Johnson lifted the restraints
on ROLLING THUNDER. Ford's remarks reflected sentiment
and pressure that had been growing for months among conservatives and their allies in the military who resented the limitations
imposed on bombing by the Johnson administration, which they
blamed for prolonging the war and jeopardizing the lives of American soldiers, and who leaked their complaints to Stennis and others who openly sympathized with their point of view.

The Southern barons who controlled key Congressional committees, like Richard Russell and Carl Vinson of Georgia and Men-
del Rivers of South Carolina, ran the Senate and House Armed
Services Committees like personal fiefdoms and maintained close
relations with the chiefs, whose budgets they controlled and in
whose districts many servicemen lived, worked—and voted. Accustomed to horse-trading behind closed doors over bourbon and
branch water, these Capitol veterans—like Stennis—expected deference from cabinet officers whose names and photos appeared on

newspaper front pages and in magazines but who would come and go while *they* remained in Congress for decades. "In both House and Senate," wrote a journalist who spent years covering Congress in the 1950s and 1960s, "were petty, arrogant men who [saw] sport in cowing officials of the Executive Branch."[35]

McNamara had a low threshold of tolerance for backslapping and schmoozing; in a political fishbowl, he was out of water. "Gene, I don't understand why you waste so much time servicing the Hill," he told his old Harvard Business School colleague and now secretary of the air force, Eugene Zuckert. "Except for Dick Russell and a few others, most of those people are really stupid."[36] It was a contemptuously sweeping statement; though many (not all) representatives and senators knew precious little about international issues, they intimately understood the concerns of their constituents. McNamara did his homework, sacrificed an extraordinary amount of sleep to his job, anticipated the questions he would be asked by the press and Congress, and spent four or five hours in preparation for each hour as a witness before House and Senate committees, always answering questions directly—even curtly—hiding his sense of humor beneath a mask of crisp, professorial logic. Unwilling to lubricate relationships by sharing a few drinks with prickly and egotistical congressional potentates, he refused to engage in the habitual flattery that is a way of life for politicians because he considered it not only demeaning to himself but also to the person on whom the adulation is bestowed and found it hard to believe that anyone would not recognize it for what it was. He felt he could avoid the little games one must play to be successful in Washington because he never felt it necessary to cover his rear in case things went wrong, to take defensive measures to make things more palatable politically, to plead for agreement when his position was clear and his logic sensible. In this sense, there was some arrogance at play, too. All of this rankled the "good ol' boys." They considered McNamara "perhaps a little too smart," noted David Halberstam, "and when Southerners say someone is smart, they are not necessarily being complimentary."[37]

Stennis and his colleagues did not forgive or forget McNamara's rigidity and, as they saw it, condescension—and decided to go hunting for bear. The Hearings on the Air War Against North Vietnam began at 10 A.M. on August 9 in Room 224 of the Old Senate Office Building (now the Russell Senate Office Building). Subcommittee chairman Stennis made clear his intent in his opening statement, when he said, "The question is growing in Congress as to whether it is wise to send more men if we are going to just leave them at the mercy of the guerrilla war without trying to cut off the enemy's supplies more effectively . . . My own personal opinion, which I have expressed many times in the past, is that it would be a tragic and perhaps fatal mistake for us to suspend or restrict the bombing."[38] Asserting that "recommendations by our military leaders have gone unheeded," Stennis made a point of opening the hearings with testimony from McNamara's arch critics: frustrated and unhappy admirals and generals who had invested their reputations in the war and resented what they considered civilian meddling that stood in the way of victory and got men killed.

First to testify was Admiral U. S. Grant Sharp, commander of air operations over Vietnam, who had flown in from Honolulu for the occasion, full of pent-up bitterness and personal animosity for the defense secretary. Sharp had fought McNamara for years over ROLLING THUNDER,* insisting that quicker and heavier bombing, such as attacking Hanoi and mining Haiphong, would force North Vietnam to crack. "This war is a dirty business, like all wars," he had written to Wheeler nine months before. "We need to get hard-headed about it. That is the only kind of action these tough-minded Communists will respect . . . When Hanoi screams, hit them again."[39] A true believer in the decisive importance of air power—which was his operational bailiwick as commander of air operations in Vietnam—Sharp remained wedded to this belief despite the now voluminous evidence to the contrary laid out in

---

* Sharp later accused McNamara of causing "needless casualties" by misusing American air power: "The air campaign of 1965 was characterized by excessive restrictions from Washington which limited us to piddling strikes against generally unimportant targets." See *New York Times*, December 18, 2001.

numerous CIA assessments, and told the subcommittee so. "Although initiated with modest efforts and slowly expanded under carefully controlled conditions," the admiral noted dismissively of ROLLING THUNDER, he declared that "the growing weight of our efforts has brought extensive destruction or disruption of North Vietnam's war-supporting resources." Emotion overcame logic and evidence. Again contending that "we have begun to hurt the enemy in his home territory—he is suffering painful military, economic, and psychological strains," Sharp urged that "now, when the enemy is hurting, we should increase our pressures." Thus, "we could make Ho Chi Minh decide that this is not a very useful war for him." Insisting, again without any evidence, that "our air campaign puts a ceiling on the troops that they can employ down there [in South Vietnam] and the level of effort," the admiral said, "they are at that ceiling . . . I think that they are struggling to maintain the level of action that they are now accomplishing"—an assessment that would be spectacularly contradicted by the massive Tet Offensive less than six months in the offing.[40]

The next witness, JCS chairman General Earle Wheeler, took his seat at the table a week later, on August 16. Wheeler offered a more balanced assessment than had Sharp. He conceded that "North Vietnam has shown marked ability to recuperate from and accommodate to our air attacks" and acknowledged the two fundamental problems plaguing the bombing program: North Vietnam's external sources of war materiel and the Communists' ability to choose when, where, and how long to fight. Because the Soviet Union and China supplied Hanoi's weapons of war, the losses inflicted by ROLLING THUNDER could constantly be replenished. "It is not like it was in Germany [during World War II] when the war resources were being fabricated in the country," Wheeler explained. "This is the reason that the targets regenerate all the time in North Vietnam." And because the enemy "won't stand and fight, . . . you can't put a strain on his logistics." Despite these fundamental problems, Wheeler nonetheless persuaded himself and told the committee "the air campaign is going well" and recommended expanding it.[41]

The chiefs of the air force and the navy, General John McConnell and Admiral Thomas Moorer, followed a week later, on August 22 and 23. McConnell expressed considerable frustration at Hanoi's recuperative ability. "You knock a bridge out and in a week those characters have the bridge back in shape, so you have to knock it out again, and the same thing applies to their airfields, to their water shipping and everything else." The intense vexation that Mc-Connell felt had erupted earlier that summer at a Pentagon brief-ing. After the briefing, McConnell held his head in his hands and said privately to aides, "I can't tell you how I feel . . . I'm so sick of it . . . I have never been so goddamn frustrated by it all . . . I'm so sick of it."[42] But his frustration led the general to emphasize what should happen, rather than what had happened. Insisting "there are many valuable targets remaining unstruck," McConnell—like Sharp before him—asserted rather than adduced evidence that an intensified bombing campaign "should . . . impose a prohibitive drain on his economy and his military assets" and that "he cannot escape the reality that we have the controlling instrument of mili-tary power." McConnell's wishful thinking extended to Russia's and China's support of Hanoi, which he rightly saw as a crucial factor. "The best way to win the war in my opinion would be to negotiate with the Soviets and the Chicoms [Chinese Communists] . . . to stop furnishing equipment and supplies to North Vietnam," the general said. "With that, the war couldn't possibly last very long." Indeed. But Moscow and Beijing had no such intention, and Washington had no ability to change their thinking, short of starting a war be-tween thermonuclear superpowers that could be apocalyptic.[43]

Admiral Moorer echoed Sharp and McConnell in his testimony by explaining that "we were not bombing to the extent that we were capable of doing, and in my view should have done" because ROLLING THUNDER had been overly burdened with restrictions and prohibited targets.[44] It was the wrong record stuck in a deep groove: for these commanders that bombing could be decisive was unquestioned dogma rather than corroborated fact. One intelli-gence study after another showed in sobering detail that bombing had not significantly affected either the will of the North Vietnamese to continue supporting the war in the South or their ability to infiltrate the necessary supplies and manpower, and little could be accomplished by increasing its scope and intensity.* With the end of Moorer's testimony, however, a parade of four-star admirals and generals had gone on record against the administration's bombing program. Each had earned headlines the day after his testimony, producing days of news stories on the military's strong feelings in favor of air escalation.

Two days later, shortly after 10 A.M. on August 25, Robert Mc-Namara began what he later described as "one of the most stressful episodes of my life."[45] The subcommittee had pitched softball questions to the admirals and generals. McNamara faced a hostile panel primed to attack and knew whatever he said would get back to the president. Yet, compelled to speak frankly, McNamara deliberately had not cleared his presentation in advance with the White House because he knew he would not have gotten approval. He was on his own, alone, and given the known sentiments of the subcommittee and the testimony that preceded him, he knew the deck was heavily stacked in favor of his inquisitors.

Settling his tense frame into the witness chair after being sworn in, he read aloud a statement released to the press just minutes earlier, also without prior White House clearance, something he had never done before. In it, the man who had pushed Johnson to begin bombing in early 1965 laid out the profound limitations he had come to see in an air campaign that, by this time, had involved more than 173,000 sorties, killed thousands of North Vietnamese, and led to the death and capture of hundreds of American pilots and air crewmen. "The nature of the combat in Vietnam, without established battle lines and with sporadic and relatively small-scale

---

* Several weeks later, McGeorge Bundy sent word to Johnson that "Dick Helms told me solemnly today that every single member of his intelligence staff agrees with the view that bombing in the Hanoi-Haiphong area has no significant effect whatever on the level of supplies that reaches the Southern battlefield. Nor does any intelligence officer of standing believe that strategic [i.e., economic and population] bombing will break the will of Hanoi in the foreseeable future." McGeorge Bundy to the President, October 17, 1967, NSF, LBJL.

enemy action, lessens the requirement for a steady stream of logistical support and reduces the volume of logistical support needed,"
he acknowledged, then went on:

> North Vietnam's ability to continue its aggression against the
> South thus depends upon imports of war-supporting material
> and their transshipment to the South. Unfortunately for the
> chances of effective interdiction, this simple agricultural soci-
> ety has a highly diversified transportation system consisting
> of rails and roads and waterways. The North Vietnamese use
> barges and sampans, trucks and foot power, and even bicycles
> capable of carrying 500-pound loads to move goods over this
> network. The capacity of this system is very large; the vol-
> ume of traffic it is now required to carry, in relation to its
> capacity, is very small.
>
> Precise figures on the amount of infiltrated material re-
> quired to support the Vietcong and North Vietnamese forces
> in the South are not known. However, intelligence estimates
> suggest that the quantity of externally supplied material, other
> than food, required to support the VC/NVA forces in South
> Vietnam at about their current level of combat activity is very,
> very small. The reported figure is 15 tons per day, but even if
> the quantity were five times that amount, it could be trans-
> ported by only a few trucks. This is the small flow of material
> which we are attempting to prevent from entering South
> Vietnam through a pipeline which has an outlet capacity of
> more than 200 tons a day.

All of this meant one thing: "There is no basis to believe that
any bombing campaign, short of one which had population as its
target, would by itself force Ho Chi Minh's regime into submission." And no senior military officer advocated that, he noted.

But McNamara was not done. He then addressed the chiefs'
insistent demand to mine North Vietnam's harbors, a step they
claimed would prove decisive:

The great bulk of North Vietnamese imports now enters through Haiphong*—perhaps as much as 4,700 out of the 5,800 tons per day . . . [but] little if any of the imported military equipment (which is estimated by intelligence sources to total 550 tons per day) comes by sea. Moreover, this present heavy reliance on Haiphong reflects convenience rather than necessity. Haiphong represents the easiest and cheapest means of import. If it and other ports were to be closed, and on the unrealistic assumption that closing the ports would eliminate all seaborne imports, North Vietnam would still be able to import over 8,400 tons a day by rail, road, and waterway. And even if, through air strikes, its road, rail and Red River waterway capacity could all be reduced by 50 percent, North Vietnam could maintain roughly 70 percent of its current imports. Since the daily importation of military and war-supporting material totals far less than this, . . . cutting off seaborne imports would not prevent North Vietnam from continuing its present level of military operations in the South . . .

The North Vietnam seacoast runs for 400 miles. Many locations are suitable for over-the-beach operations. The mining of Haiphong or the total destruction of Haiphong port facilities would not prevent offshore unloading of foreign shipping. Effective interdiction of this lighterage, even if the inevitable damage to foreign shipping were to be accepted, would only lead to total reliance on land importation through Communist China. The common border between the two countries is about 500 miles long.†

---

* North Vietnam's main port at the mouth of the Cẩm River Delta.

† There was something else as well: McNamara did not know it at the time, but Beijing had promised Hanoi that "in case Haiphong is blockaded, and there are no other ports accessible in [North] Vietnam, foreign shipments to [North] Vietnam [would] be transported through China's ports. We have an agreement for this contingency." Meeting between Zhou En-lai and Pham Van Dong, Beijing, April 10, 1967, in Odd Arne Westad, Chen Jian, Stein Tonnesson, Nguyen Vu Tang, and James G. Hershberg, eds., *77 Conversations Between Chinese and Foreign Leaders*

To McNamara, the conclusion of all this was inescapable: heavier bombing promised no greater military results and only risked greater civilian casualties and the danger of widening the war to include China.

Tension mounted in the hearing room as McNamara spoke. Although he had written a powerful case against the bombing into the record, his analysis infuriated the conservative subcommittee members. When he finished, they pummeled him with hostile questions. Republican Strom Thurmond of South Carolina said, "Mr. Secretary, I am terribly disappointed with your statement. I think it is a statement of placating the Communists. It is a statement of appeasing the Communists. It is a statement of no-win. It seems to me that if we follow what you have recommended, we ought to get out of Vietnam at once, because we have no chance to win, and I deeply regret that a man in your position is taking that position today." It was demagogic criticism, but Thurmond's conclusion about what he'd heard was not unreasonable—McNamara's analysis pointed to the same policy verdict, but he could not bring himself to advocate withdrawal, only to limit further escalation. Democrat Howard Cannon of Nevada zeroed in on McNamara's— and by implication, Johnson's—unwillingness to unreservedly follow the military's advice about Vietnam, which the senator knew to be a politically sensitive subject in the run-up to next year's presidential election. Cannon bluntly asked whether McNamara had "confidence in the members of the Joint Chiefs and in their military recommendations, and just what the reason [was] that their recommendations on military matters and military targets are not followed." In his reply, McNamara addressed the root of civil-military tension over Vietnam, and why the Constitution resolved that tension in favor of civilians. The commander in chief was an elected civilian, he pointed out, and noted more than just "narrow military factors must be taken account of by the Commander in

---

on the Wars in Indochina, 1964–1977 (Cold War International History Project, May 1998), p. 99.

Chief in making decisions in this area, and that, of course, is what happened." It was almost classic McNamara: precise and not what his interrogators wanted to hear. "It isn't at all a question of confidence in the Chiefs," he hastened to note, then added: "If we didn't have confidence in the Chiefs, they wouldn't be Chiefs."[46]

Once his testimony was complete it was clear that while McNamara had survived the Stennis hearings—Johnson had not fired him afterward—he had been wounded, diminished politically. The hearings exposed civilian-military infighting and deepened the rift between him and Johnson. By openly criticizing intensified air strikes—something he had never done before—the administration's fissure over American strategy was now public. McNamara had thus made it harder for Johnson to approve air strikes even as the pressure on him to do just this increased, effectively boxing in the president and limiting his future options—something Johnson hated. McNamara's testimony also encouraged Congress and the press to play up his difference of opinion with Johnson as a "feud" and "controversy" and to publicize the administration's internal division. "McNamara Doubts Bombing in the North Can End the War" ran a headline in the *New York Times*. "Differs with Military Chiefs on Escalation in Testimony Before Panel of Senate—Opposes New Targets," went another.

McNamara, for his part, knew that revealing his skepticism about the air war publicly for the first time at the Stennis hearings would have consequences, and was "tremendously troubled when he had to come out with testimony that he knew would infuriate Johnson," recalled his former deputy, Roswell Gilpatric. "It was just a question of how large the explosion would be and what the denouement would be."[47]

The Oval Office had not waited for the headlines to react. Johnson lit into McNamara during a twenty-minute phone call immediately after McNamara finished his testimony, giving him "a full blast of presidential anger," in the words of John McNaughton's successor as aide to McNamara, Paul Warnke.[48] To another aide, Johnson, who in what seemed like an impossible past had once idolized McNamara, now acidly remarked, "I forgot he had only been president of Ford for one week."[*49] "Believe me, Johnson was mad," White House staffer and former McNamara aide Joseph Califano recalled.[50] It wasn't McNamara's point of view that infuriated Johnson, it was that he had aired it in plain sight. "A very important thing about Lyndon Johnson," recalled McGeorge Bundy, was that "he would hear anything if he could hear it privately."[51] He detested having internal divisions exposed to public scrutiny and therefore widespread political criticism. When *Time* published an article highlighting differences between his secretary of state and secretary of defense on an issue, Johnson referred to it as "that ugly piece."[52] When he appointed Rostow national security advisor, he told Rostow's deputy Francis Bator, who had been on the NSC since 1964, "If you two fight, OK—as long as it stays quiet. But if it gets into the newspapers . . . I'll fire both of you. And I'll fire you first because you've been here longer."[53]

When the hearings ended, the subcommittee issued a unanimous report excoriating McNamara and Johnson for micromanaging the war and having "consistently overruled the unanimous recommendations of military commanders and the Joint Chiefs of Staff." It blamed the failure of ROLLING THUNDER on "the fragmentation of our air might by overly restrictive controls, limitations, and the doctrine of 'gradualism' . . . which discounted the professional judgment of our best military experts and substituted civilian judgment in the details of target selection and the timing of strikes. We shackled the true potential of airpower." The senators concluded: "We cannot, in good conscience, ask our ground forces to continue their fight in South Vietnam unless we are prepared to press the air war in the North in the most effective way possible . . . Logic and prudence requires that the decision be with the unanimous weight of professional military judgment." The use of the word "military" was a far from unsubtle rebuke to the wis-

---

* LBJ exaggerated a bit: McNamara had become the first nonfamily president of Ford Motor Company on November 9, 1960—one month and four days before JFK selected him as secretary of defense.

dom of civilian command. "What is needed now is the hard decision to do whatever is necessary![,] take the risks that have to be
taken, and apply the force that is required to see the job through."[54]

The strain in civil-military relations exposed by the hearings
went beyond the tactical. Wheeler, pale and exhausted after more
than three years as JCS chairman during a frustrating war, began
having chest pains and a few weeks later suffered a serious heart attack, the first of many that would eventually kill him. McNamara's
bruxism and reliance on sleeping pills increased, his nervous tension made worse by his wife Margy's ulcer surgery. ("Margy got
my ulcer," he said.) McNamara made the hour's drive to Johns
Hopkins University Hospital in Baltimore each night to visit her
and still arrived early the next morning at his Pentagon office, generally exhausted and sometimes unshaven.

The military's differences with McNamara (and, by extension,
with Johnson) had been laid bare before congressional critics and
the entire world, increasing the leverage of the military and congressional critics at McNamara and Johnson's expense. McNamara's
popularity on the Hill plummeted further. Johnson realized the
hearings had diminished McNamara's influence and standing, and
his own. Several weeks later, Johnson told Wheeler, "Your generals almost destroyed us with their testimony before the Stennis
Committee. We were murdered in the hearings."[55] Johnson privately criticized the senators for pressuring him into further escalation, but McNamara's testimony felt like a rug yanked out from
under him.

Despite his anger at McNamara, Johnson continued to listen to
his defense secretary and to be influenced by him. He suspended
bombing within a ten-mile radius of Hanoi in an effort initiated
by McNamara to stimulate discussions with the North Vietnamese.* He again followed McNamara's advice when he gave a speech

---

* The secret peace initiative launched in late August, codenamed PENNSYLVANIA,
proved unsuccessful—Hanoi still would have no part of a conditional cessation of
the bombing. In its view, the United States was committing an act of aggression
against a sovereign state—its homeland—and had no right to ask for conditions
under which the bombing would be stopped. After Hanoi delivered a final no to the

in San Antonio moderating his position on the bombing by stat-
ing that the United States would cease air attacks if Hanoi agreed
"promptly to productive discussions" and would "not take advantage" of a halt to increase the flow of men and supplies to the South.
(Johnson had previously insisted on an end to North Vietnamese
infiltration if he stopped the bombing, a trade-off that McNamara
privately criticized as asking "a horse for a rabbit."[56])* Hitherto,
Johnson had kept the chiefs at arm's length, using McNamara to
mediate between himself and them and to secure their acquiescence to his decisions, but now he also began including Wheeler at
Tuesday Lunches, meaning the civilian defense secretary no longer
solely represented the Pentagon at high-level White House meetings, as he had for more than six years. In giving his testimony,
McNamara had somewhat relieved his internal dissonance, but he
had also undermined his usefulness and made his position more
tenuous. Perhaps he understood this; Johnson certainly did. Given
the public nature of McNamara's dissent from administration policy on such a controversial subject, what seems remarkable is not
that Johnson would eventually ease him out, but that he would retain McNamara as long as he did. It bespoke much about the close
relationship between the two men.

Despite their differences, Johnson and McNamara both hoped
that nationwide elections scheduled for September 3 in South
Vietnam, following on the heels of a national constitution written
and adopted earlier that spring, would create greater legitimacy
and a solid political base for the government, show the world that
democracy could work in the war-torn land, and demonstrate a
new level of political maturity after four years of instability and
military rule. With domestic support for the war slipping, it had
become imperative for the Johnson administration to demonstrate

---

initiative in October, Johnson stepped up the bombing. See McNamara with Van-
DeMark, *In Retrospect*, pp. 295–302; and William C. Gibbons, *The U.S. Government
and the Vietnam War, Executive and Legislative Rules and Relationships: Part IV, July
1965–January 1968* (Government Printing Office, 1994), pp. 776–797, 869, and 874.

* This became known as the "San Antonio Formula." Hanoi rejected it as a "faked
desire for peace."

to the American people that the South Vietnamese were taking tangible steps toward responsible self-government. Successful elections now would also show that the Saigon government was not an American puppet, as the Vietcong and North Vietnamese claimed.

Washington's optimism about the elections was extraordinary, indeed incredible, to those who knew the political realities of South Vietnam, especially the bitter rivalry between Nguyễn Văn Thiệu and Nguyễn Cao Kỳ. For months, American officials, led by Ambassador Bunker, had been urging the two to put aside their feuding and unite against the Communists. Both men had risen through intrigue and manipulation, and each cordially hated the other. They had squabbled, clawed, and jockeyed for position the last two years, Kỳ—rash, charismatic, and mercurial—attracting most of the publicity, while Thiệu—secretive, suspicious, and calculating—quietly and methodically worked behind the scenes consolidating his power.* The two were constantly at each other's throats and flailing at one another, though on the surface it did not appear that way. Thiệu considered Kỳ a superficial showboat, while Kỳ considered Thiệu fundamentally corrupt. Neither had any intention of voluntarily relinquishing power.

President Johnson had a message for them: "It's not my place to say which one of them ought to be the [presidential] candidate . . . But do tell them . . . that whatever they do, they should make sure it doesn't upset the stability of the government. That's important to us."[57] After more cajoling by the American embassy, the rivals agreed to run on a single ticket—Thiệu as president and Kỳ as vice president—and they won a plurality of the vote. But their election hardly solved South Vietnam's political problems. For starters, their victory lacked broad-based legitimacy: several popular civilian candidates had been prevented from entering the race, and Thiệu and Kỳ received the votes of only 33 percent of South Vietnamese living in 67 percent of the country secure enough to hold

---

* Strategies remarkably similar to those adopted by Leon Trotsky and Joseph Stalin following Lenin's death in 1924—and with a similar result: Thiệu eventually edged Kỳ out, and ruled South Vietnam with an iron hand until the country fell to the Communists in April 1975.

elections—barely more than one in five South Vietnamese. In order to ensure the military's continued hold on power, the junta of ARVN generals from which Thiệu and Kỳ had emerged formed an extraconstitutional secret committee allowing them to appoint government officials and forcing the further illegitimated Thiệu and Kỳ to follow its directives. Accustomed to being the ruling clique, this committee would not subordinate itself to anyone, and what the generals did not influence, Washington did; the State Department drafted Thiệu and Kỳ's platform as well as their inaugural addresses. When the national legislature protested election irregularities and moved to invalidate the results, Thiệu and Kỳ blocked the effort with bribes and pressure from the U.S. embassy. It was thus no wonder that indifference, paralysis, and collaboration with the enemy continued to plague the country. The South Vietnamese felt little connection to a government that paid lip service to constitutional processes and made no sustained appeal to people at large.

Political discontent also gripped the United States. By the fall of 1967, antiwar sentiment in America neared a fever pitch. Growing numbers of college and university students and faculty, business leaders, mainstream politicians, and ordinary Americans viewed the war—costing more and more blood[*] with no end in sight—as a colossal mistake that must be ended as soon as possible. They were becoming increasingly vocal and aggressive in expressing their discontent, especially toward Johnson, whom they held responsible for the deepening debacle. Johnson's allies in Congress told him that Americans were turning against the war and that Democrats would lose the 1968 election if something wasn't done soon about Vietnam. Polls revealed that only 28 percent approved of his handling of the war. Nearly half wanted the United States to scale down the fighting or get out, while nearly 40 percent wanted to hit the Communists harder. Even more—46 percent—now con-

---

[*] By the fall of 1967, 10,000 American troops had been killed and 60,000 wounded in Vietnam.

sidered Vietnam a mistake, a tremendous and telling reversal from two years before, when U.S. troops first went into combat.[58] All of these things weighed heavily on Johnson, as became apparent at a White House meeting on October 3. For the first time—out of the blue—Johnson asked his advisors what effect a decision by him not to run again for president in the coming year would have on the war. "Our people will not hold out for four more years," he ruminated (accurately, it turned out), and then added in a heavy voice, "I just don't know if I want four more years of this."[59]

It was a recognizable Johnsonian outburst of self-pity but one that revealed an evolution of sorts. Being able to encounter unpleasant evidence and revise one's point of view in accordance with that new information is difficult and painful. Research has shown that opinions, once formed, are slow to change in response to new evidence.*[60] It requires an individual to fight against his or her natural tendencies and instincts and it means accepting discomforting and disconcerting facts. This, Johnson haltingly and belatedly began to do, the reports from Vietnam no longer one strain of a larger melody but the chorus. That fall of 1967, caught in a dynamic that he could not control, Johnson moved toward a clarity that was the product of a fundamental apprehension—of what lay ahead in Vietnam and his myopia. A powerful reality check came in mid-September in a long and carefully argued report by the chief of the CIA Office of National Estimates analyzing the "implications of an unfavorable outcome in Vietnam." Based on interviews with some thirty of the best-informed Vietnam experts within the agency, Helms delivered the top-secret assessment to Johnson with a covering note that read, "The attached paper is sensitive, particularly if its existence were to leak. It comes to you in a sealed envelope." Sophisticated and unsentimental, the report cut to the cold, hard bottom line:

---

* Even scientists wedded to empiricism, as Thomas Kuhn famously argued, often persist in adhering to theories long after such adherence can be justified by observable evidence. See Thomas S. Kuhn, *The Structure of Scientific Revolutions* (University of Chicago Press, 1962).

a. An unfavorable outcome in Vietnam would be a major set-back to the reputation of U.S. power which would limit U.S. influence and prejudice our other interests in some degree which cannot be reliably foreseen.

b. Probably the net effects would not be permanently damaging to this country's capacity to play its part as a world power working for order and security in many areas.

c. The worst potential damage would be of the self-inflicted kind: internal dissension which would limit our future ability to use our power and resources wisely and to full effect, and lead to a loss of confidence by others in the American capacity for leadership.

d. The destabilizing effects would be greatest in the immediate area of Southeast Asia where some states would probably face internal turmoil and heightened external pressures, and where some realignments might occur; similar effects would be unlikely elsewhere or could be more easily contained.

Those points were familiar, but there was another:

a. If the analysis here advances the discussion at all, it is in the direction of suggesting that the risks [in an unfavorable outcome] are probably more limited and controllable than most previous argument has indicated.[61]

Johnson pondered the report's implications, immediate and historical. These were predictions that might lead to pain and shame so intense he wouldn't wish them on his worst enemy. He did not share the memo with any of his senior advisors.

When Massachusetts Democratic representative Tip O'Neill, who held John F. Kennedy's old House seat and was a close ally of the president on the Hill whom Johnson considered "one of my own"—an "old school" New Deal Democrat much like himself—came out publicly against the war that autumn, Johnson initially reacted with hurt and fury. When O'Neill explained to Johnson that his opposition grew out of a sincere conviction that the war in Vietnam could not be won, Johnson "calmed down" and patiently heard O'Neill out.[62] That the secret CIA report and O'Neill's conclusion registered became clear at a Tuesday Lunch in mid-October, when Johnson plaintively asked, "How are we ever going to win?"[63] He repeated his growing doubts the following week. "It doesn't seem we can win the war militarily," he told his inner circle of Vietnam advisors. "We can't win diplomatically either."[64]

For two years, since he had reluctantly committed combat troops, Johnson had believed (or had wanted to believe) that he had acted properly—that his decision had been the right one and that American and Vietnamese lives had been sacrificed in the service of an achievable goal. Initially, popular opinion had ratified his course of action, as had the widespread conviction of his inner circle and highest-ranking military officers. He had persevered even when victory seemed increasingly implausible, retaining his wishful thinking as a hedge against regret and guilt, and from the fall of 1965 to the fall of 1967, he had remained obstinate despite growing political opposition and evidence that his Vietnam policy was failing. Sunk costs only stiffened his resolve not to have sacrificed American and Vietnamese lives in vain—or, for that matter, himself. The war had aroused his core source of self-validation, and the stakes for Lyndon Johnson transcended the moment, elections, even the war itself; the shame of failure would be broadcast and amplified across the world and generations. He would be the first president to lose a war, and that fact eclipsed a wiser strategic understanding. He had come to see himself through the prism of how he imagined others would see him—a self-consciousness common to some extent in all of us, but one more dominant in anyone whose professional worth is measurable by election results. By the fall of 1967, Johnson had spiraled to a point where he could not on his own reconstruct an inner confidence.

Mounting evidence of policy failure and political peril exposed the limits of Johnson's obduracy. Intransigence began to give way to hints of flexibility and reconsideration. He started to display openness to unpleasant information in a way and to a degree that he never had before and to confront, process, and internalize evidence that he had been wrong about Vietnam. This meant confronting significant psychic costs—the recognition that his judgment had cost the lives of many, many people—a difficult burden for anyone to bear. As the perceived consequences of the intractable problem of Vietnam became increasingly apparent and began to rival the perceived stakes, Johnson moved toward a fundamental reconsideration of his policy.

By the fall of 1967, antiwar sentiment had begun to affect Washington officials intimately and personally, and none more so than Robert McNamara. McNamara's youngest child and only son, Craig, a seventeen-year-old high school student at a New England prep school in the fall of 1967, had grown increasingly opposed to the war his father personified for an increasingly large generation of enraged and alienated young Americans exposed to the draft. McNamara never talked about Vietnam with Craig (or anyone else in the family for that matter), which only increased the tension at home. Left unaired, differences between McNamara and his children—he also had two daughters, little Margy and Kathy—over Vietnam festered. "Boy, this was a hell of a problem inside my family," he later admitted. "It tore my wife apart."[65] Craig loved his father but loathed the war, and the emotional turmoil this created expressed itself physically as well as emotionally. Like his mother, Craig developed a severe and painful ulcer and began stumbling academically at school. In the McNamara residence in the elegant Kalorama neighborhood of northwest Washington, Craig tacked a Vietcong flag to a wall of his bedroom; on another, he hung an American flag upside down. He also prominently displayed several punji sticks— sharpened bamboo stakes that Vietcong guerrillas smeared with human excrement and planted in rice fields and roads to puncture and infect the feet of U.S. soldiers—that his father had brought back from one of his many trips to South Vietnam. Such provocative expressions of discontent added to his father's burdens.

The October 21 March on the Pentagon further ramped up the pressure. Protests against the war had been underway since 1965, but in the spring of 1967, a coalition of antiwar activists had begun planning for a massive and audacious demonstration in the nation's capital for the fall that would combine constitutionally guaranteed dissent with "non-violent confrontation" designed to "create a social drama that could become the object of national focus."[66] Fundamental to this was a shift from protest to more active and direct resistance. They would not just burn draft cards, as had been the dramatic focus of most protests up to this point. They intended to make a scene, and a statement, by marching on the nerve center of a war they had come to hate and "obstruct the war machine." The antiwar movement had grown larger and angrier, as well as more anxious. Heretofore, middle-class whites could avoid the draft through college deferments. Congress was considering eliminating college deferments, which meant not just working-class whites, farm boys, and minorities, but middle-class whites could face conscription as well. This prospect, along with what many saw as the folly and immorality of the war, swelled the ranks of antiwar protestors, among them radicals who believed in confrontational resistance and who increasingly challenged older liberals for leadership of the movement (a polarization that reflected a similar trend in public opinion). Activists had participated in teach-ins, marches, and peace vigils only to see the Johnson administration widen the war and increase draft calls. Many of those against the war had hit a limit, and now wanted to do something dramatic to stop it. "Our country," wrote one leading activist, "is engaged in a war so hideous that we, in the greatest numbers possible, are going to break the laws of assembly in order to protest this impossible war."[67] March organizers announced that they planned to "shut down the Pentagon . . . We will fill the hallways and block the entrances . . . This confrontation will be massive." David Dellinger, a long-time peace activist* increasingly radicalized by the war, warned that "there will be no government building left unattacked." "We were trying to show that we were stepping up the militance," he later recalled, "that we were going to actually make it impossible for

---

* Ironically, Dellinger had been a Yale College classmate and friend of Johnson's hawkish national security advisor Walt Rostow.

them to continue business as usual." Those organizing the march had a savvy sense of political theater, and had no intention of being polite. "Once they became convinced that there was a horror show going on in Vietnam, they wanted it over," an antiwar leader later recalled. "We had all been raised in this polite milieu: 'You write to your Congressman, you rationally debate things.' And nothing changed—it just got worse. Under that pressure, a layer of the student movement was groping for some dramatic thing to do to end this fucking thing. The Pentagon demonstration was the first real expression of that on the national level. It caught a desperate, confrontational mood of a large number of people."[68]

The Johnson administration sensed what was coming. It had been monitoring the protest movement for months through wiretaps and informants inside antiwar groups. Those engaged in this not-always-legal surveillance included FBI, local police, army, and even CIA intelligence agents—the latter, a violation of the agency's charter.* Johnson authorized this surveillance because he suspected protestors' links to foreign Communist powers, a conjecture that reflected Johnson's paranoia and insecurity rather than reality. Some of the information gathered, whether by wire service or wiretap, prompted administration fears of major disruption, possibly even violence. Contacts around the country with knowledge of the March plans told the White House to expect a bloody weekend. Particularly worried about what would happen at the ultimate destination of the marchers, the Johnson administration made clear beforehand that any protestors attempting to enter the Pentagon would be arrested. The army prepared a force of 4,000 military police and active-duty troops to guard the building and the people inside it. U.S. Marshals would be stationed between them and the protestors. McNamara ordered that arrests be kept to a minimum and forbid the issuance of live ammunition and the loading of bayonets in order to avoid casualties. He did not want

---

* The CIA's 1947 founding charter explicitly prohibited the agency from participating in domestic intelligence gathering. The Nixon administration would also violate this charter, using the CIA to spy on American citizens opposed to the war.

American troops firing on or wounding American citizens. His strategy, he told Johnson, would be "just calm waiting them out."[69] Protest organizers originally hoped to attract a million demonstrators for the "Confrontation with the Warmakers." By mid-October it became clear that the number of marchers would be small, less than 100,000. But no one knew how even that number would behave and react in the crucible of confrontation. What would happen if the marchers became combative and degenerated into a riotous mob? Located just outside of Washington, D.C., in Arlington, Virginia, the Pentagon—the world's largest building when constructed during World War II—would be hard to defend.

On Saturday, October 21, a bright and sunny autumn morning in the nation's capital, nearly 70,000 Americans—the vast majority of them middle-class college and high-school-aged students— gathered in West Potomac Park between the Tidal Basin and the Lincoln Memorial and along the Reflecting Pool at the west end of the National Mall. The crowd included only a sprinkling of Americans older than thirty, in vivid contrast to the peace march in Washington a year before, when conservatively dressed, middle-aged men and women far outnumbered young militants. The difference in atmosphere from the 1963 civil rights march when Martin Luther King Jr. delivered his stirring "I Have a Dream" speech in the same spot reflected the dramatic change in national mood in just four years, provoked by Vietnam. Protestors carried a forest of placards, some reading "Get the Hell out of Vietnam!" and "Where Is Oswald When We Need Him?"[70] One participant lauded the "responsible people who thought enough to come down here in a show of protest"—then nervously added, "I just hope to God the whole day stays this way." Following several speeches, including one by Dellinger, who declared that "violence will not come from us," at 2:15 P.M. a smaller group of about 20,000 protestors streamed over Memorial Bridge toward the north parking lot of the Pentagon for a "gigantic teach-in" to educate the troops guarding the Pentagon to the miseries of the war.[71]

An asphalt road and acres of grass ringed the Pentagon's five sides. A little more than three hours later, as the late afternoon sun cast a lengthening shadow, about 3,000 of the most radical demonstrators, chanting "Hell no, we won't go!" and denouncing "white honky cops," broke down the wire fence that restrained them to the north parking lot and surged toward a large square of asphalt in front of the Pentagon's Mall Entrance steps in an attempt to storm the building. A line of 300 white-helmeted U.S. Marshals ready with nightsticks and military police armed with rifles and tear-gas grenade belts standing in front of the entrance confronted the loud and jeering demonstrators, some carrying Vietcong and North Vietnamese flags, brandishing sticks, and shoving against the line. Amid an exchange of fists and clubs, two dozen demonstrators crashed through the line and sprinted toward an auxiliary entrance, where soldiers inside forced them out with rifle butts. Marshals intercepted and beat the demonstrators as they came out, spattering the Pentagon steps with blood. Back at the line between protestors and troops, demonstrators shouted obscenities, spit in soldiers' faces, taunted them—"Hit them—they won't hit back," yelled one protestor—threw bottles and rocks, and urinated on the side of the building.[72] "It is difficult to report publicly the ugly and vulgar provocation of many of the militants," wrote James Reston in the *New York Times*.[73] Other demonstrators placed flowers in soldiers' rifle barrels, in what became an iconic image of the antiwar movement.

McNamara watched all of this at various points throughout the day from his office window, the roof, and the Mall Entrance. The Pentagon had learned that some of the protestors were armed, and security personnel tried to get McNamara to move away from these exposed positions, but he adamantly refused—he wanted to witness what was happening.[74] The clashes confirmed his warning to Johnson in May that Vietnam had begun to distort the American body politic. The scene dismayed and even scared him—an uncontrollable mob is a frightening thing—but he also thought the protestors would have been both more effective and maintained popular respect had some of them not turned to violence. He said to himself, "If they stick to Gandhi [and nonviolence], if they keep their discipline, they can stir the country and paralyze prosecution of the war."[75] He believed that if they had simply lain down on the asphalt and grass surrounding the Pentagon—it would have been impossible to remove all of them. The march had another effect on McNamara, too, further deepening his awareness of the growing discontent among young Americans toward the war and, as a result, deepened his reservations about its wisdom.

The day ended on a tragic note. Most of the demonstrators left by nightfall, but a few thousand decided to camp overnight on the plaza in front of the Mall Entrance, where they built bonfires out of wooden barricades they had broken through, lit draft cards that burned like fireflies in the night, and continued to taunt and curse soldiers and military police with self-righteous invective while some female protestors unbuttoned their blouses and pawed at soldiers' zippers under the glare of floodlights the military had wheeled up to illuminate the plaza. Around midnight—after most newspaper reporters had left and network television cameras had been turned off, meaning the country wasn't watching—U.S. Marshals backed by troops of the U.S. Army's 82nd Airborne Division moved in a wedge toward the remaining demonstrators and began clearing the plaza. At this point, some marshals who had been rapping their nightsticks against their hands and soldiers who had been glaring at protestors began brutally clubbing demonstrators, including young women, whose faces were soon covered with raw skin and blood.

The midnight beatings and the arrests that followed enraged—and further radicalized—protestors who endured and witnessed them. "Something happened to many of us there that is hard to describe, harder to explain," a demonstrator observed. "We went down to protest and returned ready to resist . . . Many who were not anti-government now are; many who were committed to using legal channels to change governmental policy now have what they consider the governmental attitude—cynicism, violence, covertness—which they may use for the same end . . . Reason is starting to slip, and like the inmates of concentration camps who gradually took on the values of their oppressors, I fear many are beginning to see violence as the only alternative to futile discussion."[76] The antiwar movement's fury at the government and military intensified dramatically, feeding their growing sense of apocalypse in national life, with consequences that would become apparent in the years to come as antiwar protestors became more radical and prone to violence. Yet the March on the Pentagon had the opposite effect of that intended by its organizers: a Harris Survey poll the following month revealed that 70 percent of Americans felt the march had hurt the antiwar cause and a nearly equal number viewed it as an act of disloyalty to American servicemen in Vietnam. Nevertheless, nearly 60 percent of the public still supported demonstrations against the war as long as they remained peaceful.[77]

The accumulated anguish, frustration, and pressure on Robert McNamara reached the tipping point in early November 1967. After years of grappling with Vietnam and struggling to make American policy there work—a policy that he, more than anyone else, had crafted and managed—the proud, self-assured man who had come to Washington at the beginning of Camelot believing every problem had a solution "finally bit the bullet,"[78] as he later put it, and concluded that the massive American military effort in Vietnam could not succeed.

McNamara had been moving toward a break with Johnson over Vietnam since his testimony at the Stennis hearings on August 25. At a staff meeting with his top aides on the morning of October 4, he expressed acute frustration at America's inability either to win or end the war. There were "no plans" for either. "How did we get into this box?" he lamented. Despairing about the situation, he confided to his aides that he intended to "change my basic policy."[79] McNamara spent the next several weeks rethinking his position on Vietnam. He contemplated what had brought the United States to this unhappy juncture, the direction in which circumstances pointed, and what to do about it. McNamara sketched his thinking at a Tuesday Lunch on October 31. Addressing a dimension of the war central to Johnson's calculations, McNamara warned that the domestic political situation made "indefinite continuation" of the status quo impossible. "We can't hold out as long as we're going the way we are now," he said. "We've got to stabilize this war." Rusk disagreed, arguing that as "indicators" of progress in the war trended up, "frustration will give way to a feeling that we're on the move." "Can we hold out with more of the same?" Johnson mused, picking up on McNamara's point. "I do not want to admit we can't win," said Wheeler, but he confessed in this private setting that the present "mix has not produced results."[80]

The concerns aired at the October 31 Tuesday Lunch reverberated in the memo McNamara gave Johnson the next day laying out his case in detail. The culmination of two years of soul-searching triggered by increasing doubts, the memorandum precipitated McNamara's departure from the Pentagon, ending a stewardship that had come closer than any before it to bringing the Pentagon under civilian control and had made him the most powerful man in Washington after President Kennedy and then President Johnson. McNamara did not mince his words—he wanted to maximize their impact. Recognizing that the views expressed in the memo "may not be compatible with your own," McNamara told Johnson he had not shown it to any of the other principals. In the memo, he argued for nothing less than a radical shift in American policy toward Vietnam. Implicitly conceding that the war could not be won at acceptable risk and cost—a devastating indictment of all the advice he had given Johnson for years—McNamara emphatically advocated leveling off the U.S. commitment and gradually turning the war over to the South Vietnamese. He told Johnson that continuing the "present course of action in Southeast Asia would be dangerous, costly in lives, and unsatisfactory to the American people," that the increase of U.S. combat forces to 525,000 already approved would not alter the dynamic of the war; it would only lead to more casualties on both sides—and that Johnson would still be faced with future demands for even more troops and increased pressure to expand the war into Laos, Cambodia, and North Vietnam itself in order to cut infiltration into the South. More bombing, more troops, and more political exhortation would make no difference unless the North Vietnamese concluded

> that the U.S. is prepared to remain in Vietnam for whatever period of time is necessary to assure the independent choice

of the South Vietnamese people . . . And the American public, frustrated by the slow rate of progress, fearing continued escalation, and doubting that all approaches to peace have been sincerely probed, does not give the appearance of having the will to persist. As the months go by, there will be both increasing pressure for widening the war and continued loss of support for American participation in the struggle. There will be calls for American withdrawal.

There is, in my opinion, a very real question whether under these circumstances it will be possible to maintain our efforts in South Vietnam for the time necessary to accomplish our objectives there.

McNamara had come to understand a fundamental truth: despite congressional dynamics and a long-standing narrative of American victory in wars, the American people's patience with Vietnam had its limits. It was not their endurance that was wanting. It was their increasing belief that the status quo was unacceptable, and nothing seemed to be changing. The Johnson administration's Vietnam policy could not withstand the acid test of American pragmatism; it failed on the basis of its practical consequences. The Stennis hearings and the March on the Pentagon, despite the vastly different political pressures they gave voice to, held this belief in common. The growing polarization of American society between hawks, who demanded intensifying the war, and doves, who demanded ending it, meant that support for the administration's middle-of-the-road approach was not sustainable. Too many lives had been lost for too little gain. The administration had attempted to command the political center, but the center was collapsing.

What, then, should be done? McNamara saw two alternatives. One option, favored by hawks, was to intensify the bombing as the chiefs preached and to invade Laos, Cambodia, and even North Vietnam as Westmoreland wished. But the equation remained the same as it had been: more bombing would not reduce infiltration below minimum requirements nor break Hanoi's will to fight, and expanding the war geographically meant increasing the risk of Chinese intervention and even more U.S. troops and casualties with no guarantee that the Communists would not shift the Hồ Chí Minh Trail further west, merely enlarging the scope of the battlefield. These were serious risks that Johnson had confronted, and rejected, before. The other option, which McNamara recommended, was to cap troop deployments at 525,000, stop the bombing in order to get negotiations with North Vietnam started, and gradually transfer the fighting to South Vietnamese forces. Leveling off the American commitment and reducing likely American casualties offered the only way to maintain public support over the long haul, he argued.[81]

Yet McNamara, despite his soul-searching, did not carry his analysis to its logical conclusion—that because America could not win the war, there was a moral imperative to get out in order to avoid pointlessly sacrificing more lives—and he never advocated this even after he left the Pentagon on February 29, 1968. Exhausted and overwhelmed by Vietnam, McNamara divorced himself from the issue—"I just turned off," he later said, retreating into silence and persuading himself that the choices were no longer his to make. Despite the enormity of the mistake for which he was greatly responsible, he refused to speak out. Such steps and rationalizations alleviated his internal strife and shielded him—for a time—from confronting the emotional and psychological trauma of Vietnam. McNamara had failed spectacularly—he had not guided America to victory in Vietnam. But in another sense, he succeeded beyond immediate appearances; his successor, Clark Clifford, Johnson, and Johnson's successor, Richard Nixon, would all eventually adopt the approach that he laid out in his memorandum: to level off the American military effort and gradually turn the war over to the South Vietnamese (a policy that later became well known as "Vietnamization"). By disconnecting and remaining silent, however, McNamara effectively placed loyalty to the presidency above loyalty to the national interest. In doing so, he implicitly if unintentionally supported the continuation of a disastrous involvement that claimed 45,000 more American lives and many hundreds of thousands more Indochinese lives until U.S. military involvement ended in 1973 and Hanoi forcibly reunified the country in 1975. Ironically, the man who had sought a precise metric for each situation could only measure his legacy by that most plaintive and nebulous claim that it "could have been worse."

McNamara later acknowledged this fateful shortcoming and rebuked himself for it. "I came to believe it wouldn't work, but I never took it to the next point and said, 'Mr. President, cut our losses, get out.' . . . I never did that." "No, you did not," McGeorge Bundy told him—then ruefully added, "I did the same thing two years earlier."[82] And neither man ever publicly urged getting out even after they left government service, still bound by the jeopardy of conflicting loyalties. This ethical dilemma, an outgrowth of the responsibilities and burdens of power—which few who have not faced it can fully appreciate—haunted McNamara for the remaining four decades of his life.

McNamara had sought through his memo to compel Johnson to make a painful decision. He wasn't just a man wringing his hands or one of the president's foreign policy experts; he was the secretary of defense proposing—not musing, but forcefully advocating—a fundamentally different course of action. A long-serving and loyal advisor had urged Johnson to change course, to accept there was *no* satisfactory solution in Vietnam and implicitly acknowledge the failure of the course that he as commander-in-chief had followed, with its known consequences in human lives and unknown consequences in political outcomes. It was a decision, moreover, that McNamara himself did not have to make.

A part of Johnson resented McNamara's memo, but another part of him paid careful attention to it. Toward his defense secretary, LBJ felt a complicated mix of admiration, gratitude, irritation, and resentment. From the beginning, the relationship between these two men had involved a process in which McNamara offered unpalatable advice about Vietnam, and Johnson initially resisted it and then over time largely—if grudgingly—embraced it. Evidence of this process emerged again at Johnson's meeting with the "Wise Men" the next day. A panel of elder statesmen whom Johnson had last consulted in July 1965 when he committed major U.S. ground combat forces to South Vietnam, Johnson wanted their counsel as he neared another important juncture.* Echoing the central premise of McNamara's memo (which he had stayed up late the night before reading), Johnson began by telling the Wise Men that he was "deeply concerned about the deterioration of public support" for the war. "I am like the steering wheel of a car without any control," he lamented. He put several questions to his guests, including one that he had not raised since crossing the Rubicon in July 1965: "Should we get out of Vietnam?" The Wise Men strongly advised against withdrawal, but the fact that Johnson had raised this fundamental question with them showed that his thinking was moving in McNamara's direction.[83]

Johnson never replied to McNamara about his memo. "Before he died, I never had one word on the goddamn thing," McNamara later said with some bitterness.[84] "He was the kind of a person that never wanted to say he was wrong. Maybe that was an explanation of it,"[85] said McNamara in hindsight. But while Johnson could not bring himself to acknowledge McNamara's considerable effect on his thinking regarding an issue of such magnitude and sensitivity, a memorandum for the file that he dictated on December 18 in response to McNamara's assessment offered proof that the November 1 memo did, indeed, considerably affect his thinking. In it, Johnson rejected McNamara's recommendation to stop the bombing, but "I would not, of course, rule out playing our bombing card under circumstances where there is reason for confidence that it would move us toward peace." Regarding the number of troops he was similarly wishy-washy. "I do not believe we should announce a so-called policy of stabilization," he stated, but then effectively endorsed this step, saying, "I see no basis for increasing U.S. forces above the current approved level." He also noted, "The

---

* This panel, somewhat different in composition from the assemblage of July 1965, included former secretary of state Dean Acheson, George Ball, retired general Omar Bradley, McGeorge Bundy, Clark Clifford, lawyer and diplomat Arthur Dean, former treasury secretary Douglas Dillon, kitchen cabinet member Abe Fortas, Averell Harriman, Henry Cabot Lodge, and former diplomat Robert Murphy.

third recommendation of Secretary McNamara has merit. I agree
that we should review the conduct of military operations in South
Vietnam with a view to reducing U.S. casualties, accelerating the
turnover of responsibility to the GVN [Government of South Viet-
nam], and working toward less destruction and fewer casualties in
South Vietnam."[86] Like McNamara, Johnson had grown skeptical
about the decisiveness of air power and the ability to prevail militarily before public support for the war collapsed. But skeptical was
as far as it went at this point.

McNamara's memo had another effect beyond pushing Johnson to acknowledge the merits of stepping back. "It raised the tension between two men who loved and respected each other to the
breaking point," McNamara later wrote, precipitating his departure from the Pentagon. "The fact is I had come to the conclusion, and had told him point-blank, that we could not achieve our
objective in Vietnam through any reasonable military means, and
we therefore should seek a lesser political objective through negotiations. President Johnson was not ready to accept that. It was
becoming clear to both of us that I would not change my judgment,
nor would he change his. Something had to give."[87] Both had become deeply frustrated with the other. Over the course of working
together they had become close partners, with less and less faith
in each other's judgment. "What had happened was we had come
to the point of a parting of ways. We were on such different paths.
And it was so obvious to both of us. And yet there was such deep affection that we didn't want to break."[88] An irony was that while the
situation had become intolerable for both men, Johnson was moving in McNamara's direction. And, incongruously, McNamara's
influence on Johnson would increase after McNamara left.

Johnson had known for some time that McNamara was exhausted and wanted to be unburdened of Vietnam. A part of Mc-
Namara had never felt comfortable overseeing a war (a telling fact
that Johnson himself recognized). "If I had any reservations about
you," Johnson once only half jokingly teased McNamara, "it was
because you weren't combative enough, that you were too much of
the professor, had too much of the professor approach . . . Rusk is

LBJ and McNamara Show the Strain of Vietnam
Yoichi Okamoto/LBJ Library

more of a militarist than McNamara."[89] He had always been reluctant to use force as some thought it had to be used, a contradiction that had become more pronounced as the casualties in Vietnam increased. His successor, Clark Clifford, wrote, "this man, who was probably our greatest minister of defense, was not as well suited to manage a war."[90] In a widely publicized speech at Montreal in May 1966, the secretary of defense of the greatest war machine in history had declared that a "purely military posture is not the central element of our security . . . It would be a gross oversimplification to regard Communism as the central factor in every conflict throughout the underdeveloped world . . . Neither conscience nor sanity itself suggests that the United States is, should, or could be the global gendarme."[91] It was the sort of address that could be seen as radically leftist by folks like Stennis and LeMay. "I gave the Montreal speech because I could not survive without giving it," he told friends, "could not survive with my own conscience." Yet he recognized his weakness in doing so: "But I shouldn't have done it . . . I am the secretary of defense. It is my job to motivate men to fight. It's not my job to say to colonels that their profession is irrelevant . . . But I felt it needed saying. So I said it."[92] Evidence of McNamara's growing fatigue and torment resurfaced in subsequent months. When Johnson sought a new number two at the State Department as George Ball prepared to leave for Wall Street in August 1966, McNamara told him, "If I didn't feel so damned tired, I'd suggest you [appoint] me. I wouldn't mind giving up a cabinet job." "I know you wouldn't," said Johnson.[93] And in a revealing footnote in his memo the following May urging Johnson to level off the American troop commitment in South Vietnam, McNamara had tellingly written, "We should not even rule out, as part of that strategy, changing key subordinates in the US Government to meet the charge that "Washington is tired and Washington is stale."[94] "Bob felt that he wanted to go, needed to go," recalled a colleague.[95]

Johnson also worried that McNamara might succumb to nervous exhaustion. That his defense secretary was under considerable stress became apparent at White House meetings that fall when McNamara would grip the edge of the Cabinet table with the whites of his knuckles showing. Johnson had always watched over McNamara "as though he were a member of his family," noted Lady Bird.[96] Now as he observed McNamara, he saw "an emotional basket case" as he privately remarked to his press secretary George Christian.[97] "He's looked worn and thin and running on sheer spirit for a long time now," Lady Bird noted in her diary.[98] Atomic Energy Commission chairman David Lilienthal saw a "harassed and puzzled look on the no longer sprightly" secretary of defense.[99] "Bob was dead tired by then, he was run out," recalled Francis Bator.[100] McNamara's brutal work schedule had taken a lot out of him. He had made many tough, complicated, and difficult decisions, and every one of them had displeased someone. He had made many powerful people in Congress and the military unhappy, and some of the powerful people he had made unhappy had become enemies. In a time of growing crisis, as opinion on Vietnam polarized, people had begun to see things in absolutes, in blacks and whites, and this made his moderate approach unpop-

ular, even reviled. He had initially approached the war with logic
and statistical analysis, but he had slowly and painfully learned that
war does not always accommodate itself to numbers and reason—
that imponderables, chaos, and unpredictability mattered too, and
this had shocked and disillusioned him. One afternoon in the fall
of 1967, McNamara and an assistant sat in his office calculating the
latest ammunition order for U.S. forces in South Vietnam. "Let's
see. That would be 2000 rounds for every enemy infiltrator," Mc-
Namara said as he paced back and forth on his office carpet. "That
oughta be enough." He stopped, his body shuddered, and he began
to weep.[101]

Most painfully of all, there were the casualties of Vietnam, for
which McNamara felt personally responsible. "I've killed people—
hundreds, thousands, tens of thousands—by my mistakes," he said
later with a heavy voice.[102] His own professional state echoed the
war itself: he felt obligated to keep putting more and more of himself into an unwinnable conflict. A part of McNamara begged for
release. "I just can't take it psychologically at this point," he privately told Johnson.[103] By the fall of 1967, American soldiers were
dying at a rate of more than 200 a week. "The kind of mail that
he would get was awful hard for an introspective man like him
to take. 'You murdered my boy'—that kind of business," recalled
Clifford. "It piled up on him . . . We were not succeeding. This was
his great worry . . . I think it preyed on him. Every day was an ordeal to him. I think he felt himself breaking under the strain, and I
think he felt he had to get out."[104]

By November of 1967, Johnson had begun to think so, too. "You
know, he's a fine man, a wonderful man, Bob McNamara," the president said to one of his aides. "He has given everything, just about
everything, and you know, we just can't afford another Forrestal."*[105] Johnson respected McNamara and worried about his emotional state, to be sure, but the fact that the man who had urged him

---

* James Forrestal, the first secretary of defense, had been driven to suicide in 1949
by personal demons and the pressures of office.

to stand firm in the spring and summer of 1965 was now effectively abandoning the war made the decision to ease McNamara out that much easier. Lyndon Johnson felt under siege and he did not want a secretary of defense who amplified that inclination. "I was driving him nuts," McNamara later said. "You just can't imagine."[106]

The presidency of the World Bank,* an international financial institution that provided loans to developing countries, became the means Johnson used to effect McNamara's departure. In the spring of 1967, the bank's outgoing president, George Woods, asked McNamara to succeed him. McNamara, who believed in the bank's mission, expressed interest and reported the conversation to Johnson while indicating his willingness to stay at the Pentagon as long as the president needed him. Johnson listened but said nothing. McNamara's loyalty to the office of the president remained undiminished. "Never once did I take the initiative to leave," he later acknowledged.[107] Instead, he left that initiative to Johnson.

During a conversation with McNamara on October 16, Johnson in passing asked, "Are you still interested in the World Bank?"[108] McNamara said yes, and from then on both men knew how the story would end. McNamara's November 1 memo hastened the denouement. (It was, as McNamara later put it, "the coup de grâce."[109]) Less than two weeks later, without telling McNamara, Johnson called treasury secretary Henry Fowler, the U.S. trustee on the World Bank board, and told him to move ahead with McNamara's nomination. On November 22, Fowler formally submitted McNamara's name to the World Bank. On November 29, the White House announced that McNamara would be leaving the Pentagon in sixty days—February 29, 1968. The news of his impending departure hit Washington "with the force of a string of Claymore mines exploding along Pennsylvania Avenue," *Newsweek* reported. The Washington press corps had not picked up any hint that McNamara might leave the administration.† The night of the an-

---

* Formally named the International Bank for Reconstruction and Development.

† Across the Atlantic, London's *Financial Times* broke the story of McNamara's nomination to the World Bank on November 27 based on a leak from a diplomatic source.

nouncement, Johnson told his wife, "Except for one [November 22, 1963], this is the hardest day I have spent in this job."[110]

While a part of him saw it coming and welcomed it with relief, another part of McNamara took it very hard. The night of the White House announcement, McNamara's former assistant Adam Yarmolinksy called him at home. "It was the only time that I've known him when he really seemed at a loss," recalled Yarmolinsky. "He said, in effect, 'I don't know where I am.'"[111] He was learning what the Roman philosopher Seneca had learned nineteen hundred years before: "that retiring from a political court is as hard as arriving in it." The tension between him and the president over Vietnam had been resolved, but the man who had entered the Pentagon with supreme confidence in the conviction that every question could be answered left the Pentagon in emotional agony, having failed to solve the largest problem confronting the United States since World War II. McNamara had become, as Clark Clifford aptly put it, a "kind of casualty of the war."[112]

Policymakers often wrestle with an issue they have addressed before, but they rarely fundamentally reexamine the problem. Nevertheless, a consistent dissenting minority voice seen as loyal can, even if he or she loses the debate, catalyze a reassessment, particularly when an undeniable gap appears between a goal and circumstances. Such a gap between the desired state and the situation at hand can provoke reappraisal of a situation, a reexamination of premises, and slowly* the development of a new perspective— not necessarily the minority's, but different from policymakers' prior view. Active consideration of alternatives is more likely to come from less aggressive but persistent confrontation with persons differing in viewpoint. Through these means, a dissenting minority can induce careful and sustained attention on the particular issue underlying the disagreement. Then—almost like

---

* "Dissent broadens thinking," notes Charlan Nemeth, but adds: "Persuasion by a dissenter is more indirect, requires more time, and follows a more subtle choreography of argument." Charlan Nemeth, *In Defense of Troublemakers: The Power of Dissent in Life and Business* (Basic Books, 2018), p. 2.

a delayed-action fuse—fundamental restructuring occurs and, with it, an implicit or explicit redirection of policy. The influence exerted by a minority may be deep and lasting, even though it may not be immediately apparent.[113] "Research repeatedly shows," one psychologist writes, "that dissenters have 'hidden' influence. In general, they change attitudes in private more than in public. They change minds—even if those in the majority . . . choose not to acknowledge the influence."[114] In this way, a stubborn decision-maker can be prodded to open his or her mind to a new way of thinking.

This is what happened as Johnson came to terms with McNamara's memo and his resulting departure. These two events compelled Johnson to fundamentally reconsider his Vietnam policy for the first time since July 1965. McNamara's November 1 memo had finally and fully driven home the failure of American policy to accomplish its desired results while inflicting fantastically disproportionate costs on the United States and the people of Southeast Asia. McNamara had been the first among equals of Johnson's advisors for four years, and now that first among equals had definitely told him that the war that had consumed so many lives could not be won at acceptable risk and cost. This advice was especially crushing coming from McNamara, but the fact that his defense secretary had evolved compelled Johnson (who had never been fully confident of his position) to reexamine his approach to Vietnam, and—more important—to redefine his way out of the problem, however tentatively and conditionally. The basic policy would have to shift back to the original premise: the South Vietnamese would eventually have to win or lose the war themselves, after all of the American sacrifices. It was a bitter pill for Johnson to swallow and a verdict that a part of him would continue to fight for the rest of his presidency because it would leave unfulfilled his deep need to justify the deaths of American troops. But Johnson gradually accepted that pursuing an elusive military solution in Vietnam could not justify more sacrifices. In this way, change was facilitated by his desire to avoid further psychic costs. Retreat on an issue of this magnitude would be difficult for any leader, and no less so for Lyndon Johnson.

Johnson's choice of Clark Clifford as McNamara's successor reflected this shift. Johnson had watched Clifford operate for more than two decades and knew how politically astute he was. LBJ's choice of Clifford signified his implicit if grudging acceptance of McNamara's plea to level off the American effort, not further deepen American involvement, and seek a negotiated rather than a military solution. Both Johnson and Clifford were aware that protracted war frustrated the American people and were deeply troubled by increasing dissent on the Right and the Left, which reflected the public's mounting impatience with the war and growing popular demands to "Win or Get Out!" In short, both men sensed that the war was not going well and that it could be ended only by a political settlement. Johnson knew that Clifford, despite his hawkishness since 1965, had never been comfortable with American involvement in Vietnam and had never viewed military force as a way to victory but as the most expeditious way to get out. During the year to come, Johnson would sometimes disagree vehemently with Clifford over the tactics of achieving a negotiated settlement leading to disengagement from Vietnam—particularly whether and under what conditions to stop the bombing—but he would no longer define the problem as prevailing militarily in the war. And above it all hovered Johnson's desire to "keep his options open," a Washington phrase that meant never letting anyone know what you were going to do until you have done it.

Johnson's intention in selecting Clifford came through clearly in a remark the latter made at the White House just a few months before being chosen to succeed McNamara. Speaking with Francis Bator, who oversaw Soviet policy on the NSC, Clifford told him that Washington "will need Moscow's help in extricating ourselves from this God-damned mess we've got ourselves into in Vietnam. We've got to find a way to get out. It's deeply damaging to the country." "That was a surprise to me," recalled Bator, "because the picture I had of Clifford was of a locked-in hawk." Did Johnson know of Clifford's attitude? "Of course he did—and he wanted someone who had a very Presidential interest-minded view of his choices, which Clifford had to a T," recalled Bator.[115]

Johnson's larger purpose became clear to Westmoreland during the general's visit to Washington in mid-November. In the words of one of Westmoreland's principal subordinates, Lieutenant General Bruce Palmer, Westmoreland realized then "that President Johnson would not change the way the war was being prosecuted, and that [his] job was to concentrate on improving South Vietnamese performance so that U.S. forces could disengage."[116]

An experienced and influential Washington consigliere to Democratic Party potentates, Clifford understood how to manage big egos, how power flowed through the hallways of the capital, and, most important, how to get things done—who to talk to, who to work with, who to flatter, and who to cajole in the courtly and soothing cadences of his genteel border-state accent. As a first-rate lawyer (the most famous one in town), he also knew how to get to the heart of a problem in order to start fixing it. Not accidentally—for he was always conscious of appearances—Clifford looked every inch the part in the meticulously tailored double-breasted suits that covered his tall frame and with a matinee idol face topped with perfectly combed silver hair—the embodiment of the dis-

Clark Clifford and JCS Chairman General Earle Wheeler
Yoichi Okamoto/LBJ Library

creet, knowing, and influential éminence grise whom Democratic presidents invariably turned to when seeking advice about how to get out of trouble. Johnson trusted him politically because he was not close to LBJ's nemesis, Bobby Kennedy, and he could not be cowed by generals and admirals—or presidents, for that matter. An independent-minded and experienced advisor, Clifford told Johnson what he needed to hear, not what he wanted to hear. Johnson did not always like Clifford's advice, but he always listened to him.

A Cold War liberal dating back to his days as counsel to President Truman from 1945 to 1950, Clifford believed in the benevolence of American involvement in the world, but he harbored no illusions about the limitations of American military power and no doubt about the fundamentally political nature of the Vietnam War and the domestic dangers it posed. He had witnessed how the Korean War had damaged Truman's effectiveness and the popularity of the Democratic Party, and now he saw the same thing happening to Johnson and the Democrats as a result of the Vietnam War. Clifford's political acuity had made him leery about Vietnam from the start. As early as May 1965, he warned his friend in the White House of a potential "quagmire"[117] should the United States take over the fighting. "I hate this war," he told Johnson at Camp David that summer as the president deliberated the commitment of major U.S. combat forces. "I do not believe we can win . . . It will ruin us. Five years, 50,000 men killed, hundreds of billions of dollars—it is just not for us."[118] Johnson remembered these words and reviewed them carefully shortly before selecting him in November 1967 to succeed McNamara. Even after Johnson made his fateful decision in July of 1965, Clifford made it clear to the president that he still wanted the United States to get out of Vietnam, but he became persuaded that the American military effort provided the best way and quickest way to terminate the Southeast Asian fiasco. "I went along with that, hoping and believing that the policy was going to bring us out where we wanted to be—that is, our exit from Vietnam," he later said.[119] Following that course, Clifford steadfastly opposed bombing halts from late 1965 through late

1967, a position that earned him the misleading label of hawk in the press and the public imagination.

The progress reports that Clifford received as chairman of the President's Foreign Intelligence Advisory Board reinforced this accommodation—until his fact-finding trip with White House advisor Maxwell Taylor to Southeast Asia in the summer of 1967. The leaders of Australia, Singapore, and Thailand with whom he and Taylor spoke that summer saw Vietnam very differently than Washington did. They did not accept the domino theory because they saw the conflict as a civil war between North and South Vietnam and, aware of the historic antipathy between Vietnam and China, they did not believe Hanoi would cooperate with Beijing in an aggressive sweep through the region. "I want to tell you, Mr. Clifford," confided a Thai official, "that the countries of Southeast Asia do not fear North Vietnam. Obviously, if there were to be Chinese expansionism in the area, that would be a matter of the deepest concern, but we don't see that . . . We don't think that makes any sense, so we don't have a fear of that." Unwilling to contribute further to the military effort in South Vietnam, the Thais (as well as Singaporeans and Australians) were beginning to distance themselves from America's efforts in Vietnam, although they would not say so publicly. All of this "gave me a feeling of considerable uneasiness," recalled Clifford, and reawakened his doubts of 1965.[120] Clifford related his deep dismay and concern with great candor to Johnson upon his return. If countries much closer to Vietnam than the United States did not see their interests sufficiently threatened by the Vietnamese Communists, what did this say about American national interests at stake? "The trip buried for me, once and for all, Washington's treasured domino theory," Clifford later wrote in his memoirs.[121]

Yet again this was a lesson in how differently outsiders can assess a fraught situation more dispassionately because they are not saddled by their previous recommendations and therefore are not vulnerable to internal and external needs to justify costly past mistakes. They do "not carry the same mental accounts," notes Kahneman, and therefore are "better able to ignore the sunk costs of past investments in evaluating current opportunities."[122] This fact made it easier for Clifford to separate himself from the prior course of action in Vietnam—unlike McNamara, Rusk, Rostow, Westmoreland, and Wheeler in the fall of 1967, he was not burdened by responsibility for earlier Vietnam decisions. The escalation decisions of 1965 had not been of his choosing—in fact, he had strenuously opposed them in several meetings with Johnson— therefore their consequences, especially the sunk costs in American lives, did not constrain Clifford from reconsidering the problem as it had those before him (including the president) for so long. A part of Johnson understood this, which helped explain why he chose Clifford to succeed McNamara at the Pentagon.

The drama of McNamara's announced departure coincided with Westmoreland's highly publicized visit to Washington in mid-November. President Johnson had summoned the general home from Saigon, ostensibly for consultations, but in reality to bolster public and congressional opinion on Vietnam through a carefully orchestrated public relations campaign to win time for his disengagement strategy. Although half a world away in Saigon, Westmoreland had remained well attuned to developments in the United States. He therefore recognized one fact—that domestic support for the war was rapidly eroding—and accepted another— that because of this, his commander in chief aimed to begin the process of American disengagement by gradually handing over responsibility for the war to the South Vietnamese. Westmoreland understood the pressures confronting Johnson and sought to accommodate the president. But though he knew what Johnson wanted him to say, the approach that Westmoreland adopted to alleviate those pressures reflected his own initiative and choices— particularly his desire, as he told his new deputy, General Creighton Abrams,* to "portray to the American people 'some light at the end of the tunnel.'"[123]

. Westmoreland began his public relations campaign on Novem-

---

* Abrams had been appointed Westmoreland's deputy in May 1967.

ber 15 with an appearance before the House and Senate Armed
Services Committees. The following evening, he met with a large
group of Democratic House members at the White House. Three
days later, he and Ambassador Ellsworth Bunker spoke to the nation on NBC's Sunday morning national news show, *Meet the Press*.
There, Westmoreland declared "that we are making progress and
we are winning" in Vietnam, explaining "that the enemy has very
serious manpower problems in the South" and that "he is unable
to recruit the guerrillas that he needs."[124] Two days later, on November 21, Westmoreland made what he later called "my most important public appearance during this visit" before the National
Press Club in downtown Washington, where "I permitted myself
the most optimistic appraisal of the way the war was going that
I had yet made."[125] Amplifying this enthusiasm, Westmoreland
said, "We have reached an important point when the end begins
to come into view." He based this upbeat conclusion on the confident assumption that "infiltration will slow" and that "the [South]
Vietnamese Army will show that it can handle the Vietcong."[126]
Westmoreland reiterated this in his year-end report, noting a decline
in the Communists' combat effectiveness and their control of
area and population and making it appear that the United States
wouldn't need more troops in Vietnam.[127] Westmoreland delivered
these claims because he believed them to be potentially true. Certainly, he *wanted* to believe them to be true because they boosted
the morale of both American soldiers in Vietnam and the American people, because they quenched popular thirst for news that
an end to the protracted and bloody war was in sight, and because
they addressed the pressures on his commander in chief. Emily
Dickinson's classic lines come to mind: "Tell all the truth but tell it
slant—Success in circuit lies," except in this case the truth did not
dazzle, and by making these assertions, Westmoreland created an
impression and expectations that would prove politically devastating for the Johnson administration when events just two months
hence spectacularly contradicted them. The army chief of staff,
General Harold Johnson, sensed this danger at the time Westmore-

land made his remarks. "I only hope that he has not dug a hole for himself with regard to his prognostications," Johnson said in a back-channel cable to Abrams in Saigon.[128]

Westmoreland's priority as MACV commander centered on American military operations in South Vietnam. Earle Wheeler's priority as JCS chairman centered on the worldwide military posture of the United States. Ever since Johnson had committed combat troops to Vietnam in the spring and summer of 1965, Wheeler had repeatedly urged the president to call up the reserves in order to create a sufficient reservoir of soldiers for deployment to Vietnam *and* elsewhere, such as NATO commitments in Western Europe, where the quality of army units suffered as they had been stripped of personnel assigned to Southeast Asia. The majority of combat units outside of Vietnam had deteriorated to a level of either C-3 (marginally ready) or C-4 (not ready).[129] Johnson had repeatedly refused Wheeler's request because he feared that national mobilization would stoke war fever and thus popular pressure to widen the war, while also undermining congressional attention and resources to his ambitious and expensive Great Society agenda. Wheeler went along with the president's decision because of his respect for civilian authority, but he felt caught between Johnson's reservations and what he considered the U.S. military's global needs as well as the chiefs, who continued to lobby for a reserve call-up and a wartime footing.

Skilled in Pentagon politics, Wheeler affected a modest, low-key style far different from the personal bluster of many generals and admirals. He had spent most of his career in staff jobs, so he knew how to manage the chiefs, calm their frustration and restlessness, and keep them on board while ensuring McNamara and Johnson were happy by averting damaging confrontations between the military and civilian leaders. Because of these qualities, he would serve longer than any other JCS chairman in history. He was also a sagacious bureaucrat skilled in office machinations who favored compromise over confrontation and learned to soft-pedal his disappointment with Johnson's decisions, assuming that one day events might well force Johnson into doing what he wanted. Wheeler realized, wrote JCS chronicler Mark Perry, that "by agreeing to an ever-larger commitment of U.S. forces," LBJ "was slowly moving closer to the upper limit of U.S. troop availability; when he reached the upper limit, Wheeler believed, Lyndon Johnson would have little choice but to mobilize the nation."[130] Wheeler revealed his approach in a back-channel message to Westmoreland, counseling him to accept less than what he wanted in order to get a "foot in the door, a situation I have found most useful in other areas." In the interim, Wheeler considered it an "absolute necessity," as he told Westmoreland and Sharp in another message, "for every military man to keep his mouth shut and get on with the war."[131] Wheeler's comments reflected a dutiful soldier's obedience to civilian authority, but also a willingness to continue pursuing his agenda through indirection even after the president had considered and rejected it. Civilian authority had said no to national mobilization and a reserve call-up, but Wheeler quietly kept pursuing his goal nonetheless. What justified such a Machiavellian approach in Wheeler's mind? Pentagon official Morton Halperin, who knew Wheeler well, explained the mindset: "Everybody thought the stakes" in regard to Vietnam "were high enough that you did what you had to do."[132]

By the late fall of 1967, Wheeler had become convinced that swelling troop deployments to Vietnam—nearing a half million—had reached a critical point in terms of seriously draining both the strategic reserves* and America's global military strength. General Lyman Lemnitzer, the U.S. NATO commander and former JCS chairman, privately remarked that the U.S. Army in Europe had become "damn near non-existent. Vietnam was eating up everything."[133] "We had not a single unit that was deployable," Wheeler later noted. "Not one that could be sent to Vietnam."[134] Wheeler

---

* The strategic reserves comprised active-duty forces in the continental United States, Hawaii, and Okinawa. By late 1967, it had shrunk to the point that the only combat-ready deployable forces consisted of the 82nd Airborne Division—down to one-third of its regular strength—and one marine division.

believed such a situation made a reserve call-up imperative and accelerated his efforts to achieve this goal. In November, Wheeler directed the Joint Staff under his command to study precisely how many more American troops "above and beyond the 525,000 limit" already approved by Johnson would need to be requested in order to trigger a reserve call-up.* (He knew how to do his math; he had once been a mathematics instructor at the U.S. Military Academy at West Point.) Wheeler awaited a spark, an event that would trigger what he confidentially called "the arithmetic of Vietnam."[135]

Since the arrival of the Americans, the Vietcong and North Vietnamese had followed Chinese Communist leader Mao Zedong's "three stages" of revolutionary struggle. The first stage involved protracted guerrilla warfare, attacking enemy forces at places, times, and durations of one's own choosing. The enemy would be exhausted "little by little by small victories." Losses were to be avoided "even at the cost of losing ground."[136] This enabled the Vietcong and the North Vietnamese to control their casualties and, as a result, to draw out the war and thereby sap U.S. public support for an increasingly long and costly struggle. The second stage involved achieving a military stalemate with the more powerful Americans, which the Vietcong and the North Vietnamese had done by 1967. This would be followed by the third and final stage, when the Communists would take the offensive in a decisive effort to end the war on their terms.

Hanoi's defense minister and head of the armed forces, General Võ Nguyên Giáp, had studied the three stages strategy in China in 1940 and then returned to Vietnam, where he applied it first against the Japanese occupation, then against the colonial French for independence, and now against the Americans. Yet, the second stage now achieved, a long-standing split within the Hanoi leadership led to a fierce debate over when to shift to the third stage of revolutionary struggle. A moderate, "North-first" faction, led by

---

* Wheeler had more on his mind than just foreign theaters. He also wanted troops to deal with growing urban unrest and race riots.

Giáp, whose influence was considerable but not as great as it had
been during the war against the French, favored winning the war
through diplomatic and political means and therefore preferred
continuing the strategy of protracted guerrilla war, which had
proven itself effective at countering the American strategy of attrition and sapping U.S. public support for the war. A more militant,
"South-first" faction, led by Lê Duẩn and including Lê Đức Thọ[*]
and Nguyễn Chí Thanh[†] (the Communist military commander in
South Vietnam who competed with Giáp for control of military
strategy), believed armed conflict constituted the only way to win
the war and reunify the country, and therefore preferred shifting
to the third stage in 1968, expecting it to trigger a popular uprising
in South Vietnam leading to the collapse of the Saigon government and the expulsion of the Americans. The popular uprising in
Danang during the spring 1966 Buddhist crisis seemed evidence to
the South-first faction that South Vietnam's urban areas were ripe
for insurrection sparked by a Communist military offensive.[137] Lê
Duẩn and his faction were so confident of success that they printed
money and made new uniforms for police to wear once they took
control of South Vietnam. For his part, Hồ Chí Minh leaned toward the moderate, North-first position of guerrilla over big-unit
warfare and cautioned against a "general offensive, general uprising"[‡] (*tổng công kích, tổng khởi nghĩa*), but aging and in failing
health, he no longer dominated the deliberations of the Politburo.

   Fearful that NVA officers loyal to Giáp might sink their plan, the
more militant South-first faction attacked the North-first faction
as "revisionists" (that is, counterrevolutionaries) and even went so

---

[*] Thọ controlled appointments to the party bureaucracy and would later become
North Vietnam's chief negotiator at the Paris Peace Talks to end the war, which
dragged on from May 1968 to January 1973.

[†] Thanh served on the Politburo and headed the Vietcong Military Command,
COSVN (Central Office for South Vietnam). He died of a heart attack in July 1967
while back in Hanoi from the jungles of South Vietnam for consultations.

[‡] This concept of popular uprising echoed the urban insurrections of the "August
Revolution" that had brought the Vietnam Workers Party to power against a
Japanese-installed administration in the late summer of 1945.

far as to place senior generals on Giáp's staff under house arrest,* effectively locking Giáp out of military planning.†[138] With Lê Duẩn and the South-first faction's triumph, Hanoi began doubling the number of troops and supplies sent to the South and recruiting new Vietcong cadres in preparation for a general offensive. In October 1967, it began smuggling weapons, food, and medicines into South Vietnam's cities and conducting secret training exercises in urban fighting. In November, NVA troops launched a preliminary diversionary operation intended to lure American forces into the remote border region of far northwestern South Vietnam, drawing them far away from the urban areas that comprised the main goal of the offensive.

As part of this diversionary operation, NVA troops prepared to besiege the isolated U.S. Marine firebase at Khe Sanh near the demilitarized zone and the Laotian border that had been established to block the Communists' infiltration corridor through the mist-covered Annamese Mountains. The NVA would take Khe Sanh if they could, but they would limit the price they were willing to pay for it. They certainly wanted to inflict casualties on U.S. troops, but isolating them far from the cities was the greater aim. The North Vietnamese attacked. Taking the bait and fearing another Điện Biên Phủ,‡ Westmoreland—with the anxious encouragement of President Johnson, who forced the chiefs to swear they could hold Khe Sanh and would himself follow the fighting there on a sand table constructed in the White House Situation Room— reinforced the marine garrison at Khe Sanh in order to avoid a humiliating U.S. defeat and force a conclusive showdown with the Communists. The MACV commander instructed subordinates "to

---

* The detainees ended up in Hỏa Lò Prison, which also housed American prisoners of war, who sarcastically nicknamed it the "Hanoi Hilton."

† Giáp reacted by leaving Hanoi for Eastern Europe, where he spent much of the latter part of 1967 while planning for the Tet Offensive took place. Hồ implicitly registered his own dissatisfaction by traveling to China for several months for medical treatment.

‡ A remote French Foreign Legion outpost that the Việtminh besieged and overran in the spring of 1954, leading to France's withdrawal from Indochina later that year.

ascertain that we are taking all countering actions possible in relationship to the analogous Khe Sanh situation."[139] In total, Westmoreland moved half of all his combat forces to northernmost
South Vietnam. Meanwhile, the Politburo approved the final plan
for the urban offensive in December. Hanoi-appointed military
commanders would oversee Vietcong rank-and-file comprising
the attacking force. To achieve surprise, the Politburo decided to
launch the offensive during Tết Mậu Thân (the Vietnamese Lunar
New Year holidays) beginning in late January, when a temporary
cease-fire (implicitly agreed to by all sides, including U.S. forces)
would be in effect, people throughout the country would be on the
move to their ancestral homes, ARVN soldiers would be on leave,
and families would be celebrating with fireworks. More optimistic
North Vietnamese expected Tet to spark a general uprising that
would render ARVN impotent and overthrow the Saigon government, and (mirroring Westmoreland) produce a decisive victory
that would change the balance of forces on the battlefield, break
America's will to continue the war by inflicting heavy casualties
on U.S. forces, and lead to its withdrawal from Vietnam. Less optimistic North Vietnamese aimed to demonstrate to Washington
that victory in Vietnam would be prohibitively costly and to further
demoralize the American and South Vietnamese publics—to deliver a crushing psychological blow rather than to achieve a military victory. Either outcome would increase Hanoi's leverage
against Washington at the conference table. (The Communists
reasonably assumed that political considerations in a Presidential
election year would make the Johnson Administration amenable
to negotiations.) No one in Hanoi knew that Johnson had already
decided to level off the commitment and begin the gradual process
of de-escalation and disengagement.

Vietnamese ushered in the Year of the Monkey at midnight of
the new day, January 30, 1968, with traditional *giao thua* family
altar rites. Everyone believed the events of the first day of Tet anticipated the year to come. Twenty-four hours later, the Vietcong
launched a massive, coordinated assault against cities and towns

throughout South Vietnam. Its audacity and magnitude took the Americans by surprise. Brigadier General John Chaisson, director of MACV's Combat Operations Center, called it "surprisingly well-coordinated, surprisingly intensive, and launched with a surprising amount of audacity."[140] More than 80,000 Communist cadres attacked thirty-six of forty-four provincial capitals and five of six major cities, including Saigon and the old imperial capital of Huế. Heretofore, Americans back home had seen images of troops stepping from helicopters, slowly moving through thick jungles, and crossing rice paddies—far away from centers of American power. Now, television networks broadcast vivid footage—in color no less—of the U.S. embassy in downtown Saigon under siege. Vietcong sappers blew a hole through the wall of the embassy compound, military police dashed to and fro in a frantic effort to repel the surprise attack, while General Westmoreland spoke to reporters as shells struck MACV headquarters. Marine guards hustled Ambassador Bunker in his pajamas and bathrobe in an armored personnel carrier from the ambassador's residence to a safer location. With a half million American soldiers in the country, how could the Communists attack the U.S. embassy, a symbol of seemingly invulnerable American power? But there they were.

It was impossible to scrim the chaos and violence. American newspapers printed on their front pages Associated Press photographer Eddie Adams's photo of South Vietnam's police chief, General Nguyễn Ngọc Loan, executing a bound Vietcong prisoner, firing his pistol point-blank at the right temple of the prisoner, whose limp body collapsed in a bloody mess on a Saigon street. In Huế, the historic Citadel and the Thai Hoa Palace on the north bank of the Perfume River fell into the hands of the NVA and the Vietcong, who raised their flag atop Ngọ Môn—the Meridian Gate (the main entrance into the walled Nguyễn-dynasty fortified palace grounds). The NVA and the Vietcong held the Citadel and most of the newer city for twenty-five days until intense block-by-block fighting by U.S. marines finally dislodged them at the cost of hundreds of American and thousands of Vietnamese lives. During their occupation of

Huế, the Communists went door to door with a blacklist, round-
ing up nearly 3,000 civilians, mostly government functionaries,
foreign doctors, schoolteachers, and missionaries—"reactionaries
and tyrants,"[141] the Communists called them—whom they shot, be-
headed, clubbed to death with axes and shovels, and buried alive.
Huế, noted Mark Bowden in his exhaustively detailed account of
the fighting, was "the single bloodiest battle of the war . . . and one
of the most intense urban battles in American history."[142] In the
Mekong Delta town of Bến Tre, air strikes were called in to root out
Communists controlling residential districts. The bombing devastated Bến Tre—both buildings and its civilian population. A U.S.
Army major expressed a metaphor for the entire war when he told
a reporter, "It became necessary to destroy the town to save it."[143]

Tet did not take Westmoreland completely by surprise. MACV
had some forewarning of impending enemy activity—General Frederick Weyand, commander of U.S. forces around Saigon, moved
the 25th "Tropic Lightning" Division nearer the capital—but not
enough: because the Communists carefully compartmentalized
planning for the offensive, local South Vietnamese gave no warning as tens of thousands of armed Vietcong moved through their
midst (a troubling fact in and of itself).* Furthermore, American
analysts in Saigon and Washington, despite captured enemy documents and intercepted enemy signal communications regarding the offensive, discounted this intelligence as so much wishful
thinking because they did not perceive their adversary as capable of
accomplishing their stated goals and the intelligence contradicted
prevailing assumptions and preconceived notions about Communist strength. Even this far into the war, with so much observation of the Communists' effectiveness, these Americans evaluated
the intelligence evidence through the prism of their preexisting
beliefs—another (and, in this instance, spectacular) example of seriously underestimating their adversary.[144] Because they had not

---

* The Vietcong infiltrated five battalions into Saigon alone disguised as farmers
carrying produce on sampans, flower carts, and false-bottomed trucks—and not
one citizen of Saigon alerted the government.

bothered to closely study Vietnamese history (or to countenance Chinese military philosopher Sun Tzu's emphasis on the element of surprise in war), they did not know that the Vietnamese had followed a similar course before: during Tet in 1789, Emperor Quang Trung overwhelmed a Chinese army of occupation blithely celebrating the holidays in Hanoi—not unlike George Washington's nighttime crossing of the Delaware River on Christmas Day 1776 to attack the British and Hessian mercenaries at Trenton, New Jersey. Westmoreland had expected the Communists to attack before or after, not during, the Tet holidays.[145] But it was the offensive's timing, extent, and intensity that took Westmoreland, and the American military in general, most by surprise. "I would say that no one really expected the enemy to launch the attack during Tet," Wheeler admitted two years later. "While we knew something was going to happen, we didn't know exactly when, nor did we know how extensive the attack was going to be."[146] Westmoreland later acknowledged that he failed to anticipate the "true nature or the scope" of the attacks.[147] The Americans saw parts but could not imagine their enemy deciding to sum.

After several weeks of fierce fighting that inflicted heavy casualties on the Vietcong, who surfaced in large numbers for the first time in the war—their casualties totaled 50,000, a stunning 80 percent of the fighting force*[148]—American troops eventually drove the enemy out of most of South Vietnam's towns and cities. In this sense, Tet proved a military defeat for the Communists because they failed to achieve their tactical and immediate operational objectives. (A senior Communist general later admitted that the goal of a general uprising had been "unrealistic and beyond our reach."[149]) However, the American public concentrated not on Vietcong casualties, but on American ones, and the dramatic spike in the U.S. casualty rate during Tet—at one point in February nearing

---

* Estimates are that the Communists suffered more than 110,000 casualties over the three waves of "general offensive-general uprising" in January/February, May, and August/September 1968. See Lien-Hang T. Nguyen, *Hanoi's War: An International History of the War for Peace in Vietnam* (University of North Carolina Press, 2012), p. 338, n. 7.

500 a week—led Americans to question what the United States had
to show for all that it had poured into Vietnam.*

Tet also dealt the Saigon government a "severe blow," in Westmoreland's own words, by bringing the war into the towns and
cities—supposedly impregnable areas presumably beyond their
reach—and inflicting costly damage and casualties on the country's urban population, who comprised the bulk of South Vietnamese sympathetic to the regime. Tet left more than 14,000 civilians
dead, 72,000 homes destroyed, and more than 700,000 new refugees. It greatly set back the pacification program, reducing the
secure population by 1.3 million people.[150] The South Vietnamese
government had been badly weakened. Its already diminished
prestige had suffered from the shock of the offensive; the enemy
had struck fear in the hearts of urban dwellers who witnessed the
regime's inability to protect them. Its control over the countryside and therefore its ability to provide security in the hamlets and
villages—the most important long-term aspect of the war—had
been sharply reduced. It had failed to exhibit energetic, confident
leadership and act decisively in an emergency. Thiệu and Kỳ occupied most of their time and effort criticizing each other's response
to the offensive. The province chief for Huế, Colonel Phạm Văn,
spent the first six days of the offensive hiding in the city hospital
and organizing his cronies to steal emergency shipments of rice
sent to avert starvation in the area's swelling refugee camps.[151]

Beyond the theft and avarice, Tet had also failed to inspire more
than a million ARVN troops to mount a strong effort against the
Communists (a troubling fact that the South Vietnamese people did
not miss), or to stimulate a sense of national unity and purpose.
ARVN troops stationed in Tuy Hoa, the capital of Phu Yen province, disappeared as the fighting started. Looting by other ARVN
soldiers only compounded the army's credibility crisis. People's faith
in the long-term viability of the American-supported government

---

* The North Vietnamese siege of Khe Sanh would eventually be lifted in April 1968
through a massive U.S. tactical air operation, codenamed NIAGARA, that dropped
more than 100,000 tons of bombs on enemy positions surrounding the marine firebase. U.S. forces abandoned Khe Sanh on July 5.

and army had been badly shaken. South Vietnamese now feared that ARVN, incapable of repulsing the attacks,* would be unable to withstand future Communist assaults if the Americans withdrew (a prospect borne out by later events). Widespread rumors that the United States had actually conspired with the Communists—some initially even thought another coup was underway—reflected deep cynicism and war-weariness on the part of besieged South Vietnamese. Suspicion, distrust, fearfulness, and passivity became even more dominant—a mortal threat to long-term success. A U.S. official in Saigon summed things up. "In six weeks here," he said, "we have seen that the government cannot protect the people, or control them, or administer them or help them recover."[152] If some Americans saw that, most South Vietnamese surely did, and psychological wounds ran increasingly deep.

Equally important, coming so soon on the heels of Westmoreland's widely publicized claim ·to the American people that "we have reached an important point when the end begins to come into view," the strength of the Tet Offensive—the ability of the Communists to attack everywhere in South Vietnam, at once and in force—profoundly shocked and disillusioned Americans who had been conditioned to believe that the Communists had been defanged and, in Westmoreland's own words, that there was "some light at the end of the tunnel." Tet directly belied Westmoreland's confident public assertion "that the enemy has very serious manpower problems in the South" and that "he is unable to recruit the guerrillas that he needs." It contradicted his declaration that "the [South] Vietnamese Army will show that it can handle the Vietcong." It undermined the credibility of his—and the administration's—judgments on progress in the war. And it reawakened the American public's lurking fear of an interminable, and now ever costlier, conflict. In this sense, the Tet Offensive proved a great victory for the Communists. It demonstrated that America's progress in the war had been grossly overstated and that America's foes remained

---

* A substantial number of ARVN units had been at half strength when Tet began because many soldiers had gone home on leave for the holidays.

much stronger than Westmoreland and the administration had assured the American public. The image of near victory carefully nurtured by the aggressive public relations campaign in November 1967 had been discredited, making it virtually impossible to persuade the American people of such an outcome in the future, whatever the circumstances. As one chronicler of the offensive concluded, "The North Vietnamese and Vietcong lost a battle. The United States Government lost something even more important— the confidence of its people at home."[153]

McNamara perceived most of these consequences almost immediately. During a telephone conversation on the morning of January 31, Washington time—twelve hours after the Tet attacks started—Johnson asked his outgoing defense secretary how he interpreted the surprise attacks. McNamara replied:

> I think it shows two things, Mr. President: first, that they have more power than some credit them with. I don't think it's a last-gasp action. I do think it represents a maximum effort in a sense that they've poured on all of their assets and my guess is we will inflict very heavy losses on them, both in terms of personnel and materiel and this will set them back some, but that after they absorb the losses, they will remain a substantial force. I don't anticipate that we'll hit them so hard that they'll be knocked out for an extended period or forced way back in level of effort against us . . . I don't believe they're going to be successful. I think that in Khe Sanh, where we're going to have a real military engagement, I believe we'll deal them a heavy defeat. I think in the other areas, it's largely a propaganda effort and publicity effort and I think they'll gain that way. People across the country this morning will feel they're much stronger than they previously anticipated they were, and in that sense, they gain.[154]

The Tet attacks, McNamara realized, had not changed the underlying stalemate that defined the war; both sides had been battered and bloodied by the offensive, but neither had been decisively crippled. "I don't believe" reports that "we knocked [the Communists] on [their] ass," he told his Pentagon staff on February 9, and "I don't believe" reports that the Communists knocked us "on our ass and we need [immediate] help" to survive the onslaught.[155] Whatever its political effects, Tet had not altered the basic military dynamic.

Westmoreland, on the other hand, initially reacted to the offensive with bewilderment. Richard Holbrooke, then special assistant to deputy secretary of state Nicholas Katzenbach, went to Saigon as part of a group to appraise the situation. He saw Westmoreland during the early days of Tet and described him as appearing "dispirited, deeply shaken, almost a broken man—stunned that the Communists had been able to coordinate so many attacks in such secrecy."[156] William DePuy, Westmoreland's friend and former operations chief, described MACV headquarters as "a picture of confusion, uncertainty, not understanding exactly how they could have done all that, and what it meant."[157] Struggling to do just that, Westmoreland concluded that the urban attacks represented a feint. "In my opinion this is a diversionary effort to take attention away from the north, an attack on Khe Sanh," he cabled Wheeler on February 12, characterizing both operations as a "last gasp" effort by the Communists. "We are now in a new ball game where we face a determined, highly disciplined enemy, fully mobilized to achieve a quick victory," he cabled Washington. "He is in the process of throwing in all of his 'military chips to go for broke.'"[158] He further compared Tet to the Battle of the Bulge, the last-ditch German offensive on the western front in World War II.

But Westmoreland had badly misjudged both the Communists' intentions and the effects of their actions. By forcing him to redeploy his forces to urban areas in order to put down an uprising he had failed to anticipate and ARVN had failed to contain, the South Vietnam countryside—where a majority of the country's population lived—lay open to a new round of Vietcong replenishment and taxation. The Vietcong offset their heavy losses during Tet with new recruits from the countryside during the same period, while inflicting serious damage on the crucial pacification program that Washington relied on to win the people. Richard Helms

stressed this point in a White House meeting on February 20. The
Communists "are busy in the countryside," he told the president.
"They have a manpower pool out there to draw on." "How did
they get the countryside?" Johnson asked. "All of the ARVN and
U.S. forces have come in to protect the cities," replied Helms. "Not
all," Wheeler said. "Most," shot back Helms, whom Wheeler did
not contradict.[159] In addition, the vast majority of Communist casualties during Tet involved Vietcong guerrillas—not North Vietnamese regulars—who, other than at Khe Sanh and Hué, largely
remained out of the fighting and therefore largely undiminished
as a military force.* Contrary to Westmoreland's assessment, the
Communists had not put in all of their "military chips to go for
broke." For the rest of 1968, they continued to bleed the Americans, albeit at enormous cost to themselves, with relations between Washington and Saigon continuing their deterioration as
the United States increased the pressure on South Vietnam to take
over the fighting.

The intensity of Tet engagements led to a sharp increase in American casualties. In the last quarter of 1967, U.S. deaths averaged 796
per month. In the first quarter of 1968, the U.S. death rate more
than doubled to 1,623 per month. During one week in February, the
casualty toll reached 543 Americans killed and 2,547 wounded.
The war had now claimed more than 20,000 Americans killed and
more than 50,000 wounded—shocking numbers. Such casualties
not only eroded already fragile popular support for the war, but
increased pressure for replacements. Nearly 850,000 young men
had been drafted into the army by the end of 1967. In January 1968,
the draft call rose to 33,000 per month. Still, this was not enough
to meet the military's manpower requirements in Vietnam and
throughout the world. Tet had triggered the arithmetic of Vietnam, in Wheeler's mind; it had made a reserve call-up imperative.

   With this in mind, Wheeler reached out to Westmoreland in

---

* This led many Vietcong to conclude that Hanoi wantonly, and cynically, sacrificed the southern insurgent movement.

Saigon, implicitly encouraging him to request more troops. "In summary, if you need more troops, ask for them," Wheeler said in his first cable, on February 7.[160] He artfully reinforced the hint two days later. "Please understand that I am not trying to sell you on the deployment of additional forces," he explained to Westmoreland. "However, my sensing is that the critical phase of the war is upon us, and I do not believe that you should refrain from asking for what you believe is required under the circumstances."[161] Concerned that Westmoreland might miss the insinuation or fail to factor the chairman's desire into his request, Wheeler shifted tactics. In another message the same day, he told Westmoreland, "I believe it imperative that you hold up on the front channel submission of your supplemental requirements for the coming year until at least the early part of March," which would be after Wheeler talked with Westmoreland during an intended visit he planned to Saigon later in February.[162]

To meet immediate needs, Westmoreland urged Washington to send him the final installment of troops the president had approved months earlier—a marine regiment and a brigade of the 82nd Airborne Division, 10,500 new troops—that would bring total U.S. forces to 525,000. "I need these 525,000 troops now," he insisted.[163] McNamara urged granting Westmoreland's emergency request, which Johnson did. The next day, February 13, the chiefs told McNamara that "the 82nd Airborne Division represents the only readily deployable Army division in the CONUS [continental United States]-based active strategic reserve." They then deliberately added an even darker warning: "The impending reduction of this division by one-third to meet approved deployments establishes an immediate requirement for its prompt reconstitution *which is possible only by the callup of Reserve units* [emphasis added]."[164] Hesitant to approve a reserve call-up, Johnson ordered Wheeler to Saigon for his already planned trip to look at the situation firsthand and determine what Westmoreland needed.

Wheeler arrived in South Vietnam on February 23 and held three days of intensive meetings with Westmoreland and his MACV staff. Wheeler focused on the issue of more troops, urging

Westmoreland to use the opportunity created by McNamara's departure and Johnson's anxiety about Tet to request an increase in troops—significant enough to trigger a reserve call-up and national mobilization. It was a "hard sell," recalled a general on Wheeler's staff who attended the meetings.[165] Westmoreland later told an interviewer that Wheeler had "conned" him.[166] "General Wheeler came over and he was actually begging me to ask for more troops," he told another interviewer. "Really, just begging me. He told me the President was ready to call up the Reserves"—Johnson had expressed no such readiness—"and if that were to happen, how many men would I need, how many men would I use?" An officer who accompanied Wheeler concluded, "I think General Westmoreland may have felt . . . somewhat trapped on that."[167] "Wheeler and I talked about it" some more, Westmoreland elaborated, "and came up with the troop dispositions." The total came to the precise number of additional troops that the Joint Staff had computed it would take to "trigger" a reserve call-up "and that's the figure he took back to Washington."[168] And while Wheeler reached a "clear understanding"[169] with Westmoreland that only half of the 205,000 would be earmarked for Vietnam—the other 100,000 would be used to reconstitute the strategic reserve—he further persuaded his subordinate to tell Washington that he needed all 205,000 reinforcements for Vietnam. The "fact is," said a flag-rank JCS army officer, "asking for those troops wasn't [Westmoreland's] idea, it was Wheeler's."[170]

Wheeler cabled his report to Washington on February 27, the day before he returned. He (unlike Westmoreland and others) did not describe an American triumph: "the margin of victory—in some places survival—was very, very small indeed." He noted the offensive "has by no means run its course" and acknowledged "the scope and severity of his attacks and the extent of his reinforcements are presenting us with serious and immediate problems." Although the Vietcong had suffered heavy casualties, he said the enemy could fight on because it was recruiting replacements in the countryside and infiltrating more troops and supplies from the North. He questioned whether "the South Vietnamese Armed

Forces have the stamina to withstand the pressure of a prolonged enemy offensive"—an insight that would be confirmed in the spring of 1975, when Hanoi launched its final invasion to reunify the country.[171]

Wheeler then turned to Westmoreland's request for 205,000 more troops. He characterized it not as a move to reinforce success but, rather, as a move to forestall a future setback. "If the enemy synchronizes his expected major attacks with increased pressure throughout the country, General Westmoreland's margin will be paper thin . . . For these reasons, he is asking for additional forces as soon as possible during this calendar year."[172] Tellingly, Wheeler did not mention what he had agreed with Westmoreland in Saigon: that only half of the additional 205,000 troops would be earmarked for Vietnam. Instead, he stressed Westmoreland's lack of flexibility and capability without additional forces.* "I talked about going on the offensive," Wheeler told an interviewer a few years later, "but I didn't necessarily spell out the strategic options."[173] Wheeler finessed the issue through indirection. In his mind, how he got to his goal was less important than getting there. "I wanted the capability," he later explained.[174] It is difficult to escape the conclusion that Wheeler engaged in some obfuscation—if not deception—of his superiors, the secretary of defense, and the president of the United States. As Clifford later put it, Wheeler "transfer[ed] that burden to Westmoreland as field commander" because he knew Johnson would feel more pressure to grant a field commander's request.[175]

That afternoon, McNamara went over Wheeler's report with other senior advisors during lunch at the State Department. Though leaving the Pentagon in just two days, McNamara seemed "obviously on edge" to one of the attendees. Visibly haggard, McNamara reviewed the report in detail, spelling out the implications of committing more troops to Vietnam. He expressed "grave doubts"

---

* Wheeler repeated these same comments—with the same telling omission—in a meeting with President Johnson on the morning of February 28. See Tom Johnson's Notes of Meetings, February 28, 1968, *Foreign Relations of the United States, 1964–1968, Volume VI: Vietnam, January-August 1968* (Government Printing Office, 2002), pp. 267–275.

about the request, declaring that 205,000 more troops would not change anything, since North Vietnam would match our increase. The number of additional forces that should be sent, he said, "was zero." Washington should get back to first principles and get Saigon to fight its own war.

Rostow sharply disagreed. Arguing the enemy had in fact taken a decisive beating, he urged granting Westmoreland's request and intensifying the bombing in order to exploit the recent success. "Let's not delude ourselves into thinking [the enemy] cannot maintain pressure" after the offensive, McNamara shot back,* supporting his point by reciting gloomy statistics: the air force had dropped more bombs on North and South Vietnam during the last year than the Allies had dropped on all of Europe during the last year of World War II. "It's not just that [bombing] isn't preventing the supplies from getting down the Trail," he said, grinding out the words and pounding his hand on the table. "It's destroying the countryside in the South. It's making lasting enemies. And still the damned Air Force wants more!" "There were tears in his eyes and his voice," an attendee recalled—a man full of "rage and grief and almost disorientation."[176] It was clear that McNamara had reached an end. As McNamara spoke, Rusk poured another drink of scotch. Rostow was quiet. Finally, McNamara turned to Clifford and said in a faltering voice, "We simply have to end this thing. I just hope you can get hold of it. It is out of control."[177] "McNamara was weeping," said an attendee. "He was speaking in sobs . . . and he was shaking."[178]

The disintegration of a man once hailed as the most glittering of Kennedy's men had an immense effect on Clifford. "Look at the situation from the point of view of the American public," the incoming defense secretary finally said. "How do we gain support" for 205,000 more troops "if we have told people things are going well? How do we avoid creating the feeling that we are pounding troops down a rat-hole? What is achievable?"[179] Others in the room responded with telling silence.

---

* The second and third waves of Vietcong attacks on urban areas of South Vietnam, in May and August/September 1968, bore out McNamara's warning.

Late in the morning the next day, February 28, McNamara's next-to-last day in office, Johnson walked with McNamara from the Cabinet Room in the West Wing to the East Room in the Executive Mansion, where seven years before McNamara had proudly taken the oath of office as secretary of defense under the gaze of the new president. Then, McNamara had been ebullient, confident, full of energy and optimism about tackling America's military problems. Now, he looked ashen, drawn, and spent, his formidable intellect having failed his commander in chief, his country, and, as he had become so well aware, countless innocents. Congressional leaders of both parties—allies and adversaries alike—Supreme Court justices, government colleagues, personal friends, and the press had gathered for a ceremony in which the president would award McNamara the nation's highest civilian honor, the Medal of Freedom. The ceremony was like no other. "There was an electric feeling in the room," Lady Bird noted in her diary that evening. "If I have ever sensed emotion, it was there today."[180] To the side of a podium at the south end of the room Margy and the three McNamara children stood in front of the military services' battle flags. In the front row of gold chairs set out before them sat the great and powerful of Washington surrounded by a flood of television lights. Many seated in the audience, friends and acquaintances of McNamara who had watched him and worked for him and with him, considered him the most gifted and dedicated man in the government, the greatest cabinet officer in American history. They felt sympathy and sadness.

Johnson stepped to the podium and quickly began. He made no mention of Vietnam. His continuing affection for McNamara shone through when he said, "America is giving to the world, and if I may be very personal, I am giving to the world, the very best that we have to win the most important war of all." ("I have never admired or enjoyed anyone more than your husband," he had written Margy three weeks before.[181]) He described McNamara as an "intensely loyal, brilliant, and good man." "That simple word 'good' almost undid me," noted Lady Bird, "and it did not help to look around the room. There were stricken faces, tight composure, and frank tears."[182] Then Johnson presented to McNamara the Medal of Freedom as a barrage of camera clicks and flashes recorded the moment.

McNamara approached the podium, tightly gripped its edges, and looked around the room to a sustained ovation. Clifford, standing in the front row next to his wife, Marny, later wrote: "For seven years [McNamara] had dominated Washington as few people ever do. To antiwar activists he had become a symbol of the war, to hard-liners, a symbol of ineffective half measures . . . His failure to achieve our objectives, either through military means or negotiations, had almost torn him apart." Through Lady Bird's mind kept ringing the words "seven years, seven years" and "what it takes out of blood and bone and heart."[183] McNamara tried to speak but halted for several long moments as no words came out. The gathered dignitaries sat stunned, silently watching his transparent pain. He paused for a moment and cleared his throat. Tears welled up in his eyes. He coughed and raised his hand to his mouth as he tried to gain control of himself. "I choked back conflicting feelings of pride, gratitude, frustration, sadness, and failure," McNamara later wrote.[184] Craig stared at his father as if seeing him for the first time. Finally, in a voice thick with emotion, he said, "Mr. President, I cannot find words to express what lies in my heart today. I think—I think that I had better respond on another occasion." Johnson came over to McNamara, put his arm around him, and led him out of the East Room as hushed whispers filled the air.

Johnson's and McNamara's troubles the following day—February 29, McNamara's 2,585th as secretary of defense, the longest unbroken tenure in history—seemed an allegory for those that Vietnam had caused the two men and the nation throughout their years together in Washington. Arriving in the Pentagon garage at noon for McNamara's formal departure ceremony, Johnson and McNamara boarded the executive elevator—numbered unlucky 13—to the River Entrance one floor above. As they rode up, the elevator refused to stop and got stuck just below the fourth floor, trapping its occupants. Army sergeant Clifford Potter, operating the elevator, immediately picked up the emergency phone. "Do you have a full load?" the maintenance man asked. "We sure do," Sergeant Potter nervously answered. For twelve minutes, the elevator remained stuck as Secret Service agents frantically attempted to rescue the president as Pentagon maintenance men worked to force open the doors. Finally, an agent climbed down the elevator shaft, pried open the elevator ceiling, and secured its occupants' release. Johnson emerged looking stern but rattled, yet more trouble lay ahead. Johnson and McNamara took the stairs down to the small parade ground on a raised lawn in front of the River Entrance. The military, ever sensitive to ritual, had organized a full-fledged farewell ceremony complete with an all-service honor guard, massed colors and battle streamers, band, artillery salute, and ceremonial flyover by air force and navy jets. A driving, late-winter storm of sleet and rain soaked Johnson, in topcoat and Stetson hat, and McNamara, hatless and coatless, his glasses spotted with rain, as they reviewed the 150 soldiers, sailors, marines, air force men, and coast guardsmen who comprised the honor guard. The sleet and rain also short-circuited the public address system set up for the occasion. Johnson attempted to pay tribute to McNamara but his words were inaudible. A grim, low overcast forced the cancellation of the flyover. McNamara left the Pentagon. Americans killed in Vietnam had reached 18,709.

With his departure, Robert McNamara believed he had left the burden of Vietnam behind. But Vietnam had not left him behind. And the problem of Vietnam that had beset McNamara for so long continued to beset Johnson and his other advisors after McNamara departed. Foremost among them was the immense challenge of achieving a political settlement leading to American disengagement from Vietnam, even after Johnson made the fundamental decision to begin doing so in the last months of 1967. Johnson and those around him would learn during the tumultuous year of 1968 how hard it would be to make the turn from a military to a diplomatic resolution of the war—how difficult it is to redirect a big, heavy train with immense momentum hurtling down the tracks. They would discover—awash in mounting desperation—as Clifford warned, looking back, "It is a thousand times easier to get into a war than it is to get out of one."[185]

CHAPTER 7

The Difficulty of Ending War

(March 1968–January 1969)

Wars have their own rules that are not determined solely by human will. Once underway, a war can be exceedingly difficult to stop, the effort to end it a slow, frustrating, arduous, and agonizing process. The blood and treasure expended, as well as the fears and passions raised, create pressures, momentum, and obstacles that can put decision-makers at the mercy of events rather than in control of them. This is doubly true for a belligerent, even a "great world power," whose ally is weak and insecure—and therefore desperately dependent on maintaining its patron's largesse—and whose adversary is fanatically determined and resilient, and enjoys strategic advantages that make it reluctant, if not unwilling, to substantively compromise. The "fog of peacemaking" can be just as thick and confusing as the "fog of war."

By March 1968, the conflict in Vietnam had consumed so many lives and caused so much domestic turmoil that President Johnson had concluded he must seek a political rather than a military resolution of the war. A negotiated settlement seemed the only way short of unilateral withdrawal to get out of Vietnam. But there was no agreement within the administration on what the terms of a settlement should be. And Johnson soon discovered that seeking a negotiated settlement would be far more difficult than he, his advisors, and the American people ever imagined, marked by

hidden corners and dead ends. Even *beginning* the process proved
a challenge. "Talks about talks" in which the protagonists directly
debated how formal discussions would be held, who would be involved in the negotiations, on what basis—even the shape of the
negotiating table—went on for months. All the while, the American military resisted the cessation of bombing that was demanded by
North Vietnam, the South Vietnamese felt threatened and undermined by U.S. compromises and suspected the conditions under
which the war would be ended (rightly concluding that they would
lose out because they would be unable to stand on their own), and
the North Vietnamese felt little compulsion to make serious concessions (rightly concluding that they had the upper hand and that
time was on their side). As a result, sticking points and acrimony
over a compromise solution that addressed the demands of all the
warring parties constantly threatened any progress. Each party
had a different perspective and a different agenda arising from different interests. Victory is not just on the field but in the lingering
narrative, and everyone wanted a settlement with a self-serving
story. Disagreement over the terms of an acceptable peace, exacer-
bated by Richard Nixon's exploitation of friction between Washington and Saigon for partisan advantage in the closing days of
the presidential election, pushed the opening of negotiations to the
point of breakdown in October 1968. Johnson's problem would remain America's problem for years to come.

The United States found it hard to craft a compromise political settlement acceptable to all parties in the Vietnam conflict because what Hanoi would accept would never satisfy Saigon, and
vice versa. The North Vietnamese would not make peace as long
as the Americans stayed and the South Vietnamese sensed that
they could not survive long if the Americans left. As a result, the
North and South Vietnamese—not the Americans—effectively
controlled the terms of diplomatic debate: Hanoi refused to make
substantive concessions, confident that it could win the waiting
game by continuing to expend manpower, maximizing American
casualties, and waiting for American public opinion to turn against
the war, while Saigon balked at cooperating with Washington out

of fear for its survival even though its leader, Nguyễn Văn Thiệu, could do nothing without U.S. support. ("The American Gulliver tied down by the South Vietnamese Lilliputians," in the words of one administration official.[1]) These constraints severely hampered America's ability to disengage from Vietnam even after its leaders determined that doing so served national interests. They would haunt both President Johnson and President Nixon. The war would not end in 1968, as many—including Johnson—in Washington expected in the spring of that year. Instead, it would take another four years, a tragic doubling of American casualties, and a profound polarization of American society before the United States finally disengaged militarily from Vietnam in March 1973 and Saigon fell two years and one month later. The long and wrenching effort to get out of Vietnam, like America's later travails in disengaging from Afghanistan and Iraq, confirmed Machiavelli's sobering maxim that "wars begin when you will, but they do not end when you please."[2]

At the White House breakfast on February 28, 1968, that marked McNamara's final meeting on Vietnam as secretary of defense, Johnson directed Clifford to conduct an "A to Z" review of the 205,000 troop request. Saying he wanted a "new pair of eyes and a fresh outlook," he told Clifford plaintively, "Give me the lesser of the evils."[3] Johnson's reluctance to commit any more troops came through in a cable that Wheeler sent Westmoreland the next day. Among other questions, Wheeler asked Westmoreland, "What alternative strategies can you adopt with [current] forces, plus the [10,500] recently deployed, which would defend adequately the essential areas and population of South Vietnam?"[4] Johnson may not have picked up on Wheeler's gambit in requesting 205,000 more troops, but his intuition and antennae told him something was amiss. Just two weeks earlier, Johnson told Clifford that Wheeler "is deteriorating very rapidly with me . . . I'm losing confidence in what he says and the way he thinks."[5] Johnson counted on Clifford to manage Wheeler and the military while helping him find a way to begin the process of de-escalation and disengagement.

It was a tough assignment for the newly confirmed defense secretary, made more so by the skepticism of those who greeted him
upon his arrival at the Pentagon. "It is not an exaggeration to say
that President Johnson's designation of Clark McAdams Clifford as
Secretary of Defense to succeed Robert S. McNamara was accepted
without enthusiasm," Pentagon press secretary Phil Goulding later
wrote.[6] Many Pentagon staffers like Goulding had been with Mc-
Namara for seven years; they could not imagine their idealistic
and tormented leader replaced by a presidential crony and back-
stairs advisor, a Washington fixer with no significant managerial
experience. They shared the opinion of a journalist who described
Clifford as "the prototype of the rich man's Washington lobbyist,
the supersmooth, urbane lawyer who knows where every body
is buried, the former high official who works for the government
just long enough to know where the weak spots are."[7] Outsiders
criticized Clifford's appointment as well. Connecticut's Republican
Party chairman complained that Johnson had handed over control
of the Pentagon to a "political operator" with "no apparent qualifications for the job."[8]

But critics misjudged Clifford and underestimated his experience. Clifford had long exposure to the military establishment and
military culture. He had served as a naval staff officer during World
War II, had helped draft the National Security Act of 1947 that created the Defense Department, and had gotten to know many four-
and five-star generals and admirals as an advisor to Democratic
presidents. He respected the military services, but stars on shoulder boards and the men who wore them did not intimidate him.
A man with formidable self-confidence, Clifford felt comfortable
speaking truth to powerful clients, whether they were corporate
CEOs or presidents. He preferred to "state with complete frankness" what he thought "and that fact had existed between LBJ and
me for quite a long time." Johnson "had learned to expect it, and I
think, to a certain extent, he learned to rely on it."[9] Finally, like the
president from Missouri whom he had served twenty years before,
he had a Midwesterner's common sense.

In contrast to McNamara's analytical intelligence, Clifford possessed emotional intelligence—and political wisdom. Perceptive in his dealings with powerful egos, he understood better than McNamara how to handle and manage the chiefs, grasping that they would accept being overruled as long as he did two things: (1) he ensured the president understood their position—what they wanted him to do and why they wanted him to do it; and (2) it was made clear that the president overruled them because he had responsibilities beyond theirs, not because he second-guessed them or their military expertise. McNamara had been unable to appreciate that this twisting path could also be the straightest. Clifford did, and made it a habit to bring the chiefs into the discussion, let them say their piece, and overrule them on broader grounds. "Our objective," Clifford told Pentagon staffers accustomed to a different style, "is not to prove to anyone how wrong he is. Our objective is to get them to do it our way."[10]

Clifford also understood how to prioritize his efforts. McNamara had tried to do everything as secretary of defense. "He thought his job was running the building *and* doing the war as well," said Morton Halperin, "so he ended up spending much less time on Vietnam than he should have." Clifford, on the other hand, focused solely on Vietnam and left all other Defense Department business to his deputy secretary, Paul Nitze. ("My job is to get us out of Vietnam," Clifford told his staff the first day.[11])

He approached the Wheeler-Westmoreland request like the skilled courtroom attorney he was—by gathering and studying the facts, not just about the request but about the whole war. Thus began "three weeks of the most exhausting, pressure-filled days" Clifford had ever experienced.[12] He and other senior advisors spent many sandwich-and-coffee hours in his Pentagon dining room during the first days of March, longer breaks near impossible to wedge into the workload. "He walked the halls of the building all hours of day and night," one officer remembered. "All he did was ask questions."[13] "Every one of those days was practically a month," Clifford said later. It was "the most concentrated, exhaustive period." "I was getting a compressed education in a very short period of time."[14] Some nights he slept on a cot in his cavernous office. He spent hours in "the Tank" interrogating the chiefs as he would cross-examine witnesses, posing fundamental, if uncomfortable, questions in order to get at the truth, so much of which lay encrusted beneath unquestioned assumptions and unexamined premises. Such searching and provocative questions had not been asked since Johnson had committed U.S. combat forces to Vietnam in the spring and summer of 1965. Thus began the first basic reexamination of the war in three years. Clifford could lead such a reexamination because he had no public record to defend, a fact that Johnson well understood when he assigned the task to him. Politely but firmly, Clifford pressed the chiefs:

- "Will 205,000 more do the job?" *They could give me no assurance that they would.*
- "If 205,000 might not be sufficient, how many more troops might be needed—and when?" *There was no way of knowing.*
- "Can the enemy respond with a buildup of his own?" *He could.**
- "Can bombing stop the war?" *No. Bombing was inflicting heavy personnel and materiel losses, but by itself it would not stop the war.*
- "Will stepping up the bombing decrease American casualties?" *Very little, if at all. Our casualties are a result of the intensity of the ground fighting in the South.*
- "How long must we keep on sending our men and carrying the main burden of combat?" *We do not know when, if ever, the South Vietnamese will be ready to carry the main burden of the war.*[15]

All of this disturbed Clifford. "We could see whether we were losing," he recalled, "but I couldn't see whether we were winning."[16]

---

* CIA analysts independently reached the same conclusion. When asked how Hanoi and the Vietcong would respond to increasing U.S. troop strength by another 205,000, they answered: "We would expect the Communists to continue the war. They still have resources available in North Vietnam and within South Vietnam to increase their troop strength. Their strong logistical effort and their ability to organize and exploit the people under their control in the South enable them to counter US increases." CIA Memorandum, "Questions Concerning the Situation in Vietnam," March 1, 1968, *Foreign Relations of the United States, 1964–1968, Volume VI: Vietnam, January-August 1968*, p. 290.

So he asked the chiefs, "What is your plan for victory?" They replied, "We don't have any. We'll just stay with it until the enemy gives up." "When will that be?" asked Clifford. "Will that happen next year?" "We don't know," they answered.[17] When finally he asked them, "How many troops for how long do you need to guarantee me that you will win the war?" they answered, "There is no number."[18] Their answers shocked and sobered Clifford. "I was appalled," he later wrote. "Nothing had prepared me for the weakness of the military's case."[19]

After such exchanges, it was impossible for Clifford to retain confidence in the chiefs' judgment about the war. "I thought to myself, 'Oh my God, this is hopeless. It is absolute folly for us to go on." Although an architect of the original containment policy that had done much to draw America into Vietnam two decades earlier, Clifford unequivocally concluded the United States was now on the wrong path. "I felt so strongly about it that I was not even sleeping very well at night."[20] America could not win the war at reasonable risk and cost, and therefore must begin to seek deescalation and disengagement through negotiations. His goal, he told a senior army general later in the spring, was to "bring this thing to an end on the best terms we can get."[21]

Clifford laid out his conclusion to Johnson on the evening of March 4, first in a private one-on-one meeting in the Oval Office, then before a larger group of senior advisors in the Cabinet Room. At that gathering, Johnson knew what Clifford intended to say and wanted the others to hear it. Seeking to blunt the push for more troops and reduce the pressure to approve it, Clifford recommended sending 20,000 additional men to meet immediate contingencies and implementing a limited reserve call-up, but opposed the 205,000 request. He also suggested reviewing the ground strategy and shifting from search and destroy to population security in which American troops would be deployed to protect major population centers and ARVN would be forced to assume greater responsibility for the war—all in an effort to limit America's liability and achieve a negotiated settlement, not a military victory. Clifford made his case in a careful, deliberate, lawyerly fashion, presenting point after point to the judge (Johnson) and opposing counsels (Rostow, Wheeler, and Taylor; Rusk had begun to move Clifford's way). The note taker at the meeting recorded Clifford's words, many of them in italics, reflecting the new secretary's emphasis:

> *There is a concern that if we say, yes, and step up with the addi-tion of 205,000 more men that we might continue down the road as we have been without accomplishing our purpose . . . There are* grave doubts that we have made the type of progress we had hoped to have made by this time. *As we build up our forces, they build up theirs. We continue to fight at a higher level of intensity.* Even if we were to meet this full request of 205,000 men, and the pattern continues as it has, he may want another 200,000 to 300,000 men with no end in sight . . . *We recommend that you meet the requirement for only those forces that may be needed to deal with any exigencies of the next 3–4 months . . . This is as far as we are willing to go . . .* We seem to have a sinkhole. We put in more—they match it. We put in more—they match it . . . *I see more and more fighting with more and more casualties on the U.S. side and no end in sight to the action . . .* I am not sure we can ever find our way out if we continue to shovel men into Vietnam.

Johnson, tellingly, did not challenge any part of Clifford's analy-sis, but instead let him make his case without interruption.[22]

Secretary of State Rusk had begun to change too, influenced not only by the pressure of events but also by his relatives back in Cherokee County, Georgia, who told him, "Dean, if you can't tell us when this war is going to end, well then maybe we just ought to chuck it." "The fact was," Rusk said, looking back, "we could not, in any good faith, tell them."[23] Rusk knew that if his own kinfolk felt this way, many grassroots Americans throughout the country were losing heart in the war effort. "I had come to realize with Clifford that many Americans had changed their minds about the war," Rusk later explained. To achieve this new objective, Rusk favored setting a limit on U.S. forces and gradually turning the fighting over to the South Vietnamese.[24] "Clifford and I sim-

ply came together on what we must do."[25] Thus swayed, he told
South Vietnam's ambassador, Bùi Diễm, after the meeting, "Now
we have to win not a military victory but an honorable peace."[26] He
also proposed stopping the bombing above the twentieth parallel
during the rainy season to get Hanoi to start negotiating. Johnson
quickly seized on the idea. Sensitive as ever to criticism from influential senators like Richard Russell who opposed bigger force
commitments unless the administration pursued a "winning strategy" and aware of how rapidly popular support for the war was
waning, Johnson was anxious to begin the process of de-escalation
and disengagement. He understood that initiating negotiations
with the North Vietnamese constituted a big part of this process,
and that bombing—whatever leverage he believed it offered him—
posed an impediment to Hanoi. "Dean, I want you to *really* get on
your horse on that one—right away," he commanded.[27]

At the next day's Tuesday Lunch, Rusk pulled a piece of paper
from his coat pocket and read a draft presidential statement he
had prepared. "I have directed that U.S. bombing attacks on North
Vietnam be limited to those areas which are integrally related to
the battlefield . . . Whether this step I have taken can be a step toward peace is for Hanoi to determine." Rusk advised Johnson: "Just
take the action, and see whether anybody is able to make anything
out of it."[28] Rusk's partial bombing halt idea mirrored McNamara's
proposal the previous May to limit bombing to the funnel south
of the twentieth parallel as a way to continue the interdiction of
men and supplies to the South while hopefully sparking negotiations with Hanoi, which Johnson had rejected. This time, Johnson
encouraged Rusk to pursue the idea, though he remained opposed
to a complete bombing halt (a position he would maintain until
mid-October) because he believed, as Francis Bator explained,
"that the way to get Hanoi to engage [in negotiations] was to keep
the pressure on" in part.[29] But because Hanoi continued to insist
that it would not negotiate as long as the bombing continued, a
considerable and growing segment of the American public saw a
partial bombing halt as evidence of the administration's *refusal* to
negotiate, feeding domestic dissent.

Continued tough talk in public constituted another part of Johnson's strategy. On March 16, he told a meeting in Washington of
the National Alliance of Businessmen, "We must meet our commitments in the world and in Vietnam . . . We shall and we are
going to win." In remarks two days later to the National Farmers
Union in Minneapolis, he declared, "We hope to achieve an honorable peace and a just peace at the negotiating table. But wanting
peace, praying for peace, and desiring peace, as Chamberlain found
out, doesn't always give you peace. If the enemy continues to insist,
as he does now—when he refuses to sit down and accept the fair
proposition we made, that we would stop our bombing if he would
sit down and talk promptly and productively—if he continues to
insist, as he does now, that the outcome must be determined on the
battlefield, then we will win our peace on the battlefield by supporting our men who are doing that job there now."[30] Such tough talk
seemed to contradict Johnson's commitment to de-escalation and
disengagement. In part, this reflected the emotions of a president
still desperate to validate the sacrifice of more than 18,000 American lives, as well as stubborn insecurity (and not a little pride) that
made him abidingly reluctant to admit error and defeat. But Johnson's public hawkishness had a calculated purpose as well. Convinced by his generals that the Vietcong had taken a beating in the
Tet Offensive, he thought Hanoi might soon be ready to sit down
and talk. Playing into that, Johnson wanted the North Vietnamese
to think that, despite the growing domestic opposition he faced, its
best hope lay through negotiations. Johnson hinted as much to his
advisors at a White House meeting on March 20. "I want war like
I want polio," he told them. "What you want and what your image
is are two different things."[31]

The final part of Johnson's strategy he kept to himself for the
time being: his growing inclination not to seek reelection as president in 1968. Johnson held back because a part of him worried
American troops in Vietnam would grumble, "You can get out,
but we can't." He was also sensitive about leaks, especially of his
forthcoming decisions. But Johnson had been contemplating such
a move for some time, and events precipitated his decision. "I do

not believe I can unite this country,"[32] he had admitted privately, almost shamefully, to family and close friends over the previous several months, and the increasing obviousness of that fact to him and those who supported him[*] led Johnson to acknowledge reality. The war had undermined his credibility, sapped momentum for the Great Society, divided the Democratic Party, and triggered rampant inflation.[†] The country seemed in disarray with deepening racial tensions and growing alienation between antiwar protestors and blue-collar workers. (In March, Johnson's Vietnam approval rating fell to just 26 percent, with more than twice that number—63 percent—expressing dissatisfaction over his handling of the war.) Lyndon Johnson, who so loved to control events, had lost control of the country.

The decision not to seek reelection was a bitter and painful one for a quintessentially political animal like Lyndon Johnson to make—"giving up the job he had sought almost his entire life," as Clifford put it—almost like committing seppuku, as an act of atonement. Johnson saw the war as "a blot on his administration he wanted to remove," recalled his close aide Jim Jones, who heard him muse one night in March, "I want my hands free to do what's necessary to end this thing." "I've goofed and made a lot of errors," LBJ told his old Senate colleague and current Senate critic, William Fulbright, adding: "I had rather find a way to stop killing any people—ours and theirs—than anything else in the world."[33]

Lady Bird had never been eager to see her husband run again. His health concerned her—he had barely survived a severe heart attack in 1955—and she knew that no vice president had ever succeeded to the presidency and then run for two full terms. Lady Bird had hoped that he would serve one full term, then return home to

---

[*] As early as September 1967, Johnson's oldest and closest political ally, Governor John Connally of Texas, told him that he did not think that Johnson could get reelected.

[†] Greatly increased government spending on the war beginning in mid-1965 produced upward pressure on prices. Because Johnson, Congress, and the Federal Reserve failed to institute corrective measures such as a war surtax or an increase in the interest rate, inflation had accelerated rapidly by 1968.

Texas. Again and again, she talked about "how to get out and when." She viewed the prospect of another campaign "like an open-ended stay in a concentration camp,"[34] and did not hide her feelings from the man she married. Vietnam had worn down the indefatigable McNamara, and now it was wearing down her famously energetic husband, aging him physically and taxing him emotionally. Those close to Johnson noticed the change. An old friend who visited him at the White House in early March said "he looked absolutely terrible . . . so tired, exhausted," with sunken eyes and deep lines sketched into the loose skin of his ashen face.[35] His younger brother, Sam, who saw him frequently during this period, said he felt "tired and lonely."[36] The president's long-time navy physician "did not see the bounce, the laughter, the teasing quality" that he had witnessed in Johnson over the years and thought he had grown "bone tired."[37] He got less and less sleep, often shuffling downstairs in the middle of the night to the Situation Room in his bathrobe and slippers for the latest reports from Vietnam. In private moments, with the few he felt genuinely close to and whose discretion he trusted, he would unburden himself, then put on his game face and go out and face the world.

Political realities reinforced his inclination. Johnson's fortunes had been in decline since the 1964 election. Southern whites had reacted to his signing of the Civil Rights Act and Voting Rights Act legislating equality for African Americans by abandoning the Democratic Party in droves. The 1966 midterm elections had accelerated this trend, which was compounded by growing popular frustration over Vietnam (in Washington and across the nation) and riots in many of America's cities. Having lost southern whites and now an increasing number of northern blue-collar whites—key elements of the New Deal coalition that had provided Democrats with an assortment of electoral majorities since 1932—Johnson knew his prospects in 1968 were uncertain at best.

He also confronted the problem of Robert Kennedy, his long-time rival and nemesis. Kennedy's increasing dovishness, combined with the war's increasing unpopularity, suggested that the senator might enter the Democratic primaries against him—and win. The results of the New Hampshire primary on March 12 lent credence to this prospect. Although Johnson won a plurality of votes (49 percent) as a write-in candidate, the antiwar senator Eugene McCarthy of Minnesota, the sole Democrat to challenge him, received 42 percent of the vote—far more than expected, and a sign that the president was vulnerable among voters of his own party.* Johnson himself privately called the New Hampshire results a "victory" for McCarthy.[38] It was becoming increasingly clear to Johnson that his electoral prospects were doomed. In four short years, Vietnam had reduced LBJ from the winner of the biggest election landslide in American history to a polarizing figure within his own party. "I will go down the drain," he said two weeks later.[39]

The trend in Johnson's thinking became clear when he lunched with former secretary of state Dean Acheson on March 14. An architect of the containment strategy who had persuaded President Truman to finance the French conflict in Indochina two decades earlier and had stood by Truman during the tough times of the Korean War, Acheson possessed the credentials, experience, and hard-boiled realism that commanded Johnson's respect. Acheson also spoke bluntly *and* didn't tattle to the press, which increased his credibility with Johnson, who listened carefully to him. He had asked Acheson to review the administration's Vietnam policy and arranged access to all top-secret intelligence information as well as the full cooperation of the State and Defense Departments, the CIA, and the Joint Chiefs in order to do so. In November, Acheson had strongly supported the administration policy and had counseled Johnson to persevere. Now, in the White House private dining room, he told Johnson that the American public would not support another major troop increase—they had reached the limit of their patience with an ever bigger war—and "we should launch ourselves on a path looking towards progressive disengagement" before public support for American military involvement in Vietnam

---

* Later studies revealed that many who voted for McCarthy did so as a gesture of protest against Johnson for *not doing enough* in Vietnam—corroboration of Johnson's anxiety that the most serious threat came from the Right, not the Left.

evaporated. The United States must begin to cut its losses and bring the war to a conclusion.[40] A part of Johnson did not want to hear this, and pushed back almost desperately. The military remains optimistic about the war, he plaintively told his guest. But Acheson, who had heard MacArthur tell Truman much the same in the weeks before China intervened in Korea in the fall of 1950, would have none of what he called "adrenalin [sic] infusion from the brass."[41] He told Johnson the chiefs were leading him "down the garden path."[42] He recommended reducing the American effort and insisting the South Vietnamese do more. If they would not, or could not, do more, then the United States should disengage. Reluctantly, Johnson "agreed with this and said that he thought Dean Rusk and Clark Clifford would agree also," Acheson wrote in a private memorandum after the meeting.[43] Tellingly, Johnson read from his own notes of this meeting at the Tuesday Lunch the following week.[44]

Despite his private comments to Acheson, LBJ's recent tough talk in public alarmed Clifford, who understood his old friend's mercurial temperament—"He was given to saying things that suited his mood at the moment," he recalled of Johnson—and worried that the president might be backing away from his intention to seek negotiations leading to disengagement. Indeed, those hard-line speeches "reminded me that we were engaged in a tense struggle for the soul and mind of Lyndon Johnson," Clifford later wrote. "I believed I had to try harder to persuade him."[45] Clifford set out to do so in a phone call on the morning of March 20. Carefully and deliberately, he coaxed and cajoled Johnson to maintain his commitment to a negotiated settlement. "We are out to win," he patiently told the president, "but we are not out to win the war—we are out to win the peace." "That is right," said Johnson, backing away from his public remarks. "If there is some program of gradual deescalation that the parties could get into," Clifford continued, "we could then be in a better posture." Johnson picked up on the theme. "My own thought is that we ought to stress this peace thing and we ought to stress the permanence of it," he said, to let people know that "we are willing to sit down and pull our troops out of there as soon as the violence subsides." Clifford encouraged him: "I think we have to work out some kind of arrangement where we start some kind of negotiation . . . There is a good chance to do that if it is prepared properly and if we work up to it."[46] Clifford also urged Johnson to reconvene the Wise Men, whom he had last consulted in early November—knowing that many of them had also changed their opinion on the war from holding course to beginning the process of de-escalation and disengagement. Although Johnson had recently met with one of these giants (Acheson), he doubted the efficacy of another such plenary consultation. "Nothing much comes out of these big meetings," he muttered. But Rusk endorsed Clifford's suggestion, "not only because of their great experience but because most had not been involved in the daily decision making on Vietnam and now were somewhat removed from its detail and theology."[47] So, too, did Wheeler—unaware of the changes in opinion among the Wise Men—who told Johnson their "reappraisal might be important indicators of public opinion."[48] Johnson agreed and set the meeting for March 26.

On the evening of March 25, Acheson and a dozen other member of "the Cold War Knighthood,'"* in the words of journalists Walter Isaacson and Evan Thomas, gathered for dinner in the Secretary's Dining Room on the eighth floor of the State Department. They began by reading background papers prepared by State and Defense. They then questioned Clifford, Rusk, and CIA director Helms. Clifford sketched three alternatives before the United States: (1) grant the 205,000 troop increase, increase the bombing, and expand the ground war into North Vietnam, Laos, and Cambodia to try to win militarily; (2) muddle along with the current strategy; and (3) reduce or halt the bombing to start negotiations with Hanoi, shift from attrition to a population security strategy, and gradually transfer the fighting to the South Vietnamese to dis-

---

* The composition of this meeting of the Wise Men included Dean Acheson, George Ball, McGeorge Bundy, Omar Bradley, Arthur Dean, Douglas Dillon, Arthur Goldberg, Henry Cabot Lodge Jr., Robert Murphy, Matthew Ridgway, Maxwell Taylor, and Cyrus Vance.

engage the United States from the war. Clifford recommended the third course for all of the reasons he had explained to Johnson on March 4. After dinner, the group moved to the Operations Center one floor below, where they received detailed briefings from the government's top Vietnam experts, all with substantial firsthand experience: Major General William DePuy, Westmoreland's former operations officer and now Vietnam advisor to the Joint Chiefs (chosen by Wheeler); George Carver, the CIA's chief Vietnam analyst (chosen by Helms); and Philip Habib, senior political officer at the American embassy in Saigon (chosen by Rusk). "We all tried to be factual," DePuy later said. "There was very little speculation on the part of any of us in those briefings." DePuy told the "Wise Men" that the Vietcong had suffered staggering losses during Tet. Despite this, the general projected Communist force levels would increase from 647,000 to more than 800,000 in the next two years and conceded that attrition would never catch up with infiltration. Carver told them the crucial pacification campaign had suffered and would take much longer than previously estimated. Habib told them the Saigon government was unlikely to pull itself together within any reasonable amount of time. When Habib finished, Clifford asked "one critical question," DePuy remembered: "Can the war be won militarily?"—the same question he had put to the chiefs during his first days at the Pentagon. "Not under present circumstances," said Habib. "I think all of us wondered whether it could be won militarily at that time," DePuy recalled, "even those of us who had been chasing VCs around . . . I'm not sure that any amount of optimism would have made a hell of a lot of difference." Before the meeting ended, Clifford turned to Habib and asked him a final question: "What would you do if the decision was yours to make?" "Stop the bombing and negotiate," Habib replied.[49]

Still, Johnson equivocated. Clifford's efforts to reinforce Johnson's commitment to negotiations leading to disengagement reflected his awareness of his friend's nagging sense of inadequacy, which sometimes led Johnson into a whirlpool of second-guessing and, when criticized, lashing out at his critics with chilled outrage in which every word had a vicious edge. That undertow was again evident on March 22, when Johnson had complained to Clifford "that a lot of people are . . . ready to surrender without knowing they are following a party line." Two days later, he had told Senator Russell that Pentagon civilians "practically all want us to surrender."* His bitterness peaked during a conference with Generals Wheeler and Abrams† on the morning of March 26, when he told them that these same Pentagon "civilians are cutting our guts out . . . Senator Mc-Carthy and Senator Kennedy and the left wing have informers in the departments. The *Times* and the *Post* are all against us. Most of the press is against us . . . I would give Westmoreland 206,000 men if he said he needed them and if we could get them." Such remarks betrayed Johnson's paranoia and anger at circumstances, but there was another explanation, too, which Clifford wrote of later: Johnson seemed to be "pleading for understanding, even forgiveness, from these two military officers to whom he could no longer send reinforcements."⁵⁰ He sought to ameliorate their disappointment (and potential criticism) by playing to their sympathy.

That afternoon, the Wise Men met with Johnson and his senior advisors around the same oblong table where the president and Acheson had lunched twelve days earlier. This time, Acheson sat next to Johnson. Wheeler and Abrams sat at the opposite end and began by briefing the group. Wheeler reiterated that the Vietcong had suffered "great casualties." He saw "no reason for all the gloom and doom we see in the United States press"—but then conceded that infiltration had increased and that "we face additional hard fighting." Abrams agreed, saying that while he had seen improve-

---

* Johnson had been informed of deputy defense secretary Paul Nitze's and assistant secretary of defense for international security affairs Paul Warnke's pessimism and dovishness about the war by Walt Rostow, who attended meetings of the "Non-Group"—a candid deliberation of second-level officials that met every Thursday afternoon in deputy secretary of state Nicholas Katzenbach's office. Rostow violated the ground rules of the meetings, which required participants to respect the strictly "off the record" nature of what was said in order to encourage open and frank discussion. See Nicholas deB. Katzenbach, *Some of It Was Fun: Working with RFK and LBJ* (W. W. Norton, 2008), p. 264.

† General Creighton Abrams, who was then Westmoreland's deputy, would replace him as American military commander in Vietnam in June 1968.

ment in some ARVN units, desertions exceeded casualties in others and that pacification had been set back because militia forces had been drawn from the countryside into the urban areas to repel Vietcong attacks. The Wise Men asked Abrams if ARVN could take on more of the fighting. "I feel quite certain of that," Abrams said. "I would have to quit if I didn't believe that."[51] That the Wise Men had even posed the question was a slivered indication of the direction of their thinking.

McGeorge Bundy, speaking for the unofficial visitors, led off by acknowledging there had been a "very significant shift" in their attitude since November. "When we last met," they'd seen reasons for hope because "slow but steady progress" seemed to be being made. Now they saw none. At this point, Acheson took over and summed up the majority opinion. He spoke on behalf of an Establishment that had soured on the war. The briefings these men had received had focused on events in Vietnam, but they weighed conditions in America as well. The war-related inflation was potentially ruinous. The country was more politically polarized than anytime since the Civil War. And—perhaps worst of all—the war was alienating an entire generation of the nation's youth, including the Wise Men's own sons and daughters, against the traditions and values that they embodied and cherished. The costs of Vietnam—not just military ones, but deeper cultural ones—had become wildly, senselessly disproportionate to the national interests at stake there.

As usual, Acheson did not mince his words. He turned toward Johnson and bluntly said, "In the time the American people will allow this President or any other President to continue operations in Vietnam, the belligerency there cannot be brought to a point where the GVN can handle it . . . Our broader interests require a decision now to disengage within a limited time." Communist forces could move freely while avoiding American forces (thereby continuing to control their casualties); the all-important pacification program had been badly disrupted; and—most crucially—the South Vietnamese population, while "not attracted to the Vietcong . . . do not dare risk attaching themselves to the government. In other words, what is lacking in South Vietnam is a missing component—

i.e., popular support—which the United States of America cannot supply." This had been the root problem all along.

It was a cogent and devastating appraisal that Acheson drove home with a final remark. "One thing seems sure," he told the president. "The old slogan that success is just around the corner won't work."[52] A military victory at acceptable cost and risk was unattainable. Wheeler took exception, denying the military was "bent on victory." The general's remark infuriated Acheson. "What in the name of God are 500,000 men out there doing—chasing girls?" he asked acidly. "If the deployment of all those men is not an effort to gain a military victory, then words have lost all meaning. It won't happen—at least not in any time the American people will permit."[53]

Acheson had spoken on behalf of astute men intimately familiar with Vietnam and very close to Johnson: George Ball, McGeorge Bundy, Arthur Goldberg, and Cyrus Vance. It was not a unanimous verdict: a dissenting minority recommended staying the course and believed the war still winnable. That splinter group included only one man intimately familiar with Vietnam—retired general Maxwell Taylor. The architects of the containment policy, the blueprint of American foreign policy during the Cold War, had reinforced the conclusion Johnson had privately reached, however reluctantly, bitterly, and painfully.* That it had taken the men so long to see clearly was no consolation.

Meanwhile, Johnson moved toward publicly announcing his shift in policy and the steps he planned to take related to it. At 8 P.M. on

---

* Johnson tacitly admitted as much in a handwritten note to Acheson two weeks later on the occasion of Acheson's seventy-fifth birthday. "You and I both know there have been a number of times when I did not like the advice you gave me. I am aware that you were aware that I would not like it when you gave it to me—and I am also aware that as you define your duty, my dislike was, and had to be, an irrelevancy." It was as close as the perceptive but insecure and tormented Johnson could bring himself to admit that he had made a fundamental and grievous misjudgment. "I had quite a birthday letter from LBJ—an extraordinary man," Acheson wrote his daughter Jane a few days later. "A real Centaur—part man part horse's ass. A rough appraisal, but curiously true." President Johnson to Dean Acheson, April 11, 1968, Dean Acheson Papers, Manuscripts and Archives, Yale University Library.

March 28, he met with Rusk in the Oval Office and told his secretary of state to inform Thiệu through Ambassador Bunker of the
impending bombing halt above the twentieth parallel. Later that
night, presidential speechwriter Harry McPherson sent Johnson the
latest draft of the president's address scheduled for delivery to the
nation and the world on March 31. It began with the sentence, "Tonight, I wish to speak to you of the prospects for peace in Vietnam
and Southeast Asia." On the afternoon of the 30th, Johnson, conceding that he felt "worn down," spent more than three hours with
his closest advisors at the Cabinet Room table in shirtsleeves, his
tie loosened, carefully going over every word of the speech. "The
President looked exhausted and lacked his usual sparkle," wrote a
participant at the session.[54] As the meeting ended, Johnson asked
McPherson why the draft lacked an ending. "It was too long, and
it doesn't fit the speech anymore," McPherson replied. "I'll write
a new ending that won't be so long." "Go ahead, but don't worry
about the length of it," Johnson said, adding cryptically, "I may
have a little ending of my own."[55]

Johnson rose early the next morning, Sunday, March 31, to greet
his elder daughter, Lynda, upon her return from the West Coast,
where she had said goodbye to her new husband, Chuck Robb, as
he shipped out with the marines to Vietnam. A morning chill was
in the air and sullen clouds sat low on the horizon as the car carrying Lynda pulled up to the entrance of the Diplomatic Reception Room facing the South Lawn around five o'clock. The irony
of circumstances—the president's son-in-law was going into the
war as Johnson prepared to begin leading the United States out
of it, combined with his decision about his political future—was
a final emotional straw so painful that when Lady Bird returned
to their bedroom after bidding Lynda good night, she found her
husband weeping for the first time since his mother Rebekah's death
ten years earlier. Johnson continued to cry as he dressed, then,
composing himself, he accompanied his younger daughter, Luci,
and her husband, Pat Nugent, to Sunday services at St. Dominic
Catholic Church in southwest Washington, whose rituals and
"little monks," as Johnson called them, had become a "haven for

Lyndon," in Lady Bird's words, from the psychological burdens of office. On the way back from church, Johnson stopped at Hubert Humphrey's home, where he confided to the vice president what he would announce that night. Back at the White House, he directed Clifford to order the chiefs to halt all bombing of North Vietnam north of the twentieth parallel effective at 7 P.M. He then huddled with his close friend and former aide Horace Busby in the Treaty Room on the second floor to craft the surprise ending to the night's speech. In the midafternoon, he called McPherson and told him, "I've got an ending." An overcome McPherson took a moment to recover. "So I've heard," he said (Busby had told him). "What do you think?" Johnson asked. "I'm very sorry, Mr. President." "Okay," Johnson replied in his slow Texas drawl. "So long, pardner."[56] He then summoned Lady Bird to the family quarters of the Executive Mansion, sat her down, and told her what he would say. "It was hard for me to hear," she noted, but there was "a calm finality in Lyndon's voice, and maybe [I] believed him for the first time." Then he told his two daughters, who became emotional. "Chuck will hear this on his way to Vietnam," Lynda said bitterly. "What will this do to the boys" serving in Southeast Asia? Luci asked. "Will they think, 'What have I been out here for?' 'Can I believe in what I've been fighting for?'" His daughters' comments cut to the bone. But "Lyndon seemed to be congealing into a calm, quiet state of mind," said Lady Bird, "out of the reach of us." It was as loud as a hushed moment could be. "I kept looking at the hands of the clock, and counting how long it was until nine."[57]

At 9:01 P.M. EST, the television camera and klieg lights that had been set up in front of the president's desk in the Oval Office came to life. Looking tired and haggard behind his glasses, his sallow skin accentuated by heavy bags under his eyes, Johnson began his address to the nation with the words, "Tonight I want to speak to you of peace in Vietnam and Southeast Asia." He said nothing about the 205,000 troop request, instead announcing the dispatch of only 13,500 support personnel. For the first time since committing American combat troops in the spring and summer of 1965, Johnson stressed that "the main burden of preserving" South Vietnam "must be carried by the South Vietnamese themselves . . . On their efforts—their determination and resourcefulness—the outcome will ultimately depend." Emphasizing his desire to "move immediately toward peace through negotiations," he declared, "I am taking the first step to de-escalate the conflict . . . in the hope that this action will lead to early talks." He announced the cessation of bombing north of the twentieth parallel,* noting that, "even this very limited bombing of the North could come to an early end if our restraint is matched by restraint in Hanoi." He expressed the "fervent hope" that North Vietnam would agree to join the United States at the peace table. "He was no longer saying to the American people, 'I am going to nail the coonskin on the wall in Vietnam,'" explained Clifford, looking back. "He was saying, 'I've gone as far as I'm going to go, and now we're going to do our best to start negotiations.'" Johnson "had crossed a bridge."[58]

Finally, Johnson turned to Vietnam's consequences for himself. The man who had privately confessed to his family and friends "I do not believe I can unite this country" acknowledged that "the ultimate strength of our country" lay "in the unity of our people." Then, quoting Abraham Lincoln on the eve of the Civil War, he said, "It is true that a house divided against itself . . . is a house that cannot stand." It seemed an obvious, almost clichéd, rhetorical opening for a broader assessment, but that was not quite where Johnson was going. "There is division in the American house now," Johnson admitted, knowing that much of it was of his own making. "Believing this as I do," he concluded, "I shall not seek, and I will not accept, the nomination of my party for another term as your President."[59] The words hit countless viewers with tremendous force. "I never was any surer of any decision I ever made in my life," he said to friends gathered with him in the family quarters

---

* Johnson's decision lifted bombing from 90 percent of North Vietnam's population and 78 percent of its land area. Within a few days, he restricted the bombing still further, to the area south of the nineteenth parallel, and held to this restriction despite opposition from the chiefs and some of his own advisors like Rostow and Rusk.

later that night.[60] "I'm shoving in all my stack with this one."[61] Liberated, he believed (or wanted to believe) that he had started America on the road toward de-escalation and disengagement from the war and that such severance could be achieved expeditiously. "The only guys that won't be back here by the time my term ends are the guys that left [for Vietnam] in the last day or two," he naively predicted that same night.[62] Johnson had no inkling how long and hard it would be to accomplish this goal, but he would learn in the months ahead that getting out would be as excruciatingly frustrating as everything else about Vietnam.

By March 31, 1968, Washington and Hanoi had reached a painful equilibrium. Each had suffered heavy casualties without achieving a decisive victory, and therefore each had a compelling reason to start talking. So each accepted the beginning of negotiations. Yet the emerging mutual realization that the war could not be decided militarily did not mean that peace would follow quickly or that Washington and Hanoi shared the same leverage. Johnson faced increasing pressure on the political front to terminate the war, but he also faced pressure from the chiefs not to further limit the bombing and he could continue to impose costs on Hanoi through bombing south of the nineteenth parallel. The Communists, on the other hand, continued to suffer heavy casualties but resisted making concessions until and unless their goals were met, while their forces continued to inflict relatively heavy losses on the United States in the belief this would hasten America's eventual withdrawal—in essence, a strategy of waiting out the adversary.

On April 3, less than seventy-two hours after Johnson's speech, North Vietnam announced over Radio Hanoi that it would at last talk directly with the United States, even though Washington had not met its long-standing demand to unconditionally cease the bombing.* Hanoi's decision to enter into direct discussions with

---

* The next day, civil rights leader Martin Luther King Jr., was shot to death in Memphis, Tennessee, triggering riots in Washington, D.C., and more than a hundred other American cities.

Washington reflected the pain of Tet's massive casualties combined with the pressure of international opinion and behind-the-scenes cajoling by Moscow. Vietcong forces had been so crippled that "we needed to sit and talk," one North Vietnamese official later admitted.[63] But Hanoi had no intention of beginning substantive peace negotiations (*thương lượng hòa bình*) because it had no intention of repeating what it saw as the mistake made at Geneva in 1954, when a negotiated settlement of the war with the French denied the Việtminh sovereignty over considerable territory it controlled in southern Vietnam. The Politburo decided that serious talks with the United States could not begin until the bombing stopped and Communist forces achieved a "decisive victory" in South Vietnam, which would allow Hanoi to bargain from a position of strength, rather than a position of weakness as it had in 1954.[64] Hanoi strongly believed in the motto "The battlefield will decide the results obtained at the negotiating table." Lê Duẩn and other hard-liners who controlled the Politburo did not entirely walk away. Instead, adopting a strategy of *đánh và đàm, đàm và đánh*— "fighting and talking, talking and fighting"—the North Vietnamese engaged in contacts (*tiếp xúc*) with the Americans while they continued to fight (which Washington did as well). Hanoi's intent was not to compromise but to achieve its objectives. "A cease-fire in the South and a negotiated settlement were never considered to be options," North Vietnamese official Bùi Tín later noted. "Negotiations played only a tactical role in support of the military offensives."[65] Hanoi viewed discussions with the Americans as only one part of a package of instruments to realize its goal of reunification. Where Hồ Chí Minh had been flexible and pragmatic at Geneva in 1954, Lê Duẩn would be tough and unyielding when the warring parties would meet in Paris.

On May 4, Communist forces launched a second wave offensive throughout South Vietnam that lasted for more than a month. American casualties skyrocketed to an all-time weekly high: 562 killed, nearly 2,200 wounded. Total U.S. deaths rose to almost 21,000, more than doubling in less than a year. This second wave offensive proved very costly for the Vietcong as well. Once again,

as during Tet, Vietcong cadres comprised the majority of the fighting force because they could easily slip into the cities and towns,
and once again they failed to spark a general uprising among the
South Vietnamese. And the May attacks seriously depleted Vietcong main force units and wiped out a sizable proportion of its
most experienced cadres, compelling many survivors to return to
their villages and refuse to resume the fight.[66] It also increased the
dependency of Vietcong main force units on North Vietnamese
replacements. But the recuperative powers of the Vietcong, the continued political and military weaknesses of the Saigon regime, and
the early signs of disintegrating discipline in U.S. forces stationed
in Vietnam—the Mỹ Lai Massacre,[*] in which a group of American

---

[*] On March 16, 1968, soldiers of the 23rd Infantry Division (known as the Amer-
ical Division) under the command of Lieutenant William Calley Jr. killed 350 to
500 unarmed South Vietnamese civilians in two hamlets of Sơn Mỹ village—one
of them Mỹ Lai—in Quảng Ngãi province. Covered up at the time by army officers, the Mỹ Lai Massacre became public in November 1969 and led to Calley's
court-martial and conviction for premeditated murder. Calley would serve a total
of three and a half years under house arrest for his crime. This was not the first
instance of disintegrating discipline among U.S. forces stationed in Vietnam. In
recent years, evidence has emerged that Tiger Force, a long-range reconnaissance
patrol unit of the 101st Airborne Division, tortured and executed captured prisoners and mutilated bodies between May and November 1967. During one patrol in
the summer of 1967, a Tiger Force officer told his men, "There are no civilians; shoot
anything that moves." Michael Sallah and Mitchell Weiss, *Tiger Force: A True Story
of Men at War* (Little, Brown, 2007); and *The Vietnam War*, episode 5, "This Is What
We Do (July–December 1967)," directed by Ken Burns and Lynn Novick, aired on
September 21, 2017, on PBS. Additionally, the CIA's Phoenix Program, patterned on
a South Vietnamese endeavor by a similar name (*Phụng Hoàng*, after a mythical
bird associated with royal power in Vietnamese culture), was created to identify
and neutralize covert Vietcong operatives in villages, targeting them for capture,
interrogation, and assassination. Between 1965 and 1972, nearly 40,000 suspected
Vietcong were killed as a result of the program, whose effectiveness the Communists later acknowledged. U.S. military intelligence officers later testified that South
Vietnamese Provincial Reconnaissance Units, with CIA personnel and U.S. Special Forces in supervisory roles, tortured Vietcong and their family members in
Phoenix's regional interrogation centers and threw people out of flying helicopters
to coerce others to talk. Testimony of Barton Osborne and Vincent Okamoto in
Joe Allen and John Pilger, *Vietnam: The (Last) War the U.S. Lost* (Haymarket Books,
2008), p. 164; and Christian G. Appy, *Patriots: The Vietnam War Remembered from All
Sides* (Penguin Books, 2003), p. 361.

soldiers slaughtered hundreds of unarmed South Vietnamese civilians, occurred in the spring of 1968—blunted any temporary disadvantages caused by the high casualties. The bloody slugfest was beginning to degrade both sides.

On May 13, the first direct talks between Washington and Hanoi took place at the French Foreign Ministry's International Conference Center at the historic Hôtel Majestic on Avenue Kléber in Paris's elegant sixteenth arrondissement. Veteran diplomat and troubleshooter Averell Harriman and former deputy defense secretary Cyrus Vance represented the United States, supported by Philip Habib of the State Department, William Jorden of the NSC, and General Andrew Goodpaster of the JCS. Former foreign minister Xuân Thủy and Hà Văn Lâu, a military man and veteran of the 1954 and 1962 Geneva Conferences on Indochina and Laos, led the North Vietnamese team. The American delegation booked a block of rooms nearby in an expensive Paris hotel because it confidently (and naively) assumed a settlement of the war lay just weeks, or at most months, away. The North Vietnamese delegation rented a modest villa in the less expensive suburbs because it planned to be there a long time. These differing choices of accommodation revealed a great deal about Washington's and Hanoi's differing expectations and strategies.

Finding common ground proved immensely difficult. Like most initial dialogues between combatants, these talks occurred in an adversarial climate characterized by mutual suspicion and distrust. A new war began at the talks—in the words of a North Vietnamese diplomat, "a war around a green [baize table] as bombs were still exploding on the battlefield."[67] Both sides accused the other of responsibility for the bloodshed and destruction, and North Vietnam reiterated its long-standing demand that the United States stop all bombing before serious talks could begin. At the end of the first day, Harriman and Thủy agreed to hold further discussions. These talks continued for several weeks, but quickly degenerated into barren and repetitive accusatory exchanges. Despite this, at informal chats during tea breaks, both sides intimated that they saw more discreet interaction as a potential avenue toward substantive progress—the Americans, because they were anxious to end the war; the North Vietnamese, because they wanted, as foreign minister Nguyễn Duy Trinh advised Thủy, "to investigate [the other side's intentions, but] not yet to bargain,"[68] a way to gauge their adversary's diplomatic position, test its reactions, and begin to drive a wedge between Saigon and Washington, which they thought would be easier under more confidential circumstances. And so, Vance and Lâu secretly met at a CIA safehouse* on Rue Touraine in Sceaux, a few miles west of the North Vietnamese delegation's villa in Vitry-sur-Seine. There, on the night of June 27,† Vance told Lâu that the United States would stop the bombing if North Vietnam exhibited restraint by not increasing its infiltration beyond pre-March 31 levels (when the bombing had been limited), and not attacking South Vietnam's cities. Vance said that Washington would accept the participation of the NLF (the Vietcong's political wing) at the talks in return for Hanoi's acceptance of Saigon's participation as well. Lâu rejected Vance's proposals because they attached conditions to what Hanoi still considered a nonnegotiable requirement for substantive talks: a complete bombing halt.

The beginning of talks with Hanoi had opened a split within the administration over the viability and wisdom of negotiations. Clifford, along with Harriman and Vance, assumed that North Vietnam intended to bargain seriously if the United States stopped the bombing, though they expected Hanoi would continue to fight while talking. (Clifford told Johnson that "the time may come . . . with negotiations when you've got to step up and call some kind of halt" to the bombing in order to make progress toward disengagement. Johnson did not disagree.[69]) Rusk, Rostow, Wheeler, and

---

* The North Vietnamese agreed to this site because they feared the French had bugged the International Conference Center, but apparently did not fear—or care—whether the Americans had done the same at the CIA safehouse. There is no evidence that the CIA did.

† Three weeks earlier, on June 5, presidential candidate Robert Kennedy had been assassinated in Los Angeles, California. His death threw the Democratic nominating process into turmoil and eventually led to Vice President Hubert Humphrey's nomination as Johnson's successor.

Bunker on the other hand viewed negotiations more skeptically, questioning Hanoi's seriousness and favoring continued military pressure to make the North Vietnamese amenable to bargaining. Rostow (unknowingly echoing Hanoi's philosophy about the battlefield) believed that the "outcome does not depend on the negotiating table so much as what happens on the ground, in Saigon, and [American] politics."[70] He, Rusk, Wheeler, and Bunker opposed a bombing halt without a reciprocal gesture of de-escalation and wanted to go slow in any negotiations in order not to undermine South Vietnam's stability.

Par for the course, Johnson felt pulled in both directions, torn between wanting out of Vietnam and fearful of losing. A part of him sympathized with Clifford, Harriman, and Vance about rapidly eroding domestic support, the imperative to conclude a peace agreement, and the mounting deaths on both sides.[*] But another part of him appreciated Rusk, Rostow, and Wheeler's skepticism that Hanoi would negotiate seriously and their fear that it was exploiting the reduced bombing to boost infiltration. (Informed by the CIA in early May that monthly infiltration had increased 25 percent since March 31, Johnson grumbled that "Giap gets 80,000 [more troops in South Vietnam] . . . and Westmoreland gets zero. I don't know how long we can do that if I'm going to run a football team."[71]) Johnson's conflicting emotions about the Paris talks caused him to swing like a weathervane (the metaphor Clifford used privately to characterize his behavior) and for the remainder of the year, LBJ would waver back and forth between the two factions, tossing and turning within himself, desiring to end the war during his remaining time in office but at the same time questioning Hanoi's willingness to compromise. It bothered him to side with Clifford when his three other senior advisors disagreed. His anxiety only increased when he thought about his two sons-in-law

---

[*] "I'm plowing every hour I can," he told William Fulbright in early May, because "I know the killings are taking place." Telephone Conversation between President Johnson and Senator Fulbright, Tape 13002 (WH6805.01), MCWHR.

in Vietnam* and visited wounded soldiers at Walter Reed Army Medical Center. On those occasions, Johnson would become "very pissed and emotional" in Harry McPherson's words,[72] and bellow in anger that "after 21,000 boys [killed] and $70 billion [spent], we're not going to get out," that he felt "hornswoggled on the bombing pause," and that he would like to "knock Hanoi and Haiphong off the map."[73] "I'm going to hang on as long as I know how, like a god-damn bulldog . . . I'm not going to cave in to the doves," he would insist at such moments.[74] Then, after a while, he would calm down, becoming sullen, frustrated, irritable, and depressed at how hard getting out of Vietnam was proving to be.

Ongoing divisions among his advisors compounded his worries. Johnson hated friction "within the family" and the split between Clark Clifford and Walt Rostow ran deep. "We were both reaching for the mind of the President," Clifford said later, "and it was a fight to the death. No quarter asked, and none given."[75] Their duel had great consequences and was conducted with great tenacity.† At White House meetings, Clifford repeatedly stated his belief that the United States must begin to disengage from Vietnam. He took a permissive view of a bombing halt because he understood that Hanoi considered it a precondition for serious talks and, far more important, because he saw no viable alternative to a political resolution of the war. Bombing was not going to win the war or appreciably limit the infiltration, and doubling the number of troops was not going to win the war because of the constraints imposed on American military operations in order to avoid a war with China and the rapidly diminishing patience of the American people. "Can anybody tell me what our plan is if the Paris talks fail?" Clifford

---

* Lynda's husband, Chuck Robb, commanded a combat infantry company of the 1st Marine Division in I Corps; Pat Nugent, the first husband of Luci Johnson, served as a mechanic and bomb fuser with the air national guard during a one-year combat assignment at Cam Ranh Bay and Phan Rang Air Base north of Saigon.

† For his part, Rusk shared opinions with both men: he sought a way out of the war like Clifford, but questioned Hanoi's intentions and sought to keep up the military pressure like Rostow.

bluntly asked at a Tuesday Lunch on May 21. Tellingly, no one had an answer. "If Paris fails, we have no alternative but to turn back to the military—and they have no plan to bring it to an end." And there would be "hell here at home among the people." America's position was so impossible that it must look for a diplomatic way out. "Our hopes must go with Paris," Clifford concluded.*[76]

Clifford used his courtroom-honed talents for advocating a position and his infighting skills at winning supporters and splitting opponents. This allowed him to block escalatory steps proposed by others and to keep the focus on negotiations. He viewed the hawkish Rostow as a baleful influence on the president who appealed to Johnson's "nail the coonskin to the wall" sensibility—the part of Johnson that still dreamed occasionally of military victory—and thus an impediment to progress in Paris. (In a private conversation with Harriman, Clifford referred to Rostow as that "very militarist gentleman."[77]) His goal was simple: "I wanted to be sure Rostow did not persuade [Johnson] to change again."[78]

Clifford sought to neutralize his rival—if only a bit—by inviting Rostow to dinner at his elegant colonial home in suburban Bethesda one Saturday evening in late June. It was a courteous but mannered gesture, a touch too deliberate. For three hours, the two antagonists politely discussed their respective positions on Vietnam. Each was gracious and retained eye contact throughout, but neither of them flinched.

Rostow rightly saw Clifford as his chief rival for Johnson's ear, and while he was scrupulously polite to the secretary of defense, it was kindness dipped in venom. Rostow viewed Clifford as he had viewed McNamara: as an influential advisor to the president who underestimated the effectiveness of American military operations

---

* A CIA assessment in early June corroborated Clifford's concern, noting "Communist forces have expanded their force structure through an unprecedented level of infiltration from the North . . . [They] have been recruiting, refitting, and regrouping. As a result of these activities, plus intensified recruiting in the countryside, Communist forces will be capable of undertaking a series of major attacks between now and the fall." Special National Intelligence Estimate, pp. 53–68, "The Vietnam Situation," June 6, 1968, FRUS, 1964–1968, Volume VI, p. 757.

and refused to see that Hanoi was unwilling to negotiate seriously. "Rostow had turned violently against Bob at the end of his period as Secretary," said a colleague. "He was delighted to see him go."[79] Rostow never paused to ponder the telling fact that both secretaries of defense, having wrestled intimately with Vietnam, had concluded that the war could not be won at acceptable risk and cost. Instead, behind closed doors with fellow hawks, Rostow began referring to comments he considered unduly negative as "Cliffordisms," people whom he considered defeatist as "Cliffordized," and the need to "combat Cliffordism."[80] Though Rostow never dared to use these terms in front of Clifford, they inevitably made their way back to the defense secretary.

In June, Rostow instructed the State Department's executive secretary, Benjamin Read, who controlled the distribution of the department's most sensitive cables, not to pass along Harriman's and Vance's messages from Paris to Clifford. His close-quarters bureaucratic combat failed. When Read told Rusk about Rostow's request, Rusk ordered Read to continue delivering the cables to Clifford. Later that summer, Rostow created a back channel to MACV commander General Creighton Abrams through Robert Ginsburgh, an air force colonel on the NSC staff, which enabled Rostow to communicate directly with Abrams, cutting out the secretary of defense. Through this back channel, Rostow encouraged Abrams to share his concerns about a bombing halt and present evidence of American progress that countered CIA assessments, which Rostow then fed to Johnson.*

In such ways, Rostow influenced Johnson's thinking, but the president's decisions time and again confirmed Clifford's decisive influence. Johnson formally capped U.S. troop deployments to Vietnam and publicly began shifting the burden of the war back to the South Vietnamese as part of his effort to begin the process of disengagement. Knowing that the chiefs still disliked limiting

---

* Rostow's bypass gambit created a mechanism that Nixon and his national security advisor, Henry Kissinger, later used for the double bookkeeping of Operation MENU, in which the air force, at the White House's direction, deliberately hid operational evidence of the secret bombing of Cambodia in 1969–1970.

the bombing—they had voted 3 to 2 to support it and would not have done so without Wheeler's arm-twisting—and strenuously opposed stopping it, Johnson proceeded cautiously, using Clifford to announce the first formal de-escalatory steps in order to limit pressure and criticism from the chiefs and their allies on the Hill. On April 11, Clifford publicly announced that the U.S. troop level in Vietnam "will be brought up to some 549,500," and deliberately stressed, "it is the President's intention not to increase those forces." He made certain to add, "When the South Vietnamese troops were ready they could be moved into areas where combat was taking place so that they could supplant some of the American troops." The implications were clear: for the first time, the military had been told unequivocally "this much and no more," the South Vietnamese had been told, "This is it, do more yourselves," and the North Vietnamese had been told, "Our people now know this is no longer a bottomless pit." The New York Times headline the next morning read: "U.S. Sets G.I. Ceiling at 549,500, Giving Saigon Major Role."[81] Publicly, Clifford had gotten out in front of the president—this was a more aggressive position than LBJ had encouraged. Johnson could have overruled Clifford at any time, but the White House quickly confirmed Clifford's statements as administration policy, proof that he had spoken with Johnson's consent.

The announcement unsurprisingly did almost nothing to diminish the near-constant resistance from the chiefs, whose overriding goal remained applying unrelenting military pressure against the enemy. Convinced the Communists had indeed suffered a colossal defeat during Tet, they saw no point in making concessions at the peace table. "We are smashing" the enemy "wherever he appears," said one military officer. "Peace talks be damned."[82] Such remarks led Clifford to conclude that the military, unlike Johnson, was not anxious to end the war.* Johnson and the chiefs' differing goals

---

* Clifford's military assistant, air force colonel Robert Pursley, told him that applied to "high levels only." Another air force officer—a major in planning—told an army colleague, "If we win the war without bombing in the north, the Air Force does not want to win it" because that would invalidate air force doctrine. Notes of

led them to view the bombing through differing prisms. Johnson saw the bombing as a military *and* a political instrument—both a means to inhibit the infiltration of men and supplies but also as a bargaining lever in pursuit of a negotiated settlement. The chiefs put the political element completely to the side, seeing the bombing solely as a military instrument that inhibited infiltration, aided the ground war, and protected the lives of American soldiers in the South. A bombing halt would be, they thought, a disaster without establishing conditions that would keep the North Vietnamese from taking advantage of it and thereby endangering U.S. troops. The chiefs told Johnson that a complete bombing halt would permit 30 percent more troops and supplies to reach the South.[83]

The split in perspective surfaced in a dispute between Johnson's emissary, Averell Harriman, and the chiefs' representative on his team, General Andrew Goodpaster, during their flight to Paris in early May. Harriman gathered his team on the plane and told them their mission was to pursue the president's objective of ending the war—as he put it (echoing Clifford), "To get the best terms we can, but to end the war." "That's not my understanding," Goodpaster shot back, insisting their mission was to negotiate with the North Vietnamese without compromising American pressure on the battlefield. "That's not right, general," Harriman responded politely but firmly. "It's clear what our position is: what the President ordered."[84] The attitude expressed by Goodpaster reinforced Johnson's sensitivity to the chiefs' repeated urgings to resume the bombing throughout all of North Vietnam, fed his reluctance to stop it completely even though Hanoi had made it a precondition for substantive talks, and thus made success in Paris more problematic. Johnson was moving forward, but in stutter step, his compass needle whirled by his indecision.

In mid-July, Johnson ordered Clifford to Saigon to assess the current state of South Vietnam's government and military, then to join

"8:30 Group," July 22, 1968, Personal Papers of Robert Pursley; and author's interview with Clark Clifford and Herbert Schandler, August 2, 1988, Tape One.

him in Honolulu for a summit conference with Thiệu. Increasingly concerned about his ability to conclude a deal with Hanoi before his term in office ended—he had grown "impatient and jittery" about the Paris talks, Clifford told his staff[85]—Johnson sought to jump-start the process of disengagement by more forcefully shifting more responsibility for war-fighting to ARVN. Johnson based his plan on Abrams's confidence that this could be done as well as on a report by former army advisor turned pacification specialist John Paul Vann that had been passed to him by Harry McPherson, who had met Vann during a visit to South Vietnam the previous summer. In his report (which Vann dictated over the phone to McPherson while back in the States for medical treatment) Vann said that ARVN forces were "getting much better and they will get better still if we start to reduce the size of our presence in Vietnam."[86] Vann believed that the number of American forces "in country" could be substantially trimmed because of "almost unbelievable layering of headquarters and the proliferation of many nice-to-have (but not essential) units and activities." Vann's target was more than half the current troop involvement, considering "it entirely feasible to phase down . . . to a level of 200,000 by mid-1971," he wrote another Washington official. Such reduction "would provide the necessary stimulus to the GVN" to tackle its endemic corruption and incompetence.[87] Vann's conclusions played to Johnson's hopes, and he read portions of Vann's report to the Cabinet on July 10.

Clifford shared Johnson's anxiousness to begin the process of disengagement. But it was not the prospect of progress in South Vietnam that motivated Clifford, but its absence. Clifford had made this clear when he met with South Vietnamese ambassador Bùi Diễm on March 20. "We have run out of time for diplomatic niceties," Clifford told him in the privacy of his Pentagon office that afternoon. "We are sick to death of their feuding," referring to Thiệu and Kỳ's bickering, which he considered unfathomably irresponsible. "Our people are discouraged and our support is limited."[88] Clifford felt the most important part of his upcoming trip

would be to tell these two men that Saigon could no longer afford
the luxury of political jockeying because U.S. patience was growing very thin.[89]

Clifford flew into Saigon on July 14. It was his maiden trip to
South Vietnam as secretary of defense and his first since canvass-
ing Southeast Asian heads of state with Maxwell Taylor the previous summer. Clifford began by visiting U.S. troops at Danang
and in the Mekong Delta, who had carried the burden of fighting
during the Tet and May Offensives. To him, Vietnam seemed the
"worst place in the world to fight a war."[90] At a press conference,
he stressed the growing importance of ARVN assuming more of
the war fighting. Clifford reiterated these points to Thiệu and Kỳ
when he met with them at the Independence Palace on July 16. At a
long rectangular table in a second-floor conference room at the top
of the palace's grandiose staircase, Thiệu and Kỳ sat on one side,
Clifford and Ambassador Bunker on the other. It was a cold, tense
atmosphere. "You might just as well have been in a meat locker,"
said a member of the American party.[91] Although Johnson had sent
Bunker to Saigon to help get the United States out of Vietnam,*
Clifford sensed that Bunker had "gone native," seeing things from
Saigon's rather than Washington's point of view and interests.

A proper and reserved diplomat of the old school, Bunker typically held bland and formal conversations with Thiệu and, as one
observer noted, "didn't 'call' Thieu when he knew Thieu was con-
ning him."[92] Clifford, on the other hand, did not mince words—he
was there to deliver strong medicine on behalf of the president—
and bluntly related the American people's impatience and frustration to Thiệu and Kỳ, telling them that the U.S. public simply
would not support the war effort much longer, and therefore the
South Vietnamese must begin to do more.† "Saigon's weakness

---

* "I had gotten him out of the Dominican Republic," Bunker told an associate, "and
he wanted me to do the same in South Vietnam." Quoted in Stephen B. Young,
"The Birth of 'Vietnamization,'" *New York Times*, April 28, 2017.

† When Vice President Humphrey had called on Thiệu the previous autumn and
told him essentially the same thing, Thiệu had responded blandly that the United

was the major cause of our dilemma," he later wrote, "and I saw
no reason to indulge it." "It was one of the very first times," said a
member of Clifford's traveling party, "that a U.S. official at a very
high level had talked to them in very hard, graphic terms about
what the future looked like and what their responsibilities were going to be in terms that visibly shook them."[93]

An exchange between Clifford and Kỳ epitomized the ruinous
association. He asked Kỳ what the United States could do to make
ARVN more effective, a request for more recruits, more weapons,
more training. Instead, Kỳ emphasized "improving material conditions," specifically "pay and pensions." "Some of the money
[you] spend for thousands of bombs," said Kỳ, "could be given to
the South Vietnamese for that purpose."[94] No wonder, thought
Clifford, "that Saigon appeared to oppose *any* agreement with
Hanoi"—it would mean turning off the immense flow of American spending in South Vietnam—$750 million a day—which Thiệu
and Kỳ themselves had made their priority.[95] During the meeting,
Thiệu and Kỳ's prime minister, Trần Văn Hương—whom Clifford
considered "the most realistic" of all South Vietnamese leaders,
candidly conceded without the least hint of irony that if the government "were to put in jail all the petty corrupt officials, they
would not have enough jails, and if they sought to expel the small
fry from the government, they would run out of people. Quite a
few would like to leave the administration because they now have
enough wealth."[96] "We were pouring" immense amounts of treasure "into Vietnam per month," noted Clifford. "It was a golden
avalanche."[97] The corruption he had witnessed intensified his belief
in the imperative of disengagement at the same time that he more
sharply grasped its difficulty. "If I needed any additional proof that
we should get out" of Vietnam, Clifford told his Pentagon staff after he returned to Washington, "this trip did it."[98]

"Most of the [South] Vietnamese we worked with had really

States would be there for a long time and had no option but to keep its forces at
current levels. See Hubert H. Humphrey, *The Education of a Public Man: My Life and
Politics* (Doubleday, 1976), p. 349.

no faith that the war would be won or could be won," the CIA's George Allen, who had witnessed events in the country since the 1950s, later observed. "Most of them were going along with us only to the extent that they saw our involvement as a means of enriching themselves, getting a slice of the pie or skimming off some of the cream for themselves . . . I said on numerous occasions over the years, 'Those people, ARVN and Thieu and company, are going to continue to fight only until it becomes clear to them that it's over, that the U.S. aid has ended, that there'll be no more B-52s; our firepower is no longer there to bail them out. And when this becomes apparent, stand aside, because the flood is just going to be overwhelming as the exodus takes place.'"[99] Such an attitude made those who governed South Vietnam unenthusiastic about any peace settlement that would see the Americans go, and thus made Johnson's goal of ending the war infinitely harder.

The fundamental malfunction remained as it always had been: the South Vietnamese leadership resented the Americans but they needed them. They did not want to see the Americans go because they benefited enormously from U.S. assistance and feared they could not stand up to the Vietcong and North Vietnamese without them. Yet, as had been the case throughout the war, there was dependency on both sides, each side having come to rely on the other while each, at some level, distrusted and resented the other. This made compromise very difficult. And in delivering his stiff message on President Johnson's behalf, Clifford had, as one long-time Vietnam hand put it, "broken a cardinal rule—never lecture a Vietnamese. The resentment generated always obscured the message, no matter how reasonable."[100] Although Clifford's tough talk to the South Vietnamese was understandable, it also created an obstacle, as explained by Fisher and Ury:

> For a negotiator to reach an agreement that meets his self-interest he needs to develop a solution which also appeals to the self-interest of the other. Yet emotional involvement on one side of an issue makes it difficult to achieve the detachment necessary to think up wise ways of meeting the interests

of both sides: "We've got enough problems of our own; they can look after theirs." There also frequently exists a psychological reluctance to accord any legitimacy to the views of the other side; it seems disloyal to think up ways to satisfy them. Short-sighted self-concern thus leads a negotiator to develop only partisan positions, partisan arguments, and one-sided solutions.[101]

Such short-sightedness would come back to haunt Clifford and the rest of the Johnson administration in the fall.

Clifford left Saigon on July 18 and arranged a meeting upon his arrival in Honolulu with Johnson, Rusk, and Rostow before the president's summit conference with Thiệu the next morning. There, Clifford stressed his beliefs that there was "no way we can terminate the war militarily" at acceptable risk and cost, that the Saigon government did not want the conflict to end while it was protected by 540,000 American troops—"they'll let it drag on forever"; that South Vietnam was riddled with greed and corruption abetted by the deluge of American dollars flowing into the country; and therefore that the president should make an all-out effort to settle the war before his term of office ended because Saigon would never agree to a settlement until it became convinced of U.S. disengagement. Getting the United States out of Vietnam pronto had become Clifford's goal. He took the objective Johnson had defined and sought to put it into fast-forward. Focusing on the politics of the war—something always on his mind—Clifford reminded Johnson that the presumptive Republican presidential nominee, Richard Nixon (one of the strongest proponents for U.S. military involvement in Vietnam through 1965), had referred to "phasing out" U.S. troops and turning over more of the war to the South Vietnamese and the Republican Party's convention platform urged "de-Americanizing" the conflict. Every candidate except right-wing demagogue governor George Wallace of Alabama was moving away from the war. Rusk expressed disapproval of Clifford's emphasis on politics and disagreement with his proposed pace of disengagement. Rostow said nothing, but his frosty glare said everything. Johnson, ever sensitive to disagreement among his advisors, showed obvious discomfort, but after his one-on-one conference with Thiệu the next morning, he pulled Clifford aside, told him, "I am impressed by the points you made," and "I took them up with Thieu." Once again, Johnson had sided with Clifford in pursuit of disengagement.[102]

At that one-on-one meeting, Thiệu urged Johnson to take a hard line with Hanoi and insist the United States would not stop the bombing until all North Vietnamese troops withdrew from the South.* Johnson had never entertained such a condition because he and his advisors—both civilian and military—knew Hanoi would never accept it. But Thiệu pushed the idea, perhaps because he thought Johnson would agree, certainly because it served his interests. It was troubling evidence, a red flag—ignored by Johnson at the time (and later by Nixon)—that Thiệu might oppose any settlement crafted by the United States and reflecting U.S. interests. Americans overlooked this red flag because they had difficulty seeing the situation as Thiệu saw it. The ability to put oneself in another's shoes "is one of the most important skills a negotiator can possess," note Fisher and Ury. "It is not enough to know that they see things differently. If you want to influence them, you also need to understand empathetically the power of their point of view and to feel the emotional force with which they believe it. It is not enough to study them like beetles under a microscope; you need to know what it feels like to be a beetle."[103]

The Honolulu communiqué issued at the end of the two presidents' summit meeting diplomatically omitted any mention of Thiệu's proposal because Johnson did not want a confrontation with his South Vietnamese counterpart, whose cooperation he needed. But the issue would not go away just because it had been finessed, resurfacing in the months and years to come and serve as a powerful reminder that a great power's ability to get out of a war—

---

* Thiệu would cling tenaciously to a hard-line position for the next four years—a sign of how vulnerable Saigon felt about its ability to cope with the Communists on its own, and of how inadequate for the task ARVN was and would remain.

however much it wishes to do so—can be significantly affected by its subordinate partner's recalcitrance, which can produce a paradoxical tyranny of the weak, in which the tail wags the dog.

Johnson returned to a capital shifting its focus to the upcoming election. Robert Kennedy's assassination in June had ensured Hubert Humphrey's nomination as the Democratic presidential candidate. Unlike today, when caucus and primary voters determine the nominee, in 1968 state and local party leaders effectively controlled the nominating process. They would not accept the iconoclastic antiwar candidate Senator Eugene McCarthy, and Humphrey had been a leading light of the party since his stirring civil rights speech at the 1948 Democratic National Convention, then as senator from Minnesota, and finally as Johnson's vice president. Humphrey had not shaped administration policy on Vietnam, but he, too, had become hostage to it by the summer of 1968. The war's increasing unpopularity put pressure on Humphrey to distance himself from Johnson on Vietnam in order to win in November. Humphrey's advisors urged him to support a bombing halt to convince antiwar voters that he would be more ready to compromise than the president.

Johnson bristled at the thought that Humphrey might move away from him and even repudiate administration policy by urging greater concessions to Hanoi in pursuit of peace, which Johnson considered unwise and that, in his pride and insecurity, he considered a personal affront by the man whom he had made vice president. Clifford, who knew Johnson well, explained how LBJ's self-pity catalyzed a vindictive undermining of the ticket. "The Presidency meant so much to Johnson . . . He wasn't just the President, he had brought the Presidency to its final flower, and the Presidency and Johnson were indistinguishable. To have a Democrat, one whom the President considered infinitely junior to him, come in and become President, become the most important Democrat in the country, would relegate Johnson to a small, unimportant role from then on. However, should Nixon win, Johnson would remain the leading Democrat in the country. Humphrey would be relegated to the backwash of defeated candidates who are nothing, and Johnson would continue to be the ex-President and would be consulted by Nixon and others. All of that was very appealing to him."[104]

His ego again getting in the way of wisdom, Johnson acted accordingly. He told his advisors at a Tuesday Lunch on July 24 that "when [Nixon] gets the [Republican] nomination, he may be more responsible . . . The GOP may be of more help to [the country] than the Democrats."[105] Johnson decided to meet with Nixon to sound out his position on Vietnam. At their meeting two days later, Johnson called rumors that Humphrey might support a bombing halt "a very bad thing," given that Hanoi had made no reciprocal concessions since the president's March 31st speech and MACV reported evidence of an impending third wave Communist offensive. "We have taken the first step [and] if [Hanoi] will take a step, we will take other steps. But they are not doing that," he said. Stirred by his own words, Johnson blurted that "we're not losing the war, . . . we're very close to winning it," then backpedaled as his anger and emotions subsided and reality once again set in, forcing him to

LBJ Meets with Republican Candidate Richard Nixon
World History Archive/Alamy Stock Photo

admit to Nixon that he "wouldn't say that exactly." Nixon cagily encouraged Johnson without indicating what he would say and do during the fall election campaign, skillfully portraying himself as more sympathetic than Humphrey to the president's position on Vietnam.[106] The Republican's clever tactic worked: Johnson told a White House aide that "it would be better for the country" for Nixon to win if Humphrey "didn't stick firm on Vietnam."[107]

Johnson's frustration with Humphrey echoed his frustration with the larger dilemma he confronted. "God, I want to be a hero, I want to get the war over," he told New Jersey governor Richard Hughes in a phone conversation on July 30, but "I just can't do any more than I'm doing that I know of." Johnson remained open, as he had said in San Antonio the previous September, to stopping the bombing if it led to negotiations and Hanoi promised not to take advantage of it. But at present Hanoi "wanted something for nothing, and that I will not give them," and he could not bring himself to "say to the men at the DMZ [demilitarized zone] and all through I Corps that I'm going to increase the weight you're carrying . . . by taking away from you your most important weapon."[108] To Clifford, he seemed "all wound up" and determined not to capitulate.[109] Having insisted that Hanoi concede something in return for an American bombing halt, Johnson found it hard to bend.

LBJ's position on the bombing reflected a tendency of people known to behavioral economists and decision theorists as the "reluctance to trade" or the "endowment effect." "What one side is willing to give up," notes Thomas Gilovich, "tends to loom larger to that side than to the side receiving it, with the result that agreements with which both sides would be happy are difficult to achieve."[110] Daniel Kahneman and Richard Thaler conducted an experiment that illustrated this principle at work. They gave a mug worth $6 to half of the participants, whom they designated the Sellers. The other half of the participants were designated the Buyers. The results were dramatic: the Sellers only agreed to part with their mugs for $12—and the number of sales was less than half what was expected. Then, Kahneman and Thaler added a third group to the experiment, the Choosers, who, unlike the Buyers, could either receive a mug without paying or get an amount of money they thought the mug was worth. The Choosers set a value for a mug at less than half what the Sellers did—even though they faced the same choice: going home with either a mug or money.[111] "The disadvantages of a change," concluded Kahneman, "loom larger than its advantages, inducing a bias that favors the status quo."[112] Johnson exhibited a similar bias. The high value that he attached to the bombing made him reluctant to give it up. His reluctance was reinforced by his concern about the danger to American troops, his irritation at Humphrey's deviation, and his sensitivity to the chiefs' opposition to a halt.

Johnson's stubbornness on the bombing also reflected his fear and insecurity about de-escalation and disengagement, which meant not only accepting a step—the cessation of bombing—whose consequences he could neither anticipate nor control, but accepting personal failure as commander in chief and involving himself in a peace process in which he could not be sure of controlling the results. Johnson hated the unknown. "He wanted to control everything," presidential aide Joseph Califano recalled. "His greatest outbursts of anger were triggered by people or situations that escaped his control."[113] He also hated giving up the last military card in his already weak hand. When repeatedly pushed by Clifford to do just that in order to get things off diplomatic dead center, Johnson would fly into fits of rage, convinced that his defense secretary was intriguing with others in the Pentagon and the White House to tie his hands. He told Clifford he would not succumb to the "campaign" against his view and to "lay off the line" that a bombing halt would have negligible military consequences.[114] On those occasions, "he was colder than a whore's heart," recalled Clifford. "He'd say, 'Here is Clifford, he's a dependable guy, but he turned out to be kind of a Judas.' He was listening to me, but, oh boy, the relationship was really deteriorating every day."[115] Johnson's rage toward his old friend reflected his anxiety over the uncertainty that de-escalation and disengagement entailed, his obstinacy expressing itself through his mantra, "Stopping the bombing would be too dangerous."

LBJ's hardened position on the bombing worried Clifford, who understood a halt's central importance to breaking the logjam in Paris. "The President understood why I was doing what I had to do," Clifford reflected, "but there was still a sense of resentment because it made life so difficult for him."[116] Clifford believed the president would come around, that he could settle it all with Johnson if the two of them could just sit down and talk—the only alternative, Clifford told Rusk, was to "keep on fighting and having our men killed indefinitely."[117] (In 1968, an average of 45 Americans died in Vietnam every day.) But Clifford could not do so unless and until Johnson asked.

It was not the stubborn man who clung desperately to the bombing as his only leverage with Hanoi, but the anguished man longing for a peace agreement who invited Clifford to his Texas ranch the weekend of August 3–4. (When Clifford received Johnson's invitation, he quipped to his staff, "Well, I guess I've got to look at those goddamn cows one more time."[118]) Clifford flew down on a government jet—the ranch had its own airstrip—Saturday afternoon. The following evening, the two men sat down together in the wood-paneled living room of the main ranch house for their first one-on-one conversation on Vietnam in months. Johnson had "left his rage behind in Washington, and seemed prepared to listen," Clifford later wrote.[119] Seeking to assuage Johnson's distress and self-doubt, Clifford approached his old friend like he would any client, patiently talking him through his quandary. He told the president that he had fulfilled his obligations to the South Vietnamese many times over—the country had been saved from subjugation, the Communists had been prevented from taking over the cities, ARVN had been strengthened. But another reality also had to be acknowledged: North Vietnam could continue the war indefinitely but the United States could not because of declining domestic support. It was imperative to recognize these facts and to begin the process of disengagement in Paris.

Knowing a bombing halt was the main obstacle in Paris, Clifford carefully explained why a halt would not put U.S. troops in additional jeopardy. It would not lead to increased infiltration be-

cause bombing had interdicted a mere 7 percent of men and materiel even before it had been limited on March 31. The air campaign
in North Vietnam had never determined the scale of fighting in
South Vietnam and never would. Infiltration levels depended not
on the bombing but on the amount of effort exerted by the North
Vietnamese, and while bombing undoubtedly raised the cost to
North Vietnam of moving men and materiel into South Vietnam,
it did not significantly reduce the flow reaching South Vietnam.*
As had been the pattern for more than three years, the more the
U.S. bombed, the more trucks and men Hanoi sent South,† with
the Soviet Union and China providing the supplies and paying the
bills. Stop the bombing, Clifford told Johnson—it would either lead
to substantive talks to end the war or expose Hanoi's insincerity, in
which case the bombing could be resumed immediately. The alternative was continuing on a path that Clifford considered hopeless
and senseless.

When he finished, Johnson, who had been patiently listening
with a darkening face, said in a pleasant voice, "Clark, that's all
very interesting, but I don't agree with a word that you have said."
It was a courteously cutting remark made by a bitter man. But a
part of Johnson—the anguished realist rather than the stubborn
and insecure fighting cock—refused to slam the door. He told Clifford to put his ideas in writing and discuss them with Rusk.[120] "The
trouble," Johnson later told Clifford in a private Oval Office conversation, "is I think you are wrong, but when you begin to tell me
about it, then I don't think you're as wrong as I think you ought to
be . . . I just prefer that you tell me instead of telling it in front of

---

* The cost of bombing for the United States was not insignificant: measured in 2018
dollars, the U.S. inflicted $2.1 billion of damage on North Vietnam, but it expended
$6.4 billion doing so.

† After March 31, U.S. bombing sorties increased 260 percent and the concentration
of bombs and shells increased 2,000 percent. Despite this, the quantity of supplies
that North Vietnam shipped to the South doubled and the number of troops increased 70 percent. See *U.S. Air Force Magazine,* April 1969; and Military History
Institute of Vietnam, *Victory in Vietnam: The Official History of the People's Army of
Vietnam, 1954–1975* (University of Kansas Press, 2002), p. 227.

everybody." Johnson continued to give Clifford a chance, as Clifford said, looking back, "to make the argument that I knew ahead of time he didn't want to hear."[121]

Whatever headway Clifford made at the ranch was undercut by Hanoi's third wave offensive* that began two weeks later. Pressure from the chiefs to maintain—even increase—the bombing flared again, and Johnson concluded that a halt in the midst of this latest assault would increase U.S. losses and prolong, rather than shorten, the war. The Communists' offensive continued through the end of September, but the attacks again failed to spark a general uprising among the South Vietnamese people, and the Vietcong and U.S. forces sustained another punishing round of casualties (approximately 20,000). The number of American deaths rose to 308 and 408 in successive weeks, and by late August, polls showed that more than twice as many Americans (61 percent†) opposed a bombing halt as favored one (24 percent) even as antiwar activists grew increasingly disaffected. Meanwhile, since the March on the Pentagon in November, a part of the antiwar movement had grown more radicalized, not only siding with the Vietnamese but the Communists who were killing Americans. These increasingly fanatic groups, like Johnson, were becoming imprisoned by emotion.

This domestic division played out in Chicago during the Democratic National Convention in late August. Radical protestors—many of them middle-class college students angered by the war and passionately opposed to Johnson and Humphrey—vowed to disrupt the proceedings. The Democratic mayor of Chicago, Rich-

---

* The third and final phase of the Communists' 1968 offensive, which began on August 17 and lasted for five weeks.

† Much of this "silent majority" would vote in November for Nixon and the third-party populist candidate, segregationist George Wallace, whose appeal to blue-collar voters in the North and South drew many more votes away from Nixon than Humphrey. The only two senators who voted against the Tonkin Gulf Resolution in 1964—Ernest Gruening of Alaska and Wayne Morse of Oregon—both lost their reelection bids in 1968. No comparable penalties befell senators and representatives who staunchly supported the war.

ard Daley, vowed to maintain law and order with his 12,000-man police force. Chain-link fencing topped with barbed wire went up around the convention site at the International Amphitheater just south of downtown. National Guardsmen and U.S. Army troops went on high alert as thousands of antiwar protestors gathered in the city. Machine-gun emplacements went up along Michigan Avenue, the main downtown thoroughfare paralleling the lake. Within the downtown Loop, police—nearly all working-class and preemptively allergic to those they saw as coddled elites—were stationed on every corner and in the middle of every block. Helicopters patrolled over the city as firefighters stood ready to deal with bomb throwers.

On August 25, the day before the convention began, hundreds of protestors—some of them waving Vietcong flags—assembled in Lincoln Park a mile north of the Loop and began heckling and taunting the police, chanting "Fuck the pigs!," "Ho-Ho-Ho Chi Minh, NLF is Gonna Win!," and "Two-Four-Six-Eight, Organize and Smash the State!" Helmeted police armed with billy clubs and tear gas charged into the crowd and brutally drove protestors out of the park, sparking a running street battle that lasted well into the night. Skirmishes continued for the next several days, police wielding batons, protestors throwing rocks and bottles, shouting "Sieg, Heil!" and "Kill the pigs!" The climax (or low point) came on August 28, when protestors chanting "Fuck you, LBJ!" started out from Grant Park toward the International Amphitheater on the night of the presidential balloting. At the intersection of Michigan Avenue and East Balbo Drive, across the street from the Hilton Hotel housing convention delegates, a triple line of angry policemen awaited them. TV trucks covering the convention recorded the melee that followed. Nightsticks and rocks flew through the air as police teargassed demonstrators, reporters, and bystanders and dragged protestors kicking and screaming, blood running down their faces, to waiting paddy wagons while the wounded and terrified shouted, "The whole world is watching!" The images of helpless demonstrators beaten senseless swept live across a stunned and disbelieving nation. As civil order collapsed in the streets,

Democratic unity in the convention hall fractured as well. Liberal senator Abraham Ribicoff of Connecticut condemned "Gestapo tactics in the streets of Chicago," sparking Daley and his aides on the convention floor to shake their fists at him and shout back obscenities. "How hard it is to accept the truth," retorted Ribicoff, staring down at Daley from the podium. "How hard it is."* The Vietnam War had become a war within the Democratic Party and America itself.

The nationally publicized debacle in Chicago revealed how precipitously Johnson and the Democratic Party had fallen since his landslide election just four years before because of Vietnam. The violence also stoked Johnson's anger and paranoia about antiwar protestors whom he saw as "Communist infiltrated, Communist supported, and aggravated"[122] and reignited his hard line on the bombing.† A distressed Clifford set out once more to persuade the president. During a five-and-a-half-hour dinner at the White House on September 24—arranged, tellingly, at Johnson's request—Clifford again pleaded with him to test Hanoi's earnestness by stopping the bombing (resuming it if Hanoi did not respond) as a way to lower the level of hostilities and look toward a resolution of the conflict. "Only five percent of our [military] assets is the bombing" of North Vietnam, he told the president, pointing out that troop activity and B-52 strikes in South Vietnam "are what is doing things. We keep 95 percent of our strength and give up only five percent to get movement in Paris." Johnson again grumbled about stopping the bombing without any reciprocal concession, but he seemed to Clifford "more friendly" and "less emotional" than he had been in months. "Instead of a rough, brutal, and adamant position," Clifford recounted to his Pentagon staff the next morn-

---

* Two months later, the presidentially appointed National Violence Commission's *Walker Report* characterized what had taken place as a "police riot."

† Johnson was far from alone in his suspicions and antipathies; letters poured into Chicago City Hall commending the police for giving the demonstrators "what they deserved." A Gallup poll revealed that 56 percent of Americans approved of what the Chicago police had done.

ing, "he heard me out." Johnson even directed Clifford to repeat his points to Rostow and Wheeler at an NSC meeting the next day. Clifford's arguments were sinking in with the president.[*][123]

Despite North Vietnam's adamant stance on bombing, Hanoi's offensive had failed in its overall objectives, the Vietcong had suffered more heavy losses, and Politburo leaders increasingly realized they could not achieve the decisive military breakthrough they had doggedly sought since Tet. Lê Duẩn and his Politburo colleagues anticipated that Johnson would feel pressure to stop the bombing as the presidential election neared because he wanted to be viewed by history as a peace president who would end the war as rapidly as the French-Indochina War had ended at Geneva in 1954. They also assumed he wanted to help Humphrey's chances in a tightening race with Richard Nixon, whom Politburo leaders considered more "obstinate" (*ngoan cố*) and hawkish on the war. Since the spring, Hanoi had been marking time in Paris, but now it shifted tactics, prioritizing negotiating efforts over military ones,[†] and decided to move ahead quickly into substantive discussions once the bombing ceased. The Politburo instructed its negotiators in Paris to adopt a more flexible line in order to facilitate America's disengagement.

On October 11, Xuân Thủy and another envoy recently dispatched to Paris, Lê Đức Thọ, asked Harriman and Vance if Washington would stop the bombing if Hanoi agreed to Saigon's participation at the talks—something that Washington had always demanded

---

[*] Unbeknownst to Clifford, Johnson told Senate Majority Leader Mike Mansfield in a telephone call later that "I really wish I had Clifford in those negotiations because, God, he's smart and able and tough." Telephone Conversation between President Johnson and Senator Mike Mansfield, October 16, 1968, 9:34 A.M., *Foreign Relations of the United States, 1964–1968, Volume VII: Vietnam, September 1968–January 1969*, pp. 213–216.

[†] Henceforward, the Vietcong and the NVA (unlike the Vietcong, largely undiminished by the 1968 offensives) would rebuild their strength and revert to harassing actions and guerrilla warfare in which they once again controlled their casualties and played the waiting game. They would maintain this posture until the Americans left—then adopt conventional warfare against the inferior South Vietnamese army, which they decisively defeated in a conventional invasion in the spring of 1975.

and that Hanoi had always refused for fear that Saigon's presence would complicate the negotiations and delay the withdrawal of U.S. forces. Thủy and Thọ concluded by saying that serious discussions could now begin and rapid progress made if Washington was determined to move toward peace.[124] Hanoi had finally offered what Johnson had been seeking since March 31: a reciprocal concession for a bombing halt.

The election was less than a month away. Johnson knew some Americans would think he was stopping the bombing to influence the outcome, that Nixon would be disappointed and suspect a political trick, that opponents of the war would chastise him for not having done it much sooner, and that supporters of the war would accuse him of risking the lives of American boys. But there was no way he could gauge how seriously Hanoi wanted a settlement until both sides got down to bargaining. "If this isn't the way of stopping [the war]," he told his advisors, "I don't have another way to end it."[125] The global struggle against Communism sometimes felt almost irrelevant when compared to the tragedy of sending more Americans to their doom. After once seeing off soldiers of the army's 82nd Airborne Division at Fort Bragg, North Carolina, LBJ had told his advisors, "Those boys . . . it was obvious to me that none of them was happy to be going." From Fort Bragg he had traveled on to Southern California, where he had seen off marines gathered in a hangar at Marine Corps Air Station El Toro, waiting to board transport planes for Vietnam. "I walked down rows of men. I told myself—I am at heart a sentimental guy at times like those—that I sure regret having to send those men. One soldier really melted me and brought me to my knees. I asked a boy from Ohio if he had been to Vietnam before. He said yes, he had been there four times. I asked him if he had a family. He said, yes sir, he had a little baby boy born yesterday. There wasn't a tear in his eye. No bitterness showed on his face. But I can assure you I sure stopped asking any men questions for a while."*[126] Johnson's

---

* He had told Harriman and Vance weeks earlier, "For God's sake, try to get some kind of peace in my time, I have given up everything to try to do it, and I want it

thoughts and feelings boiled down to: "I don't want to be the one to have it said about [him] that one man died tomorrow who could have been saved because of this." He added, "I'm going to get peace any day I can if it's right up to the night of the election 'cause I got a lot of boys out there and I want to stop killing them when I can."[127]

Word went out to Saigon, and Bunker and Abrams cabled back that "a complete cessation of bombing . . . need not worry us excessively." Vietcong operations had declined significantly since the third wave offensive and the monsoon rains had begun, making the military effects of a halt negligible because low cloud cover made identifying targets on the ground almost impossible. Also, NVA forces had regrouped to sanctuaries in Laos and Cambodia, so bombing efforts could be shifted outside of Vietnamese borders.* "We can handle whatever they send down," the two men said.[128] Abrams's assurance relieved Johnson, alleviating his long-standing anxiety that U.S. forces might be put in jeopardy by a halt.†

A thoughtful military officer despite his tough image and gruff demeanor—he chewed cigars (of good quality) but listened to Mozart and Wagner—"Abe" Abrams understood the political dimensions of the war far better than Westmoreland, who had been his classmate in the West Point Class of 1936 and whom he had succeeded as MACV commander in June.‡ Clifford considered Abrams "quiet, logical, and unemotional"—a distinct improvement over his predecessor, of whom Clifford observed, "the more you got to

---

honorable but I want it." Telephone Conversation between President Johnson and Senator Mike Mansfield, October 16, 1968, 9:34 A.M., *FRUS, 1964–1968, Volume VII*, pp. 213–216.

* After the bombing halt, U.S. sorties in Laos in November 1968 nearly tripled to 12,000 from 4,400 in November 1967.

† Johnson received Wheeler's and the chiefs' support as well—for similar reasons—at an NSC meeting on October 14. He wanted them on the record so that they couldn't criticize him later. See Notes of Meeting, October 14, 1968, *FRUS, 1964–1968, Volume VII*, pp. 185–196.

‡ Westmoreland returned to Washington and became army chief of staff, a position he held until his retirement in July 1972.

know Westy, the more you found out that he was a nice man and had the appearance of exactly the kind of general you would want, but you go beyond that and you don't find anything."[129] Abrams was reticent rather than talkative and photogenic. "He would call a spade a spade, and if things looked bad, he would say they looked bad," said a military colleague.[130] He moved out of Westmoreland's high-ceilinged, French-style villa shaded by tall trees into a smaller, simpler bungalow near MACV headquarters. When he visited ARVN headquarters, he drove his own jeep, eschewing West-moreland's multivehicle procession complete with sirens. He also habitually wore rumpled field fatigues and a soft cap rather than Westmoreland's usual crisply starched spit-and-polish uniform. Abrams's responsibility for the advisory relationship with ARVN forces during his tenure as Westmoreland's deputy had sensitized him to the South Vietnamese point of view, and he interacted with ARVN generals with restraint and candor, not with his predecessor's stiff formality and barely disguised impatience. Instead of opening with a bland statement about how well things were going, as Westmoreland customarily did, Abrams began by sharing his

General Creighton Abrams
Yoichi Okamoto/LBJ Library

problems in a frank and personal way, which encouraged his South Vietnamese counterparts to do the same.

Since taking command, Abrams had implemented the recommendations of the PROVN study two years earlier, shifting the strategy away from attrition and body counts to protecting the population while minimizing civilian casualties, moving from large-unit sweeps to small-unit patrols in order to eliminate enemy forces in hamlets and villages, and building up ARVN. He realized that indiscriminate destruction alienated the population, undermining whatever results might be achieved by combat operations. Abrams also understood that the American public's patience was running out and the president wanted to begin disengagement. He, too, believed the war "ought to be ended at the conference table."[131] Abrams knew he would not be getting any more American troops, so he pursued Johnson's program of expanding, equipping, and training ARVN and assigning them an ever-increasing combat role. "We have to get ARVN ready to stand on their own feet," he told his staff at meeting after meeting. "If we're ever going to get out of here, we've got to do more to get them ready to take over."[132] It was a difficult situation for an American general in the field, but Abrams accepted it and made the most of it.

Bunker also sought and received Thiệu's agreement to the bombing halt. "Thieu concurs in instructions to be given Harriman-Vance," he informed Washington on October 13. Bunker sent a more detailed message the following day. "I must confess I thought Thieu would want to think over-night before providing an answer," the ambassador cabled, "but he responded immediately and unequivocally . . . Thieu said so long as we are going to press the offensive in the South and in Laos, and so long as we are prepared to resume the bombing if they violate the DMZ or attack the cities, he is ready to go along. 'After all,' he said, 'the main problem is not to stop the bombing but to stop the war, and we must try this path to see if they are serious.' I thought this a statesman's view."[133] But while Thiệu seemed to be in favor of Washington's plan without reservations, he and Washington had not discussed or agreed on the *goal* to be sought at Paris.

Then, Hanoi unexpectedly hardened its position. Washington
had suggested a twenty-four-hour interval between a bombing halt
and the start of negotiations. But on October 15, Lê Duẩn and other
Politburo hardliners, not wanting to appear too eager, began drag-
ging their feet on setting a date for the beginning of talks following
a halt. Thủy parried Harriman and Vance's requests to set a start
date until he received further instructions from Hanoi, which told
its delegation, "We should go step by step, lest the U.S. think that
we accept too easily."[134] At Washington's urging, Moscow pressed
the North Vietnamese to begin negotiations, and on October 20
Hanoi instructed Thủy and Thọ to start serious talks within seven
to ten days of a bombing halt—that is, before the U.S. presidential
election on November 5. Agreement finally came on October 27,
when the North Vietnamese proposed, and the United States accepted, stopping the bombing on October 30 and beginning talks
on November 3.[135] Everything, it seemed, was now back on track.

It was not. Washington and Hanoi's disagreement over how
quickly to begin negotiations had created a fateful delay. During
this interim period, the wily and increasingly anxious Thiệu re-
neged on his promise to attend the Paris talks. On October 18, he
informed the United States that he would not participate if the NLF
attended as well, even though it had been he who had originally
suggested the "our side-your side" formula as a way to bring all
sides in the Vietnamese conflict to the table.[136] Sitting down with
the ostensibly independent South Vietnamese NLF had always
bothered Thiệu, who feared doing so would bestow recognition
and respectability on what he considered a tool of Hanoi (the mirror image of how Hanoi viewed him: a tool of Washington) while
undermining his legitimacy and increasing the prospects of a coalition government. He was no dummy: the South Vietnamese embassy in Washington had been following the presidential campaign
with growing alarm as Humphrey's poll numbers increased the
more he appealed to the gathering tide of antiwar sentiment. On
September 30, Humphrey made a major speech in Salt Lake City in
which he advocated a bombing halt and the "de-Americanization"

of the war as "an acceptable risk for peace," which Thiệu interpreted as a departure from established policy and even a trial bal-
loon by the Johnson administration. A few days later, Humphrey
advocated a "systematic reduction of the American forces" in
South Vietnam. These statements made Thiệu nervous and distrustful of the Johnson administration and the Democratic Party.
Yet as Humphrey moved leftward on the war, he began narrowing
Nixon's once commanding lead in the polls—from 43 percent for
Nixon, 28 percent for Humphrey, and 15 percent for Wallace in
mid-September to 44 percent for Nixon, 36 percent for Humphrey,
and 15 percent for Wallace in mid-October. Undecided voters were
breaking for Humphrey.

Anyone following the news could see that Nixon's position on
Vietnam, though vague—Nixon implied that he had a plan to end
the war (even touching his breast pocket as if the plan were right
there) but said he didn't want to do anything that might "prejudice the Paris negotiations"—was more hawkish than Humphrey's.
This included Thiệu, who worried that in their anxiety the Democrats would concede too much. Fearing the Paris talks and having
played no part in arranging them, Thiệu recognized the military
and economic advantages in America's continued involvement and
he knew he would be more vulnerable if Washington achieved a
settlement with Hanoi and departed. With seemingly little to gain
by an American withdrawal, Thiệu calculated that he would get
a better settlement the longer he waited—so long as the United
States continued to carry the brunt of the fighting and to expend
vast sums of money on its South Vietnamese ally. Concluding that
Nixon's position on Vietnam—an "honorable peace," achieved by
unspecified actions—more closely aligned with his own interests,
he decided to thwart the negotiations in the hope that Nixon would
succeed Johnson.

Nixon, for his part, believed Johnson's motivation and timing
regarding the Paris talks reflected more than diplomatic considerations alone. He suspected Johnson of plotting an "October surprise" to tip the election to his fellow Democrat. Nixon's concern
centered mostly on the actions of Humphrey's chief foreign policy

advisor, George Ball (recently resigned as Johnson's U.N. ambassador). In late September, Ball had sent a partner, George Fitzgibbon,
in his Manhattan investment banking firm, Lehman Brothers, to
Paris to consult with Harriman and Vance about Humphrey's
Salt Lake City speech advocating a bombing halt, which the two
American negotiators also strongly favored as a way to get talks
started and to help elect Humphrey.* Johnson learned of the Ball-
Fitzgibbon channel from Vance when Vance returned to Washington for consultations in early October. Johnson told Vance that
he disapproved of U.S. government negotiators collaborating with
the Humphrey campaign, but he did not recall Vance or Harriman from Paris, nor did he inform Nixon of the Ball-Fitzgibbon
channel.[137]

Nixon got wind of the Ball-Fitzgibbon channel through Bryce
Harlow, a Republican lobbyist in Washington and Nixon campaign
advisor who had worked with Vice President Nixon as a staffer in
the Eisenhower White House and who, as an Oklahoman, maintained close contacts with Texans in the Johnson administration.†
Harlow had "a double agent working in the White House," he
later recalled. "I knew what their next move was going to be. I
kept Nixon informed." Harlow told Nixon that Johnson's "going to
dump on you" by announcing a bombing halt that would tip the
election to Humphrey.[138] Although Nixon had concurred with
the importance of getting the South Vietnamese to the conference
table,[139] and had vowed that he did "not want to play politics with
peace,"[140] he did not trust Johnson or his motives. Viewing (then
and later) election ethics as an oxymoron, Nixon began secretly
lobbying Thiệu to stall as a way to counter Johnson's "political maneuver." He did so using a secret channel he had set up earlier in
the year that included his campaign manager (and later attorney

---

* Around this time, Harriman told a reporter on the record, "We're engaged in negotiations and in that capacity I'm taking no part in the campaign." See Telephone
Conversation between President Johnson and Secretary of State Rusk, October 3,
1968, *FRUS, 1964–1968, Volume VII*, p. 131.

† Harlow later became one of Nixon's first White House appointments—counselor
to the president, with Cabinet rank.

general) John Mitchell; Anna Chan Chennault, a prominent Republican fund-raiser, Washington hostess, and leading figure in the pro-Taiwan "China Lobby" as the widow of Flying Tigers* leader General Claire Chennault; and South Vietnamese ambassador to Washington Bùi Diễm. Mitchell had become a close friend of the candidate during their six years together at a Manhattan law firm, and Nixon trusted his stony-faced, tight-lipped associate with his most sensitive political assignments. A small, intense, and energetic woman, Chennault maintained close contacts with the Saigon government (among them, her sister Connie, the wife of Taiwan's commercial affairs officer in Saigon, and Thiệu's brother Nguyễn Văn Hiếu, South Vietnam's ambassador to Taiwan). Like most supporters of the Nationalist Chinese, Chennault blamed Washington, rather than the corruption and incompetence of Chiang Kai Shek, for the "loss" of her beloved China to Mao's Communists, and she opposed peace negotiations with Hanoi because she believed Washington would abandon Thiệu just as she believed it had abandoned Chiang in 1949. Bùi Diễm, a small, wiry, affable, and canny man who had turned from journalism to diplomacy, represented Thiệu in Washington, where he met regularly with top Johnson administration officials, who kept him informed of the Paris negotiations, and came to know leading Republicans through Anna Chennault's salon in her Watergate penthouse apartment. Nixon told Bùi Diễm to convey messages from Thiệu through Chennault, and she would relay them from Nixon through Mitchell. In this way, Nixon could maintain "plausible deniability," preventing anyone from directly linking him to the caper. The South Vietnamese ambassador agreed to participate in this back channel because he, too, believed Nixon would secure Saigon a better deal.

On October 15, Thiệu informed Bùi Diễm that a breakthrough in Paris was imminent. Bùi Diễm passed the information on to Chennault, who notified Nixon through Mitchell using a private

---

* The Flying Tigers was an American volunteer air squadron that flew combat missions in China against invading Japanese forces in the years before Pearl Harbor brought the United States into the war on December 7, 1941.

phone number that Mitchell changed every few days to avoid surveillance. On October 22, Nixon instructed his close aide (and later White House chief of staff) H. R. Haldeman to tell Mitchell to "keep Anna Chennault working on" Thiệu and urge him—in Nixon's words—to secretly "monkey wrench" the peace talks in Paris.[141] (Cognizant of the impropriety of their conversations, Mitchell told Chennault, "Call me from a pay phone. Don't talk in your office.") His message to her: "Don't let him [Thiệu] go" to Paris.[142] Nixon also lobbied Thiệu through Bùi Diễm. On October 23, Bùi Diễm cabled Saigon: "Many Republican friends have contacted me and encouraged us to stand firm."[143] The information was transferred to Thiệu, who soon informed Chennault that he "would much prefer to have the peace talks after [Nixon's] election" and that she should "convey this message to your candidate."[144] On October 27, Bùi Diễm informed Thiệu that he had "explained discreetly to our partisan friends our firm attitude" and "plan to adhere to that position." He hastened to add, "The longer the impasse continues, the more "difficulties" Johnson would have "in forcing our hand."[145]

Johnson learned of Nixon's skullduggery on October 29 through National Security Agency intercepts of Bùi Diễm's cables to Thiệu and a CIA bug in Thiệu's office. The next day, he ordered the FBI to tap Anna Chennault's phone based on possible violation of federal laws dealing with contacts between private citizens and foreign governments. He informed Humphrey about Chennault and Bùi Diễm's activities on November 1, four days before Election Day. An incensed Johnson spoke to Nixon by phone and asked him point-blank if he was involved. "My God," Nixon replied, "I would never do anything to encourage . . . Saigon not to come to the table because . . . we want them over in Paris. We've got to get them to Paris, or you can't have a peace."[146] Whatever Chennault had done had been on her own, without his knowledge or approval. (This falsehood followed on the heels of a statement Nixon had released just days earlier addressing rumors about "a cynical, last-minute attempt by President Johnson to salvage the candidacy of Mr. Humphrey," saying he did "not believe" them[147]—Nixon's time-tested technique of making a statement full of sly insinuations and then denying them through pious disassociation.) Clifford told Johnson that releasing the evidence publicly would justifiably ruin Nixon's chances to get elected, but the absence of absolute proof of Nixon's culpability militated against distribution. "No matter how completely we could implicate Anna Chennault," Clifford later explained, "we could not tie it to Dick Nixon or anybody high up in his campaign."[148] Rusk concurred for different reasons; he feared exposure would reveal the strains between Saigon and Washington, thus stiffening Hanoi's position and disrupting the negotiations, while also damaging Thiệu's standing with the American public so severely that it might endanger U.S. support for South Vietnam. Humphrey decided not to make it an issue in the final days of the campaign for the same reasons that Johnson didn't— Bunker might still be able to change Thiệu's mind, there was no evidence of Nixon's direct involvement (which came to light only in 2017), and it might lead to exposure of the Humphrey campaign's secret Ball-Fitzgibbons channel to Harriman and Vance in Paris. Johnson (who privately called the affair "the damndest mess you ever saw"[149]) decided not to release the evidence of Thiệu's complicity with Nixon.

Johnson remained livid at the "son-of-a-bitch" Thiệu, whose behavior he considered "absolutely disgraceful," and Nixon, who he told aides was guilty of "treason."*[150] Johnson has "worked so hard" to get peace talks started, Clifford told his staff. "He's snake-bitten."[151] "Just as soon as we got sight of the promised land, they [Thiệu and Nixon] blew it," Johnson said.[152] He instructed Bunker to deliver a message to Saigon: "If President Thieu makes himself responsible for preventing the very peace talks which have cost so

---

* The 1799 Logan Act made it a felony for a private American citizen to interfere in diplomatic negotiations with a foreign government: "Any citizen of the United States, wherever he may be, who, without authority of the United States, directly or indirectly commences or carries on any correspondence or intercourse with any foreign government or any officer or agent thereof, with intent to influence the measures or conduct of any foreign government or of any officer or agent thereof, in relation to any disputes or controversies with the United States, or to defeat the measures of the United States, shall be fined under this title or imprisoned."

much to obtain, the people of this country would never forget the man responsible . . . If President Thieu keeps us from moving at this moment of opportunity, God help South Vietnam, because no President could maintain the support of the American people."[153]

In the end, Johnson decided to proceed without Thiệu. In a speech broadcast nationally at 8 P.M. on October 31, he announced that U.S. bombing of North Vietnam would stop in twelve hours and that serious talks with Hanoi would begin the day after the election, in which Saigon would be "free to participate." Johnson's departing-train strategy implied that talks would go forward whether or not Saigon joined them. The pressure did not work. Thiệu promptly branded Johnson's announcement a "unilateral" decision and said flatly he would not send anyone to Paris, telling journalists, "South Vietnam is not a truck to be attached to a locomotive which will pull it wherever it likes."[154] Thiệu would filibuster while awaiting a change of administrations. The spoiler had called his patron's bluff.

A deflated Johnson did not press the issue because, as Rusk later wrote, Washington "couldn't name a South Vietnamese delegation, tie its members into an airplane, and fly them to Paris in handcuffs when Thiệu gritted his teeth and refused to participate."[155] Nor did Johnson try to coerce Thiệu—for example, by threatening to cut off all U.S. military and economic aid, as some of his advisors recommended—for fear that such attempted coercion would shatter the alliance between Washington and Saigon, embolden Hanoi, and jeopardize a peace settlement. He knew that the peace process could not continue without everyone on board, so yet again Washington continued to support Saigon despite its behavior.

Later that night, Nixon solemnly declared at a rally in Madison Square Garden that neither he nor his vice presidential candidate would "say anything that might destroy the chance to have peace." Nixon even went so far as to have his staff tell reporters that he had been surprised by Thiệu's rejection and asked "why we didn't have the agreement worked out with our allies" since Johnson had led him to believe that "all the diplomatic ducks were in a row."[156] A few days later, he expressed sorrow that the "outlook was so bleak" and on NBC's *Meet the Press* two days before the American public went to the polls he even volunteered to go to Saigon or Paris after the election to "get these talks off dead center." A triumphant-feeling Thiệu told his private secretary, "This is nice. Now at least we have bought ourselves some time . . . We have some more rope to play with."[157]

Six days later, on November 5, Nixon won election as president with 43.4 percent of the vote to Humphrey's 42.7 percent—a margin of less than 500,000 votes out of more than 63 million cast.* The next day, Washington—its hand forced by the South Vietnamese—and Hanoi announced postponement of the Paris talks. They would not begin until January 25, 1969, after several more weeks of delay and deadlock caused by Saigon's objections to the shape of the negotiating table. Even then, little agreement existed within the executive branch on basic policy questions like America's negotiating position, how to define America's ultimate goal(s) in Vietnam, and what, specifically, Washington sought to achieve in the talks.

Did Nixon's deviousness and dishonesty—aspects of his character that would eventually prove his undoing during the Watergate crisis—substantively change things? It seems unlikely. The South Vietnamese president did not need to be lobbied very hard to balk at joining peace talks that he considered inherently disadvantageous, though, as William Bundy later wrote, "if he had not been told that he would have Nixon's support in holding back, he would surely have had to give greater weight to what refusing to go along could do to his chances of full support from any American President."[158] Thiệu doubted Hanoi's intentions and feared for his future in any negotiations even before he made and broke his promise to Johnson, and his doubts and fears persisted long after Nixon became president and negotiations in Paris eventually got underway. "I did not base my policy on a single personality but

---

* Nixon won the Electoral College by a larger margin—302 to 191. Wallace and his running mate, retired air force general Curtis LeMay, received nearly 10 million votes (13.5 percent)—most of which would have gone to Nixon if Wallace, who also appealed to hard-line opinion, had not been a candidate.

on the U.S. policy," he later explained. "I understood that U.S. policy was to negotiate a coalition [government] for South Vietnam, not win a military victory."[159] Thiệu always believed that he stood to lose in any settlement that ended a war in which he could not stand on his own militarily against the Vietcong and the North Vietnamese. As a result, he never saw the peace process as the best means for resolving the conflict. His sabotaging of the negotiations reflected self-protection, latent hostility at his own dependence on the United States, and—most important—the limitations that had always plagued Saigon and that made the prospects of a peace deal in which the American role would be substantially reduced highly problematic for Saigon. It was a position that made for great intransigence, as Nixon would discover to his own frustration in the years to come.

Johnson's problem would become Nixon's for the same underlying reasons: the tyranny of the weak would persist. Nixon's significant contribution was to make the problem worse. After four more years of war and 21,000 more American (and hundreds of thousands more Vietnamese) deaths, a period in which the United States would be torn apart by the worst internal strife in a century, Thiệu would defy Nixon (who had never clearly articulated to the South Vietnamese leader the hard limits of his own interests) on the eve of the 1972 election in a similar manner for similar reasons, refusing to sign a cease-fire agreement negotiated by the United States that allowed North Vietnamese forces to remain in South Vietnam after America's withdrawal, which Thiệu viewed as a crippling disadvantage. This led to Washington's attempt to revise the cease-fire terms, Hanoi's refusal to do so, and the "Christmas bombing"* that followed. After the Christmas bombing forced Hanoi back to the negotiating table, Washington pressured Thiệu to accept a fundamentally unchanged cease-fire agreement—or the

---

* Conducted December 18–29, 1972, Operation LINEBACKER II (as it was code-named) comprised the most concentrated U.S. bombing of the war. B-52s flying from U.S. air bases in Guam and Thailand targeted sites in Hanoi, Haiphong, and surrounding areas. The bombing destroyed war-related infrastructure, killed more than 1,500 civilians, and generated considerable international criticism.

United States would proceed on its own. Through these means, a peace treaty finally ending American involvement in the Vietnam War would not come until January 23, 1973.

Lyndon Johnson spent his final days as president a frustrated and humbled man. His political career and his party's electoral majority had been shattered by the war. Vietnam had deflected America's attention from other problems, torn the nation's social and political fabric, sapped its confidence in itself, soiled the country's reputation abroad, and led America's allies to question its strategic wisdom. (In a final insult, Saigon waited until five days after Johnson left the White House before joining the talks in Paris.) The hope and expectation Johnson had nursed since March 31 that he would bring American boys home from Vietnam by the time his term in office ended had proven a tragic illusion. Rather than a year of peace, 1968 had been one of unprecedented bloodshed. More American servicemen were killed in Vietnam in 1968—nearly 17,000—than in any other year of the war. By the end of 1968, as Johnson's days in the Oval Office rapidly dwindled, almost 37,000 Americans had perished in the conflict. That number had stood at 200 when Johnson had assumed the presidency, and responsibility for the war, in late November 1963. Hundreds of thousands of Vietnamese—North and South—died during the bloody year of 1968 as well, adding to the staggering death toll of Indochinese that had already surpassed a million, as the war continued to wreak immense destruction on the countries of Southeast Asia. America's snowballing military involvement in the war had been stopped, but America was no nearer extricating itself from Vietnam and the war raged unabated.

All of this remained on Johnson's mind when he gave his last public speech at the National Press Club only a few blocks from the White House, on Friday, January 17, 1969. The outgoing president began by harkening back to old days of campaigning, and as he reflected, the visibly drained Johnson, unexpectedly drawing energy from the audience, seemed to come to life for a moment, offering warm remarks and even demonstrating flashes of his earthy humor. But as he neared the end of his speech, he grew quiet and somber. Nevermore running for office, for the first time in nearly thirty years he wasn't seeking to win over voters with hyperbole or hokum. Instead, in his final public appearance, Johnson did something he had rarely done before—he spoke from the heart about his limitations and failures, inadequacies and uncertainties. His greatest disappointment about leaving the Oval Office the following Monday at noon, he confessed to those gathered before him, was "that peace has eluded me" and that he had failed "to bring back every boy I sent out there to Vietnam."[160] No one in the National Press Club audience listening to Johnson's painful words knew quite what to say. What could one say? It was as far as this proud, stubborn, sensitive, but deeply insecure man could go in confessing that he had made a terrible mistake, as far as he could go in making a public apology for it—the burdens and disappointments were just too great. He called it failure, because to call it regret would be too unbearable.

The Burden of Regret

Some regrets entail more burdens than others. Yet we can gain insights and wisdom by consciously registering the meaning of our choices, acknowledging regret to ourselves, and reflecting on the consequences in a way that shines instructional light on the future. This is the power of "backward thinking."[1]

Those principally responsible for Vietnam decision-making during the Kennedy and Johnson years wrestled with this burden, in varying degrees and in varying ways, throughout the remaining years of their lives. Of course there was no action to be taken that would bring back those who had perished or been scarred physically by wounds or emotionally by post-traumatic stress disorder. Exhausted, Lyndon Johnson returned to his beloved ranch on the Pedernales River in the Texas Hill Country. There, surrounded by oaks and cattle and the vast sky, he recuperated by spending time with his family, visiting with friends, and running the ranch from behind the wheel of his white Lincoln convertible, which gave him, however modest, a sense of control and allowed him to again bend at least some things to his will. At the same time, because of the war's unpopularity and his own—the hawks blamed him for not crushing North Vietnam and the doves detested the war and held him responsible for every ugly aspect of it—his retirement became a kind of exile suffused with the pain of diminished stature and public rejection.

The decisions on Vietnam had, ultimately, been his. He had lost the presidency, his political standing, his dreams of further domestic reform, his historical reputation as a war leader—the yardsticks by which he had always judged success in life. Because of Vietnam, Johnson became such a pariah in his own party that top officials made it clear they did not want him to attend the 1972 Democratic National Convention in Miami Beach that nominated an antiwar candidate, Senator George McGovern of South Dakota, a vocal Johnson critic, for the presidency. No image of Johnson as president appeared at the convention, only a small portrait of him as Senate majority leader in the 1950s that hung in a back room. "Lyndon just doesn't carry any weight in the party anymore, and he knows it," said a friend. "It's a miserable fact for a man who only four years ago was President of the United States. But it is a fact."[2] "My daddy committed political suicide for that war in Vietnam," his younger daughter, Luci, later said. "And since politics was his life, it was like committing actual suicide."[3]

Johnson's personal habits reflected his burden. Moody and hypersensitive to criticism all his life, out of office he became restless and suffered periodic fits of depression. When he reminisced, it was about the early days—helping build FDR's New Deal in Depression-era Texas—much less often about Vietnam, and then only in shielded tones. He grew his now white hair long—almost shoulder-length, swept back and curled on the ends like an Old Testament prophet—as if in silent sympathy with the young student radicals who had turned so vehemently against him and the war. For the first time since his heart attack in 1955, he resumed drinking more than moderately, started chain smoking again (two to three packs of cigarettes a day), and put on considerable weight—even after he suffered an episode of angina (a hardening of the arteries carrying blood from the heart)—dangerously and tellingly self-destructive behavior for a man in his sixties with a serious heart condition. He took to showing ranch visitors the carefully tended little family cemetery containing the graves of his mother and father, telling them here, too, he planned to be laid to rest.

Outside of his close circle, Johnson found it nearly impossible to speak from the heart about the war and to reflect on it with hindsight. Like many human beings, he avoided contemplating unpleasant things about himself in the interest of self-protectiveness, denying regret and hiding it from himself. Instead, he muffled the memory of Vietnam by defensive maneuvers. He published a bland and guarded memoir of his presidency, *The Vantage Point* (1971), in which the colorful, flesh-and-blood LBJ was largely absent. "What do you think this is," Johnson railed to an aide during the drafting, "the tale of an uneducated cowboy? It's a presidential memoir, damn it, and I've got to come out looking like a statesman, not some backwoods politician."[34] His insecurity never went away. As a result, the book's Vietnam sections reflected more of ghostwriter William Jorden, who had served on the NSC staff under Walt Rostow, than they did LBJ himself: a detailed but dry defense of judgment calls rather than a personal account of how and why he made them.

But implicitly, Johnson wanted to share the burden and tragedy of Vietnam with his countrymen, and to have others draw lessons—not flattering to him, as he well knew—from the worst foreign policy disaster in the country's history that divided the nation more deeply than any event since the Civil War (and, in a sense, continues to divide the nation to this day). On the eastern edge of the University of Texas campus in Austin he created a presidential library in which "it's all here, the story of our time—with the bark off," as he said at the library's dedication ceremony in May 1971. "There is no record of a mistake, nothing critical, ugly, or unpleasant that is not included in the files here." He was right. He encouraged the federal government and its agencies to expedite declassification of the records of his administration's decision-making on Vietnam, and the Johnson library became one of the most open presidential libraries in the country.

Johnson suffered another major heart attack in the spring of 1972. He survived this one, too, but afterward chest pains began hitting him every day and he started swallowing nitroglycerin tablets and gulping air from a portable oxygen tank. On the afternoon of January 22, 1973, alone in the bedroom at his Texas ranch, he died of a massive coronary at the age of sixty-four. He did not live to witness the signing of the peace agreement in Paris, only three days later, that finally ended American involvement in the Vietnam War.

After eight years in office, Dean Rusk left Foggy Bottom in January 1969 "bone-tired" after serving the second longest term as secretary of state in American history.* Before Rusk departed Washington for his native Georgia, Soviet ambassador Anatoly Dobrynin hosted a farewell dinner for him at the new Soviet embassy on Mount Alto in northwest D.C. Dobrynin found Rusk sad but stoic about Vietnam. Rusk conceded that mistakes had been committed, for which he felt considerable responsibility, but he offered no explanations or excuses. "What's done cannot be undone," said Rusk.[5] He would leave it to historians to pass their verdict.

Out of power, out of work, and lacking independent means like many of his government colleagues with a Wall Street background, Rusk struggled to adjust to his newly diminished circumstances and his unpopularity among liberals, many of whose views he had shared and championed as president of the Rockefeller Foundation in the 1950s. "I had trouble trying to wind down from the job," he confessed, looking back many years later.[6] Having survived his last year as secretary of state largely on pertinacity, cigarettes, and scotch, he seemed to his family emotionally exhausted, depressed, and "com[ing] apart at the seams," in the words of his younger son, Richard, who wrote that his father "had all the appearances of a deeply troubled man."[7] He rarely discussed the war and its legacy with family or friends—the sensitivity and, one imagines, the embarrassment, simply ran too deep.

A pariah on many American college campuses, where opposition to the war intensified during the early 1970s, Rusk eventually found work as an academic in his native South. Overcoming resistance from conservative regents who hated his progressive views on

---

* Only Cordell Hull, Franklin Roosevelt's first secretary of state from 1933 to 1944, served longer.

race and "internationalism," the University of Georgia appointed him in 1970 a professor at its law school in Athens, where Rusk educated a generation of students about his passion: international law. He settled quietly into academic life, which allowed him some measure of peace and which he found a welcome respite from the unceasing pressure and criticism of life in the fishbowl of high politics. "The students I was privileged to teach helped rejuvenate my life and make a new start after those hard years in Washington," he later wrote.[8] Accessible and unassuming, he became popular with students surprised to find the former great man genuinely and disarmingly modest. He didn't rail those with antiwar fervor who harshly criticized him, still less questioned their motives. He didn't publish and he didn't teach from textbooks, preferring instead to pose Socratic questions and draw on examples from personal experience. He became known as an "easy mark" who graded student exams and papers A and B far more often than C, D, or F.

Rusk's door was always open, even after he retired from teaching in 1984. Visitors to the rustic campus dotted with neoclassical buildings forty-five miles southeast of his native Cherokee County would find the aging man seated behind a simple desk in the far corner of the little cottage that served as his office. Just to his right, on a window ledge, sat large black-and-white photographic portraits of John F. Kennedy and Lyndon B. Johnson, the men he had served with unbending loyalty and affection if not imagination and critical detachment. Rusk would field questions readily and directly, speaking in a courtly manner and a soft Georgia accent, but he remained laconic about the war and its consequences. Publicly, he would concede that he made two errors of judgment: "to underestimate the tenacity of the North Vietnamese and to overestimate the patience of the American people." Privately, on occasion the stoic facade would crack a bit and he would make telling, if implicit, comments that revealed his anguish and regret.

Having forsworn writing a memoir upon leaving office, after many years and with the help of Richard, with whom he reconciled after a long period of estrangement over Vietnam, Rusk finally did just that in 1991. In the memoir, *As I Saw It*, he acknowledged that his years as secretary of state "were filled with excitement, accomplishment and failure, and a healthy dose of tragedy."[9] But this acknowledgment was of a lunchtime sort, not midnight.

When I trekked to Athens in 1988 to interview Rusk, I asked him, "If you had known what the costs of the war would ultimately become in terms of U.S. lives and resources expended and domestic divisions sowed by the war, would you, first, have given President Kennedy and President Johnson the advice you did and, second, would President Johnson have committed the country as deeply as he did?" Rusk answered: "I've been offered several opportunities to present a mea culpa on Vietnam, and I've not done so because I thought that the principal decisions made by Kennedy and Johnson were right at the time." He paused, then added, "They're not here to speak for themselves, so I'll just live with it. I don't want to say or do anything that would cause any of the men and women in uniform who carried the fight for us to think that they were engaged in some unseemly or disgraceful action, and so I've not presented a recantation on Vietnam. I'll live with that responsibility. There's nothing I can say now that would mitigate, in any way, the degree of responsibility I had for the events of those days, and so I just will take the view that while I was there I did my duty as I saw it, and let the chips fall where they may."[10] Dean Rusk died of heart failure at his home in Athens on December 20, 1994, at the age of eight-five.

Vietnam destroyed many things, not least the Establishment's dominance of American foreign policy. As national security advisor to Kennedy and Johnson from 1961 to 1966, McGeorge Bundy, the brilliant, self-confident scion of Groton, Yale, and Harvard, properly embodied the capacity—and what most considered the appropriateness—of a well-educated East Coast aristocrat to define U.S. foreign policy. The disaster of Vietnam fatally undermined this heretofore unassailable assumption about the elite and helped drive a frustrated Bundy from the White House, his stature diminished and tarnished, though he continued to informally advise President Johnson. Afterward, the direct descendant of Puritans pursued good works as president of the Ford Foundation, at the time the world's wealthiest philanthropy, during the late 1960s and 1970s and then taught and wrote about the history he had helped make as a professor at New York University (NYU) during the 1980s, though twenty-four faculty members had tried to block his appointment, calling him a "war criminal."

Politically unsympathetic and culturally uncomfortable with Johnson's successor, Bundy had little influence with the Nixon White House, even though Nixon's national security advisor Henry Kissinger had been a junior colleague of Bundy's in Harvard's government department for many years. Bundy faulted the Nixon administration's slow pace of disengagement, but how could he publicly complain as one who had a substantial role in the original escalation? In private settings like the grand second-floor meeting room of the Council on Foreign Relations on the East Side of Manhattan, where the febrile antiwar climate of the early 1970s held lesser sway, Bundy candidly acknowledged the negative consequences of a policy he had heavily influenced. In May 1971, he told a council audience that "there has been very much more cost and pain than most of us would have thought justified if we had perceived [the war] as inevitable in 1965."[11] But that was as far as Bundy could and would go. He, in his own words, "deliberately put aside for decades" public discussion of how the tragedy happened and what could be learned from it. To a persistent questioner at a Harvard cocktail reception for Nieman Fellows in 1976 who said, "Mac, you fucked it up, didn't you?" he snapped, "Yes I did. But I'm not going to waste the rest of my life feeling guilty about it."[12] Bundy's acerbic reply reflected the defensiveness of wounded pride, but also an awareness that the passions and controversy stirred by the war were simply too great, the personal anger and pain of those affected by Vietnam too raw and deep. "To take account of feelings is not necessarily to ease them," he admitted in a note to himself.[13]

But Vietnam never went away for Bundy. "I had the war on my mind ever since I left the government in 1966," he later confessed.[14] Beneath his reserved New England mien that eschewed emotional displays in favor of cold, crisp logic lurked a heart with feelings like any other human being's. Bundy never stopped mulling the impact of the decisions he helped make both on the nation he loved and those touched by the war. Nothing illustrated this more tellingly than Bundy's regular, but unpublicized, visits to the Vietnam Veterans Memorial at the west end of the National Mall in Washington. Like everything else about the war, architect Maya Lin's long, low, black gabbro wall engraved with the names of 58,318 fallen U.S. service members triggered intense controversy when constructed in 1982. It eventually became a shrine for millions of annual visitors, Bundy among them, who left flowers and letters for the dead and made rubbings of the names of loved ones as treasured mementos. He made these visits because he felt "a heavy obligation," as he wrote in a note to himself, "to salute the lasting contributions of the sacrifice of those men whose names are on that long wall." He could not bring them back, but he could try to "honor the meaning and value of their sacrifice."[15]

Bundy began the difficult and painful process of publicly addressing his role in Vietnam soon after Robert McNamara published *In Retrospect* in the spring of 1995. Since leaving the White House, Bundy had discussed Vietnam with journalists and academics through correspondence and in interviews at his office at the Ford Foundation, then NYU, and finally the Carnegie Corporation, where he perched in retirement, and he had lectured on the war at Harvard, Yale, NYU, and the Kennedy library. But he had never fundamentally reconsidered Vietnam and widely acknowledged his part in it until his former colleague and close friend inspired him to do the same. McNamara's book reopened the floodgates of debate, provoking considerable emotion and anger among Americans. Bundy concluded that the remedy to such emotion and anger was *more* discussion, and he would contribute to it by wrestling with his own demons and offering his own reflections. Over the years, he had had too many arguments with too many different critics to believe that he could address Vietnam without the prospect of heated disagreement. But he also knew that wars—especially lost ones—offer many lessons and now fully recognized that the performance of those responsible for the war, like himself, had been so wanting that they had an obligation to explain what went wrong and why. "I have now been out of government for 30 years, the subject is still open—and I can try to help," he mused. "I had a part in a great failure, and if I have learned anything, I should share."[16]

Bundy set out to write a memoir with the research help of Columbia University graduate student Gordon Goldstein. "The errors I know best by now are my own," he wrote, and so he would "give them special attention." This meant beginning with the "*mea culpa*" that he did not see that the American effort was doomed and had been "reluctant to give up" once he did. He acknowledged "mistakes of perception, recommendation and execution." But he believed "the cardinal error was getting too far in, in terms of U.S. combat troops." He concluded with thirty years of hindsight that "more would not have succeeded, so less would have been better" and that "the domino effect so deeply feared could have been contained just about as well as it was at much lower cost." The once proudly self-confident Bundy—one of the war's chief architects—brought himself to humbly admit, flatly and unequivocally, that "I was wrong" about a war that cost so many American and Vietnamese lives.[17] He was no longer a prisoner of unacknowledged regret.

Sadly, Bundy did not live to complete his confessional memoir. He died on September 16, 1996, of a heart attack at his vacation home in Manchester-by-the-Sea, Massachusetts, at the age of seventy-seven. Among the small number of papers found lying on his desk at the Carnegie Corporation in New York after his death included a handwritten list of points he had penned more than three years before in which he listed "my own main exposures" concerning Vietnam: "(1) escalation to a war of attrition, (2) joining in the overthrow of Diem, (3) pretending there was a negotiable settlement, (4) not leveling with the country on the decision to fight." He pleaded "guilty in various ways on all 4." Bundy had continued to wrestle with these exposures, to ponder their human costs, and to reformulate the meaning of his past to the last day of his life.[18]

The years after 1968 proved difficult for Robert McNamara. A fugitive from his past, he had no intention of becoming morbidly introspective. Preoccupation with the busyness of a peripatetic life as president of the World Bank from 1968 to 1981 filled with travel, speeches, and conferences helped keep thoughts and feelings of regret at bay. "He's running fast so the ghosts don't catch him," noted a long-time acquaintance.[19] He also keyed on the successful aspects of his career before and after his tenure as secretary of defense, which were many. He recoiled when people pressed him about Vietnam, bypassing regret by avoiding the reminders.

But submerging the past proved as hard and exhausting for him as one who constantly tries to immerse an inflated ball deep underwater. The criticism of commentators and scholars during the 1970s and 1980s served as an unceasing reminder of all of his bad judgments, of all that had gone wrong and could not be undone. The criticism was hard to bear, the hardest of it all because he knew there was some truth to it. So, too, were occasional encounters with angry pedestrians—many of them former servicemen and antiwar protestors—who accosted him during his daily walk between his home in the Kalorama neighborhood of Washington and the World Bank and later his retirement office next to the Willard Hotel. "I had some confrontations you wouldn't believe," he later admitted.[20] But there was no turning back the clock. He could not change the past. Life had to go on.

Slowly, however, the past worked its way to the surface. The tacit regret he had harbored for so long became increasingly conscious. As the years passed and the distance from Vietnam grew, he inched closer to the truth and acknowledging it. Gradually, tentatively—even reluctantly—he stopped fleeing his ghosts and started confronting them. When the Vietnam Veterans Memorial opened, McNamara had been unable to appear at it publicly. "It was absolutely impossible for me," he later said—the personal pain and shame at that stage was simply too great. By the end of the 1980s, though, he made regular nocturnal visits to the memorial, "but not in a way that anybody could observe me doing it." After hours, "I'd just walk down in the dark," and quietly study the thousands of names inscribed on a mournful facade that echoed the night sky above him. It was a "tremendous" experience for him. He felt "a sense of honor for those who served and a sense of continuing questioning of those who caused them to serve"—not least himself.[21]

In the early 1990s, he resolved to finally reckon with Vietnam and his part in it. Before it was too late, he wanted to acknowledge that "I was wrong" rather "than go down in history as a guy who was wrong and refused to admit it." He was "willing to pay the price of being charged with failure and having caused all of these fatalities" because, then, "at least I could begin to correct my error before I left."[22] Writing *In Retrospect* became a kind of therapy, an effort to understand and explain himself. The story of his involvement with Vietnam was not simple and he did not make it seem so. The resulting memoir was a meditation on his mistakes and the losses they entailed. It allowed him to form intellectual judgments and to share the emotional pain of regret. It also helped him air grief long kept tightly contained. He enlisted my assistance to ensure accuracy by basing his account on the contemporaneous record rather than fallible (and sometimes wishful) memory. Such assistance enhanced the historical validity and analytic nature of *In Retrospect* at the cost of a more personal approach. Yet of all those who led the charge into Vietnam, perhaps McNamara best understood that life is about making imperfect choices, and this trade-off, in some ways par for his course, was one he was willing to make. He tried to be faithful to the record and to understand its meaning, primarily for the benefit of posterity. He understood that was how his memoir would live on after his death—by continuing to inform and instruct future generations.

It had taken McNamara a long time—thirty years—but as he wrote he finally stopped the emotional distancing and disengagement and started consciously regretting, rather than continually suppressing, his thoughts and feelings about Vietnam. He achieved resolution of regret through acceptance. Critics on the Left (many of them former antiwar protestors) and on the Right (many of them Vietnam veterans) perceived *In Retrospect* not as an act of self-revelation but as contrived contrition, too little, too late—thirty years too late. Some thought it revealed no genuine change of mind and heart, only the weakness of a man whose advancing age made him feel vulnerable. Such critics felt no apology could ever be sufficient and would never let him forget the anger and hurt he had caused others. In the end then, McNamara discovered only a balm, not a cure for his own pain and the pain of all those Americans and Southeast Asians touched by the war.

After the publication of *In Retrospect*, McNamara visited Vietnam, first in the fall of 1995 and again in the summer of 1997. These visits—ostensibly to attend scholarly conferences in Hanoi but, in a deeper sense, personal pilgrimages as well—represented his effort to come to terms with the war's impact in Indochina as well as in the United States. The trips became, as one journalist who covered them wrote, "a lonely journey into a regretful past."[23] The seniormost policymaker of the Kennedy and Johnson administrations to visit Hanoi, McNamara met with old adversaries like General Võ Nguyên Giáp and acknowledged that what Americans called the Vietnam War and Vietnamese called the American War should not have been fought and could not have been won at reasonable risk and cost. McNamara's efforts surprised—even confounded—the Vietnamese, whose long history of foreign domination bred a habit of keeping secrets to defend themselves and for whom open debate on the war remained (and largely remains) taboo.* As a result, McNamara had only limited success in his effort to persuade

---

* When asked about divisions within the Politburo during the war, former foreign minister Nguyễn Cơ Thạch said quietly, "There were discussions, but we are not permitted to publicize them." "Sometimes we cannot even get access to our own secrets, so how can we share that with others?" Quoted in David K. Shipler, "Robert McNamara and the Ghosts of Vietnam," *New York Times Magazine*, August 10, 1997, p. 34.

Hanoi* to open up official documentation of North Vietnamese decision-making anywhere near as fully as had been official U.S. documentation of the Kennedy and Johnson years. At the same time, McNamara's sojourns angered the fraternity of retired senior American military officers like William Westmoreland, who told an interviewer, "I can just imagine the attitude of my troops when they read in the paper that the old man goes to Hanoi."[24] At the conferences, McNamara demonstrated admirable self-criticism and a relentless spirit of inquiry while stressing the theme of missed diplomatic opportunities, a generic (and in its specifics) debatable thesis designed to convince himself and others that all of the bloodshed could have been averted. "He's asking a lot of history," noted a former Johnson administration official at the 1997 conference.[25]

At the turn of the twenty-first century, McNamara conducted lengthy interviews with filmmaker Errol Morris for a documentary of his life and decisions as secretary of defense, titled *The Fog of War*. In these up-close interviews, McNamara explored the moral dimensions of his participation in the bombing of German and Japanese cities as an army air corps officer during World War II, the Cuban Missile Crisis, and the Vietnam War in a frank and emotional way that allowed viewers to catch a glimpse of the flesh-and-blood human being behind the famously rational facade. The film was a candid and intimate journey through his life and some of the most significant events of twentieth-century history, and it won the Academy Award for Best Documentary Feature in 2003.

McNamara continued to wrestle with the war and its consequences for the rest of his life. He spent his final years quietly as his health slowly but inexorably deteriorated. Unknown to most, he embraced religion with renewed passion and study. Raised a Presbyterian, he became an active elder in his local Washington church, assisting in the preparation and serving of communion, visiting the sick at their homes, comforting the bereaved, and performing other pastoral duties. These duties gave him a measure

---

* The Vietnam Foreign Ministry's Institute for International Relations sponsored the conferences.

of solace that he desperately sought in the twilight of his life, part of his search for redemption amid sad thoughts of mortality. But the war remained his personal nightmare. His worst enemy now existed inside of him: his regrets and the doubts created by them, the perils of his own past, his predicament illustrating the insight of Albert Camus, who wrote "that a man is always a prey to his truths. Once he has admitted them, he cannot free himself from them."[26] The long-ago secretary of defense remained a man with an unquiet heart that gave him no rest and that he could not escape. He insisted that after his death there be no memorial service of any kind and no burial in Arlington National Cemetery.* Robert McNamara died of heart failure at his home in Washington on July 6, 2009, at the age of ninety-three. On his deathbed, he confessed to his son, Craig, that he felt God had abandoned him.[27]

More than fifty years have passed since McNamara and his colleagues led America into the Bay of Pigs, to the brink of nuclear war over missiles in Cuba, and into the quagmire of Vietnam during the 1960s. In the intervening half century, the iconic nature of their cautionary tale has lost none of its extraordinary power to attract, to move, and, most important, to sober those who contemplate it and the lessons it teaches. Their experience transcends the particularities of their story, as does the educative power of their cognitive foibles. And it continues to fascinate and frighten—as it always will—because their story is, at heart, a tale of very capable and well-intentioned men with very human limitations who confronted complex and difficult problems that led to disaster and in the end brought them low, as it did the country they served and loved. The story of the Bay of Pigs, the Cuban Missile Crisis, and the Vietnam War proved that even the best—and they *were* the best—have limitations that beset all human beings. It is a basic and disconcerting truth that each of us understands deep down, even if we are at the same time chastened by it.

In a fundamental sense, brilliant men not only lost the war in

---

* His family later arranged for the burial of his remains in Arlington.

Southeast Asia, they lost the war against themselves because they were unable to surmount deeply ingrained cognitive patterns that channeled them into the abyss. They had no one like Daniel Kahneman to read, so they had no map to their biases and no compass to help them navigate toward a more objective assessment of reality. It would have taken enormous self-awareness and self-reflection to go against the heuristics and biases their minds were programmed to revert to when confronting the complex problem of Vietnam—but the benefits would have been massive. We need strategies for overcoming the quicksand within all of us and how it can be avoided, especially by those who prosecute future wars. We need to look for the patterns of our recurrent mistakes and devise solutions for them. Developing such strategies helps give redemptive meaning to the suffering and sacrifices caused by Vietnam.

The first step in avoiding future quagmires is to acknowledge the hazards of high-level decision-making. Fiercely ambitious and self-confident people, presidents and their advisors like to think of themselves as in control—of events, of outcomes, of consequences. But what, really, is in their control and what is not? More than they know—or care to admit—they are like mountaineers on the upper reaches of Mount Everest whose fixation on the summit can dull them to the dangers of their surroundings. In both instances, the vistas are breathtaking. But the air is thin, the winds are strong, the hidden crevasses are deep, and if one slips and falls, the slopes are steep. Both environments are notoriously unforgiving of mistakes and misjudgments. The demands of high-level decision-making are intensified by information overload under pressure of circumstances. Social psychologists Jacob Jacoby of New York University and Carol Kohn and Donald Speller of Purdue University showed that increases in information load cause decision-makers to pay less attention to relevant data.[28] This leads them to examine only a small proportion of available information, making it less likely that they will tend to some critical facts.[29] On any given day, Johnson and his advisors dealt not just with Vietnam (as Kennedy and his advisors had dealt not just with Cuba), but troubles in Europe, China, India, and the Middle East—all of which had to be dealt with expeditiously. They confronted a myriad of problems, moreover, with incomplete information and a rapidly ticking clock, which gave them limited time for reflection. Crises, with all of their uncertainties, unknowns, and risks, had to be solved now. Such circumstances often led to reactive little decisions when creative big decisions were imperative.

There is no way to change the frenetic nature of high-level decision-making. Being bombarded with a multitude of pressing issues, day in and day out, is par for the course in the West Wing of the White House. All of this discourages the self-awareness and self-reflection necessary to offset heuristics and biases the human mind adopts when seeking solutions to problems. When faced with issues, we rarely deviate from past approaches, becoming entrenched in our own point of view and overconfident in our assumptions. A powerful antidote is to regularly ask oneself, "What if I'm wrong in clinging to my assumptions without reexamining them and in reaching conclusions without questioning them?" "Self-critical thinkers," notes political psychologist Philip Tetlock of the University of Pennsylvania, "are better at figuring out the contradictory dynamics of evolving situations, more circumspect about their forecasting prowess, more accurate in recalling mistakes, less prone to rationalize those mistakes, more likely to update their beliefs in a timely fashion and—as a cumulative result of these advantages—better positioned to affix realistic probabilities in the next round of events."[30]

Harnessing cognitive diversity is another part of the answer. One important step is to enlist a range of thinkers in the collaborative task of crafting creative solutions by networking minds to tap varied perspectives. "It's the difference in how we think [and] what perspectives we bring to a problem . . . that, when combined, unlock breakthrough results," notes Amy Wilkinson of Stanford's Graduate School of Business. She cites the paradigmatic example of Bletchley Park, the British code-breaking center during World War II that assembled an improbable mix of crossword-puzzlers, cryptographers, engineers, linguists, and mathematicians to break the Enigma Code protecting Nazi military communications, thereby saving thousands of Allied lives.[31] Brainstorming can help because it separates imagination from judgment, the creative act from the evaluative one. "A brainstorming session is designed to produce as many ideas as possible to solve the problem at hand," Roger Fisher and William Ury write. "The key ground rule is to postpone all criticism and evaluation of ideas. The group simply invents ideas without pausing to consider whether they are good or bad, realistic or unrealistic. With those inhibitions removed, one idea should stimulate another like firecrackers setting off one another."[32] Having invented the widest possible range of options, decision-makers can *then* choose among alternatives for action. Prior to the famously successful July 1976 raid on Entebbe Airport in Uganda that ended a hostage crisis, Israeli defense minister Shimon Peres convened what one member called a "fantasy council" that brought together creative thinkers to consider every known option, boldly imagine others, and game out all scenarios, no matter how fanciful. Daring thinking—envisioning the unimagined—led to innovation and success. Yet it only did so because Peres saw value in gathering unconventional perspectives, and because he was both humble enough to know he might be wrong and confident enough to know that if presented with radical ideas that contradicted his assumptions it was a sign of strength to change one's mind.[33] Decision-making and problem-solving benefit from an open-minded search for information and an open-minded consideration of alternatives.

Even when not harried by circumstances, decision-makers generally lack the capacity to think outside of hardened molds, recognize the parameters of a situation early on, and ponder consequences in a systematic and probing way. No one person can synthesize all the information around us and even very bright people fall into mental ruts and cling to old strategies. One way to overcome these limits is to seek outside expertise from varying disciplines—for example, historians, linguists, and cultural anthropologists—whose analysis is unencumbered by the political and bureaucratic constraints of insider status, in which the norm is not to rock the boat and which inhibits advisors from pushing decision-makers out of fear of getting fired or exiled. The sources of regional expertise, moreover, are more abundant than they were fifty years ago. America's increasingly diverse population means that today's Vietnam specialists, for example, are more likely to be Vietnamese Americans, which can mean deeper, richer insights and thus better advice. There is no disputing the value of knowledge and understanding that comes from integrating expertise from across different fields. Having such outside expertise at hand requires supporting the education and recruitment of such experts early on, before problems become acute and far less tractable. Creating a bench of available outside experts is not cheap, but the cost of doing so is a tiny fraction of the costs of war. And timing is crucial. During the Vietnam War, Washington began utilizing a cadre of outside experts on Southeast Asia after it had plunged into the conflict—firefighters, rung only after the embers had become a conflagration. Much the same proved true in 2001 and 2003: Washington did not think to cultivate a cohort of outside experts on Afghan and Iraqi issues and utilize their expertise until after the invasions of Afghanistan and Iraq were underway. The time to do so is before the tinder begins to smoke. Outside experts can help dampen the embers, even to the point of extinction.

Utilizing them requires opening oneself to new ideas. Embracing innovative thinking involves breaking established routines, which most decision-makers resist doing because they are very busy and so they are inclined to listen to their existing information suppliers, who ferociously defend established procedures. Their reliance becomes institutionalized in bureaucratic processes (daily intelligence briefings, national estimates) in which organizational missions channel attention, affect the selection of information, and make it difficult to seek out and embrace new ideas. Harvard Business School professor Clayton M. Christensen has shown that innovations often begin as small-scale experiments, placing a small bet to test a big idea in a trial-and-error process.[34] One such experiment might be to create an independent office operating under the protection of the president to explore and exploit innovating thinking. Being open to new ideas can make decision-makers more accurate in their predictions and more thoughtful in their judgments.

Another step is to adopt "a cognitive net" that puts in place a system to catch flaws of assumptions, reasoning, and thoroughness inherent in decision-making. Good decisions require looking at so many different factors in so many ways that even the smartest individual can make mistakes. Such a cognitive net would mandate communication across the board to deal with the unexpected and uncertain. This proved essential—and successful—in improving the safety of surgical procedures, as Atul Gawande of the Harvard Medical School detailed in his book, *The Checklist Manifesto*. A blizzard of things occur whenever a patient is wheeled into an operating room: allergies are identified, medicines are given, anesthesia is administered, surgical instruments are laid out, equipment is prepared, specialists are summoned, among many other things. All of this can lead to overlooked errors: in one hospital, a third of appendectomy patients failed to receive the right antibiotic at the right time. To remedy this problem, the hospital's administrator created a verbal checklist for operating room staffs. The checklist was greeted with skepticism and resistance at first out of fear that it would consume precious time and increase an already heavy workload, but surgical teams quickly learned the benefits of orally confirming a series of steps before the first incision was made. After three months, 89 percent of appendectomy patients received the right antibiotic at the right time; after ten months, all such patients did. When a similar checklist was adopted by the World Health Organization and applied in eight hospitals in both developed and underdeveloped countries, the results were equally dramatic: major complications for surgical patients fell by 36 percent, deaths by 47 percent, and infections by almost half.[35]

The same can be done by high-level decision-makers prone to cognitive error if they go through a checklist of steps including rigorously and ruthlessly questioning assumptions, candidly acknowledging unforeseen developments, and open-mindedly exploring the widest possible range of options. "While no one [can] anticipate all problems," observes Gawande, adopting a cognitive net could allow decision-makers to "foresee where and when they might occur . . . If you got the right people together and had them take a moment to talk things over as a team rather than as individuals, serious problems could be identified and averted."[36] A checklist will not be foolproof and it may slow down the decision-making process up front, but unlike a haphazard process, it may encourage people to talk through hard and unexpected problems, see subtleties, flag potential traps, and thus yield wiser decisions in far less time overall. As Gawande concludes, "Under conditions of complexity, not only are checklists a help, they are *required* for success. There must always be room for judgment, but judgment aided—and even enhanced—by procedure."[37] Dealing with immensely complex problems like Vietnam demands a disciplined routine in which decision-makers acknowledge their fallibility, talk frankly with one another—most especially, share their apprehensions (which Johnson, McNamara, and the chiefs never really did)—and adopt methodical teamwork to catch problems and increase the probability that they have the critical information they need when they need it in order to craft solutions to the problems facing them. Doing so could improve decision outcomes with no increase in an individual decision-maker's skills. All of this may seem obvious, but it pushes against two abiding facts of Washington life: powerful egos who believe they have the right stuff, consider themselves to be their own experts, and don't need checklists, and the strong bureaucratic culture of turf-consciousness and turf-protection.

Perhaps the most difficult problem to overcome in decision-making is the problem of immediacy. Most policymakers unsurprisingly prioritize the short term. They find it difficult to look beyond the moment—not the minute, but the span of a few days or weeks. Short-term thinking helps them deal with crises and rapid change, and cope with an uncertain future. But it has costs. In a large survey of corporate chief financial officers, researchers found that 80 percent of them turned down lucrative projects because doing so would lower their companies' quarterly earnings.[38] A similar dynamic affects decision-makers when dealing with complex, fast-moving problems. President Johnson and his advisors fell into this trap. Preoccupied by Vietnam's daily vexations, they paid scant attention to signals that their assumptions were dangerously obsolete or to the war's long-term implications. When they did, it was only in fits and starts. The first of them to really do so in a systematic way, Robert McNamara, took two agonizingly long years from the fall of 1965 to the fall of 1967 to change his outlook on the war.

Long-term thinking can be difficult, but it can also be transformational. What might look like weakness and failure now might later be seen as enlightened leadership. The examples of BASF and Unilever Corporations are two cases in point. In the early 1990s, BASF decided to stop manufacturing highly profitable plastic products that contained a flame retardant suspected of causing cancer. This decision by BASF's president, Carles Navarro, was highly unpopular with employees and shareholders, and resulted in a sharp drop in revenue. After two years, however, BASF returned to the market with substitute products, using different chemicals, which eventually allowed BASF to recoup—and exceed—its prior sales. Navarro's decision resulted in short-term pain but long-term gain.[39] In 2010, Unilever announced that it would henceforth release semiannual, rather than the customary quarterly, earnings statements. The company's share price plummeted in the wake of the announcement. But two years later, Unilever's stock had risen 35 percent above its preannouncement level. Through long-term action, the company had actually attracted more capital.[40] Sometimes, looking far down the road is a necessity. As Amy Wilkinson observes, "Race-car drivers . . . go too fast to navigate by the lines on the pavement or the position of their fellow drivers. Instead, they focus on the horizon."[41] Decision-making at the highest level is not that different: policymakers move very fast on a shifting course and face the ever-present chance of a crash. Presidents and their advisors, like race-car drivers, must keep their eyes fixed on the horizon.

The challenges of strategic thinking are real, however. The revolution in communications technology means that problems are now identified—and on decision-makers' plates—faster than ever, creating even greater pressure for immediate action or mere improvisation than in the past. It's hard to think strategically when

trying to solve immediate problems. Taking the long view, moreover, is a tall order to ask of elected leaders in a democracy, where
polls and electoral accountability necessarily focus the mind and
dull attention to longer-term considerations. The future casts no
vote. In the day-to-day process of Washington decision-making,
problems usually manifest themselves in the form of immediate
pressures, and busy and harried decision-makers tend to look for
correspondingly immediate solutions, quick-working remedies that
tide them over a crisis. They tend to act in terms of the seen, with less
attention to the unseen. They are discouraged from making politically risky decisions because the short-term pain is often obvious
while the long-term gain is something avoided. Johnson wrestled
with this dilemma during the critical years 1964–1965, and it powerfully and fatally reinforced his short-term thinking. But short-term
thinking, as the tragic unspooling of Vietnam showed, can lead to
immensely damaging and destructive consequences. If decision-
makers consciously strive to weigh the effect of what they do on
the more distant future, they are more likely to see their choices
in a clearer light. This is true of what *not* to do as well. "Making
'don't do' lists," notes Wilkinson, helps "overcome hubris . . . that
can hold people back."[42] It is well to remember that making history
means understanding that history is sometimes made years after
an action itself, and that leaders are ultimately judged not by their
day-to-day choices but by the long-term consequences of their decisions.

Acknowledgments

"Feeling gratitude and not expressing it is like wrapping a present and not giving it," a writer once noted. In that spirit, I acknowledge accumulating many presents while writing this book and I happily share them now with recipients and readers alike. It's nice feeling like Santa Claus.

I owe a considerable debt to the John F. Kennedy and Lyndon B. Johnson presidential libraries, where I have conducted archival research periodically for more than thirty years. The friendly, professional staffs at both libraries labor diligently to share their rich holdings with the public in the belief that the past offers lessons and that an informed citizenry is the bedrock of a democracy. At the JFK library in Boston, I wish to thank David Castillo, Stacey Chandler, Michael Desmond, Megan Desnoyers, Maryrose Grossman, Rachael Guadagni, Catherine Shaw, and Ronald Whelan. At the LBJ library in Austin, I thank Claudia Anderson, Regina Greenwell, Margaret Harman, and in particular David Humphrey and John Wilson, the past and present archivists responsible for the library's national security files, who patiently and capably fielded my many requests, large and small.

Several officials of the Kennedy and Johnson administrations kindly agreed to share their memories and insights of those now distant years with me, along with their incomparable perspectives as eyewitnesses to history. They include Francis Bator, Robert Gard, and Morton Halperin. I am deeply grateful for their time and help, as I am to the veterans, antiwar protestors, and Vietnamese who have reached out to me over the years and helped me better understand the complexities of Vietnam and its enduring legacy.

Sincere thanks, too, are due to Clark Clifford's daughters, Joyce Clifford Burland and Randall Clifford Wight, and Robert Mc-Namara's widow, Diana Masieri McNamara, who generously and graciously allowed me to quote from my extensive interviews with their father and husband, without restriction, in the belief that others—especially the current and future generations—could learn from the tragedy of Vietnam. I deeply appreciate their trust and faith.

While writing this book, I tested several ideas and insights with my students at the United States Naval Academy in Annapolis. The perceptiveness of their questions and the directness of their answers reminded me, again and again, what a responsibility— and privilege—it is to teach at Annapolis. Helping midshipmen learn, through the study of history, how to deal wisely with the challenges that lie ahead for them is an important reason I undertook this book.

Historians benefit from the perspective of other scholars. I imposed on two distinguished and experienced ones—Robert Dallek and George Herring—to read the manuscript in its entirety and offer me critical feedback. Dallek and Herring came through splendidly. They closely read the manuscript, offered detailed and constructive comments, and—most important—helped me see where I might make things better and clearer for the reader. I am deeply grateful to both; their professional example has inspired me for a long time and still does. I am also indebted to fellow author Craig Mullaney for reading and critiquing several chapters from the point of view of a combat veteran (of Afghanistan).

At an early stage, as I wrestled with defining and framing this book, I received invaluable help from freelance editor Sarah Flynn. Sarah pushed me to clarify my thinking and objectives and offered valuable feedback with just the right mix of candor and commitment. Her enthusiasm and support for the project inspired and sustained me along the way.

My literary agent, Michael Carlisle of Inkwell Management,

excelled in many crucial ways, as an advocate, a receptive ear, and—not least—simply a friend. From beginning to end, Michael understood and embraced my goals and helped me realize them with unfailing professionalism and grace. Michael is the best agent an author can have, and a gentleman to boot. Thank you, Michael.

The person who impacted this book the most is Geoff Shandler, executive director and vice president of HarperCollins's Custom House imprint. Geoff is one of the most talented and tactful editors with whom I have ever been privileged to work. He trusted, pushed, inspired, cajoled, and guided me to produce the best possible book I could. Just when I thought I had done my best, he encouraged me to do even better, and by doing so, helped make the book more than I thought it could be. What more can one ask of an editor? He is a singular talent whom I feel privileged to also call a friend. I am abidingly grateful to you, Geoff. Thanks, too, to Geoff's editorial assistant, Vedika Khanna, who happily fielded many queries and helped guide me through production issues.

Finally, and most importantly, I thank my lovely wife, Donna. She suffered the fate of a writer's widow for a long time—too long—yet demonstrated patience, understanding, and support in equal, cheerful measure, sometimes filling the hours sailing the waters of Chesapeake Bay, where she feels so at home and at peace. She brightens my life in many ways, some she can scarcely imagine. Thank you for being my partner and my best friend, Donna. I cherish you as both.

Notes

PROLOGUE: A VERY HUMAN CULPRIT

1. Amos Tversky and Daniel Kahneman, "Rational Choice and the Framing of Decisions," in Robin M. Hogarth and Melvin W. Reder, eds., *Rational Choice: The Contrast Between Economics and Psychology* (University of Chicago Press, 1987), p. 68.

2. Jonathan Bendor, *Bounded Rationality and Politics* (University of California Press, 2010).

3. Herbert Simon, *Models of Man: Social and Rational* (John Wiley & Sons, 1957), p. 198.

4. Daniel Kahneman, *Thinking, Fast and Slow* (Farrar, Straus and Giroux, 2011), pp. 13–14.

5. Quoted in Michael E. Ruane, "Vietnam Critic's End Was the Start of Family's Pain," *Washington Post*, November 1, 2015.

6. Kahneman, *Thinking, Fast and Slow*, pp. 13–14.

7. Susan T. Fiske and Shelley E. Taylor, *Social Cognition* (Random House, 1984), p. 284.

8. Richard Nisbett and Lee Ross, *Human Inference: Strategies and Shortcomings of Social Judgment* (Prentice-Hall, 1980), p. 41.

9. Author's interviews with Robert McNamara, July 18, 1994; Ernest May, Robert McNamara, and Richard Neustadt, May 5, 1994; and Robert McNamara, September 16, 1994.

CHAPTER 1: THE DANGER OF UNQUESTIONED ASSUMPTIONS (JANUARY–APRIL 1961)

1. David Halberstam, *The Best and the Brightest* (Random House, 1972).

2. Amos Tversky and Daniel Kahneman, "Availability: A Heuristic for Judging Frequency and Probability," *Cognitive Psychology* 5 (1973): pp. 207–232; and Amos Tversky and Daniel Kahneman, "Judgment under Uncertainty: Heuristics and Biases," *Science* 185 (1974): pp. 1124–1131.

3. Dean Rusk, *As I Saw It* (W. W. Norton, 1990), p. 203.

4. Preface to Robert Kennedy, *Thirteen Days: A Memoir of the Cuban Missile Crisis* (W. W. Norton, 1969), p. 13.

5. McGeorge Bundy draft manuscript on Vietnam (hereafter cited as MBDMVN), May 6, 1996, Personal Papers of McGeorge Bundy (hereafter cited as PPMB), Box 223, John F. Kennedy Library (hereafter cited as JFKL).

6.   Author's interview with Clark Clifford, September 13, 1988, Tape Two.

7.   Evelyn Lincoln, *My Twelve Years with John F. Kennedy* (David McKay, 1965), p. 239.

8.   Quoted in Halberstam, *Best and the Brightest*, p. 41.

9.   Arthur M. Schlesinger Jr., *A Thousand Days: John F. Kennedy in the White House* (Houghton Mifflin, 1965), pp. 206–207, 210, and 214. Schlesinger was a special assistant to the president.

10. Author's interview with Clark Clifford, October 17, 1988, Tape Two; Clark Clifford Oral History Interview (hereafter cited as OHI), JFKL.

11. Baruch Fischhoff, Paul Slovic, and Sarah Lichtenstein, "Knowing with Certainty: The Appropriateness of Extreme Confidence," *Journal of Experimental Psychology: Human Perception and Performance* 3, n. 4 (1977): p. 562; and Thomas Gilovich, *How We Know What Isn't So: The Fallibility of Human Reason in Everyday Life* (Free Press, 1991), p. 15. See also G. Pitz, "Subjective Probability Distributions for Imperfectly Known Quantities," in G.W. Gregg, ed., *Knowledge and Cognition* (John Wiley & Sons, 1974); and M.L. Johnson-Abercrombie, *The Anatomy of Judgment* (Basic Books, 1960).

12. MBDMVN, "Draft #3/Chapter I—June 1996," June 12, 1996, p. 2, PPMB, Box 223, JFKL.

13. MBDMVN, Chapter I, and 1995 Draft, typed in February 1996, p. 2, ibid.

14. Quoted in Jonathan Haslam, *No Virtue Like Necessity: Realist Thought in International Relations Since Machiavelli* (Yale University Press, 2002), p. 4.

15. Gilovich, *How We Know What Isn't So*, p. 50.

16. Edward Engel, "Binocular Methods in Psychological Research," in Franklin P. Kilpatrick, ed., *Explorations in Transactional Psychology* (New York University Press, 1961), p. 303.

17. Quotation is at dansimons.com. For a fuller explication of "inattentional blindness," see Christopher Chabris and Daniel Simons, *The Invisible Gorilla: How Our Intuitions Deceive Us* (Crown, 2010).

18. N. S. Khrushchev, "For New Victories of the World Communist Movement," Meeting of the Higher Party School, Academy of Social Sciences and the Institute for Marxism-Leninism, Moscow, January 6, 1961.

19. *Public Papers of the President: John F. Kennedy, 1961* (Government Printing Office, 1962), pp. 1–3.

20. Ibid., pp. 22–23.

21. Peter Kornbluh, ed., *Bay of Pigs Declassified: The Secret CIA Report on the Invasion of Cuba* (New Press, 1998), p. 2.

22. John F. Kennedy, October 7 and 16, 1960, quoted in Piero Gleijeses, "Ships in the Night: The CIA, the White House and the Bay of Pigs," *Journal of Latin American Studies*, February 1995.

23. *New York Times*, October 7, 1960.

24. Clark Clifford with Richard Holbrooke, *Counsel to the President: A Memoir* (Random House, 1991), p. 344; and Robert Amory OHI, Part II, p. 32, JFKL. Robert Amory was the CIA's deputy director for intelligence—the analytical counterpart of the Directorate for Plans, which ran covert action programs.

25. Alexander Fursenko and Timothy Naftali, *"One Hell of a Gamble": Khrushchev, Castro, and Kennedy, 1958–1964* (W. W. Norton, 1997), p. 71.

26. Javier Felipe Pazos Vea, "Cuba—'Long Live the Revolution!'" *New Republic*, November 3, 1962.

27. The phrase is Roswell Gilpatric's, quoted in Peter Wyden, *Bay of Pigs: The Untold Story* (Simon & Schuster, 1979), p. 315.

28. Quoted in Ibid, p. 95.

29. Quoted in James G. Blight and Peter Kornbluh, eds., *Politics of Illusion: The Bay of Pigs Invasion Reexamined* (Lynne Rienner, 1998), p. 65.

30. Richard M. Bissell Jr., with Jonathan E. Lewis and Frances T. Pudlo, *Reflections of a Cold Warrior: From Yalta to the Bay of Pigs* (Yale University Press, 1996), p. 157.

31. Quotes are in Harris Wofford, *Of Kennedys and Kings: Making Sense of the Sixties* (Farrar, Straus & Giroux, 1980; reprint ed., University of Pittsburgh Press, 1992) p. 359; and Robert Amory OHI, Part II, p. 30, JFKL.

32. CIA Board of National Estimates, "Is Time on Our Side in Cuba?" January 27, 1961, and "Is Time on Our Side in Cuba?" March 10, 1961, National Security Archives, Washington, D.C.

33. McGeorge Bundy to the President, February 25, 1961, President's Office Files (hereafter cited as POF) Staff Memo, Bundy, Box 62, JFKL.

34. Richard Bissell OHI, Part I, p. 7, JFKL.

35. Susan S. Lang, "The Power of Wishful Thinking: It Influences What People See," *Cornell Chronicle*, July 3, 2006; and Emily Balcetis and David Dunning, "See What You Want to See: Motivational Influences on Visual Perception," *Journal of Personality and Social Psychology* 91, n. 4 (2006): pp. 612–625.

36. David Rosenhan and Samuel Messick, "Affect and Expectation," *Journal of Personality and Social Psychology* 3 (1966): pp. 38–44; Francis Irwin, "Stated Expectations as Functions of Probability and Desirability of Outcomes," *Journal of Personality* 21 (1953): pp. 329–353; Francis Irwin and Marsha Metzger, "Effects of Independent Outcome-Values of Past Events upon Subsequent Choices," *Psychonomic Science* 9 (1967): pp. 613–614; and Richard Jessor and Joel Readio, "The Influence of the Value of an Event upon the Expectancy of Its Occurrence," *Journal of General Psychology* 56 (1957): pp. 219–228.

37. Quoted in Amory OHI, Part I, p. 5, JFKL; and Schlesinger, *Thousand Days*, p. 258.

38. Kornbluh, *Bay of Pigs Declassified*, p. 291; Wyden, *Bay of Pigs*, p. 139.

39. Robert Amory OHI, JFKL; *Foreign Relations of the United States, 1961–1963, Volume X: Cuba* (hereafter cited as *FRUS, 1961–1963, Volume X*) (Government Printing Office, 1997); Richard N. Goodwin, *Remembering America: A Voice from the Sixties* (Little, Brown, 1988), p. 172; Theodore C. Sorensen, *Kennedy* (Harper & Row, 1965), p. 296; and Stewart Alsop, "The Lessons of the Cuban Disaster," *Saturday Evening Post*, June 24, 1961, p. 68.

40. Quoted in Wyden, *Bay of Pigs*, p. 307.

41. Quoted in Bissell, *Reflections of a Cold Warrior*, p. 167.

42. Quoted in Lucien S. Vandenbroucke, *Perilous Options: Special Operations as an Instrument of U.S. Foreign Policy* (Oxford University Press, 1993), p. 23.

43. Earle Wheeler OHI, JFKL.

44. MBDMVN, "Draft #3/Chapter I—June 1996," June 12, 1996, p. 4, PPMB, Box 223, JFKL.

45. Memorandum for McNamara from JCS, "Military Evaluation of the CIA Para-Military Plan," February 3, 1961, *FRUS, 1961–1963, Volume X*, pp. 67–78; and Dean Rusk, *As I Saw It* (W. W. Norton, 1990), p. 211.

46. Bissell, *Reflections of a Cold Warrior*, p. 167.

47. Stanley Beerli, quoted in ibid.

48. See Morton H. Halperin and Arnold Kanter, "The Bureaucratic Perspective," in Robert J. Art and Robert Jervis, eds., *International Politics* (Harper-Collins, 1992).

49. Quoted in Bissell, *Reflections of a Cold Warrior*, p. 198.

50. General Lyman Lemnitzer to McNamara, March 11, 1961, Taylor Report, Annex 10, JFKL; and Paul L. Kesaris, ed., *Operation ZAPATA: The "Ultrasensitive" Report and Testimony of the Board of Inquiry on the Bay of Pigs* (University Publications of America, 1981).

51. Author's interview with Robert McNamara, September 8, 1992.

52. Quoted in "JFK's McGeorge Bundy," *Newsweek*, March 4, 1963, p. 24.

53. Dean Rusk OHI, Interview 3, pp. 90–91, JFKL.

54. Robert S. McNamara with Brian VanDeMark, *In Retrospect: The Tragedy and Lessons of Vietnam* (Times Books, 1995), p. 26.

55. Bissell, *Reflections of a Cold Warrior*, p. 166.

56. Author's interview with Robert McNamara, September 8, 1992.

57. Robert S. McNamara OHI, pp. 19–20, JFKL.

58. Arthur Schlesinger to the President, *FRUS, 1961–1963, Volume X*, pp. 92–93; and Wyden, *Bay of Pigs*, p. 102.

59. Quotes are in Wyden, *Bay of Pigs*, pp. 102–103.

60. Quoted in Richard N. Goodwin, *Remembering America: A Voice from the Sixties* (Little, Brown, 1988), p. 183.

61. Quoted in Vandenbroucke, *Perilous Options*, p. 27.

62. CIA Information Report, March 16, 1961, cited in Bissell, *Reflections of a Cold Warrior*, p. 180; Schlesinger, *Thousand Days*, p. 270; and McGeorge Bundy to the president, March 15, 1961, *FRUS, 1961–1963, Volume X*, p. 158.

63. Lyman Kirkpatrick OHI, p. 15, JFKL.

64. Lyman B. Kirkpatrick, Jr., "Paramilitary Case Study—The Bay of Pigs," *Naval War College Review*, November–December 1972.

65. Dean Acheson OHI, pp. 13–14, JFKL.

66. Quoted in Blight and Kornbluh, eds., *Politics of Illusion*, p. 64.

67. Schlesinger, *Thousand Days*, p. 246.

68. Sorensen, *Kennedy*, p. 304.

69. Author's interview with Clark Clifford, September 12, 1988, Tape Three; and Schlesinger, *Thousand Days*, p. 259.

70. Quoted in Blight and Kornbluh, eds., *Politics of Illusion*.

71. Wyden, *Bay of Pigs*, p. 160; and Evan Thomas, *The Very Best Men: The Early Years of the CIA* (Simon & Schuster, 1995), p. 253.

72. Quoted in Thomas, *Very Best Men*, pp. 247–248.

73. Handwritten Notes, Box 244, Allen W. Dulles Papers, Seeley G. Mudd Library, Princeton University.

74. Haynes Johnson, *The Bay of Pigs: The Leaders' Story of Brigade 2506* (W. W. Norton, 1964), p. 75.

75.   Quoted in Thomas, *Very Best Men*, p. 249.

76.   Quoted in Michael R. Beschloss, *The Crisis Years: Kennedy and Khrushchev, 1960–1963* (HarperCollins, 1991), p. 114.

77.   Text of Emergency Cable Traffic of 13 April 1961 between Jacob Esterline and Colonel Jack Hawkins, Puerto Cabezas, Nicaragua, in Blight and Kornbluh, eds., *Politics of Illusion*, pp. 224–225.

78.   Quoted in Bissell, *Reflections of a Cold Warrior*, p. 183.

79.   Kornbluh, ed., *Bay of Pigs Declassified*, pp. 271 and 276.

80.   Meyer and Szulc, *Cuban Invasion*, p. 155.

81.   Ibid., pp. 277–282, 295, 301; and Wyden, *Bay of Pigs*, pp. 46, 153–155.

82.   Robert Lovett OHI, JFKL.

83.   Richard Bissell OHI, Part II, pp. 42–43, JFKL; Robert Amory OHI, Part II, p. 31, JFKL; Bissell, *Reflections of a Cold Warrior*, p. 173; and Kornbluh, ed., *Bay of Pigs Declassified*, p. 55.

84.   Quoted Vandenbroucke, *Perilous Options*, p. 46.

85.   Quoted in Tad Szulc, *Fidel: A Critical Portrait* (William Morrow, 1986), p. 556.

86.   Quoted in Sorensen, *Kennedy*, p. 294.

87.   Robert Lovett OHI, JFKL.

88.   Theodore Draper, *Castro's Revolution: Myths and Realities* (Frederick A. Praeger, 1962), p. 59.

89.   Maxwell Taylor, quoted in Memorandum for the File, May 19, 1961, "First Meeting of the President's Foreign Intelligence Advisory Board, May 15, 1961," President's Foreign Intelligence Advisory Board Records (hereafter cited as PFIABR), Washington, D.C.

90.   Quoted in Beschloss, *Crisis Years*, p. 131.

91.   Author's interview with Robert McNamara, September 8, 1992.

92.   Quoted in Bissell, *Reflections of a Cold Warrior*, p. 191.

CHAPTER 2: THE LIMITS OF IMAGINATION (APRIL 1961–OCTOBER 1962)

1.   Quoted in James G. Blight, Bruce J. Allyn, and David A. Welch, eds., *Cuba on the Brink: Castro, the Missile Crisis, and the Soviet Collapse* (Pantheon Books, 1993), p. 41.

2.   Goodwin, *Remembering America*, p. 184.

3.   Arthur Schlesinger Jr. Memorandum to the President, May 3, 1961, in Blight and Kornbluh, eds., *Politics of Illusion*, p. 272.

4.   Quoted in Halberstam, *Best and Brightest*, p. 76.

5.   Quoted in Schlesinger, *Thousand Days*, p. 292; and Wofford, *Of Kennedys and Kings*, p. 363.

6.   Rusk quoted in Beschloss, *Crisis Years*, p. 375; Richard Helms with William Hood, *A Look over My Shoulder: A Life in the Central Intelligence Agency* (Random House, 2003), p. 181; and Bundy quoted in Thomas, *Very Best Men*, p. 270.

7.   Quoted in Gus Russo and Stephen Molton, *Brothers in Arms: The Kennedys, the Castros, and the Politics of Murder* (Bloomsbury, 2008), p. 125.

8.   Goodwin, *Remembering America*, p. 187.

9.   Robert McNamara, July 11, 1975, quoted in Frank Church, *Alleged Assassination Plots Involving Foreign Leaders* (W. W. Norton, 1976), pp. 157–158.

10. Ibid., p. 141; and Thomas Powers, *The Man Who Kept the Secrets: Richard Helms & the CIA* (Alfred A. Knopf, 1979), p. 154.

11. Bissell, *Reflections of a Cold Warrior*, p. 201.

12. Helms quotes are in Beschloss, *Crisis Years*, pp. 5 and 376; Memorandum for the Director of Central Intelligence (John McCone), Subject: Meeting with the Attorney General of the United States Concerning Cuba, 19 January 1962, reprinted in Blight and Kornbluh, eds., *Politics of Illusion*, pp. 246–247; Church, *Alleged Assassination Plots*, p. 141; John H. Davis, *The Kennedys: Dynasty and Disaster* (McGraw-Hill, 1984), p. 394; Richard Reeves, *President Kennedy: Profile of Power* (Simon & Schuster, 1993), p. 265; Michael Dobbs, *One Minute to Midnight: Kennedy, Khrushchev, and Castro on the Brink of Nuclear War* (Alfred A. Knopf, 2008), p. 10; and Dean Rusk OHI, JFKL.

13. Laurence Chang, ed., *The Cuban Missile Crisis, 1962* (National Security Archive), p. 42.

14. CIA Special National Intelligence Estimate, April 10, 1962, JFKL.

15. Bissell, *Reflections of a Cold Warrior*, p. 201.

16. Quoted in Beschloss, *Crisis Years*, p. 376.

17. Quoted in Powers, *Man Who Kept the Secrets*, p. 138.

18. Quoted by Sam Halpern in Blight and Kornbluh, eds., *Politics of Illusion*, p. 118.

19. Goodwin, *Remembering America*, pp. 200–201.

20. Quoted in Frederick Kempe, *Berlin 1961: Kennedy, Khrushchev, and the Most Dangerous Place on Earth* (G. P. Putnam's Sons, 2011), p. 486.

21. Fursenko and Naftali, *"One Hell of a Gamble,"* p. 139.

22. Quoted in ibid., p. 146.

23. Ibid., pp. 151–154.

24. Edward Crankshaw and Strobe Talbott, eds., *Khrushchev Remembers* (Little, Brown, 1970), pp. 492–493.

25. Anatoly Dobrynin, *In Confidence: Moscow's Ambassador to America's Six Cold War Presidents* (Times Books, 1995), p. 73n.

26. William Taubman, *Khrushchev: The Man and His Era* (W. W. Norton, 2003), p. 541.

27. Fursenko and Naftali, *"One Hell of a Gamble,"* p. 182.

28. Dobrynin, *In Confidence*, p. 51; and Crankshaw and Talbott, eds., *Khrushchev Remembers*, pp. 493–494.

29. Anatoli I. Gribkov and William Y. Smith, *Operation Anadyr: U.S. and Soviet Generals Recount the Cuban Missile Crisis* (Edition Q, 1994), pp. 7–10.

30. Taubman, *Khrushchev*, p. 544.

31. See Gilovich, *How We Know What Isn't So*; and Margit E. Oswald and Stefan Grosjean, "Confirmation Bias," in Rudiger F. Pohl, ed., *Cognitive Illusions: A Handbook on Fallacies and Biases in Thinking, Judgement and Memory* (Psychology Press, 2005), pp. 79–96.

32. Peter Wason, "On the Failure to Eliminate Hypotheses in a Conceptual Task," *Quarterly Journal of Experimental Psychology* 12, n. 3 (1960): pp. 129–140.

33. Dobrynin, *In Confidence*, p. 72.

34. See Matthias Uhl and Vladimir I. Ivkin, "Operation Atom: The Soviet Union's Stationing of Nuclear Missiles in the German Democratic Repub-

lic, 1959," *Cold War International History Bulletin* (hereafter cited as CWIHB), Fall/Winter 2001, pp. 299–306.

35. Taubman, *Khrushchev*, p. 546.

36. Quoted in Powers, *Man Who Kept the Secrets*, p. 129.

37. Author's interview with Roswell Gilpatric, New York, November 5, 1992.

38. Helms, *A Look over My Shoulder*, p. 202.

39. Author's interview with Alfred Goldberg and Robert McNamara, April 29, 1994.

40. Quoted in Blight and Kornbluh, eds., *Politics of Illusion*, p. 123.

41. Reprinted in Timothy Naftali and Philip Zelikow, eds., *The Presidential Recordings: John F. Kennedy*, Vol. 2, *The Great Crises, September–October 1962* (W. W. Norton, 2001) (hereafter cited as *PR: JFK*), p. 80.

42. Dobrynin Diary, September 13, 1962, quoted in Aleksandr Fursenko and Timothy Naftali, *Khrushchev's Cold War: The Inside Story of an American Adversary* (W. W. Norton, 2006), p. 454; and Dobrynin, *In Confidence*, pp. 68–69.

43. Dobrynin, *In Confidence*, p. 69.

44. *FRUS, 1961–1963, Volume X*, pp. 1047–1048.

45. Roger Fisher and William Ury, *Getting to Yes: Negotiating Agreement Without Giving In* (Houghton Mifflin, 1981).

46. Mike Mansfield to President Kennedy, September 12, 1962, Box 31, President's Office File (hereafter cited as POF), JFKL.

47. *Public Papers of the President: John F. Kennedy, 1962* (Government Printing Office, 1963), p. 674.

48. Fursenko and Naftali, *"One Hell of a Gamble,"* p. 219.

49. Quoted in Beschloss, *Crisis Years*, p. 6.

50. Roswell Gilpatric OHI, JFKL.

51. This and all subsequent White House meeting quotes during the thirteen days of the Missile Crisis are from presidential recordings reproduced in Sheldon M. Stern, *Averting "The Final Failure": John F. Kennedy and the Secret Cuban Missile Crisis Meetings* (Stanford University Press, 2003).

52. Emile G. Bruneau, Nicholas Dufour, and Rebecca Saxe, "Social Cognition in Members of Conflict Groups: Behavioural and Neural Responses in Arabs, Israelis, and South Americans to Each Other's Misfortunes," *Philosophical Transactions of the Royal Society B (Biological Sciences)*, January 23, 2012.

53. Stevenson to Kennedy, October 17, 1962, reprinted in Laurence Chang and Peter Kornbluh, eds., *The Cuban Missile Crisis, 1962: A National Security Archives Documents Reader* (New Press, 1992), pp. 119–120.

54. Robert Lovett OHI, JFKL.

55. Robert McNamara OHI, JFKL.

56. Author's interview with Robert McNamara, Washington, D.C., July 10, 1992.

57. Quoted by Arthur Schlesinger in Blight and Kornbluh, eds., *Politics of Illusion*, p. 66.

58. The following account is based on "Memorandum of Conversation, October 18, 1962, 5 P.M.," *Foreign Relations of the United States, 1961–1963, Volume XI: Cuban Missile Crisis and Aftermath* (hereafter cited as *FRUS, 1961–163, Volume XI*) (Government Printing Office, 1996); pp. 110–114; Dean Rusk OHI, JFKL; and Andrei Gromyko, *Memoirs* (Doubleday, 1989), pp. 176–181.

59. Remarks at Indianapolis, Indiana, October 13, 1962, *PPP: JFK, 1962*, p. 772.

60. Jerrold L. Schecter with Vyacheslav V. Luchkov, eds., *Khrushchev Remembers: The Glasnost Tapes* (Little, Brown, 1990), p. 174.

61. Quoted in Dino Brugioni, *Eyeball to Eyeball: The Inside Story of the Cuban Missile Crisis* (Random House, 1991), pp. 453–457.

62. Notes Taken from Transcripts of Meetings of the JCS, October 1962, Cuban Missile Crisis Collection, National Security Archives (hereafter cited as CMCC, NSA), Washington, D.C.

63. Quoted in Brugioni, *Eyeball to Eyeball*, p. 262.

64. Quoted in Kenneth O'Donnell and David Powers, *Johnny, We Hardly Knew Ye* (Little, Brown, 1970), p. 318.

65. Quotes are in Brugioni, *Eyeball to Eyeball*, p. 314; and Reeves, *President Kennedy*, p. 388.

66. The following account is based on NSC Executive Secretary Bromley Smith's notes, reprinted in *FRUS, 1961–1963, Volume XI*, pp. 126–136.

67. Notes Taken from Transcripts of Meetings of the JCS, October 1962, CMCC, NSA.

68. Theodore Sorensen OHI, JFKL; and Sorensen, *Kennedy*, pp. 2–3.

69. Quoted in Beschloss, *Crisis Years*, p. 493.

70. Sir David Ormsby-Gore to Prime Minister Harold Macmillan, October 22 and 23, 1962, Public Records Office, Kew, England.

71. The following account is based on Minutes of the 507th Meeting of the National Security Council, Washington, October 22, 1962, 3 P.M., *FRUS, 1961–1963, Volume XI*, pp. 152–156; and Stern, *Averting "The Final Failure."*

72. Kennedy, *Thirteen Days*, pp. 53–55.

73. Radio and Television Report to the American People on the Soviet Arms Buildup in Cuba, October 22, 1962, *PPP: JFK, 1962*, pp. 484–486.

74. Letter from President Kennedy to Chairman Khrushchev, October 22, 1962, *FRUS, 1961–1963, Volume XI*, pp. 162–163.

75. Quotes are in Fursenko and Naftali, *"One Hell of a Gamble,"* p. 241; and Taubman, *Khrushchev*, p 561.

76. Crankshaw and Talbott, eds., *Khrushchev Remembers*, p. 497.

77. Rusk OHI, JFKL.

78. Kennedy to Khrushchev, October 23, 1962, *Foreign Relations of the United States, 1961–1963, Volume VI: Kennedy-Khrushchev Exchanges* (hereafter cited as *FRUS, 1961–1963, Volume VI*) (Government Printing Office, 1996), p. 168.

79. Evelyn Lincoln Appointments Book, October 23, 1962; and Fursenko and Naftali, *"One Hell of a Gamble,"* pp. 250–252.

80. Dobrynin, *In Confidence*, pp. 81–82; Dobrynin cable to Moscow, October 24, 1962, *CWIHPB*, v. 5, Spring 1995, pp. 71–75; and Fursenko and Naftali, *"One Hell of a Gamble,"* pp. 252–253.

81. Quoted in Arthur M. Schlesinger, Jr., *Robert Kennedy and His Times* (Houghton Mifflin, 1978), p. 514.

82. William Knox OHI, JFKL; and William Knox, "Close Up of Khrushchev during a Crisis," *New York Times Magazine*, November 18, 1962, pp. 32, 128–129.

83. James G. Blight and David A. Welch, *On the Brink: Americans and Soviets Reexamine the Cuban Missile Crisis* (Hill and Wang, 1989), p. 306.

84.   Rusk OHI, JFKL.

85.   Kennedy, *Thirteen Days*, p. 55.

86.   Quoted in Brugioni, *Eyeball to Eyeball*, p. 400.

87.   Blight and Welch, *On the Brink*, pp. 63–64; Roswell Gilpatric OHI, JFKL; Deborah Shapley, *Promise and Power: The Life and Times of Robert McNamara* (Little, Brown, 1993), pp. 176–178; and Robert Dallek, *Unfinished Life: John F. Kennedy, 1917–1963* (Little, Brown, 2003), pp. 562–563.

88.   Khrushchev to Kennedy, October 24, 1962; and Kennedy to Khrushchev, October 25, 1962, *FRUS, 1961–1963, Volume VI*, pp. 169–171.

89.   Fursenko and Naftali, *"One Hell of a Gamble,"* pp. 259–260; and Crankshaw and Talbott, eds., *Khrushchev Remembers*, p. 497.

90.   Quoted in O'Donnell and Powers, *"Johnny, We Hardly Knew Ye,"* p. 323.

91.   Khrushchev to Kennedy, October 26, 1962, *FRUS, 1961–1963, Volume VI*, pp. 172–177.

92.   Quotes are in Beschloss, *Crisis Years*, pp. 521–523; and Brugioni, *Eyeball to Eyeball*, p. 448.

93.   Fursenko and Naftali, *"One Hell of a Gamble,"* pp. 272–273; James G. Blight, Bruce J. Allyn, and David A. Welch, eds., *Cuba on the Brink: Castro, the Missile Crisis, and the Soviet Collapse* (Pantheon Books, 1993), pp. 108–109; and Schecter and Luchkov, eds., *Khrushchev Remembers: The Glasnost Tapes*, p. 177.

94.   Fursenko and Naftali, *"One Hell of a Gamble,"* p. 274.

95.   Quoted in Paul Ghali article in *New Orleans Times-Picayune*, November 2, 1962.

96.   Final quote is in Bromley Smith's Summary Record of the Seventh Meeting of the Executive Committee of the National Security Council, October 27, 1962, *FRUS, 1961–1963, Volume XI*, p. 256.

97.   Quoted in Hilsman, *To Move a Nation*, p. 221.

98.   President's Appointments Books and Gilpatric OHI, JFKL.

99.   Quoted in Blight, Allyn, and Welch, eds., *Cuba on the Brink*, p. 378.

100. Khrushchev to Kennedy, October 27, 1962, *FRUS, 1961–1963, Volume VI*, pp. 178–181.

101. Fursenko and Naftali, *"One Hell of a Gamble,"* pp. 276–277.

102. Muriel Maignan Wilkins, "Signs That You're Being Too Stubborn," *Harvard Business Review*, May 21, 2015.

103. Fursenko and Naftali, *"One Hell of a Gamble,"* pp. 281–282; Taubman, *Khrushchev*, pp. 573–574; Beschloss, *Crisis Years*, pp. 536–537; Kennedy, *Thirteen Days*, pp. 80–84; and Dobrynin, *In Confidence*, pp. 86–88.

104. Alexander Mozgovoi, *Kubinskaya Samba Kvarteta Foxtrotov* [The Cuban Samba of the Foxtrot Quartet] (Moscow: Voennyi Parad 2002), and Dobbs, *One Minute to Midnight*, pp. 303, 317–318.

105. Quoted in Taubman, *Khrushchev*, p. 574.

106. Dobrynin, *In Confidence*, p. 89; and Oleg Troyanovsky, quoted in Fursenko and Naftali, *"One Hell of a Gamble,"* p. 285.

107. Quoted in Fursenko and Naftali, *"One Hell of a Gamble,"* pp. 286–289.

108. Summary Record of the Tenth Meeting of the Executive Committee of the National Security Council, October 28, 1962, *FRUS, 1961–1963, Volume XI*, p. 283.

109. Quotes are in Beschloss, *Crisis Years*, pp. 540–542.

110. JCS to President Kennedy, JCSM-844-62, October 28, 1962, Records of the Office of the Secretary of Defense, 71-A-2896, National Records Center, Washington, D.C.

111. Maxwell Taylor OHI, JFKL.

112. Quoted in O'Donnell and Powers, *"Johnny, We Hardly Knew Ye,"* p. 341.

113. Quoted in Beschloss, *Crisis Years*, p. 544.

114. Cyrus Vance OHI, Lyndon B. Johnson Library (hereafter cited as LBJL).

115. MBDMVN, PPMB, Box 224, JFKL.

CHAPTER 3: THE FAILURE OF ANTICIPATION (OCTOBER 1962—NOVEMBER 1963)

1. Søren Kierkegaard, *Journals and Papers* (1843), Volume I.

2. Quoted in Francis Steegmuller, *Maupassant: A Lion in the Path* (Macmillan, 1949), p. 60.

3. Fredrik Logevall, *Embers of War: The Fall of an Empire and the Making of America's Vietnam* (Random House, 2012), p. xvi.

4. William J. Duiker, *Ho Chi Minh* (Hyperion, 2000), p. 638, n. 41.

5. Kahneman, *Thinking, Fast and Slow*, pp. 122–123.

6. Tversky and Kahneman, "Availability," pp. 207–232.

7. Kahneman, *Thinking, Fast and Slow*, p. 8.

8. Ibid., p. 277.

9. Thomas Kuhn, *The Structure of Scientific Revolutions* (University of Chicago Press, 1962); and Robert Jervis, *Perception and Misperception in International Politics* (Princeton University Press, 1976).

10. Kahneman, *Thinking, Fast and Slow*, pp. 85–88, and 201.

11. Lyle A. Brenner, Derek J. Koehler, and Amos Tversky, "On the Evaluation of One-Sided Evidence," *Journal of Behavioral Decision Making* 9 (1996): pp. 59–70.

12. *Public Papers of the Presidents: Dwight D. Eisenhower, 1954* (Government Printing Office, 1960), pp. 382–384.

13. See Agreement on the Cessation of Hostilities in Vietnam, July 20, 1954; and Final Declaration of the Geneva Conference, July 21, 1954, in *Further Documents Relating to the Discussion of Indochina at the Geneva Conference* (Great Britain Parliamentary Sessional Papers) 31 (1953–54), pp. 27–38 and 9–11. For Washington's position, see Closing Remarks of the Geneva Conference, pp. 5–9.

14. William Colby OHI, LBJL.

15. Quoted in David L. Anderson, *Trapped by Success: The Eisenhower Administration and Vietnam, 1953–1961* (Columbia University Press, 1991), p. 133; and Memorandum of Conversation, John Foster Dulles and Guy La Chambre, September 6, 1954, *Foreign Relations of the United States, 1952–1954, Volume XIII: Indochina*, Part 2, pp. 2007–2010.

16. Quoted in Frances FitzGerald, *Fire in the Lake: The Vietnamese and the Americans in Vietnam* (Atlantic—Little, Brown, 1972), p. 87.

17. Quoted in Bernard Fall, *The Two Vietnams: A Political and Military Analysis* (Praeger, 1963), p. 236.

18. Dwight D. Eisenhower, *Mandate for Change, 1953–1956* (Doubleday, 1963), p. 372.

19. Gareth Porter, "The Tonkin Gulf Crisis Reconsidered: Unwitting Provocation in U.S. Coercive Diplomacy," October 28, 1988, p. 2, PPMB, JFKL.

20. Quoted in John C. Donnell, Guy J. Pauker, and J. Joseph Zasloff, *Viet Cong Motivation and Morale in 1964: A Preliminary Report* (RAND Corporation, March 1965), pp. vii-ix.

21. JFK Travel Journal, October–November 1951; Halberstam, *Best and the Brightest*, p. 94; JFK Radio Broadcast, November 14, 1951, Pre-Presidential Papers, JFKL; and JFK on the Senate floor, April 6, 1954, in John Galloway, ed., *The Kennedys and Vietnam* (Facts on File, 1971), p. 11.

22. *Congressional Record*, v. 95, pt. 1, January 3, 1949 to February 17, 1949, pp. 532–533.

23. Remarks at the Conference on Vietnam Luncheon in the Hotel Willard, Washington, D.C., June 1, 1956, Senate Speech File, John F. Kennedy Pre-Presidential Papers, JFKL.

24. McNamara with VanDeMark, *In Retrospect*, p. 39.

25. Author's interview with David Ginsburg and Robert McNamara, April 14, 1994.

26. Author's interview with Robert McNamara, September 16, 1994.

27. MBDMVN, PPMB, Box 225, JFKL.

28. Author's interview with Robert McNamara, July 12, 1993.

29. See William Bundy to McGeorge Bundy, September 14, 1994, PPMB, Box 223, JFKL.

30. Richard Helms with William Hood, *A Look Over My Shoulder: A Life in the Central Intelligence Agency* (Random House, 2003), p. 319.

31. See WGBH transcript of Vietnam Debate between McGeorge Bundy and Stanley Hoffmann, Harvard University, March 10, 1968, PPMB, Box 225, JFKL.

32. Author's interview with Robert McNamara, January 14, 1993.

33. MBDMVN, Chapter I, April 27, 1996, pp. 2 and 5, PPMB, Box 223, JFKL.

34. Quoted in Wofford, *Of Kennedys and Kings*, p. 379.

35. See excerpts of the Taylor Report, reprinted in *The Pentagon Papers: The Defense Department History of United States Decisionmaking on Vietnam*, Senator Gravel Edition (hereafter cited as *Pentagon Papers*) (Beacon, 1971), vol. 2, pp. 87–98, 652–654.

36. Quoted in Schlesinger, *A Thousand Days*, p. 547.

37. Author's interview with Robert McNamara, July 12, 1993.

38. MBDMVN, Chapter I, Kennedy's Basic Decisions (from Manchester), Friday, August 9, 1996, p. 1, PPMB, Box 223, JFKL.

39. Author's interview with Robert McNamara, July 12, 1993.

40. Robert F. Kennedy OHI, JKFL.

41. Roswell Gilpatric OHI, JFKL.

42. Author's interview with Robert McNamara, July 12, 1993.

43. Deposition of George A. Carver Jr., William Westmoreland v. CBS, Inc. et al., November 1983.

44. Amos Tversky and Daniel Kahneman, "Belief in the Law of Small Numbers," *Psychological Bulletin* 76, n. 2 (1971): pp. 105–110; and Daniel Kahneman and Amos Tversky, "Subjective Probability: A Judgment of Representativeness," *Cognitive Psychology* 3 (1972): pp. 430–454.

45. Amos Tversky and Daniel Kahneman, "On the Psychology of Prediction," *Psychological Review* 80, n. 4 (1973): pp. 237–251; and Tversky and Kahneman, "Judgment under Uncertainty," pp. 1124–1131.

46. This anecdote is recounted in Rufus Phillips, *Why Vietnam Matters: An Eyewitness Account of Lessons Not Learned* (Naval Institute Press, 2008), p. xiii; and Max Boot, *The Road Not Taken: Edward Lansdale and the American Tragedy in Vietnam* (Liveright, 2018), pp. 366–367.

47. Roswell Gilpatric OHI, JFKL.

48. Victor Krulak OHI, JFKL.

49. Author's interview with Robert McNamara, July 12, 1993.

50. Record of the Sixth Secretary of Defense Conference, Camp Smith, Hawaii, July 23, 1962, *Foreign Relations of the United States, 1961–1963, Volume II: Vietnam, 1962 (hereafter cited as FRUS, 1961–1963, Volume II* (Government Printing Office, 1990), pp. 546–556.

51. Quoted in Neil Sheehan, *A Bright Shining Lie: John Paul Vann and America in Vietnam* (Random House, 1988), p. 290.

52. Phillips, *Why Vietnam Matters*, p. 183.

53. John McCone to Dean Rusk, January 7, 1964, *Foreign Relations of the United States, 1964–1968, Volume I: Vietnam 1964* (Government Printing Office, 1992), p. 5; and Halberstam, *Best and the Brightest*, p. 297.

54. Gilovich, *How We Know What Isn't So*, pp. 90 and 111.

55. Halberstam, *Best and the Brightest*, p. 183.

56. George Allen, quoted in William J. Rust, *Kennedy in Vietnam* (Charles Scribner's Sons, 1985), p. 78.

57. Victor Krulak OHI, JFKL.

58. Michael Forrestal OHI, JFKL.

59. Quoted in Stanley Karnow, *Vietnam: A History*, rev. ed. (Viking, 1991), p. 275.

60. Quoted in Phillips, *Why Vietnam Matters*, p. 178.

61. Quoted in Harvey Neese and John O'Donnell, eds., *Prelude to Tragedy: Vietnam, 1960–1965* (Naval Institute Press, 2001), p. 45.

62. *Vital Speeches*, December 15, 1962, pp. 157–160.

63. Quoted in David Kaiser, *American Tragedy: Kennedy, Johnson, and the Origins of the Vietnam War* (Belknap Press of Harvard University Press, 2000), p. 68.

64. Victor Krulak OHI, JFKL.

65. Author's interview with Robert McNamara, July 12, 1993.

66. Richard Stilwell OHI, LBJL.

67. Quoted in Rust, *Kennedy in Vietnam*, p. 38.

68. Homer Bigart in *New York Times*, March 29, 1962, p. 1; and Sheehan, *Bright Shining Lie*, p. 310.

69. Charles Bartlett OHI, LBJL.

70. Mike Mansfield OHI, JFKL.

71. Report by the Senate Majority Leader, Southeast Asia—Vietnam, December 18, 1962, *FRUS, 1961–1963, Volume II*, pp. 779–787.

72. Quotes are in O'Donnell and Powers, *"Johnny, We Hardly Knew Ye,"* pp. 15–16.

73. Author's interviews with Clark Clifford, September 12 and 20, 1988.

74. Author's interview with Ernest May, Robert McNamara, and Richard Neustadt, May 5, 1994.

75.   Quoted in Marvin E. Gettleman, *Vietnam: History, Documents, and Opinions on a Major World Crisis* (Penguin Books, 1966).

76.   Michael Forrestal OHI, JFKL.

77.   Quoted in Clarence R. Wyatt, *Paper Soldiers: The American Press and the Vietnam War* (University of Chicago Press, 1993), p. 112.

78.   Quoted in Benjamin C. Bradlee, *Conversations with Kennedy* (W. W. Norton, 1975), p. 59.

79.   Karnow, *Vietnam*, p. 281; Vo Van Hai and Nguyen Dinh Thuan, quoted in Phillips, *Why Vietnam Matters*, pp. 155, 157; and Frank Valeo, "Meeting with the Ambassador of Viet Nam and Madame Tran Van Chuong," October 30, 1962, Mike Mansfield Archive, Box 105, University of Montana, Missoula.

80.   Quoted in Rudy Abramson, *Spanning the Century: The Life of W. Averell Harriman, 1891–1986* (William Morrow, 1992), p. 609.

81.   O'Donnell and Powers, *"Johnny, We Hardly Knew Ye,"* p. 16.

82.   Rusk, *As I Saw It*, p. 440.

83.   William Colby OHI, LBJL.

84.   Quoted in Karnow, *Vietnam*, p. 304.

85.   Phillips, *Why Vietnam Matters*, p. 207.

86.   Hồ Chí Minh, quoted in Ellen Hammer, *A Death in November: America in Vietnam, 1963*, reprint ed. (Oxford University Press, 1988), p. 222; and Colonel Trần Ngọc Châu, quoted in Harvey C. Neese and John O'Donnell, eds., *Prelude to Tragedy: Vietnam, 1960–1965* (Naval Institute Press, 2000), pp. 197–198.

87.   Telegram 243, Washington to Saigon, August 24, 1963, *Foreign Relations of the United States, 1961–1963, Volume III: Vietnam, January–August 1963* (hereafter cited as *FRUS, 1961–1963, Volume III*), (Government Printing Office, 1991), pp. 628–629.

88.   Author's interview with McGeorge Bundy and Robert McNamara, March 18, 1994.

89.   Quoted in Rust, *Kennedy in Vietnam*, p. 114.

90.   Quoted in George W. Ball, *The Past Has Another Pattern: Memoirs* (W. W. Norton, 1982), p. 371.

91.   Roswell Gilpatric OHI, JFKL.

92.   Maxwell Taylor, *Swords and Ploughshares* (W. W. Norton, 1972), p. 292; Presidential Recordings, November 4, 1963, JFKL; and Robert F. Kennedy OHI, JFKL.

93.   Author's interview with Robert McNamara, August 18, 1993.

94.   Amos Tversky and Eldar Shafir, "The Disjunction Effect in Choice Under Uncertainty," *Psychological Science* 3 (1992): pp. 358–361.

95.   Tape 107/A42, Meeting on Vietnam, 26 August 1963, Presidential Recordings Collection (hereafter cited as PRC), POF, JFKL.

96.   Tape 107/A42, Meeting on Vietnam, 27 August 1963, Ibid.

97.   Tapes 107/A42 and 108, Meeting on Vietnam, 28 August 1963, PRC, POF, JFKL; and Arthur M. Schlesinger Jr., *Robert Kennedy and His Times* (Houghton Mifflin, 1978), p. 714.

98.   Tape 108, Meetings on Vietnam and Civil Rights, 28 August–3 September 1963, PRC, POF, JFKL; and *Newsweek*, September 23, 1963, pp. 25–26.

99. Robert S. McNamara, James G. Blight, and Robert K. Brigham with Thomas J. Biersteker and Colonel Herbert Y. Schandler, *Argument Without End: In Search of Answers to the Vietnam Tragedy* (PublicAffairs, 1999), p. 102.

100. Message from the President to the Ambassador in Vietnam, August 29, 1963, *Foreign Relations of the United States, 1961–1963, Volume IV: Vietnam, August–December 1963* (hereafter cited as *FRUS, 1961–1963, Volume IV*) (Government Printing Office, 1991), pp. 35–36.

101. *Public Papers of the Presidents: John F. Kennedy, 1963* (hereafter cited as *PPP, JFK, 1963*) (Government Printing Office, 1964), pp. 650–653.

102. Transcript of broadcast on NBC's "Huntley-Brinkley Report," September 9, 1963, ibid., 658–660.

103. Report by the Joint Chiefs of Staff's Special Assistant for Counterinsurgency and Special Activities (Krulak), September 10, 1963, *FRUS, 1961–1963, Volume IV*, pp. 153–160; and Victor Krulak OHI, JFKL.

104. Tape 109, Meetings on Balance of Payments; Nuclear Test Ban; Vietnam [Entire Tape], PRC, POF, JFKL.

105. Meetings: Tape 110, Meeting on Vietnam, 11 September 1963, ibid; and Church, *Alleged Assassination Plots*, p. 221.

106. Meetings: Tape 111, Vietnam, 17 September 1963, PRC, POF, JFKL.

107. Memorandum of a Conversation, Department of State, April 1, 1963, Noon, *FRUS, 1961–1963, Volume III*, p. 193; and Memorandum for the Record of the Secretary of Defense Conference, Honolulu, May 6, 1963, ibid., pp. 265–270.

108. Meetings: Tape 111, Vietnam, 19 September 1963, PRC, POF, JFKL.

109. Meetings: Tape 112, Vietnam, 23 September 1963, PRC, POF, JFKL.

110. William Bundy, quoted in Phillips, *Why Vietnam Matters*, p. 197.

111. The exchange between the major and McNamara in Long An province is related in Halberstam, *Best and the Brightest*, p. 284. A detailed and insightful study of Long An province during the war is Jeffrey Race, *War Comes to Long An: Revolutionary Conflict in a Vietnamese Village* (University of California Press, 1972).

112. McNamara with VanDeMark, *In Retrospect*, p. 74.

113. Report by the Secretary of Defense, September 26, 1963, *FRUS, 1961–1963, Volume IV*, pp. 293–295.

114. Report of McNamara's 27 September 63 interview with Richardson, *FRUS, 1961–1963, Volume IV*, pp. 301–303.

115. Author's interview with Robert McNamara, July 12, 1993.

116. McNamara with VanDeMark, *In Retrospect*, pp. 75–77; Rust, *Kennedy in Vietnam*, p. 143; and Meetings: Tape 114/A49, Meeting on Malaysia, Meeting on Vietnam, 2 October 1963, PRC, POF, JFKL.

117. Author's interview with Robert McNamara, August 18, 1993.

118. Memorandum from the Chairman of the Joint Chiefs of Staff and the Secretary of Defense to the President, October 2, 1963, *FRUS, 1961–1963, Volume IV*, pp. 336–346.

119. David Dunning and Emily Balcetis, "Wishful Seeing: How Preferences Shape Visual Perception," *Current Directions in Psychological Science* 22 (2013): pp. 33–37.

120.   Ziva Kunda, "The Case for Motivated Reasoning," *Psychological Bulletin* 108 (1990): pp. 480–498.

121.   Meetings: Tape 114/A49, Meeting on Malaysia, Meeting on Vietnam, 2 October 1963, PRC, POF, JFKL.

122.   Author's interview with Robert McNamara, July 12, 1993.

123.   Author's interview with Robert McNamara, August 18, 1993.

124.   Anthony Bastardi, Eric Luis Uhlmann, and Lee Ross, "Wishful Thinking: Belief, Decision, and the Motivated Evaluation of Scientific Evidence," *Psychological Science*, April 22, 2011. See also Kunda, "The Case for Motivated Reasoning."

125.   Meetings: Tape 114/A49, NSC Meeting on McNamara-Taylor Report on Vietnam, 2 October 1963, PRC, POF, JFKL.

126.   Office of Current Intelligence Memorandum 2703/63, "Cast of Characters in South Vietnam," August 28, 1963, Microfiche (Carrollton Press, 1977).

127.   Quoted in Rust, *Kennedy in Vietnam*, p. 154.

128.   Embassy telegram (hereafter cited as Embtel) 1964, Lodge to Bundy, October 25, 1963, Box 201, National Security Files (hereafter cited as NSF), JFKL.

129.   Meetings: Tape 117/A53, Meeting on Vietnam, 25 October 1963, PRC, POF, JFKL.

130.   Kennedy emphasized this point in his Dictated Memoir Entry of November 4, 1963.

131.   Meetings: Tape 118/A54, Meeting on Vietnam, 29 October 1963, PRC, POF, JFKL.

132.   Embtel 805, October 28, 1963, *FRUS, 1961–1963, Volume IV*, pp. 442–446.

133.   Quoted in Hammer, *A Death in November*, p. 269.

134.   Phillips, *Why Vietnam Matters*, pp. 201–202.

135.   Hammer, *A Death in November*, p. 273.

136.   Lodge to Department of State, October 30, 1963, *FRUS, 1961–1963, Volume IV*, pp. 484–488.

137.   Quoted in William Colby with James McCargar, *Lost Victory: A Firsthand Account of America's Sixteen-Year Involvement in Vietnam* (Contemporary Books, 1989), p. 151.

138.   Harkins to Taylor, October 30, 1963, ibid., pp. 479–482.

139.   Meetings: Tape 118/A54, Meeting on Vietnam, 30 October 1963, PRC, POF, JFKL.

140.   Quoted by Lodge in Rust, *Kennedy in Vietnam*, p. 162.

141.   Embtel 841, Lodge to Rusk, November 1, 1963, *FRUS, 1961–1963, Volume IV*, pp. 516–517.

142.   Quoted in Hammer, *A Death in November*, p. 287.

143.   Embtel 860, Saigon to Washington, November 1, 1963, *FRUS, 1961–1963, Volume IV*, p. 513.

144.   Quoted in Hammer, *A Death in November*, p. 297.

145.   Quoted in Trần Văn Đôn, *Our Endless War* (Presidio Press, 1978), p. 111; and Sheehan, *Bright Shining Lie*, p. 371.

146.   Forrestal interview in *NBC White Paper, Death of Diem*, December 22, 1971; Schlesinger, *Thousand Days*, pp. 997–998; Taylor, *Swords and Ploughshares*,

p. 301; and Meetings, Tape 119/A55. Meeting on Vietnam, 2 November 1963, PRC, POF, JFKL.

147. Meetings: Tape 119/A55, Meeting on Vietnam, 2 November 1963, PRC, POF, JFKL.

148. CIA Far East Division director William Colby, quoted in Rust, *Kennedy in Vietnam*, p. 148.

149. Telephone recordings: Dictation Belt 52.1. Dictated Memoir Entries, November 4, 1963, PRC, POF, JFKL.

150. Author's interview with Robert McNamara, August 18, 1993.

151. Quoted in Schlesinger, *Robert Kennedy*, p. 722.

152. McGeorge Bundy, "The History-Maker," *Proceedings of the Massachusetts Historical Society* 90 (1978): pp. 82 and 84; McGeorge Bundy, "Starting from Vietnam," February 23, 1993, Box 232, PPMB, JFKL; Mike Mansfield OHI, JFKL; and McGeorge Bundy Memoir Fragment (hereafter cited as MBMF), No. 71, pp. 4–5.

153. Meetings: Tape 117/A53, Meeting on Vietnam, 25 October 1963, PRC, POF, JFKL.

154. National Liberation Front (NLF) president Nguyễn Hữu Thọ, quoted in Hammer, *A Death in November*, p. 309.

155. Quoted by William Colby in Colby OHI, LBJL.

156. Edgar Snow, "Talking of South Vietnam," *Sunday Times* (London), February 14, 1965; and author's interview with Ernest May, Robert McNamara, and Richard Neustadt, May 5, 1994.

157. Quoted in Daniel Ellsberg, *Secrets: A Memoir of Vietnam and the Pentagon Papers* (Viking, 2002), p. 195.

158. Author's interviews with Clark Clifford, June 3, September 14, and October 17, 1988.

159. Schlesinger, *Robert Kennedy*, p. 722.

160. Author's interviews with Robert McNamara, July 12, 1993, July 18, 1994, and September 16, 1994.

161. *PPP, JFK, 1963*, pp. 846, 848.

162. MBDMVN, "More Notes on JFK," July 9, 1996, PPMB, Box 226, JFKL.

CHAPTER 4: THE PERIL OF SHORT-TERM THINKING (NOVEMBER 1963–JULY 1965)

1. MBDMVN, "FEB 20," PPMB, Box 226, JFKL.

2. Author's interview with Robert McNamara, November 3, 1993.

3. Horace Busby, *The Thirty-First of March: An Intimate Portrait of Lyndon Johnson's Final Days in Office* (Farrar, Straus and Giroux, 2005), p. 14.

4. Quoted by Bill Moyers at Lady Bird's 2007 memorial service.

5. Gerald Siegel, quoted in Merle Miller, *Lyndon: An Oral Biography* (G. P. Putnam's Sons, 1980), p. 534.

6. Author's interview with Clark Clifford, June 3, 1988, Tape One.

7. Busby, *The Thirty-First of March*, pp. 103–104.

8. Author's interview with Harry McPherson, July 20, 1988.

9. Author's interview with Clark Clifford and Benjamin Read, August 18, 1988.

10. Author's interview with Clark Clifford, September 12, 1988, Tape Two.

11. Author's interview with McGeorge Bundy and Robert McNamara, March 18, 1994.

12. Author's interview with Clark Clifford, June 27, 1988, Tape One.

13. McGeorge Bundy OHI 07–13, LBJL; and Eric F. Goldman, *The Tragedy of Lyndon Johnson* (Alfred A. Knopf, 1969), pp. 447–448.

14. Lyndon Baines Johnson, *The Vantage Point: Perspectives of the Presidency, 1963–1969* (Holt, Rinehart and Winston, 1971), pp. 12 and 18.

15. Author's interview with Adam Yarmolinsky, April 1, 1993.

16. Cabinet Meeting, November 23, 1963, Cabinet Papers, LBJL.

17. Quoted in Doris Kearns, *Lyndon Johnson and the American Dream* (Harper & Row, 1976), pp. 177–178.

18. Quoted by Richard Holbrooke during author's interview with Clark Clifford, October 17, 1988, Tape Two.

19. Jack Valenti, cited in Don Oberdorfer, *Senator Mansfield: The Extraordinary Life of a Great American Statesman and Diplomat* (Smithsonian Books, 2003), p. 216.

20. McGeorge Bundy OHI 07–13, LBJL.

21. Bill Moyers, quoted in Robert Dallek, *Flawed Giant: Lyndon Johnson and His Times, 1961–1973* (Oxford University Press, 1999), p. 88.

22. Telephone conversation with John Knight, February 3, 1964, in Michael Beschloss, ed., *Taking Charge: The Johnson White House Tapes, 1963–1964* (Simon & Schuster, 1997), p. 213.

23. Author's interview with Clark Clifford, July 20, 1988, Tape Two.

24. Quoted in Halberstam, *Best and the Brightest*, pp. 41 and 305.

25. Author's interview with Robert McNamara, July 18, 1994.

26. Lady Bird Audio Diary Transcripts (hereafter cited as LBADT), April 15, 1965, LBJL; Lady Bird Johnson Diary Entry, February 14, 1965, in Beschloss, ed., *Taking Charge*, p. 178.

27. LBADT, July 25, 1965, LBJL.

28. Author's interview with Francis Bator, May 18, 2016.

29. McGeorge Bundy OHI 07–13, LBJL.

30. MBDMVN, Tues. 23 MAY, PPMB, Box 226, JFKL.

31. Telephone conversation with Abe Fortas, May 23, 1965, in Michael Beschloss, ed., *Reaching for Glory: Lyndon Johnson's Secret White House Tapes, 1964–1965* (Simon & Schuster, 2001), p. 339.

32. Quoted in Henry F. Graff, *The Tuesday Cabinet: Deliberation and Decision on Peace and War under Lyndon B. Johnson* (Prentice-Hall, 1970), p. 56.

33. Halberstam, *Best and the Brightest*, pp. 517–518 and 305.

34. Johnson to Kennedy, May 23, 1961, "Southeast Asia," Aides File, McGeorge Bundy (hereafter cited as AF, MB), Box 18/19, NSF, LBJL.

35. MBMF, December 12, 1995, p. 14.

36. LBADT, July 25, 1965, LBJL.

37. Quoted in Karnow, *Vietnam*, p. 339.

38. Author's interview with Robert McNamara and McGeorge Bundy, March 18, 1994.

39. McNamara with VanDeMark, *In Retrospect*, p. 101.

40. Bill Moyers, "Flashbacks," *Newsweek*, February 10, 1975.

41.   Sheehan, *Bright Shining Lie*, p. 372.

42.   Bùi Diễm with David Chanoff, *In the Jaws of History* (Houghton Mifflin, 1987), p. 114; and Phillips, *Why Vietnam Matters*, p. 218.

43.   Memorandum for the President, December 21, 1963, *FRUS, 1961–1963, Volume IV*, pp. 732–735.

44.   Quoted in Halberstam, *Best and the Brightest*, p. 292.

45.   Telephone conversation with Senator Richard Russell, May 27, 1964, in Beschloss, ed., *Taking Charge*, p. 366.

46.   Mansfield to Johnson, January 6, 1964; McNamara to Johnson, January 7, 1964; and Bundy and Rusk to Johnson, January 9, 1964, *FRUS, 1964–1968, Volume I*, pp. 2–3; 8–13.

47.   Author's interview with Robert McNamara, October 9, 1993.

48.   Quoted in Halberstam, *Best and the Brightest*, p. 434.

49.   Telephone conversation with Robert McNamara, March 2, 1964, in Beschloss, ed., *Taking Charge*, p. 257.

50.   Telephone conversation with Senator Fulbright, March 2, 1964, ibid., p. 264.

51.   Quoted in Karnow, *Vietnam*, p. 341.

52.   Author's interview with McGeorge Bundy and Robert McNamara, March 18, 1994.

53.   JCSM-46–64, January 22, 1964, *Pentagon Papers*, vol. 3, pp. 496–499.

54.   Author's interview with Clark Clifford and Herbert Schandler, August 2, 1998, Tape One.

55.   JCSM-174–64, March 2, 1964, *FRUS, 1964–1968, Volume I*, pp. 112–118; and Memorandum of Conversation between the Joint Chiefs of Staff and the President, March 4, 1964, *FRUS, 1964–1968, Volume I*, pp. 129–130.

56.   Taylor, *Swords and Ploughshares*, p. 329; and Bùi Diễm with Chanoff, *In the Jaws of History*, p. 109.

57.   Halberstam, *Best and the Brightest*, p. 352; Memorandum of Conversation between the Joint Chiefs of Staff and the President, March 4, 1964, *FRUS, 1964–1968, Volume I*, p. 129; and McNamara with VanDeMark, *In Retrospect*, p. 112.

58.   Bùi Diễm with Chanoff, *In the Jaws of History*, pp. 114–115; and Đôn, *Our Endless War*, p. 126.

59.   Quoted in Wilfred Burchett, *Vietnam: Inside Story of the Guerrilla War* (International Publishers, 1965), p. 219.

60.   Memorandum from the Joint Chiefs of Staff to the Secretary of Defense, March 14, 1964, *FRUS, 1964–1968, Volume I*, pp. 149–150; Memorandum from the Secretary of Defense to the President, March 16, 1964, ibid., pp. 153–167; Summary Record of the 524th Meeting of the National Security Council, March 17, 1964, ibid., pp. 170–172; Telephone Conversation with Robert McNamara, March 21, 1964, in Beschloss, ed., *Taking Charge*, p. 293; and Telephone conversation with McGeorge Bundy, April 14, 1964, ibid., p. 319.

61.   Telephone conversation with Robert McNamara, April 30, 1964, in Beschloss, ed., *Taking Charge*, p. 338.

62.   McNamara with VanDeMark, *In Retrospect*, p. 114.

63.   Memorandum Prepared by the Directorate of Intelligence, CIA, May 15, 1964, *FRUS, 1964–1968, Volume I*, p. 336.

64. Memorandum from the Board of National Estimates to the Director of Central Intelligence, June 9, 1964, *FRUS, 1964–1968, Volume I*, pp. 484–487.

65. Michael I. Norton, Daniel Mochon, and Dan Ariely, "The 'IKEA Effect': When Labor Leads to Love," *Journal of Consumer Psychology* 22, n. 3, pp. 453–460.

66. *Personal Statements of Robert S. McNamara, Secretary of Defense, 1964*, vol. 3, p. 1210. [Private volume]

67. Telephone conversation with Richard Russell, June 11, 1964, and Telephone conversation with Robert McNamara, June 16, 1964, in Beschloss, ed., *Taking Charge*, pp. 401 and 411.

68. Telephone conversation with Hubert Humphrey, June 9, 1964, in ibid., p. 395.

69. Embtel 2052, Taylor to Johnson, January 6, 1965, *Foreign Relations of the United States, 1964–1968, Volume II: Vietnam, January–June 1965* (hereafter cited as *FRUS, 1964–1968, Volume II*) (Government Printing Office, 1996), pp. 12–19.

70. Memorandum from the President's Special Assistant for National Security Affairs to the President, May 22, 1964, in Beschloss, ed., *Taking Charge*, pp. 349–351.

71. Author's interview with Robert McNamara, September 10, 1993.

72. See Asselin, *Hanoi's Road*, pp. 148–168.

73. Quoted in Halberstam, *Best and the Brightest*, p. 368.

74. Telephone conversations with Adlai Stevenson, Richard Russell, and McGeorge Bundy, May 27, 1964, in Beschloss, ed., *Taking Charge*, pp. 363–372.

75. Quoted in Frank E. Vandiver, *Shadows of Vietnam: Lyndon Johnson's Wars* (Texas A&M University Press, 1997), p. 18.

76. Resolution of the Ninth Plenum of the Central Committee of the Vietnam Workers' Party: Strive to Struggle, Rush Forward to Win New Victories in the South, December 1963, quoted in Asselin, *Hanoi's Road*, p. 165.

77. Summary of 1964 Seaborn Conversations, in George C. Herring, ed., *The Secret Diplomacy of the Vietnam War: The Negotiating Volumes of the Pentagon Papers* (University of Texas Press, 1983), p. 11.

78. Quoted in Asselin, *Hanoi's Road*, p. 191.

79. Roger Fisher and William Ury, *Getting to Yes: Negotiating Agreement Without Giving In* (Houghton Mifflin, 1981), pp. 59–60.

80. Memorandum from the Joint Chiefs of Staff to the Secretary of Defense, JCSM-471–64, June 2, 1964, *FRUS, 1964–1968, Volume I*, pp. 437–440.

81. Memorandum from the Joint Chiefs of Staff to the Secretary of Defense, JCSM-426–64, ibid., pp. 338–340.

82. U. S. Grant Sharp OHI, LBJL.

83. This was confirmed at a Vietnamese-American conference on the war held in Hanoi in November 1995. Robert S. McNamara et al., *Argument Without End: In Search of Answers to the Vietnam Tragedy* (PublicAffairs, 1999), p. 185.

84. Thomas Hughes, in Ted Gittinger, ed., *The Johnson Years: A Vietnam Roundtable* (Lyndon Baines Johnson Library, 1993), p. 33.

85. Embtel 282, Taylor to Rusk, August 3, 1964, *FRUS, 1964–1968, Volume I*, pp. 593–594.

86. Telephone conversation with Robert McNamara, 10:20 A.M., August 3, 1964, in Beschloss, ed., *Taking Charge*, p. 495.

87. Author's interview with Robert McNamara, September 20, 1993.

88. Quoted in Dallek, *Flawed Giant*, p. 150; and MBMF, No. 71, pp. 7–8.

89. 041727Z, Department of State, Central Files, POL 27 VIET S., cited in *FRUS, 1964–1968, Volume I*, p. 609.

90. McNamara with VanDeMark, *In Retrospect*, pp. 133–134.

91. MBMF, No. 84, Manchester, Massachusetts, August 20, 1996, and No. 71, October 11, 1995, p. 10.

92. McGeorge Bundy in Gittinger, ed., *Johnson Years*, pp. 31–32.

93. Author's interview with Robert McNamara and McGeorge Bundy, March 18, 1994.

94. "Outside Westgate," Radiolab, National Public Radio, November 29, 2014.

95. Gilovich, *How We Know What Isn't So*, pp. 3 and 30.

96. Ibid., p. 33.

97. Peter C. Wason, "Reasoning," in B. M. Foss, ed., *New Horizons in Psychology* (Penguin, 1966); and Peter C. Wason, "Reasoning About a Rule," *Quarterly Journal of Experimental Psychology*, 20, n. 3 (1968): pp. 273–281.

98. Hugo Mercier and Dan Sperber, *The Enigma of Reason* (Harvard University Press, 2017); and D. N. Perkins, M. Faraday, and B. Bushey, "Everyday Reasoning and the Roots of Intelligence," in J. F. Voss, D. N. Perkins, and J. W. Segal, eds., *Informal Reasoning and Education* (Erlbaum, 1991), pp. 83–106.

99. Steven Sloman and Philip Fernbach, *The Knowledge Illusion: Why We Never Think Alone* (Riverhead Books, 2017).

100. Scott H. Young, "The Bicycle Problem: How the Illusion of Explanatory Depth Tricks Your Brain," *Scott H. Young* (blog), December 2015, https://www.scotthyoung.com/blog/2015/12/22/illusion-of-explanatory-depth/.

101. Raymond S. Nickerson, "Confirmation Bias: A Ubiquitous Phenomenon in Many Guises," *Review of General Psychology* 2, n. 2 (1998): p. 176.

102. Tim Larimer, "McNamara and Giap Revisit Gulf of Tonkin," *International Herald-Tribune*, November 10, 1995, p. 1.

103. Telephone conversation with Mike Mansfield, June 9, 1964, in Beschloss, ed., *Taking Charge*, pp. 394–395.

104. Quoted in Halberstam, *Best and the Brightest*, p. 422.

105. MBMF, Fragment 84, Manchester, Massachusetts, August 20, 1996.

106. Gareth Porter, "Coercive Diplomacy in Vietnam: The Tonkin Gulf Crisis Reconsidered," in Jayne Werner and David Hunt, eds., *The American War in Vietnam* (Cornell University Southeast Asia Program, 1993), pp. 19–20.

107. Cited in Halberstam, *Best and the Brightest*, p. 425.

108. Quoted in Tom Wicker, *JFK and LBJ: The Influence of Personality Upon Politics* (Penguin, 1968), p. 205.

109. Quoted in Kearns, *Lyndon Johnson and the American Dream*, pp. 252–253.

110. *Public Papers of the Presidents: Lyndon B. Johnson, 1963–64* (Government Printing Office, 1965), Book II, pp. 952–955.

111. Ibid., pp. 1019–1024, 1122–1128, 1160–1169, and 1387–1393.

112. Quoted in Halberstam, *Best and the Brightest*, p. 424.

113. Author's interview with Robert McNamara, October 19, 1993.

114. Author's interview with Clark Clifford, October 17, 1988, Tape Two.

115. Quoted in Halberstam, *Best and the Brightest*, pp. 424–425.

116.   Telephone conversation with Martin Luther King Jr., January 15, 1965, in Beschloss, ed., *Reaching for Glory*, p. 160.

117.   President's Daily Diary, November 3, 1964, LBJL.

118.   Telephone conversation with Robert McNamara, September 21, 1964, in Beschloss, ed., *Reaching for Glory*, p. 41.

119.   Halberstam, *Best and the Brightest*, p. 462; and Jack Shulimson, *History of the Joint Chiefs of Staff: The Joint Chiefs of Staff and the War in Vietnam, 1960–1968*, Part I (Office of Joint History, 2011), Chapter 12, pp. 14–16.

120.   Colonel Quach Hai Luong, quoted in McNamara, et al., *Argument Without End*, p. 194.

121.   Appendix A to JCSM-729-64, August 24, 1964, JCS Files, Record Group 218, National Archives and Records Administration; and Memorandum from the Joint Chiefs of Staff to the Secretary of Defense, August 27, 1964, *FRUS, 1964–1968, Volume I*, pp. 713–717.

122.   Notes of Meeting with General Wheeler, November 1, 1964, Robert S. McNamara Papers, Department of Defense, cited in McNamara with Van-DeMark, *In Retrospect*, p. 159; and Sigma II-64 Final Report, pp. D14–15, LBJL.

123.   Author's interview with Ernest May, Robert McNamara, and Richard Neustadt, May 5, 1994.

124.   Bùi Diễm with Chanoff, *In the Jaws of History*, p. 121.

125.   Unpublished William Bundy Manuscript on Vietnam, Chapter 18, p. 1, LBJL.

126.   Richard H. Thaler, Cass R. Sunstein, and John P. Balz, "Choice Architecture," *SSRN*, April 2, 2010.

127.   Cass R. Sunstein, "The Law of Group Polarization," *Journal of Political Philosophy* 10, n. 2 (2002): pp. 175–195.

128.   L. Ross, M. R. Lepper, and M. Hubbard, "Perseverance in Self-Perception and Social Perception: Biased Attributional Processes in the Debriefing Paradigm," *Journal of Personality and Social Psychology* 32 (1975): pp. 888–892.

129.   Author's interviews with Robert McNamara, December 14, 1993, and October 19, 1993.

130.   John McNaughton and McGeorge Bundy Notes, Meeting Notes File (hereafter cited as MNF), Box 1, LBJL; and PPMB, LBJL.

131.   CAP64375, Johnson to Taylor, December 30, 1964, *FRUS, 1964–1968, Volume I*, pp. 1057–1059.

132.   Embtel 2052, Taylor to Johnson, January 6, 1965, *FRUS, 1964–1968, Volume II*, pp. 12–19.

133.   Author's interview with Robert McNamara and McGeorge Bundy, March 18, 1994.

134.   MBDMVN, Draft #1/65—Important miscellaneous, May 3, 1996, p. 2, PPMB, Box 224, JFKL.

135.   Author's interview with Robert McNamara, December 14, 1993.

136.   McGeorge Bundy OHI 07–18, LBJL.

137.   Telephone Conversation between President Johnson and Robert McNamara, January 17, 1966, Tape 9502 (WH 6601.08), Miller Center White House Recordings (hereafter cited as MCWHR)

138.   Bundy to Johnson, January 27, 1965, *FRUS, 1964–1968, Volume II*, pp. 95–97.

139.   McGeorge Bundy OHI 07–18, LBJL.

140.   Author's interview with Robert McNamara, July 18, 1994.

141.   Rusk to Johnson, February 23, 1965, *FRUS, 1964–1968, Volume II*, pp. 355–359.

142.   Lady Bird Johnson Tape-Recorded Diary Entry, January 29, 1965, in Beschloss, ed., *Reaching for Glory*, p. 170.

143.   McGeorge Bundy's notes of January 27, 1965, meeting in PPMB, LBJL.

144.   Quoted in Halberstam, *Best and the Brightest*, p. 530.

145.   Luu Doan Huynh, quoted in McNamara et al., *Argument Without End*, p. 228.

146.   Quoted in Ellsberg, *Secrets*, p. 52.

147.   Quoted in Halberstam, *Best and the Brightest*, p. 528.

148.   McGeorge Bundy OHI 07–18, LBJL.

149.   MBDMVN, PPMB, Box 225, JFKL.

150.   Author's interview with Robert McNamara, November 3, 1993.

151.   Bundy to McCone, February 4, 1965, *FRUS, 1964–1968, Volume II*, pp. 140–141.

152.   Bromley Smith's Summary Notes of 545th National Security Council Meeting, February 6, 1965, ibid.; and Johnson, *Vantage Point*, pp. 124–125.

153.   Bundy to Johnson, February 7, 1965, *FRUS, 1964–1968, Volume II*, pp. 174–181.

154.   Summary Notes of 547th NSC Meeting, February 8, 1965, ibid., pp. 188–192.

155.   Quoted in McNamara et al., *Argument Without End*, p. 209.

156.   *Washington Post*, February 23, 1965, p. A9.

157.   Quoted in Mark Lorell, Charles Kelley Jr., and Deborah Hensler, *Casualties, Public Opinion, and Presidential Policy Making During the Vietnam War* (Rand Corporation, 1985), p. 45; and Clifford with Holbrooke, *Counsel to the President*, p. 417.

158.   Author's interview with Robert McNamara, November 3, 1993.

159.   Author's interview with Robert Gard, August 18, 2016.

160.   Author's interview with Robert McNamara, November 3, 1993.

161.   Taylor to Joint Chiefs of Staff, February 22, 1965, *FRUS, 1964–1968, Volume II*, pp. 347–349; and Telephone conversation with Robert McNamara, February 26, 1965, in Beschloss, ed., *Reaching for Glory*, pp. 193–195.

162.   Telephone conversation with Richard Russell, March 6, 1965, 12:05 P.M., ibid, pp. 211–212.

163.   Telephone conversation with Robert McNamara, March 6, 1965, 2:32 P.M., ibid., pp. 213–216.

164.   Quoted in *The Vietnam War*, episode 3, "The River Styx (January 1964– December 1965)," directed by Ken Burns and Lynn Novick, aired on September 19, 2017, on PBS.

165.   Telephone conversation with Robert McNamara, July 2, 1965, Beschloss, ed., *Reaching for Glory*, p. 238.

166.   Quoted in Halberstam, *Best and the Brightest*, p. 572.

167.   See McGeorge Bundy's notes of the April 1, 1965, meeting in PPMB, LBJL.

168.   J. L. Freedman and S. C. Fraser, "Compliance Without Pressure: The Foot-in-the-Door Technique," *Journal of Personality and Psychology* 4, n. 2 (1966): pp. 195–202.

169.   Jerry M. Burger, "The Foot-in-the-Door Compliance Procedure: A Multiple-Process Analysis and Review," *Personality and Social Psychology Review* 3, n. 4 (1999): pp. 303–325; and Kris Kristofferson, Katherine White, and John

Peloza, "The Nature of Slacktivism: How the Social Observability of an Initial Act of Token Support Affects Subsequent Prosocial Action," *Journal of Consumer Research*, 2013.

170. See McCone to Rusk et al., April 2, 1965, *FRUS, 1964–1968, Volume II*, pp. 522–524.

171. Quoted in Kearns, *Lyndon Johnson and the American Dream*, p. 270.

172. See Qiang Zhai, "Beijing and the Vietnam Conflict, 1964–1965: New Chinese Evidence," *Cold War International History Project Bulletin*, n. 6–7, Winter 1995/1996, pp. 233–250; and James G. Hershberg and Chen Jian, "Reading and Warning the Likely Enemy: China's Signals to the United States about Vietnam in 1965," *International History Review*, v. 27, n. 1, March 2005, p. 64, citing minutes of an April 12, 1965, Politburo meeting in China's Central Committee Archives.

173. Author's interview with Ernest May, Robert McNamara, and Richard Neustadt, May 5, 1994.

174. Jared Diamond, "Easter's End," *Discover*, August 1, 1995.

175. Author's interview with Robert McNamara, October 9, 1993.

176. First Secretary Lê Duẩn to General Nguyễn Chí Thanh, May 1965, in Le Duan, *Letters to the South* (Hanoi: Foreign Languages Press, 1986).

177. McNamara to Johnson, April 21, 1965, *FRUS, 1964–1968, Volume II*, pp. 574–576.

178. President's News Conference, April 27, 1965, *Public Papers: Lyndon B. Johnson, 1965*, Book I (Government Printing Office, 1966), pp. 448–456.

179. *New York Herald-Tribune*, May 23, 1965.

180. Kỳ interview with Brian Moynahan published in the *Sunday Mirror*, July 4, 1965, p. 9; Bùi Diễm with Chanoff, *In the Jaws of History*, p. 149; William Bundy OHI, LBJL; Greene quotes in *Newsweek*, May 10, 1965, p. 49; and Embtel 4035, Taylor to Rusk, June 3, 1965, *FRUS, 1964–1968, Volume II*, pp. 710–713.

181. McNamara with VanDeMark, *In Retrospect*, p. 188.

182. Westmoreland to Wheeler, June 7, 1965, ibid., pp. 733–736.

183. For a record of this June 8, 1965 meeting, see PPMB, LBJL.

184. Author's interview with George Ball, June 1988.

185. Telephone conversation with Mike Mansfield, June 8, 1965, 5:05 P.M., in Beschloss, ed., *Reaching for Glory*, pp. 344–348.

186. Mansfield to Johnson, June 5 and 9, 1965, *FRUS, 1964–1968, Volume II*, pp. 725–727 and 741–744.

187. For notes of this June 10, 1965, meeting, see PPMB, LBJL.

188. Telephone conversation with Robert McNamara, June 10, 1965, 6:40 P.M., in Beschloss, ed., *Reaching for Glory*, pp. 348–353.

189. See confidential Louis Harris polls in Hayes Redmon to Johnson, June 17, 1965, and "PR 16 Public Opinion Polls (April 1964–June 1965)," Boxes 71 and 80, Confidential Files (hereafter cited as CFF), White House Central Files (hereafter cited as WHCF), LBJL.

190. Telephone conversation with Robert McNamara, June 21, 1965, in Beschloss, ed., *Reaching for Glory*, pp. 364–366.

191. Author's interview with Robert McNamara and McGeorge Bundy, March 18, 1994.

192.   Telephone conversation with Robert McNamara, June 30, 1965, in Beschloss ed., *Reaching for Glory*, pp. 376–377.

193.   Lady Bird Johnson Audio Diary Transcripts, July 8, 1965, LBJL.

194.   Telephone conversation with Robert McNamara, July 2, 1965, Beschloss ed., *Reaching for Glory*, pp. 381–382.

195.   McNamara to Johnson, July 20, 1965, *Foreign Relations of the United States, 1964–1968, Volume III: Vietnam, June–December 1965 (hereafter cited as FRUS, 1964–1968, Volume III)* (U.S. Government Printing Office, 1996), pp. 171–179.

196.   Kahneman, *Thinking, Fast and Slow*, pp. 280–284.

197.   Robert H. Frank, "What Comes Next for Obamacare?: The Case for Medicare for All," *New York Times*, March 24, 2017.

198.   Daniel Kahneman and Amos Tversky, "Choices, Values, and Frames," *American Psychologist* 39, n. 4 (1984): pp. 341–350.

199.   Author's interviews with Clark Clifford, June 7, 1988, Tape One; and June 3, 1988, Tape Two.

200.   Quoted in Kearns, *Lyndon Johnson and the American Dream*, pp. 259–260; and William Bundy unpublished Vietnam manuscript, LBJL.

201.   President's News Conference, July 28, 1965, *Public Papers: Lyndon B. Johnson, 1965*, Book II (Government Printing Office, 1966), pp. 794–803.

202.   Author's interview with McGeorge Bundy and Robert McNamara, March 18, 1994.

203.   Author's interview with Ernest May, Robert McNamara, and Richard Neustadt, May 5, 1994.

204.   Clark Clifford stressed this point to Johnson at the time, in interviews with the author, and in his memoir.

205.   Quoted in Halberstam, *Best and the Brightest*, p. 507.

206.   Telephone Conversation between President Johnson and Robert McNamara, January 31, 1966, Tape 9543 (WH6601.11), MCWHR.

207.   President's News Conference, July 28, 1965, *Public Papers: Lyndon B. Johnson, 1965*, Book II (Government Printing Office, 1966), pp. 794–803.

CHAPTER 5: THE HAZARD OF SUNK COSTS (AUGUST 1965–MAY 1967)

1.   PPMB, Box 226, JFKL; McGeorge Bundy, "Starting from Vietnam," February 23, 1993, Box 232; and author's interview with Robert McNamara, July 19, 1994.

2.   See Hersh Shefrin and Meit Statman, "The Disposition to Sell Winners Too Early and Ride Losers Too Long: Theory and Evidence," *Journal of Finance* 40 (1985): pp. 777–790; and Terrance Odean, "Are Investors Reluctant to Realize Their Losses?" *Journal of Finance*, 53 (1998): pp. 1775–1798.

3.   Barry M. Staw, "The Escalation of Commitment to a Course of Action," *Academy of Management Review* v. 6, n. 4 (October 1981): pp. 557–587.

4.   Barry M. Staw, "Knee-Deep in the Big Muddy: A Study of Escalating Commitment to a Chosen Course of Action," *Organizational Behavior and Human Performance* 16 (1976): pp. 27–44.

5.   Leon Festinger, *A Theory of Cognitive Dissonance* (Stanford University Press, 1957); and J. W. Brehm and A. E. Cohen, *Explorations in Cognitive Dissonance* (Wiley, 1962).

6. Quoted in Joel Brockner and Jeffrey Z. Rubin, *Entrapment in Escalating Conflicts: A Social Psychological Analysis* (Springer-Verlag, 1985), p. 148.

7. Kahneman, *Thinking, Fast and Slow*, pp. 345–346.

8. H. Garland, "Throwing Good Money After Bad: The Effect of Sunk Costs on the Decision to Escalate Commitment to an Ongoing Project," *Journal of Applied Psychology* 75 (1990): pp. 728–731.

9. Hal R. Arkes and Peter Ayton, "The Sunk Cost and Concorde Effects: Are Humans Less Rational Than Lower Animals?" *Psychological Bulletin* 125, n. 5 (1999): pp. 591–600.

10. Kahneman, *Thinking, Fast and Slow*, pp. 318–319.

11. Richard H. Thaler and Cass R. Sunstein, *Nudge: Improving Decisions about Wealth, Health, and Happiness* (Yale University Press, 2008), p. 37.

12. Quoted in Ellsberg, *Secrets*, p. 86.

13. See Herbert A. Simon, *Models of Bounded Rationality*, 3 vols. (MIT Press, 1982, 1997) and *Reason in Human Affairs* (Stanford University Press, 1983); and Kahneman, *Thinking, Fast and Slow*, pp. 39–40.

14. Gilovich, *How We Know What Isn't So*, p. 133.

15. Bùi Diễm with Chanoff, *In the Jaws of History*, p. 153; "Bill Moyers Talks about the War and LBJ, An Interview," *The Atlantic*, July 1968; Bernard B. Fall, "Vietnam Blitz: A Report on the Impersonal War," *The New Republic*, October 9, 1965, pp. 17–21; and *Newsweek*, October 11, 1965, p. 2.

16. Cited by McGeorge Bundy in his May 1971 lecture at the Council on Foreign Relations, PPMB, Box 224, JFKL.

17. Quoted in the *Wall Street Journal*, November 26–27, 2016, p. C7.

18. Quoted in Sheehan, *Bright Shining Lie*, p. 643.

19. Roger Buehler, Dale Griffin, and Michael Ross, "Exploring the 'Planning Fallacy': Why People Underestimate Their Task Completion Times," *Journal of Personality and Social Psychology* 67, n. 3 (1994): pp. 366–381.

20. Kahneman, *Thinking, Fast and Slow*, p. 252. See also Daniel Kahneman and Amos Tversky, "Intuitive Prediction: Biases and Corrective Procedures," *Management Science* 12 (1979): pp. 313–327; and Daniel Kahneman and Dan Lovallo, "Delusions of Success: How Optimism Undermines Executives' Decisions," *Harvard Business Review* 81 (2003): pp. 56–63.

21. Quoted in Peer de Silva, *Sub Rosa: The CIA and the Uses of Intelligence* (Times Books, 1978), p. 224.

22. Quoted in Sheehan, *Bright Shining Lie*, p. 568; and William Conrad Gibbons, *The U.S. Government and the Vietnam War: Executive and Legislative Roles and Relationships, Part IV, July 1965–January 1968* (Government Printing Office, 1994), p. 50.

23. Author's interview with Ernest May, Robert McNamara, and Richard Neustadt, May 5, 1994.

24. Quoted in Lewis Sorley, *Honorable Warrior: General Harold K. Johnson and the Ethics of Command* (University Press of Kansas, 1998), p. 290.

25. Admiral Charles K. Duncan, USN (Retired), United States Naval Institute Oral History, vol. 2, p. 656.

26. Quoted in James Cannon to Adam Yarmolinsky, July 29, 1963, McNamara files in author's possession.

27.   Author's interview with Robert Gard, August 18, 2016.

28.   Author's interview with Morton Halperin, October 17, 2016.

29.   Henry Glass, quoted in Shapley, *Promise and Power*, p. 357; Bundy quoted in Gibbons, *U.S. Government and the Vietnam War, Volume IV*, p. 54; and MBDMVN, PPMB, Box 224, JFKL.

30.   Author's interview with Alfred Goldberg and Robert McNamara, April 29, 1994.

31.   Quoted in John Mason Glen, "Was America Duped at Khe Sanh?" *New York Times*, January 1, 2018.

32.   Thomas C. Thayer, *War Without Fronts: The American Experience in Vietnam* (Westview Press, 1985), p. 46.

33.   Vo Nguyen Giap, "People's War, People's Army," in Russell Stetler, ed., *The Military Art of People's War: Selected Writings of Vo Nguyen Giap* (Monthly Review Press, 1970), pp. 104–106.

34.   Quoted in Neil Sheehan, "David and Goliath in Vietnam," *New York Times*, May 26, 2017.

35.   Reprinted in Bui Tin, *From Enemy to Friend: A North Vietnamese Perspective on the War* (Naval Institute Press, 2002), pp. 19–20.

36.   Quoted in Andrew F. Krepinevich Jr., *The Army and Vietnam* (Johns Hopkins University Press, 1986), p. 190.

37.   Cited in *Congressional Record*, v. 118, n. 76, May 10, 1972, p. E4978.

38.   Author's interview with Clark Clifford, October 17, 1988.

39.   Tin, *From Enemy to Friend*, p. 4.

40.   Richard Stilwell OHI, LBJL.

41.   Ho Chi Minh, *Collected Works*, v. 2 (Truth Publishing House, 1980), p. 376.

42.   Interview with Nguyễn Cơ Thạch, cited in Porter, "The Tonkin Gulf Crisis Reconsidered," p. 22, n. 55.

43.   Mats Alvesson and Andre Spicer, *The Stupidity Paradox: The Power and Pitfalls of Functional Stupidity at Work* (Profile Books, 2016), p. 192.

44.   Colby with McCargar, *Lost Victory*, p. 179.

45.   Telephone Conversation between President Johnson and Robert McNamara, September 12, 1965, Tape 8851 (WH6509.03), MCWHR.

46.   William Ehrhart, quoted in Karnow, *Vietnam*, p. 482.

47.   President Johnson's Notes on Conversation with Secretary McNamara, November 30, 1965, Recordings and Transcripts of Telephone Conversations and Meetings (hereafter cited as RTTCM), Box 7, LBJL.

48.   General Harold K. Johnson, quoted by Colonel Sidney Berry in Sorley, *Honorable Warrior*, p. 224.

49.   McNamara with VanDeMark, *In Retrospect*, p. 222; and Chet Cooper quoted in Shapley, *Promise and Power*, p. 358.

50.   Memorandum from Secretary of Defense McNamara to President Johnson, November 30, 1965, *FRUS, 1964–1968, Volume III*, pp. 591–594; and Notes of Meeting with McNamara et al., November 30, 1965, PPMB, LBJL.

51.   Telephone Conversation between President Johnson and Robert McNamara, November 2, 1965, Tape 9103 (WH6511.01), MCWHR.

52.   Jean-Leon Beauvois, Robert-Vincent Joule, and Fabien Brunetti, "Cognitive

Rationalization and Act Rationalization in an Escalation of Commitment," *Basic and Applied Social Psychology* 14 (1993): pp. 1–17.

53. Telephone Conversation between President Johnson and Robert McNamara, December 2, 1965, Tape 9305 (WH6512.01), MCWHR.

54. Telephone Conversation between President Johnson and McGeorge Bundy, December 11, 1965, Tape 9314 (WH6512.02), MCWHR.

55. Notes of December 6, 1965, White House Meeting, PPMB, LBJL.

56. Author's interview with Robert McNamara, April 1, 1994.

57. Notes of December 7, 1965, Meeting at the Johnson Ranch, PPMB, LBJL.

58. Notes of Meeting, December 17, 1965, *FRUS, 1964–1968, Volume III*, pp. 644–647.

59. Telephone Conversation between President Johnson and Dean Rusk, February 20, 1966, Tape 9649 (WH6602.05), MCWHR.

60. Notes of December 18, 1965, meeting, *FRUS, 1964–1968, Volume III*, pp. 658–669; and Clifford with Holbrooke, *Counsel to the President*, pp. 434–435.

61. Telephone Conversation between President Johnson and Dean Rusk, January 21, 1966, Tape 9522 (WHG6601.10), MCWHR; and Chester Cooper, *In the Shadows of History: Fifty Years Behind the Scenes of Cold War Diplomacy* (Prometheus Books, 2005), p. 229.

62. Telephone Conversation between President Johnson and Robert McNamara, January 17, 1966, Tape 9502 (WH6601.08), MCWHR.

63. Quoted in Cooper, *In the Shadows of History,* p. 255.

64. Quoted in ibid., p. 259.

65. Quoted in McNamara, et al., *Argument Without End,* p. 260.

66. Richard Helms with William Hood, *A Look over My Shoulder: A Life in the Central Intelligence Agency* (Random House, 2003), p. 318.

67. Douglas Pike, "Watching Hanoi," in Edward Doyle, Samuel Lipsman, Terrence Maitland, and the editors of Boston Publishing Company, *The Vietnam Experience: The North* (Boston Publishing Company, 1986), p. 30.

68. Telephone Conversation between President Johnson and Dean Rusk, February 20, 1966, Tape 9649 (WH6602.05), MCWHR; and author's interview with Robert McNamara, April 1, 1994.

69. Quoted in McNamara et al., *Argument Without End,* p. 243.

70. General Nguyễn Đình Ước, head of Vietnam's Institute of Military History; and Christopher Goscha, *Vietnam: A New History* (Basic Books, 2016), p. 329.

71. Schlesinger, *Robert F. Kennedy and His Times,* pp. 734–735.

72. Benjamin T. Harrison and Christopher L. Mosher, "The Secret Diary of McNamara's Dove: The Long-Lost Story of John T. McNaughton's Opposition to the Vietnam War," *Diplomatic History* 35, n. 3 (June 2011): p. 519.

73. Postscript to Memorandum of Conversation with Secretary McNamara, June 23, 1966, Averell Harriman Papers, Manuscript Division, Library of Congress.

74. LBADT, February 4, 1966, LBJL.

75. Johnson to Mansfield, June 22, 1966, WHCF; and President Johnson's Notes on Conversation with Walker Stone, February 22, 1966, 5 PM, RTTCM, Box 8, LBJL.

76. Telephone Conversation between President Johnson and Maxwell Taylor, December 27, 1965, Tape 9339 (WH6512.05), MCWHR.

77. President Johnson's Notes on Conversation with Henry Luce, February 21, 1966, 9:35 A.M., MCWHR.

78. Merriman Smith to President Johnson, February 19, 1966, LBJL.

79. President Johnson's Notes on Conversation with Walker Stone, February 22, 1966, 5 P.M., RTTCM, Box 8, ibid.

80. President Johnson to Senator Robert Kennedy, January 27, 1966, LBJL.

81. Telephone Conversation between President Johnson and Dwight Eisenhower, January 25, 1966, Tape 9533 (WH6601.10); and Telephone Conversation between President Johnson and McGeorge Bundy, February 22, 1966, Tape 9656 (WH6602.07), MCWHR.

82. Quoted in Bùi Diễm with Chanoff, In the Jaws of History, p. 161; and Karnow, Vietnam, p. 459.

83. Halberstam, Best and the Brightest, p. 623.

84. MBDMVN, "My Parting with Lyndon Johnson," PPMB, Box 226, JFKL.

85. Author's interview with Ernest May, Robert McNamara, and Richard Neustadt, May 5, 1994; and Telephone Conversation between President Johnson and George Ball, March 10, 1966, Tape 9876 (WH6603.06), MCWHR.

86. Telephone Conversation between President Johnson and McGeorge Bundy, December 3, 1965, Tape 9307 (WH6512.01), MCWHR.

87. Quoted in Kai Bird, The Color of Truth: McGeorge Bundy and William Bundy Brothers in Arms (Simon & Schuster, 1998), pp. 344 and 346.

88. Author's interview with Robert McNamara, July 18, 1994.

89. Author's interview with George Ball, June 9, 1988.

90. Author's interview with Francis Bator, May 18, 2016.

91. Telephone Conversation between President Johnson and Dean Rusk, November 29, 1965, Tape 9198 (WH6511.09), MCWHR.

92. Author's interview with Francis Bator, May 18, 2016.

93. Quoted in Ellsberg, Secrets, p. 184.

94. McGeorge Bundy to Robert McNamara, March 25, 1994, PPMB, Box 189, JFKL.

95. Halberstam, Best and the Brightest, p. 637.

96. Author's interview with Clark Clifford and Benjamin Read, August 18, 1988.

97. George W. Allen, None So Blind: A Personal Account of the Intelligence Failure in Vietnam (Ivan R. Dee, 2001), pp. 236–237; and George Allen OHI, pp. 55–57, LBJL.

98. Telephone Conversation between President Johnson and Dean Rusk, March 18, 1966, Tape 9918 (WH6603.09), MCWHR.

99. McNamara with VanDeMark, In Retrospect, p. 261.

100. FitzGerald, Fire in the Lake, p. 294.

101. U. S. Grant Sharp, Strategy for Defeat: Vietnam in Retrospect (Presidio Press, 1978), p. 269.

102. Quoted in Karnow, Vietnam, p. 512.

103. "Memorandum for the File, Subject: Board Meeting, May 26–27, 1966," PFIAB Records.

104. Board of National Estimates Special Memorandum, cited in Gibbons, U.S.

Government and the Vietnam War, Volume IV, July 1965–January 1968, p. 153; Jack Valenti's Notes of White House Meeting, January 22, 1966, MNF, LBJL; and Military History Institute of Vietnam, *Victory in Vietnam: The Official History of the People's Army of Vietnam, 1954–1975* (University of Kansas Press, 2002), p. 182.

105.   Telephone Conversation between President Johnson and McGeorge Bundy, February 22, 1966, Tape 9655 (WH6602.07), MCWHR.

106.   *Congressional Record*, v. 112, January 24, 1966, pp. 965–966.

107.   *Washington Post*, January 31, 1966.

108.   "Petroleum in North Vietnam at the Outset of 1967 (A Review of Developments During 1966)," February 1967, CIA Memos, 1967, Box 180, NSF, Vietnam, LBJL.

109.   Gallup Poll, July 24, 1966, WHCF, LBJL.

110.   Carl Berger, ed., *The United States Air Force in Southeast Asia, 1961–1973* (Office of Air Force History, 1977), p. 366.

111.   See Tin, *From Enemy to Friend*, p. 75.

112.   Author's interview with Robert McNamara and Paul Warnke, March 28, 1994.

113.   Pierre Asselin, "Hanoi and Americanization of the War in Vietnam: New Evidence from Vietnam," *Pacific Historical Review* 74, n. 3 (2005): p. 430.

114.   Mark Clodfelter, *The Limits of Air Power: The American Bombing of North Vietnam* (Free Press, 1989), p. 136.

115.   Ibid., p. 135.

116.   Military History Institute of Vietnam, *Victory in Vietnam*, p. 170.

117.   Ibid., pp. xiii-xiv, 174, and 182.

118.   Ibid., p. 156; and William J. Duiker, *Ho Chi Minh: A Life* (Hyperion, 2000), p. 548.

119.   These hazards are vividly described in Bùi Tín, *Following Ho Chi Minh: Memoirs of a North Vietnamese Colonel* (University of Hawaii Press, 1995), pp. 47–51. Tín first made the trek down the Hồ Chí Minh Trail in 1964.

120.   Military History Institute of Vietnam, *Victory in Vietnam*, p. 182.

121.   Krepinevich, *Army and Vietnam*, pp. 180–183; and Douglas Kinnard, *The War Managers* (University Press of New England, 1977), p. 69.

122.   Sheehan, *Bright Shining Lie*, p. 683.

123.   Quoted in Krepinevich, *Army and Vietnam*, p. 197.

124.   *Newsweek*, March 27, 1967.

125.   Lieutenant General John Tolson, *Vietnam Studies: Airmobility, 1961–1971* (Government Printing Office, 1973), p. 117.

126.   A detailed discussion of the PROVN study is in Sorley, *Honorable Warrior*, pp. 227–241.

127.   Statistical Information about Fatal Casualties of the Vietnam War, Military Records, National Archives, Washington, D.C.

128.   Congressional Research Service Reports and Department of Defense Personnel Statistics.

129.   Gerald F. Goodwin, "Black and White in Vietnam," *New York Times*, July 18, 2017; and Deborah Paredez, "Soldiers in La Guerra," *New York Times*, January 5, 2018.

130. McNamara with VanDeMark, *In Retrospect*, pp. 242–243.

131. Westmoreland, *A Soldier Reports*, p. 295.

132. Lieutenant Colonel Dave Grossman, *On Killing: The Psychological Cost of Learning to Kill in War and Society* (revised ed., Back Bay Books, 2009), p. xxxi.

133. Karl Marlantes, *What It Is Like to Go to War* (Atlantic Monthly Press, 2011), pp. xi, 3, and 44.

134. Peter Fossel, "PTSD Does Not Mean You're Weak," *New York Times*, September 26, 2017.

135. Grossman, *On Killing*, p. xxxv.

136. R. A. Gilbert, *No More Heroes: Madness and Psychiatry in War* (Hill and Wang, 1987).

137. Guenter Lewy, *America in Vietnam: Illusion, Myth, and Reality* (Oxford University Press, 1978), p. 152.

138. Quoted in *The Vietnam War*, episode 4, "Resolve (January 1966–June 1967)," directed by Ken Burns and Lynn Novick, aired on September 20, 2017, on PBS.

139. Krepinevich, *Army and Vietnam*, pp. 222–223, 199–200, and 203; and Douglas Kinnard, *The War Managers* (University Press of New Hampshire, 1977), pp. 54–55.

140. See Office of the Assistant Secretary of Defense for Systems Analysis, Working Paper on the War in South Vietnam, August 14, 1967, Papers of Alain Enthoven (hereafter cited as PAE), Box 24, LBJL.

141. Quoted in *Honorable Warrior*, p. 255.

142. Quoted in *The Vietnam War*, episode 5, "This Is What We Do (July–December 1967)," directed by Ken Burns and Lynn Novick, aired on September 21, 2017, on PBS.

143. Quoted in Ellsberg, *Secrets*, p. 165.

144. Sorley, *Honorable Warrior*, p. 234.

145. Cincinnatus, *Self-Destruction* (W. W. Norton, 1981), pp. 83–84.

146. Quoted in Krepinevich, *Army and Vietnam*, p. 204.

147. Ibid., p. 199.

148. Thayer, *War Without Fronts*, p. 79; Raphael Littauer and Norman Uphoff, eds., *Air War in Indochina* (Beacon Press, 1972), p. 11; and Carl Berger, ed., *The United States Air Force in Southeast Asia, 1961–1973* (Office of Air Force History, 1984), p. 89.

149. John Wheeler, "U.S. Bombs Kill Innocents," *Washington Evening Star*, July 19, 1965.

150. Phillips, *Why Vietnam Matters*, p. 271.

151. Mai Elliott, "The Terrible Violence of 'Pacification," *New York Times*, January 18, 2018.

152. These quotes are in Westmoreland's taped interview as part of Peter Davis's 1974 documentary film, *Hearts and Minds*.

153. Quoted in *Vietnam War*, episode 5.

154. Quoted in Sheehan, *Bright Shining Lie*, p. 619.

155. Quotes are in Karnow, *Vietnam*, pp. 452–453.

156. Anthony J. Russo, "A Statistical Analysis of the US Crop Spraying Program in South Vietnam," RM-5450-I-ISAARPA (Rand Corporation, 1967).

157.   Alain C. Enthoven and K. Wayne Smith, *How Much Is Enough?: Shaping the Defense Program, 1961–1969* (Harper & Row, 1971), p. 294.

158.   Quoted in Cecil B. Currey, *Edward Lansdale: The Unquiet American* (Houghton Mifflin, 1989), p. 306.

159.   Phillips, *Why Vietnam Matters*, p. 267.

160.   Quoted in FitzGerald, *Fire in the Lake*, p. 464.

161.   George Allen OHI, I, pp. 38–39, LBJL.

162.   Ibid., p. 318; and Phillips, *Why Vietnam Matters*, p. 253.

163.   David Halberstam, "Return to Vietnam," *Harper's*, December 1967, p. 53.

164.   Quoted in Ellsberg, *Secrets*, p. 169.

165.   Rufus Phillips, "'Peace and Prosperity' Village, Gia Dinh Province: The Political War," August 21, 1966, Edward Lansdale Collection, Box 56, Hoover Institution, Stanford, California.

166.   John McNaughton Diary, April 6, 1966, quoted in Harrison and Mosher, "The Secret Diary of McNamara's Dove," p. 525.

167.   Telephone Conversation between President Johnson and Richard Russell, June 2, 1966, Tape 10204 (WH6606.01), MCWHR; and *Washington Post*, June 19, 1966.

168.   Telephone Conversation between President Johnson and Robert McNamara, June 28, 1966, Tape 10266 (WH6606.06), MCWHR.

169.   "Memorandum for the File: Subject: Board Meeting, September 29–30, 1966," PFIAB Records.

170.   Allen, *None So Blind*, pp. 211–217.

171.   Quoted in Dallek, *Flawed Giant*, p. 385.

172.   Address before the Tennessee Legislature, March 15, 1967, *Public Papers of the Presidents, Lyndon B. Johnson, 1967* (Government Printing Office, 1968), pp. 348–354.

173.   Author's interviews with Clark Clifford, August 2, 1988, Tape Two; October 17, 1988, Tape Two; and June 3, 1988, Tape Two.

174.   McNamara to JCS, "CINCPAC CY 1966 Adjusted Requirements & CY 1967 Requirements," August 5, 1966, *Pentagon Papers*, vol. 4, p. 326.

175.   Telephone Conversation between President Johnson and Robert McNamara, September 19, 1966, Tape 10808 (WH6609.10), MCWHR.

176.   Transcript of McChristian Briefing, MACV Records (microfilm), U.S. Army Military History Institute, Carlisle Barracks, Pennsylvania.

177.   Memorandum from Secretary of Defense McNamara to President Johnson, October 14, 1966, *Foreign Relations of the United States, 1964–1968, Volume IV: Vietnam, 1966* (hereafter cited as *FRUS, 1964–1968, Volume IV*) (Government Printing Office, 1998), pp. 727–738.

178.   Author's interview with Robert McNamara, September 16, 1994.

179.   Author's interview with Robert McNamara, January 9, 1994.

180.   Author's interview with Robert McNamara, July 18, 1994.

181.   Memorandum from the Joint Chiefs of Staff to Secretary of Defense McNamara, JCSM-672–66, October 14, 1966, *FRUS, 1964–1968, Volume IV*, pp. 738–742.

182.   "Recommended FY 67 Southeast Asia Supplemental Appropriation," November 17, 1966, McNaughton Files, Paul Warnke Papers (hereafter cited as PWP), LBJL.

183. Telephone Conversation between President Johnson and Robert McNamara, January 25, 1967, Tape 11406 (WH6701.08), MCWHR.

184. John McNaughton Diary, December 11, 1966, quoted in Harrison and Mosher, "The Secret Diary of McNamara's Dove," pp. 529–530.

185. Bernard William Rogers, *Cedar Falls—Junction City: A Turning Point* (Government Printing Office, 1974), p. 157.

186. Senate Judiciary Committee, *Civilian Casualty, Social Welfare, and Refugee Problems in South Vietnam* (Government Printing Office, 1968).

187. COMUSMACV 09101 to CINCPAC, "Force Requirements," March 18, 1967, McNaughton Files, PWP, LBJL.

188. Notes on Discussion with the President, April 27, 1967, ibid.

189. Draft Memorandum from Secretary of Defense McNamara to President Johnson, May 19, 1967, *FRUS, 1964–1968, Volume V: Vietnam, 1967* (Government Printing Office, 2002), pp. 423–438.

190. McNamara with VanDeMark, *In Retrospect*, p. 269.

191. See note 189 above.

CHAPTER 6: THE JEOPARDY OF CONFLICTING LOYALTIES (MAY 1967–FEBRUARY 1968)

1. Author's interview with Adam Yarmolinsky, April 1, 1993.

2. Quoted in Henry L. Trewhitt, *McNamara: His Ordeal in the Pentagon* (Harper & Row, 1971), p. 237.

3. Author's interview with Robert McNamara, September 16, 1994.

4. Quoted in Trewhitt, *McNamara*, p. 270.

5. Author's interview with Morton Halperin, October 17, 2016.

6. Author's interview with Robert McNamara, September 16, 1994.

7. Eric Anicich and Jacob Hirsh, "The Psychology of Middle Power: Vertical Code-Switching, Role Conflict, and Behavioral Inhibition," *Academy of Management Review* 42, n. 2 (April 2017); and Eric M. Anicich and Jacob B. Hirsh, "Why Being a Middle Manager Is So Exhausting, *Harvard Business Review*, March 22, 2017.

8. Quoted in Trewhitt, *McNamara*, p. 267.

9. Military History Institute of Vietnam, *Victory in Vietnam*, p. 211.

10. Quoted in Halberstam, *Best and the Brightest*, p. 633.

11. CIA, "Synthesis of the Vietnam Situation: An Analysis and Estimate," May 23, 1967, NSF, Box 187, LBJL.

12. CIA Directorate of Intelligence, "Consequences of Mining the Seaports and Water Approaches to North Vietnam and Bombing the Northern Railroads and Roads" and "The Effectiveness of the Rolling Thunder Program," May 23, 1967, NSF, Box 180, LBJL.

13. Author's interview with Robert McNamara and Paul Warnke, March 28, 1994.

14. Author's interview with Robert Gard, August 18, 2016.

15. McNamara with VanDeMark, *In Retrospect*, p. 280.

16. Leslie Gelb, quoted in John Prados and Margaret Pratt Porter, eds., *Inside the Pentagon Papers* (University Press of Kansas, 2004), p. 18.

17. Author's interview with Morton Halperin, October 17, 2016.

18. Quoted in Halberstam, *Best and the Brightest*, p. 633.

19. General Douglas Kinnard, quoted in Gibbons, *U.S. Government and the Vietnam War, Part IV*, p. 726.

20. Bùi Diễm with Chanoff, *In the Jaws of History*, p. 188.

21. *Pentagon Papers, vol. 4*, pp. 517–518.

22. Author's interview with Robert Gard, August 18, 2016.

23. Quoted in Gibbons, *U.S. Government and the Vietnam War, Part IV*, p. 728.

24. President's Daily Diary, May 12, 1967, LBJL.

25. Harris Surveys, *New York Times*, May 17, 1967; and Fred Panzer to President Johnson, July 28, 1967, WHCF, LBJL.

26. Tom Johnson's Notes of Meetings, July 12, 1967, LBJL; Memorandum for the Record, July 12, 1967, Maxwell Taylor Papers, National Defense University; and McNamara with VanDeMark, *In Retrospect*, p. 283.

27. Quoted by McNamara in *New York Times*, July 13, 1967.

28. Author's interview with Robert McNamara, December 14, 1993.

29. Charlan Nemeth: *In Defense of Troublemakers: The Power of Dissent in Life and Business* (Basic Books, 2018), pp. 2–3.

30. Tom Johnson's Notes of Meetings, July 13, 1967, LBJL.

31. Author's interview with Francis Bator, May 18, 2016.

32. See Karnow, *Vietnam*, p. 559.

33. Tom Johnson's Notes of Meetings, August 8, 1967, LBJL.

34. Quoted in Trewhitt, *McNamara*, p. 272.

35. Phil G. Goulding, *Confirm or Deny: Informing the People on National Security* (Harper & Row, 1970), p. 181.

36. Author's interview with Eugene Zuckert, October 29, 1992.

37. Halberstam, *Best and the Brightest*, p. 246.

38. *Air War Against North Vietnam: Hearings before the Preparedness Investigating Subcommittee of the Committee on Armed Services, United States Senate*, Ninetieth Congress, First Session (Government Printing Office, 1967), Part 1, p. 2.

39. Admiral Sharp to General Wheeler, December 24, 1966, Backchannel Message File, William Westmoreland/CBS Litigation Records (hereafter cited as BMF, WW/CBSLR), Record Group 407, Box 17, Federal Records Center (hereafter cited as FRC), Suitland, Maryland.

40. *Air War Against North Vietnam*, Part 1, pp. 6, 8, 10, and 83.

41. Ibid., Part 2, pp. 126–127 and 143–144.

42. Quoted in Halberstam, *Best and the Brightest*, p. 647.

43. *Air War Against North Vietnam*, Part 3, pp. 205, 214, and 234.

44. Ibid., pp. 246 and 259.

45. McNamara with VanDeMark, *In Retrospect*, p. 284.

46. *Air War Against North Vietnam*, Part 4, pp. 276–277, 281, 297, and 304–305.

47. Quoted in Gibbons, *U.S. Government and the Vietnam War, Part IV*, p. 751.

48. Author's interview with Robert McNamara and Paul Warnke, March 28, 1994.

49. Quoted in Halberstam, *Best and the Brightest*, p. 218.

50. Quoted in Shapley, *Promise and Power*, p. 432.

51. McGeorge Bundy interview with Fredrik Logevall, March 15, 1994, PPMB, Box 225, JFKL.

52. Author's interview with Robert McNamara and Paul Warnke, March 28, 1994.

53.   Author's interview with Francis Bator, May 18, 2016.

54.   Quoted in Gibbons, *U.S. Government and the Vietnam War, Part IV*, pp. 752–753.

55.   Tom Johnson's Notes of Meetings, October 17, 1967, LBJL.

56.   Author's interview with Robert McNamara, April 1, 1994.

57.   Quoted in Bùi Diễm with Chanoff, *In the Jaws of History*, p. 195.

58.   Gallup Polls, October 7 and 25, 1967, WHCF, LBJL.

59.   Tom Johnson's Notes of Meetings, October 3, 1967, LBJL.

60.   C. I. Hovland, I. L. Janis, and H. H. Kelley, *Communication and Persuasion* (Yale University Press, 1953); and A. S. Luchins, "Experimental Attempts to Minimize the Impact of First Impressions," in C. I. Hovland, ed., *The Order of Presentation in Persuasion* (Yale University Press, 1957).

61.   Richard Helms, Memorandum for the President, September 12, 1967, VN, Box 259/260, LBJL.

62.   See Tip O'Neill, *Man of the House* (Random House, 1987), pp. 189–199.

63.   Tom Johnson's Notes of Meetings, October 16, 1967, LBJL.

64.   Tom Johnson's Notes of Meetings, October 23, 1967, LBJL.

65.   Author's interview with Robert McNamara, July 18, 1994.

66.   Quoted in Tom Wells, *The War Within: America's Battle over Vietnam* (University of California Press, 1994), p. 174.

67.   Quoted in Norman Mailer, *The Armies of the Night: History as a Novel, the Novel as History* (New American Library, 1968), p. 240.

68.   Ibid., pp. 175–178.

69.   Transcript of Telephone Conversation between President Johnson and Robert McNamara, October 21, 1967, 5:43 P.M., LBJL.

70.   *Time*, October 27, 1967.

71.   Joseph Loftus, "Guards Repulse War Protesters at the Pentagon," *New York Times*, October 22, 1967, pp. 1 and 58; and William Chapman, "152 Arrested as Violence Takes Over," *Washington Post*, October 22, 1967, pp. A1 and A10.

72.   Quoted in Jimmy Breslin, "Quiet Rally Turns Vicious," *Washington Post*, October 22, 1967, pp. A1 and A10.

73.   James Reston in the *New York Times*, October 23, 1967.

74.   Author's interview with Robert Gard, August 18, 2016.

75.   Quoted in Wofford, *Of Kennedys and Kings*, p. 448.

76.   Quoted in Bruce Jackson, "The Battle of the Pentagon," *The Atlantic*, January 1968, p. 41.

77.   *Washington Post*, December 18, 1967.

78.   Quoted in Trewhitt, *McNamara*, p. 244.

79.   0815, 10/4/67, Robert Pursley's Notes of Secretaries of Defense Robert McNamara's and Clark Clifford's Morning Staff Conferences, October 1967–January 1969, Personal Papers of Robert Pursley (hereafter cited as PPRP).

80.   Handwritten Notes of October 31, 1967 Meeting, Personal Papers of Tom Johnson, Box 6, LBJL.

81.   Draft Memorandum from Secretary of Defense McNamara to President Johnson, November 1, 1967, *Foreign Relations of the United States, 1964–1968, Volume V: Vietnam 1967* (Government Printing Office, 2002), pp. 943–950.

82.   Author's interview with McGeorge Bundy and Robert McNamara, March 18, 1994.

83.   Jim Jones's Notes of November 2, 1967, Meeting, MNF, LBJL.

84.   Author's interview with Robert McNamara, April 1, 1994.

85.   Author's interview with Robert McNamara, July 19, 1994.

86.   Memorandum of the President for the File, December 18, 1967, NSF, LBJL.

87.   McNamara with VanDeMark, *In Retrospect*, pp. 311 and 313.

88.   Author's interview with Robert McNamara, April 29, 1994.

89.   Telephone Conversation between President Johnson and Robert McNamara, March 4, 1966, Tape 9829 (WH6603.02), MCWHR.

90.   Clifford with Holbrooke, *Counsel to the President*, p. 460.

91.   Robert McNamara, "Security in the Contemporary World," Speech before American Society of Newspaper Editors, Montreal, Canada, May 18, 1966.

92.   Quoted in Halberstam, *Best and the Brightest*, p. 220; and Shapley, *Promise and Power*, p. 384.

93.   Telephone Conversation between President Johnson and Robert McNamara, August 10, 1966, Tape 10604 (WH6608.09), MCWHR.

94.   Draft Memorandum from Secretary of Defense McNamara to President Johnson, May 19, 1967, *FRUS, 1964–1968, Volume V*, p. 434.

95.   Author's interview with Francis Bator, May 18, 2016.

96.   LBADT, March 5, 1965, LBJL.

97.   Quoted in Sheehan, *Bright Shining Lie*, p. 692.

98.   LBADT, October 29, 1967, LBJL.

99.   David Eli Lilienthal, *The Journals of David E. Lilienthal*, vol. 6, *Creativity and Conflict, 1964–1967* (Harper & Row, 1976), p. 418.

100. Author's interview with Francis Bator, May 18, 2016.

101. Quoted in Shapley, *Promise and Power*, p. 415.

102. Author's interview with Robert McNamara, December 14, 1993.

103. Telephone Conversation between President Johnson and Robert McNamara, January 24, 1968, Tape 12610 (WH6801.01), MCWHR.

104. Author's interview with Clark Clifford, July 27, 1988.

105. Quoted in Shapley, *Promise and Power*, p. 427.

106. Author's interview with Robert McNamara, September 16, 1994.

107. Author's interview with Robert McNamara, July 19, 1994.

108. Quoted in Trewhitt, *McNamara*, p. 273.

109. Author's interview with Robert McNamara, July 19, 1994.

110. LBADT, October 29, 1967, LBJL.

111. Author's interview with Adam Yarmolinsky, April 1, 1993.

112. Author's interview with Clark Clifford, July 27, 1988.

113. Robert S. Billings and Charles F. Hermann, "Problem Identification in Sequential Policy Decision Making: The Re-Representation of Problems," in Donald A. Sylvan and James F. Voss, eds., *Problem Representation in Foreign Policy Decision Making* (Cambridge University Press, 1998), pp. 53–79; John M. Levine and Eileen M. Russo, "Majority and Minority Influence," in Clyde Hendrick, ed., *Group Processes* (Sage Publications, 1987), pp. 13–51; S. Moscovici, "Toward a Theory of Conversion Behavior," in L. Berkowitz, ed., *Advances in Experimental Social Psychology* (Academic Press, 1980), pp. 209–239; and Charlan Jeanne Nemeth, "Differential Contributions of Majority and Minority Influence," *Psychological Review* 93, n. 1 (1986): pp. 23–32.

114.   Nemeth, *In Defense of Troublemakers*, p. 68.

115.   Author's interview with Francis Bator, May 18, 2016.

116.   Bruce Palmer to Harry Middleton, in Gittinger, ed., *Johnson Years*, p. 161.

117.   Clark Clifford to President Johnson, May 17, 1965, NSF, LBJL.

118.   Jack Valenti's Notes of July 25, 1965, Camp David Meeting, MNF, Box 1, LBJL.

119.   Author's interview with Clark Clifford, August 5, 1988.

120.   Author's interview with Clark Clifford, July 14, 1988.

121.   Clifford with Holbrooke, *Counsel to the President*, p. 452.

122.   Kahneman, *Thinking, Fast and Slow*, p. 346.

123.   See Westmoreland to Abrams, November 26, 1967, HWA 3445, Message Files, Westmoreland Papers, Center for Military History (hereafter cited as CMH), Carlisle Barracks, Pennsylvania.

124.   Transcript of *Meet the Press*, aired November 19, 1967, on NBC.

125.   Westmoreland, *A Soldier Reports*, p. 234.

126.   William C. Westmoreland, National Press Club Address, November 21, 1967, quoted in George Wilson, "War's End in View—Westmoreland," *Washington Post*, November 22, 1967.

127.   Westmoreland to Sharp, "Military Operations in Vietnam," December 10, 1967, Message Files, Westmoreland Papers, CMH.

128.   Johnson to Abrams, WDC 15663, 221857Z, November 1967, ibid.

129.   Lieutenant General Joseph M. Heiser Jr., *Logistic Support* (Department of the Army, 1974), p. 251.

130.   Mark Perry, *Four Stars* (Houghton Mifflin, 1989), pp. 158–159.

131.   General Wheeler to General Westmoreland, June 2, 1966; and General Wheeler to Admiral Sharp and General Westmoreland, March 6, 1967, BMF, WW/CBSLR, Boxes 15 and 17, FRC.

132.   Author's interview with Morton Halperin, October 17, 2016.

133.   Quoted in Perry, *Four Stars*, p. 176.

134.   Earle Wheeler OHI, LBJL.

135.   Quoted in Perry, *Four Stars*, pp. 173–174.

136.   "People's War, People's Army" in Russell Stetler, ed., *The Military Art of People's War: Selected Writings of General Vo Nguyen Giap* (Monthly Review Press, 1970), pp. 104–106.

137.   The split within Hanoi's Politburo over proper military strategy is thoroughly analyzed in Lien-Hang T. Nguyen, "The War Politburo: North Vietnam's Diplomatic and Political Road to the Tet Offensive," *Journal of Vietnamese Studies* 1, n. 1–2 (2006): pp. 4–58.

138.   See Christopher Goscha, *Vietnam: A New History* (Basic Books, 2016), p. 331.

139.   MACV memo, quoted in Glen, "Was America Duped at Khe Sanh?"

140.   Quoted in Clark Dougan, Stephen Weiss, and the editors of Boston Publishing Company, *The Vietnam Experience: Nineteen Sixty-Eight* (Boston Publishing, 1983), p. 12.

141.   Quoted in Military History Institute of Vietnam, *Victory in Vietnam*, p. 218.

142.   Mark Bowden, *Hue 1968: A Turning Point of the American War in Vietnam* (Atlantic Monthly Press, 2017), p. 520.

143.   "Major Describes Move," *New York Times*, February 8, 1968.

144.   See Richard Helms to Maxwell Taylor, April 1, 1968, cited in *Foreign Rela-*

tions of the United States, 1964–1968, Volume VI: Vietnam, January–August 1968 (hereafter cited as *FRUS, 1964–1968, Volume VI*) (Government Printing Office, 2002), pp. 240–241.

145. Memorandum from Maxwell Taylor to President Johnson, June 7, 1968, "Evaluation of the Quality of U.S. Intelligence Bearing on the Tet Offensive, January 1968, PFIABR.

146. Earle Wheeler OHI, LBJL.

147. Quoted in Karnow, *Vietnam*, p. 556.

148. See Lien-Hang T. Nguyen, "The War Politburo: North Vietnam's Diplomatic and Political Road to the Tet Offensive," *Journal of Vietnamese Studies* 1, n. 1 (2006): p. 57.

149. Tran Van Tra, "Tet: The 1968 General Offensive and General Uprising," in Jayne S. Werner and Luu Doan Huynh, eds., *The Vietnam War: Vietnamese and American Perspectives* (M.E. Sharpe, 1993), p. 52.

150. "The War in Vietnam—Post-Tet," May 31, 1968, PAE, Box 24, LBJL.

151. See FitzGerald, *Fire in the Lake*, p. 397.

152. Quoted in ibid., p. 396.

153. Don Oberdorfer, *Tet!: The Turning Point in the Vietnam War* (Doubleday, 1971), p. 329.

154. Telephone Conversation between President Johnson and Robert McNamara, January 31, 1968, Tape 12617 (WH6801.02), MCWHR.

155. 2/9/68, Robert Pursley's Notes of Secretaries of Defense Robert McNamara's and Clark Clifford's Morning Staff Conferences, October 1967–January 1969, PPRP.

156. Quoted in Karnow, *Vietnam*, p. 562.

157. William DePuy OHI, LBJL.

158. MAC 01975, Westmoreland to Sharp and Wheeler, February 12, 1968, *FRUS, 1964–1968, Volume VI*, pp. 183–185.

159. Notes of President's Luncheon Meeting with Foreign Policy Advisors, February 20, 1968, Tom Johnson's Notes of Meetings, LBJL.

160. JCS 1529, Wheeler to Westmoreland, February 7, 1968, William C. Westmoreland Papers (hereafter cited as WCWP), LBJL.

161. JCS 1590, Wheeler to Westmoreland, February 9, 1968, WCWP, LBJL.

162. JCS 1589, Wheeler to Westmoreland, February 9, 1968; and JCS 1695, Wheeler to Westmoreland, February 12, 1968, WCWP, LBJL.

163. Stevenson to Kennedy, October 17, 1962, reprinted in Chang and Kornbluh, eds., *Cuban Missile Crisis*, pp. 119–120.

164. Quoted in *Pentagon Papers*, vol. 4, p. 542.

165. Quoted in Perry, *Four Stars*, p. 187.

166. Quoted in Karnow, *Vietnam*, p. 564.

167. William DePuy OHI, LBJL.

168. Quoted in Perry, *Four Stars*, pp. 187–188.

169. Quoted in John B. Henry II, "February 1968," *Foreign Policy*, Autumn 1971, p. 16.

170. Quoted in Perry, *Four Stars*, p. 188.

171. Memorandum from the Chairman of the Joint Chiefs of Staff to President Johnson, February 27, 1968, *FRUS, 1964–1968, Volume VI*, pp. 263–266.

172. Ibid.

173. Quoted in Henry, "February 1968," p. 24.

174. Ibid., p. 21.

175. Author's interview with Clark Clifford, August 5, 1988.

176. Quoted in Shapley, *Promise and Power*, p. 444; author's interview with Harry McPherson, July 20, 1988; and Karnow, *Vietnam*, p. 512.

177. Quoted in Clifford with Holbrooke, *Counsel to the President*, p. 485.

178. Author's interview with Harry McPherson, July 20, 1988.

179. Harry McPherson's Notes of Meeting, February 27, 1968, *FRUS, 1964–1968, Volume VI*, pp. 260–262; and Harry McPherson, *A Political Education* (Atlantic–Little, Brown, 1972), p. 431.

180. LBADT, February 28, 1968, LBJL.

181. President Johnson to Margy McNamara, February 7, 1968, Name File, WHCF, Box 318, LBJL.

182. LBADT, February 28, 1968.

183. Ibid.; and Clifford with Holbrooke, *Counsel to the President*, p. 486.

184. McNamara with VanDeMark, *In Retrospect*, pp. 316–317.

185. Author's interview with Clark Clifford.

CHAPTER 7: THE DIFFICULTY OF ENDING WAR (MARCH 1968–JANUARY 1969)

1. Harry McPherson to Clark Clifford, August 13, 1968, Aides Files/Harry McPherson, Box 53, LBJL.

2. Niccolo Machiavelli, *The Florentine History* (Harper & Row, 1960), p. 68.

3. Quoted in George C. Herring, *LBJ and Vietnam: A Different Kind of War* (University of Texas Press, 1994), p. 158; and Karnow, *Vietnam*, p. 565.

4. Quoted in Henry, "February 1968," p. 26.

5. Telephone Conversation between President Johnson and Clark Clifford, February 14, 1968, Tape 12716 (WH6802.02), MCWHR.

6. Goulding, *Confirm or Deny*, p. 306.

7. Halberstam, *Best and the Brightest*, p. 650.

8. Quoted in Goulding, *Confirm or Deny*, p. 309.

9. Author's interview with Clark Clifford, August 5, 1988.

10. Goulding, *Confirm or Deny*, p. 312.

11. Author's interview with Morton Halperin, October 17, 2016.

12. Author's interview with Clark Clifford, July 20, 1988, Tape One.

13. Quoted in Perry, *Four Stars*, p. 190.

14. Author's interview with Clark Clifford, July 29, 1988, Tape One.

15. Quoted in Clifford with Holbrooke, *Counsel to the President*, p. 493.

16. Author's interview with Clark Clifford, August 5, 1988.

17. Author's interview with Clark Clifford, June 7, 1988.

18. Author's interview with Morton Halperin, October 17, 2016.

19. Clifford with Holbrooke, *Counsel to the President*, pp. 493–494.

20. Author's interview with Clark Clifford, June 7, 1988, Tape Two.

21. Harold Johnson Notes of Meetings, May 1968, Box 127, Harold K. Johnson Papers, U.S. Army Military History Institute, Carlisle Barracks, Pennsylvania.

22. Notes of Meeting, March 4, 1968, *FRUS, 1964–1968, Volume VI*, pp. 316–327.

23. Quoted in Karnow, *Vietnam*, p. 561.

24. *FRUS, 1964–1968, Volume VI*, p. 313.

25. Rusk, *As I Saw It*, pp. 477 and 482.

26. Quoted in Bùi Diễm with Chanoff, *In the Jaws of History*, p. 225.

27. Notes of Meeting, March 4, 1968, *FRUS, 1964–1968, Volume VI*, pp. 316–327; and Clifford with Holbrooke, *Counsel to the President*, p. 496.

28. Quoted in Karnow, *Vietnam*, p. 570.

29. Author's interview with Francis Bator, May 18, 2016.

30. *Public Papers of the Presidents: Lyndon B. Johnson, 1968, Book 1* (Government Printing Office, 1969), pp. 402–413.

31. Notes of Meetings, March 20, 1968, 5:08–7:20 P.M., *FRUS, 1964–1968, Volume VI*, p. 433.

32. LBADT, March 31, 1968, LBJL.

33. Clifford with Holbrooke, *Counsel to the President*, p. 524; Telephone Conversation between President Johnson and William Fulbright, April 1, 1968, Tape 12901 (WH6804.01), MCWHR; and James R. Jones, "Behind LBJ's Decision Not to Run in '68," *New York Times*, April 16, 1988.

34. Quoted in Dallek, *Flawed Giant*, p. 523.

35. Elizabeth Wickenden, quoted in ibid., p. 528.

36. Sam Houston Johnson, *My Brother Lyndon* (Cowles, 1969), p. 4.

37. Lady Bird Johnson, *A White House Diary* (Holt, Rinehart, and Winston, 1970), p. 573.

38. Telephone Conversation between President Johnson and Senator Richard Russell, March 22, 1968, 4:49 P.M., *FRUS, 1964–1968, Volume VI*, p. 449.

39. Notes of the President's Meeting with General Earle Wheeler, JCS, and General Creighton Abrams, March 26, 1968, ibid., p. 463.

40. See Memorandum for the Record, "SUBJECT: Summary of Dean Acheson's Proposal," March 14, 1968, ibid., pp. 378–379.

41. Dean Acheson to Jane Acheson Brown, April 13, 1968, in David S. McLellan and David C. Acheson, eds., *Among Friends: Personal Letters of Dean Acheson* (Dodd, Mead, 1980), p. 297.

42. Quoted in Douglas Brinkley, *Dean Acheson: The Cold War Years, 1953–1971* (Yale University Press, 1992), p. 258.

43. McLellan and Acheson, eds., *Among Friends*, p. 293.

44. See Notes of the President's Meeting with His Foreign Policy Advisers at the Tuesday Luncheon, March 19, 1968, *FRUS, 1964–1968, Volume VI*, p. 413.

45. Clifford with Holbrooke, *Counsel to the President*, p. 507.

46. Telephone Conversation between President Johnson and Secretary of Defense Clifford, March 20, 1968, 8:44 A.M., *FRUS, 1964–1968, Volume VI*, pp. 428–431.

47. Rusk, *As I Saw It*, pp. 480–481.

48. Notes of President's Meeting with His Foreign Policy Advisers at the Tuesday Luncheon, March 19, 1968, *FRUS, 1964–1968, Volume VI*, pp. 412–418.

49. William DePuy OHI, Tape I, p. 48, LBJL; Notes of Meeting, March 27, 1968; *FRUS, 1964–1968, Volume VI*, p. 481; and Clifford with Holbrooke, *Counsel to the President*, pp. 512–514.

50. Notes of Meeting, March 22, 1968, *FRUS, 1964–1968, Volume VI*, p. 444; Telephone Conversation between President Johnson and Senator Richard Russell,

March 22, 1968, 4:49 P.M., ibid., pp. 447–451; Notes of the President's Meeting with General Earle Wheeler, JCS, and General Creighton Abrams, March 26, 1968, 10:30 A.M.—12:15 P.M., ibid., pp. 459–465; and Clifford with Holbrooke, *Counsel to the President*, p. 515.

51.   Notes of the President's Meeting with His Foreign Policy Advisers," March 26, 1968, 1:15–3:05 P.M., *FRUS, 1964–1968, Volume VI*, pp. 466–470.

52.   Summary of Notes, March 26, 1968, ibid., p. 471; and Confidential Memorandum, DA's Views regarding Vietnam as of March 26, 1968, in McLellan and Acheson, eds., *Among Friends*, pp. 295–296.

53.   Summary of Notes, March 26, 1968, *FRUS, 1964–1968, Volume VI*, pp. 471–474; Clifford with Holbrooke, *Counsel to the President*, pp. 517–518; and Karnow, *Vietnam*, p. 577.

54.   Katzenbach, *Some of It Was Fun*, p. 275.

55.   Transcripts of Meetings in the Cabinet Room, LBJL; and Clifford with Holbrooke, *Counsel to the President*, pp. 520–522.

56.   Quoted in Karnow, *Vietnam*, p. 579.

57.   LBADT, March 31, 1968, LBJL.

58.   Author's interviews with Clark Clifford, July 29, 1988, Tape One; and August 2, 1988, Tape One.

59.   Address to the Nation, March 31, 1968, *Public Papers of the President: Lyndon B. Johnson, 1968–69*, Book I (Government Printing Office, 1970), pp. 469–476.

60.   President's Daily Diary for March 31, 1968, LBJL.

61.   Quoted in Busby, *The Thirty-First of March*, p. 9.

62.   President's Daily Diary for March 31, 1968, LBJL.

63.   Quoted in Pierre Asselin, *A Bitter Peace: Washington, Hanoi, and the Making of the Paris Agreement* (University of North Carolina Press, 2002), p. 5.

64.   See Nguyen, *Hanoi's War*, p. 90.

65.   Tin, *From Enemy to Friend*, pp. 32 and 93.

66.   See David Elliott, *The Vietnamese War: Revolutionary and Social Change in the Mekong Delta, 1930–1975* (M. E. Sharpe, 2003), v. 2, pp. 1113–1114.

67.   Luu Van Loi, quoted in Nguyen, *Hanoi's War*, p. 115.

68.   Quoted in Asselin, *Bitter Peace*, p. 6. See also Ang Cheng Guan, *Ending the Vietnam War: The Vietnamese Communists' Perspective* (RoutledgeCurzon, 2004), p. 11.

69.   Telephone Conversation between President Johnson and Clark Clifford, May 4, 1968, Tape 13006 (WH6805.02), MCWHR.

70.   Telephone Conversation between President Johnson and Walt Rostow, May 3, 1968, Tape 13004 (WH6805.01), MCWHR.

71.   Quoted in Blight and Kornbluh, eds., *Politics of Illusion*, p. 64.

72.   Notes of "8:30 Group" Meeting, July 27, 1968, Personal Papers of George Elsey (hereafter cited as PPGE).

73.   Notes of "8:30 Group" Meetings, May 18 and June 12, 1968, PPGE and PPRP.

74.   Telephone Conversation between President Johnson and Clark Clifford, May 4, 1968, Tape 13007 (WH6805.02), WCWHR.

75.   Author's interview with Clark Clifford, July 20, 1988.

76.   Clifford with Holbrooke, *Counsel to the President*, p. 541; and Notes of "8:30 Group" Meeting, May 29, 1968, PPGE.

77. Notes on Telephone Conversation between Secretary of Defense Clifford and Ambassador Harriman, June 21, 1968, 7:05 P.M., *FRUS, 1964–1968, Volume VI*, p. 800.

78. Author's interview with Clark Clifford, August 2, 1988, Tape One.

79. Author's interview with Clark Clifford and Benjamin Read, August 18, 1988.

80. Quoted in Halberstam, *Best and the Brightest*, p. 638.

81. Clifford with Holbrooke, *Counsel to the President*, p. 535.

82. Quoted in Herring, *LBJ and Vietnam*, p. 168.

83. See Notes of the President's Meeting with Foreign Policy Advisers, July 30, 1968, *FRUS, 1964–1968, Volume VI*, p. 921.

84. Quoted in Perry, *Four Stars*, p. 196.

85. Notes of "8:30 Group" Meeting, June 7, 1968, PPGE.

86. Memorandum from the President's Special Counsel (McPherson) to President Johnson, July 3, 1968, *FRUS, 1964–1968, Volume VI*, pp. 835–836.

87. Quoted in Sheehan, *Bright Shining Lie*, pp. 724–725.

88. Quoted in Bùi Diễm with Chanoff, *In the Jaws of History*, p. 225.

89. Notes of "8:30 Group" Meeting, June 25, 1968, PPGE.

90. Notes of "8:30 Group" Meeting, July 22, 1968, PPRP.

91. Author's interview with Clark Clifford and Robert Pursley, August 17, 1988, Tape Two.

92. Phillips, *Why Vietnam Matters*, p. 286.

93. Author's interview with Clark Clifford and Robert Pursley, August 17, 1988, Tape Two.

94. "Meeting with President Thieu and His Colleagues," July 16, 1968, "South Vietnam Trip, July 13–19, 1968: Memos to the President from Clifford," Clifford Papers, LBJL.

95. Clifford with Holbrooke, *Counsel to the President*, p. 551.

96. "Meeting with President Thieu and His Colleagues," July 16, 1968, Clifford Papers, LBJL.

97. Author's interview with Clark Clifford and Robert Pursley, August 17, 1988, Tape Two.

98. Notes of "8:30 Group" Meeting, July 22, 1968, PPGE.

99. George Allen OHI, I, p. 35, LBJL.

100. Phillips, *Why Vietnam Matters*, p. 297.

101. Fisher and Ury, *Getting to Yes*, pp. 61–62.

102. Notes of "8:30 Group" Meeting, July 22, 1968, PPGE and PPRP.

103. Fisher and Ury, *Getting to Yes*, pp. 23–24.

104. Author's interview with Clark Clifford, September 12, 1988, Tape One.

105. Notes of Meeting of the President with His Foreign Policy Advisers at Lunch, July 24, 1968, *FRUS, 1964–1968, Volume VI*, p. 889.

106. President Johnson's Notes on Meeting in Cabinet Room with Richard Nixon, Joined Later by Secretary Rusk, Tom Johnson, and Walt Rostow, July 26, 1968, 6–7:35 P.M., ibid., pp. 893–909.

107. Notes of "8:30 Group" Meeting, August 12, 1968, PPGE.

108. Telephone Conversation between President Johnson and Governor Richard Hughes, July 30, 1968, Tape 13222 (WH6807.02), MCHWR.

109. Notes of "8:30 Group" Meeting, July 31, 1968, PPRP.

110.   Gilovich, *How We Know What Isn't So*, p. 76.

111.   Kahneman, *Thinking, Fast and Slow*, pp. 295–296.

112.   Ibid., p. 292.

113.   Joseph Califano, *The Triumph and Tragedy of Lyndon Johnson: The White House Years* (Simon & Schuster, 1992), p. 11.

114.   Notes of "8:30 Group" Meeting, July 31, 1968, PPRP.

115.   Author's interview with Clark Clifford, June 7, 1988, Tape Two; and author's interview with Clark Clifford and Benjamin Read, August 18, 1988.

116.   Ibid.

117.   Clifford with Holbrooke, *Counsel to the President*, p. 569; and Notes of "8:30 Group" Meeting, August 8, 1968, PPGE.

118.   Author's interview with Clark Clifford and Robert Pursley, August 17, 1988, Tape One.

119.   Clifford with Holbrooke, *Counsel to the President*, p. 568.

120.   Ibid.; and Notes of "8:30 Group" Meeting, August 5, 1968, PPGE and PPRP.

121.   Author's interview with Clark Clifford and Robert Pursley, August 17, 1988, Tape One.

122.   Quoted in Dallek, *Flawed Giant*, p. 577.

123.   Notes of "8:30 Group" Meetings, September 16, 24, and 25, 1968, PPGE.

124.   See Nguyen, *Hanoi's War*, pp. 124–125; and Harriman and Vance to Rusk, October 11, 1968, *Foreign Relations of the United States, 1964–1968, Volume VII: Vietnam, September 1968–January 1969* (hereafter cited as *FRUS, 1964–1968, Volume VII*) (Government Printing Office, 2003), pp. 155–158.

125.   Tom Johnson's Notes of Meetings, October 14, 1968, LBJL.

126.   Notes of the President's Luncheon Meeting with Foreign Policy Advisors, February 20, 1968, *FRUS, 1964–1968, Volume VI*, pp. 223–224.

127.   Notes of Meetings, October 14, 1968; and Telephone Conversation with Senator Everett Dirksen, October 16, 1968, 3:27 P.M., *FRUS, 1964–1968, Volume VII*, pp. 195, 198, and 227.

128.   Saigon 40117, Bunker and Abrams to Rusk, October 12, 1968; and Saigon 40178, Bunker to Rusk, October 13, 1968, ibid., pp. 162–164.

129.   Author's interviews with Clark Clifford and Robert Pursley, August 17, 1988, Tapes One and Three.

130.   Author's interview with Clark Clifford and Robert Pursley, August 17, 1988, Tape Three.

131.   Quoted in Henry Brandon: *Anatomy of Error: The Inside Story of the Asian War on the Potomac, 1954–1969* (Gambit, 1969), p. 150.

132.   Quoted in Lewis Sorley, *Thunderbolt: General Creighton Abrams and the Army of His Times* (Simon & Schuster, 1992), p. 200.

133.   Saigon 40220, Bunker to Rusk, October 14, 1968, Vietnam Country File, Box 124, NSF, LBJL.

134.   Quoted in Guan, *Ending the Vietnam War*, p. 15.

135.   See Nguyen, *Hanoi's War*, pp. 126–128.

136.   See Saigon 40627, Bunker to Rusk, October 18, 1968, *FRUS, 1964–1968, Volume VII*, pp. 240–241.

137.   See Telephone Conversation between President Johnson and Secretary of State Rusk, October 6, 1968, *FRUS, 1964–1968, Volume VII*, pp. 137–144.

138. Bryce Harlow OHI, LBJL.

139. Telephone Conversation between President Johnson and Secretary of State Dean Rusk, October 7, 1968, *FRUS, 1964–1968, Volume VII*, p. 145.

140. Carroll Kilpatrick, "Nixon Backs Quest for Bomb Halt," *Washington Post*, October 18, 1968.

141. Quoted in Peter Baker, "Nixon Sought 'Monkey Wrench' in Vietnam Talks," *New York Times*, January 3, 2017, p. A1.

142. Quoted in Nguyen Tien Hung and Jerrold L. Schechter, *The Palace File* (Harper & Row, 1986), p. 24.

143. Bùi Diễm with Chanoff, *In the Jaws of History*, pp. 239–245.

144. Anna Chennault, *The Education of Anna* (Times Books, 1980), p. 186.

145. Quoted in William Bundy, *A Tangled Web: The Making of Foreign Policy in the Nixon Presidency* (Hill and Wang, 1998), p. 42.

146. Telephone Conversation between President Johnson and Richard Nixon, November 3, 1968, Tape 13710 (WH6811.01), MCWHR.

147. Richard Nixon, *The Memoirs of Richard Nixon* (Grosset & Dunlap, 1978), p. 327.

148. Author's interview with Clark Clifford, September 12, 1988, Tape One.

149. Telephone Conversation between President Johnson and Robert McNamara, November 1, 1968, *FRUS, 1964–1968, Volume VII*, p. 497.

150. Telephone Conversation between President Johnson and Secretary of State Rusk, October 17, 1968, *FRUS, 1964–1968, Volume VII*, p. 239; and Dallek, *Flawed Giant*, p. 588.

151. Notes of "8:30 Group" Meeting, October 30, 1968, PPGE.

152. Notes on Foreign Policy Meeting, October 29, 1968, 6:28–7:40 P.M., *FRUS, 1964–1968, Volume VII*, p. 440.

153. Telegram 263699 from the Department of State to the Embassy in Vietnam, October 30, 1968, ibid., p. 442.

154. Excerpted in *Kessing's Contemporary Archives*, September 6–13, 1969, pp. 23549–23550.

155. Rusk, *As I Saw It*, p. 488.

156. Nixon, *Memoirs*, pp. 328–329.

157. Quoted in Hung and Schechter, *Palace File*, p. 29.

158. Bundy, *Tangled Web*, p. 47.

159. Quoted in *Palace File*, p. 30.

160. LBADT, January 17, 1969, LBJL.

EPILOGUE: THE BURDEN OF REGRET

1. Daniel Kahneman and D. T. Miller, "Norm Theory: Comparing Reality to Its Alternatives," *Psychological Review* 93 (1986): p. 137.

2. Quoted in Leo Janos, "The Last Days of the President: LBJ in Retirement," *The Atlantic*, July 1973.

3. Quoted in Dallek, *Flawed Giant*, p. 601.

4. Quoted in Tom Johnson OHI, April 11, 1974, LBJL.

5. Quoted in Dobrynin, *In Confidence*, p. 188.

6. Rusk, *As I Saw It*, p. 595.

7. Quoted in ibid.

8. Ibid., p. 607.

9.   Ibid., p. 610.

10. Author's interview with Dean Rusk, November 14, 1988.

11. MBDMVN, PPMB, Box 224, JFKL.

12. Quoted in Bird, *Color of Truth*, p. 403.

13. MBDMVN, PPMB, Box 223, JFKL.

14. Ibid.

15. Draft #2, May 1, 1996, ibid.

16. "16 August" and Draft #1 Introduction, May 6, 1996, Boxes 223–225, ibid.

17. Draft #1/Introduction #2, June 3, 1996, Fragment #10 (January 1996), "22 Feb," Boxes 224–226, ibid.

18. "June 26 93," Box 250, ibid.

19. Quoted in David K. Shipler, "Robert McNamara and the Ghosts of Vietnam," *New York Times Magazine*, August 10, 1997, p. 57.

20. Author's interview with Robert McNamara, September 16, 1994.

21. Ibid.

22. Author's interview with Robert McNamara, July 19, 1994.

23. Shipler, "Robert McNamara and the Ghosts of Vietnam," p. 30.

24. Quoted in ibid., p. 33.

25. Chester Cooper, quoted in ibid., p. 57.

26. Albert Camus, *The Myth of Sisyphus and Other Essays* (Alfred A. Knopf, 1955), p. 31.

27. Cited in Seymour M. Hersh, "The Scene of the Crime," *The New Yorker*, March 30, 2015, p. 61.

28. Jacob Jacoby, Carol A. Kohn, and Donald E. Speller, "Time Spent Acquiring Information as a Function of Information Load and Organization," *Proceedings of the American Psychological Association's 81st Annual Convention*, Washington, D.C., 1973, pp. 813–814.

29. Jacob Jacoby, "Perspectives on Information Overload," *Journal of Consumer Research* 10, n. 4 (March 1984): pp. 432–435.

30. Philip E. Tetlock, *Expert Political Judgment: How Good Is It? How Can We Know?* (Princeton University Press, 2005).

31. Amy Wilkinson, *The Creator's Code: The Six Essential Skills of Extraordinary Entrepreneurs* (Simon & Schuster, 2015), pp. 134–135.

32. Fisher and Ury, *Getting to Yes*, pp. 62–63.

33. Shimon Peres, *No Room for Small Dreams: Courage, Imagination, and the Making of Modern Israel* (HarperCollins, 2017).

34. Clayton M. Christensen, Michael E. Raynor, and Rory McDonald, "What Is Disruptive Innovation?" *Harvard Business Review*, December 2015.

35. Atul Gawande, *The Checklist Manifesto: How to Get Things Right* (Metropolitan Books, 2009), pp. 98–100, 153–154.

36. Ibid., pp. 65–66.

37. Ibid., p. 79.

38. J. R. Graham, C. R. Harvey, and S. Rajgopal, "The Economic Implications of Corporate Financial Reporting," *Journal of Accounting and Economics* 40, n. 1 (2005): pp. 3–73.

39. David Souder, Greg Reilly, and Rebecca Ranucci, "Long-Term Thinking in a

Short-Term World: A Guide for Executives," Network for Business Sustainability, Canada, nbs.net.

40.   P. Bansal and M. R. DesJardine, "Business Sustainability: It Is about Time," *Strategic Organization* 12, n. 1 (2014): pp. 70–78.

41.   Wilkinson, *Creator's Code*, p. 51.

42.   Ibid., p. 72.

Select Bibliography of Published Sources

Abramson, Rudy. *Spanning the Century: The Life of W. Averell Harriman, 1891–1986.* William Morrow, 1992.

Acacia, John. *Clark Clifford: The Wise Man of Washington.* University Press of Kentucky, 2009.

Allen, George W. *None So Blind: A Personal Account of the Intelligence Failure in Vietnam.* Ivan R. Dee, 2001.

Allison, Graham and Philip Zelikow. *Essence of Decision: Explaining the Cuban Missile Crisis.* 2nd ed., Longman, 1999.

Alsop, Stewart and Charles Bartlett. "In Time of Crisis," *Saturday Evening Post*, December 8, 1962, pp. 15–21.

Ang, Cheng Guan. *Ending the Vietnam War: The Vietnamese Communists' Perspective.* RoutledgeCurzon, 2004.

Ariely, Dan. *Predictably Irrational: The Hidden Forces That Shape Our Decisions.* HarperCollins, 2008.

Arkes, Hal R. and Catherine Blumer, "The Psychology of Sunk Cost," *Organizational Behavior and Human Decision Processes*, v. 35, 1985, pp. 124–140.

Asselin, Pierre. *A Bitter Peace: Washington, Hanoi, and the Making of the Paris Agreement.* University of North Carolina Press, 2002.

_____. "Hanoi and Americanization of the War in Vietnam: New Evidence from Vietnam," *Pacific Historical Review*, v. 74, n. 3, 2005, pp. 427–439.

_____. *Hanoi's Road to the Vietnam War, 1954–1965.* University of California Press, 2013.

Ball, George W. *The Past Has Another Pattern: Memoirs.* W. W. Norton, 1982.

Bator, Francis M. *No Good Choices: LBJ and the Vietnam/Great Society Connection.* American Academy of Arts and Sciences, 2007.

Bendor, Jonathan. *Bounded Rationality and Politics.* University of California Press, 2010.

Beschloss, Michael R. *The Crisis Years: Kennedy and Khrushchev, 1960–1963.* HarperCollins, 1991.

_____, ed. *Reaching for Glory: Lyndon Johnson's Secret White House Tapes, 1964–1965.* Simon & Schuster, 2001.

_____, ed. *Taking Charge: The Johnson White House Tapes, 1963–1964.* Simon & Schuster, 1997.

Bird, Kai. *The Color of Truth: McGeorge Bundy and William Bundy, Brothers in Arms.* Simon & Schuster, 1998.

Bissell, Richard M., Jr. *Reflections of a Cold Warrior: From Yalta to the Bay of Pigs.* Yale University Press, 1996.

Blair, Anne. *Lodge in Vietnam: A Patriot Abroad.* Yale University Press, 1995.

Blight, James G., Bruce J. Allyn, and David A. Welch. *Cuba on the Brink: Castro, the Missile Crisis, and the Soviet Collapse.* Pantheon, 1993.

Blight, James G. and David A. Welch. *On the Brink: Americans and Soviets Reexamine the Cuban Missile Crisis.* Hill and Wang, 1989.

Blight, James G. and Peter Kornbluh, eds. *Politics of Illusion: The Bay of Pigs Reexamined.* Lynne Rienner, 1998.

Bohlen, Charles E. *Witness to History, 1929–1969.* W. W. Norton, 1973.

Boot, Max. *Invisible Armies: An Epic History of Guerrilla Warfare from Ancient Times to the Present.* Liveright, 2013.

_____. *The Road Not Taken: Edward Lansdale and the American Tragedy in Vietnam.* Liveright, 2018.

Boston Publishing Company. *The Vietnam Experience.* 20 vols., Boston Publishing Company, 1981–1986.

Bowden, Mark. *Hue 1968: A Turning Point of the American War in Vietnam.* Atlantic Monthly Press, 2017.

Bradley, Mark Phillip. *Vietnam at War.* Oxford University Press, 2009.

Brandon, Henry. *Anatomy of Error: The Inside Story of the Asian War on the Potomac, 1954–1969.* Gambit, 1969.

Brigham, Robert K. *ARVN: Life and Death in the South Vietnamese Army.* University Press of Kansas, 2006.

Brinkley, Douglas. *Dean Acheson: The Cold War Years, 1953–1971.* Yale University Press, 1992.

Brockner, Joel. "The Escalation of Commitment to a Failing Course of Action: Toward Theoretical Progress," *Academy of Management Review,* v. 17, n. 1, January 1992, pp. 39–61.

_____ and J. Z. Rubin. *Entrapment in Escalating Conflicts: A Social Psychological Analysis.* Springer-Verlag, 1985.

Brodie, Bernard. *War and Politics.* Macmillan, 1973.

Brugioni, Dino A. *Eyeball to Eyeball: The Inside Story of the Cuban Missile Crisis.* Random House: 1991.

Bundy, William. *A Tangled Web: The Making of Foreign Policy in the Nixon Presidency.* Hill and Wang, 1998.

Busby, Horace. *The Thirty-First of March: An Intimate Portrait of Lyndon Johnson's Final Days in Office.* Farrar, Straus and Giroux, 2005.

Caro, Robert A. *The Years of Lyndon Johnson: The Passage of Power.* Alfred A. Knopf, 2012.

Castro, Fidel and Ignacio Ramonet. *Fidel Castro: My Life, A Spoken Autobiography.* Scribner, 2006.

Chabris, Christopher and Daniel Simons. *The Invisible Gorilla: How Our Intuitions Deceive Us.* MJF Books, 2010.

Chennault, Anna. *The Education of Anna.* Times Books, 1980.

Church, Frank. *Alleged Assassination Plots Involving Foreign Leaders: An Interim Report of the Select Committee to Study Governmental Operations with Respect to Intelligence Activities.* W. W. Norton, 1976.

Clifford, Clark with Richard Holbrooke. *Counsel to the President: A Memoir.* Random House, 1991.

Clodfelter, Mark. *The Limits of Air Power: The American Bombing of North Vietnam.* Free Press, 1989.

Cochrane, Feargal. *Ending Wars.* Polity, 2008.

Cohen, Warren I. *Dean Rusk.* Cooper Square Publishers, 1980.

Colby, William with James McCargar. *Lost Victory: A Firsthand Account of America's Sixteen-Year Involvement in Vietnam.* Contemporary Books, 1989.

Cooper, Chester L. *In the Shadows of History: 50 Years Behind the Scenes of Cold War Diplomacy.* Prometheus Books, 2005.

_____. *The Lost Crusade: America in Vietnam.* Dodd, Mead, and Company, 1970.

Cosmas, Graham A. *History of the Joint Chiefs of Staff: The Joint Chiefs of Staff and the War in Vietnam, 1960–1968, Part 2.* Office of Joint History, 2012.

_____. *History of the Joint Chiefs of Staff: The Joint Chiefs of Staff and the War in Vietnam, 1960–1968, Part 3.* Office of Joint History, 2009.

Crankshaw, Edward and Strobe Talbott, eds., *Khrushchev Remembers.* Little, Brown, 1970.

Daddis, Gregory A. *No Sure Victory: Measuring U.S. Army Effectiveness and Progress in the Vietnam War.* Oxford University Press, 2011.

_____. *Westmoreland's War: Reassessing American Strategy in Vietnam.* Oxford University Press, 2015.

Dallek, Robert. *An Unfinished Life: John F. Kennedy, 1917–1963.* Little, Brown, 2003.

_____. *Flawed Giant: Lyndon Johnson and His Times, 1961–1973.* Oxford University Press, 1998.

de Silva, Peer. *Sub Rosa: The CIA and the Uses of Intelligence.* Times Books, 1978.

Destatte, Robert J. and Merle L. Pribbenow. *The 1968 Tet Offensive and Uprising in the Tri-Thien-Hué Theater.* United States Army Center of Military History, 2001.

Diem, Bui with David Chanoff. *In the Jaws of History.* Houghton Mifflin, 1987.

Dobbs, Michael. *One Minute to Midnight: Kennedy, Khrushchev, and Castro on the Brink of Nuclear War.* Alfred A. Knopf, 2008.

Dobrynin, Anatoly. *In Confidence: Moscow's Ambassador to America's Six Cold War Presidents.* Times Books, 1995.

Drea, Edward J. *McNamara, Clifford, and the Burdens of Vietnam, 1965–69.* Office of the Secretary of Defense Historical Office, 2011.

Duiker, William J. *Ho Chi Minh: A Life.* Hyperion, 2000.

Elliott, David W. P. *The Vietnamese War: Revolution and Social Change in the Mekong Delta, 1930–1975.* 2 Vols., M. E. Sharpe, 2003.

Elliott, Mai. *RAND in Southeast Asia: A History of the Vietnam War Era.* RAND Corporation, 2010.

Ellsberg, Daniel. *Secrets: A Memoir of Vietnam and the Pentagon Papers.* Viking, 2002.

Engel, Edward. "Binocular Methods in Psychological Research," in Franklin P. Kilpatrick, ed., *Explorations in Transactional Psychology.* New York University Press, 1961.

Enthoven, Alain C. and K. Wayne Smith. *How Much is Enough?: Shaping the Defense Program, 1961–1969.* Harper & Row, 1971.

Fall, Bernard. *The Two Vietnams: A Political and Military Analysis.* Praeger, 1963.

Farnham, Barbara, ed. *Avoiding Losses/Taking Risks: Prospect Theory and International Conflict*. University of Michigan Press, 1994.

Ferguson, Niall. *Kissinger, 1923–1968: The Idealist*. Penguin Press, 2015.

Festinger, Leon. *A Theory of Cognitive Dissonance*. Stanford University Press, 1957.

Fisher, Roger and William Ury. *Getting to YES: Negotiating Agreement Without Giving In*. Houghton Mifflin, 1981.

FitzGerald, Frances. *Fire in the Lake: The Vietnamese and the Americans in Vietnam*. Atlantic–Little, Brown, 1972.

Fletcher, George P. *Loyalty: An Essay on the Morality of Relationships*. Oxford University Press, 1993.

Freedman, Lawrence. *Kennedy's Wars: Berlin, Cuba, Laos, and Vietnam*. Oxford University Press, 2000.

_____. *Strategy: A History*. Oxford University Press, 2013.

Fursenko, Aleksandr and Timothy Naftali. *Khrushchev's Cold War: The Inside Story of an American Adversary*. W. W. Norton, 2006.

_____. *"One Hell of a Gamble": Khrushchev, Castro, and Kennedy, 1958–1964*. W. W. Norton, 1997.

Gaiduk, Ilya V. *Confronting Vietnam: Soviet Policy toward the Indochina Conflict, 1954–1963*. Woodrow Wilson Center Press, 2003.

_____. *The Soviet Union and the Vietnam War*. Ivan R. Dee, 1996.

Gawande, Atul. *The Checklist Manifesto: How to Get Things Right*. Metropolitan Books, Henry Holt and Company, 2009.

Gibbons, William Conrad. *The U.S. Government and the Vietnam War: Executive and Legislative Roles and Relationships*. 4 Vols., Government Printing Office, 1984–1994.

Gilovich, Thomas. *How We Know What Isn't So: The Fallibility of Human Reason in Everyday Life*. Free Press, 1991.

Gittinger, Ted, ed. *The Johnson Years: A Vietnam Roundtable*. Lyndon Baines Johnson Library, 1993.

Goldstein, Gordon M. *Lessons in Disaster: McGeorge Bundy and the Path to War in Vietnam*. Times Books, Henry Holt and Company, 2009.

Goodwin, Richard N. *Remembering America: A Voice from the Sixties*. Little, Brown, 1988.

Goscha, Christopher. *Vietnam: A New History*. Basic Books, 2016.

Goulding, Phil C. *Confirm or Deny: Informing the People on National Security*. Harper & Row, 1970.

Gravel, Senator Mike, ed. *The Pentagon Papers: The Defense Department History of United States Decisionmaking on Vietnam*. 5 Vols. Beacon Press, 1971.

Gromyko, Andrei. *Memoirs*. Doubleday, 1989.

Grossman, Lt. Col. Dave. *On Killing: The Psychological Cost of Learning to Kill in War and Society*. Rev. ed. Back Bay Books, 2009.

Guan, Ang Cheng. "Decision-Making Leading to the Tet Offensive (1968): The Vietnamese Communist Perspective," *Journal of Contemporary History*, v. 33, n. 3, July 1998, pp. 341–353.

_____. "The Vietnam War, 1962–64: The Vietnamese Communist Perspective," *Journal of Contemporary History*, v. 35, n. 4, October 2000.

Halberstam, David. *The Best and the Brightest*. Random House, 1972.

Hammer, Ellen J. *A Death in November: America in Vietnam, 1963*. E. P. Dutton, 1987; reprint ed. Oxford University Press, 1988.

Hanyok, Robert J. "Skunks, Bogies, Silent Hounds, and the Flying Fish: The Gulf of Tonkin Mystery, 2–4 August 1964," *Cryptologic Quarterly*, Winter 2000/Spring 2001.

Harrison, Benjamin T. and Christopher L. Mosher. "The Secret Diary of McNamara's Dove: The Long-Lost Story of John T. McNaughton's Opposition to the Vietnam War," *Diplomatic History*, v. 35, n. 3, June 2011, pp. 505–534.

Helms, Richard with William Hood. *A Look Over My Shoulder: A Life in the Central Intelligence Agency*. Random House, 2003.

Hendrickson, Paul. *The Living and the Dead: Robert McNamara and Five Lives of a Lost War*. Alfred A. Knopf, 1996.

Henry, John B., II. "February, 1968," *Foreign Policy*, n. 4, Autumn 1971, pp. 3–33.

Herring, George C. *LBJ and Vietnam: A Different Kind of War*. University of Texas Press, 1994.

_____, ed. *The Secret Diplomacy of the Vietnam War: The Negotiating Volumes of the Pentagon Papers*. University of Texas Press, 1983.

Hershberg, James G. *Marigold: The Lost Chance for Peace in Vietnam*. Woodrow Wilson Center Press, 2012.

_____ and Chen Jian. "Reading and Warning the Likely Enemy: China's Signals to the United States about Vietnam in 1965," *International History Review*, v. 27, n. 1, March 2005, pp. 47–84.

Higgins, Trumbull. *A Perfect Failure: Kennedy, Eisenhower, and the CIA at the Bay of Pigs*. W. W. Norton, 1987.

Hilsman, Roger. *To Move a Nation: The Politics of Foreign Policy in the Administration of John F. Kennedy*. Doubleday & Company, 1967.

Historical Division, Joint Secretariat, Joint Chiefs of Staff. *The History of the Joint Chiefs of Staff: The Joint Chiefs of Staff and the War in Vietnam, 1960–1968* (1970).

Hughes, Ken. *Chasing Shadows: The Nixon Tapes, the Chennault Affair, and the Origins of Watergate*. University of Virginia Press, 2014.

Hung, Nguyen Tien and Jerrold L. Schecter. *The Palace File*. Harper & Row, 1986.

Jackson, Bruce. "The Battle of the Pentagon," *Atlantic*, January 1968, pp. 35–42.

Jervis, Robert. *How Statesmen Think: The Psychology of International Politics*. Princeton University Press, 2017.

_____. *Perception and Misperception in International Politics*. Princeton University Press, 1976.

Jian, Chen. "China's Involvement in the Vietnam War, 1964–1969," *China Quarterly*, June 1995, pp. 356–385.

Johnson, Haynes. *The Bay of Pigs: The Leaders' Story of Brigade 2506*. W. W. Norton, 1964.

Johnson, Lyndon Baines. *The Vantage Point: Perspectives of the Presidency, 1963–1969*. Holt, Rinehart, and Winston, 1971.

Jones, Howard. *The Bay of Pigs*. Oxford University Press, 2008.

_____. *Death of a Generation: How the Assassinations of Diem and JFK Prolonged the Vietnam War*. Oxford University Press, 2003.

Kaiser, David. *American Tragedy: Kennedy, Johnson, and the Origins of the Vietnam War.* Belknap Press of Harvard University Press, 2000.

Kahneman, Daniel. *Thinking, Fast and Slow.* Farrar, Straus and Giroux, 2011.

Kaplan, Lawrence, Ronald D. Landa, and Edward J. Drea. *The McNamara Ascendancy, 1961–1965.* Historical Office, Office of the Secretary of Defense, 2006.

Karnow, Stanley. *Vietnam: A History.* Viking, 1983.

Katzenbach, Nicholas deB. *Some of It Was Fun: Working with RFK and LBJ.* W. W. Norton, 2008.

Kearns, Doris. *Lyndon Johnson and the American Dream.* Harper and Row, 1976.

Kempe, Frederick. *Berlin 1961: Kennedy, Khrushchev, and the Most Dangerous Place on Earth.* G. P. Putnam's Sons, 2011.

Khong, Yuen Foong. "Mind Games," *Foreign Affairs,* May/June 2017.

Kiernan, Ben. *Viet Nam: A History from Earliest Times to the Present.* Oxford University Press, 2017.

Kirkpatrick, Lyman B., Jr. *The Real CIA.* Macmillan, 1968.

Kornbluh, Peter, ed. *Bay of Pigs Declassified: The Secret CIA Report on the Invasion of Cuba.* New Press, 1998.

Ky, Nguyen Cao. *Twenty Years and Twenty Days.* Stein and Day, 1976.

Landman, Janet. *Regret: The Persistence of the Possible.* Oxford University Press, 1993.

Langguth, A. J. *Our Vietnam: The War, 1954–1975.* Simon & Schuster, 2000.

Lewis, Michael. *The Undoing Project: A Friendship That Changed Our Minds.* W. W. Norton, 2017.

Lobel, Aaron, ed. *Presidential Judgment: Foreign Policy Decision Making in the White House.* Hollis Publishing, 2001.

Logevall, Fredrik. *Choosing War: The Lost Chance for Peace and the Escalation of the Vietnam War.* University of California Press, 1999.

_____. *Embers of War: The Fall of an Empire and the Making of America's Vietnam.* Random House, 2012.

Macmillan, Harold. *At the End of the Day, 1961–1963.* Harper & Row, 1973.

Mailer, Norman. *The Armies of the Night.* New American Library, 1968.

Manning, Robert, ed. *The Vietnam Experience.* 20 vols. Boston Publishing Company, 1981–1986.

McLellan, David S. and David C. Acheson, eds., *Among Friends: Personal Letters of Dean Acheson.* Dodd, Mead, 1980.

McMaster, H. R. *Dereliction of Duty: Lyndon Johnson, Robert McNamara, the Joint Chiefs of Staff, and the Lies That Led to Vietnam.* HarperCollins, 1997.

McNamara, Robert S. with James Blight, Robert Brigham, Thomas Biersteker, and Col. Herbert Schandler. *Argument Without End: In Search of Answers to the Vietnam Tragedy.* PublicAffairs, 1999.

McNamara, Robert S. with Brian VanDeMark. *In Retrospect: The Tragedy and Lessons of Vietnam.* Times Books, 1995.

Meyer, Karl E. and Tad Szulc. *The Cuban Invasion: The Chronicle of a Disaster.* Frederick A. Praeger, 1962.

Military History Institute of Vietnam. *Victory in Vietnam: The Official History of the People's Army of Vietnam, 1954–1975.* University of Kansas Press, 2002.

Miller, Edward. *Misalliance: Ngo Dinh Diem, the United States, and the Fate of South Vietnam.* Harvard University Press, 2013.

Moaz, Zeev. *Paradoxes of War: On the Art of National Self-Entrapment.* Unwin Hyman, 1990.

Moïse, Edwin E. *Tonkin Gulf and the Escalation of the Vietnam War.* University of North Carolina Press, 1996.

Moore, Harold G. and Joseph L. Galloway. *We Were Soldiers Once . . . And Young.* HarperCollins, 1993.

Moyar, Mark. *Triumph Forsaken: The Vietnam War, 1954–1965.* Cambridge University Press, 2006.

Nemeth, Charlan. *In Defense of Troublemakers: The Power of Dissent in Life and Business.* Basic Books, 2018.

Neese, Harvey and John O'Donnell, eds. *Prelude to Tragedy: Vietnam, 1960–1965.* Naval Institute Press, 2001.

Mueller, John E. *War, Presidents and Public Opinion.* Wiley, 1973.

Nguyen, Lien-Hang T. *Hanoi's War: An International History of the War for Peace in Vietnam.* University of North Carolina Press, 2012.

_____. "The War Politburo: North Vietnam's Diplomatic and Political Road to the Tet Offensive," *Journal of Vietnamese Studies,* Fall 2006, pp. 4–58.

Nisbett, Richard E. and Lee Ross. *Human Inference: Strategies and Shortcomings in Social Judgment.* Prentice-Hall, 1980.

Nixon, Richard. *The Memoirs of Richard Nixon.* Grosset & Dunlap, 1978.

Nolting, Frederick. *From Trust to Tragedy: The Political Memoirs of Frederick Nolting, Kennedy's Ambassador to Diem's Vietnam.* Praeger, 1988.

Oberdorfer, Don. *Senator Mansfield: The Extraordinary Life of a Great American Statesman and Diplomat.* Smithsonian Books, 2003.

_____. *Tet!: The Turning Point in the Vietnam War.* Doubleday, 1971.

Perry, Mark. *Four Stars.* Houghton Mifflin, 1989.

Phillips, David Atlee. *The Night Watch.* Atheneum, 1977.

Phillips, Rufus. *Why Vietnam Matters: An Eyewitness Account of Lessons Not Learned.* Naval Institute Press, 2008.

Porter, Gareth. "The Tonkin Gulf Crisis Reconsidered: Unwitting Provocation in U.S. Coercive Diplomacy," October 28, 1988.

Powers, Thomas. *The Man Who Kept the Secrets: Richard Helms & the CIA.* Alfred A. Knopf, 1979.

Preston, Andrew. *The War Council: McGeorge Bundy, the NSC, and Vietnam.* Harvard University Press, 2006.

Pribbenow, Merle. "General Vo Nguyen Giap and the Mysterious Evolution of the Plan for the 1968 Tet Offensive," *Journal of Vietnamese Studies,* Summer 2008, pp. 1–33.

Qiang Zhai. "Beijing and the Vietnam Conflict, 1964–1965," prepared for the Wilson Center Conference in Hong Kong, January 1996.

Quinn-Judge, Sophie. "The Ideological Debate in the DRV and the Significance of the Anti-Party Affair, 1967–1968," *Cold War History,* v. 5, n. 4, 2005, pp. 479–500.

Race, Jeffrey. *War Comes to Long An: Revolutionary Conflict in a Vietnamese Province.* University of California Press, 1972.

Rasenberger, Jim. *The Brilliant Disaster: JFK, Castro, and America's Doomed Invasion of Cuba's Bay of Pigs.* Scribner, 2011.

Reedy, George E. *The Twilight of the Presidency.* World Publishing, 1970.

Reeves, Richard. *President Kennedy: Profile of Power.* Simon & Schuster, 1993.

Rostow, W. W. *The Diffusion of Power: An Essay in Recent History.* Macmillan, 1972.

Rusk, Dean, as told to Richard Rusk. *As I Saw It.* W. W. Norton, 1991.

Rust, William J. *Before the Quagmire: American Intervention in Laos, 1954–1961.* University Press of Kentucky, 2012.

_____. *Kennedy in Vietnam: American Vietnam Policy, 1960–63.* Scribner, 1985.

_____. *So Much to Lose: John F. Kennedy and American Policy in Laos.* University Press of Kentucky, 2014.

Schandler, Herbert Y. *Lyndon Johnson and Vietnam: The Unmaking of a President.* Princeton University Press, 1977.

_____. "The Pentagon and Peace Negotiations after March 31, 1968," in Lloyd C. Gardner and Ted Gittinger, eds., *The Search for Peace in Vietnam, 1964–1968.* Texas A&M University Press, 2004. pp. 321–354.

Schell, Johnathan. *The Military Half: An Account of Destruction in Quang Ngai and Quang Tin.* Alfred A. Knopf, 1968.

_____. *The Village of Ben Suc.* Alfred A. Knopf, 1967.

Schecter, Jerrold L. with Vyacheslav V. Luchkov, eds. *Khrushchev Remembers: The Glasnost Tapes.* Little, Brown, 1990.

Schelling, Thomas C. "Experimental Games and Bargaining Theory," in Klaus Knorr and Sidney Verba, eds., *The International System: Theoretical Essays.* Princeton University Press, 1961, pp. 47–68.

Schlesinger, Arthur M., Jr. *A Thousand Days: John F. Kennedy in the White House.* Houghton Mifflin, 1965.

_____. *Robert Kennedy and His Times.* Houghton Mifflin, 1978.

Schulimson, Jack. *History of the Joint Chiefs of Staff: The Joint Chiefs of Staff and the War in Vietnam, 1960–1968, Part 1.* Office of Joint History, 2011.

Shapley, Deborah. *Promise and Power: The Life and Times of Robert McNamara.* Little, Brown, 1993.

Sharp, U. S. Grant. *Strategy for Defeat: Vietnam in Retrospect.* Presidio Press, 1978.

Sheehan, Neil. *A Bright Shining Lie: John Paul Vann and America in Vietnam.* Random House, 1988.

Shipler, David K. "McNamara and the Ghosts of Vietnam," *New York Times Magazine,* August 10, 1997.

Sorensen, Theodore C. *Kennedy.* Harper & Row, 1965.

Sorley, Lewis. *Honorable Warrior: General Harold K. Johnson and the Ethics of Command.* University Press of Kansas, 1998.

_____. *Thunderbolt: General Creighton Abrams and the Army of His Times.* Simon & Schuster, 1992.

Spector, Ronald H. *After Tet: The Bloodiest Year in Vietnam.* Free Press, 1993.

Staw, Barry M. "Knee-Deep in the Big Muddy: A Study of Escalating Commitment to a Chosen Course of Action," *Organizational Behavior and Human Performance,* v. 16, 1976, pp. 27–44.

_____. "The Escalation of Commitment to a Course of Action," *Academy of Management Review,* v. 6, n. 4, 1981, pp. 577–587.

_____ and Jerry Ross. "Understanding Behavior in Escalation Situations," *Science,* v. 246, n. 4,927, October 13, 1989, pp. 216–220.

Stern, Sheldon. *Averting "The Final Failure": John F. Kennedy and the Secret Cuban Missile Crisis Meetings*. Stanford University Press, 2003.

Szule, Tad. *Fidel: A Critical Portrait*. William Morrow, 1986.

Taubman, William. *Khrushchev: The Man and His Era*. W. W. Norton, 2003.

Taylor, K. W. *A History of the Vietnamese*. Cambridge University Press, 2013.

Taylor, Maxwell D. *Swords and Ploughshares*. W. W. Norton, 1972.

Teger, Allan I. *Too Much Invested to Quit*. Pergamon Press, 1980.

Thaler, Richard H. and Cass R Sunstein. *Nudge: Improving Decisions about Health, Wealth, and Happiness*. Yale University Press, 2008.

Thayer, Thomas C. *War Without Fronts: The American Experience in Vietnam*. Westview Press, 1985.

Thies, Wallace J. *When Governments Collide: Coercion and Diplomacy in the Vietnam Conflict, 1964–1968*. University of California Press, 1980.

Thomas, Evan. *The Very Best Men: Four Who Dared, The Early Years of the CIA*. Simon & Schuster, 1995.

Thomson, James C. Jr. "How Could Vietnam Happen?: An Autopsy," *Atlantic*, April 1968, pp. 47–53.

Tin, Bui. *Following Ho Chi Minh: Memoirs of a North Vietnamese Colonel*. University of Hawaii Press, 1999.

_____. *From Enemy to Friend*. Naval Institute Press, 2002.

Tra, Tran Van. "Tet: The 1968 General Offensive and General Uprising," in Jayne S. Werner and Luu Doan Huynh, *The Vietnam War: Vietnamese and American Perspectives*. M. E. Sharpe, 1993.

Trewhitt, Henry L. *McNamara: His Ordeal in the Pentagon*. Harper & Row, 1971.

Tung, Nguyen Vu, "Hanoi's Search for an Effective Strategy," in Peter Lowe, ed., *The Vietnam War*. MacMillan Press, 1998.

Turley, William S. *The Second Indochina War: A Concise Political and Military History*. 2nd ed., Rowman & Littlefield, 2009.

Unger, Sanford J. *The Papers and the Papers: An Account of the Legal and Political Battle over the Pentagon Papers*. Dutton, 1972.

U.S. Department of State. *Foreign Relations of the United States, Vietnam, 1961–1968*. 11 Vols. United States Government Printing Office, 1988–2003.

VanDeMark, Brian. "A Way of Thinking: The Kennedy Administration's Initial Assumptions about Vietnam and Their Consequences," in Lloyd C. Gardner and Ted Gittinger, eds., *Vietnam: The Early Decisions*. University of Texas Press, 1997.

_____. *Into the Quagmire: Lyndon Johnson and the Escalation of the Vietnam War*. Oxford University Press, 1991.

Vandenbroucke, Lucien S. *Perilous Options: Special Operations as an Instrument of U.S. Foreign Policy*. Oxford University Press, 1993.

Wells, Tom. *The War Within: America's Battle over Vietnam*. University of California Press, 1994.

Westad, Odd Arne, Chen Jian, Stein Tonnesson, Nguyen Vu Tung, and James G. Hershberg, eds. *77 Conversations Between Chinese and Foreign Leaders on the Wars in Indochina, 1964–1977*. Cold War International History Project, May 1998.

Westmoreland, General William C. *A Soldier Reports*. Doubleday, 1976.

Willbanks, James H. *The Tet Offensive: A Concise History*. Columbia University Press, 2007.

Womack, Brantly. *China and Vietnam: The Politics of Asymmetry*. Cambridge University Press, 2006.

Wyden, Peter. *Bay of Pigs: The Untold Story*. Simon & Schuster, 1979.

Zaffiri, Samuel. *Westmoreland: A Biography of General William C. Westmoreland*. William Morrow, 1994.

Zhai, Qiang. *China and the Vietnam Wars, 1950–1975*. University of North Carolina Press, 2000.

Zubok, Vladislav M. *A Failed Empire: The Soviet Union in the Cold War from Stalin to Gorbachev*. University of North Carolina Press, 2007.

Index

Brian VanDeMark teaches history at the United States Naval Academy in Annapolis, where for more than twenty-five years he has educated students about the Vietnam War. A Ph.D. graduate of UCLA and an elected visiting fellow at Oxford University, he served as research assistant on Clark Clifford's bestselling autobiography, *Counsel to the President*, and coauthor of Robert McNamara's number one bestseller, *In Retrospect*. A Texas native, he now lives in Maryland.